Using
Novell NetWare®

Bill Lawrence

Technical Review by
David Horwatt
Business Computer Resources
Los Angeles, California

CORPORATION
LEADING COMPUTER KNOWLEDGE

Using Novell NetWare®

To my wife, Jenny, without whom this book never would have been finished,
and

To my children, Hannah, Dan, Peter, and Mary, without whom this book would
have been finished six months earlier.

—BL

Publishing Director

Lloyd J. Short

Acquisitions Editor

Karen A. Bluestein

Product Director

David Maguiness

Book Design and Production

Dan Armstrong
Bill Basham
Brad Chinn
Don Clemons
Sally Copenhaver
Tom Emrick
Dennis Hager
Corinne Harmon
Tami Hughes
Bill Hurley
Becky Imel
Jodi Jensen
David Kline
Larry Lynch
Lori A. Lyons
Jennifer Matthews
Cindy Phipps
Joe Ramon
Dennis Sheehan
Louise Shinault
Bruce D. Steed
Mary Beth Wakefield
Jenny Watson
Nora Westlake

Production Editor

Gregory Robertson

Editors

Sara Allaei
Jo Anna Arnott
Mary Arthur
Luanne R. Blackburn
Sandra Blackthorn
Fran Blauw
Kelly Currie
Jeannine Freudenberger
Joseph P. Goodwin
Julia Knispel
Daniel Schnake
Mary Stansifer
Richard Turner

Technical Editor

David Horwatt

Indexers

Hilary Adams
Joelynn Gifford

Editorial Assistant

Renee Ackermann

Composed in Garamond and Excellent No. 47
by Que Corporation.

ABOUT THE AUTHOR

Bill Lawrence

B ill Lawrence has been involved actively in micro-computer networking since its inception, and he writes and speaks extensively about networking and other computing issues. He is a network engineer for a major utility, and is part of the team that manages a NetWare-based LAN of more than 1200 workstations. Lawrence also has served as a consultant to major corporations and institutions and has assisted a wide range of clients in the implementation of local area networks.

CONTENTS AT A GLANCE ▼

Introduction 1

Part I   Networking Basics

Chapter 1   Exploring the Benefits of Networking 5
Chapter 2   Understanding the Components of a Network 13
Chapter 3   Introducing NetWare.......................... 21

Part II   Installing NetWare

Chapter 4   Selecting Software and Hardware 33
Chapter 5   Generating NetWare 286 53
Chapter 6   Installing NetWare 286 74
Chapter 7   Installing NetWare 386 127
Chapter 8   Activating Workstations.......................155

Part III   Organizing Your Server

Chapter 9   Organizing Information with NetWare 183
Chapter 10   Adding Users 197
Chapter 11   Understanding NetWare Rights 229
Chapter 12   Managing Files..............................265
Chapter 13   Establishing Real-World Security 319
Chapter 14   Implementing Shared Printing 337
Chapter 15   Using Shared Printers........................361
Chapter 16   Creating Login Scripts 413
Chapter 17   Implementing NetWare Accounting 465

Part IV   Managing Your Network

Chapter 18   Using NetWare's Network-Management
                Commands..................................487
Chapter 19   Server Console Commands and Loadable
                Modules 535
Chapter 20   Establishing a Network-Management Plan 581

Part V   Advanced Topics

Chapter 21 Building Menus................................607
Chapter 22 Installing Network Versions of Software..........625

Appendix A NetWare Command, Rights, and Attributes
                   Summary....................................651
Appendix B Special Keys for Menued Utility Commands 669
Appendix C Important NetWare Files and Directories 671
Appendix D Network Node Address Reference Chart.........673
Appendix E Shortcuts for Managing Users...................681
Appendix F Working with ELS NetWare 689
Appendix G NetWare and OS/2 695
Appendix H NetWare for Macintosh—An Overview 701
Appendix I Winning at Network Snipes 705

Index...711

TABLE OF CONTENTS

Introduction 1

I   Networking Basics

1   Exploring the Benefits of Networking 5

Hardware Sharing.. 6
   Sharing Disk Space 6
   Sharing Printers....................................... 7
   Accessing Other Computer Systems 8
   Sharing Communication Devices 8
Software Sharing.. 9
   Sharing Software Packages............................. 10
   Sharing Data.. 10
Multiuser Systems 11
Chapter Summary 12

2   Understanding the Components
of a Network................................. 13

Exploring the Hardware Components 14
   Servers 14
   Workstations 16
   The Network Communication System.................... 16
Examining the Software Component: The NetWare
   Operating System..................................... 18
Chapter Summary 19

3   Introducing NetWare........................ 21

The History of NetWare.................................... 21
Linking Your PC to a File Server 22
Providing Security... 23
   Controlling Logins and Passwords 23
   Controlling Trustee Security and Rights................. 23
Making the Network Easy To Use.......................... 27
Handling Network Printing 28
Chapter Summary 29

II   Installing NetWare

4   Selecting Software and Hardware   33

Choosing the Appropriate Version of NetWare   33
   NetWare 286   35
   Advanced NetWare   35
      SFT NetWare   36
   NetWare 386   37
   ELS NetWare   38
   Choosing NetWare for Special Situations   38
Selecting File Servers   39
   The Central Processing Unit   40
   The Hard Disk and Controller   41
   Random-Access Memory   43
      Considering Clock Speed   43
      How NetWare Uses Memory   43
   The Hardware Bus   45
Selecting Your Network Communication System   46
Designing Your Network   48
   Multiple Servers   49
   Multiple Networks   49
Chapter Summary   52

5   Generating NetWare 286   53

Installing and Configuring Your Server Hardware   54
Generating NetWare   54
   Starting NETGEN   56
   Choosing NETGEN's Default or Custom Level   56
   Choosing Where NETGEN Looks for Files   59
   Uploading Configuration Files to a Disk   60
   Configuring Your Server Using the Default Mode   62
      Setting Operating System Options   62
      Selecting LAN Drivers   63
      Selecting Disk Drivers   64
      Selecting Other Drivers   65
   Saving Your Selections and Generating NetWare   66
   Configuring Your Server Using the Custom Mode   68
      Resources and Resource Sets   68
      Setting Operating System Options   69
      Selecting Resource Sets   69
      Selecting LAN Drivers   71
      Selecting Disk Drivers   71

Selecting Other Drivers. 72
Configuring Drivers and Resources. 72
Configuring Resource Sets 72
Configuring LAN Drivers. 73
Entering Server Information. 74
Editing the Resource List and Resource Sets 74
Saving Your Selections and Generating NetWare. 76
Starting NETGEN with Custom Options 77
Installing Network Adapter Cards. 78
Chapter Summary 78

6   Installing NetWare 286.   79
Assembling Your Server's Hardware. 80
Starting NETGEN. 81
Choosing NETGEN's Default or Custom Level 82
Starting NETGEN with Command Line Options. 83
Using NETGEN To Prepare the Server Disks 83
Running DISKSET 84
Running COMPSURF. 86
Understanding COMPSURF. 88
Selecting COMPSURF's Operation Parameters. 90
Using NETGEN To Install NetWare 93
Installing NetWare with NETGEN's Default Mode 93
Disk Mirroring and Duplexing with
SFT NetWare 286. 95
Viewing the Volume List. 97
Entering the File Server Name. 98
Viewing the Server Configuration 98
Defining Network Printers 99
Installing NetWare's Files 100
NETGEN Bugs 101
Installing and Customizing NetWare with NETGEN's
Custom Mode 101
About Partition Tables. 104
Creating and Modifying Disk Partition Tables. 105
Setting Up a Hot Fix Area. 107
Disk Mirroring and Duplexing. 108
Initializing Disks. 109
The Miscellaneous Maintenance Option 114
Installing NetWare's Files 119
Booting the File Server 120
Booting a Dedicated Server 120
Booting a Nondedicated Server. 122

Understanding the Server Boot Messages 123
Downing the Server 125
Placing Your Server in a Good Operating Environment 125
Chapter Summary 126

7   Installing NetWare 386 . . . . **127**
Understanding Differences between
NetWare 286 and 386 128
Assembling Your Server's Hardware 129
Booting the Server 130
Creating a Server Boot Disk 131
Creating a DOS Partition for Server Booting 131
Starting NetWare 386 for the First Time 133
Viewing Start-Up Information and Processor Speed 133
Naming the Server 134
Entering the IPX Internal Number 134
Activating the Server Disks 135
Activating Network Adapters 136
Preparing the Server Disks 137
Using Diskset 138
Starting and Using INSTALL 139
Deciding Whether To Format a Disk 139
Partitioning Disks 140
Performing a Disk Surface Test 142
Mirroring Disks 143
Creating NetWare Volumes 144
Determining Your Volume Strategy 145
Creating Volumes with INSTALL 146
Naming the Volume 146
Choosing a Volume Block Size 147
Specifying the Volume Size 147
Adding Another Disk Segment to an Existing
Volume 148
Deleting a Volume 148
Mounting Your Volumes 148
Completing the Installation Process 149
Copying System and Public Files 149
Handling Password Encryption 149
Creating the AUTOEXEC.NCF File 150
Preparing for Non-DOS Files 151
Creating the STARTUP.NCF File 152
Stopping and Starting the Server 152
Placing Your Server in a Good Operating Environment 153
Chapter Summary 154

8 **Activating Workstations** **155**

The Very Important NetWare Shell 155
Creating the NetWare Shell 157
  Preparing for Floppy-Based Shell Generation 158
  Preparing for Hard Disk or Network-Volume-Based Shell
    Generation 158
    NetWare 286 158
    NetWare 386 158
  Starting SHGEN 160
  Using NetWare 286 SHGEN 160
    Using the Default Level 161
    Using the Intermediate Level 162
    Using the Custom Level 164
    Using NetWare 386 SHGEN 171
    Printing a Configuration Record 172
  Installing Network Adapter Cards 173
    Starting SHGEN with Custom Options 173
    Preparing To Use the NetWare shell 173
    Loading the NetWare Shell 175
    Logging into the Server 177
    Attaching to Multiple Servers 178
  Chapter Summary 180

III **Organizing Your Server**

9 **Organizing Information with NetWare** **183**

Examining the Information Hierarchy 183
  Disk Drives and Volumes 184
  Directories and Subdirectories 185
  NetWare's Version of the Hierarchy 185
Using the MAP Command 188
  Displaying a List of Assigned Drives 189
  Assigning Drive Letters 189
  Deleting Drive Letters 190
  Using MAP Shortcuts 190
  Mapping Search Drives 191
  Mapping to the Root Directory with the MAP Command . . 194
Using DOS and OS/2 Commands on the
  File Server Disk 195
Chapter Summary 196

10 **Adding Users**. **197**

The Purpose of a Login Name. 197
Different Categories of Users. 198
Introducing SYSCON. 198
   Managing Login Names 200
   Using Special Login Names 202
Working with a User's Account. 203
   Login Names 204
   Passwords. 205
   Full Names 206
   Account, Station, and Time Restrictions. 206
      Account Restrictions 207
   Limiting a User's Disk Space with NetWare 386. 212
      Station Restrictions 212
      Time Restrictions. 214
      Setting Default Account and Time Restrictions 216
   Other User Information 217
   Trustee Assignments, Groups Belonged To, and Security
   Equivalences 218
      Trustee Assignments 218
      Groups Belonged To 218
      Security Equivalence 219
Working With Groups of Users. 219
   Adding, Deleting, and Renaming Groups 219
   Working with a Group Account. 220
      Enter a Full Name for the Group 220
      Adding Users to a Group 221
      Viewing Information about the Group. 222
      Working with the Group's Trustee Assignments 222
      Another Way To Add a User to a Group. 222
   The Everyone Group 223
NetWare 386's Advanced-User and Group-Management
Features. 223
   Creating Workgroup Managers. 223
   Assigning Users or Groups to Manage Other Users
   and Groups 224
   Viewing a User's or Group's Managers 225
Other NetWare Utilities and Commands that Control
User Accounts 225
   Changing your Password with SETPASS 225
   Using DSPACE to Manage Disk Space Restrictions
   (NetWare 386 only). 226
Chapter Summary 227

11   Understanding NetWare Rights 229

Examining the Eight NetWare Directory Rights 230
   Granting Rights to Individual Files 234
   Combining Directory and File Rights 235
Using the Right Combination of Rights 235
Knowing Which Rights To Give 238
Using NetWare Commands That Control Trustee Rights 238
   Controlling Rights with SYSCON 238
      Making Users Directory Trustees 239
      Adding or Deleting Directory Rights 242
      Making Users File Trustees 243
      Adding or Deleting File Rights 245
      Adding Rights to Groups of Users 246
      The Everyone Group 248
      Adding Rights Using Security Equivalence 249
   Controlling Rights with TLIST, GRANT, REVOKE,
      and REMOVE 250
Setting Rights Masks 256
   Setting NetWare 286's Maximum Rights Mask 256
   Setting NetWare 386's Inherited Rights Mask 257
   Setting Rights Masks with FILER 257
Understanding Effective Rights 261
Shortcuts for Adding Users and Granting Rights 262
Chapter Summary 263

12   Managing Files 265

File Attributes 266
   NetWare 286 File Attributes 268
   NetWare 386 File Attributes 270
   Directory Attributes 270
   Rules for Using Attributes 272
File and Directory Information 272
Controlling File Attributes 272
   FLAG 272
      Using FLAG To View Attribute Settings 273
      Viewing Attribute Settings for Files
         in Subdirectories 275
      Using FLAG to Change Attribute Settings 275
   FLAGDIR 278
   FILER 279
      Selecting the Current Directory 280
      Setting Filer's Default Options 281
      Viewing and Changing Current Directory Information .. 283

Working with Files in the Current Directory 287
Working with Multiple Files. 292
Working with Subdirectories 293
Working with Multiple Subdirectories 297
Volume Information. 298
File and Directory Commands. 298
HIDEFILE and SHOWFILE (NetWare 286 Only) 299
SALVAGE and PURGE. 299
NetWare 286 SALVAGE and PURGE Commands 300
NetWare 386 SALVAGE and PURGECommands 300
NCOPY 304
Extra Features of NetWare 386's NCOPY 305
NDIR 306
Listing Files Only or Directories Only 307
Listing by File Name 308
Listing by Attribute 308
Listing by Date 309
Listing by Owner 310
Listing by Size. 310
Sorting with NDIR 311
Combining Options 312
Printing Results or Sending Results to a File. 312
Getting NDIR Help 312
NetWare 386 NDIR Menu 312
LISTDIR. 313
DSPACE (NetWare 386 Only) 314
SMODE 316
Chapter Summary 318

13 **Establishing Real-World Security** 319

Using Security in Real Situations. 320
Setting Up Personal Directories 320
Naming Each Directory. 320
Designing the Right Directory Structure 321
Assigning Rights 322
Restrictions 322
Setting Up a File-Sharing Pool. 323
Creating and Mapping to the Directory. 324
Assigning Rights 324
Managing the Shared-File Pool. 326
Using File Attributes 326
Setting Up a Shared Database 328
Which Files Go Where 329

	Access to Program Files	329
	Access Rights to Data Files	330
	File Attributes for Data Files	332
	Examining Netware Security from the Inside	333
	Chapter Summary	335

14 | **Implementing Shared Printing** | **337**

	The Shared-Printing Process	338
	Step One: Redirecting Printer Output	338
	Step Two: Waiting in a Print Queue	339
	Step Three: Moving from the Queue to the Printer	339
	Setting Up Shared Printing	341
	Creating Print Queues	341
	Adding Queue Operators and Users	343
	Assigning Queues to Printers	345
	Assigning Queues with NetWare 286	345
	Assigning Queues with NetWare 386's Print Server Module	347
	Starting a NetWare 386 Print Server	356
	Starting a Workstation-Based Shared Printer	357
	Chapter Summary	359

15 | **Using Shared Printers** | **361**

	Sending Print Requests to Shared Printers	361
	Using CAPTURE without Parameters	366
	Choosing How Your Output Should Be Redirected	366
	Setting Output and Format Options	367
	Using Banner Options	369
	Using End-of-Job Options	370
	Using Notification Options (NetWare 386 Only)	371
	Showing CAPTURE's Current Status	371
	Printing Files with NPRINT	372
	Using Advanced Printer Configuration Options	374
	Using PRINTDEF	376
	Working with Print Devices	376
	Defining Forms	382
	Using PRINTCON	383
	Creating Print Job Configurations	384
	Choosing a Default Print Job Configuration	387
	Sending Print Job Configurations to Other Users	388
	Storing Printer Configurations	388
	Managing Shared Printing	389
	Using PCONSOLE To Manage Shared Printing	390

Managing Queued Print Jobs 390
Controlling Print Queues 395
Using PCONSOLE To Control Printers
(NetWare 386 Only) 397
Controlling NetWare 386 Print Servers 399
Using NetWare 386's PSC Command
To Manage Printing 401
Starting and Stopping a Printer 402
Controlling Paper Type and Alignment 403
Controlling or Showing Print Server Status 404
Making Remote Printers Private or Shared 405
Using Console Commands To Manage
Shared Printing 405
Controlling Printers with NetWare 286
Console Commands 406
Controlling Queues with NetWare 286
Console Commands 409
Assigning Printer Numbers to Queues 411
Chapter Summary 412

16 Creating Login Scripts 413

The Two Types of Login Scripts 414
The System Login Script 414
The User Login Script 414
The Default User Login Script 415
Working with Login Scripts 416
Creating Login Scripts 416
Using SYSCON's Login Script Editor 417
Creating a System Login Script 420
Login Script Commands 420
MAP 424
Using Map With Variables 428
Setting a Default Drive with the Drive Command 437
Login Script Commands that Display Information 438
WRITE 438
Using Variables with WRITE 440
DISPLAY and FDISPLAY 441
Commands that Control Login Script Flow 442
IF and THEN 443
Compound Conditions 443
Multiple Commands 444
Rules for Comparing Variables to Literal Values 444
Rules for Building Compound Conditional Statements .. 446

BREAK. 446
PAUSE and WAIT 447
Commands that Execute External Programs. 447
EXECUTE 448
Rules for Using EXECUTE. 449
EXIT 450
Attaching to Other Servers from a Login Script. 451
Using Commands from an External File 452
Special-Purpose Login Script Commands. 453
DOS SET. 453
DOS VERIFY. 454
DOS BREAK 455
COMSPEC. 456
Workstation Information Commands. 456
Placing Comments in Your Login Scripts 458
Working with Login Command Line Parameters. 459
A Command that Makes Noise 460
Managing Login Scripts. 461
Distributing the Same Script to Multiple Users 462
How Netware Stores Login Scripts. 463
Chapter Summary 464

17   **Implementing NetWare Accounting** 465

Accounting Strategy. 466
Installing NetWare Accounting 467
Selecting Accounting Servers. 468
Setting Up Server Charge Rates. 469
Understanding Disk Blocks 469
Chargeable Items 470
Understanding Charge Rates 471
Assigning Charge Rates with SYSCON. 472
Setting the Charge Rate for Disk Storage 475
Establishing Account Balances and Credit Status. 478
Setting Account Balances for Individual Users. 478
Setting Account Balances for Multiple Users 479
Default Account Balances for Future Users 480
Giving Unlimited Credit to All Users. 481
Managing NetWare Accounting. 481
PAUDIT. 482
ATOTAL 483
Removing NetWare Accounting 484
Chapter Summary 484

IV Managing Your Network

18 Using NetWare's Network-Management Commands **487**

Introducing FCONSOLE 488
Starting FCONSOLE 488
Creating Console Operators 489
FCONSOLE and NetWare 386 490
Choosing the Server To Work With 490
Managing Server Availability and Information 491
Listing All Servers with SLIST 491
Displaying File Server Information with SYSCON 492
Displaying File Server Information with NVER 493
Viewing and Controlling Server Status
with FCONSOLE 494
Downing the File Server 494
Controlling User Access to the Server 495
Setting the Server's Date and Time 495
Viewing the Server's LAN Driver Information 496
Viewing the Server's NetWare
Version Information 496
Managing the Server's Disk Space 497
Checking Disk Space Usage on All Volumes with
VOLINFO 497
Checking Disk Space Usage with CHKVOL 499
Checking Directory Sizes with CHKDIR 500
Checking a User's Disk Space Usage with DSPACE 501
Checking a User's Disk Space Usage with SYSCON 501
Managing User Connections 502
Listing User Connections with USERLIST 502
Managing User Connections with FCONSOLE 504
Sending Messages to the User Connection 504
Broadcasting Messages to Multiple Users 505
Clearing a Connection 505
Clearing Multiple Connections 506
Viewing a Connection's Open Files, Locks, and
Semaphores 506
Viewing Assorted Information
about the Connection 507
Managing File Usage and Record Locking 508
Using FCONSOLE To View File and Record Lock
Information 509

Viewing File and Physical Record
   Lock Information 510
Viewing Logical Lock Information. 512
Viewing Information about Semaphores. 512
Using FCONSOLE To Purge Files. 513
Viewing Advanced File-Server Performance and
Configuration with FCONSOLE 514
Viewing a Summary of Server Statistics. 515
Viewing Cache Statistics 519
Viewing Disk Statistics 521
Viewing File System Statistics. 522
Viewing LAN I/O Statistics. 524
Viewing Transaction Tracking Statistics 526
Viewing Volume Information 527
Communicating with Other Workstations. 529
Using SEND 529
Blocking Messages with CASTOFF. 530
Unblocking Messages with CASTON 531
Managing Your Personal Session. 531
Sending Messages 532
Viewing User Information 532
Working with Drive Mappings 533
Chapter Summary 534

**19 Server Console Commands and Loadable
Modules** **535**

Running Console Commands and NLMs 536
Getting to the Console on a Nondedicated Server 537
Console Commands that Display Server Information 537
NAME (NetWare 286 and 386) 538
CONFIG (NetWare 286 and 386) 538
TRACK (NetWare 286 and 386) 538
DISPLAY SERVERS (NetWare 286 and 386). 539
DISPLAY NETWORKS (NetWare 286 and 386). 539
TIME (NetWare 286 and 386). 539
VERSION (NetWare 286 and 386) 540
MONITOR (NetWare 286) 540
Server Utilization Statistics 540
Connection Information 541
Looking at Different Connections 543
SPEED (NetWare 386) 544
PROTOCOL (NetWare 386) 544
Controlling Access to the Server 544

DISABLE LOGIN (NetWare 286 and 386) 544
ENABLE LOGIN (NetWare 286 and 386) 545
CLEAR STATION 545
Sending Messages to Users 545
BROADCAST (NetWare 286 and 386) 545
SEND (NetWare 286 and 386) 546
Stopping the Server 547
DOWN (NetWare 286 and 386) 547
EXIT (NetWare 386) 547
Controlling the Console Display 548
OFF (NetWare 286 and 386) 548
CLS (NetWare 386) 548
CLEAR MESSAGE (NetWare 286) 548
Controlling Disks 548
DISK (NetWare 286) 549
UNMIRROR and REMIRROR (NetWare 286) 551
MOUNT and DISMOUNT (NetWare 286) 551
MOUNT and DISMOUNT (NetWare 386) 552
VOLUME (NetWare 386) 552
Reconfiguring the Server 552
SET (NetWare 386) 552
SET TIME (NetWare 286 and 386) 562
RESET ROUTER (NetWare 286 and 386) 562
DISABLE TTS (NetWare 386) 562
ENABLE TTS (NetWare 386) 563
ADD NAME SPACE (NetWare 386) 563
BIND and UNBIND (NetWare 386) 563
Working with NetWare 386 NetWare
Loadable Modules 564
Loading an NLM 565
Unloading an NLM 565
Using the MONITOR NLM 566
Starting MONITOR 566
Working with Server Connections 568
Viewing Disk Information 569
Viewing LAN Information 570
Viewing the List of Loaded NLMs 571
Locking and Unlocking the Server
Console Keyboard 571
Viewing File Status Information 572
Viewing Memory Usage Information 573
NLMs Discussed in Other Chapters 574
Managing NLMs 574

MODULES 575
SEARCH 575
SECURE CONSOLE. 576
REMOVE DOS. 576
NetWare 286 VAPs—A Special Situation 577
Running Console Commands Automatically 578
Special Server-Management Situations 579
Chapter Summary 579

20   Establishing a Network-Management Plan **581**

What Should a Network Management Plan Accomplish? 582
Monitoring and Controlling Hard Disk Space Usage. 583
Monitoring Server Performance 585
Maintaining User Login IDs and Workstation Information. . 586
Checking and Resetting Network Devices 588
Maintaining Network Databases and Other Software 589
Making Regular Backups 590
Choosing a Backup Device. 591
Implementing a Backup Strategy. 591
Backing Up Open Files 593
Netware's Backup Utilities 593
Backup Options 597
Restore Options 602
Chapter Summary 604

V   Advanced Topics

21   Building Menus. **607**

Preparing To Use NetWare's Menu Builder 608
Designing Your Menus 608
Creating and Running Your First Menu. 611
Running A Script. 611
Examining Script File Structure 612
Creating Submenus. 613
Prompting for User Input 616
Controlling Menu Window Position 617
Determining Menu Width and Height. 618
Changing Menu Colors. 619
Using COLORPAL to Create Your Own Palettes 620
Handling Special Color Configurations. 621
Running The Menu Utility without a Network 621
Handling Special Situations 622
Chapter Summary 624

22   Installing Network Versions of Software **625**

The Benefits of LAN-Based Software...................... 626
Installation Strategies for Network Software............... 627
   Choosing the Servers on Which To Store Shared Programs
.... 627
   Choosing a Directory Structure for Shared Programs...... 629
   Installing Your Program............................... 630
Controlling Access to Shared Programs.................... 631
   Choosing Which Netware Rights To Grant 632
   Granting Rights to Groups instead of Individuals 632
   Setting the Program File Attributes 633
Making Shared Programs Easy To Use 634
   Starting Shared Programs with Batch Files.............. 634
   Starting Shared Programs from a Menu................. 636
Installing Shared Software—Three Case Studies............. 636
   WordPerfect.. 637
      Buying a WordPerfect Network License 637
      WordPerfect's Network-Specific Features.............. 637
      Creating a Directory for WordPerfect 637
      Turning On File Attributes.......................... 639
      Giving Users Rights to the WordPerfect Directories.... 639
      Configuring WordPerfect 639
      Storing and Updating Individual Configuration Files 640
      Starting WordPerfect............................... 641
   Lotus 1-2-3... 642
      Buying a Network License for 1-2-3.................. 642
      1-2-3's Network-Specific Features 642
      Creating Directories for 1-2-3 643
      Giving Users Rights to 1-2-3'S Directories............ 644
      Installing the Program Files and Configuring the
        License Count.................................. 644
      Setting File Attributes 644
      Starting 1-2-3..................................... 645
      Establishing a Default Configuration.................. 645
   Paradox.. 647
      Buying a Network License for Paradox 647
      Creating Directories To Store Paradox's Files.......... 647
      Granting Rights to Users........................... 648
      Setting File Attributes 648
      Configuring Paradox 649
      Starting Paradox................................... 649
Chapter Summary 650

A **NetWare Command, Rights, and Attributes Summary** **651**

NetWare Commands 651
NetWare Rights 664
File and Directory Attributes............................ 665
   NetWare 286 File Attributes........................... 665
   NetWare 386 File Attributes........................... 667
   Directory Attributes 667

B **Special Keys Menued Utility Commands** **669**

C **Important NetWare Files and Directories** **671**

D **Network Node Address Reference Chart** **673**

E **Shortcuts for Managing Users** **681**

Using USERDEF 682
   Creating a Template................................. 682
      Editing the Template's Parameters 683
      Editing the Template's Login Script 685
   Adding Users with USERDEF.......................... 686
Using MAKEUSER...................................... 686

F **Working with ELS NetWare** **689**

Designing an ELS NetWare Network 690
   Design Considerations with ELS NetWare Level I......... 690
   Design Considerations with ELS NetWare Level II 691
Installing ELS NetWare 691
   Tips for Installing ELS NetWare Level I 691
   Tips for Installing ELS NetWare Level II................ 692
Examining the Differences Between ELS NetWare and
   NetWare 286 Version 2.1............................. 693

G **NetWare and OS/2** **695**

The NetWare OS/2 Requester 696
   Installing OS/2 Versions of NetWare Commands.......... 696
   Activating OS/2 Workstations 697
NetWare'S OS/2-Specific Features 698
   Running Commands in Global or Private Mode 699
   Special Rules for Running NetWare OS/2 Commands 700

H **NetWare for Macintosh—An Overview** **701**

How NetWare for Macintosh Works 702
Hardware and Software Requirements.................... 702
Special Instructions...................................... 703

I **Winning at Network Snipes** **705**

Starting NSNIPES 705
Starting Multiuser Snipes 706
The Rules of the Game................................. 707
Shooting.. 707
Moving Your Player.................................... 708
Playing at Higher Levels............................... 708
Advanced Features..................................... 708
   Electric Walls....................................... 709
   Ghosts.. 709
   Ricochet Shooting................................... 709
Stopping SNIPES....................................... 710
Erasing NSNIPES's Data Files........................... 710
Removing NSNIPES from a Server 710

Index **711**

ACKNOWLEDGMENTS

Many distinguished networkers have influenced this book.

This book would not have been possible without the extensive cooperation and assistance of many Novell employees. Gordon Smith took time out of an incredibly busy schedule to provide a first look at NetWare 386. Patty Heisser provided many NetWare products on short notice, and went the extra mile to make sure that my versions of NetWare were always up to date. Bob Gimigliano and Faye Pentecost provided much moral support and let me rifle their well-stocked NetWare literature racks. Novell's advanced support group was kind enough to work writer's hours (nights and weekends).

Vitek Distribution Group provided assistance and advice concerning the equipment required to complete this project. Larry Lasky steered me to a fine choice for a file server. I am indebted to Tom Pine, the president of Vitek, for having the foresight to see what computer networking would become and for letting me ride along.

Many great network supervisors, designers, and installers have shared ideas that have influenced this book. They are Jim Yee, Tom Giangreco, Bert Du Mars, Paul Singer, Kathy Strother, Rich Walters, Rod Hildreth, Stan Bridgeford, Claude Lane, Rick Narramore, Vito Palozolo, Dr. Stephen Franklin, Walter Thompson, Bob Greene, Stephen McQuarry, Scott Norton, Dave Cheatham, Scott Cheatham, Dennis Passavoy, Nathan Roseman, Randy Wise, and C.W. Rogers. I also have had the privilege of working with courageous people who have sponsored and spearheaded major network projects in their organizations, people who have had the vision to see that networking computers really means networking people. These insightful people are Russ Henderson, Jim Groves, Walt Harshman, Bill True, and John LaFare.

Several people shared specialized expertise. Vic Sangveraphunsiri of Advanced Logic Research provided much useful information about server hardware. Paul Singer helped me master the NetWare OS/2 Requester. Rich Walters helped me research facts about hard disk types. Dan and Hannah Lawrence extensively researched Network Snipes.

Mike Durr, my mentor in the writing business and one of the industry's most effective communicators about networking subjects, helped conceive this project and encouraged me to tackle it. Dick

Ridington and Marc Scapicchio also have played a major role in shaping my writing skills and keeping me aware of current computing issues.

Many capable staff members at Que Corporation provided encouragement and guidance as this project progressed. David Maguiness pulled together the team and kept the encouragement coming when it seemed like we would never finish. Greg Robertson and Sandy Blackthorn managed the very talented editing team.

A very special thanks goes to David Horwatt, this book's technical editor. Dave's real-world perspective and continual flow of good ideas played a vital role in keeping this book well organized and accurate. Dave would be a great writer in his own right if he weren't in such demand as a network designer. How he found the time to devote to this project is a great mystery to me.

TRADEMARK ACKNOWLEDGMENTS

Que Corporation has made every effort to supply trademark information about company names, products, and services mentioned in this book. Trademarks indicated below were derived from various sources. Que Corporation cannot attest to the accuracy of this information.

1-2-3 and Lotus are registered trademarks of Lotus Development Corporation.

Apple and Macintosh are registered trademarks of Apple Computer, Inc.

ARCNet and Datapoint are registered trademarks of Datapoint Corporation.

CompuServe is a registered trademark of CompuServe, Inc. and H & R Block, Inc.

dBASE is a registered trademark and dBASE IV is a trademark of Ashton-Tate Corporation.

DEC is a registered trademark and VAX is a trademark of Digital Equipment Corporation.

EtherNet is a trademark of 3Com Corporation.

Harvard Graphics is a trademark of Software Publishing Corporation.

IBM, OS/2, and PS/2 are registered trademarks and ProPrinter and Micro Channel are trademarks of International Business Machines Corporation.

LaserJet is a trademark of Hewlett-Packard Co.

MCI Mail is a registered service mark of MCI Communications Corporation.

NetWare and Novell are registered trademarks of Novell, Inc.

Paradox and SideKick are registered trademarks of Borland International.

Prime Computer is a registered trademark of Prime Computer, Inc.

R:BASE is a registered trademark of Microrim, Inc.

The Source is a service mark of Source Telecomputing Corporation, a subsidiary of The Reader's Digest Association, Inc.

WordPerfect is a registered trademark of WordPerfect Corporation.

XENIX and MS-DOS are registered trademarks of Microsoft Corporation.

CONVENTIONS USED IN THIS BOOK ▼

The conventions used in this book have been established to help you learn to use the program quickly and easily.

1. Menu names and options begin with capital letters.

2. Screen messages appear in a `special typeface`.

3. The names of screens and windows appear with initial capital letters.

4. Words or commands that the user should type are italicized or on a line by themselves.

5. DOS and NetWare commands are in all capital letters.

Introduction

NetWare is running on more local area networks (LANs) today than any other network operating system. The networks using NetWare range in size from just a few PCs to thousands of workstations. NetWare has become a key player in the computing strategy of many major corporations, as well as in small- and medium-sized businesses, government agencies, and educational institutions.

NetWare's phenomenal success is a direct result of its speed, dependability, and flexibility. Although many newcomers have come into the network operating system world, NetWare is a mature veteran. Today's NetWare is the result of many years of development, refinement, and real-world experience.

Using Novell NetWare tells how to use NetWare as the cornerstone of your PC network. Every version of NetWare is discussed and compared. NetWare 386, the most recent addition to the NetWare family, is covered fully.

Using Novell NetWare is not just a "how to" book about NetWare. The "how to" of using NetWare is covered in detail, but in conjunction with every "how to" is a corresponding "why," so that you will understand the purpose and real-life application of every NetWare command and utility.

You can follow *Using Novell NetWare* like a road map as you plan and build your network. If you are new to networking, you will find Part I, "Networking Basics," a good "Networking 101" course. This section familiarizes you with the components of a network and introduces NetWare's major features and functions.

1

Part II, "Installing NetWare," guides you through designing and installing your network. You will learn how to choose the version of NetWare that best suits your situation and how to combine NetWare with a hardware and network design to ensure maximum network performance. You will walk through installing NetWare on a server PC and activating workstations.

Part III, "Organizing Your Server," details how to configure a NetWare server so that it can do real work. You will learn how to use a server to store, retrieve, and share files. You also will learn how to add users to the server and personalize NetWare for them. Printer sharing is discussed, as is using NetWare security to make your servers a safe place for important applications and data.

In Part IV, "Managing Your Network," you will learn about the NetWare commands and utilities that enable you to keep your network operating at an optimum performance level. This section contains techniques that experienced NetWare supervisors have developed to make their LANs useful, trouble-free, responsive, and easy to manage.

Part V, "Advanced Topics," describes how to add network versions of software to your servers and how to create menus that make your network's resources easy to use.

The appendixes contain useful reference information and details about using NetWare with Macintosh and OS/2 computers.

Using Novell NetWare can be used as a comprehensive NetWare reference. After your network is up and running, you can refer to this book for the details about using NetWare's many commands and utilities.

Don't be intimidated by the size of *Using Novell NetWare*. Although virtually all of NetWare's utilities and commands are covered in detail, you are free to skip those you don't need. In fact, this book honestly tells you about the relative importance of each NetWare command and utility and distinguishes between those that are essential and those that are optional.

Whether you are a network installer, supervisor, or administrator, or a curious user who wants to get the most out of NetWare, this book has been written with you in mind.

Part I

Networking
Basics

Includes

Exploring the Benefits of Networking
Understanding the Components of a Network
Introducing NetWare

Exploring the Benefits of Networking

If you're new to the subject of PC networks, you may not be aware of the variety of benefits you can reap from connecting the PCs in your company. Before you learn the specifics of how networks work and how you can effectively use NetWare, you should examine the ways in which PC networks are being used in many organizations.

The personal computer, for all its usefulness and user friendliness, has a serious shortcoming. Unlike its mainframe and minicomputer cousins, the personal computer is essentially a single-user device. Because it is meant to accommodate one user at a time, the personal computer is not designed to share its resources. Instead, the personal computer insists on having its own copy of everything it uses. If you want to run a particular software package, you must purchase your own copy of that package. And using a printer means connecting it exclusively to your PC's parallel port.

This isolation results in duplication. If your company has 50 PCs and all 50 PC users want to run a particular spreadsheet package, you must buy 50 individual copies of that program for things to remain legal. Similarly, each user must be provided with a printer as well as other peripherals, such as modems, plotters, and scanners.

Duplication isn't the only price paid. Imagine the following scenario. Your company develops a database application to manage its inventory and runs this application on a PC in the accounting department. In the beginning, everything works fine. One person enters inventory updates, and others occasionally use the PC to look up the stock level of a particular item or run a special report. The application proves useful and soon the demand to use the database PC increases. And the company decides to expand its

5

product line, so more and more inventory items must be entered and tracked. Because only one user at a time can access the database application, there aren't enough hours in a day to keep the database updated properly.

A local area network (LAN) running the NetWare operating system can change a group of isolated PCs into a coordinated multiuser computer system. A LAN-connected PC user is not subject to the limitations described in the preceding example. A LAN-connected user can easily and legally share copies of software packages with other users, as well as access LAN-connected printers, plotters, modems, and other peripherals. A PC-based inventory management system, when implemented on a LAN, can be accessed by many users at the same time.

A LAN makes all these opportunities possible by connecting PCs together. In the next chapter, you will examine the particular components of a network that make this possible, but for now you will learn about some of the benefits you can gain by installing and using a LAN.

LANs are being put to many creative uses in many companies, and most of these uses fall into one of three categories: sharing hardware, sharing software, and running multiuser systems.

Hardware Sharing

A LAN enables users to share a wide variety of hardware devices. The most frequently shared items are hard disks, printers, and communication devices.

Sharing Disk Space

LANs were originally designed to enable PCs to share hardware. In the early days of personal computing, hard disks were expensive items, often costing several times more than the PC itself. Connecting more than one PC to a hard disk to spread this cost over more than one user made sense. Early LANs were primarily disk-sharing systems.

Today's LANs are still based on the concept of sharing access to one or more common hard disks. These hard disks are installed in the LAN's special PCs called *file servers*, which are discussed in detail in the next chapter.

Sharing access to a common hard disk has many benefits. The most obvious advantage is cost. If users can share the hard disk on a file server, they may not need hard disks of their own. Having all files stored on the file server also simplifies data backups. The LAN administrator can use one tape backup unit to archive shared hard disks—a far easier proposition than trying to back up the hard disks of many individual PCs.

Sharing Printers

LANs make sharing printers easy. If a printer is connected to a file server, all LAN users can access it. You also can trade quantity for quality. Instead of providing each user with a low-cost personal printer, you can consolidate your expenditure and provide a few high-quality printers. With a LAN, for example, you may find that installing a high-speed laser printer is economically feasible because the cost of that printer can be spread over many users.

LAN users can have access to a wider variety of printers because they can be shared. If you need to print a spreadsheet that is more than 80 characters wide, you're in luck as long as a wide-carriage printer is connected to a file server on your LAN. If your LAN has five different types of shared printers connected to it, you can send print jobs to any one of the printers almost as easily as if it were connected directly to your PC. Figure 1.1 shows shared printers connected to a file server.

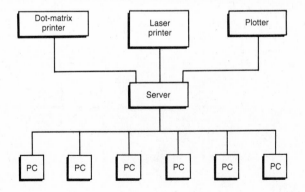

Fig. 1.1.
Shared printers connected to a file server.

With a little more creativity, you also can use a LAN to share other types of input/output devices, such as plotters, scanners, or peripherals that produce slides and overheads.

Accessing Other Computer Systems

PC users on a LAN may need to communicate with other types of computer systems. In many large companies, PCs have replaced the data terminals originally used for accessing the company mainframe or minicomputer. To replace a data terminal, a PC generally must be equipped with special boards that enable it to communicate directly with the mainframe or minicomputer in the same way that the terminal did. This process is called *terminal emulation* because the PC emulates a terminal, or looks like a terminal to the host computer.

The cost of making a PC look like a terminal can be steep. If you factor in the costs of the behind-the-scenes equipment (such as cabling to the host computer as well as communication controllers and multiplexers), the total can exceed the original cost of the PC itself! This expenditure is even more painful when you consider that many users may use their host connections for only a few hours a week.

Consolidating this cost in a single LAN-based connection makes economic sense. A device that uses a LAN to provide PCs with access to other computer systems is called a *gateway* (see fig. 1.2). A gateway is typically a dedicated or nondedicated PC somewhere on the LAN that is connected to the host computer. The gateway serves as the translator between LAN PCs and the host computer so that any PC on the LAN can access the host. Because the cost of terminal emulation for a single PC can be rather high, the savings resulting from installing a gateway can be dramatic.

Fig. 1.2.
A gateway.

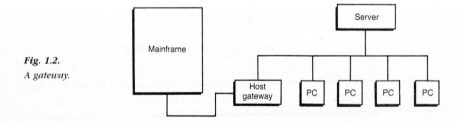

Sharing Communication Devices

In addition to communicating with mainframes and minicomputers, PC users often use modems to transmit data to other PCs or to access services such as bulletin boards. A *modem* is a device that enables computers to send information across telephone lines. Modem gateways are available, so LAN users can share modems in a manner similar to the way host connections are shared with a host gateway.

A newer use of LANs is the sharing of facsimile (fax) equipment. Fax communication is gaining wide acceptance as a method for sending documents over telephone lines, and a LAN can make sending and receiving fax messages more convenient. A LAN-based fax enables you to create a document with your word processor and send that document over the LAN to your fax machine, which in turn sends the document to the destination fax machine. Similarly, when an incoming fax is received for you, you can print it on your nearest LAN printer or perhaps display it on your PC.

The benefits of sharing hardware are clear. Not only are costs reduced as duplicate peripheral purchases are minimized, but LAN users can access an astonishing array of equipment. Think of a LAN as being able to provide all hardware services on one cable (see fig. 1.3).

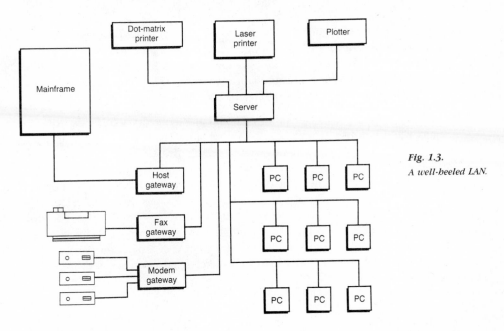

Fig. 1.3.
A well-heeled LAN.

Software Sharing

Several types of software sharing are made possible by a LAN. You can share software packages by purchasing LAN versions of your most widely used programs. Users also can share access to data, making it possible to build "libraries" of files that contain useful information. You also can create multiuser applications so that data can be accessed and updated by many users at the same time.

Sharing Software Packages

You have already read about the expense and inconvenience of providing software packages to large numbers of stand-alone PCs. In many companies, the result is a great deal of illegal software duplication. Someone also has to do a tremendous amount of recordkeeping so that when a new version of a popular package becomes available, every copy (that is, every *legal* copy) of that particular package is accounted for and properly upgraded.

Configuration control also becomes messy. If a vendor sends your company a bug fix that corrects a problem with a particular package, making sure that the fix is installed on every PC running the package can be difficult.

Using LAN versions of your favorite software packages is an elegant solution to all these problems. Configuration control and upgrades become easy because the LAN copy of the package is stored in one place—on the hard disk of a file server. The motivation to make illegal copies is reduced because all LAN users have the ability to use the package.

Depending on the package, you may or may not realize a significant cost savings when you use the package's LAN version. Many companies offer network versions of their software at reasonable prices, but with other programs, you end up paying about what you would pay for the equivalent number of single PC copies. (In other words, if you buy a network version that enables 20 users to access the package at the same time, the price may be the same as if you purchased 20 single copies.) Even if you end up paying the equivalent multiple of the single-copy price, chances are you can still reap an economic benefit: a 20-user copy of a package may take care of a LAN of 100 users because it's unlikely that everyone will use the package at the same time.

Sharing Data

Because all LAN users can access common disks, it becomes possible to share access to data files on those disks. On a particular LAN, for example, the engineering department has a large shared library of spreadsheets stored on its file server, and each spreadsheet performs a series of technical calculations. Because the library is LAN based, any engineer in the department can use his or her PC to "check out" a copy of the particular spreadsheet needed. The training organization has a directory of lesson plans that various instructors can access as a resource in planning training classes.

In almost any organization, being able to share data files will prove useful at times. Some PC software packages, particularly database managers, are designed to permit more than one user to access and update a file simultaneously. Other packages, such as word processors and spreadsheets, are designed so that only one user at a time should access the file.

Multiuser Systems

Certain software packages are designed with a LAN in mind. Instead of being LAN adaptations of single-user programs, these packages are designed specifically for use by multiple users and for generating data that is shared.

Electronic mail (E-mail) is a common example. A full-featured electronic mail package enables you to send messages as well as files and graphs to other LAN users. E-mail is particularly useful on larger LANs that span several buildings, where it is an effective alternative to sending paper memos and playing telephone tag. E-mail is surprisingly worthwhile on a small LAN as well.

A related category of LAN software has been dubbed *groupware*. Usually a groupware package has electronic mail, a multiuser appointment manager (so you can manage your own calendar as well as view others' calendars to schedule meetings), and also a feature that lets you circulate documents that others can annotate with comments. Groupware is a software category that is still being defined, so watch for some interesting new ideas and features to emerge in future groupware packages.

You also can use LANs to run more traditional types of multiuser software that in the past could only be run on minicomputers or mainframes. A LAN can be an effective host system for multiuser accounting software, where processes such as order entry, invoicing, payroll processing, and journal updates can be performed concurrently on different PCs on the LAN. Multiuser database applications also lend themselves well to use on a LAN, and a wide array of LAN-compatible database managers are available to help you create these types of applications.

Chapter Summary

In this chapter, you learned that a LAN can be a cost-effective productivity and data-processing tool. As with any tool, a LAN must be used properly to be of benefit. The first step to using a LAN wisely is understanding how it works. In the next chapter, you will examine the pieces that fit together to make a LAN. You also will begin to explore the important role that NetWare plays.

2

Understanding the
Components of a
Network

If you are just beginning to study local area networks, you probably find much of the terminology confusing. In this chapter, you will learn about the basic building blocks shared by all PC LANs that use NetWare.

When you boil things down to the essentials, a LAN has only one basic function: to move information among shared computers on the network (called *servers*) and the PC workstations of the network users. Usually this information is in the form of files. Suppose that you are a network user, and you want to run the network version of Lotus 1-2-3. Type *lotus*, and the network hardware and operating system go to work to retrieve the files needed to start 1-2-3 and move them from the file server into the memory of your PC. The network hardware and operating system cooperate to make these actions occur invisibly, just as if you were using the program from your own computer's hard disk.

The components of a network can be divided into two categories: *hardware* (consisting of the network communication boards, cables, workstations, and servers) and *software* (the network operating system).

Exploring the Hardware Components

Figure 2.1 illustrates the hardware components of a basic network. The hardware in a LAN can be divided into three major categories: servers, workstations, and the boards and cables that handle communication between them. In this section, you will examine these components individually.

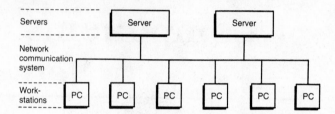

Fig. 2.1.

The three hardware components of a network.

Servers

Servers are computers on a network that can be accessed by network users. These computers contain some resource that they "serve" to network users who request that resource.

By far the most common type of server is the *file server*. Every LAN using NetWare as its operating system has at least one, and larger LANs may have many. As the name implies, a file server's resource is the files it contains. In the previous example describing the use of the LAN version of 1-2-3, the file server "served" the files for the Lotus program to the workstation that requested them.

Nothing is special about the hardware that makes up a file server; it is just a computer with one or more hard disks. The hard disk on a file server is typically of a larger capacity than the hard disk you would put in your own computer, because the file server's hard disk is shared. (A size of several hundred megabytes is not uncommon.) Similarly, because multiple users access a file server, you may want to use a higher performance computer for the server. Although the workstations on your network can be XT- and AT-type PCs, you may want to make your file servers 80386-based computers or 80486-based computers.

Network users can store files to and retrieve files from file servers as if the users were using their own hard disks. NetWare, the network operating system, makes sure that this process is rapid and safe. Because multiple users can access the files on a file server, sharing programs and data becomes possible. In cases in which sharing is not desirable, private areas can be set up for individual users.

File servers perform another important function on a network. Printers connected to file servers can be accessed by all network users. At first, you may think that this capability has nothing to do with file serving, but it is closely related. When you send output from your PC to a network printer, NetWare converts the output into a file as it arrives at the file server. The contents of the file are then sent to the printer connected to the file server. If several users are sending output to the printer at the same time, each user's output is converted to an individual file. These files "wait in line" in what is called a *print queue* and are fed to the printer one at a time.

File servers are the most common but not the only type of server you can have on a network. Any computer on your LAN that has a shareable resource can be called a server. For example, a PC that houses modems that can be used by network users is called a *modem server*. A PC that is connected to a shared facsimile machine is a *fax server*. *Gateways*, which are devices that connect a LAN to other types of systems such as mainframes and minicomputers, are also servers.

When you set up a file server, you assign a unique name to it. This name enables network users to distinguish the file server from other servers when using the file server's disk space or sending jobs to one of its printers. A common strategy in multiserver networks is to use names corresponding to the departments that use each particular server (resulting in names like ACCTING, SALES, and WAREHSE) or to use names that describe the server's function. For example, a server that stores electronic mail may be called E-MAIL.

Servers can be dedicated or nondedicated. A dedicated file server is a PC that is used only as a file server and nothing else. A nondedicated file server can be used as a server and workstation at the same time. Obviously, dedicated servers are better in terms of stability and performance because the PC processor does not have to divide its time between two tasks. For a small network, or in a situation in which an extra PC is hard to justify, however, the nondedicated approach can be worthwhile.

Workstations

Connecting a PC to a LAN does not dramatically alter the way the PC is used; a LAN-connected PC merely has more places from which it can retrieve files. The PC still uses its normal operating system. LANs that use NetWare can have both IBM-compatible and Macintosh workstations. IBM-compatible workstations can run either DOS or OS/2.

The PC workstation's job is to execute the program files retrieved from the LAN, and the server's job is to deliver those files to the workstation. On a typical LAN, PC workstations do most of the processing, and the file servers deliver the files to be processed. This arrangement is not exclusively the case, however. Programs are now being designed to enable servers and workstations to share the processing load. The most common example is called a database server or database engine.

The Network Communication System

You already know basically how workstations and servers communicate with each other. Workstations request files stored on file servers or send print jobs to network printers. Network PCs communicate with the gateway to exchange information with a mainframe or minicomputer. Some type of system has to be in place to make this communication possible.

When you connect computers to create a network, you install a special board in each PC and server and then connect the boards with cable. This board is called a *network adapter*, or *network interface board*. Many different types and brands of network adapters are available, but they all perform the same function: enabling you to transmit large amounts of data at high speeds between computers.

High-speed data transmission is important to the success of a network. If starting a copy of 1-2-3 stored on your personal hard disk takes two seconds, then network users expect the time required to start a copy stored on the file server to be comparable. The only way it will be comparable is if your network adapters and cable system are capable of high-speed performance.

Most types of network communication systems are capable of communication speeds ranging from 1 million to 16 million bits per second. Thus the time to transmit a 100,000-byte file (which is 800,000 bits of information) takes less than 2 seconds on even the slowest type of network. Compare these speeds to those you get when you use a modem over a telephone line, where the best speeds possible are 9,600 bits per second in most circumstances.

Because a cable must connect every computer on a network, you have limits to the distance your network can span. For this reason, networks generally must be confined to buildings or campuses where you can run cable. (As you may have guessed, this restriction is where the "local area" part of the term "local area network" originates.)

You may have heard of certain types of network communication systems. Ethernet, Token Ring, and ARCnet are commonly used types of network adapters. They vary in terms of the type of cable used and the method by which they transfer data, but they have enough in common to enable you to study in general terms how all network communication systems work.

The process used to transmit a file from a file server to a network PC works as follows. First the file is conveyed to the file server's network adapter card, where the file is translated into *data packets*. (These packets are of a fixed size, which varies depending on the network adapter type. Most adapters use packet sizes ranging from 500 to 2,000 bytes. If the file is too big to fit in one packet, it is sent in multiple packets.) The file server's network adapter card places the data packets on the network cable, where they are transmitted to the network adapter of the workstation that requested the file.

A data packet can be likened to the envelope you use to send a letter. The data packet contains the "address" of the PC on the network to which the data contained in the packet should be sent. Just as every house on a particular street must have a unique number to guarantee that the postal service delivers mail properly, every PC on your network must have a unique address. With some types of network adapters, you set this address with switches when you install the adapter card. With others, a unique address is set at the factory. Figure 2.2 shows a diagram of a data packet.

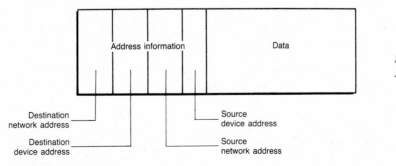

Fig. 2.2.
A data packet.

Most network communication systems allow up to 256 uniquely addressed PCs to exist on one network. (Those of you who are programmers will instantly ascertain the reason: 1 byte of the data packet is used to store the address, and 256 is the largest number that can be stored in a byte.) Although this number is more than enough for most LANs, in some cases you may need to network more than 256 PCs. How do you do so, given the 256 PC limit? If you carry the analogy to house numbers a step further, you will see how. Two houses cannot have the same number if they are on the same street, but they can if they are on different streets. You can network more than 256 PCs by creating a second network and joining it to the first.

You can join networks by using bridges or routers. A *router*, or *bridge*, is a PC or other device that has two or more network adapters inside, one for each network that is being joined or bridged. If a PC on one network needs to send data packets to a PC on another network, the packets are delivered to the bridge, which receives them, readdresses them, and sends them to the correct address on the second network. NetWare allows you to combine bridging and file serving by placing two or more network adapters in a file server (this design is called an *internal bridge*). Or you can use a separate PC, called an *external bridge*, for this function.

Examining the Software Component: The NetWare Operating System

The complex processes that take place on the network hardware have to be directed by some form of intelligence. The hardware components need a set of instructions to follow. Just as your PC needs an operating system (PC DOS or OS/2 on an IBM PC; System on a Macintosh) to work properly, your network needs one also.

NetWare is a network operating system, which is designed to perform two important tasks. It controls the operation of the file server, and it cooperates with the workstation operating system to make network resources easy to use.

In many ways, NetWare does the same work for the file server that your PC's operating system does for your PC. Like your PC's operating system,

NetWare manages disk access, file storage, and memory utilization. But NetWare has some additional responsibilities.

NetWare must manage file server security. It provides the network administrator with the tools to control which network users are allowed to use the server, and enables the administrator to control who can access file directories on the server's hard disks. For example, you may want to permit all users to access the file directory that stores electronic mail but allow only users from the accounting department to access the directories containing the company's accounting system.

NetWare controls not only *what* a user can access, but also *how*. For example, a user can be given unlimited access to his or her personal worksheet storage area, with the ability to create, delete, and modify files. On the other hand, the user should have restricted access to 1-2-3's program files, located in the network 1-2-3 directory, and be able to use them but not modify or delete them.

The NetWare operating system also must cooperate with your PC's operating system so that using network resources is a natural extension of using your PC. For example, in an IBM PC environment, you address different disk drives by using drive letters. With NetWare, you assign drive letters to the file server disk volumes so that accessing them is just like using the disk drives on your PC. You also can use PC DOS and OS/2 commands to work with files stored on a NetWare file server, just as if the files were stored on your personal hard disk. Similarly, on a MacIntosh you use icons to access server-based software and printers.

Chapter Summary

In this chapter, you learned that a typical LAN consists of several hardware components (servers, workstations, and the network communication system) and a network operating system to coordinate the interaction of the hardware components. Now that you have some idea of what comprises a network and how the components work together, you're ready to take a closer look at NetWare itself. The next chapter examines the NetWare family in more depth.

3

Introducing NetWare

You will be studying each aspect of NetWare in detail in the following chapters. But before looking at the trees, you should be aware of the forest. This chapter takes a quick look at NetWare as a whole. The discussion begins with the basics: linking your PC to a file server and logging in. That text is followed by an overview of NetWare security and rights. You also will look at how using a NetWare disk compares with using the disks on your own PC and how printer sharing works.

The History of NetWare

NetWare came into being at about the same time as the IBM PC. NetWare was developed to allow groups of microcomputers to share access to the files stored on a file server and to share peripherals connected to that file server.

In the early days, most network operating systems were notoriously slow and unreliable. NetWare steadily gained acceptance as a fast and stable alternative. Today it is the most widely used network operating system on the market.

NetWare has continued to mature and improve, and many new features have been added. Perhaps the best indicator of its increased sophistication is the fact that the original NetWare was shipped on 5 disks, compared to more than 20 for today's versions.

Linking Your PC to a File Server

You already have learned how the LAN communication system establishes a hardware connection between networked PCs and one or more file servers. This hardware link must be activated on each PC, a process called attaching, by a special piece of NetWare software called the *NetWare shell*.

The NetWare shell is the one part of NetWare that runs on your PC (rather than on a file server). Connecting the PC to the server involves two steps: attaching and logging in. *Attaching* establishes a hardware connection between the PC and the file server. *Logging in* allows you to access the file server's resources.

When you start the shell program, your PC's network adapter broadcasts a request over the network cable system, asking a file server to respond. Your PC is linked, or attached, to the first file server that answers. The NetWare shell stays in the memory of your PC and serves as the software link between your PC's operating system and NetWare on the file server (see fig. 3.1).

Fig. 3.1.
The NetWare shell.

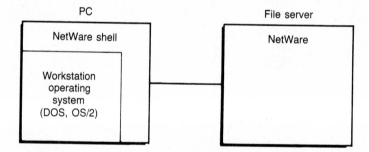

The next job performed by the shell is to provide you with a way to log into a network file server. On an IBM PC running PC DOS, the shell creates a new drive letter (F in most cases) on which you will find a directory of the linked server. This directory contains the LOGIN command, which you can use to log into a file server. (For more information on logging in, see "Controlling Logins and Passwords," elsewhere in this chapter.)

Chapter 8 discusses the NetWare shell in greater detail, but for now you need to know that it is the software link between NetWare and your PC. Loading the shell is the first step to using NetWare.

Providing Security

The cornerstone of the safe sharing of network resources is security. Security is not a big issue on your own stand-alone PC. You can add and delete files and directories at will, and you have complete access to all disk contents because they are yours exclusively. That is not the case on a network.

You are permitted to share access to the files and directories on network disks, but this sharing must be governed by a set of rules. If not, you would have the freedom to delete—whether accidentally or intentionally—someone else's files, and they could do the same to you. Another user could copy copious amounts of information to the file server disk, filling it up and leaving you with no room for your own files. Even sabotage becomes a possibility. Without some type of control, a network-based accounting system is subject to deliberate tampering or outright destruction.

NetWare provides the tools to prevent uncontrolled sharing. Each file server has at least one user who has supervisory control, and this network supervisor has the responsibility to use NetWare's security tools to create a safe network environment.

Controlling Logins and Passwords

The most basic security tool is login and password control. It governs which users are allowed to log into a file server. The supervisor creates a unique login name for each user who is to be permitted to log into the server. At the supervisor's option, those users also may be required to use passwords each time they log in.

Logging into a file server is the first step to using its resources. If you do not have a login name, you cannot access any of the server's files, run any of the programs it stores, or send jobs to its connected printers.

Logging in is simple. Type *login* and then receive the response ENTER YOUR LOGIN NAME. If your network has just one file server, enter your login name. If you have multiple file servers, respond by typing the name of the file server to which you want to log in, followed by either a slash (/) or a backslash (\) and your login name. If your server is called SERV1 and your login name on that server is ADAM, for example, respond with

SERV1/ADAM

or

SERV1\ADAM

If you are using a password, the system asks you to enter it. What you enter is not displayed, so someone looking over your shoulder cannot learn your password.

You can shorten the process slightly by typing everything on one line:

LOGIN SERV1/ADAM

After you are logged into a server, you also can log into additional ones. A separate command called ATTACH is used for this purpose. Using ATTACH is just like using LOGIN. You start by typing *attach*, to which you receive the response ENTER YOUR LOGIN NAME. Respond by typing the name of the file server to which you want to attach, a slash or backslash, and your login name. If you are attaching to a server called SERV2 and your login name on that server is GUEST, for example, respond with

SERV2/GUEST

If you are using a password, the system asks you to enter it.

As with LOGIN, you can shorten the process by typing everything on one line:

ATTACH SERV2/GUEST

Controlling Trustee Security and Rights

After you are logged into a server, should you have complete access to its disk contents, as you do on your PC's disk drives? The answer depends on your needs. If you are the network supervisor, then you should have full access. Because the disk is being shared, NetWare allows the network supervisor to grant varying levels of access to different areas of the disk.

NetWare disks, like the hard disks on PCs, are divided into directories. Each directory stores a group of related files. Directories themselves can be divided further into subdirectories. For example, your file server's disk may have one directory called USERS where each user is given a separate subdirectory for personal storage. Another directory, called SOFTWARE, may store network versions of software, such as Lotus 1-2-3, WordPerfect, and dBASE IV. Another directory called ACCTING may store your company's accounting system. Figure 3.2 shows a sample diagram of these directories on a file server's disk.

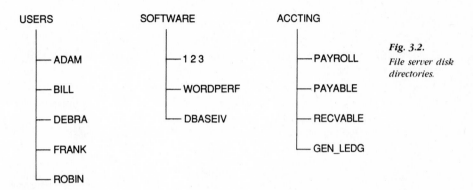

Fig. 3.2.
File server disk directories.

All users do not need the same type of access to each of these directories. In your personal subdirectory in USERS, you need *unlimited* access, with the ability to create, delete, and modify files as you want. But perhaps you should have *limited* access to the SOFTWARE directory, where you need only to be able to run programs, not delete or modify program files. Finally, unless you happen to work in the accounting department, you need *no* access to the ACCTING directory. Figure 3.3 shows the type of access the user named Adam should have to each of the directories on the server disk.

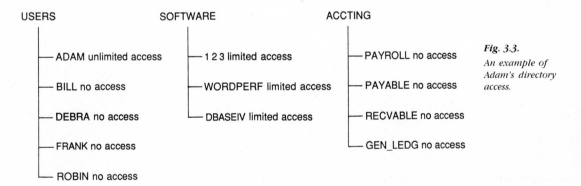

Fig. 3.3.
An example of Adam's directory access.

How does the network supervisor grant these varying levels of control? The supervisor uses a NetWare feature called *trustee security*. To grant a user access to a directory, the supervisor makes that user a trustee to that directory. Being a trustee allows the user to see and use the files in a particular directory. In the example shown in figure 3.3, Adam is a trustee in the ADAM subdirectory under USERS and a trustee to all subdirectories under SOFTWARE. He is not a trustee to the ACCTING directory or to the subdirectories of other users.

The NetWare supervisor can further customize Adam's access by limiting the way in which he can use the files in the SOFTWARE subdirectories. Adam should not be able to delete accidentally the files for the dBASE IV program or to change the default printer selections for WordPerfect. When a user becomes a trustee to a directory, NetWare lets the supervisor give or withhold eight different directory access rights. By deciding which rights to grant, the supervisor can fine-tune Adam's access to the programs in the SOFTWARE directory. The access rights are listed in table 3.1.

Table 3.1
Access Rights

Access right	Allows user to
READ	Read from (or run) files
WRITE	Write to existing files
OPEN	Open existing files
CREATE	Create new files
DELETE or ERASE	Delete files
PARENTAL or ACCESS CONTROL	Create new subdirectories and be a "minisupervisor" to that directory, granting rights to other users
SEARCH or FILE SCAN	Search the directory's file list
MODIFY	Change file attributes and names
SUPERVISORY	Grants all the above rights

The ability to control NetWare trustee rights is one of the most powerful security tools at the network supervisor's disposal, but it is also one of the most complicated. In Chapter 11, you can study NetWare rights in exhaustive detail.

Making the Network Easy To Use

In addition to making the sharing of resources safe, NetWare also makes it easy. The first step to making network files easy to access is to make file server disks look just like local disks to your PC. The disks on your PC are automatically assigned drive letters. Your first floppy disk is designated with the letter A and is referred to as *drive A*. The hard disk on your PC is assigned letter C.

When you load the NetWare shell, it automatically creates a new drive letter, which points to the disk on the file server to which the shell links. On most PCs, that drive letter is F. PC DOS Versions 3.0 and later automatically reserve letters A through E for local drives, so NetWare assigns F because it is the next available letter. If you have more local disks than A through E, the shell picks the next available letter.

After you are logged in, NetWare's MAP command permits you to assign the drive letter of your choosing to any disk on any file server to which you are logged in (the MAP command is discussed in detail in Chapter 9). To run WordPerfect, for example, you can use the MAP command to make the network disk and directory where WordPerfect is stored drive F and make your personal network storage area drive G.

The process of manually using MAP to create drive letters can get tedious in time. If you generally use the same mappings every time you log in, you can create a *login script* that sets up your favorite drive mappings automatically at login. The login script, which is similar in function to the AUTOEXEC.BAT file in DOS, has other uses and is the number one tool for creating a friendly environment once you log into a file server. An entire chapter of this book is devoted to creating useful login scripts (see Chapter 16, "Creating Login Scripts").

In addition to drive letters, you will find other aspects of using network disks to be familiar. Nearly all the standard DOS and OS/2 commands you use to manipulate files and move among directories can be used on NetWare file server disks just as you use the commands on your local drives.

NetWare also includes a powerful menu-building utility. With this feature, you can create menus that look professional but are surprisingly easy to create and modify. Menus are an excellent way to make network resources such as programs and printers easy to use, especially for less-experienced users. Menu building is discussed in Chapter 21.

Handling Network Printing

A network makes sharing many types of hardware possible, including modems, facsimile machines, and host gateways. By far the most common category of shared network hardware is printers. Just as a printer is the first peripheral you buy when you purchase a PC, a printer is probably the first shared peripheral you install when you set up a network.

Almost all types of PC software are designed to produce printed output. For network printer sharing to be useful, it must work no matter what word processor, database, spreadsheet, or graphics package you decide to throw at the printer. Printing through the network must be no different from printing to a locally attached printer, as far as your software is concerned. In other words, when you use a network printer, your software must be "fooled" into thinking that a real printer is attached to your PC.

The NetWare shell plays a big role in making this process work. When you decide to use a network printer, you execute a NetWare command called CAPTURE. It tells the NetWare shell to "capture" the output that would normally go to a local printer and to redirect that output to the network printer you select. The software doing the actual printing is unaware of this redirection and sends its output normally.

Your print output is redirected to the file server to which the network printer is attached. The output is converted to a file as it is received and stored on the file server disk. When your print output is complete, the file is closed.

If the printer is not busy, your job immediately starts printing. If another user's job currently has the printer occupied, your job file is stored in what is called a *print queue* and is printed when the printer becomes available. Figure 3.4 illustrates how the process of printing to a network printer works.

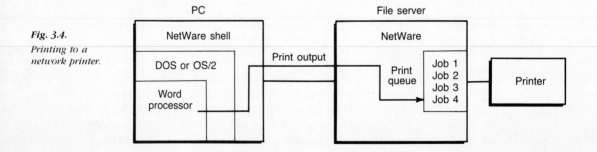

Fig. 3.4.
Printing to a network printer.

NetWare lets you manage print queues in interesting ways. If your boss has just finished sending print output to the print queue and is upset because 10 print jobs are in the queue ahead of his, you can easily move his job to the front of the line. If another user accidentally outputs to the print queue a 300-page report rather than the 3-page letter that was supposed to be sent, you can cancel that print job and save paper and printer time. If you need to print a detailed graph that you know will tie up the printer for a long time, you can tell the print queue not to release your job to the network printer until after working hours. Because of the control over the print queue that NetWare gives you, using a network printer can be more convenient in many ways than using a local printer. (For more information on these printing options, see Chapter 15.)

Chapter Summary

In this chapter, you learned that NetWare is a complex and multifaceted product. Thanks to its security features, users can safely share access to file server disks. You also learned that you can use NetWare's MAP command and login script feature to make server-based programs and files easy to access and use. Using a shared printer is also easy and gives you the added benefit of greater control over when your job is printed.

In the hands of a well-informed and creative network supervisor, Netware offers abundant possibilities and can be the foundation on which you can build a productive LAN. The next chapter will help you learn to make good decisions in selecting other software and hardware for your network.

Part II

Installing NetWare

Includes

Selecting Software and Hardware
Generating NetWare 286
Installing NetWare 286
Installing NetWare 386
Activating Workstations

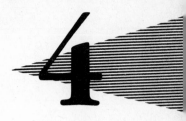

Selecting Software and Hardware

Creating a successful network starts with making some important hardware and software decisions. This chapter steps you through the factors you need to consider in order to make an intelligent selection of your operating system, file server, and network communication system.

Choosing the Appropriate Version of NetWare

If you are reading this book, you have probably already decided that NetWare will be your network operating system. But your choice does not end there; you have to select the version of NetWare that is best suited to your needs.

Three major versions of NetWare are available. *NetWare 286* has long been the mainstay of the NetWare family and is probably the most widely used network operating system in the world. *NetWare 386* is the most recent addition to the NetWare family. NetWare 386 is designed to run on 80386 or 80486 server PCs and is the most capable, flexible, and robust network operating system that you can buy. Servers running both NetWare 286 and NetWare 386 can coexist on the same network.

ELS NetWare is a third version of NetWare designed for small networks. Providing many of the same features as NetWare 286 and 386, ELS NetWare limits the number of users who can connect to the server to either four or eight. Table 4.1 compares NetWare versions feature-by-feature. Each version of NetWare is discussed in the following sections.

Table 4.1
Comparing NetWare Versions

	Netware 386	NetWare 286 Advanced	NetWare 286 SFT	ELS NetWare Level II	ELS NetWare Level I
Maximum Concurrent Users per Server	250	100	100	8	4
Maximum Disks	1,024	32	32	2	2
Maximum Files per Volume	2,097,152	32,000	32,000	32,000	24,000
Maximum Files Concurrently Open	100,000	1,000	1,000	1,000	1,000
Volumes per Server	32	32	32	32	32
Maximum Volume Size	32T*	255M	255M	255M	255M
Maximum Number of Disks per Volume	32	1	1	1	1
Maximum Server Memory	4G*	12M	12M	8M	8M
Minimum Server Memory	2M	2M	2M	640K	1.2M (dedicated) 1 M (non-dedicated)
Server CPU Types Supported	80386 80486	80286 80386 80486	80286 80386 80486	80286 80386 80386	80286 80386 80486

	Netware 386	NetWare 286 Advanced	NetWare 286 SFT	ELS NetWare Level II	ELS NetWare Level I
Nondedicated Servers	no	yes	no	yes	yes (except 8088/ 8086)
Hot Fix	yes	yes	yes	yes	yes
Disk Mirroring	yes	no	yes	no	no
Transaction Tracking	yes	no	yes	no	no
Printers per Server	16	5	5	5	5

* *Terabytes.* 1T = 1000G.
** *Gigabytes.* 1G = 1000M.

NetWare 286

Two versions of NetWare 286 are available: Advanced NetWare and SFT NetWare. Advanced NetWare is the most frequently used of the two versions, so it will be discussed first.

Advanced NetWare

Advanced NetWare is the mainstay of the NetWare family and is the version of NetWare most often used for medium- to large-size networks. It permits 100 users to access a file server simultaneously and allows multiple servers to exist on the same LAN. You have the choice of operating the server as dedicated or nondedicated (see Chapter 2).

Advanced NetWare is rich in features. It comes with an extremely powerful security and access accounting system and gives you tools to make file servers easy for the people on your network to use. All these features are discussed in later chapters.

Advanced NetWare also protects you from certain types of disk failure with a feature called Hot Fix. This feature checks all data after it has been written to the file server disk (this process is called *read after write verification*). If data written to a certain area of the disk fails this check, Advanced NetWare rewrites the data to another part of the disk and marks the failed area as unusable.

Advanced NetWare 286 is designed to run on PCs that use the 80286 or 80386 CPU. To maximize performance, this NetWare version uses what is called the protected mode of the 80286, meaning that the CPU's full capability is used. PC DOS, on the other hand, uses the real mode of the 80286, which is a slower mode designed to make the 80286 compatible with the less capable 8088 of the IBM XT. If none of this information makes sense to you, don't worry. CPUs are discussed in detail later in this chapter (see the section entitled "The Central Processing Unit").

SFT NetWare

SFT stands for System Fault Tolerant, and SFT NetWare is true to its name. It adds two features to Advanced NetWare that enhance system reliability. First, SFT NetWare enables you to "mirror" file server hard disks. Mirrored hard disks exist in pairs, and each disk is an exact duplicate of the other.

Hard disks are mechanical devices and are more prone to failure than most other PC components. The consequences of hard disk failure are quite severe; you lose not only your disk but also the data it contains. SFT NetWare gives you extra insurance against data loss because your data exists on two disks rather than one. SFT NetWare also minimizes the disruption of disk failure. If one disk fails, the other continues to operate until you have the opportunity to down the server and correct the problem.

Novell provides disk fault tolerance with two options: *disk duplexing*, in which both hard disks and controllers are backed up by spares, and *disk mirroring*, in which only the hard disk drives, not the controllers, are duplicated.

SFT's second reliability enhancement is called the Transaction Tracking System (TTS). TTS is a software feature that allows you to protect network database applications from data corruption due to incomplete or aborted transactions. Database files can be damaged because of an event such as a workstation crash in the middle of a database update. TTS allows you to "back out" of an incomplete transaction and restore the data file to its condition before it was corrupted.

You have the choice when you install SFT NetWare of using or not using disk mirroring and TTS. If you need TTS but don't want to invest in an extra hard disk for disk mirroring, for example, SFT NetWare allows you to use TTS but run on only one hard disk. Conversely, you can implement disk mirroring without TTS.

NetWare 386

NetWare 386 is a recent addition to the NetWare family. It offers all the features of Advanced and SFT NetWare 286, and enhances some of the features in useful ways. Like NetWare 286, NetWare 386 has a powerful security and access accounting system and abundant tools to enable you to make file servers easy to use. NetWare 386 also offers the same data-protection features of SFT NetWare 286, including Hot Fix, disk mirroring, and NetWare's Transaction Tracking System.

NetWare 386 outperforms NetWare 286 in two key areas: capacity and flexibility. Although NetWare 286 limits the maximum number of users to 100, NetWare 386 permits 250 users to be logged in to a single server. NetWare 386 also can use more memory and enables you to have extremely large amounts of file-server disk space.

If you are already familiar with NetWare 286, you will appreciate NetWare 386's increased flexibility. With NetWare 286, you often have to stop the server and run special programs to make even minor configuration changes. NetWare 386 enables you to make these changes while the server continues running and remains available to its users. NetWare 386 also is designed to work with a wide variety of communication protocols, so that you probably will be able to connect NetWare 386 servers to an interesting assortment of communication networks. NetWare 286 is limited to NetWare's own IPX (Internetwork Packet Exchange) protocol.

The chief source of NetWare 386's power and flexibility is its use of the protected mode of the 80386 and 80486 processors. Just as NetWare 286 uses the full capability of the 80286 processor, NetWare 386 uses the full capability of the more powerful 80386.

You will read in later chapters about NetWare 386's ability to run programs called *NetWare Loadable Modules* (or NLMs) on the server. This capability increases NetWare 386's usefulness in some interesting ways. Like NetWare 386 itself, NLMs use the full capability of the 80386 processor, making it possible for vendors and in-house programmers to create powerful server-based applications, such as database servers and communication gateways, that operate with an efficiency level that cannot be matched by workstation-based programs.

ELS NetWare

ELS stands for Entry Level Solution. As the name implies, ELS NetWare is designed for small networks. ELS NetWare Level I is for networks of no more than four users and is priced with the budget-conscious buyer in mind. Like Advanced NetWare, ELS NetWare requires an 80286-based file server and permits you to run the file server as a nondedicated PC (as both a server and a workstation simultaneously).

Because it is an older release level of NetWare (Version 2.0), ELS NetWare Level I does not have some of the features and commands described in this book. It is chiefly lacking in network-management utilities, but perhaps that issue is not a big one when your maximum network size is four users.

ELS NetWare Level II, on the other hand, is current with the latest NetWare release level (2.1x). This version includes all the features and commands of Advanced NetWare. With Level II, you can have double the number of users (eight). You can operate the server as either dedicated or nondedicated.

Neither version of ELS NetWare allows you to use more than one file server per network, which is probably unnecessary anyway on four- and eight-user systems. ELS NetWare can be a cost-effective way to begin a network. If your system grows beyond its capabilities, you can easily upgrade to Advanced NetWare or SFT NetWare.

Choosing NetWare for Special Situations

NetWare typically uses IBM-compatible 80286 or 80386 PCs as file servers. A special version of NetWare called NetWare VMS, however, uses a DEC VAX minicomputer as a file server. This version is the first of perhaps many implementations of Portable NetWare, which is designed to run on minicomputer and mainframe hosts. (NCR, Prime Computer Corp., Hewlett-Packard, and 22 other vendors have announced support for Portable NetWare.)

NetWare was originally designed to network only IBM-compatible workstations. A new Novell product called NetWare for Macintosh permits Apple Macintosh computers to be networked as well. Special software, called a *value-added process*, or VAP, is added to your file server to enable Macintoshes to access it. Macintoshes can then share most network resources, such as printers and files, with users who have IBM-compatible workstations.

Selecting File Servers

File servers play an important role in determining your network's performance. Simple mathematics tells you that the file server's workload is much higher than that of a typical stand-alone PC. Although a stand-alone PC takes care of the needs of one user at a time, a file server often has to handle the requests of many users simultaneously. NetWare is designed to handle this workload with amazing efficiency, but you can help by making wise hardware decisions as you configure your file server.

In Chapter 2 you learned that a server can be either dedicated or nondedicated. Remember that a nondedicated server functions as both a workstation and server at the same time. You need to be aware of a few cautions about using nondedicated servers.

First, a nondedicated server will be noticeably slower than its dedicated counterpart because the nondedicated server is doing two jobs. Second, running in nondedicated mode is a real test of IBM AT compatibility, so not all AT look-alikes can work as nondedicated servers. The best approach is to check with your NetWare vendor to confirm whether the PC model you plan to use is certified by Novell as working in nondedicated mode.

For larger networks, your file server needs to be the fastest and most efficient PC that you can afford. The following sections examine the factors that govern file server performance.

Figure 4.1 diagrams the major hardware components of the file server. These parts are identical to the components of the typical PC (which should come as no surprise because the file server is nothing more than a computer running the network operating system). These components, the

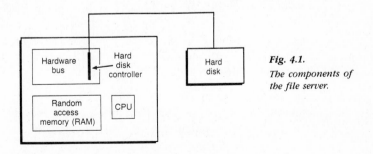

Fig. 4.1.

The components of the file server.

central processing unit, the hard disk and controller, random-access memory (RAM), and the hardware bus, play significant roles in determining the efficiency of your file server.

The Central Processing Unit

The *central processing unit* (CPU) is the component in your PC that performs all processing tasks. The CPU executes the programs you run and controls the operation of all the hardware components of your PC.

PCs are categorized by the types of CPUs they use. For example, XT types of computers use a CPU called the Intel 8088. (Intel is the manufacturer, and 8088 is the model number for the processor chip itself.) AT-compatible computers use a CPU called the Intel 80286. The fastest IBM-compatible computers now use a CPU called the Intel 80386.

Two important factors govern CPU performance. The first is the CPU's data bus size. The *bus* is an electrical pathway for data that connects the CPU with the network card, floppy and hard disk controllers, the video adapter, and other boards in the computer. The size of the data bus determines how much information the CPU can access in one processing cycle. The 8-bit data bus of the 8088 CPU can access 8 bits of data in each processing cycle. The size of the pathway doubles for each successive model of the Intel processors. The 80286 has a 16-bit bus; the 80386, a 32-bit bus. CPUs are often described by this specification. For example, the 80286 is called a "16-bit processor."

As you probably have guessed, the bigger the data bus, the better the performance. Just as you can dig a hole more quickly with a shovel than with a spoon, you can process more information in the same amount of time with a 32-bit processor than you can with a 16- or 8-bit processor.

For the CPU to get the maximum benefit of the data bus, the peripheral boards plugged into the computer—the video, hard disk, memory, and network boards—must also use the maximum size of the pathway. But many video and network cards are designed to work in the oldest Intel models running the 8088 chip, which only supports an 8-bit bus. Most peripherals can work with the newer model CPUs but move data at a speed slower than that which the CPU can handle.

The second performance factor is the CPU's *clock speed*. Although the data bus determines how much data can be accessed in one cycle, the clock speed determines how frequently these cycles occur. The clock speed is measured in megahertz (MHz), or millions of cycles per second. The 8088 CPU in an IBM XT has a clock speed of 4.77 MHz, and 80286 CPUs are available in speeds from 6 to 20 MHz. 80386 CPUs range in speed from 16 to 33 MHz.

Clock speed, data bus, and CPU specifications provide benchmarks for comparing file servers. This comparison is important because CPU performance has a direct bearing on how fast the file server will be able to execute NetWare. Table 4.2 summarizes the comparison of the 8088, 80286, and 80386 CPUs.

Table 4.2
Comparing CPUs

CPU	Data Bus Size	Clock Speeds Available	Can Be Used as Server CPU for These NetWare Versions
8086	8 bits	4.77–10 MHz	ELS Level II (versions previous to 2.15)
80286	16 bits	6–20 MHz	ELS Level I & II NetWare 286
80386	32 bits	16–33 MHz	All

The Hard Disk and Controller

It is not difficult to understand why hard disk performance is critical to the overall efficiency of a file server. Because the file server's primary job is to deliver files to network users, the speed at which files can be retrieved from the server's disk is crucial.

Predicting hard disk performance is a two-part equation. The hard disk and hard disk controller work as a team to respond to read and write requests from NetWare. The *hard disk* itself is a mechanical device consisting of stacked metal platters that can store information magnetically. Information is stored and retrieved by read/write heads that travel across the platter surfaces while the platters rotate.

The *hard disk controller* is a circuit board that, as its name implies, directs the operation of the hard disk. This device controls the travel of the disk's read/write heads so that the correct information is written or read as requested by NetWare.

The speed at which information travels from the hard disk into the file server is relatively slow compared to how fast data moves inside the file server itself. Although information moves inside an 80386 file server at speeds of up to 10 million bits per second, data moves from the hard disk into the file server at only about 1/20 of that at best. Data transfer rates from a hard disk range from 250,000 bits per second to 600,000 bits per second, depending on the type of disk and controller combination you are using. Minimizing this bottleneck by choosing the fastest hard disk system you can afford is obviously in your best interests.

As with CPUs, you need to follow several guidelines in judging hard disk performance. For the hard disk itself, the specification to be aware of is access speed. *Access speed* is a measure of the average time the disk takes to find and read one unit of information. Most drives on the market today have access speeds ranging between 15 and 80 milliseconds (thousandths of a second).

Hard disk controllers are not so simple to rate. NetWare supports three categories of hard disk controllers: ST506 (the standard type of controller used in IBM AT types of computers), ESDI (for Enhanced Small Device Interface, available as an option on some models of the IBM PS/2), and SCSI (for Small Computer System Interface, commonly pronounced "scuzzy").

These three categories vary in both performance and the number and sizes of hard disks that you can attach. The ST506 type of controller has a data transfer rate of 5–7 megabits per second and can support a maximum of two disk drives. The drives that you can connect can be up to 150M in size. ESDI controllers have a data transfer rate of 10 megabits and can support a maximum of four disk drives. These controllers can deal with larger disks. Sizes of 100M to 300M are common, and you can use disks up to 600M on the high end.

Novell offers its own high-speed SCSI controller option. Called the *disk coprocessor board*, it improves disk performance by placing a special processor in the file server to relieve the CPU of disk-management tasks. Using this option, you can achieve a data transfer rate of 10 megabits, and you can use up to 32 disk drives. Currently, you can find hard disk drives as large as 700M that have a SCSI interface.

When selecting a disk configuration, you need to consider another factor besides performance. You need to choose a setup that gives you enough capacity to meet your long-term file storage needs. Although no hard and fast rule is available for predicting your future requirements for disk space, an experienced LAN supervisor has a good guiding principle: calculate your worst case requirements and double them!

The next chapter returns to the subject of disks when it discusses preparing file server disks for the installation of NetWare.

Random-Access Memory

Random-access memory (RAM) is used in a PC as an area to store information for the CPU to read. The CPU cannot read information directly from a hard disk but can direct the disk controller to move information from the hard disk into memory. When you talk about CPU cycles and clock speed, you are referring to the process whereby the CPU periodically looks into memory.

Considering Clock Speed

Like the CPU, memory has a clock speed, which affects the speed at which information moves to and from RAM to the CPU. For this reason, RAM chip costs rise with the speed of the chip. The clock speed of memory is a combination of measurements:

❑ The speed of the bus
❑ The width of the bus
❑ The number of wait states
❑ The speed of the memory chips

Most PCs are designed to permit the use of slower RAM chips with a faster CPU. The CPU compensates for the slowness of the RAM by using *wait states*—skipping a cycle or two between memory accesses to give the slower RAM the opportunity to "catch up." When a PC is advertised as operating with one wait state, the CPU skips one cycle between each memory access. When RAM is at zero wait states, the CPU accesses memory on every cycle, which is obviously more efficient (and probably more expensive). If you can afford it, make sure that the PC you use as a file server has RAM with zero wait states.

How NetWare Uses Memory

In addition to memory *quality*, as discussed in the previous section, you need to consider memory *quantity*. Memory is the key to NetWare's capacity to give many users fast access to one file server disk. Thanks to NetWare's clever use of memory, the performance when you're accessing the file server's disk compares favorably with the access speed you enjoy when you're using a local hard disk.

NetWare uses memory as a high-speed buffer for the file server hard disk. The hard disk's directory (the list of files the disk contains) and file allocation table, or FAT (the table that tells where each file is stored on the disk), are stored completely in server memory. This method is called *directory caching*. When you use the DOS or OS/2 DIR command to list the files on an IBM-compatible PC's disk, notice that the disk access light comes on because the directory must be read from the disk itself. If you repeat the same operation on a NetWare disk, the disk light on the server does not come on, because the directory is read from server memory.

What does directory caching do to improve performance? Because the disk directory and FAT are in memory, the server's CPU can access them instantly. The simple process of learning the location of a file on the server's hard disk is almost immediate because, unlike DOS or OS/2, a NetWare server does not need to look at its disk just to learn where to find a file.

NetWare further capitalizes on this technique by using what is called *directory hashing*. When a user requests a file on a file server, NetWare does not start at the top of the directory list and search until finding the directory entry for the requested file. Instead, the system intelligently divides the directory list into smaller parts and searches only a subset of the whole list. You do a form of hashing when you look up a name in a phone book. Rather than start with the first name in the book and read until you find the right name, you begin looking in the section that contains last names starting with the same letter as the name you are looking for.

In addition to directory caching and hashing, which speed up the process of initially locating a file, NetWare also uses a technique called *file caching* to speed up the use of the file after it's found. The parts of the file you are using are kept in server memory on a space-available basis. If you use your word processor to retrieve a large document, NetWare intelligently caches parts of that file in memory. As you page through the document, your word processor reads more and more of the file from the server. Chances are you will be reading from memory instead of disk, thanks to NetWare's file caching. If you make changes to the file and save it, you are writing the file to server memory first (and your word processor may tell you it is finished saving the file sooner than you expect). While you and your word processor move on to other business, NetWare moves the file from memory to disk. (For safety's sake, NetWare makes sure that this move happens within a few seconds.)

To use caching and hashing to optimum benefit, you must have memory in proportion to the amount of disk space and the number of files you expect to store on your server.

The Hardware Bus

If you have ever opened a PC to add a new board, you have worked with the hardware bus. The hardware bus facilitates the communication between the PC and its added boards, including network adapters, disk controllers, parallel and serial ports, and add-in memory boards.

The hardware bus plays an important role in server efficiency. Because it is the medium that handles all communication between the central processing unit and the server PC's add-in boards and devices, the bus's performance dictates how efficiently information can be moved from the server memory and hard disk to its network adapter. The faster that information can move from the server disk and memory to its network adapter, the faster network users receive information they request from the server.

Like the CPU, the two factors that govern the performance of the hardware bus are its data bus size and its speed. The data bus size is a measure of how much information can be moved across the hardware bus in one cycle, and the speed is a measure of how rapidly the hardware bus can transmit information.

Three standard types of buses are currently used in 80286, 80386, and 80486 PCs. The Industry Standard Architecture (ISA) bus is found in AT-compatible PCs. The ISA bus supports data bus sizes of 8 and 16 bits, and can transmit information at speeds ranging up to 1.6 megabits per second. Two higher performance hardware buses have been introduced recently. The Micro Channel Architecture (MCA) bus supports data bus sizes of 16 and 32 megabits and can use an advanced technique called bus mastering to achieve a speed of up to 40 megabits per second. The MCA bus is found in IBM PS/2 computers. The Extended Industry Standard Architecture (EISA) bus supports data bus sizes of 8, 16, and 32 bits and also can use bus mastering to achieve speeds of up to 32 megabits per second.

Experts are divided about whether the MCA or EISA hardware bus is a better choice when a high-performance server PC is needed (although no one disputes the fact that PCs with these buses are significantly more expensive than ISA bus PCs). If you are in a position to afford the higher cost of an MCA or EISA bus server PC, make sure that the network adapter type you plan to use is available for the hardware bus that you choose. (You will learn about choosing network adapters and a communication system later in this chapter.)

Fast file servers result in happy network users. By correctly choosing the best file server components and matching them to the best version of NetWare, the prospects for having satisfied users are excellent.

Selecting Your Network Communication System

Discussing all network communication systems in detail is beyond the scope of this book, for the subject is at least as involved as NetWare itself. This chapter, however, covers a few things you should consider as you select a network communication system.

The network communication system consists of network adapters, which are installed in each PC and file server on your LAN, and the cable and other devices that connect the adapters. Many products are available, and you may find the variety quite confusing. If you don't have the budget to recable your facility, your choice may be dictated by the type of cable that is already available, or your company may have already standardized on a particular type of system. Fortunately, NetWare is designed to run on almost any type of network communication system.

If the decision is not already made for you, then you need to consider a few factors as you make your choice. First, will this network communication system support enough connections to meet your long-term needs? All network communication systems specify a maximum number of users, which is usually indicative of how robust the system is. Some permit as few as 50, most can handle 100 to 250, and a few are unlimited. Network communication systems also advertise a data transfer rate, which is a measure of how many bits of information are transmitted in a certain amount of time. For example, EtherNet networks have a data transfer rate of 10 megabits per second, and IBM's Token Ring network transfers at 4 or 16 megabits per second.

Obviously, the more bits transmitted, the faster the network. But this figure is a dangerous specification to rely on solely, because much of the transfer rate can be used up with overhead functions like network-address management and sending acknowledgments. Experts point out that EtherNet and IBM Token Ring use as much as half of their data transfer rate in this way, leaving only the other half for the transmission of real data.

You also should consider whether the network communication system will permit cable runs long enough to meet your long-term needs. Nearly all systems can handle networking one floor, but if you are networking an entire building or campus, you need a system capable of handling long-distance connections.

Most network communication systems use one of three topologies. (*Topology* refers to the physical pattern of the network cable and communication devices.) These topologies—linear bus, ring, and distributed star—are diagrammed in figure 4.2.

Four different cable types are used: coaxial (also used by IBM terminals), unshielded twisted-pair (the same as is used for telephones), shielded twisted-pair, and fiber-optic cable. Fortunately, enough variety exists in the world of network communication systems that you are bound to have at least one good choice for the type of cable you have or plan to install.

Currently, the three most popular networks are EtherNet, ARCnet, and IBM Token Ring. EtherNet and ARCnet use coaxial, twisted-pair, or fiber-optic cable; IBM Token Ring supports either twisted-pair or fiber-optic. All three of these networks work well and provide reliable, fast transmission—just how reliable and how fast is determined by design and workmanship.

Cable is a major source of network-management problems. Problems can be caused when the wrong materials are used, the connections are fabricated improperly, or out-of-spec wiring standards are used. Be sure to employ experienced installers who will test the cable system for you.

When comparing the costs of alternative systems and components, consider the costs of operation and the system limits, not just the up-front costs. You cannot predict the winner of the Indianapolis 500 by choosing the car with the most horsepower. Likewise, you cannot pick the fastest LAN by choosing the system with the highest transmission speed. Other considerations are involved. You need to think about throughput versus transmission speed, the type of traffic the network will support, the impact of network performance on the users (such as the effect on productivity and user satisfaction), the system's reliability, and the cost per node through one year of operation.

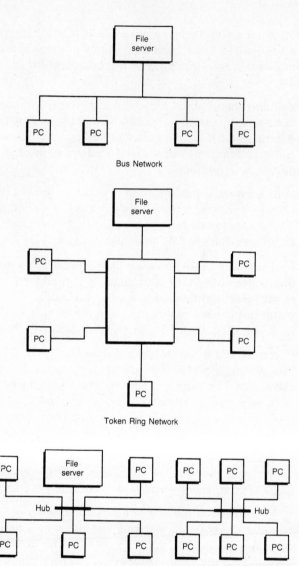

Fig. 4.2.
Comparing cable topologies.

Designing Your Network

After you have chosen the communication system, server types, and version of NetWare to include in your network, you need to combine these components into one efficient and responsive system. These individual components are like soldiers in an army, and you are the commanding general. You must decide how many soldiers to put on the various fronts in your ongoing war against slow network performance.

Multiple Servers

Based on your previous reading, you already know that NetWare enables you to use multiple servers on one network. Dividing your network's workload among several servers may be a useful way to improve performance. If your network is the host system to a particularly busy database application called on to produce numerous reports and respond quickly to on-line queries for information, for example, you may be wise to dedicate a server to that task. Doing so accomplishes two goals: the database application will run more quickly because all the server's resources are dedicated to it, and other tasks, such as electronic mail and personal user storage, will not be affected during those times when the database application "thrashes" the server disk (such as when it is rebuilding indexes or running complex reports).

You also can mix NetWare 286 and NetWare 386 on one LAN to your advantage. NetWare 286 can be used for those situations in which good performance and a maximum of 100 users are enough. NetWare 386 can be used for bigger and tougher jobs, such as on the server for the previously mentioned database or in cases in which up to 250 users must use the same server. NetWare 386's capacity to combine disks to create one volume can be selectively used when you must store very large amounts of data.

Figure 4.3 shows a planning worksheet for a network that will consist of five servers. Three of the servers will be used by members of individual departments, and two will be used by everyone.

Multiple Networks

NetWare lets you divide the workload of the network communication system by separating your network into individual physical networks. Each network is a separate communication system, but the network is linked or "bridged" to all others so that the users on one network can access all the servers and resources on another.

```
SERV1
USERS:                    Accting Dept (47 workstations)
APPLICATIONS:             Personal storage
                          Electronic mail
                          Company accounting system
NETWARE VERSION:          286 Advanced
DISK STORAGE:             2 disks, 200M each
PRINTERS:                 1 laser printer


SERV2
USERS:                    Sales Dept (65 workstations)
APPLICATIONS:             Personal storage
                          Electronic mail
NETWARE VERSION:          286 Advanced
DISK STORAGE:             1 disk, 200M
PRINTERS:                 1 laser printer
                          1 dot-matrix printer

SERV3
USERS:                    Marketing Dept (53 workstations)
APPLICATIONS:             Personal storage
                          Electronic mail
NETWARE VERSION:          286 Advanced
DISK STORAGE:             2 disks, 200M each
PRINTERS:                 1 laser printer
                          1 plotter


SERV4
USERS:                    Everyone
APPLICATIONS:             Inventory database
NETWARE VERSION:          386
DISK STORAGE:             2 mirrored disks, 150M each

SERV5
USERS:                    Everyone
APPLICATIONS:             Shared software
                            Word processor
                            Spreadsheet
                            Database manager
                            Graphics package
                          Archived transaction records
NETWARE VERSION:          386
DISK STORAGE:             2 disks, 200M each, linked as
                          one volume
```

Fig. 4.3.

A planning worksheet for a network that will consist of five servers.

Dividing a large network into smaller individual networks has several advantages. The first advantage is performance. The response time on a smaller network is improved because fewer workstations are being handled by each network. Dividing your network communication system also makes sense from a reliability standpoint. When a network adapter in one workstation fails, the entire network communication system is often affected, making it impossible for users to access servers until the problem is resolved. If you split your network into several smaller networks, then a network adapter or cable failure will affect only the users on that network; the rest of the users can use their networks normally.

You link networks together by placing two or more network adapters in a file server or in a separate PC called a bridge. A file server that links multiple networks by using two or more network adapters is called an *internal bridge*. A separate PC used for this function is called an *external bridge*.

Figures 4.4 and 4.5 show two possible designs for the five-server network planned in figure 4.3. Figure 4.4 shows all users connected to one network, and figure 4.5 shows three individual networks bridged together. Notice that SERV4 and SERV5 are internal bridges, linking networks 1, 2, and 3 to each other.

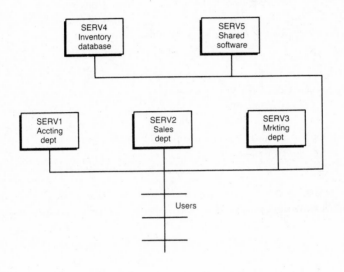

Fig. 4.4.

Placing all users and servers on one common network.

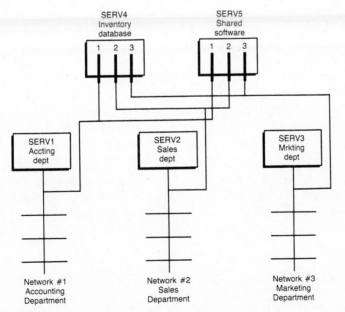

Fig. 4.5.

The same network redesigned to divide the network communication system into separate networks.

Bridging has one major disadvantage. Network supervisors report that users who access a server on another network instead of their own experience 30 percent less performance than when accessing a server on their own networks. Look at the design shown in figure 4.5 for an example. A user in the accounting department (network #1) will experience good performance on SERV1, SERV4, and SERV5 because these servers are all on the user's network. The user will experience poorer performance when accessing SERV2 and SERV3 because these servers are on network #2 and network #3, respectively. Fortunately, users in the accounting department seldom or never have to use SERV2 and SERV3, because they contain only the personal storage and electronic mail for users in other departments.

There is a use for bridging networks other than for fine-tuning network performance. Bridging offers a method whereby two different communication system types, such as EtherNet and Token Ring, can be joined. If you have an EtherNet communication system and you want to link your LAN to the network in another department (which happens to have a Token Ring communication system), you can do so by using a bridge.

When you create a network, NetWare asks that you give each physical network a unique number. In figure 4.5, the numbers 1, 2, and 3 are used.

Chapter Summary

In this chapter, you learned that the choices you make as you plan your network determine whether it will be responsive and able to handle the growth that almost inevitably will occur as your LAN provides useful benefits to its users. NetWare itself is designed to provide almost amazing performance. You should choose the other components of your LAN to do the same, insofar as your budget permits. Develop a well thought-out network design that will enable those components to work together with peak efficiency.

Now that you have learned the ingredients that make up a good network, you should be able to make an informed choice of your software and hardware components. The next chapter tells you how to generate NetWare 286.

Generating
NetWare 286

Installing NetWare 286 on a server is a process with many steps. If you are installing NetWare for the first time, you may feel intimidated by the many pages of documentation and stacks of disks that confront you as you open NetWare 286's big red box.

You can combat this uneasiness by taking a little time to plan your installation. You probably need to take the following steps as part of your installation strategy:

1. Design your network cabling and server layout.

2. Install and configure your server hardware.

3. Make backup copies of your NetWare disks, upload them to a hard disk or file server, or do both.

4. Generate NetWare so that it is configured to match your network and server specifications.

5. Install NetWare on your servers.

6. Place your servers in a safe operating environment.

7. Install network adapters in workstations and create NetWare workstation shells for these adapters.

In the previous chapter, you learned about the first step: designing your network communication system and server layout. In this chapter, you will learn about installing and configuring your server and using NetWare's

53

NETGEN utility to generate a copy of NetWare 286 to match your configuration. In the next chapter, you will explore the steps required to install NetWare 286 on a server. If you are installing NetWare 386, you can skip Chapter 6 and move to Chapter 7, "Installing NetWare 386."

Installing and Configuring Your Server Hardware

Depending on how your organization handles the procurement and installation of computer equipment, the PC that is to become your file server may arrive in varying stages of preparation. The computer may have everything ready to go, or it may arrive in bits and pieces.

Preparing a PC for NetWare installation is similar to preparing a PC for installing DOS or OS/2. The PC must have all floppy and hard drives connected. Memory must be installed; the display adapter and serial and parallel ports required to run the printers you plan to connect to the server must be in place. Finally, you must run the PC's setup program to make sure that it recognizes the memory and disk drives that are installed.

If you are using a SCSI disk drive configuration in combination with Novell's disk coprocessor board, your disks are not recognized by DOS or OS/2, and you cannot verify that they work until you try to install NetWare. You should follow the manufacturer's instructions closely or arrange for the assistance of an experienced installer.

At some point, you also need to install the network adapter in your server. If you know how the network adapter should be configured, you can install it when you first configure the server. Because you are shown a number of options for configuring your network adapter during the steps you follow to generate NetWare, you may want to install the adapter later. Waiting is suggested if you are using your server as an internal bridge and installing multiple network adapters (see Chapter 4) or if you are installing network adapters of different types (such as Token Ring and ARCnet).

When the server PC is configured, you are ready to begin generating NetWare 286.

Generating NetWare

NetWare 286 can work with a wide variety of network adapters and hard disk types. Because of its flexibility, you must generate (or "gen" in the lingo of veteran network supervisors) a customized copy of NetWare 286 to match the server configuration you plan to use.

Perhaps you are a bit stunned by the many disks included in the NetWare 286 package. These disks fall into two categories: disks used to generate NetWare and disks containing the NetWare operating system commands and files. These files are copied to the server disk in the final stages of installation. Disks are also included to enable you to create external bridges. (For more information on external bridges, see Chapter 4.)

Use the DOS DISKCOPY command to make working copies of all the NetWare disks. Because the 5 1/4-inch version of NetWare 286 consists of almost 40 disks, this requirement may seem cumbersome. If you own only one copy of NetWare, making a backup copy is worth the investment in time and disks. If you own several copies of NetWare, you can depend on the safety-in-numbers principle to protect you from the consequences of disk failure. One complete backup copy of your NetWare operating system disks should be stored in a safe place.

Regardless of whether you decide to back up some or all of the NetWare disks, you must make working copies of the following disks:

- ❏ NETGEN
- ❏ AUXGEN
- ❏ SUPPORT
- ❏ OSEXE-1
- ❏ OSEXE-2
- ❏ UTILEXE-1
- ❏ UTILEXE-2

Label your working copies with the same name as the original disks, because you are prompted to use these disks by name many times during the installation process.

If you are using NetWare Version 2.15 or later, you also should use DISKCOPY to back up the disk labeled GENDATA. With NetWare versions before 2.15, the GENDATA disk cannot be backed up. In all versions of NetWare, the GENDATA disk is used for preventing illegal copying of NetWare and creates a unique identification number for the NetWare operating system files you generate. If you use the same GENDATA to create two sets of operating system files, you are violating your license agreement for NetWare. Rumors abound as to what happens when two servers with the same identification number are on the same LAN. The rumor is that the users on the offending servers receive about every two minutes error messages identifying the violation. These messages interrupt whatever the user is working on and render the network virtually unusable.

You should label your GENDATA disk with the name of the server the disk was used to generate so that no possibility exists for inadvertently using the disk to generate another one.

To generate NetWare, use a PC with at least one floppy drive and 640K of RAM. Boot the PC with your DOS CONFIG.SYS file set to FILES = 20 and BUFFERS = 15. You have four options when deciding how to work with the disks and files used to generate NetWare. You can work entirely with floppies, work with floppies and a RAM disk, copy the generation files to a local hard disk, or copy them to a server disk.

If possible, copy the files to a local hard disk or server volume. If you use the floppy-only or RAM-drive method, you will be astounded at the number of times you switch disks in your floppy drive. The process is very slow and must be repeated any time a major change occurs to your server (such as when you add another network adapter to make it an internal bridge or change to another disk drive type). Loading the files to a hard disk or server is easy and gives you an instantly available copy of the NetWare files so that you easily can make configuration changes or generate new servers. A working copy of the files requires approximately 5M on your hard drive.

Starting NETGEN

NETGEN is the NetWare utility you use to configure and generate copies of NetWare. To start NETGEN, insert your working copy of the NetWare disk labeled NETGEN into a floppy drive. Make that drive the default drive (for example, type *a:* and then press Enter if you are using drive A). Type

    NETGEN

and press Enter to start NETGEN.

If you are using a NetWare utility for the first time, you are getting your first taste of NetWare's menu interface. To execute a menu option, use the up- and down-arrow keys to highlight the option; then press Enter. To leave a menu or display window, press the Esc key.

Choosing NETGEN's Default or Custom Level

The first screen prompts you to choose to use NETGEN at either the default or custom level (see fig. 5.1). The default level of NETGEN handles almost all server configuration requirements with a minimum of complexity and time and is the best choice for beginners or for situations where no unusual configurations are built.

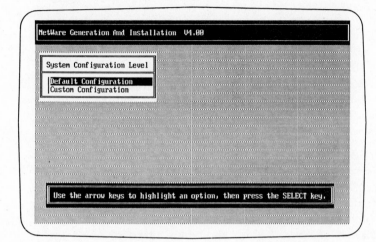

Fig. 5.1.

The System Configuration Level menu.

The default level of NETGEN does not allow you to specify settings for the network adapters that are installed in your server. When you specify a network adapter's settings, you designate which memory address, I/O (Input/Output) ports, interrupts, and DMA (Direct Memory Access) channels the adapter uses. Each type of adapter uses at least one of these methods to communicate with the PC in which it is installed, and some use two or three. Many other common PC devices use these methods also. You do not have to know how these methods work; you only need to know that, in most cases, no two devices in your server can use the same interrupt, memory address, I/O port, or DMA channel.

How Network Adapters Talk to PCs

You do not have to be an expert on the methods network adapters use to communicate with the PC in which they are installed, but knowing what each method is and how it is used helps. Each type of network adapter uses one or more of the following methods:

Memory address: If your network adapter has its own ROM instructions, your PC must allocate a memory address to store the instructions. When you configure NetWare for a network adapter that uses a memory address, you must specify the address to be used, and that address cannot be used by any other device in the PC. The IBM Token Ring adapter and most ARCnet adapters use memory addresses for ROM instructions. Memory addresses are expressed as four-digit hexadecimal numbers, such as D000 or C800.

I/O ports: I/O ports are a standard method PCs use to communicate with input/output devices, such as network adapters, serial ports, and disk controllers. I/O ports are like mailing addresses used by the device and the PC to send messages to each other. Each device using an I/O port must have its own address. An I/O port address is expressed as a range of three-digit hexadecimal numbers, showing both the starting (low) and ending (high) addresses, such as 2F8–2FF.

Interrupts: An interrupt is a method whereby a device can request the services of the PC's processor. Interrupts are shown as decimal digits, such as 2, 5, or 7. Most network adapters require an interrupt address, and each device must have its own interrupt. Most eight-bit network cards can use interrupts 2, 3, 5, or 7. Sixteen-bit network cards can use these plus interrupts 9, 10, 11, and 12. Table 5.1 lists the interrupts used by standard PC devices.

Table 5.1
Typical Interrupt Assignments

Device	*Assignment*
LPT1	7
LPT2	5
COM1	4
COM2	3
AT Hard Disk Controller	14

DMA channels: DMA, or Direct Memory Access, is used by a device to access memory without "bothering" the CPU. DMA is not widely used by network adapters; neither the IBM Token Ring adapter nor the ARCnet adapter uses it, but some types of EtherNet adapters do. In most cases, a device must have exclusive use of its assigned DMA channel. DMA channels are numbered with the use of decimal integers.

You need to customize these settings only if the server has a number of other devices whose addresses cannot be used. If your server is going to have four printers attached to it, two using parallel ports (LPT1 and LPT2) and two using serial ports (COM1 and COM2), four interrupts (7, 5, 4, and 3) are unavailable for use by network adapters. Rather than dig out your PC's technical reference manual to find this information, you can use the custom level of NETGEN to designate which devices will be installed in the server. If you tell NETGEN that printer ports LPT1, LPT2, COM1, and COM2 will be in use, it automatically reserves the addresses used by these devices and does not pick the same addresses for your network adapters.

To choose the custom or default level of NETGEN, highlight your selection and press Enter.

Choosing Where NETGEN Looks for Files

NETGEN next prompts you to choose one of its four run options:

❏ Standard (floppy disks)
❏ RAM disk
❏ Hard disk
❏ Network drive

Your selection determines whether NETGEN uses floppies, floppies and a RAM disk, a local disk, or a server drive as the source of its configuration and generation files.

Select Standard (floppy disks) if you have prepared working copies of NetWare's disks and you do not want to copy configuration and generation files to a local hard disk or server volume. Select RAM Disk if you have used DOS's VDISK driver or a similar method to create a RAM disk of at least 1M in size, and you want to use it to augment the floppy-based method of configuration. The RAM disk method eliminates some of the disk swapping because the RAM drive is used for temporarily storing some of the configuration files. Either of these first two methods involves extensive disk swapping and is slow. (If you sense a strong recommendation not to use these methods, you have sensed correctly!)

If you select Standard (floppy disks), you are prompted to begin inserting the appropriate disks during the configuration process. If you select RAM Disk, you are prompted to enter the drive letter of the RAM disk you plan to use.

Uploading Configuration Files to a Disk

If you plan to select Hard Disk or Network Drive from NETGEN's Run Options menu, you first need to be aware of how and where NETGEN uploads its configuration files. When you select either option, you are prompted to enter the drive letter for the disk you plan to use. That disk's default directory is the starting point for the uploading of NetWare files. Under that directory, a subdirectory called NETWARE is created, followed by a series of subdirectories, as shown in figure 5.2. The default directory on the drive you select must be the directory where you want these subdirectories created.

NETWARE

Fig. 5.2.

NetWare
subdirectories
created by NETGEN.

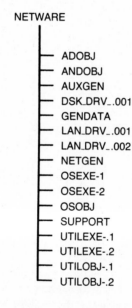

- ADOBJ
- ANDOBJ
- AUXGEN
- DSK_DRV_.001
- GENDATA
- LAN_DRV_.001
- LAN_DRV_.002
- NETGEN
- OSEXE-1
- OSEXE-2
- OSOBJ
- SUPPORT
- UTILEXE-.1
- UTILEXE-.2
- UTILOBJ-.1
- UTILOBJ-.2

You may want to exit NETGEN for a moment and change to or create the directory you want to use. To exit NETGEN, press Esc. Change to the drive on which you plan to upload your files (for example, if the drive you plan to use is C, switch to it by typing *c:* and pressing Enter). Change to the directory you plan to use as the beginning of the subdirectory structure shown in figure 5.2 or create the directory by using the DOS MD (MAKE DIRECTORY) command. You may want to make this directory name correspond to the NetWare version number you are uploading, such as ANET215 for Advanced NetWare Version 2.15. (To create a directory by this name, type *md\anet215* and then press Enter.)

Make the new directory your default; then return to your floppy disk and restart NETGEN by typing *netgen* and then pressing Enter. From the opening menu, select either the default or custom level of operation, as previously discussed, and from the next menu, select Hard Disk or Network Drive. You are prompted to enter the appropriate drive letter, after which you are prompted to insert selected NetWare disks to upload files to the selected drive.

After the standard list of disks has been uploaded, you are asked whether you want to upload additional disks. If a vendor or manufacturer has supplied a disk with special files to be added to the NetWare configuration files, you should press Y to answer yes and insert the appropriate disk. This disk should have a volume name similar to one of the following:

❏ LAN_DRV_.AAA (for a disk containing additional network adapter configuration files)

❏ DSK_DRV_.AAA (for a disk containing additional disk drive configuration files)

❏ OTH_DRV_.AAA (for a disk containing configuration files for miscellaneous devices)

You also can add configuration files to generate NetWare workstation shells and external bridges by uploading the files from the following disks:

❏ SHGEN-1
❏ SHGEN-2
❏ BRGEN-1
❏ BRGEN-2
❏ BRGEN-3
❏ BRUTILS

Note: When you upload NetWare's configuration files, subdirectory GENDATA is created. You already have read an ominous warning about using the same GENDATA disk to create two sets of server operating system files. If you will be using these files to generate NetWare for more than one server, be sure to delete the GENDATA directory and its files. To do so, make the NETWARE directory the default and type

   DEL GENDATA

and then press Enter. Next, type

   RD GENDATA

and then press Enter. When you have deleted the GENDATA subdirectory, the NETGEN program prompts you to use the GENDATA disk instead. You need to use a different GENDATA disk for each server that you install.

Configuring Your Server Using the Default Mode

When your working copies of disks are made, and you have optionally uploaded your disks to a hard disk, you are ready to generate NetWare.

If you are not still in NETGEN from the previous steps, and you are working from floppies, insert the NETGEN disk into a floppy disk drive, make that floppy disk drive the default, type *netgen*, and then press Enter. If you have uploaded the NetWare files to a disk, make the NETWARE subdirectory (created during the upload process) the default, type *netgen*, and then press Enter.

NETGEN's opening screen prompts you to choose either the default or custom mode of using NETGEN (again see fig. 5.1). In this section of the chapter, you examine the default mode, so select Default Configuration.

After choosing the default mode, you are prompted to specify whether you are generating NetWare using floppies, floppies with a RAM disk, a hard disk, or a server drive. Enter the appropriate choice. If you are using floppies with a RAM disk, you are prompted to enter the letter of the drive assigned to your RAM disk. If you are working with files uploaded to a hard disk or server drive, you are prompted to enter the drive and directory containing the uploaded files.

The next screen asks whether you want to select the network configuration or exit NETGEN (a pointless question because you would not have started NETGEN if you didn't want to configure NetWare in some way). Choose the Select Network Configuration option.

You are shown NETGEN's Available Options configuration menu (see fig. 5.3). Configuring NetWare is simply a matter of stepping through the menu options and making selections from the choices each offers. Each menu option is examined individually in the following sections.

Setting Operating System Options

When you select the first menu option (Set Operating System Options), you are prompted to choose generating NetWare 286 for a dedicated server or nondedicated server. A dedicated server acts as a server only; a nondedicated server can be used as a workstation and a server at the same time. For a discussion of the pros and cons of each configuration, see Chapter 4.

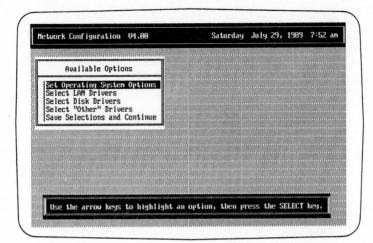

Fig. 5.3.

The default mode Available Options menu.

Highlight Advanced NetWare 286/Dedicated or Advanced NetWare 286/ Nondedicated, and press Enter. You are returned to NETGEN's Available Options configuration menu.

Selecting LAN Drivers

The next option is Select LAN Drivers, which allows you to choose the type of network adapter that will be installed in the server. If you are going to use the server as an internal bridge, you can select up to four network adapter drivers and configurations for this purpose (see Chapter 4 for more information about bridging).

Highlight the Select LAN Drivers menu option and press Enter. You are taken to a menu offering two options: to select a loaded item or to load and select an item. *Loaded item* refers to NetWare's standard list of network adapter drivers, and the most widely used network adapters are listed there. Highlight the Select Loaded Item option and press Enter. You are shown a list of network adapter drivers. Scroll through the list by using the up- and down-arrow keys. Highlight the driver that matches the description of your network adapter and press Enter. The selected driver is shown in the Selected LAN Drivers window (see fig. 5.4). If you plan to have additional network adapters in your server (because your server is going to be a bridge), select the LAN drivers for each by highlighting the correct driver name and pressing Enter.

If you are using a network adapter that requires a driver supplied by the manufacturer, copy the driver to your NetWare configuration files

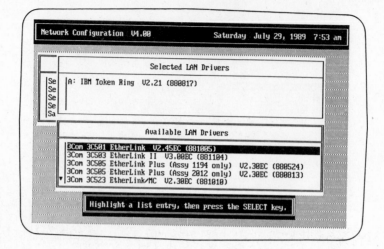

Fig. 5.4.

The Selected LAN Drivers window.

directory or to the working copy of one of your disks, according to the manufacturer's instructions. Use the Load and Select Item option to select this driver.

If you select the wrong network adapter driver, use the Deselect an Item option to remove the driver. When your LAN driver list is complete, press Esc to return to the NETGEN Available Options configuration menu.

Selecting Disk Drivers

Use the next menu option, Select Disk Drivers, to choose the type of hard disk(s) to be used with your server. Highlight the Select Disk Drivers option and press Enter.

Again, you are offered two options: to select a loaded item or to load and select an item. *Loaded item* refers to NetWare's standard list of disk drivers, which covers standard AT and PS/2 hard disk controllers and Novell's disk coprocessors.

When you pick a disk driver, you are specifying the type of controller the disk will be using. (For a discussion of the various controller options available with NetWare, see Chapter 4.) A NetWare server can use disks connected to as many as five channels, numbered 0 to 4. Channel 0 is usually the native controller that comes with an AT-compatible computer or IBM PS/2 type of computer and can be an ST506 or ESDI controller. Channels 1 through 4 are used by Novell disk coprocessor boards (DCBs).

Highlight the Select Loaded Item option and press Enter. You are asked to enter the disk channel number. If your controller is the native controller normally used by the PC to run DOS or OS/2, press 0. If your disk controller is a Novell DCB, press 1. You are shown a list of disk drivers through which you can scroll by using the up- and down-arrow keys. Highlight the driver that matches the description of your disk controller and press Enter. The driver is displayed in the Selected Disk Drivers window, as shown in figure 5.5. If you are using more than one disk controller type in your server or more than one Novell DCB (to implement disk duplexing, for example), select the correct disk driver for each channel.

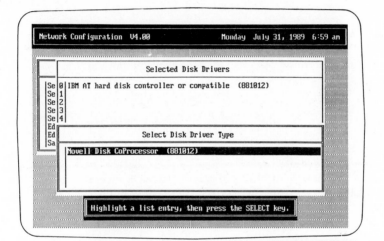

Fig. 5.5.
The Selected Disk Drivers window.

If you are using a disk that requires a driver supplied by the manufacturer, copy the driver to your NetWare configuration files directory or to the working copy of one of your disks, according to the manufacturer's instructions. Use the Load and Select Item option to select this disk driver.

If you select the wrong disk driver, use the Deselect an Item option to remove the driver. When your disk driver list is complete, press Esc to return to the NETGEN Available Options configuration menu.

Selecting Other Drivers

The Select "Other" Drivers menu option is for the specialized drivers that must be included in the installation process. More than likely, you will not have to use this option because it is designed to handle unusual situations, such as a tape controller card that is installed within the file server.

If you have purchased an item that requires that its driver be included in the server configuration process, follow the manufacturer's instructions to load its driver files to a working copy of one of your NetWare disks or into a subdirectory of your NetWare files. Choose the Select "Other" Drivers option to load and select that driver.

Saving Your Selections and Generating NetWare

When you have selected your network adapter and disk drivers and have chosen between creating a dedicated or nondedicated server, choose the Save Selections and Continue option. You are taken to the File Server Information window, as shown in figure 5.6. In this window, enter the number you are assigning to the network used by each of the server's network adapters. The network number(s) you use must be consistent on all servers on the same physical network, so check your entries carefully. (For more information on physical networks and network numbers, see Chapter 4.) If you are creating a nondedicated server, you also must assign it a unique network number (because the link between DOS and NetWare in the nondedicated server is treated as a separate network).

Fig. 5.6.

The File Server Information window.

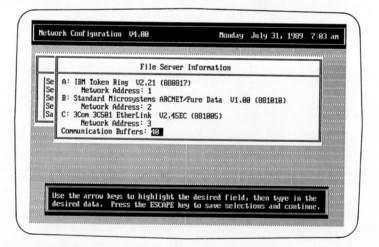

Enter the number of communication buffers to be used by the server. You can specify between 10 and 150 buffers. A communication buffer is approximately 500 bytes and holds incoming communication packets from workstations until the packets can be processed. An inadequate number of communication buffers results in communication packets having to be re-sent by workstations, and an excessive number results in wasted memory. You should allocate a minimum of 40 communication buffers, plus 1 additional buffer for each workstation that is to be connected to the file server. If 50 PCs will be connected to the server, for example, your communication buffers number should be 90 (40 + 50).

When the information in the File Server Information window is complete, press Esc to save the information. You are shown a window called Selected Configurations. The information shown in this window is useful and should be recorded or printed for future reference. (Configuration sheets are supplied in your NetWare manuals for this purpose.) You may want to store a printed copy of this screen with the GENDATA disk for the server you are installing.

Press Esc to exit the Selected Configurations window. You are prompted to confirm that you want to continue network generation using the configuration options you have selected. Press Y to respond yes, and the server operating system files are automatically generated, a process that takes several minutes if you are using uploaded files. If you are using the floppy-based method, the process takes much longer, and you are prompted to insert various NetWare disks a number of times.

When the files have been generated, you are returned to a NETGEN menu that gives you the options to exit NETGEN or to select a network configuration. If you use the floppy-based method of generation, the files needed to install NetWare have been automatically placed on the following disks:

- ❏ NETGEN
- ❏ SUPPORT
- ❏ OSEXE-1
- ❏ OSEXE-2
- ❏ UTILEXE-1
- ❏ UTILEXE-2

If you use files uploaded to a disk or network drive, when you select the option to exit NETGEN, you are asked whether you want to download the newly generated files to disks. NETGEN has placed these files in the subdirectories whose names match the disks given in the preceding list. Have working copies of the preceding disks on hand and press Y to answer yes.

The steps to generate the NetWare operating system are complete, and you are ready to use the files you have created to install NetWare on a server.

Configuring Your Server Using the Custom Mode

NETGEN's default mode is excellent for quick and easy NetWare configuration. You may, however, want to know the technical details of the choices you are making, even if gaining this information means more effort on your part.

NETGEN's custom mode gives you the opportunity to expend more effort and control the technical details. Custom mode lets you choose which interrupts, I/O ports, memory addresses, and DMA channels your network adapters use. The custom mode also lets you designate which resource sets are to be installed in your file server. (*Resource sets*, in NETGEN terminology, are items such as printer ports, display adapters, hard disk controllers, and so on.) NETGEN tracks the interrupts and addresses used by the resources you have selected and does not allow you to choose a network adapter configuration that conflicts with them.

If you are using NETGEN from floppies or from floppies and a RAM disk, insert the NETGEN disk into a floppy drive, make that floppy drive the current drive, type *netgen*, and press Enter. If you are using files uploaded to a disk or network drive, make the NETWARE subdirectory the current directory, type *netgen*, and press Enter.

To use NETGEN's custom mode, select Custom Configuration from NETGEN's opening menu. As with the default mode, you are taken to a menu that prompts you to choose whether you are using floppies, floppies and a RAM disk, a hard disk, or a network drive as the work area for generating NetWare. Make the appropriate selection and enter the drive letter of your RAM disk, hard disk, or network volume, if required. You see a menu that has two options: selecting a network configuration or exiting NETGEN. Select the first option.

NETGEN's custom configuration Available Options menu appears (see fig. 5.7). It offers several more selections than the default configuration menu, and each new option allows you to configure network adapter drivers or resource sets.

Resources and Resource Sets

NETGEN defines as a resource any item you install in your PC that requires a memory address, I/O port, interrupt, or DMA channel. For example, parallel and serial ports, display adapters, and hard and floppy

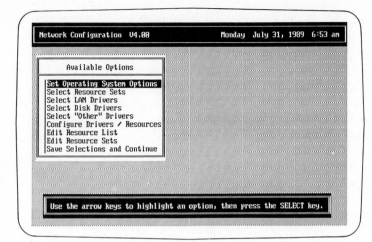

Fig. 5.7.
*The custom
configuration
Available Options
menu.*

disk controllers are all resources. NETGEN lets you group resources into resource sets. A resource set consists of one to six resources. For example, if you have a favorite server configuration that consists of a monochrome adapter, a Western digital floppy controller, two parallel ports (LPT1 and LPT2), and a serial port, you can group these resources into a set called Standard Server. The addresses used by all the items in the Standard Server set are tracked by NETGEN, and you are not permitted to choose a network adapter configuration that conflicts with any of the resources.

Using resource sets can be helpful if you are not conversant with addresses and ports but know which items will be installed in your server. Resource sets also can provide a quick way to know which addresses, interrupts, and ports are used by a particular item.

Setting Operating System Options

The first option on the custom configuration Available Options menu is identical to its counterpart in the default configuration menu. When you select Set Operating System Options, you are prompted to choose between generating NetWare 286 for a dedicated server and a nondedicated server.

Highlight Advanced NetWare 286/Dedicated or Advanced NetWare 286/ Nondedicated and press Enter. The Available Options menu returns to the screen.

Selecting Resource Sets

Choose the Select Resource Sets option to select items to be installed in your file server that use memory addresses, I/O ports, interrupts, or DMA channels. NETGEN tracks the addresses used and does not let you select a network adapter configuration that uses the same address.

When you highlight Select Resource Sets and press Enter, you see a menu offering two options: to select a loaded item or to load and select an item. *Loaded item* refers to NetWare's standard lists of resource sets. These sets include COM1, COM2, LPT1, LPT2, Hercules Mono Adapter, Enhanced Graphics Adapter, and AT Compatible File Server. Highlight the Select Loaded Item option and press Enter. You are shown a list of resource sets. Highlight a set that matches the item being installed in your server and press Enter. The item is shown in the Selected Resource Sets window, as shown in figure 5.8. Continue to select resource sets until you have chosen all the items you are installing in your server.

Note: If you are installing Netware in an IBM PS/2 model, *do not* select AT Compatible File Server as a resource set, because Netware will not load.

Fig. 5.8.
The Selected Resource Sets window.

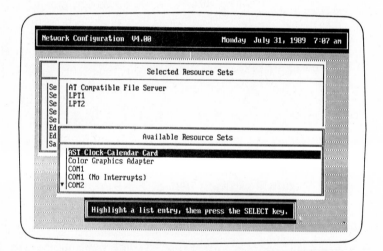

If you need to work with a resource set supplied by a manufacturer or vendor, you must copy the resource set to your NetWare configuration files directory or to the working copy of one of your disks, according to the supplier's instructions. You then can activate that set by using the Load and Select Item option. Network supervisors report that few, if any, manufacturers are actively supporting NETGEN's resource set feature, so you probably will never need to go through this procedure.

If you select the wrong resource set, use the Deselect an Item option to remove the resource set. When your resource set list is complete, press Esc to return to the NETGEN Available Options configuration menu.

Selecting LAN Drivers

The Select LAN Drivers option is identical to its counterpart in the default configuration menu. When you select this option, you are prompted to choose the drivers for the network adapters that will be installed in your server. You must select one driver for each network adapter to be installed in the server (up to a maximum of four).

Highlight the Select LAN Drivers option and press Enter. You see a menu offering two options: to select a loaded item or to load and select an item. *Loaded item* refers to NetWare's standard list of network adapter drivers; the driver you need is likely to be among them. Highlight the Select Loaded Item option and press Enter. You are shown a list of network adapter drivers, through which you can scroll by using the up- and down-arrow keys. Highlight the driver that matches the description of your network adapter and press Enter.

Be sure to select a driver that exactly matches the manufacturer and model number of your network card. Network cards of the same type, like EtherNet, but with different manufacturers or model numbers may require different drivers. The item is shown in the Selected LAN Drivers window (see fig. 5.4). If you plan to have additional network adapters in your server (because your server is going to be a bridge), select the LAN drivers for each by highlighting the correct driver name and pressing Enter. When your LAN driver list is complete, press Esc to return to the NETGEN Available Options configuration menu.

Selecting Disk Drivers

The Select Disk Drivers option is identical to its counterpart in the default configuration menu. This option is used to indicate the type of hard disk(s) used with your server. Highlight the Select Disk Drivers option and press Enter.

The menu you see next offers two options: to select a loaded item or to load and select an item. Highlight the Select Loaded Item option and press Enter. You are asked to enter the disk channel number. If your controller is the native controller normally used by the PC to run DOS or OS/2, press 0. Channels 1 through 4 can be used by Novell disk coprocessor boards (DCBs), third-party SCSI interface adapters, and other third-party disk drive interface adapters. Novell DCB boards are preset to use a specific channel number. If you are using a Novell DCB, set the channel number to that used by your DCB board. (The number is listed on the DCB box). Normally, the first DCB is set to channel 1. If you are using SFT

NetWare with disk duplexing and Novell DCBs, you will have two DCBs, using channels 1 and 2. You are shown a list of disk drivers. You can scroll through the list by using the up- and down-arrow keys. Highlight the driver that matches the description of your disk controller and press Enter. The driver is shown in the Selected Disk Drivers window (see fig. 5.5). If you plan to use more than one disk controller type in your server or plan to use more than one Novell DCB (to implement disk duplexing, for example), select the correct disk driver for each channel.

If you select the wrong disk driver, use the Deselect an Item option to remove the driver. When your disk driver list is complete, press Esc to return to the NETGEN Available Options configuration menu.

Selecting Other Drivers

The Select "Other" Drivers option is for specialized drivers that must be included in the installation process. More than likely, you will not need to use this option because it is designed to handle unusual situations, such as a tape controller card that is installed within the file server.

If you have purchased an item that requires its driver to be included in the server configuration process, follow the manufacturer's instructions to load its driver files to a working copy of one of your NetWare disks or into a subdirectory on the uploaded copies of your NetWare files. Then choose the Select "Other" Drivers option to load and select that driver.

Configuring Drivers and Resources

The menu option Configure Drivers/Resources lets you choose the configuration for network adapters or resources that can be set to more than one address, port, interrupt, or DMA channel. You also use this option to assign network addresses to your network adapters and to set the number of communication buffers for your server.

Configuring Resource Sets

Highlight the Configure Drivers/Resources option and press Enter. The menu shown in figure 5.9 appears. (If you haven't selected any resource sets that require configuration, the first option, Choose Resource Set Configuration, does not appear.) Highlight the first option and press Enter. A list of resource sets including unconfigured resources appears. Highlight the first listing and press Enter. You are shown the individual resources that need to be configured. Highlight the first resource and press Enter. You see a list of the configuration options; highlight the appropriate option and press Enter. Repeat this procedure for every other resource on the list.

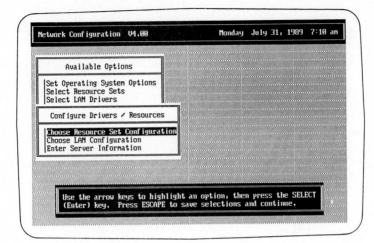

Fig. 5.9.
The Configure
Drivers/Resources
menu.

When you complete the configuration of each resource set, the Configure Drivers/Resources menu returns to the screen. The Release Resource Set Configuration option appears. You select this option to undo any resource set configurations you need to change.

Configuring LAN Drivers

When you use the custom level of NETGEN, you must indicate the configuration for each network adapter you want to install in your server. The menu option Choose LAN Configuration enables you to specify these configurations. Highlight this selection and press Enter. You see a list of the network adapters that you have selected using the Select LAN Drivers option.

Highlight the first driver and press Enter. A list of possible configurations appears, similar to that shown in figure 5.10. Highlight the configuration you want to use and press Enter. Only configurations that do not conflict with the resource sets, disk drivers, and any other LAN adapters selected are displayed. If you are installing only one LAN adapter, you probably can select Configuration Option 0, which usually corresponds to the manufacturer's default settings on the LAN adapter. You are returned to the list of network adapters. Repeat this process for every other adapter until each one has been configured.

Next, you are returned to the Configure Drivers/Resources menu. The Release LAN Configuration option appears. Select this option to undo any network adapter configurations you need to change.

Fig. 5.10.

The Available LAN Configurations selection screen.

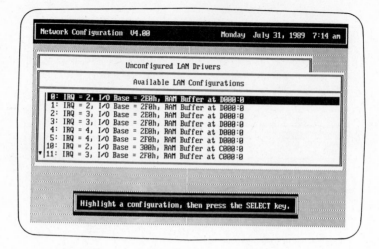

```
Network Configuration  V4.00              Monday  July 31, 1989  7:14 am

                        Unconfigured LAN Drivers

                       Available LAN Configurations

      0:  IRQ = 2,  I/O Base = 2E0h,  RAM Buffer at D000:0
      1:  IRQ = 2,  I/O Base = 2F0h,  RAM Buffer at D000:0
      2:  IRQ = 3,  I/O Base = 2E0h,  RAM Buffer at D000:0
      3:  IRQ = 3,  I/O Base = 2F0h,  RAM Buffer at D000:0
      4:  IRQ = 4,  I/O Base = 2E0h,  RAM Buffer at D000:0
      5:  IRQ = 4,  I/O Base = 2F0h,  RAM Buffer at D000:0
     10:  IRQ = 2,  I/O Base = 300h,  RAM Buffer at C000:0
     11:  IRQ = 3,  I/O Base = 2F0h,  RAM Buffer at C000:0


            Highlight a configuration, then press the SELECT key.
```

Entering Server Information

Selecting the Enter Server Information option takes you to the File Server Information window. This step is identical to entering information in the File Server Information window by using the default level of NETGEN. Enter the number(s) you want to assign to the networks used by each network adapter in the server. The network number(s) you use must be consistent on all servers on the same physical network, so check your entries carefully. If you are creating a nondedicated server, also assign it a unique network number.

Enter the number of communication buffers to be used by the server. You can specify between 10 and 150 buffers. You should allocate a minimum of 40 communication buffers plus one additional buffer for each workstation that will be connected to the file server.

When the information in the File Server Information window is complete, press Esc to save the information. The Configure Drivers/Resources menu returns to the screen. Press Esc to return to the Available Options configuration menu.

Editing the Resource List and Resource Sets

Two more resource-related options are available on the custom level configuration menu. Most network supervisors report never using either, and many do not even know what these options do. Both options enable you to create your own resource and resource-set definitions and modify the existing list. If you don't plan to customize resources or resource sets, you may skip this section.

The Edit Resource List option lets you work with the list of individual resources. Highlight this option and press Enter; you see a list of the defined resources. Highlight a particular resource and press Enter; you receive a list of the possible configurations for that resource. After you select a configuration; you see a detail screen that shows complete information about the memory address, I/O port, interrupt, and DMA channel usage for that resource (see fig. 5.11).

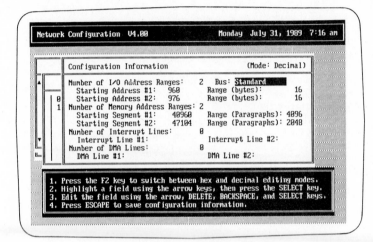

Fig. 5.11.

The Configuration Information screen.

You also can use this option to create your own resource definitions. With the list of resources on-screen, press Ins. You are prompted to enter the name of your resource. After typing your resource name and pressing Enter, you see an empty window called Resource Configurations. This window lists the various configuration options for your resource. To add the first one, press Ins. You are prompted to enter a number and a description for this configuration (such as *0: Configuration 0 - IRQ 5, DMA 3*). After you enter the resource number and name, the detail screen shown in figure 5.11 appears. On this screen, you enter the configuration details for your resource configuration.

You can delete resource definitions from the resource list. Highlight the resource you want to remove and press Del. You also can highlight multiple resource definitions with the F5 key and delete all of them at the same time by pressing Del.

The Edit Resource Sets option enables you to create your own resource sets by grouping individual resources. When you select this option, a list of currently defined resource sets is shown. To create a new resource set, press Ins, and you are prompted to enter the name of your new resource set. After you enter the name, the resource set is added to the resource set list. Highlight the new name and press Enter; you see an empty window called Selected Resources. When you press Ins, a list of individual resources appears. To add a resource to your new set, highlight the resource name and press Enter. Repeat the process to add additional resources, up to a maximum of six. When your list of resources is complete, press Esc to save your resource set definition and return to the list of resource sets.

You can edit an existing resource set by highlighting its name and pressing Enter. A list of its resources appears on-screen. You can add a resource by pressing Ins to display a list of resources. Highlight the one you want to add and press Enter. The resource is added to the resource set.

You can delete a resource set by highlighting its name and pressing Del. You can delete more than one at a time by marking each resource set name with F5 and then pressing Del.

When you are finished working with the resource set list, press Esc to return to the Configure Drivers/Resources menu. Press Esc to return to the Available Options configuration menu.

Saving Your Selections and Generating NetWare

When all drivers have been selected and configured, select Review Selected Configurations and record the information on the network configuration sheets found at the back of the Netware Installation Manual. You are then ready to choose the Save Selections and Continue option. If you see the disconcerting prompt ABANDON NETWORK GENERATION and Exit!, you have overlooked one or more steps in the configuration process. Select No to go back and review your selection of drivers and configuration options. Be sure that you have selected at least one LAN driver and one disk driver and that you have used the Set Operating Systems Options selection to choose between creating a dedicated or nondedicated server. If you have made all these selections, check that all selected LAN drivers and resource sets have been configured with the Configure Drivers/Resources option and that you have entered network numbers for each network adapter and have selected the number of communication buffers.

If all these tasks have been performed, choosing the Save Selections and Continue option results in a prompt that asks Continue Network Generation

Using Selected Configuration? Pressing Y to answer yes to this prompt results in NetWare operating system files being generated according to the configuration you defined. This process takes several minutes, and longer if you are using the floppy-based method (you are also prompted to insert various NetWare disks a number of times).

When all files have been generated, you are returned to a NETGEN menu that gives you the options to exit NETGEN or to select a network configuration. If you are using the floppy-based method of generation, the files needed to install NetWare have been placed on the following disks:

❏ NETGEN
❏ SUPPORT
❏ OSEXE-1
❏ OSEXE-2
❏ UTILEXE-1
❏ UTILEXE-2

If you are using files uploaded to a disk or network drive, when you select the option to exit NETGEN, you are asked whether you want to download the newly generated files to disks. Have your working copies of the preceding disks on hand and press Y to answer yes. The files you have generated also reside under the NetWare subdirectory in subdirectories that correspond to the names in the preceding list.

When you have used NETGEN to create and generate a server configuration, the program "remembers" your previous settings. If you start NETGEN again (using the same disks or disk area), it assumes that you may not want to repeat the selection process and gives you the option of recreating operating system files and utilities using your existing selections.

Starting NETGEN with Custom Options

Several command line parameter options are available when you start NETGEN. You can use them to bypass some of the opening menus. The command line options are the following:

❏ NETGEN-N (ignores the previous configuration and starts a new configuration)

❏ NETGEN-D (selects the default mode of NETGEN)

❏ NETGEN-C (selects the custom mode of NETGEN)

❏ NETGEN-S (selects the standard floppy mode for working with files)

You can combine these parameters; for example, using

NETGEN-NC

and then pressing Enter starts a new configuration using the custom level of NETGEN.

Installing Network Adapter Cards

When NetWare is generated, you should have a record of the configuration required for your network adapter (or adapters if you are making your server an internal bridge). Using the information generated by NETGEN, you can consult the manufacturer's instructions and set network adapter switches to match your NetWare configuration. You then can install the network adapter(s) in the PC you plan to use as the server.

Chapter Summary

Generating NetWare is a fairly complex process. If you are a beginner, you should consider using the default level of NETGEN until you begin to feel comfortable with the flow of the installation process. In fact, you may want to use the default most of the time and reserve the custom level only for special situations, such as when you must configure the server as an internal bridge using multiple network adapters. When you have completed the steps required to generate the NetWare operating system, you are ready to use the files you have created to install NetWare on a server. Installing NetWare is examined in the next chapter.

6

Installing NetWare 286

In the last chapter you learned about generating NetWare 286 and you prepared the files needed to install it. Now you are ready to use those files to bring up a file server.

After you have generated NetWare 286, you usually follow these steps to install it:

1. Assemble the server hardware.

2. Prepare the server disk or disks with NETGEN.

3. Run NETGEN to select the server installation options.

4. Copy NetWare's command files to the server.

5. Boot the server.

6. Place the server in a safe operating environment.

Some of these steps may have been performed for you already. For example, your computer dealer may have delivered the server PC already assembled, or you may have purchased a disk drive that is advertised as NetWare prepared.

If possible, take your time installing NetWare so that you can learn and thoroughly understand each step. As your network grows, you probably will be called upon to add servers as your network grows. Even if there is no possibility of adding servers to your LAN, you probably will use NETGEN again to change the configuration of your server in some way.

Now, look further at the steps you take to install NetWare 286.

Assembling Your Server's Hardware

Prior to being able to install NetWare, your server must be able to boot PC DOS, which requires that the server be completely assembled. All memory must be installed and properly configured. The display adapter must be installed and operating properly. If your server is going to be used to run network printers, the ports to which the printers will connect must be in place, and PC DOS must be able to recognize them.

Especially important is the installation of the hard disk (or disks) that will serve as the shared disk space. If you are converting a PC that has been used to run DOS or OS/2 into a server, and you need to keep its files, back up its disk. The disk's current contents are erased during NetWare installation.

You may be using a disk configuration that cannot be used with DOS or OS/2. If this is the case, install the disk controller and disks exactly according to the manufacturer's instructions. Pay close attention to switch and jumper settings. For example, Novell's disk coprocessor board used with a SCSI controller cannot be used by any operating system except NetWare. Therefore, you cannot test these disks prior to installing the server.

You also need to install the network adapter or adapters that belong in the server. Use the information that you recorded or printed while generating NetWare and make sure that the network adapters are configured properly. With some types of adapters, you must set a unique node address. Choose an address that is not to be used by any other device, and record it so that you do not accidentally use it again.

Write down the drive type and manufacturer's model number, network card model and revision number, network card configuration, and serial and parallel ports installed on the server. You may need to refer to this information during the installation of NetWare.

When all hardware is assembled and properly configured, run the setup program that comes with the server PC and properly enter all the server PC's hardware settings. Test the server by booting it with DOS.

Finally, store in a safe place all the manuals that come with the server PC and its peripherals. You are likely to need to consult them later if you decide to add new items to the server PC.

After the server PC is properly assembled and it boots DOS without errors, you are ready to prepare the server hard disk or disks for NetWare. You do this with NETGEN, the same utility that you used to generate NetWare's installation files.

Starting NETGEN

When you used NETGEN *to create the files* needed to install NetWare, you could run it from any PC. You also had the option of using NETGEN from floppy disk, hard disk, or network drive. When you use NETGEN *for the actual installation* of NetWare, you must run it from the server PC. If you are installing your first server, you must use NETGEN from a floppy disk. If you are adding a server to an existing LAN, you have the option of booting the new server as a workstation and using NETGEN stored on another server to install NetWare.

To start NETGEN from floppies, locate the working copies of the NetWare disks that you created and used to generate NetWare. These disks must contain the configuration files created when you generated NetWare. If you used the hard disk or network drive method to create these files, you must use the disks to which you downloaded those files.

Boot the server PC with DOS. Your boot disk must contain a CONFIG.SYS file that sets the number of files that can be opened (make it at least 10). In other words, your CONFIG.SYS file must include the statement FILES = 10. Insert the working copy of the disk labeled NETGEN into the floppy drive, make that drive your default, type *netgen*, and press Enter. If you have a second floppy drive, place the SUPPORT or AUXGEN disk in it to minimize disk swapping. Use SUPPORT for NetWare on 5 1/4-inch disks, and use AUXGEN for NetWare on 3 1/2-inch disks.

If you are going to use NETGEN from the drive of an existing server, you must be sure that the files you created when you generated NetWare are still located in the subdirectories that contain NetWare's files. Make sure that another user has not modified or deleted them after you generated NetWare. Boot the server PC with DOS, and load the NetWare shell. (See Chapter 8 for complete information about creating and using the NetWare shell.) Log in to that server and make the NETWARE subdirectory the default. Type *netgen*, then press Enter.

Choosing NETGEN's Default or Custom Level

When you used NETGEN to generate NetWare 286, you chose between two levels of operation, which were the default level and the custom level. It is the same when you use NETGEN to install NetWare.

You need to use NETGEN to prepare the server disks and install NetWare on them. For the first task (preparing server disks), use NETGEN's custom mode.

When you actually install NetWare, either the default or custom mode will work. The default level is easy to use, and it enables you to complete your installation with a minimum of hassle. The default level is the best way to go if you are installing NetWare for the first time. However, it severely limits your configuration flexibility. You can safely use the default level if all of the following descriptions reflect your situation:

1. You plan to use all of each disk drive for NetWare. (On a nondedicated server, you might want to use part of a file server disk as a DOS partition; you cannot do this with the default level of NETGEN.)

2. You don't mind using NetWare's default server configuration settings for the number of open files, file and directory entries, and indexed files.

3. You do not plan to limit each user's disk space.

4. If you install NetWare using the default level of NETGEN, you can run NETGEN later with the custom level, changing the default settings as needed. However, you cannot easily "undo" disk partition information. If you need to use part of a disk for NetWare and part for DOS, or if you must subdivide one disk into separate NetWare volumes, then you have no choice but to use the custom level.

5. If you are using a disk that has not been "COMPSURFed" (NETGEN's disk surface analysis has not been run), you can start NETGEN in the custom mode and perform this test. You can then exit NETGEN and restart NETGEN in default mode to perform the server installation. This is a good strategy if you are a first-time installer.

Starting NETGEN with Command Line Options

The first menu that you see when you start NETGEN prompts you to choose between its default and custom levels. The second menu prompts you to choose between running NETGEN from floppies, floppies and a RAM disk, a hard disk, or a network drive. You can bypass these menus by starting NETGEN with command line parameters. The command line options are the following:

1. NETGEN-D (selects the default mode)

2. NETGEN-C (selects the custom mode)

3. NETGEN-S (selects the standard floppy mode for working with files)

You can combine these parameters. For example, you could use command-line option NETGEN-CS, which designates the custom mode using floppies.

Caution: You may remember from the previous chapter that NETGEN accepts the additional command line option N for starting a new configuration. Do not use this option when you are using NETGEN to install NetWare, because it deletes the configuration information required to complete the installation. The N option should be used only when you are generating Netware 286.

Using NETGEN To Prepare the Server Disks

The server hard disks have an important job. They store your server's most important product—its files. It is vital that the server hard disks do this in a safe, reliable manner. Your best assurance that they will is to choose a disk configuration with a proven track record of reliability, and then test that configuration thoroughly before putting it into production. When NetWare writes information to a server disk, it reads that information after it has been written to ensure that it is correct. If this read-after-write verification fails, that part of the disk is flagged as unusable, and the information is written on another section of the disk. Unfortunately, this is not a "bullet-proof" method. If a part of the disk fails where information is already written, that information is subsequently lost.

The best way to prevent this loss of information is to exercise the disk thoroughly before using it to store live data. Unless a vendor or manufacturer has done this for you, the first thing you need to do is perform this test. A utility called COMPSURF (COMPrehensive SURFace analysis) is used to perform the disk test. If you are using Novell's disk coprocessor board in your server, you need to run the DISKSET utility before you run COMPSURF.

Running DISKSET

The Novell disk coprocessor board is a high-performance SCSI (small computer system interface) disk interface that allows you to attach up to 32 disks to the file server. Depending on the configuration of the hardware and network card(s) in a file server, you can install up to four DCBs in one server, and each DCB can have up to eight disk controllers attached. Two DCBs are often used in file servers where disk mirroring is implemented (one set of disks and controllers duplicates another to ensure continuous operation and to prevent the loss of data if one fails). If you are not using DCBs in your server, you can skip this section and proceed to "Running COMPSURF."

DISKSET is used to specify the types of controllers and hard disks that are attached to each of the Novell disk coprocessor boards installed in your server. There are two ways to start DISKSET. You can run it from NETGEN's configure file server utilities menus if you started NETGEN in the custom mode, or you can run it directly from the working copy of the DSK_DRV_.001 disk.

To start it from NETGEN's menus, start NETGEN with one of the methods described above and select its custom level. Specify whether you are using it from floppies, floppies and a RAM disk, or from a network drive. You are prompted to enter a drive letter if you are running NETGEN from floppies and a RAM disk or from a network drive. Finally, you see the Network Generation Options menu (see fig. 6.1). Highlight the option called Configure File Server Utilities and press Enter. From the resulting Configuration Utilities menu, select DISKSET.

To start DISKSET from DSK_DRV_.001, place your working copy of this disk in the server PC's floppy drive. Make that drive the default, type *diskset*, and press Enter. If you are equipped to run NETGEN from a network drive, you also can run DISKSET directly from it. Boot the server PC as a workstation, load the NetWare shell, log in to the server that has NetWare's installation files, and make the DSK_DRV_.001 subdirectory under the NETWARE directory the default. Type *diskset* and press Enter.

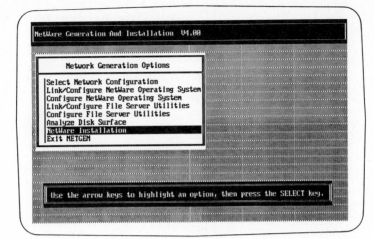

Fig. 6.1.
Starting NETGEN in
the custom mode.

As you run DISKSET, you need to know your exact disk drive configuration. You can have one to four DCBs, and each one is set for a channel from 1 to 4. The DCB's channel is determined by the PAL (Programmable Array Logic) chips and jumper settings on the DCB card. You can have only one DCB per channel number, although you do not have to begin with channel 1. Each DCB also has one or more controllers and disk drives attached to it, and you need to know the manufacturer and model number for each.

DISKSET's menu displays the following options:

Change Current Channel Number
Display Current Channel Configuration

Each Disk Coprocessor Board is assigned to one channel. The channel that you are currently working with is displayed at the top of the screen. To change to another channel, select Change Current Channel Number, and choose the appropriate channel from the list that is displayed.

After the correct channel is selected, choose the menu option called Display Current Channel Configuration. A screen appears, showing the currently selected controllers, disk types, and each controller's address. Each controller and its connected disks are shown on a separate line. If you are working with a new DCB, the list is blank. If the DCB has been used before, and you need to delete some or all of its current configuration, highlight the controller and disk configuration that you want to remove, and press Del. You are prompted to confirm that you want to delete the selected configuration line. Press Y to respond with yes, and the line showing that controller and disk configuration is removed.

To select a controller and disk configuration to add, press Ins. A list of all available configuration options appears. Highlight the one that matches the controller(s) and disk(s) attached to the DCB, and press Enter. Carefully check your choice, because many options look alike. When making a selection, you are prompted to enter the address for the controller you selected. Highlight the correct number and press Enter. Don't confuse the controller address with the DCB channel number. You can have multiple DCBs, and each DCB can have multiple controllers (up to eight). Each controller is given a unique address; the first controller always uses address 0, the second uses address 1, and so on. The configuration window is updated to show the new controller and drive combination that you specify. Repeat the process if you need to define additional controllers and drives for the currently selected DCB channel number.

Some controllers are separate from disk drives, but others are installed on the bottom of the drive and are called *embedded* SCSI controllers. To set properly the controller address and correct disk drives, you need the documentation for the controllers and drives you plan to attach to the server. Otherwise, have your vendor set up the disk subsystem for you. If you need to learn this procedure, see if you can watch an experienced installer configure the system.

When you have finished, press Esc, and you are prompted to confirm that you want to save the configuration. Answer yes and DISKSET's opening menu returns to the screen. If necessary, you can select another disk channel to specify the configuration for another DCB.

After you have completed the configuration definitions for each DCB that is installed in the server, press Esc from DISKSET's opening menu. If you run DISKSET from NETGEN's menus, NETGEN's menu returns to the screen.

After you have properly configured the Disk Coprocessor Boards in your server, you are ready to run COMPSURF to test the hard disks.

Running COMPSURF

COMPSURF can take hours to run, particularly if you have a large hard disk or multiple disks in your server. Fortunately, after you start it, it runs unattended. Veteran NetWare installers often let COMPSURF run overnight. You also can find disks already "COMPSURFed" for NetWare from companies such as Storage Dimensions, ADIC, and CORE.

COMPSURF ends by producing a list of the bad disk areas or *blocks* that it has found. If you have a printer connected to the parallel port of the server PC, you can print this list. If you do not have a printer or parallel port available, you should be prepared to copy the list by hand. Good practice dictates that you record the bad block list and store it for future reference. After the server is up and running, you will want to use a NetWare command periodically to see how many bad blocks have currently been located. You can compare this information with COMPSURF's original bad block count and listing to see if the count is increasing at an inordinately fast rate.

You can start COMPSURF in two ways. You can run it from NETGEN's menus if you started NETGEN in the custom mode, or you can run it directly from the UTILEXE-1 (NetWare on 5 1/4-inch disks) or UTILEXE (NetWare on 3 1/2-inch disks) disk.

To start COMPSURF from NETGEN's menus, start NETGEN with one of the methods previously discussed, and select the custom level. Next, specify whether you are using NETGEN from floppies, floppies and a RAM disk, or a network drive. You are prompted to enter a drive letter if you are running NETGEN from floppies and a RAM disk or from a network drive. Finally, you see the menu shown in figure 6.1. Highlight the option called Analyze Disk Surface and press Enter.

To start COMPSURF from UTILEXE-1 or UTILEXE, place your working copy of this disk in the server PC's floppy drive. Make that drive the default, type *compsurf*, and press Enter. If you are equipped to run NETGEN from a network drive, you can run COMPSURF directly from it as well. Boot the server PC as a workstation, load the NetWare shell, log in to the server that has NetWare's installation files, and make the UTILEXE-1 or UTILEXE subdirectory under the NETWARE directory the default. Type *compsurf* and press Enter.

COMPSURF begins with a warning that it will destroy all data on the disk you are testing and gives you the option to exit. Answer yes to continue running COMPSURF. Next, you see a list of the hard disks installed in the server PC, similar to the list shown in figure 6.2. If this list is incomplete or incorrect in any way, it indicates that your hardware is not properly assembled, or that the setup utility on the server PC has not been run. If you are using Novell's disk coprocessor board, it could mean that you have not run the DISKSET utility discussed in the preceding section. Pressing Esc enables you to exit the COMPSURF utility if you need to recheck your hard disk and controller configuration. If you have more than one disk installed in the server, use the arrow keys to highlight the one you want to COMPSURF, then press Enter.

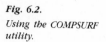

Fig. 6.2.

Using the COMPSURF utility.

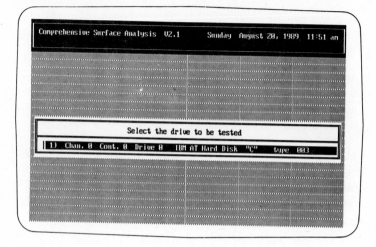

Understanding COMPSURF

After you have selected the disk that you plan to COMPSURF, you see a screen that prompts you to select the tasks that COMPSURF should perform. You specify the following conditions:

❑ Whether the disk will be formatted

❑ The hard disk interleave factor

❑ Whether the current media defect list should be retained

❑ Whether you will enter a list of known bad blocks or media defects

❑ The number of sequential disk test passes that COMPSURF should make

❑ The number of random input/output operations that should be performed

These choices are confusing unless you know how hard disks work. The first thing you need to know is what COMPSURF does and the implications of your choices.

COMPSURF performs three operations. First, it *formats* the disk (unless you tell it not to), which organizes the disk into 4096-byte blocks that NetWare uses as the unit of storage when it reads or writes to the disk. If you are running COMPSURF on a disk that has never been used for NetWare, in most cases you must format it (unless the disk manufacturer's or NetWare's instructions explicitly say not to, which is the case with some types of ESDI drives). Even though the disk already has been formatted by DOS or from a previous COMPSURF run, it does not hurt to format it again. Formatting does not take much time compared to COMPSURF's other operations.

After COMPSURF formats the disk, it performs a *sequential disk test*. Beginning with the first block of the disk, COMPSURF writes a test pattern to each disk block and then reads that block to make sure that the disk has stored the information correctly. If a particular block fails the test, it is marked as bad, and NetWare does not use it to store information. When you start COMPSURF, you can specify that it perform from zero to five sets of sequential disk passes. NetWare experts recommend three sets for a first-time COMPSURF operation. The sequential disk test is COMPSURF's biggest time consumer; one set of passes takes approximately forty minutes on a 30M hard disk. The time increases proportionately if you are using a larger hard disk, or if you are doing more test passes.

COMPSURF's third operation is called the *random I/O test*. Test patterns are read and written to and from random disk blocks in rapid succession. This test simulates the way your server disk operates as it receives requests to retrieve information scattered throughout the disk. When you start COMPSURF, it suggests a default number of I/O tests based on the number of blocks on your disk. You are free to increase or decrease this number. Entering zero results in no random I/O test being performed, but it is not a good idea to skip this test.

In addition to choosing whether or not to run these operations, COMPSURF prompts you to set the disk interleave factor. A hard disk platter is divided into areas called *sectors*, which are divisions shaped like pie slices on each disk platter. As the disk platter rotates, each sector area travels past the read/write heads, at which point data can be read from or written to that sector. After the data is read or written, the disk read/write head is directed to read or write from another sector. Ideally, that same sector is traveling past the read/write head at the precise moment that this instruction is received; if it is not, however, the read/write head waits until it is before executing the instruction.

Setting the interleave factor enables you to coordinate the rotation speed of the disk platters with the speed at which the disk controller can issue instructions to the read/write heads. An interleave factor of 1 means that the disk controller can be ready with a new instruction for every sector that travels past the read/write heads. If the controller needs a little more time, then a higher interleave factor can be chosen. The interleave factor determines how many sectors travel past the read/write heads between instructions from the disk controller. For example, an interleave factor of 3 means that data is written to the disk on every third sector, and a factor of 2 means that data is written to every other sector.

Don't worry if you don't completely understand this concept. As a general rule, the ST506 disk and controller types that are common in IBM AT-compatibles should have an interleave factor of 2. Disks with ESDI controllers (such as those commonly used in IBM PS/2 machines) should have an interleave factor of 1. If you are using another type of disk, the hard disk vendor or manufacturer may have a suggested interleave factor. Do not use a lower interleave factor than recommended by the dealer or manufacturer. Setting the interleave factor lower than a drive and controller are designed for dramatically slows down disk performance.

COMPSURF also asks you to designate whether you are going to retain the disk's current bad block list. This question is often answered incorrectly. When COMPSURF is run, it builds a list of known bad blocks and stores them on the disk itself. If you have never run COMPSURF on the disk you are testing, answer no, because there is no bad block list to retain. If you are running COMPSURF to recheck a disk that has already been COMPSURFed, press Y to answer yes, because a bad block list exists.

You also are asked if you want to enter bad block locations. With most disks, a printed list of the bad blocks discovered during the manufacturer's testing is supplied. Usually this information is on a sticker attached to the disk itself. If such a list exists for the disk you are using, answer yes, and enter the manufacturer's list of bad blocks so that COMPSURF does not have to rediscover them.

Selecting COMPSURF's Operation Parameters

With a good understanding of what COMPSURF does, you are ready to select the operations that you want it to perform. You are asked to choose them one at a time, and the Program Operation Parameters window is updated to display your selections (see fig. 6.3).

You first are asked whether you want to *format the disk*. Answer yes (in most cases) or no, and the Program Operation Parameters screen shows your choice. If you want to change your decision, press Esc, and you are asked again whether you want to format the disk.

If you opt to format the disk, you are asked to *select the interleave factor* and the screen shows a list of possible interleave factors from 1 to 8. Highlight the appropriate choice and press Enter. An updated Program Operation Parameters window shows your choice, and you can cancel it by pressing Esc.

Next, the program asks whether you want to *maintain the current media defect list*. If you already COMPSURFed the disk you are working with and you know it already has a valid bad block list, answer yes. Answer no if this is the first time the disk is being COMPSURFed.

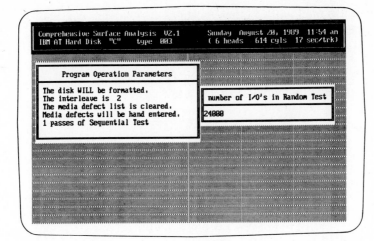

Fig. 6.3.

Choosing the COMPSURF Program Operation Parameters.

If you answered no, you are asked whether you want to enter media defects. If you have a list of the manufacturer's bad blocks for the disk, answer yes. After you have specified COMPSURF's other operating parameters, a prompt tells you to enter the bad block locations.

Next, you are prompted to select the *number of sequential test passes* that should be performed, and you are offered choices ranging from 0 to 5. The recommended number for a first time test is 3. Highlight your choice and press Enter.

You also need to enter the *number of random I/O tests* that should be performed, and a suggested default number of tests is displayed. Normally, you should accept the default recommendation, but if you don't, backspace over this number, type your choice, and press Enter (if you want no random I/O tests performed, enter 0). If you enter a number lower than the suggested default, you receive a warning message that you should use the default number for best results. Press Esc to bypass this message and continue.

Finally, you are asked to confirm that your choices are correct. Review your selections as shown in the Program Operation Parameters window. If you need to change one, answer no at the confirmation prompt; all your selections disappear, and you are prompted to reenter them. If your selections are correct, answer yes.

If you previously opted to enter bad block locations manually, you are taken to a screen similar to the one shown in figure 6.4. Locate the bad block list supplied by your disk manufacturer. To enter one of its listed bad blocks, press Ins. A prompt tells you to enter the head number. After entering the head number, you are asked to enter the cylinder number.

Continue this process until all bad block locations are entered. Recheck your entries carefully by comparing them to the manufacturer's list. If one of your entries is incorrect, highlight it and press Del. You then can press Ins to reenter it correctly. When you are finished entering the bad blocks, press Esc. You are told to confirm that your entries are correct. Answer yes, and the COMPSURF operations that you want begin.

Fig. 6.4.

Entering the list of bad blocks.

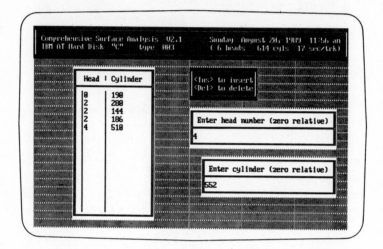

If you opted to format the disk, the first message you see is The drive is being formatted. The hard disk activity light (if your server PC is equipped with one) shows almost continuous disk access during this step. After formatting, it begins the sequential test and displays information similar to the following, showing the block number that is being tested, the pattern of information that is being used for the test, the pass numbers (current and total), and the number of bad blocks located so far:

Block #	Pattern	Pass	BadBlocks
4456	db6d	1/3	34

You also have the option to display or print the bad block table and turn the screen update on or off. Turning off the screen update may save you some time by saving the server PC's processor a little work.

After the sequential tests are finished, the random I/O tests begin. A screen display similar to the one above appears to show you the progress of the tests.

After the tests are complete, you should select the option to print the bad block table, if you have a parallel port in the server PC and a printer available. Otherwise, you should display the bad block table and copy its contents by hand. Store this list with your other server documentation in case you need to refer to it again.

After you have printed or copied the bad block table, press Esc to exit COMPSURF. If COMPSURF was started from a NETGEN's menu, it returns to that menu.

If you have more than one disk in your file server, you should run COMPSURF on each. For each disk installed in or attached to your server, repeat the steps previously listed.

After all disks have been COMPSURFed, you are ready to install NetWare on the server.

Using NETGEN To Install NetWare

You already have read about the factors that govern your choice concerning whether to use NETGEN's default or custom mode. The default mode is best for a first-time installer, and the custom mode is good for an experienced installer who needs to vary from the default installation parameters. You also can restart NETGEN in the custom mode if you need to change any of the configuration options established when you installed NetWare using the default mode.

If at all possible, your first experience with installing NetWare should come from using NETGEN's default mode. NETGEN's custom mode is renowned for its complexity—when network supervisors get together and tell computer war stories, NETGEN's custom mode is often the main topic of conversation. The custom mode is less intimidating if you are familiar with DOS and understand how the hard disks work.

The default mode is discussed first, and you will learn how to use the custom mode to change the server configuration after NetWare has been installed.

Installing NetWare with NETGEN's Default Mode

Start NETGEN with one of the methods described in this chapter's section called "Starting NETGEN." You have several options, depending on whether you are working with floppies or with NETGEN's files stored on an existing server. In either case, make sure that you use the same working copies of NETGEN's files that you used to generate NetWare for your server.

From NETGEN's initial menu, choose Default Configuration when you are prompted to select the configuration level. (You can bypass this step by starting NETGEN with the -D command line parameter, as described earlier in this chapter.) From the next menu, specify whether you are using NETGEN from floppies, floppies and a RAM drive, or a network drive.

After you have made the proper preliminary selections, NETGEN displays the menu shown in figure 6.5. If you follow these steps and arrive at this menu, but the option NetWare Installation does not appear, it means that you are not working with the same set of floppies you used to generate NetWare or that NetWare has not been generated yet. To correct this problem, exit NETGEN and restart it, using those files. If for some reason you cannot locate them, or if you never generated NetWare, you need to do so before going any further. (See the preceding chapter for complete instructions on generating NetWare.)

Fig. 6.5.

Installing NetWare by using NETGEN's default mode.

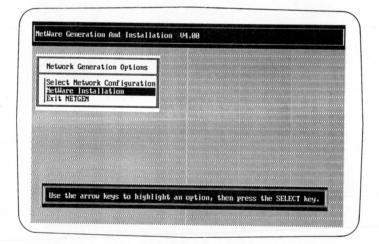

NetWare's default installation option prompts you to complete the following steps:

1. Confirm that the disk configuration is correct.

2. Overwrite your disk's current partition table with one that makes the entire disk usable for NetWare.

3. Pick a name for the file server.

4. Select which ports on the file server should be used for network printers.

5. Copy NetWare's files to the server disk.

These steps are easy to follow. To begin, select NetWare Installation from the menu shown in figure 6.5. You see a list of all the disks installed in the server PC. Examine this list to confirm that it is correct and is the same list that you used when generating NetWare and running DISKSET and COMPSURF. Press Esc when you have finished examining the list, and you are prompted to confirm that the drive list is correct. If it is not, select Drive List Is Not Correct, and NETGEN's main menu returns to the screen, from which you can exit the program and correct the problem. For example, if a particular drive that should be on the list is not, check for proper connection or that the disk subsystem is turned on. After correcting the problem, restart NETGEN and follow the same steps to continue installing NetWare.

Disk Mirroring and Duplexing with SFT NetWare 286

If you are using SFT NetWare 286, a special installation option becomes available if you have two or more disks attached to your server that are identical to each other in size. SFT NetWare enables you to designate that two disks become a *mirrored* or *duplexed* pair so that whatever is written to one is automatically written to the other.

Two disks are *mirrored* if they are on the same disk channel (which means they are attached to the same disk coprocessor board, SCSI interface adapter, or controller). They are *duplexed* if they are on different disk channels (which means they are each attached to separate DCBs, SCSI adapters, or controllers). When two disks become a mirrored pair, an extra level of protection against disk failure is put into place. If one disk in the mirrored pair fails, no data is lost because the other disk in the pair contains the same information. No interruption in server availability occurs either because the server continues to operate. When two disks become a duplexed pair, the level of redundancy extends not only to the disks themselves, but also to their controllers and DCBs. With a mirrored pair, a failure of the controller or DCB that they share results in server failure and possible data loss or corruption. With a duplexed pair, controller or DCB failure is not a problem, because duplicates of each exist.

Mirroring and duplexing each affect disk performance. If two drives are mirrored, disk writes can take up to twice as long because the disk controller must first write to one disk and then the other. This problem does not occur with disk duplexing because each disk has its own controller, and disk writes can be performed simultaneously. Disk reads can be affected positively by disk duplexing or mirroring. When the controller requests information from a pair of disks, each disk seeks the information. Because of differing read/write head and sector positioning, one of the two disks is likely to find the information a little more quickly than the other, and that disk will be the one used by the controller to satisfy the read request. With a mirrored or duplexed pair of disks, your disk read performance should improve slightly.

Creating a Mirrored Pair

If you have the equipment installed in your PC to make mirroring or duplexing possible, a Mirroring Options menu automatically appears after you have confirmed that your disk drive configuration is correct. This menu shows the list of disks that can be mirrored or duplexed, and offers you the following options:

    Establish Mirror Pair
    Done, Continue Installation

If you choose not to mirror or duplex any drives, you can highlight Done, Continue Installation and press Enter. You then see the next installation step.

If you want to mirror or duplex a drive pair, highlight *Establish Mirror Pair* and press Enter. Highlight the disk that you want to designate as the primary one in the pair and press Enter. NETGEN then lists the disks that are the same size as the disk that you have selected. Highlight the drive that you want to make the other half of the pair and press Enter. (If there is only one disk that matches, it is selected automatically.) In future installation operations, the mirrored or duplexed pair is treated as if the drives are one disk. In the window that lists the available drives, the primary disk has a P in its status column, and the secondary disk has an S in its status column.

When NETGEN returns to the Mirroring Options menu, a new option, Un-mirror Existing Mirror Pair, appears. Repeat the preceding steps if you want to establish another duplexed or mirrored pair, or select Done, Continue Installation to leave the Mirroring Options menu. If you need to unmirror or unduplex a disk pair, follow the directions given in the following section.

Unmirroring a Disk Pair

To *unmirror* or *unduplex* a disk pair, select Un-Mirror Existing Mirror Pair from the Mirroring Options menu. A list of mirrored drives appears. Highlight the primary disk (which shows a P in its status column) and press Enter. The disk pair is unmirrored and you can establish separate disk volumes on each disk.

The program now returns to the Mirroring Options menu. Repeat the preceding steps if you want to establish another duplexed or mirrored pair, or select Done, Continue Installation to leave the Mirroring Options menu and continue installing NetWare.

Viewing the Volume List

When you are finished working with the list of disk drives, highlight Drive List Is Correct and then press Enter. You see a menu that prompts you to either Select Default Installation Options or Continue Installation. You want to choose Select Default Installation Options, because selecting Continue Installation at this point only returns you to NETGEN's main menu.

After choosing Select Default Installation Options, NETGEN automatically assigns volume names to your available disks, and you are shown a list of the NetWare volumes to be created. NetWare 286 has two rules that it follows for creating volumes: a volume must be on one disk only (unlike NetWare 386, where volumes can consist of more than one disk), and a volume cannot exceed 255M in size. If you have only one disk in the server PC of less than 255M in size, only one volume is created, and it is called SYS (the name that NetWare always assigns to the first volume).

Based on those two rules, if there are multiple disks attached to your server PC and all of them are smaller than 255M, the first is called SYS, the second VOL1, the third VOL2, and so on. If your first disk in the server is larger than 255M, then the first 255M is called volume SYS, and the next 255M (or whatever disk space remains) is called VOL1. The next disk or 255M of space is called VOL2, and the next is VOL3.

You cannot change the volume information, although you can use the custom mode of NETGEN to change volume names later. To continue the installation process, press Esc after you have viewed the volume list.

Entering the File Server Name

Next, you are prompted to choose a file server name and enter it in an entry box similar to the one shown in figure 6.6. Your server name must be between 2 and 45 characters in length. Choose a name that is brief and meaningful, such as the name of the department that is using the server (such as SALES or ACCTING), the server's location (such as WAREHSE or FLOOR2) or the server's primary application (such as EMAIL or INVENTORY). If you have more than one file server in your local area network, each must be given a unique name. The server name cannot begin with a period (.) and cannot include spaces or the following characters:

" * + , / \ ¦ : ; = < > ? [ ]

Type the name of the server that you want to use and press Enter.

Fig. 6.6.

Entering the file server name.

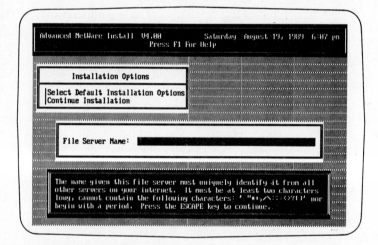

Viewing the Server Configuration

On-screen you see a list of the server configuration parameters, as shown in figure 6.7. You are shown the server name and the total number of files that can be open on the server at the same time by all users. You also are advised that the maximum number of indexed files is set to 0 (indexed files are discussed in Chapter 12) and the option to limit disk space is not activated (limiting disk space is discussed in Chapter 10). If you have SFT NetWare, you see two parameters for the Transaction Tracking System

(TTS): the transaction backout volume (where data for transactions in progress is stored) and the maximum number of transactions that can be in progress at any one time. You also are shown the maximum number of Bindery objects. The Bindery is a group of files where NetWare stores its user and security information. You will learn about the Bindery and NetWare security in Chapters 10, 11, and 13. Unless you opt to limit disk space, you do not have to set a maximum number of Bindery objects.

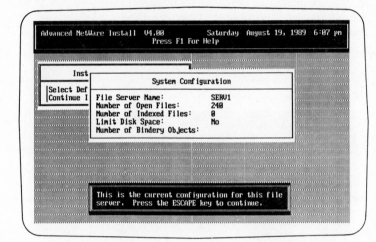

Fig. 6.7.
NETGEN's default settings for the file server's configuration parameters.

You cannot change any of these options now, but later you can use NETGEN's custom mode to modify them. Press Esc to leave this screen and continue installing NetWare.

Defining Network Printers

If there are any parallel and serial ports in the server PC, NETGEN offers you the opportunity to use them as connections for shared network printers. Like DOS and OS/2, NETGEN refers to serial and parallel ports by their device names (COM1 and COM2 for serial ports and LPT1, LPT2, and LPT3 for parallel ports). NetWare 286 permits up to two serial ports and three parallel ports to be used to connect network printers (five per server).

For each port in your server PC, NETGEN asks you to respond to a prompt similar to the following:

```
Use COM1 for a Network Printer?
```

Only if you plan to connect a printer to the COM1 port should you respond yes.

After you have responded to NETGEN's prompt for every port, you see a list of every port and its status as a network printer connection (see fig. 6.8). Every network printer is given a number, starting with 0 for the first printer. Serial ports are automatically set to the following communication parameters: 9600 baud, 8 data bits, 1 stop bit, no parity, and XON/XOFF protocol disabled. You can set your serial printers to match this configuration, or use NETGEN's custom mode to modify the port's settings after installation. Similarly, if you made a mistake in your port assignments, or want to change your selections, you must use NETGEN's custom mode after installation.

Fig. 6.8.

Specifying printer ports.

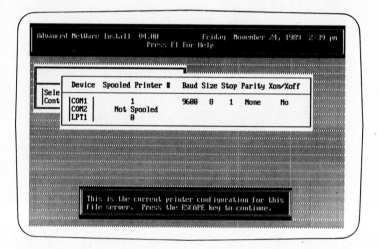

You should record your printer port configuration for future reference. After you have done so, press Esc to leave the printer port information screen and to continue installing NetWare.

Installing NetWare's Files

The steps you have followed so far have defined your server's installation parameters. You have defined the disk and volume configuration, chosen a file server name, and defined the network printer ports. You are now ready to copy NetWare's operating system and command files to the disk that is volume SYS.

When you pressed Esc after viewing the network printer port configuration list, you returned to NETGEN's Installation Options menu. This menu offers you two choices: Select Default Installation Options and Continue Installation. You can choose Select Default Installation Options if you want to view your previous selections, but you are only permitted to change the file server name. To continue the installation and copy NetWare's files to the server PC, select Continue Installation. A prompt asks you to confirm that you want to install NetWare's files on the server. Answer yes. If you answer no, you are given the opportunity to abandon the installation process and exit NETGEN.

You are prompted to place NetWare's disks in the server one at a time, and NetWare's files are copied to the server disk from each one. You need your working copies of the OSEXE disks for this operation, as well as the disks labeled SYSTEM and PUBLIC. With NetWare Version 2.15, you also are prompted to insert a disk called PROGRAMS-1. It's easy to miss this disk because it is not packaged in the same boxes as NetWare's regulars disks. It is the disk that contains the files for NetWare's help system.

In addition to copying NetWare's files, this step also installs what NetWare calls *cold boot loaders* to the first server disk. These cold boot loaders are used to boot the server if your disk configuration permits booting from a hard disk.

When the last disk's files have been copied, you see the message System files successfully installed and you are prompted to press a key to continue. After pressing a key, the Network Generation Options menu returns to the screen. One of your options from this menu is to exit NETGEN. Select this option, and the DOS prompt returns to the screen.

Congratulations! You have successfully installed NetWare. At this point, you may need to change some of the defaults by using NETGEN's custom options, or you may want to boot the server to test it. In the next section, you will learn how to use NETGEN's custom mode to install and customize NetWare. You may want to skip the following section for now and proceed directly to this chapter's section called "Booting the File Server."

If your experience with NETGEN was not successful, read the next section to see if you have encountered one of NETGEN's common bugs. You also may want to have your NetWare vendor or other experienced help available in case something unexpected happens.

NETGEN Bugs

A bug may occur when you are installing NetWare on a server with an unusually large amount of disk space. NETGEN attempts to store the volume information for this disk space in memory, but it runs out of memory space and aborts. Veteran NetWare installers report that this occurs in cases where five or more large volumes are being assigned for one server.

To work around this bug, temporarily disconnect some of the disk volumes (you also may have to run DISKSET to temporarily remove those disks from your DCB configurations). Run NETGEN and install NetWare as you usual. Now reconnect the additional volumes, and run NETGEN again in the custom mode to activate them.

Hopefully, you will not encounter this bug or any other problem. The impact of unexpected problems can be minimized by working with an experienced NetWare vendor who is aware of any possible anomalies and can warn you about them.

Installing and Customizing NetWare with NETGEN's Custom Mode

Using NETGEN's default mode to install NetWare is like going to a restaurant that only serves seven-course meals. You must take what you are served, and you have no freedom to change the side dishes. Using NETGEN's custom mode is more like going to a cafeteria. You can have a seven-course meal if you like, but you also can have salad and a dessert if that is all you prefer. Because NETGEN's custom mode lets you select and perform installation and configuration tasks individually, it is the method of choice for NetWare installers who need to vary NetWare's installation defaults. It is also the method that you must use if you want to change some of the server's configuration options after NetWare has been installed.

Start NETGEN with one of the methods described in the section in this chapter called "Starting NETGEN." You have several options, depending on whether you are working with floppies or with NETGEN's files stored on an existing server. In either case, make sure that you use the same working copies of NETGEN's files that you used to generate NetWare for your server.

From NETGEN's initial menu, choose Custom Configuration when you are prompted to select the configuration level (or you can bypass this step by starting NETGEN with the -C command line parameter as previously described). From the next menu, specify whether you are using NETGEN from floppies, floppies and a RAM drive, or from a network drive.

After you have made the proper preliminary selections, NETGEN displays the menu shown in figure 6.1. If you follow these steps and arrive at this menu but the option NetWare Installation does not appear, it means that you are not working with the same set of floppies you used to generate NetWare. To correct this problem, exit NETGEN and restart it using those files. If for some reason you cannot locate them, or you never generated NetWare, you need to do so before going any further (see the previous chapter for complete instructions on generating NetWare).

Select NetWare Installation from the menu shown in figure 6.1. If you are working with a server disk on which NetWare has not been installed, you are prompted to perform the following steps:

1. Confirm that the disk drive configuration is correct.

2. Create a partition table on the server disks.

3. Set up disk drive mirrored pairs (if applicable).

You are first shown the list of the disks installed in the server PC. Examine this list to confirm that it is correct and is the same list that you used when generating NetWare and running DISKSET. Press Esc when you have finished examining the list, and you are prompted to confirm that the drive list is correct. If it is not, highlight Drive List Is Not Correct, and NETGEN's main menu returns, from which you can exit the program and correct the problem. For example, if a particular drive that should be on the list is not, check to see that it is connected properly. After correcting the problem, restart NETGEN and follow the same steps to continue installing NetWare.

You now see the Installation Options menu, which offers the following three options:

Select Default Installation Options
Select Custom Installation Options
Continue Installation

If you select the first option, you are prompted to follow exactly the same steps that you follow when installing NetWare using NETGEN's default mode. You automatically choose default settings for volume assignments, printers, and other server options and are prompted to enter the file server name. These steps are not discussed here because the previous section covers them in detail. You may want to use this method to quickly configure the server, and then choose the Installation Option menu's second selection (Select Custom Installation Options) to modify a few aspects of the configuration.

Some NetWare installers skip the first option and go directly to the second (Select Custom Installation Options). When you select this option, you are taken through the following tasks:

❑ Creating a disk partition table entry for NetWare

❑ Setting up a "Hot Fix" area on each disk

❑ Choosing the server volume arrangement

❑ Setting various server configuration options

❑ Choosing which NetWare files should be copied to the server disks

❑ Choosing which ports should be used for shared printers

About Partition Tables

If you are working with a disk that does not have NetWare already installed, and it is a type that uses partition tables, choosing Select Custom Installation Options from NETGEN's Installation Options menu takes you to a menu that offers two options: Modify Partition Table and Return To Previous Menu. Disks attached to the server using the Novell DCB do not use partition tables, but disks that use ST506 or ESDI controllers usually do. A disk partition is a physical area of the disk reserved for a particular operating system.

When you define a partition table, you designate its operating system type, whether or not it is bootable, and its starting and ending cylinders. If you have several partitions on a disk, only one can be defined as bootable, and that is the one that the server PC tries to boot from when it is first started.

The starting and ending cylinder settings define the partition's size. A hard disk consists of a stack of metallic circular platters. Each platter is formatted into a series of tracks, which radiate from the center of the platter, starting from track zero. A cylinder is a grouping of every track on every platter with the same number. For example, if your disk has 3 platters, cylinder number 15 consists of the tracks numbered 15 on all 3 of the platters. A partition table beginning at cylinder 15 and ending at cylinder 100 consists of all tracks from 15 to 100 on all disk platters. If your memories of high school geometry are distant and blurred, and you have trouble understanding this, don't worry. Just remember that a cylinder is a unit of disk space used to define partition sizes. If your disk has 1000 cylinders, a partition table of 500 cylinders consists of exactly half of the available disk space.

Obviously, you must know the number of cylinders on your disks to know how to best prepare your disk's partition table. When you ran your server PC's setup program, it probably listed the number of cylinders for your disk when you specified which disk type number to use. The reference manual for your server PC's setup program also may have a table showing the cylinder count for each disk type. COMPSURF also displays this information, and NETGEN displays the highest cylinder number when it prompts you to enter the ending cylinder for a partition.

If you plan to use all of your server disk space for NetWare, then each disk should have only one partition for NetWare. If you plan to use the server PC as both a server and a workstation, you may want to have two types of disk partitions—one for NetWare and the other for DOS. The DOS partition is available only to the person who uses the server PC as a workstation, but the NetWare partition is available to all network users.

There are several rules that govern creating partitions. First, the NetWare partition must be the first partition (starting on cylinder zero). Second, there can only be one NetWare partition per disk. If you plan to use part of the disk for DOS, a primary DOS partition must be located within the first 32M of the disk, and should be at least 2M in size. That means that your NetWare partition on that disk can be no greater than 30M because it must coexist with the primary DOS partition within the first 32M of disk space. Finally, no more than four partitions can be created on a single disk.

Creating and Modifying Disk Partition Tables

To configure the partitions on your server disks, select Modify Partition Table from the Custom Installation menu. If you have more than one disk in your server, a list of disks appears. Highlight the disk that you want to partition and press Enter. A window opens, showing the current partition table information. On a newly COMPSURFed disk, the window is empty.

To add a new partition, press Ins. The window shown in figure 6.9 appears. You are prompted to choose four attributes of the partition: the operating system type, the status (bootable or nonbootable), its starting cylinder, and its ending cylinder. By default, this window suggests a partition that uses the entire disk for NetWare. If you want to use the entire disk for NetWare, press Esc to accept the defaults. The partition window is updated to show the NetWare partition.

If you want to use part of the disk for DOS, change the ending cylinder number to something other than the last cylinder. For example, if you want to use one half of the disk for NetWare and the other half for DOS, highlight the entry box next to End Cylinder and enter the cylinder number that is exactly halfway between the first cylinder (zero) and the last. If you are going to make the server nondedicated (where it is used both for NetWare and as a DOS workstation), make the NetWare partition

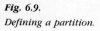

Fig. 6.9.

Defining a partition.

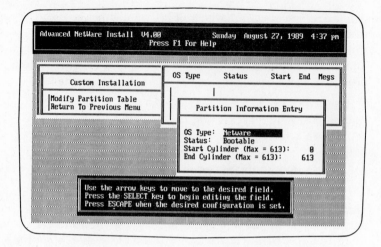

nonbootable. For a nondedicated server, you need to boot from a DOS partition or a DOS floppy, so the NetWare partition should be nonbootable. After the partition information is set the way you want it, press Esc, and the partition window is updated to show your selection.

If you used only part of the disk for NetWare, you need to add one or more additional partitions so that all disk cylinders are used. Press Ins to add another partition. Again, a window similar to the one in figure 6.9 appears. This time, the operating system type is displayed as Undefined. To specify the operating system type, highlight the entry box next to DOS Type and press Enter. The entry box lists the following operating system options:

DOS 12-Bit FATs
DOS 16-Bit FATs
Extended DOS
NetWare
Other

If you are defining the primary DOS partition, choose the first option if your disk is 10M or less in size (which is unlikely because that leaves little room for either NetWare or DOS, let alone both of them). Choose DOS 16-Bit FATs in the more likely event that you are using a disk more than 10M in size. Remember that the primary DOS partition must be contained within the first 32M of disk space.

Select Extended DOS if you are defining a DOS partition other than the first. The extended DOS partition does not have to be contained within the disk's first 32M, but you cannot have an extended DOS partition without first creating a primary DOS partition. Select Other if you need to create a partition for a non-DOS operating system, such as XENIX.

After you have selected the partition's operating-system type, you need to define its starting and ending cylinders. Pick a starting cylinder that is one greater than the ending cylinder of the previous partition. Choose an ending cylinder based on how large you want the partition to be. If you are creating the final partition on the disk, choose the highest cylinder number as the ending cylinder.

After defining each partition, press Esc to leave the partition entry box. The partition table window is updated to show the partition you have defined.

When all partitions have been defined, press Esc to leave the partition table window. You are prompted to confirm that you want to save the partition table. Answer yes to save your changes, no to cancel your entries and return to the installation menu, or press Esc to return to the partition table window. If you opt to save the partition table information, you may receive warning messages indicating problems with your partition entries. For example, if two partitions have overlapping starting and ending cylinders, or if you forgot to define a NetWare partition, you need to make corrections. You also receive a warning message if you marked the NetWare partition as nonbootable. This is allowed if you are using a nondedicated server.

After the partition table has been saved, the screen returns to the list of disks installed in the server PC (unless there is only one). Select the next disk and configure its partition table. After all disks have their partition tables established, press Esc. You are taken to a menu, and it prompts you to set up a Hot Fix area on each disk.

Setting Up a Hot Fix Area

After working with the disk partition tables, you are brought to a menu, which lists the following options:

    Hot Fix Drives To Default
    Modify Hot Fix
    Redirection Tables
    Modify Partition Table
    Return To Previous Menu

The first two options enable you to establish a Hot Fix area on each disk drive.

You have already learned about using COMPSURF to find bad blocks on your server disks and mark them as unusable. Unfortunately, it is not unusual for a disk to develop additional bad blocks as it is being used.

Rather than living a perfect life and then suddenly failing, most disks gradually wear out, developing an increasing number of bad blocks during the process.

NetWare's Hot Fix feature is designed to minimize the problems caused by this gradual decline. It is like an ongoing COMPSURF; after a disk block is written to, it is read to see if the information was written accurately. If the disk block fails the test, it is marked as unusable and replaced by another disk block.

When you establish a Hot Fix area, you are setting aside a pool of disk blocks that are available to replace blocks that fail NetWare's read-after-write test. NETGEN suggests a default area that is equal to between two and three percent of the disk's total block count. This means that two or three percent of your disk space is unavailable for regular use.

Select the Hot Fix Drives To Default option on the Custom Installation menu to automatically allocate this much of each disk as a Hot Fix area. Between two and three percent of each disk attached to the server PC is automatically allocated as a Hot Fix area.

Another menu option, Modify Hot Fix Redirection Tables, enables you to increase or decrease the size of the Hot Fix area. When you select this option, a list of the disks attached to the server is displayed. Disks that have been Hot Fixed have an asterisk (*) displayed under the heading Hot Fixed. You are allowed to use as little as one percent or as much as two-thirds of the disk as a Hot Fix area if you want. There are not many good reasons to increase or decrease the size of the Hot Fix area. In virtually every case, using the default size is adequate.

To modify the size of a disk's Hot Fix area, highlight the disk from the drive list and press Enter, NETGEN displays the disk's physical size (the actual number of physical blocks available on the disk) and prompts you to enter the logical disk size (the actual amount of disk space to be used for storing information). The difference between the physical and logical disk sizes is the Hot Fix area. These are shown in units of disk blocks (4096 bytes). Enter the logical disk size of your choice, and press Esc to save this information. Repeat these steps for each disk for which you want to customize the Hot Fix area size. When you have finished working with the Hot Fix areas for each disk, press Esc to leave the disk list and return to the Custom Installation menu.

Disk Mirroring and Duplexing

If you are using SFT NetWare 286, after establishing a Hot Fix area on all disks, a special installation option becomes available if you have two or more disks attached to your server that are identical to each other in size. SFT NetWare enables you to designate that two disks become a mirrored or duplexed pair so that whatever is written to one is automatically written to the other.

If you have the equipment installed in your PC to make mirroring or duplexing possible, a Mirroring Options menu appears along with the list of disks that can be mirrored or duplexed. If you want to activate disk mirroring or duplexing, select the Establish Mirror Pair option and read the section in this chapter called "Disk Mirroring and Duplexing with SFT NetWare 286" for details on setting up a mirrored or duplexed disk pair. Otherwise, select Done, Continue Installation to bypass this menu.

Initializing Disks

After you have established a Hot Fix area on each disk and established mirrored disk pairs (if applicable), a new option called Initialize appears on the Custom Installation menu. Selecting this option results in the following on-screen prompts:

Choose A File Server Name
Specify File Server Configuration Information
Define Volume Information For The Disk

Highlight the Initialize a Disk option and press Enter. You see a list of the hard disks attached to the server. Highlight the first and press Enter. This disk becomes the hard disk that stores the file server configuration information. For this drive only, you are prompted to enter the file server configuration information.

Entering the File Server Configuration

When you initialize the first hard disk on your file server, the System Configuration window appears (see fig. 6.10), and you are prompted to enter the server's system configuration information.

The file server configuration information consists of the following items:

1. The file server name

2. The maximum number of files that can be open at any one time

3. The maximum number of indexed files that can be stored on the server

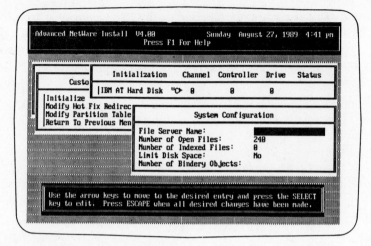

Fig. 6.10.
Initializing the first
server disk.

4. Whether to limit disk space per user

5. The maximum number of bindery objects

The settings that you enter now can be changed later if necessary.

The first item that you are prompted to enter in the System Configuration window is the file server name. If you have more than one file server on your network, each file server name must be unique. Your server name must be between 2 and 45 characters in length. Choose a name that is brief and meaningful, such as the name of the department that is using the server (such as SALES or ACCTING), the server's location (such as WAREHSE or FLOOR2), or the server's primary application (such as EMAIL or INVENTORY). The server name cannot begin with a period (.), cannot include spaces, and cannot employ any of the following characters:

" * + , / \ ¦ : ; = < > ? [ ]

Type the server name that you want to use and press Enter.

After entering the server name, the highlight moves to the Number of Open Files setting. This configuration option determines how many files can be open simultaneously by all file server users. NETGEN suggests a default of 240, which is usually adequate. If you know how many users will be connecting to the file server at one time and the average number of files each will open, you can compare the total number of files to this setting and increase it if necessary. If it is too high, you can decrease it and free up file server memory for other purposes. Any setting from 20 to 1000 is allowed.

To change the maximum number of open files, make sure that the current number is highlighted and press Enter. Press Backspace to remove the current setting, type the number that you want to use, and press Enter.

After entering the maximum number of open files, the highlight moves to the Number of Indexed Files setting. INDEXED is a special NetWare file attribute, which you will learn about in detail in Chapter 12. It is used for files that are at least several megabytes in size, and can improve the speed at which data within those files can be retrieved. The application creating the files must set the INDEXED attribute when the file is created. Network supervisors report that few applications are taking advantage of this feature, so it is unlikely that you will be using it. If you are not aware of any applications that use the INDEXED attribute, leave this option at the default setting of zero. To change the setting, highlight the current setting, press Enter, Backspace, and type a number from 0 to 1000. Press Enter to update the setting.

If you have SFT NetWare, you are shown two parameters for the Transaction Tracking System (TTS): the transaction backout volume (where data for transactions in progress is stored) and the maximum number of transactions that can be in progress at any one time. In most cases, a *transaction* is an update performed to a series of database files. To protect the data files from being corrupted as a result of being partially updated (as would be the case if a power failure occurred during an update), transactions are "staged" on the backout volume, and then written to the actual data files only after they have been completed. To take advantage of this feature, your application must be written to use TTS.

The backout volume is the NetWare volume where staged transactions are stored. For now, because you are defining your first volume, you have no choice but to accept the default backout volume, SYS (the first NetWare volume is always called SYS). During a later step after other volumes are defined, you can change this. Use the down-arrow key or press Enter to bypass this setting for now.

Next you must define the number of transactions that can be in progress and tracked by TTS at any one time. If you know which applications on the server will be taking advantage of TTS and how many users will be using the system and performing updates at any given time, you should be able to calculate this number fairly accurately.

To change the number of transactions, highlight the current setting and press Enter. Backspace over the current setting, and type the number of your choice. Press Enter to update the setting.

The Limit Disk Space option lets you specify whether the network supervisor can limit each user to a particular amount of disk space. This is a useful management tool on servers where users are given the freedom to store personal files on the server disks. To prevent users from using up the server disk, set this option to yes (this feature is covered in Chapter 10).

Set the current Limit Disk Space setting. Press Y to change the setting to yes. You can press N to return the setting to no if you want.

When you change the Limit Disk Space option to yes, NETGEN supplies a default setting for the number of bindery objects. NetWare's *Bindery* is a group of files that store user and security information. The default setting of 500 is the minimum setting and is adequate in most situations, but this number can be increased if necessary to an upper limit of 5000.

To change the number of Bindery objects allowed, highlight the current setting and press Enter. Backspace over the current setting and type the number of your choice. Press Enter to update the setting.

After you have entered the desired settings for each configuration option, press Esc to leave the System Configuration window. You are ready for the next step: entering the disk volume information.

Defining Disk Volumes

After setting each of the System Configuration options, the next step is to divide the hard disk into volumes. When you leave the System Configuration screen, the Volume Table window automatically appears on-screen.

A volume is similar to a disk partition in that it is a physical area on a disk. The NetWare partition that you placed on the disk can be subdivided into as many as 16 volumes. It is generally best to divide the disk into as few volumes as possible so that you have the freedom to allocate disk space as you want. NetWare volumes can be as large as 255M, so if your disk is less than 255M in size, you can make the disk one NetWare volume. If your disk is larger than this limit, you need to subdivide the disk into volumes of 255M or less.

To create the first volume, press Ins. The Volume Definition window opens (see fig. 6.11), prompting you to enter the volume name and size, as well as the number of directory entries and whether the directory should be cached. For the first volume you create, the name is automatically SYS, and you cannot change it. On subsequent volumes, you can enter the name of your choice.

A volume name can be from 2 to 15 characters long, cannot begin with a period, and cannot include any of the following characters:

" * + , / \ ¦ : ; = < > ? [ ]

If you have multiple servers with more than one volume, you may want to use a consistent volume-naming scheme on all servers. For example, you may want to call all second volumes VOL2, and third volumes VOL3.

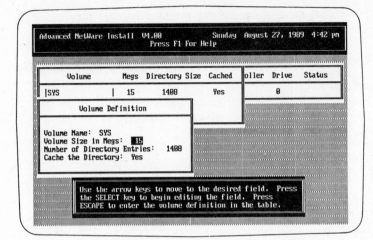

Fig. 6.11.
Defining a NetWare
volume.

To enter the *volume size*, highlight the current volume size setting. NETGEN inserts the maximum possible size as the default. To change this setting, press Enter, backspace over the current setting and type the desired volume size in megabytes (from 5 to 255 or the maximum disk size, whichever is smaller). Press Enter to update the volume size setting. After you establish the volume size, you cannot change it without reinitializing the disk and erasing all of the files it contains.

The next option to set is the *number of directory entries*. This refers simply to the number of directories, subdirectories, and files that the disk volume can store. NETGEN calculates the default setting for this based on the size of the volume. You can raise it or lower it in increments of 128 entries. Occasionally an application creates unusually large numbers of files and directories. If this is the case for the volume you are working with, you may want to increase the entry. However, the default setting is adequate in the vast majority of cases, and can be changed at any time. Each block of 128 directory entries requires 5120 bytes of server memory.

To change the number of directory entries, highlight the current setting and press Enter. Backspace over the current setting and type the number of your choice. Press Enter to update the setting. The number you select is updated automatically to the next highest multiple of 128.

The Cache the Directory setting may not have much meaning for you. Directory caching is a term that refers to NetWare's keeping a volume's file and directory listings in memory after the server is booted. When a user requests a file that is stored on a volume where directory caching is activated, NetWare can search for the file's location in memory, which is substantially quicker than reading the disk volume itself to get the information. Directory caching is one of NetWare's primary methods of improving disk and server performance. It should only be disabled when you must conserve memory for other purposes. Leave directory caching set to yes whenever possible.

To turn off directory caching (which is not recommended), highlight the current Cache the Directory setting and press N to change the setting to no. You can press Y to return the setting to yes if you want.

After you have configured the volume, press Esc to leave the Volume Definition window and return to the Volume Table screen. It is updated to show the volume you have added.

To add another volume, press Ins and repeat the preceding steps. To delete a volume, highlight it on the Volume Table Screen and press Del. You cannot delete the SYS volume, but you can modify its configuration or that of any other volume by highlighting that volume's name and pressing Enter. The Volume Definition window returns to the screen.

After you have configured the disk volumes as desired, review the information in the Volume Table window carefully. You cannot change the volume sizes or delete or add volumes later without reinitializing the disk and erasing all the files it contains. Press Esc to save your changes. You are prompted to confirm that you want to create the volumes. Answer yes. If there are additional disks to be initialized, a list of disk drives comes back on-screen. Select the next disk to initialize, and repeat the steps you followed to initialize the first disk.

When you have initialized all disks, the Custom Installation menu shown in figure 6.12 appears. A new option, called Miscellaneous Maintenance, appears. You use this option to specify the final installation steps. This menu also offers you the capability to redo any of the previously performed tasks, such as modifying the partition table and the Hot Fix areas. You should use these options with caution. For example, changing the NetWare partition's size destroys the volume definition work that you have done. Selecting the Reinitialize a Disk option has the same effect.

At this point, you should select the Miscellaneous Maintenance option to perform the final steps prior to copying NetWare's files to your server.

The Miscellaneous Maintenance Option

The Miscellaneous Maintenance option from NETGEN's Custom Installation menu takes you through the final tasks in the server installation. This menu

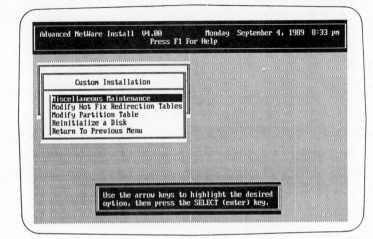

```
        Custom Installation
Miscellaneous Maintenance
Modify Hot Fix Redirection Tables
Modify Partition Table
Reinitialize a Disk
Return To Previous Menu
```

```
Use the arrow keys to highlight the desired
option, then press the SELECT (enter) key.
```

Fig. 6.12.
Using the
Miscellaneous
Maintenance option.

is also the one you use when you are running NETGEN after installing NetWare for the purpose of modifying some of the server's configuration parameters.

When you select this option, a submenu appears that offers you the following choices:

Load Operating System
Load System & Public Files
System Configuration
Volume Information
Printer Maintenance

Each selection corresponds to a basic task that must be performed to install NetWare on a server. These are the same tasks that are performed automatically when you select NETGEN's default mode. You also can return to this menu to change the server configuration after NetWare has been installed.

During a first-time installation of NetWare, you must select and review each option. Each option will be discussed individually in the following sections.

Load Operating System

When you select this option, NETGEN sets a flag to prompt you to install NetWare's operating system files. These files are stored on your working copies of the OSEXE disks. The operating system files are named

NET$OS.EXE, NET$OS.EX1, and NET$OS.EX2. When you install NetWare, they are copied and combined into one file called NET$OS.EXE in a directory called SYSTEM on the server's first volume.

If you are doing a full installation of NetWare on the server, you must select this menu option. When you do so, you are prompted to confirm that you want to set a flag for operating system load.

Normally, you do not select this option if you are not doing a full installation and are only customizing server configuration options. An exception is when you have created new operating system files for an existing server, perhaps to implement a "patch" provided to fix a bug, or to change your server from dedicated to nondedicated operation (or vice versa).

Load System & Public Files

When this option is selected, NETGEN sets a flag to prompt you to install NetWare's system and public files. These files are stored on the disks labeled SYSTEM, PUBLIC-1, PUBLIC-2, PUBLIC-3, and so on. These files are the NetWare commands that users and the network supervisor employ when they are logged in to the server. They are placed in three directories on the server's SYS volume, which are SYSTEM, PUBLIC, and LOGIN.

If you are doing a full installation of NetWare on the server, you must select this menu option. When you do, you are prompted to confirm that you want to set a flag for system and public file load. You normally do not select this option if you are not doing a full installation but are only customizing server configuration options.

System Configuration

The System Configuration menu option enables you to change the server configuration options that you set when initializing the first file server disk. You can change the file server name, the number of files that can be opened simultaneously by all server users, and the number of indexed files. It also lets you choose whether or not you can limit each user to a particular amount of disk space. If you are using SFT NetWare 286, you also are given the opportunity to choose the operating parameters for NetWare's Transaction Tracking System.

When you select the System Configuration option, a window appears similar to the one shown in figure 6.10. You can use the arrow keys to move to and then modify any of the window's entries. For a complete explanation of each option, see the section in this chapter called "System Configuration."

After you have entered the desired settings for each System Configuration option, press Esc to leave the window and return to the Miscellaneous Options menu.

Volume Information

For every disk volume, there are three settings that you can modify: the volume name (except in the case of the first server volume, which is always named SYS), the number of directory entries, and whether the directory is cached.

To work with these settings for a particular volume, highlight Volume Information from the Miscellaneous Maintenance menu and press Enter. A list of volumes appears; highlight the one with which you want to work and press Enter. A window opens, showing the current name, number of directory entries, and directory cache setting for the selected volume. You can use the arrow keys to move the highlight bar next to each setting in order to modify it. For example, to change the volume name, move the highlight bar to the current name and enter the new name.

As previously described, the number of directory entries refers simply to the number of directories, subdirectories, and files that the disk volume can store. NETGEN calculates the default setting for this, based on the size of the volume. You can raise or lower it in increments of 128 entries. Occasionally an application creates unusually large numbers of files and directories. If this is the case for the volume you are working with, you may want to increase the entry. However, the default setting is adequate in the vast majority of cases, and can be changed at any time using this menu option.

The Cache the Directory setting refers to NetWare's keeping a volume's file and directory listings in memory after the server is booted. It should only be disabled when you are trying to conserve memory. Leave directory caching set to yes whenever possible.

After you have finished working with the settings for a particular volume, press Esc to leave the Volume Definition window and return to the list of volumes. Press Esc from the list of volumes to return to the Miscellaneous Maintenance menu.

Printer Maintenance

The Printer Maintenance option lets you choose which printer ports in the file server should support shared printers. If there are any parallel and serial ports in the server PC, NETGEN offers you the opportunity to use them as connections for shared network printers. Like DOS and OS/2, NETGEN refers to serial and parallel ports using their device names (COM1 and COM2 for serial ports and LPT1, LPT2 and LPT3 for parallel ports). NetWare 286 permits up to two serial ports and three parallel ports to be used to connect network printers, for a total number of five per server.

When you select the Printer Maintenance menu option, you are shown a list of every port and its status as a network printer connection (fig. 6.13). By default, no printer ports are assigned to be used for network printers, and all show the status Not Spooled (*spooled* refers to the sharing of one printer by many users). To assign a printer port for use as a network printer connection, highlight it and press Enter. If the port you selected is a parallel port, you see a window displaying the device name (such as LPT1) and the assigned printer number (0-4). You can type a new printer number if you want, and then press Esc to return to the printer list. It is updated to show the addition of a new printer.

Fig. 6.13.

Configuring server ports for shared printers.

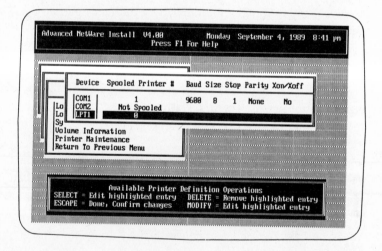

You should assign printer number 0 to the port that you expect to be the most heavily used. When users connect to a network printer, printer 0 is the one selected by default.

If you are assigning a serial port for use as a network printer, you see a window listing the device name, the assigned printer number, and the communication settings for the port. The following default communication settings are shown:

Baud Rate:	9600
Word Length:	8 bits
Stop Bits:	1 bit
Parity:	None
Xon/Xoff Protocol:	No

With the arrow keys, you can highlight each of the communication parameters and change them to whatever setting you need to use. You also can change the assigned printer number with the same method. When you have changed the settings to the desired configuration, press Esc to return to the spooled printer list. The spooled printer list is updated to show your changes.

To delete a spooled printer from the list, highlight it and press Del. It's status on the printer list is changed to show that it is no longer a network printer.

You should record your printer port configuration for future reference. After you have done so, press Esc to leave the printer port information screen. When you are prompted to confirm that you want to use the new printer definitions, answer yes, and you again see the Miscellaneous Maintenance menu.

Installing NetWare's Files

When you have finished working with the Miscellaneous Maintenance options, you should be ready to install NetWare's files on the SYS volume of your server. Select Return To Previous Menu, or press Esc to return to the Custom Installation menu. Select Return To Previous Menu, or press Esc again, and the Installation Options menu returns to the screen.

From the Installation Options menu, select the Continue Installation option. You are prompted to confirm that you want to install networking software on the file server. You need your working copies of the OSEXE disks for this operation, as well as the disks labeled SYSTEM and PUBLIC. In addition to copying NetWare's files, this step also installs the cold boot loader to the first server disk. It is used to boot the server if your disk configuration permits booting from a hard disk.

When the last disk's files have been copied, you see the message, System files successfully installed, and you are prompted to press a key to continue. After doing so, you are returned to the Network Generation Options menu. One of your options from this menu is to exit NETGEN. Select this option and you see a DOS prompt.

You have now completed one of the most complicated installation processes known to modern computing—you have installed NetWare 286 using NETGEN's custom mode! At this point, you may feel like you have earned a vacation. But, like most network installers, you are probably anxious to find out whether your installation was successful, so it's time to boot the server. Booting the server is discussed in the next section.

If for some reason your experience with NETGEN was not successful, read the previous section in this chapter, called "NETGEN Bugs." You also may want to have your NetWare vendor or other experienced help available in case something unexpected happens.

Booting the File Server

Booting is a term used for starting a computer and loading its operating system. When you boot a NetWare file server, you are starting it so that others can use it.

How you boot your newly installed file server depends on the following two factors:

1. Whether the file server is dedicated or nondedicated

2. Whether your file server has a bootable hard disk

Booting both a dedicated and a nondedicated server is covered next.

Booting a Dedicated Server

If you are running your server in dedicated mode, how you boot it depends on whether it has a self-booting disk drive.

Booting from a Self-Booting Hard Disk

If your file server is equipped with a self-booting hard disk, booting it is simply a matter of turning it on, or, if it is already booted from DOS, a matter of pressing Ctrl-Alt-Del to allow it to reboot as a server from its hard disk.

The following types of disks are self-booting:

1. A disk that uses an internal ST506 controller (generally used in AT-compatible PCs)

2. A disk that uses an internal ESDI controller (generally used in a PS/2-compatible PC)

Disks that attach to the Novell disk coprocessor board are generally not self-booting (except for certain models of Novell-designed file servers, such as the 286B).

Booting from a Floppy Disk

In cases where the file server contains no self-booting disk, you must start the server from a floppy disk. The server needs to boot from a bootable floppy disk, using DOS Version 3.0 or later (you can create a self-booting disk by formatting it with the FORMAT command, using the /S parameter). After the server PC has successfully booted from DOS, place the working copy of your OSEXE-1 disk in the server PC's floppy drive and type *net$os*.

If you are using 5 1/4-inch disks, you are prompted to insert the OSEXE-2 disk.

You probably will want to create a special boot disk for the server and store your OSEXE disks for safe keeping. If your server is equipped with a high-density 5 1/4-inch floppy drive or a 3 1/2-inch disk drive, you can format a 1.2M, 5 1/4-inch disk or a 720K or 1.44M 3 1/2-inch floppy using the FORMAT command with the /S option. Next, copy all the files from your OSEXE-1 and OSEXE-2 disks to this disk (if you are using the 3 1/2-inch disk version of NetWare, you do not have an OSEXE-2 disk). Create an AUTOEXEC.BAT file on this disk that includes the following command:

    NET$OS

When the file server PC boots from this disk, it automatically loads NetWare.

If your server PC has only a low-density 5 1/4-inch floppy drive, you cannot boot it from one disk. You need to copy the files from the OSEXE-1 disk to a bootable low-density floppy disk, and the files from the OSEXE-2 disk to a second low-density disk. You can boot the server from the first disk, and then place the second disk in the floppy drive when you are prompted for the OSEXE-2 disk.

Booting a Nondedicated Server

A nondedicated file server is used as both a server and workstation at the same time. It must boot DOS first, then load the NetWare operating system files (from your OSEXE disks), and finally load the NetWare workstation shell.

You can boot DOS from a floppy, or from the server's hard disk if you created a bootable DOS partition on it. Both methods are discussed in the following sections.

Booting from a Floppy Disk

If you plan to run your server in nondedicated mode and it has no self-booting hard disk, or you opted not to create a bootable DOS partition on a server hard disk, you must start the server from a floppy disk. The server needs to boot from a bootable floppy disk, using DOS Version 3.0 or later (you can create a self-booting disk by formatting it with the FORMAT command, using the /S parameter). After the server PC has successfully booted from DOS, place the working copy of your OSEXE-1 disk in the server PC's floppy drive and type *net$os*.

If you are using 5 1/4-inch disks, you are prompted to insert the OSEXE-2 disk. The server completes the boot process and becomes available to users.

You probably will want to create a special boot disk for the server and store your OSEXE disks for safe keeping. If your server is equipped with a high-density 5 1/4-inch floppy drive or a 3 1/2-inch disk drive, you can format a 1.2M, 5 1/4-inch disk or a 720K or 1.44M, 3 1/2-inch floppy using the FORMAT command with the /S parameter. Next, copy all the files from your OSEXE-1 and OSEXE-2 disks to this disk (if you are using the 3 1/2-inch disk version of NetWare, you do not have an OSEXE-2 disk). Copy a NetWare shell to the disk as well (NET3.COM for DOS 3.x or NET4.COM for DOS 4.x—you will learn about creating the NetWare shell's files in the next chapter).

Create an AUTOEXEC.BAT file on this disk, consisting of the following commands (substitute NET4 for NET3 if you are using DOS 4.x):

    NET$OS

    NET3

    F:

When the file server PC boots from this disk, it automatically loads NetWare and starts the PC as a server. It then loads the NetWare shell and makes the network drive (F:) the default.

If your server PC has only a low-density 5 1/4-inch floppy drive, you cannot boot it from one disk. You need to copy the files from the OSEXE-1 disk to a bootable low-density floppy disk, and the files from the OSEXE-2 disk as well as a copy of the NetWare shell to a second low-density disk. You can boot the server from the first disk, and then place the second disk in floppy drive when you are prompted for the OSEXE-2 disk.

Booting from a Self-Booting Hard Disk

You can boot a nondedicated server from the server's hard disk if the disk is self-booting and you created a bootable DOS partition on it. You first need to format that partition with the FORMAT command, using the /S option to make it bootable. Next, you need to copy all the files from your OSEXE-1 and OSEXE-2 disks to this disk (if you are using the 3 1/2-inch disk version of NetWare you do not have an OSEXE-2 disk). Copy a NetWare shell to the disk as well. (NET3.COM for DOS 3.x or NET4.COM for DOS 4.x. You will learn about creating the NetWare shell's files in the next chapter.)

If you want the server PC to automatically start as a server, create an AUTOEXEC.BAT file in the root directory of the DOS portion of the server disk. The AUTOEXEC.BAT file should contain the following commands (substitute NET4 for NET3 if you are using DOS 4.x):

> NET$OS
>
> NET3

This automatically starts nondedicated NetWare 286 and loads the NetWare shell, which is a prerequisite to logging in to the server (you will learn about the NetWare shell in the next chapter).

Understanding the Server Boot Messages

You should watch the server PC's display as it boots. It gives you status messages as the server is coming up that help you understand the steps that the server follows as it boots. If any error messages are displayed, knowing at what point the error message occurred helps you know where to look to correct the error.

If you are booting a dedicated server from a self-booting hard disk, the NetWare Cold Boot Loader message appears first, showing information similar to the following:

Novell SFT NetWare File Server Cold Boot Loader

If you are booting from a floppy, or booting a nondedicated server from a DOS partition, the cold boot loader is not used, so you do not see this message.

You next see a volume mounting message for each volume that mounts. The message for volume SYS is Mounting Volume SYS.

It may take a number of seconds for each volume to mount. If a problem is encountered while mounting a particular volume, the corresponding error message is displayed after the volume mounting message.

After all volumes are mounted, the file server checks its Bindery files. The Bindery is NetWare's term for its security files. At this point, the server screen shows Checking Bindery. Any errors detected in the Bindery are shown on-screen after this message.

Next, the print queues are checked, and the message Checking Queues is displayed.

Finally, the server initializes the network adapters that are installed in the server. The following message is displayed when the first network adapter is initialized:

Initializing LAN A

The second network adapter is referred to as *LAN B*, the third as *LAN C*, and the fourth as *LAN D*. If your server is nondedicated, it also initializes *LAN E*, which is the link between the workstation part of the server and NetWare.

Problems initializing network adapters are displayed at this point. Some types of network adapters, such as EtherNet and Token Ring cards, may not initialize properly unless they are connected to a successfully terminated cable system. If your server stops booting while initializing a network adapter, check to see that it is correctly configured and connected to its cable system.

Finally, the server displays the current date and time. If you are booting a dedicated server, a colon prompt (:) is displayed on the screen, where you can enter NetWare console commands (you will learn about console commands in Chapter 19).

A nondedicated server ends at the DOS prompt from where the NET$OS command was entered, such as C:\› or A:\›.

Downing the Server

After the server has successfully booted NetWare, at some point you will need to shut it down, perhaps to move it to its permanent location. If the server is dedicated, it boots to a NetWare colon prompt (:). From this prompt, type *down* and press Enter.

The server shuts down, at which point you can turn it off.

If your server is nondedicated, it boots to a DOS prompt. Load the NetWare shell (NET3 or NET4), and then type *f:console*, and press Enter. This command brings you to the console colon prompt (:). From this prompt, type *down* and press Enter.

The server shuts down, and you can turn it off.

Placing Your Server in a Good Operating Environment

After your server has NetWare properly installed, you are ready to move it to its permanent location. Unlike its minicomputer or mainframe cousins, a server does not require a special operating environment. It should be kept in an area with good ventilation at normal room temperature below 80 degrees Fahrenheit. It should not be exposed to excessive heat, humidity or dust. If you leave your file server running 24 hours a day, make sure that the room temperature does not exceed 80 degrees during off-hours or on weekends. High ambient temperatures cause electronic components and hard drives to age prematurely and can cause failure.

The only special accommodation that you should make for a server that you might not make for a normal PC is power protection. Because the server is used to store important files and often is the host for multiuser applications, it is vital that it be protected from a sudden power loss.

A power interruption while a database file is being updated can corrupt the database file. Installing an uninterruptible power supply (UPS) is low-cost insurance against this happening. A UPS provides battery-supplied power to the server when the normal power source fails, giving you time to down the server in an orderly fashion. Some UPS devices come with monitoring equipment that can be installed in the file server. If the normal power source fails, the UPS monitoring equipment senses this fact, automatically closes all the server's open files, and downs the server so that no data is corrupted.

You also may want to place your server in a secure area so that no one can turn it off or use the server console commands to clear the connections of other users.

Chapter Summary

You now know that installing a server is a detailed and complex process, and is probably the most difficult part of using NetWare. Whenever possible, you should use the default options provided by NETGEN to make your job easier and minimize the possibility that mistakes will be made. With practice, you can master installing NetWare 286 and configuring your server.

Installing NetWare 386

If you have generated and installed NetWare 286 or read about these tasks in the last two chapters, you may be concerned that installing the more powerful NetWare 386 is an even more complex process. Fortunately, nothing could be further from the truth. Installing NetWare 386 is surprisingly easy and requires only a fraction of the time and effort involved in preparing and installing NetWare 286.

Installing NetWare 386 generally consists of the following steps:

1. Assemble the server hardware.

2. Boot the server.

3. Activate the server's disks and network adapters.

4. Prepare the server disks.

5. Configure the server.

6. Copy NetWare's command files to the server.

7. Place the server in a safe operating environment.

The order of these steps may seem odd to you if you have had experience with NetWare 286. Booting the server is the second step in installing NetWare 386, whereas booting is nearly the last step when you install NetWare 286. You run NetWare 386's installation and configuration processes after starting the server.

Understanding Differences between NetWare 286 and 386

You set "in concrete" most of NetWare 286's installation and configuration options when you generate its files and use NETGEN to install NetWare. As you prepare to generate NetWare 286's main operating system file (NET$OS.EXE), you specify the types of network adapters and disks to be installed in the server and indicate whether the server is to be dedicated or nondedicated.

NetWare 386, however, comes with a main operating system file called SERVER.EXE, which already has been created. This file provides all you need to start a NetWare 386 server. When you first execute SERVER.EXE, your server PC comes up as a NetWare server, but it cannot recognize disks or network adapters. You must use additional commands to activate them.

You use the same commands that *start* disks and network adapters to *stop* them. The capability of starting and stopping these devices without downing the server is the secret to NetWare 386's dynamism. You can set and change many other configuration options while the server is running; NetWare 286 requires that you down the server before running NETGEN.

Some of this dynamism is hard to take advantage of. Even though NetWare 386 makes it possible theoretically to activate a new network adapter without downing the server, installing a new network adapter without first turning off the server PC is hardly safe. (If you run into a technician who claims to know how to do this, check his or her references thoroughly.) On the other hand, with new advances in removable disk platters, the capability of activating new disk volumes while the server is running can be useful. NetWare 386 also enables you to activate and configure network printers while the server is running, a task that requires downing the server and running NETGEN with NetWare 286.

Besides being dynamic, NetWare 386 can run NetWare Loadable Modules (NLMs), programs that can run on the server itself. In certain situations, running a program from the server instead of a workstation has significant advantages. Programs that run on a NetWare 386 server use the full capabilities of the 80386 processor, not the 8086 mode used by DOS or the 80286 mode used by OS/2. An emerging category of software that benefits from running on the server is the database server (sometimes called a database "engine"). A database server receives requests for data from workstations and then does the required processing and file retrieval within the server itself, cutting down on the network communications necessary to satisfy the request.

As you configure NetWare 386 on a server, you use several NLMs. You can use them to fine-tune an extensive array of server operating parameters without downing the server.

The following sections discuss the steps you follow to activate and install NetWare 386.

Assembling Your Server's Hardware

Before your server can boot NetWare 386, the server must be able to boot PC DOS; in other words, your server must be completely assembled. All memory must be installed and properly configured, and the display adapter must be installed and operating properly. If you are going to use your server to run network printers, the ports to which the printers connect must be in place, and PC DOS must be able to recognize them.

Your server PC must have a high-density floppy disk drive. You need at least 2M of RAM, but more is better, especially if you plan to use large disk drives for server volumes.

Especially important is the installation of the hard disk (or disks) that serves as the shared disk space. If you are converting a PC that has been used to run DOS or OS/2 into a server and you need to keep that PC's files, back up the disk. A hard disk's contents are erased during NetWare installation.

You may be using a disk configuration that cannot be used with DOS or OS/2. In this case, install the disk controller and disks exactly according to the manufacturer's instructions, paying close attention to switch and jumper settings. For example, Novell's disk coprocessor board used with a SCSI controller cannot be used by any operating system except NetWare, so you cannot test these disks before installing the server.

You also need to install and configure the network adapter or adapters that belong in the server. If you are using multiple adapters, use extra care to make sure that their configurations do not conflict. Each adapter must have a unique interrupt, I/O port, and ROM memory address (see "How Network Adapters Talk to PCs," in Chapter 5, for more details). Use the manuals that come with your network adapters to learn how to make these settings. With some types of adapters, you must set a unique node address. Choose an address that is not to be used by any other device, and record the address so that you do not accidentally use it again.

When you have assembled and properly configured all the hardware, run the setup program that comes with the server PC and enter all the server PC's hardware settings. Next, test the server by booting it with DOS.

Finally, store in a safe place all the manuals that come with the server PC and its peripherals. You likely will need to consult them later if you decide to add new items to the server PC.

After the server PC is properly assembled so that it boots DOS without errors, you are ready to start NetWare 386 using the file SERVER.EXE.

Booting the Server

You are now ready to start using the disks that come with NetWare 386. Prudence dictates that you first make backup copies (*working copies*) of your NetWare 386 disks. You should label your working copies with the same name as the original disks because you are prompted by name to use these disks many times during the installation process. After you have made working copies, store the original NetWare 386 disks in a safe place.

You have two options for booting a NetWare 386 server. You can boot from a high-density floppy disk or from a DOS partition on a hard disk. You can create a DOS partition on the disk only if you are using a hard disk in the server connected to an ST506- or ESDI-type controller (see Chapter 4 for more information about disk controller types).

Each method has its pros and cons. If you are using hard disks that are not DOS compatible, the floppy disk method is your only choice. When you boot from a floppy disk, you can more easily modify NetWare 386's start-up files while the server is running, because you can remove the disk and work with it on another PC. Booting from a hard disk is much faster, however, and a hard disk is less prone to failure (*media failure*) than a floppy disk. The hard disk partition takes up only one or two megabytes. Even if you plan to boot from a hard disk partition, creating a bootable floppy disk as an alternate booting method is wise.

Some 386 PCs have more than one speed of operation. Of course, you should make sure that the server PC is running at its top speed. Some PCs automatically revert to a slower speed when reading from a floppy disk. If you are booting the server PC from a floppy disk, consult your manuals to make sure that your computer is running at its fastest speed while booting. After the server PC loads NetWare 386, you probably cannot change the speed. If your PC cannot be set to its highest speed while booting from a floppy disk, you should consider booting from a DOS partition instead.

Creating a Server Boot Disk

Format a high-density 5 1/4- or 3 1/2-inch disk by using the DOS FORMAT command with the /S (system) option. (If you are formatting the disk in drive A, type *format a:/s* and press Enter. The /s makes the disk bootable.) Copy all the files from the NetWare 386 disk labeled System to this floppy disk.

Your network adapter manufacturer or vendor may have supplied a driver file for your network adapter type (a file with the extension LAN). Copy this file to the boot disk also. In addition, your disk drive vendor may have supplied a driver file for your server's hard disk configuration (probably with the file extension DSK). You need to copy this file to the boot disk as well. If you begin to run low on space on the boot disk, you can delete all files with the extension LAN or DSK, except the ones you will be using.

If you want NetWare 386 to start automatically when you boot from the disk you prepared, create an AUTOEXEC.BAT file on the disk containing the following command line:

SERVER

(A boot disk's AUTOEXEC.BAT file contains commands that are executed automatically when the PC is booted. See your DOS manual for more details.)

You are now ready to boot your server PC from this disk.

Creating a DOS Partition for Server Booting

Before you create a DOS partition on a hard disk, make sure that the disk has been properly installed and has received a low-level format to prepare it for DOS partitioning and formatting. Creating a new partition on a disk generally erases its contents, so if the disk you are using contains data you need to keep, back up its files.

Boot the server PC with a DOS floppy disk; then use the FDISK utility to create a DOS partition on the beginning cylinders of the disk. (FDISK is a DOS utility that enables you to partition hard disks. See your DOS manual for complete information.) A 1- or 2-megabyte partition is adequate to store the files necessary to boot NetWare 386.

When you define a partition table, you designate its starting and ending cylinders to define the partition's size. A hard disk consists of a stack of metallic circular platters. Each platter is formatted into a series of tracks that radiate from the center of the platter, starting from track 0. A cylinder (the unit of disk space used to define partition sizes) is a grouping of every track on every platter with the same number. If your disk has 1,000 cylinders, a partition table of 500 cylinders constitutes exactly half the available disk space.

You need to know two figures in order to calculate the number of cylinders to give to this DOS partition: the total number of cylinders on your disk and the disk size in megabytes. The FDISK command displays the total number of disk cylinders. Your PC's setup program or reference manual probably shows both the cylinder count and megabyte size of the disk. To calculate the amount of space needed to make a 2-megabyte partition, divide the number of cylinders by the number of megabytes to find the number of cylinders per megabyte. Multiply this number by 2 to find the number of cylinders you should assign for a 2-megabyte partition. For example, a 40-megabyte disk with 800 cylinders has 20 cylinders per megabyte (800/40 = 20). A 2-megabyte partition requires 40 cylinders (20 × 2).

Use FDISK to create a DOS partition on the beginning cylinders of the disk, starting with cylinder 0 and ending with the cylinder number necessary to give you the total cylinders required for two megabytes. Follow FDISK's prompts to activate this partition and assign it to drive C. After saving the partition information, reboot your PC (from the DOS floppy disk as before).

You next need to format the new partition by using the FORMAT command with the /S (system) option (type *format c:/s* and press Enter). Finally, copy to drive C all the files from the NetWare 386 disk labeled System.

Your network adapter manufacturer or vendor may have supplied a driver file for your network adapter type (a file with the extension LAN). Copy this file to drive C also. In addition, your disk drive vendor may have supplied a driver file for your server's hard disk configuration (probably with the file extension DSK). You need to copy this file to drive C as well. If you begin to run low on space in the DOS partition, you can delete all files with the extension LAN or DSK except the ones you will be using.

If you want NetWare 386 to start automatically when you boot from the hard disk, create an AUTOEXEC.BAT file containing the following command line:

SERVER

You are now ready to boot your server PC from the hard disk.

Starting NetWare 386 for the First Time

Boot your server PC from the floppy disk or DOS partition you have prepared. If you didn't create an AUTOEXEC.BAT file to execute SERVER.EXE automatically, execute it manually by typing *server* at the DOS prompt and pressing Enter.

When you boot the server for the first time, you need to perform a number of special tasks. You have to identify the disks, network adapters, and configuration options you want to activate. After these are identified, you are prompted to create an AUTOEXEC.NCF file for the server. This file contains the commands you typed when booting the server for the first time. The AUTOEXEC.NCF file is read every time the server is started so that you don't have to type the commands to name the server or activate its disks and network adapters.

After you have activated the network adapters and disks, you need to place a NetWare partition on each server disk and define NetWare volumes. You also have the option of performing a surface test on the disk (NetWare 286 uses the COMPSURF command for this test). Finally, you copy NetWare 386's command files from the disks to the server disk.

Viewing Start-Up Information and Processor Speed

When you first execute SERVER.EXE, you are shown your NetWare 386 version and revision level. Next, you see NetWare 386's calculation of your processor speed. Check this figure to make sure that your server PC is set to its maximum operating speed (particularly when you are booting from a floppy disk, as discussed earlier).

A server PC running at 16 MHz with an 80386 processor should have a speed rating of approximately 120, an 80386SX processor a rating of approximately 95, and a 25 MHz 80386 processor a rating of 150 or greater. If the speed rating shown is significantly lower than these numbers, check to make sure that your server PC is configured to operate at its maximum speed.

Naming the Server

After you see the processor speed, the following screen message prompts you to enter the server name:

    File server name:

Your server name must be between 2 and 47 characters in length. Choose a name that is brief and meaningful, such as the name of the department that is using the server (SALES or ACCTING), the server's location (WAREHSE or FLOOR2), or the server's primary application (EMAIL or INVENTORY). The server name cannot begin with a period (.) and cannot include spaces or the following characters:

    " * + , / \ ¦ : ; = < > ? [ ] .

NetWare 386 does not let you type any of these illegal characters.

Type the server name you want to use and press Enter.

Entering the IPX Internal Number

After entering the server name, a prompt tells you to choose a unique internal network number for your server, as follows:

    IPX internal network number:

If you have experience with NetWare 286, you know that every physical network on your local area network has a unique number. NetWare's IPX (Internetwork Packet Exchange) protocol uses these numbers to differentiate separate networks and to route data packets from a workstation or server on one network to a workstation or server on another. (Chapter 4 provides more information about multiple networks and servers.) With NetWare 386, this identification system is expanded, and each NetWare 386 server is required to have an identification number separate from the identification numbers given to physical networks.

Giving each server a unique number paves the way for *server mirroring*, which, like disk mirroring, enables two servers to duplicate each other. If one fails, the other continues to operate.

You can enter any number not already used by a physical network or another NetWare 386 server. This number is in hexadecimal format, which allows the digits 0 through 9 as well as the letters A through F; in other words, your internal network number can be 100 or 5BF. Record the number you assign to the internal network on a diagram of your network and label the server PC itself with this information.

When you enter an internal network number, your server finishes booting and displays the current date and time followed by a colon prompt (:). As with your PC's DOS prompt, you can enter server console commands at the colon prompt. You enter several commands here during this first configuration process. You will learn about console commands that are used on a day-to-day basis in Chapter 19.

Your server is officially "up" now. However, congratulations are not yet in order because it is a server with no disk space or network communications capability. Your next step is to activate the server disks and network adapters. After that, you prepare your server disks for actual use and copy NetWare's files to them.

Activating the Server Disks

To activate a server disk, you load its NetWare 386 disk driver into server memory by using the NetWare 386 console LOAD command, which also is used to load NLMs. As discussed previously, NLMs are programs and utilities that run with NetWare 386.

NetWare 386 comes with drivers for the three standard server disk options. The ISADISK driver is used for ST506 AT-compatible disk controllers. The ESDI driver is used for ESDI disk controllers (found in PS/2 and compatible PCs). The DCB disk driver is used if Novell's disk coprocessor board is installed in your server PC. If a vendor has supplied a disk driver that you copied to your server boot disk, you need to load that driver. To load a driver, type the LOAD command followed by the name of your disk driver, such as

    LOAD ESDI

With each type of disk, you are prompted to confirm your disk controller's I/O port and interrupt settings. Every driver offers a default setting, which you should accept unless your controller is a nonstandard configuration.

Normally, you load only one disk driver. If you have multiple disk controllers (such as two Novell disk coprocessor boards or an ST506 disk controller and a Novell DCB), however, you need to load the disk driver for each controller. If you load a particular disk driver for the second time, you are prompted again to enter I/O port and interrupt settings. Settings other than the ones you selected the first time are offered.

When the appropriate disk driver or drivers are loaded, you are ready to take similar steps to activate your network adapters.

Activating Network Adapters

To activate the network adapter or adapters in your server, you need to load each adapter's NetWare 386 LAN driver into server memory by using the LOAD command.

NetWare 386 comes with drivers for several standard types of network adapters. Your network adapter manufacturer or vendor may have supplied a driver file for the type you are using; you should have copied this file to the server boot disk and to the working copy of your NetWare 386 System disk. To load a network adapter driver, type the LOAD command followed by the driver name, such as

LOAD TOKEN

With certain types of network adapters, you are prompted to confirm the I/O port, memory address, and interrupt settings. A default setting is offered for each item. Carefully check your configuration information (referring to your network adapter manual if necessary) and make sure that the settings you select match the settings of your network adapter. The defaults are generally what you should use.

If you are using your server as an internal bridge (see Chapter 4 for details about internal bridges), you need to load multiple local area network drivers: one for each of the network adapters installed in your server PC. If you load a LAN driver for the second time, you are prompted again to enter I/O port and interrupt settings; settings other than those you selected the first time are offered. Make sure that the settings you enter match the settings of your network adapters.

After you have loaded the appropriate LAN drivers, you need to *bind* a protocol to that adapter. Unlike NetWare 286, which supports only NetWare's native IPX communications protocol, NetWare 386 is designed to support a variety of protocols. After you load the LAN driver, you assign, or bind, a protocol to the driver; in other words, you specify which protocol that network adapter is to use. You use the console BIND command to perform this task.

To assign the IPX protocol to a Token Ring board, you type

BIND IPX TO TOKEN

(Substitute the protocol you are using for *IPX*, and the network adapter driver you are using for *TOKEN*.) For the IPX protocol, the following prompt tells you to enter the network number to be used by the network adapter you are configuring:

Network number:

Enter any hexadecimal number up to 12 digits in length. Remember that every physical network must have a unique number. All network adapters in servers that connect to a particular physical network must have the number of that physical network specified.

If you have two or more network adapters of the same type in a server, a list of the boards for the loaded LAN drivers is displayed when you use the BIND command to assign a protocol. Select the driver to which you want to bind the protocol.

Some types of network adapters, such as EtherNet and Token Ring cards, may not initialize properly unless they are connected to a properly terminated cable system. If your network adapter fails to initialize, check to make sure that the network adapter is properly configured and connected to its cable system.

After your network adapters are fully activated, you are ready to configure the server disks.

Preparing the Server Disks

You use an NLM called INSTALL to prepare your server disks. You use INSTALL first to add a NetWare partition to each disk and then to perform a surface test on each disk.

A special situation exists if you use disks connected to the Novell DCB. Before loading the INSTALL NLM, you need to load the DISKSET NLM to configure the DCB.

Using DISKSET

The Novell disk coprocessor board is a high-performance disk interface that enables you to run large numbers of disks in the file server. You can install up to four DCBs in one server, and each DCB can have up to eight disk controllers attached. Multiple DCBs often are used in file servers in which disk mirroring is implemented. If you are not using DCBs in your server, you can skip this section and proceed to "Partitioning Disks."

You use DISKSET to specify the types of controllers and hard disks that are attached to each Novell DCB installed in your server. You need to know the exact disk configuration of your file server because DISKSET prompts you to identify each disk from a list showing the manufacturer's name and disk model number.

To start DISKSET, type *load diskset* from the server console colon prompt and press Enter. A menu appears with the following options:

    Disk Coprocessor Board SET UP
    NetWare Ready Disk Backup/Restore
    Third Party Disk Specifications

Highlight the first option and press Enter. You see a screen showing the currently loaded disk drivers. If you have only one DCB installed in your server PC, you have only one driver on the list. Highlight the driver for the DCB with which you plan to work and press Enter. (The other two options are designed for disk manufacturers, so you don't need to be concerned about them.)

You are shown a list of controller numbers (0–7). Each DCB can have up to eight controllers attached. Highlight the number for the first controller connected to the DCB and press Enter.

A list of disk drives and disk combinations appears. Carefully select the listing that matches the type of driver connected to the controller number you previously specified (more than one disk from the same manufacturer may be listed). Press Esc to save your selection. The list of loaded disk drivers returns to the screen.

Repeat these steps until every disk connected to the DCBs in your server has been identified. When you are finished using DISKSET, press Esc to return to its main menu, and press Esc again to exit and return to the server colon prompt.

After you have configured your DCBs, you are ready to format and test the disks connected to them by using the INSTALL NLM.

Starting and Using INSTALL

You use the INSTALL NLM utility to test and prepare your server disks. To start the utility, type *load install* from the server console's colon prompt and press Enter. You are presented with the Installation Options menu, which offers the following selections:

Disk Options
Volume Options
System Options
Exit

You first need to work with the Disk Options selection. Highlight it and press Enter. The Available Disk Options menu appears with the following selections:

Format (optional)
Partition Tables
Mirroring
Surface Test (optional)
Return to Main Menu

Your first decision is whether to format any disks attached to your server PC.

Deciding To Format a Disk

If you are using a disk that has never been formatted with the type of controller to which the disk is connected, you need to format it by selecting the Format (Optional) option from INSTALL's Disk Options menu. Your vendor or the disk manufacturer may have formatted the disk already. If you are working with a disk on which you have installed a DOS partition for booting the server, formatting the disk destroys your partition. (In this case, formatting shouldn't be necessary because you could not have successfully created the DOS partition on this disk if it were not already formatted.) If your server has multiple disks, they are listed. Select the disk you want to format. You are prompted to confirm your choice, and the drive is then formatted. Repeat these steps for any disks that you need to format.

Partitioning Disks

Your next step is to use INSTALL to add a NetWare 386 partition to each of the server's disks. Each disk can contain one NetWare 386 partition. In most cases, you want to make the entire disk a NetWare partition, except when you have created a small DOS partition (using the beginning cylinders of the disk) for server booting.

To add a NetWare 386 partition to a disk, select Partition Tables from the Available Disk Options menu. If you have more than one disk that can be partitioned, a list is displayed. Select the drive that you want to work with. You are shown a partition table for that disk along with INSTALL's Partition Options menu (see fig. 7.1). The partition table display shows the current partitions, and available disk space is shown as Free Space.

Fig. 7.1.

The Partition Options menu and partition table display.

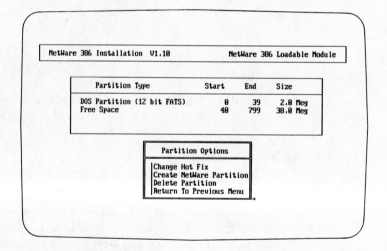

If any partitions need to be removed, select the Delete Partition option. A list of partitions is shown; highlight the partition you want to delete and press Enter.

To create the NetWare 386 partition, select Create NetWare Partition. INSTALL analyzes the existing partition table and displays a list of possible starting points for your partition. If your disk had no partitions to start with, INSTALL suggests a partition that starts on cylinder 0 and uses all available disk cylinders. If you have placed a small DOS partition on the disk, INSTALL also suggests a NetWare 386 partition starting on the first cylinder after the DOS partition.

If you want your partition to consist of the entire disk, accept the option to start on cylinder 0. If your disk has a DOS partition and you want to retain it, select the option that starts on the first cylinder after the DOS partition.

You see a window that displays the partition's default settings (see fig. 7.2). The maximum available size is shown as a default. You can decrease the size by entering a smaller number of cylinders (but little good reason exists to do so). You have the option of modifying the partition's size and the size of its Hot Fix area. INSTALL allocates two percent of the disk area for use by NetWare's Hot Fix feature.

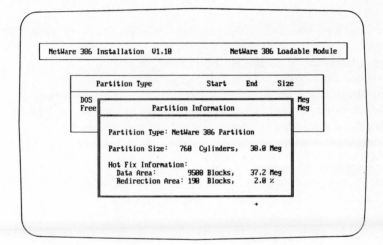

Fig. 7.2.
The partition's default settings.

Like most people, hard disks gradually wear out rather than fail suddenly. They develop an increasing number of bad blocks during the process. (A block is the smallest unit of information that NetWare reads or writes to the disk; a block contains 4,096 bytes unless you change its size.)

NetWare's Hot Fix feature is designed to minimize the problems caused by this gradual decline. After a disk block is written to, NetWare reads the block to determine whether the information was written accurately. If the disk block fails the test, the block is marked as unusable and replaced by another disk block.

When you establish a Hot Fix area, you are setting aside a pool of disk blocks to replace blocks that fail NetWare's read-after-write test. INSTALL suggests a default area from two to three percent of the disk's total block count; in other words, two to three percent of your disk space is not available for regular use. Network supervisors report that this default size is adequate for almost all situations.

You can increase or decrease the size of this area by changing the Redirection Area setting in the Partition Information screen.

When your partition settings are as you want them to be, press Esc to leave the Partition Information screen. You are prompted to confirm that you want to create the partition. Press Y to answer yes, and the partition is created.

Performing a Disk Surface Test

The server hard disks have an important job: they store your server's most important product—files. The best way to ensure that your hard disks store your files safely and reliably is to choose a disk configuration with a proven track record and then to test that configuration thoroughly before putting it "into production." Although NetWare 386's Hot Fix feature does an excellent job of detecting and compensating for disk block failures, Hot Fix cannot salvage information lost when a part of the disk fails where information is already written.

The best way to prevent this loss of information is to exercise the disk thoroughly before using it to store "live" data. Unless a vendor or manufacturer has done this test for you, you should perform a disk surface test.

The surface test is similar to NetWare 286's COMPSURF utility. If you let the test run long enough, it tests every disk block by writing and reading information to and from the block. You can choose between the destructive or nondestructive modes of the test. The destructive mode overwrites what is already on the disk, whereas the nondestructive mode reads and stores the information first before writing and reading a test pattern to and from the disk block. After the write/read test is complete for that block, the original information is restored. As you may guess, the nondestructive mode takes longer to run.

To start a surface test, select Surface Test (Optional) from the Available Disk Options menu. If you have multiple disks in your server, a list of the disks appears. Select the disk you want to test. A small menu appears with the options to begin and stop the surface test (see fig. 7.3). Select the option to begin the test. You are prompted to choose between the destructive and nondestructive tests. If you are working with a newly installed disk, select the quicker destructive test. If you are working with a disk that already has been used to store files, select the slower nondestructive test.

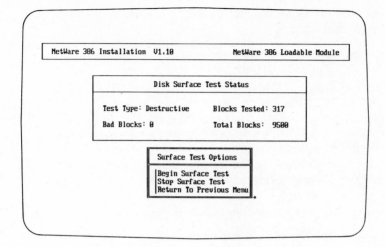

Fig. 7.3.
The Surface Test
Options menu and
status screen.

After you make this choice, the test begins, and a status screen shows the number of blocks that have been tested. To ensure that the test is comprehensive, let the test run until the total number of blocks tested is equal to at least the total number of blocks on the disk.

To stop the test, select Stop Surface Test and then Return to Previous Menu to go back to the Available Disk Options menu.

Mirroring Disks

With NetWare 386, a special configuration option is available if you have attached to your server two or more disks that are similar in size. NetWare 386 enables you to designate that two disks become a *mirrored*, or *duplexed*, pair, so that whatever is written to one disk also is written to the other.

Two disks are *mirrored* when they are on the same disk channel (attached to the same DCB or controller). They are *duplexed* when they are on different disk channels (attached to separate DCBs). When two disks become a mirrored pair, an extra level of protection against disk failure is put into place. If one disk in the mirrored pair fails, no data is lost because the other disk in the pair contains the same information. In addition, no interruption in server availability occurs because the server continues to operate. When two disks become a duplexed pair, the level of redundancy extends not only to the disks themselves but also to their controllers and DCBs. With a mirrored pair, a failure of the controller or DCB they share results in server failure and possible data loss or corruption. With a duplexed pair, controller or DCB failure is not a problem because duplicates exist of each.

Mirroring and duplexing do affect disk performance. If two drives are mirrored, disk writes can take up to twice as long because the disk controller must first write to one disk and then the other. With disk duplexing, however, each disk has its own controller, and disk writes can be performed simultaneously. Disk reads can be positively affected by disk duplexing or mirroring. When the controller requests information from a pair of disks, each disk seeks the information. Because of different read/write head and sector positions, one of the two disks is likely to find the information slightly sooner than the other, and this disk is the one used by the controller to satisfy the read request. With a mirrored or duplexed pair of disks, your disk read performance should improve slightly.

To mirror or duplex two drives, select the Mirroring option from the Available Disk Options menu. A list of all the drives installed in the server appears. Highlight the first drive you want to make a member of the mirrored or duplexed pair and press Enter. Press Ins to see a list of all other server drives that have NetWare 386 partitions equal to or greater in size than your selection. Highlight the drive you want to make the other member of the pair and press Enter.

If you pick a drive that has a larger NetWare 386 partition than the first, you receive a warning message. Press Esc to bypass this drive. When two drives of unequal sizes are paired, their net size is the size of the smaller of the two. Confirm that you want to pair the two disks, and the pair is created.

Repeat the preceding steps if you want to mirror or duplex other drive pairs. When you are finished, press Esc to return to the Available Disk Options menu.

Your disk preparations and testing are now complete, and you are ready to create NetWare volumes on the disks.

Creating NetWare Volumes

A *volume* is a physical area of disk space. With DOS or OS/2, a volume is equivalent to a disk partition and is assigned a drive letter, such as C or D. Optionally, you can give the volume a label or name. With NetWare, a partition can contain one or more volumes. Each volume is assigned a name but not a drive letter. (You assign drive letters dynamically with the MAP command, which is discussed in Chapter 9.)

If you have worked with volumes using NetWare 286, you know that it limits the volume size to 255M or less and that each volume must be contained on one disk. NetWare 386 does not impose these restraints. Its maximum volume size is 4 Terabytes, and a single volume can consist of disk space from multiple hard disks. The hard disk areas that are combined to make volumes are called *segments*.

Determining Your Volume Strategy

NetWare 386's increased volume capabilities require you to make some choices. How large should your server volumes be? Should you take advantage of NetWare 386's capability of placing one volume on multiple disks? The decisions you make now may be difficult to undo because changing the size of a volume usually results in the loss of the original data the volume stored (except when you add another disk area or segment to an existing volume). Whatever your choices, you should plan your volume layout in advance.

Most network supervisors report that for the sake of flexibility, you should make your volume sizes as large as practically possible. Suppose that you have a 300M disk in your server, and you have three departments in your company that plan to use that disk space. Each department has asked for 100M of space exclusively for its use. Should you create one 300M volume or three 100M volumes? Your first inclination may be to set up three separate volumes.

If you opt to create one large volume, however, NetWare 386 gives you the capability of using access rights and restrictions to divide the space on a disk volume in such a way that each department has exclusive use of exactly 100M. Using this method, you are in a better position to respond to future changes. For example, what if one department transfers to a new city (away from your network) and can no longer use the disk space? If you created three separate volumes, you face the messy job of changing your volume definitions for that disk, including backing up all your data, changing the volume structure, and then restoring the data to the new volumes, an extremely time-consuming process.

You also need to decide whether to place one volume on multiple disks. This approach has pros and cons. If one volume spans multiple disks and one disk fails, all the data on your volume is lost. This loss should not be great, however, if you have a regular program of making backups for your network volumes.

Using multiple disks for one volume can improve performance. If each disk is connected to a separate controller, all disks can receive or retrieve information at the same time. NetWare 386 spreads evenly across all disks each file you write to a volume. When you retrieve that file, each disk goes to work reading its part of the file, similar to going from a one-lane country road to a four-lane freeway.

When you know your server's disk arrangement, you should plan carefully how the volumes are to be set up. After you have made your plans, you are ready to create the volumes.

Creating Volumes with INSTALL

From INSTALL's Installation Options menu, select Volume Options. A small window opens, showing the current volumes (it is empty if you haven't set up any volumes yet). Press Ins to create a new volume. If you have more than one disk with unassigned space available, a list of those disks appears. Select the disk you want to use, and the New Volume Information window opens (see fig. 7.4).

Fig. 7.4.
The New Volume
Information screen.

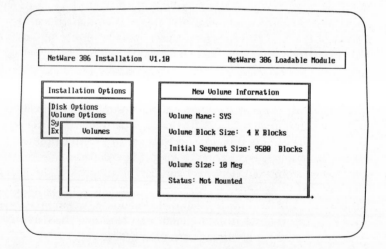

When you define a volume, you can change three options: volume name, block size, and overall size.

Naming the Volume

INSTALL automatically suggests a default name of SYS for the first volume you define; you are required to have one volume on your server with this

name. A volume name can be from 2 to 15 characters long, it cannot start
with a period, and it cannot include spaces or the following characters:

" * + , / \ ¦ : ; = < > ? [ ] .

Choosing a Volume Block Size

You also must select the volume block size. A volume block is the unit of
information that NetWare reads or writes to the disk in one operation.
INSTALL suggests a default of 4K, the size you should use unless you have
a compelling reason to do otherwise. (Your options are 4, 8, 16, 32, or
64K.)

As with most NetWare decisions, large and small block sizes have their
advantages and disadvantages. A block is the smallest unit of information
that NetWare writes to the disk. For example, if your block size is 4K and
you copy a 5K file to the volume, you need two blocks (or 8K of space)
to store that file. Similarly, if your block size is 64K and you store a 65K
file to the volume, two blocks (128K) are used. The bigger your volume
block size, the greater the space that is wasted as files are stored.

Bigger block sizes are more efficient if you generally retrieve large
amounts of information. If you have a database on your volume with
records of 61K and users typically retrieve one entire record at a time, a
block size of 64K enables a record to be retrieved in one operation. If the
block size is 4K, 16 operations are necessary to retrieve the same record.

NetWare 286 uses a volume block size of 4K, and network supervisors
report that this size has worked well. They generally consider that the
performance gained by using larger block sizes is not worth the disk space
wasted.

Specifying the Volume Size

The Initial Segment Size setting in the New Volume Information window
shows the number of volume blocks on the disk that are assigned to the
volume (see fig. 7.4). The Volume Size setting shows the same information
in megabytes. By default, INSTALL shows a setting that uses the entire disk.
If you want to use only part of the disk, enter a lower number of blocks
for the Initial Segment Size setting.

After you have entered the desired volume name, block size, and segment
size, press Esc to leave the New Volume Information window. You are
prompted to confirm that you want to create the volume; press Y to
answer yes, and the volume is created.

Adding Another Disk Segment to an Existing Volume

If you want your volume to span more than one disk, you must add disk segments to the current volume definition. From INSTALL's Installation Options screen, select Volume Options. A list of volumes appears. Highlight the volume to which you want to add a segment and press Enter. The Volume Information window appears, similar to the one shown in figure 7.4. Use the down arrow to move the highlight to Volume Segments and press Enter. A list appears that shows the disk segments currently assigned to the volume.

To add a new segment, press Ins, and a list of disks with available space appears. Highlight the disk you want to use and press Enter. A small box showing the total number of blocks available on that disk is shown. If you want to use all the space on the disk, press Enter. Otherwise, you can backspace over the number, enter a lower one, and press Enter. You are prompted to confirm that you want to add this segment to the volume; respond by pressing Y for yes, and the segment is added.

Next, you are returned to the Volume Segments screen, which has been updated to show your choice. You can press Ins to repeat the process if you want to add additional segments, or you can press Esc to return to the Volume Information window. Press Esc again to return to the volume list.

Deleting a Volume

Deleting a volume erases any information it contains, so this step should be taken with the utmost care and forethought. From INSTALL's Installation Options screen, select Volume Options. A list of volumes appears. Highlight the volume you want to delete and press Del. You are asked to confirm that you want to remove the volume; answer Yes by pressing y, and the volume is deleted.

Mounting Your Volumes

After you have created your volumes, you need to *mount* at least the SYS volume so that you can work with it as you complete the installation of NetWare 386. Mounting activates a volume and makes it available to server users. You can mount volumes by using the MOUNT command. Volumes can be dismounted by using the DISMOUNT command.

If you are currently in INSTALL, you can go to the NetWare 386 colon prompt by pressing Alt-Esc or Ctrl-Esc. From the prompt, type *mount sys* and press Enter. The SYS volume is mounted so that you can work with it. If you want to return to INSTALL, press Alt-Esc or Ctrl-Esc.

Completing the Installation Process

If you have followed the installation steps in this chapter, you need to complete only two or three more tasks to finish installing NetWare 386. You need to copy the NetWare 386 command files to the SYS volume, and you need to create AUTOEXEC.NCF and STARTUP.NCF files for the server to use so that it automatically runs all the commands you executed manually when you started NetWare 386 for the first time.

If your server is being added to an existing network that includes NetWare 286 servers, you also may need to decide how NetWare 386's password encryption is to be handled on your local area network.

Copying System and Public Files

Copying NetWare 386's command files to the server enables you and other users to use NetWare's commands and utilities when you are logged into the server. You need to locate your working copies of the NetWare disks labeled System and Utility.

From INSTALL's Installation Options menu, select System Options. Select Copy System and Public Files from the next menu, and you are prompted to place your disks one at a time into the server's floppy drive until all files have been copied.

Handling Password Encryption

If you are adding your NetWare 386 server to an existing network that has NetWare 286 servers, you may need to turn off NetWare 386's password encryption feature. By default, NetWare 386 servers expect that the passwords users enter when logging in are encrypted before they are sent over the network cable system to the server. This feature is not supported by NetWare 286 servers, however. This password encryption is performed by the NetWare 386 workstation shell (a special part of NetWare that runs at the workstation—the feature is discussed in detail in Chapter 8). If the workstations on your local area network are using the NetWare 286 workstation shell rather than the NetWare 386 version, you must enter a command to enable the NetWare 386 server to work with unencrypted passwords.

If you are in INSTALL, you can go to the NetWare 386 colon prompt by pressing Alt-Esc or Ctrl-Esc. From the prompt, type

    SET ALLOW UNENCRYPTED PASSWORDS = ON

and press Enter.

You should add this command to your server's AUTOEXEC.NCF file so that it is executed every time you start the server (you will learn how to add this command in the next section). If you want to return to INSTALL, press Alt-Esc or Ctrl-Esc.

Creating the AUTOEXEC.NCF File

The AUTOEXEC.NCF file is similar in purpose to the AUTOEXEC.BAT file on your PC. As soon as you start the server, AUTOEXEC.NCF executes the commands that are needed to start the server's disks and network adapters.

When you start NetWare 386 for the first time, the software remembers the commands you enter to activate the disks and network adapters. To look at these commands, select System Options from INSTALL's Installation Options menu. From the menu that appears, select Create AUTOEXEC.NCF File. You see an editing window that displays the AUTOEXEC.NCF file.

A typical AUTOEXEC.NCF file looks like the following:

    file server name SERV386
    ipx internal net 10A
    load RXNET port = 2E0 mem = D0000 int = 2
    bind IPX to RXNET net = 1
    mount all

Notice that the commands parallel those that you entered when you first started NetWare 386. The first line establishes the file server name; the second establishes the internal network number. The third line loads the local area network driver for the server's network adapter, and the fourth assigns the IPX protocol to that adapter. The last line mounts all server volumes. If you are particularly observant, you have noticed that the command to load the disk driver is not listed. This command is stored in the STARTUP.NCF file, which is discussed in the next section.

You can edit the AUTOEXEC.NCF file, but in many cases you don't need to; you can simply press Esc to save the file. If you need to enable the server to work with unencrypted passwords, however, you must add one line to the file. Use the down arrow to position the cursor at the next line after the end of the AUTOEXEC.NCF file, and type the following command:

SET ALLOW UNENCRYPTED PASSWORDS = ON

Press Esc to exit the editing screen and save the AUTOEXEC.NCF file. It is saved to the SYSTEM directory on the SYS volume of your server. If you need to make changes to this file in the future, you can use the Edit AUTOEXEC.NCF File selection from the Available System Options menu.

Preparing for Non-DOS Files

If you plan to store non-DOS files on a particular volume, you need to load the non-DOS file protocol's NLM and run a special console command called ADD NAME SPACE. This procedure is required to accommodate workstations such as the Macintosh.

Non-DOS file protocols have their own NLM files with the extension NAM. These NLMs are loaded just like the INSTALL NLM. For example, to load the NLM for the Macintosh file protocol, you type *load mac* and press Enter from the NetWare 386 server console.

After the file protocol NLM is loaded, you must use a command called ADD NAME SPACE to designate the volume or volumes that can be used to store non-DOS files. For example, to enable the storage of Macintosh files on the server volume called VOL1, you type

ADD NAME SPACE MAC to volume VOL1

and press Enter. (You can leave out *to volume* if you want). Execute the ADD NAME SPACE command for each volume that needs to support the non-DOS file protocol.

You probably will want to place the commands that load non-DOS file protocols and add name space in your server's AUTOEXEC.NCF file so that they are executed every time you start the server (you will learn how to do this procedure when you read the next section).

Creating the STARTUP.NCF File

The STARTUP.NCF file is stored on your server PC's boot disk and contains the command or commands to load the disk drivers for your server disks. As with the AUTOEXEC.NCF file, the software remembers the command you entered to load the disk driver. You can view and create the STARTUP.NCF file by selecting System Options from INSTALL's Installation Options menu. From the menu that appears, select the Create STARTUP.NCF File option. The name and path of your STARTUP.NCF file is shown.

If you are booting from a floppy disk, the name and path should read A:STARTUP.NCF. If you are booting from a DOS partition, the drive letter of that partition along with the file name should be shown (for example, C:STARTUP.NCF). Make sure that the correct drive letter is shown, and press Enter (or backspace over the incorrect drive letter and enter the correct drive followed by STARTUP.NCF). An editing window opens and displays the STARTUP.NCF file.

A typical STARTUP.NCF file contains a command similar to the following:

    LOAD ISADISK PORT = 1F0 INT = E

Notice that the command parallels what you entered when you first loaded the disk driver for your server disk. (If you have disks that use different controllers, you see multiple commands.)

You can change this file, but you shouldn't need to. Press Esc to exit the editing screen and save the STARTUP.NCF file. If you need to make changes to this file in the future, you can use the Edit STARTUP.NCF File selection from the Available System Options menu.

Stopping and Starting the Server

When you are finished installing and configuring the server, you are ready to stop and restart it to make sure that it boots properly. If you are currently in INSTALL, move to the NetWare colon prompt by pressing Alt-Esc or Ctrl-Esc. From this prompt, type *down* and press Enter. The server shuts down. You can turn it off, or you can return to the DOS prompt by typing *exit* and pressing Enter.

To boot the server, make sure that the boot disk is in the floppy drive (if you are booting from a floppy disk), and then boot the server PC by pressing Ctrl-Alt-Del or by turning it off and on. If you created an AUTOEXEC.BAT file that executes SERVER.EXE, NetWare boots automatically. Otherwise, type *server* and press Enter to start NetWare.

When you run SERVER.EXE, it automatically reads the STARTUP.NCF file to activate your server disks. SERVER.EXE then reads the AUTOEXEC.NCF file to activate the network adapter, mounts server volumes, and sets other server configuration options. Occasionally, you may want to activate these devices manually so that you can customize options before all the server's devices are activated.

To start the server without reading the STARTUP.NCF file on the server boot disk, type

SERVER-NS

and press Enter.

To start the server and read an alternate startup file, type

SERVER-S FILENAME.EXT

and press Enter. (Replace *FILENAME.EXT* with the name of your file).

If you want to start the server and read the STARTUP.NCF file but ignore the AUTOEXEC.NCF file, type

SERVER-NA

and press Enter.

Placing Your Server in a Good Operating Environment

After NetWare 386 has been installed on your server, you are ready to move the server to its permanent location. Unlike its minicomputer or mainframe cousins, a server does not require a special operating environment. Your server should be kept in an area with good ventilation at normal room temperature, and it should not be exposed to excessive humidity or dust.

The only special accommodation that you make for a server but may not make for a normal PC (although you should) is power protection. Because the server is used to store important files and often is the host for multiuser applications, it must be protected from a sudden power loss.

A power interruption while a database file is being updated could corrupt the database file. Installing an uninterruptible power supply (UPS) is low-cost insurance against this occurrence. A UPS provides battery-supplied power to the server when the normal power source fails, giving you time to down the server in an orderly fashion. Some UPS devices come with monitoring equipment that can be installed in the file server; this equipment senses a power failure, automatically closes all the server's open files, and downs it so that no data is corrupted.

You also may want to place your server in a secure area so that no one can inadvertently or intentionally turn it off or use the server console commands to clear the connection of other users.

Chapter Summary

Congratulations on successfully installing NetWare 386. You now know that installing a server is a detailed and complex process. In later chapters, you will learn about ways you can further configure and customize the server.

Now that your server is up and running, you are ready to activate workstations so that users can log in to the server and begin to use its resources. You will learn about this process in the next chapter.

Activating
Workstations

In the preceding two chapters you stepped through the process of installing NetWare on a file server. File servers are important, but they are useless unless PCs are connected to the servers that can access the files stored there.

In this chapter you will learn what needs to be done to make those PCs a part of your network. You first create a special part of the NetWare operating system called the NetWare shell (the NetWare shell is the one part of NetWare that is installed on the workstation). Next, you set the switches, jumpers, or both on your network adapters and install the adapters in your workstations. Finally, you connect each workstation's network adapter to the network cable system and execute, or *load*, the network shell. After these steps have been taken you can log into the file server and start using it.

The NetWare Shell

The NetWare shell is NetWare's ambassador to your PC's operating system. All communication between your PC and the file server passes through the NetWare shell. For example, if you need to use the files stored in a certain directory on a file server, the NetWare shell lets you assign a drive letter to that directory so that you can use the file server directory as you do a directory on a local disk. The shell, directories, and files on the server perform like those on your PC's local disks and you can use DOS and OS/2 commands to work with them.

When you print a word processor document on a network printer, the NetWare shell lets you redirect the print job from its normal destination (the parallel port on your PC) to a network-based printer. The NetWare shell performs this redirection so skillfully that your word processor does not even notice the difference.

Figure 8.1 illustrates the NetWare shell's interaction with your PC's operating system for handling file directories and printing. The shell performs another important task after first being loaded. The network adapter card is your PC's link to the network, but the adapter card remains dormant until activated by the NetWare shell. When you load the shell program, your PC's network adapter broadcasts a request over the network cable system, asking a file server to respond. Your PC is linked to the first file server that answers. The NetWare shell stays in the memory of your PC.

Fig. 8.1.
The NetWare shell.

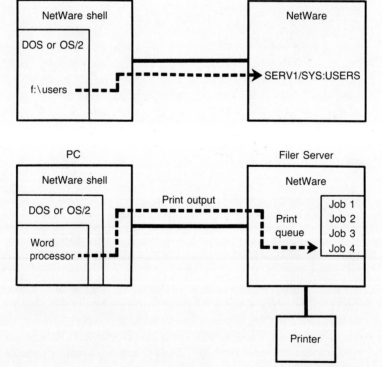

After the shell is loaded, its first job is to provide you with a way to log into a network file server. On an IBM PC running PC DOS, the shell creates a new drive letter (F, in most cases), on which you find a directory that is on the server your PC linked to when the shell was loaded. This directory contains the LOGIN command that you use to log into a file server.

The NetWare shell is a memory-resident, or "terminate-and-stay-resident" (TSR), program; the program remains in the memory of your PC after being loaded into RAM. The NetWare shell should be the first TSR loaded when you boot your PC.

Creating the NetWare Shell

A NetWare utility called SHGEN (for shell generation) is used to create the NetWare shell. When you run SHGEN, you identify the type of network adapter you are using and its configuration. When you have made your choices, the files that make up the NetWare shell are automatically created.

If you read Chapter 5's description of generating NetWare 286, or if you are otherwise familiar with the NETGEN program, you will find creating a shell to be a similar but less complicated process. Your first step is to locate the floppy disks that contain SHGEN and its related files. For NetWare 286 on 5 1/4-inch disks, the disks are labeled SHGEN-1, SHGEN-2, LAN_DRV_001, and LAN_DRV_002. The 3 1/2-inch disk format of NetWare 286 disks are SHGEN-1, LAN_DRV_.001, and LAN_DRV_.002. For NetWare 386, one disk labeled SHGEN-1 is used.

You have several options when deciding how to work with SHGEN and its files. You can upload the files to a hard disk or network volume, or you can work with floppy disks entirely. Uploading the files to a hard disk keeps a permanent copy of the SHGEN files readily available so that you can quickly create new shells as needed; creating them takes only a minute or two. You need to dedicate approximately 600K on your hard disk drive for these files with NetWare 386 and 1.5M for NetWare 286.

If you anticipate creating shells more than once, you should use the hard disk or network drive method. Using a floppy-based method is slower and with NetWare 286 involves considerable disk swapping.

SHGEN requires a PC running DOS 3.0 or later with 640K and at least one floppy disk drive. If you haven't already done so, make backup copies of your NetWare disks, or be sure that you have duplicate copies in case of disk failure.

Preparing for Floppy-Based Shell Generation

To create a NetWare shell using floppies only, you should use the DOS DISKCOPY command to make working copies of the disks that you will be using. Label the working copies with the same name as the originals, because you will be asked for the disks by name during the shell-generation process.

Preparing for Hard Disk or Network-Volume-Based Shell Generation

The method you use to upload the SHGEN files to a disk or network drive depends on whether you are using NetWare 286 or NetWare 386.

NetWare 286

If you plan to keep the SHGEN files on a hard disk or network drive, you first need to be aware of how and where SHGEN uploads them. When you start SHGEN and opt to use a hard disk or network drive, you are prompted to enter the drive letter for the disk you plan to use. That drive's default directory becomes the starting point for the upload of NetWare files. Under that directory, a subdirectory called NETWARE is created, followed by a series of subdirectories, each named for one of the NetWare disks from which you upload the files. Before starting SHGEN, be sure that the default directory on the drive you select is the one where you want these subdirectories created. You may need to create this directory first by using the DOS MD (MAKE DIRECTORY) command, and then make the newly created directory the default by using the CD (CHANGE DIRECTORY) command.

If you already have used NETGEN to upload other NetWare disks to subdirectories under a particular directory, you can add the SHGEN files to that directory. You save space by using this method because the files from the LAN_DRV_002 disks are already in place.

To upload the SHGEN files, make the default directory the one where SHGEN should create the subdirectories that will store SHGEN files. Place the SHGEN-1 disk in a floppy disk drive and change to that drive. (For example, if you placed the floppy disk in drive A, type *a:* and press Enter). Type *shgen* and press Enter. You see a menu with the following options:

Default Configuration
Intermediate Configuration
Custom Configuration

Highlight Default Configuration and press Enter. You're asked to choose between using SHGEN from floppy disks, a hard disk, or a network drive; select Hard Disk or Network Drive. You're prompted to enter the drive letter for your hard disk or network volume you are selecting. As prompted, insert the appropriate NetWare disks in your floppy drive one by one, until all the files are uploaded. After the standard list of disks is uploaded, you're asked if you want to Upload Additional Diskettes? If a vendor or manufacturer has supplied a disk with special files to be added to the SHGEN configuration files, you should answer *yes* and insert the appropriate disk. This disk should have a volume name that starts with LAN_DRV_ and has an extension consisting of three numbers.

When your files are uploaded, you can exit SHGEN by pressing Esc, or you may follow the prompts to continue creating a NetWare shell.

NetWare 386

NetWare 386 does not have a menu-assisted method of uploading SHGEN's files to a hard disk or network drive. You need to use the DOS MD command to create a directory name, and then create a subdirectory called NETWARE, followed by a subdirectory under NETWARE called SHGEN-1. If the directory you decide to create is named NET386, your directory structure should look like the following:

```
NET386
 └NETWARE
     │ shgen.exe
     └─ SHGEN-1
          files from SHGEN-1 disk
```

Use the DOS COPY command to copy all files from the SHGEN-1 disk into the SHGEN-1 subdirectory and the SHGEN.EXE file into the NETWARE subdirectory.

If a vendor or manufacturer has supplied you with a disk containing special files to be added to the SHGEN configuration files, create a subdirectory under the NETWARE subdirectory with the same name as the label on the disk (the volume name should be similar to LAN_DRV_.100).

When you have created the directory structure and copied the files from the SHGEN-1 disk, you're ready to start SHGEN and create the NetWare shell.

Starting SHGEN

If you are working with SHGEN using floppies, insert the disk labeled SHGEN-1 in a floppy drive. Make that drive the default, and type *shgen* and press Enter.

If you are working with SHGEN using a hard disk or network drive, switch to that drive and make the NETWARE directory the default. Type *shgen* and press Enter.

The SHGEN utilities for NetWare 286 and NetWare 386 are similar. The main difference is that SHGEN for NetWare 286 offers several levels of operation, and NetWare 386's SHGEN offers one level of operation. If you have both NetWare 386 and NetWare 286 servers on your LAN, you can use NetWare 386's SHGEN to generate shells that let you access either. NetWare 286-generated shells can access NetWare 386 servers only if you disable each NetWare 386 server's password encryption feature (see the section in the previous chapter called "Handling Password Encryption").

If you are using NetWare 286's SHGEN, read the next section. If you are using NetWare 386's SHGEN, skip to the section called "Using NetWare 386 SHGEN".

Using NetWare 286 SHGEN

When you first start SHGEN for NetWare 286, the opening menu prompts you to choose from three options:

    Default Configuration
    Intermediate Configuration
    Custom Configuration

You can choose the default level to quickly create a NetWare shell that matches the manufacturer's default settings for your network adapter. The intermediate level enables you to choose your own settings from a list of all possible settings. The custom level is like the custom level of NETGEN, enabling you to define and choose resource sets that identify hardware options installed in your workstation. The custom level analyzes the resource sets that you select and offers the network adapter options that are compatible.

Using the Default Level

Chapter 5 discussed the methods network adapters use to communicate with the PCs in which the adapters are installed. Most network adapters use some combination of four methods: interrupts, I/O ports, DMA, and memory addresses for ROM (see the sidebar in Chapter 5 called "How Network Adapters Talk to PCs" for a quick look at how these methods work). Other devices in your PC use these methods also, so unique addresses or settings must be assigned to your network adapter to eliminate the possibility of two devices using the same setting. With most network adapters, you change these settings using switches, jumpers, or both. Most network adapters arrive with default settings designed to work in all but the most unusual situations. The SHGEN default level of operation is designed to create automatically a NetWare shell matching these defaults. If you are not familiar with the interrupt, I/O port, DMA channel, and memory address requirements of the devices in your PC, and you don't have the time to find this information, use the default settings for your network adapter. Network supervisors who are knowledgeable about the address requirements in their workstations report that they use the manufacturer's default network adapter settings most of the time. Table 8.1 lists the SHGEN abbreviations and their meanings.

Table 8.1
SHGEN Abbreviations and Their Meanings

Abbreviation	Meaning
IRQ	Interrupts
I/O Base	I/O (Input/Output) port
RAM Buffer	Memory address for network adapter's ROM
DMA	DMA (Direct Memory Access) channel

To use SHGEN in the default mode, highlight Default Configuration from the SHGEN opening menu and press Enter. You see a menu where you are prompted to choose between using SHGEN from floppies, a hard disk, or a network drive. Make the appropriate selection. Next, you enter the letter of the disk drive where the SHGEN files are stored, if you are selecting the hard disk or network drive option.

The SHGEN Available LAN Drivers screen appears (see fig. 8.2). Highlight the network adapter driver name that matches the type you are using and press Enter. The Selected Configurations window lets you review your selection. This window shows the LAN driver name you selected and the settings and addresses that are used. A prompt asks you to confirm that you want to Continue Shell Generation Using Selected Configurations? If you respond with yes, the NetWork shell is created. If you answer no, you're asked if you want to ABANDON SHELL GENERATION and Exit! If you answer no, you return to the Available LAN Drivers window from which you can make another network adapter selection. Answering yes results in leaving SHGEN. You also can use the Esc key to return to the Available LAN Drivers window from any other window in SHGEN. If you press Esc from the Available LAN Drivers window, you are prompted to confirm that you want to exit the program.

Fig. 8.2.

The Available LAN Drivers window.

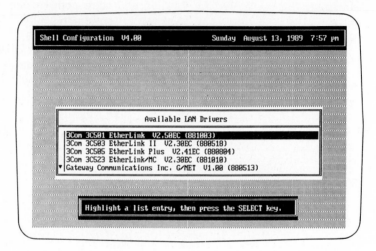

```
Shell Configuration  V4.00                   Sunday  August 13, 1989  7:57 pm




                              Available LAN Drivers
              ┌─────────────────────────────────────────────────┐
              │3Com 3C501 EtherLink   V2.50EC (881003)           │
              │3Com 3C503 EtherLink II  V2.30EC (880518)         │
              │3Com 3C505 EtherLink Plus  V2.41EC (888084)       │
              │3Com 3C523 EtherLink/MC  V2.30EC (881010)         │
              ▼Gateway Communications Inc. G/NET  V1.00 (888513)  │
              └─────────────────────────────────────────────────┘


              ┌─────────────────────────────────────────────────┐
              │ Highlight a list entry, then press the SELECT key. │
              └─────────────────────────────────────────────────┘
```

After the shell is created, SHGEN tells you that a valid shell has been placed on the SHGEN-1 or SHGEN-2 disk or in the SHGEN-1 or SHGEN-2 directory (SHGEN-2 for NetWare on 5 1/4-inch disks and SHGEN-1 for NetWare on 3 1/2-inch disks). If you are using SHGEN from a hard disk or network drive, you're asked if you want to download the newly created shell files to a floppy disk. If you answer yes, the computer tells you to put a disk in a floppy drive, and the shell files are downloaded to the floppy disk. SHGEN then returns you to the DOS prompt.

The default level of SHGEN lets you produce the files for the NetWare shell in just a few seconds and with a minimum number of keystrokes. The default level does not let you choose the addresses and settings for your network adapter, however, and cannot handle those cases when you must vary from the default configuration for your network adapter type.

Using the Intermediate Level

The intermediate level of SHGEN allows you to choose the settings that are used to configure your NetWare shell.

To use SHGEN in the intermediate mode, highlight Intermediate Configuration from the SHGEN opening menu and press Enter. A menu appears telling you to choose between using SHGEN from floppies, a hard disk, or a network drive; make the appropriate selection. You are then prompted to enter the letter of the disk drive where the SHGEN files are stored, if you are using the hard disk or network drive option.

The SHGEN Available LAN Drivers screen appears. Highlight the network adapter driver name that matches the type you are using and press Enter. The Available LAN Driver Configurations window appears (see fig. 8.3), which lists all the possible configurations for the network adapter type you are selecting. Highlight the configuration you want to use and press Enter.

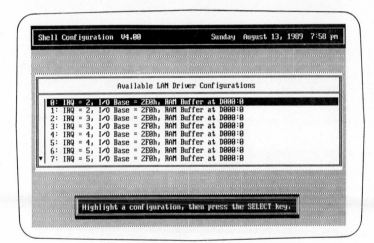

Fig. 8.3.
The Available LAN Driver Configurations window.

The Selected Configurations window opens to let you review your selection. The window shows the LAN driver name and configuration you selected. You are asked to confirm that you want to Continue Shell Generation Using Selected Configurations? If you respond with yes, the NetWork Shell is created. If you answer no, the computer asks if you want to ABANDON SHELL GENERATION and Exit! If you answer no, the Available LAN Drivers window reappears on-screen, from which you can make another network adapter selection. Answering yes results in leaving SHGEN. You also can use the Esc key to return to the Available LAN Drivers window from any other window in SHGEN. If you press Esc from the Available LAN Drivers window itself, you're prompted to confirm that you want to exit the program.

After the shell is created, SHGEN tells you that a valid shell has been placed on the SHGEN-1 or SHGEN-2 disk or in the SHGEN-1 or SHGEN-2 directory (SHGEN-2 for NetWare on 5 1/4-inch disks and SHGEN-1 for NetWare on 3 1/2-inch disks). If you are using SHGEN from a hard disk or network drive, you're asked if you want to download the newly created shell files to a floppy disk. If you answer yes, you are told to place a disk in a floppy drive, and the shell files are downloaded to the disk. SHGEN returns you to the DOS prompt.

The intermediate level of SHGEN is a favorite of network supervisors because it enables them to choose the exact shell configuration with a minimum of complication. One more level of SHGEN is available, which enables you to compare possible shell configurations with the addresses and settings used by other hardware items in your PC. The custom level is discussed in the next section.

Using the Custom Level

With the first two levels of SHGEN (default and intermediate) you specify only what type of network adapter is installed in your PC. The SHGEN custom level is the most complicated way to generate a NetWare shell. The custom level is similar to the custom level of NetWare 286's NETGEN: you define which resource sets are installed in your workstation. (As with NETGEN, a resource is any input/output device installed in your PC, such as a printer port, a hard disk controller, or a display adapter). SHGEN tracks the interrupts and addresses used by the resource sets you have selected and does not let you choose a network adapter configuration that conflicts with them.

To use SHGEN in custom mode, highlight Custom Configuration from SHGEN's opening menu and press Enter. A menu prompts you to choose between using SHGEN from floppies, a hard disk, or a network drive. Make the appropriate selection. You are prompted to enter the disk drive letter where the SHGEN files are stored, if you selected the hard disk or network drive option.

Next, a screen prompts you to choose between selecting a shell configuration or exiting SHGEN. Choose Select Shell Configuration, and you see the Available Options screen shown in figure 8.4. In addition to offering you the option to select a LAN driver, the Available Options screen also offers several selections that let you configure resources and resource sets.

Resources and Resource Sets

Many network supervisors skip using resource sets because they are already familiar with the addresses and ports used by the items in their

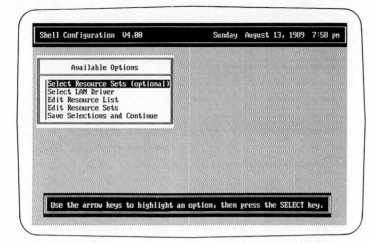

Fig. 8.4.

The shell configuration Available Options screen.

servers. Some network supervisors have found network adapter addresses that work and don't want to be bothered with the details of choosing resource sets.

SHGEN defines as a resource any item you install in your PC that requires a memory address, I/O port, interrupt, or DMA channel. SHGEN lets you group resources into resource sets; a resource set consists of one to six resources. For example, if you have a standard PC configuration consisting of a monochrome adapter, a Western digital floppy controller, two parallel ports (LPT1 and LPT2), and a serial port (COM1), you can group these resources into a set called Standard Workstation. The addresses used by all the items in the Standard Workstation set are tracked by SHGEN, and SHGEN does not let you choose a network adapter configuration that conflicts with any of them.

Using resource sets can be helpful if you are not conversant with addresses and ports, but you know which items are installed in your workstation. Resource sets also can provide a quick way to find the addresses, interrupts, and ports used by a particular resource.

Selecting Resource Sets

When you choose the Select Resource Sets option, you select the items that are to be installed in your workstations that use memory addresses, I/O ports, interrupts, or DMA channels. SHGEN tracks the addresses used and lets you select a network adapter configuration using the same address.

When you highlight Select Resource Sets and press Enter, you see a menu offering two options: to select a loaded item or to load and select an item. Loaded items consist of NetWare's standard list of resource sets. Highlight the Select Loaded Item option and press Enter. You see a list of resource sets. Highlight a set that matches the set to be installed in your workstation and press Enter. The set you selected is shown in the Selected Resource Sets window (see fig. 8.5). Continue to select resource sets until you have chosen all the resources to be installed in your workstation.

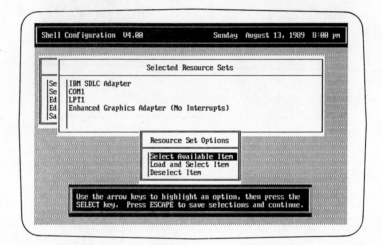

Fig. 8.5.

The Selected Resource Sets window.

If you need to work with a resource set supplied by a manufacturer or vendor, copy the set to your NetWare configuration files directory or to the working copy of one of your disks, according to the supplier's instructions. You can then activate that set by using the Load and Select Item option. Network supervisors report that few manufacturers are actively supporting SHGEN's resource set feature, so you probably will not have to do this.

If you select the wrong resource set, use the Deselect an Item option to remove it. When your resource set list is complete, press Esc to return to the SHGEN Available Topics menu.

Selecting The LAN Driver

When you choose the Select LAN Driver option, you are prompted to choose the driver for the network adapter to be installed in your workstation. When you highlight this option and press Enter, you see a menu offering two options: to select a loaded item or to load and select an item. "Loaded items" refers to NetWare's standard list of network adapter drivers, and the one you need is likely to be among them. Highlight the Select Loaded Item option and press Enter. You see a list of network adapter drivers through which you can scroll by using the up and down arrows. Highlight the driver that matches the description of your network adapter and press Enter; this driver is shown in the Selected LAN Driver window (see fig. 8.6). When you select the correct LAN driver, press Esc to return to the SHGEN configuration menu.

If you are using a network adapter that requires a driver supplied by the manufacturer, copy the driver to your NetWare configuration files directory or to the working copy of one of your disks, according to the manufacturer's instructions. Use the Load and Select Item option to select this driver.

If you select the wrong network adapter driver, use the Deselect an Item option to remove it. When your LAN driver list is complete, press Esc to return to the SHGEN Available Topics menu.

Configuring the Selected Driver and Resources

The Configure Driver/Resources menu option lets you choose the configuration for your network adapter and for resources that are capable of being set to more than one address, port, interrupt, or DMA channel. When you highlight this option and press Enter, you see two options: choosing the configuration for your network adapter and choosing the configuration for your selected resource sets (if you didn't select any resource sets that have more than one possible setting, you don't see the option to configure them).

Configuring the LAN Driver

The Choose LAN Configuration menu option allows you to pick the settings for your network adapter. Highlight this selection and press Enter. The screen shows the network adapter driver you selected by using the Select LAN Drivers option (see fig. 8.6). Press Enter and you see a list of possible configurations similar to that shown earlier in figure 8.3. Highlight the one you want to use and press Enter. The Configure Driver/Resources menu appears with a new option called Release LAN Configuration. You can select this option to "undo" any network adapter configurations you need to change.

Configuring Resource Sets

If you select a resource set with more than one possible configuration, the menu option Choose Resource Configuration is displayed. Highlight this option and press Enter. A list of resource sets that includes unconfigured resources appears. Highlight the first listing and press Enter. You then see individual resources that need to be configured. Highlight the first one and press Enter. A list of the configuration options appears; highlight the appropriate one and press Enter. Repeat this procedure for every other

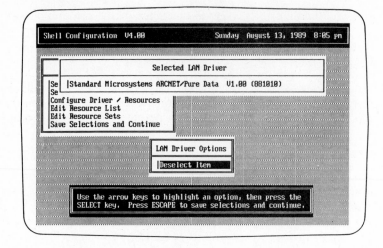

Fig. 8.6.

The Selected LAN Driver window.

resource on the list. When you complete the configuration of each resource set, the Configure Driver/Resources menu appears. A new option called Release Resource Set Configuration appears. Select this option to "undo" any resource set configurations you need to change.

When your network adapter driver and resource set configuration is complete, a menu option called Review Selected Configurations appears. When you highlight Review Selected Configurations and press Enter, you see a summary of your configuration selections (see fig. 8.7). Press Esc to leave this screen and return to the Configure Driver/Resources menu. Press Esc again to return to the SHGEN Available Options menu.

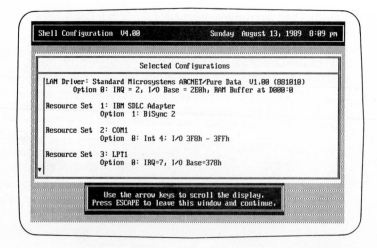

Fig. 8.7.

The Selected Configurations summary screen.

Editing the Resource List and Resource Sets

Two more resource-related options are available on the SHGEN custom level configuration menu. Most network supervisors report never using either option and many do not even know what these options do. Both options enable you to create your own resource and resource set definitions and modify the existing list. These options are identical to the options with the same titles on the NETGEN custom configuration menu. If you don't plan to customize resources or resource sets, or if you have already read the discussion of the NETGEN version of these options in Chapter 5, you can skip this section.

The Edit Resource List option lets you work with the list of individual resources. When you highlight this option and press Enter, you see a list of the defined resources. Highlight a particular one and press Enter; a list of that resource's possible configurations appears. Select a configuration; a detail screen (see fig. 8.8) is displayed showing complete information about that resource's memory address, I/O port, interrupt, and DMA channel usage.

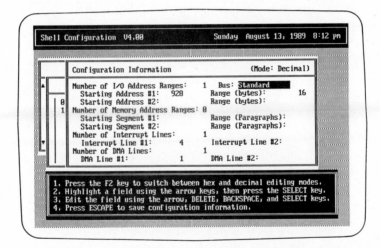

Fig. 8.8.
The Configuration Information window.

You can use the Edit Resource List option to create your own resource definitions. With the list of resources on the screen, press Ins. A prompt tells you to enter the name of your resource. After typing your resource name and pressing Enter, an empty window called Resource Configurations appears. This window lists the various configuration options for your resource. To add the first one, press Ins, and you are prompted to enter a number and a description for this particular configuration (such as 0: Configuration 0 - IRQ 5, DMA 3). After entering the configuration number and description, the detail screen shown in figure 8.8 appears, where you enter the configuration details for your resource configuration.

You can delete resource definitions from the resource list. Highlight the resource you want to remove and press Del. You can highlight multiple resource definitions with the F5 key, and delete all of them at the same time by pressing Del.

The Edit Resource Sets option enables you to create your own resource sets by grouping individual resources. When you select this option, a list of currently defined resource sets is shown. To create a new one, press Ins and you are prompted to enter the name of your new resource set. After entering its name, the set is added to the resource set list. Highlight the new name and press Enter; an empty window called Selected Resources appears. Press Ins and a list of individual resources appears. To add a resource to your newly created set, highlight the resource and press Enter. Repeat the process to add more resources, up to a maximum of six. When your list of resources is complete, press Esc to save your resource set definition and return to the list of resource sets.

You can edit an existing resource set by highlighting its name and pressing Enter. A list of its resources appears on-screen. You can add a resource by pressing Ins to display a list of resources. Highlight the one you want to add and press Enter. You can delete a resource by highlighting it and pressing Del, or you can delete several at a time by marking each one with the F5 key and pressing Del. When your list of resources is complete, press Esc to save your resource set definition and return to the list of resource sets.

You can delete a resource set by highlighting its name and pressing Del. You can delete more than one at a time by marking a group of resource set names with the F5 key and pressing Del.

When you are finished working with the resource set list, press Esc to return to the custom level Available Options menu.

Saving Your Selections and Creating the NetWare Shell

When you have chosen the configuration for your network adapter, you are ready to create the NetWare shell. Start by selecting the Save Selections and Continue menu option. You are asked to confirm that you want to continue generating the shell. Press Y to answer yes; answering no results in a prompt to leave SHGEN, and pressing Esc returns you to the SHGEN Available Options menu.

A menu appears prompting you to "link" the NetWare shell, or to select a new shell configuration. Linking is a process in which separate files are combined into one file. Choose the option to link the NetWare shell. If you are running SHGEN from floppies, you're prompted to swap disks so that SHGEN can find the files needing to be linked. After the shell files are linked, a menu prompts you to configure the NetWare shell. Select this option, and the NetWare shell files are created and placed in the SHGEN-1 subdirectory or on the SHGEN-1 disk (for NetWare on 3 1/2-inch disks) or in the SHGEN-2 subdirectory or on the SHGEN-2 disk (for NetWare on 5 1/4-inch disks). You are then prompted to exit SHGEN. When you answer yes, the program asks whether you want to download the shell files to a floppy disk. If you answer yes, a screen message tells you to place a disk in a floppy drive, and the shell files are copied to the floppy disk. The DOS prompt returns to the screen.

The custom level of SHGEN offers a complex approach to creating the NetWare shell. You can probably achieve satisfactory results using the default or intermediate level, however, because most network adapters come with default settings that do not conflict with the commonly installed input/output devices in PC workstations. In those cases where you have to install an unusual device (such as an IBM SDLC adapter), the custom level might be a good way to ensure that you choose a working network adapter configuration. The custom level also can serve as an on-line reference where you can look up the interrupts and addresses used by various devices.

Using NetWare 386 SHGEN

NetWare 386's SHGEN is very similar to the intermediate level of NetWare 286 SHGEN. NetWare 386 SHGEN allows you to choose your network adapter's configuration from a list of all possible settings. Unlike the default level of NetWare 286 SHGEN, NetWare 386 SHGEN does not identify a default setting, and unlike the custom level, does not let you cross-reference your network adapter's configuration to the adapter configuration of other devices in your workstation.

If you are using NetWare 386 SHGEN from a floppy disk, insert your working copy of the SHGEN-1 disk into a floppy drive and make that floppy drive your default. (For example, if you are using the A drive, type *a:* and press Enter.) Type *shgen* and press Enter.

If you have uploaded the SHGEN file to a hard disk or network drive, switch to that drive, make the NETWARE subdirectory the default, and type *shgen* and press Enter.

The opening menu for SHGEN appears and offers you two options:

Select LAN Driver from List
Load into List from LAN_DRV_???

If you select the first option, the Available LAN Drivers window appears. Highlight the network adapter type you are using and press Enter. Your selection appears in the Selected LAN Driver window. Press Esc to save your selection and continue, or choose the Change Selection option to cancel your choice and make another one.

After you save your selection, the Available LAN Driver Configurations window opens, showing a list of all possible configurations. The configuration at the top of the list is generally the manufacturer's default, and is probably your best setting. Highlight your choice and press Enter. A window opens showing your selected configuration and a prompt asks you to confirm your selection. Respond with yes and the Network Shell files are automatically created (if you respond with no or press Esc, the SHGEN beginning menu reappears).

After the files are created, a message appears on-screen stating that the shell files have been placed on SHGEN-1. If you are working with SHGEN from a floppy, these files are placed on your SHGEN-1 disk. If you have uploaded the SHGEN files to a hard disk or network drive, the files are located in the SHGEN-1 subdirectory.

Printing a Configuration Record

It is important for you to know the configuration of the NetWare shell you have created. You can copy this information easily from the screen while you are running SHGEN, but a better way is available for printing this information. After the NetWare shell is created, a file called CONFIG.DAT is created in the SHGEN-1 subdirectory. CONFIG.DAT is in ASCII format and can be printed by issuing the following command from the SHGEN-1 subdirectory:

COPY CONFIG.DAT LPT1:

and press enter. The contents of a typical CONFIG.DAT created by using NetWare 286's custom level of SHGEN are shown in figure 8.9.

Fig. 8.9.

The CONFIG.DAT file contents.

LAN Driver: Standard Microsystems ARCNET/Pure Data V1.00 (881010)
    Option 0: IRQ = 2, I/O Base = 2E0h, RAM Buffer at D000:0

Resource Set 1: COM1
    Option 0: Int 4; I/O 3F8h - 3FFh

Resource Set 2: IBM SDLC Adapter
    Option 1: BiSync 2

Resource Set 3: LPT1
    Option 0: IRQ = 7, I/O Base = 378h

Resource Set 4: Enhanced Graphics Adapter (No Interrupts)
    Option 0: Attached to Color/EGA monitor

Installing Network Adapter Cards

When the NetWare shell is generated, you are ready to configure and install network adapters in your workstations. Using the configuration information obtained from SHGEN, consult the manufacturer's instructions and set network adapter switches to match your NetWare configuration (with some types of network adapters and with some versions of NetWare, you also can consult the installation guide supplied with NetWare's documentation).

With some types of network adapters, you also must set a unique address for each workstation. If that step is required for the type of network adapter you are using, choose a unique address for each workstation and set the switches on the network adapters accordingly. Record these addresses (so that you know which addresses are available for future workstations) and label each workstation with its network adapter configuration and address. You then can install network adapters in your workstations and connect each one to the network cable system.

Starting SHGEN with Custom Options

Several command line parameter options are available when you start SHGEN. You can use them to bypass some of the opening menus. The command line options are

SHGEN-N (ignores the previous configuration and starts a new configuration)

SHGEN-D (selects the default mode of SHGEN)

SHGEN-I (selects the intermediate mode of SHGEN)

SHGEN-C (selects the custom mode of SHGEN)

SHGEN-S (selects the standard floppy mode for working with files)

You can combine these parameters; for example, type *shgen-nc* and press Enter to start a new configuration using the custom level of SHGEN.

Preparing To Use the NetWare Shell

With the network adapter installed and connected, you're ready to use the NetWare shell. You need to copy the appropriate shell files to the boot disk of the workstation.

SHGEN creates six files when you generate the NetWare shell. Several of these files must be copied to the workstation, and the particular files you copy depend on the workstation's DOS version and the network services that will be used. Each of these six files and its function is described below.

File Name	Description
IPX.COM	All workstations must have IPX.COM installed on their boot disks. IPX (Internetwork Packet Exchange) is the primary protocol used by NetWare workstations and file servers to communicate with each other. Loading IPX.COM activates your network adapter, making the adapter capable of communicating with other devices that use the IPX protocol. IPX.COM is the first part of the NetWare shell to be loaded.
NET2.COM NET3.COM NET4.COM	The NETx.COM file serves as the software interface between NetWare and PC DOS. It makes using the file server's disk and printing resources just like using their equivalents on a DOS workstation. NET2.COM is used on workstations running DOS 2.x, NET3.COM on those running DOS 3.x, and NET4.COM on those running DOS 4.x. NETx.COM is loaded immediately after IPX.COM. All workstations must have the appropriate NETx.COM file installed on their boot disks.
NETBIOS.EXE	NETBIOS is a protocol developed by IBM to facilitate communication between networked devices. Certain network products, especially gateways and other resource-sharing devices, use NETBIOS as a communication method. IBM provides NETBIOS with its Token Ring network adapter. If you need to use a product that requires NETBIOS, and you are using a non-IBM network adapter, you can load NETBIOS.EXE. NETBIOS.EXE is NetWare's emulation of IBM's NETBIOS.
INT2F.COM	INT2F.COM is a small memory-resident program that must be loaded after you load NETBIOS.EXE. INT2F.COM "hooks" interrupt 2F, which is required for full NETBIOS emulation.

You need to copy IPX.COM and the appropriate NETx.COM file to the boot disk of each workstation. If your network has a gateway or similar device requiring NETBIOS, also copy NETBIOS.EXE and INT2F.COM to the boot disk. Most network supervisors create a special directory on each workstation (with a name such as NETWORK or SHELLS) to store these files.

Loading the NetWare Shell

The NetWare shell files have to be loaded in the following order:

IPX.COM
NETx.COM
NETBIOS.EXE
INT2F.COM

Remember that NETBIOS.EXE and INT2F.COM only need to be loaded in special situations.

After you boot your workstation with DOS, you can load IPX.COM by changing to the directory on your boot disk where it is stored, typing *ipx* and pressing Enter. You see a message similar to the following after loading IPX.COM:

```
Novell IPX/SPX V2.15 (C) Copyright 1985, 1988 Novell Inc. All
Rights Reserved.

LAN Option: Standard Microsystems ARCNET/Pure Data V1.00 (881010)
Hardware Configuration: IRQ = 2, I/O Base = 2E0h, RAM Buffer at
D000:0
```

Notice that the message tells you the IPX.COM version number, the type of network adapter it is configured for, and the expected hardware settings on the adapter.

After loading IPX, you need to load the correct NETx.COM file (NET2.COM if you are using DOS 2.x, NET3.COM for DOS 3.x, and NET4.COM for DOS 4.x). Type

NETx

where x is the correct DOS version number, and press Enter, and you see a message similar to the following:

```
NetWare V2.15 rev. A - Workstation Shell for PC DOS V3.x (C)
Copyright 1983, 1988 Novell, Inc. All Rights Reserved.

Attached to server SERV1 Sunday, August 13, 1989  1:48:46 am
```

This message tells you which server you are attached to and the date and time of the attachment. Loading NETx.COM broadcasts a request to all servers on your network. The first server to respond is the one whose name is shown.

If you plan to use a device that requires NETBIOS, you can load the NetWare NETBIOS emulator by typing *netbios* and pressing Enter, followed by typing *int2f* and pressing Enter.

When the Shell Doesn't Load

Loading the shell successfully from the first workstation is an intensely exhilarating experience that proves you have installed your network properly. Sometimes your exhilaration is postponed; when you execute the shell files, one or all of them do not load properly. The problem often is easy to correct.

If IPX.COM does not load, but causes your PC to "hang" or "freeze," it indicates that the configuration you specified when using SHGEN does not match the actual settings on your network adapter. Recheck the switch and jumper settings on your network adapter, and review the information you printed from the CONFIG.DAT file to make sure that your shell and network adapter configurations match exactly.

If IPX.COM loads, but NETx.com does not, you may have a problem with the cable connection between the workstation you are testing and the server or servers. Sometimes the error message File server could not be found is returned. Start by checking the obvious: Is the cable connected to your network adapter and to your file servers? Is the file server turned on? If the answer to these questions is yes, you may want to try connecting one workstation directly to a file server using a short cable run. If this works, but the regular cable connection doesn't, you probably have a cable problem. If a direct connection doesn't work, check the configuration of both your shell and the LAN drivers used to configure the server; be sure both match the actual settings of your network adapters.

Memory Usage

When you load IPX.COM and NETx.COM, both files remain in memory and consume about 50,000 bytes of available space. These programs should be the first memory-resident programs executed.

Loading NETBIOS consumes approximately 14,000 additional bytes of RAM.

The only way to unload the NetWork shell and to free the memory the shell uses is to reboot your computer.

Displaying Shell Configuration Information

You can display the load message information of an IPX.COM or NETx.COM file without loading them by typing the file name followed by the letter I (for information). For example, to display the configuration information for an IPX.COM file, type

    IPX.COM I

and press Enter.

Logging into the Server

With your workstations connected and the NetWare shell loaded, you are ready to log into a server and start using it. When you load the NetWare shell, a new drive letter is automatically created. This drive letter is the first letter not reserved for use by a local disk drive. With DOS Versions 3.x and 4.x, this is usually drive FV, because letters A through E are reserved for floppy and hard drives and RAM disks. With DOS 2.x, the letter used is the first unused letter.

If you have used the LASTDRIVE= statement in your PC's CONFIG.SYS file, the NetWare shell creates the drive letter after the drive you specify. Occasionally a user has the statement LASTDRIVE = Z in his CONFIG.SYS file, which causes the NetWare shell to create an unusable drive beyond drive Z.

When you switch to the drive created by the shell (in most cases by typing *f:* and pressing Enter), you see that the drive contains two files: LOGIN.EXE and SLIST.EXE. LOGIN.EXE is used to log into a server. To log into a server, you must have a login name on it. When you first install a server, two login names are automatically created: SUPERVISOR and GUEST. Neither has a password (you will learn more about adding login names and passwords in Chapter 10). SUPERVISOR has the ability to use all server files and directories and to add other users to the network. GUEST is only allowed limited use of the server files and connected printers.

To log into a server, type *login* and press Enter, and you see the following prompt:

    Enter your login name:

Type the name of the server you want to log into, followed by a slash (/) and a login name. For example, to log into server SERV1 using the login name SUPERVISOR, type

    SERV1/SUPERVISOR

and press Enter.

If the login name you use has a password assigned to it, you are prompted to enter the password.

If your network has only one server, you do not have to enter the server name; you can type *supervisor* and press Enter and you are logged into the server automatically.

If your network has multiple servers, you can list them using the SLIST (Server List) command. From the drive letter the network shell creates, type *slist*, press Enter, and all available servers are listed.

Instead of typing *login* and waiting for its prompt, you can type *login* followed by your server and login name, such as

    LOGIN SERV1/SUPERVISOR

and press Enter.

This is handy when you want to place the LOGIN command in a batch file. You can also enter just the server name followed by a slash, such as

    LOGIN SERV1/

and the login name you type in response to the Enter your login name: prompt is presumed to be on the SERV1 server.

The directory containing the LOGIN.EXE and SLIST.EXE files is called LOGIN. Every server has a LOGIN directory by default. When you first load the NetWare shell, the shell sends a request to all servers on the network. The first server to respond to the request is the one on which a drive letter is created. This drive letter points to the responding server's LOGIN directory. The message shown after you have loaded the NETx.COM part of the shell shows which server you are attached to. If you use the LOGIN command without specifying a server name, the login name you enter is presumed to be on the server the shell is attached to.

Attaching to Multiple Servers

When you log into your first server, you can attach up to seven more. The ATTACH command is used for this purpose. To ATTACH to a second server, type

    ATTACH

and press Enter. You see the following prompt:

    Enter server name:

Enter the name of a file server. You are then prompted to

```
Enter user name:
```

Respond by typing a valid login name on the server. You're prompted to enter a password if one is assigned to the login name you are using.

As with the LOGIN command, you can eliminate the prompts and enter on one line all the information required to attach by following the ATTACH command with the server name and login name:

ATTACH SERV2/GUEST

Or you can type only the server name followed by a slash:

ATTACH SERV2/

You are prompted to enter only the login name.

Changing Your AUTOEXEC.BAT File

When your network is in operation, you probably will want to load the NetWare shell and be prompted to log in automatically. Placing lines similar to the following in your AUTOEXEC.BAT file accomplishes this:

```
CD\NETWORK
IPX
NET3
F:
LOGIN
```

The first line changes to the directory where the shell files are stored. The next two lines load the IPX and NET3 files. Then the current drive is set to the one created by the shell (F:) and the LOGIN command is executed, which prompts you to log in.

Customizing the NetWare Shell with the SHELL.CFG File

In most situations, when the NetWare shell is configured and created using SHGEN, no customization is necessary. However, several aspects of the shell can be fine-tuned. You can fine-tune the shell by creating an ASCII text file called SHELL.CFG, which contains customization information for the NetWare shell. When you place SHELL.CFG in the same directory where the shell files are located, SHELL.CFG is read when the shell files are loaded.

Three of the shell files (IPX.COM, NETx.COM, and NETBIOS.EXE) have configurable parameters that can be set in SHELL.CFG. You can create SHELL.CFG using any word processor or text editor that can produce an ASCII text file, or you can use the DOS EDLIN or COPY CON commands. Each line of SHELL.CFG contains a shell option that can be customized with the value you want.

Most of these items should not be changed casually. Only make these changes when you are sure that they are wise, and even then you should test the results on one or two workstations before making the change everywhere. If you purchase a special product to run on your network and its documentation suggests customizing the shell using the SHELL.CFG file, the parameters that can be set in the SHELL.CFG file are listed and explained in your NetWare documentation.

The NetWare shell is your personal computer's link to NetWare. The shell is a memory-resident program that handles all communications between your personal computer and your network's servers. NetWare's SHGEN utility is used to configure and create the NetWare shell files.

After the NetWare shell is loaded, you can log into a file server and begin using its files and resources.

Chapter Summary

Congratulations! In this chapter, you learned how to install NetWare and activate servers and workstations. You are now ready to begin a process that will last for the life of your LAN—organizing and managing your network and its servers. You will begin to learn about this task in the next chapter.

Part III

Organizing
Your Server

Includes

Organizing Information with NetWare
Adding Users
Understanding NetWare Rights
Managing Files
Establishing Real-World Security
Implementing Shared Printing
Using Shared Printers
Creating Login Scripts
Setting Up NetWare Accounting

Organizing Information with NetWare

A file server's main job is to make storing and retrieving files easy. For this reason, information placed on the file server must be logically organized, and the method of organization must be easy to understand. To the programs you are running, the files on the server must look and act just as they would if they were stored on your PC's local disks. For example, if you store a spreadsheet file on a file server disk, your spreadsheet program should be able to find and retrieve the file just as if the program were retrieving a file from your personal hard disk.

Examining the Information Hierarchy

NetWare organizes data on file server disks similar to the way that PC DOS and OS/2 organize it on a PC's hard disk. On both a NetWare server and an IBM-compatible PC, data is organized in a hierarchy of directories, such as the one diagrammed in figure 9.1. Many PC scholars call this hierarchy a tree structure (it is more like an upside-down tree). Because the PC contains all the devices that store information, the PC is at the root of the tree.

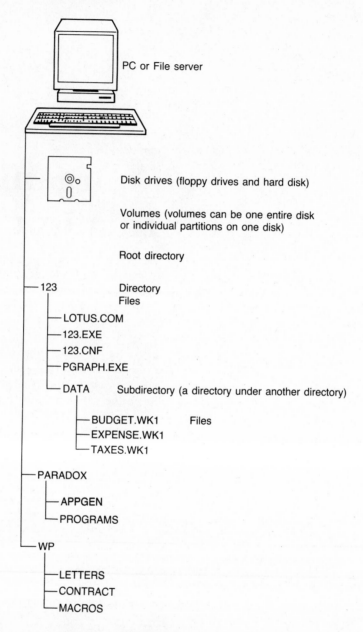

Fig. 9.1.

The information hierarchy.

Disk Drives and Volumes

The next level consists of the PC's disk drives (in most cases, one or two floppy drives and a hard disk). Each drive contains at least one volume.

With floppy drives, each disk is a separate volume, so the disks are sometimes called removable or interchangeable volumes. A PC hard disk can consist of one single volume or can be divided or partitioned into more than one.

You have the option of giving each volume a name. Each volume on an IBM PC is also assigned a drive letter. The first floppy drive is assigned the letter A and is called the A drive or drive A. The first hard disk volume is usually assigned C. You switch from one volume to another by entering at the operating system prompt the volume letter name followed by a colon. For example, to switch to drive C you type *c:* and press Enter.

Directories and Subdirectories

Volumes are further divided into directories and subdirectories. The directory at the highest level of the tree is called the *root directory*. In PC DOS and OS/2, the root directory is designated by a \ (backslash). Under the root directory are *directories*, and under the directories are *subdirectories*.

A disk drive, or volume, is something like a file cabinet made up of many file drawers. Like a label on a file cabinet that lists the contents of the cabinet, a directory lists the files and subdirectories contained in the volume. A subdirectory lists the contents of a particular drawer.

At the bottom of the hierarchy are the *files*. Here the tree analogy becomes a little misleading. You might think that files can be stored only in subdirectories because files are shown at the lowest level of the information hierarchy. But in fact you can store files anywhere on a disk volume—in the root directory or in any directory or subdirectory.

Directories exist to give you a way to organize related groups of files and store them in one place. For example, when you install Lotus 1-2-3, you can create a directory called 123 and install the program files there. You might make a subdirectory under 123 called DATA to store the spreadsheets you create.

NetWare's Version of the Hierarchy

NetWare modifies the directory hierarchy only slightly. At the root of the tree, you have a file server rather than a PC. On a network file server, because of the increased storage requirements of a group of users, several disks may be available, each with its own tree-structured directory. And remember that a network can have more than one file server.

With this capability to handle multiple drives (up to 32 in NetWare 286) and multiple directory trees, NetWare uses its own system of coordinates to identify a file's location. The first entity specified in the location of a file is the server, and the next coordinates are the volume, the directory, and the file name—in that order.

Volumes on a network, as with DOS and OS/2, are either entire disks or parts of a disk (partitions). Unlike DOS and OS/2, however, with NetWare volume names are not optional. Every volume is given a name when you install the file server. In fact, NetWare automatically names the first volume SYS.

How is this hierarchy useful? Understanding how it works helps you move quickly to the server, volume, directory, and subdirectory where a particular file is stored. For example, if you want to start Lotus 1-2-3, you first need to position yourself in its directory. On a DOS or OS/2 PC, you first move to the correct volume by typing *c:*.

You next change to the proper directory by typing *cd\123*. (CD is the command to change directories.) If someone asks you to identify completely the directory in which Lotus 1-2-3 is stored, you respond with

C:\123

where C: designates the disk drive (volume), \ is the root directory, and 123 is the name of the directory.

Similarly, if you need to identify a particular spreadsheet file called BUDGET.WK1 that you have stored in the subdirectory called DATA under the 123 directory, you identify the file as

C:\123\DATA\BUDGET.WK1

This means of file identification is called a *path*.

If Lotus 1-2-3 is stored on a file server, the information is a little more detailed. The 123 directory on a file server might be referred to as

SERV1/SYS:123

where SERV1 is the server name, SYS: is the volume, and 123 is the directory. The BUDGET.WK1 spreadsheet file would be identified as

SERV1/SYS:123\DATA\BUDGET.WK1

As you can see, the complete NetWare name of a file is similar to its DOS or OS/2 counterpart, but a few things are added. You add the server name at the beginning, and substitute the name of the NetWare volume for the drive letter. Although network users can be shielded from this additional requirement, the network supervisor must understand this naming system because many NetWare utilities and commands require its use. Figure 9.2 shows the components of the complete NetWare path for a file.

SERV1/SYS:123\DATA\BUDGET.WK1

File server   Volume   Directory   Subdirectory   File name

Fig. 9.2.
The complete
NetWare file path.

Notice that the server name is separated from the volume name with a slash (/), and that the volume name is followed by a colon (:). Directory names are separated from each other with backslashes (\). Actually, you can use either slashes or backslashes to separate directory and subdirectory names or to separate the server and volume names.

Why does the NetWare name have to be longer? Simply because there are more places to put things. The NetWare name has to accommodate the fact that files can be not only in different volumes and directories but also on different servers. Consider a network with two file servers as an example. Figure 9.3 shows a diagram of the file storage structure of this network.

The first server, which is named SERV1, has two volumes: SYS: and SYS2:. The SYS: volume is used to store each user's personal files, and each user has an individual subdirectory under the directory called USERS. The SYS2: volume is used to store the network's electronic mail. The second server is called SERV2. Its first volume (SYS:) stores the network's shared software and has directories for programs like WordPerfect, Lotus 1-2-3, and dBASE. The second volume (SYS2:) stores the company's accounting system.

Now look at how you identify the various directories on these two file servers. The directory that stores WordPerfect is on the server named SERV2 on the SYS: volume. The directory's complete NetWare path is

SERV2/SYS:WORDPERF

Perhaps the user named Jimmy has a document called REPORT.WP that is stored in his personal storage area on SERV1. That file's complete NetWare path is

SERV1/SYS:USERS\JIMMY\REPORT.WP

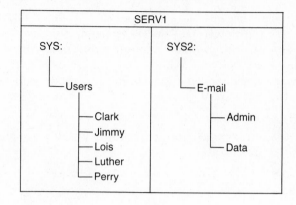

Fig. 9.3.

Directories on a two-server network.

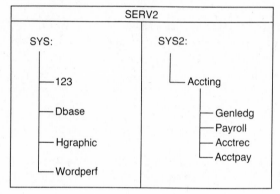

Using the MAP Command

When you are working with files on your own PC, you use drive letters as shortcuts to avoid typing the full paths of the files and directories with which you are working. If you are copying spreadsheet files from the C:\123\DATA directory to a floppy disk, you might type

    COPY C:\123\DATA*.*   A:\

But if you know that DATA is the default directory on drive C, you can save some keystrokes by just typing

    COPY C:*.*   A:

Similarly, you can refer to SERV1/SYS:USERS\JIMMY\REPORT.WP as F:REPORT.WP if you can somehow make the SERV1/SYS:USERS\JIMMY directory the default directory on drive F. How do you go about assigning a drive letter to a directory or a server?

In the last chapter, you learned that loading the NetWare shell automatically creates a new drive letter on your PC. This drive letter points to the SYS:LOGIN directory on the file server that answered the shell's request for a connection. The drive letter NetWare chooses is the first one not used by your PC, which is generally drive F.

Fortunately, your ability to assign drive letters doesn't end there. The NetWare MAP command is designed to let you assign drive letters to file server volumes. The network supervisor and sophisticated user alike will find the MAP command to be one of NetWare's most versatile and often-used tools. You use it to create a DOS- or OS/2-like environment on the file server so that you can run programs and use files on servers as if they were stored on your own hard disk.

Displaying a List of Assigned Drives

The MAP command has several uses. If you type *map* and press Enter, you see a list of the drive letters that are currently assigned. Your list probably looks similar to the following:

```
Drive A: maps to a local disk
Drive B: maps to a local disk
Drive C: maps to a local disk
Drive F: = SERV1/SYS:SYSTEM
Drive G: = SERV1/SYS:LOGIN
-----
SEARCH1: = Z:. [SERV1/SYS:PUBLIC]
```

The MAP display shows you how each drive letter is being used. If the letter is assigned to a server volume and directory, that information is listed. If a drive letter is in use for a local disk, MAP tells you that as well.

The previous list also shows a special type of drive designation called SEARCH1:. This drive is a special kind of mapping called a *search drive*, which is similar to a directory designated as part of your DOS or OS/2 search path. This topic is discussed in detail later in this chapter (see "Mapping Search Drives").

Assigning Drive Letters

You use MAP in a different way if you want to assign a new drive letter (or reassign one already in use). Suppose that you want to designate drive

H to be your private storage area, which is known by the NetWare name of SERV1/SYS:USERS\JIMMY. To make this assignment, type the following MAP command:

MAP H: = SERV1/SYS:USERS\JIMMY

and press Enter. Notice that you follow the MAP command with the drive letter you want to use (H), a colon, an equal sign, and the NetWare name of the directory to which you want to point. The NetWare name includes the server (SERV1), the volume (SYS:), the directory (USERS), and the subdirectory (JIMMY).

You also can map a drive letter to a directory on a different server, as in

MAP I: = SERV2/SYS:WORDPERF

If you are not attached to that server yet, however, NetWare prompts you to enter your login identification on that server. (For complete details on attaching to a server, see Chapter 8, "Activating Workstations.")

Deleting Drive Letters

Sometimes, when you are finished using a drive letter, you may want to delete it. In the previous example, when you are finished using WordPerfect, you can delete your mapping to its directory by typing

MAP DEL I:

You have two other ways to delete mappings. When you log out of a server, any drive letters you have mapped to that server are automatically deleted. Also, if you use MAP to assign a letter that you had already assigned in a previous command, the new assignment automatically replaces the old one.

Using MAP Shortcuts

After you become familiar with the MAP command, you can use a few keystroke-saving shortcuts. First, if your network has only one server, or if you are logged onto only one server and want to assign a drive letter on that server, you can safely omit the server name:

MAP H: = SYS:USERS\JIMMY

The MAP command assumes that because you left out the server name, you want to stay on the current server. Similarly, if you want to map a drive that is on the same server and the same volume, you can omit the volume name also, replacing it with a \ (the DOS and OS/2 symbol for the root directory). The MAP command then assumes that you want to stay on the current volume. For example, if you want to map drive I to another user's directory on the same volume, you can use the following shortened MAP command:

> MAP I: = \USERS\CLARK

If you want to make one drive letter point to exactly the same server volume and directory as another drive letter, you can tell the MAP command to make the new drive letter the same as the other. If you want to make drive J the same as drive F, for example, use this command:

> MAP J: = F:

Mapping Search Drives

As mentioned previously, you can use the MAP command to create a special kind of directory mapping called a search drive. The function of a NetWare search drive is identical to that of a directory you have declared to be a DOS or OS/2 search path.

As its name indicates, a search drive is a directory that can be searched for commands not found in your current directory. Whenever you execute a command, your PC's operating system searches for the command file in your current default directory. If it is not found, the search stops unless you have used the PATH command to establish search paths to other directories. For example, you might have a search path to the DOS directory so that you can use commands like EDLIN and FORMAT without having to switch to the DOS directory.

You can use MAP to create search paths to directories on file server disks. You already have learned that most NetWare commands are stored in a directory called PUBLIC on the SYS: volume. Some of these commands, such as MAP, ATTACH, LOGIN, and LOGOUT, are needed frequently. Having to switch to the SYS:PUBLIC directory every time you need to use one of those commands is inconvenient. For this reason, when you log into a file server, a search drive is created for SYS:PUBLIC by default, enabling you to use important NetWare commands easily and without having to switch to the directory that stores them. In Chapter 16, "Creating Login Scripts," you will learn about the process that automatically creates search drives.

Using MAP to create a search drive is similar to using the command to create a regular drive letter. To create a search drive for the 123 directory on the SERV2 server and SYS: volume, you type

MAP S1:=SERV2/SYS:123

and press Enter. As you can see, rather than designate a drive letter, you type *s* (for search) followed by a number. The number designates the search drive's place in the search order. For example, look at the following three MAP commands, which create three search drives:

MAP S1:=SERV1/SYS:PUBLIC
MAP S2:=SERV1/SYS2:EMAIL\DATA
MAP S3:=SERV2/SYS:123

The resulting search order is

1. SERV1/SYS:PUBLIC

2. SERV1/SYS2:EMAIL\DATA

3. SERV2/SYS:123

With these search paths in place, you can type *lotus* to start 1-2-3 and create a flurry of digital activity. First, your PC looks for the LOTUS command file in your default directory. The PC does not find the file there, so the system proceeds to search for the file in PUBLIC (search drive 1). Not finding the file there, the PC next looks in search drive 2, which happens to be the EMAIL\DATA directory. The system finally looks in search drive 3, the 123 directory, where it is successful. The Lotus 1-2-3 program starts. Fortunately, the whole search process takes place in milliseconds; you don't notice the delay.

But you need to note one important point about creating search drives. In the preceding example, the file server processor has to look through two other directories before getting to 123. Even though in many cases you don't perceive the delay, searching through directories does take processor time. With many users building search paths, a file server's CPU can spend a lot of time looking through search paths. You thus should design search paths to minimize the time required to find a file. Put first the drive you will most likely need to access. For example, if you are going to run Lotus often, insert 123 as the first search drive (MAP S1:=SERV2/SYS:123). If the next most likely path is to PUBLIC, then use MAP S2:=SYS:PUBLIC.

Search drives are a handy way to make file server directories easy to use. NetWare allows you to create up to 16 search drives if you allow enough DOS or OS/2 environment space to accommodate them. (See your DOS or OS/2 manual for details about environment space.) You probably will not need that many.

In one situation, using the MAP command to create search drives is dangerous. If you have already used the DOS or OS/2 PATH command to create search paths on your local disks, invoking MAP to create a network-based search drive destroys components of DOS search paths. For every search path created, one component of the DOS path is deleted. For example, if you used the DOS path

PATH = C:\;C:\DOS;C:\UTIL;

and then use

MAP S2: = SYS:PUBLIC

the DOS path loses the first component: C:\. The new path is

PATH = C:\DOS;C:\UTIL;

Previously created network search drives that you created with MAP are not removed, only those created with PATH. Fortunately, a remedy is available, and if you frequently use PATH, you should adopt this method as your standard practice. Modify your MAP command by placing the word INSERT before the search drive designation (S1:, S2:, and so on) to add the network search drive without disturbing search paths you created with PATH. Using this method, the previously listed commands to create three search drives would look like this:

```
MAP INSERT S1: = SERV1/SYS:PUBLIC
MAP INSERT S2: = SERV1/SYS2:EMAIL\DATA
MAP INSERT S3: = SERV2/SYS:123
```

You should note one other interesting fact about the relationship between the MAP and PATH commands. When you use MAP to create a search drive, NetWare automatically assigns the search drive a letter of the alphabet. The system starts at the end of the alphabet and works forward. The previous MAP commands thus not only create search mappings but also assign drive letters Z, Y, and X to SERV1/SYS:PUBLIC, SERV1/SYS2:EMAIL\DATA, and SERV2/SYS:123, respectively. When you then type *map* to list the currently used drive letters, the command lists the following information for you about these drives:

```
SEARCH1: = Z:. [SERV1/SYS:PUBLIC]
SEARCH2: = Y:. [SERV1/SYS2:EMAIL\DATA]
SEARCH3: = X:. [SERV2/SYS:123]
```

The next search drive, if you were to create one, would be assigned drive W. (You can see why veteran network supervisors are famous for their ability to recite the alphabet backwards.) This design enables the PATH command, which cannot understand NetWare directory names (because they include server and volume names), to reference network search drives by what the command can understand: a drive letter. If you are familiar with the PATH command, you know that when you type *path*, you are shown a list of the search paths that you have created. The list you would see might be similar to the following:

```
PATH=C:\DOS;C:\UTILITY;
```

After you use MAP to insert the three search drives in the previous example, PATH's list is modified:

```
PATH=Z:.;Y:.;X:.;C:\DOS;C:\UTILITY;
```

The supervisor often uses the MAP command as part of batch files and menus to make using the network easy for others. Some of these uses are discussed in future chapters, and you will also see how the MAP command plays an important role in another NetWare tool called the login script. (You will learn about login scripts in Chapter 16.)

Mapping to the Root Directory with the MAP Command

NetWare 386's MAP command provides a special option that enables you to make a server directory a "fake root" directory. Suppose that you want to map the directory called SERV1/SYS:PRIVATE\SMITHFD as drive F, and you want it to appear as if it is the root directory (the directory at the top of the directory tree structure) on drive F. You can accomplish this by following the MAP command with the special parameter named ROOT, as shown in this example:

```
MAP ROOT F:=SERV1/SYS:PRIVATE\SMITHFD
```

After executing this MAP command, drive F appears to be mapped to a root directory (F:\), but the root directory actually is SERV1/SYS:PRIVATE\SMITHFD.

Using DOS and OS/2 Commands on the File Server Disk

Knowing how to use the MAP command enables you to "navigate" file server volumes and directories, but you will be glad to know that most of your favorite DOS or OS/2 commands can be used freely on the file server disk, just as you use them on your PC's local disks. For example, if you want to see a list of files in a file server directory, you do not have to use a NetWare command (although you could). You can simply use DIR, which is the DOS and OS/2 command that lists a directory's files. All the normal parameters that you use with the DIR command also work, such as /P and /W, as well as qualifiers and wild-card characters, such as *.* and ??????.EXE.

Similarly, you can use commands such as CD (change directory), MD (make directory), and RD (remove directory) to manipulate directories on file server disks. If you are in the WordPerfect directory and want to switch to the dBASE directory on the same server volume, you can simply type *cd\dbase*.

You also can change to a different volume on the same file server by typing *cd sys2:*, which moves you from the SYS: volume to the SYS2: volume.

Two DOS and OS/2 commands do not work. For obvious security reasons (as well as a few technical ones) you cannot use the FORMAT command to reformat a server disk. You also cannot use CHKDSK to check the size of a server disk, although similar NetWare commands called CHKVOL and VOLINFO are available.

Other commands, such as COPY and ERASE, work as they do on your local disks. NetWare also provides enhanced commands in some cases. For example, a command called NCOPY is available to do high-speed copies from one directory on a server to another on the same server.

Sometimes, your ability to use a DOS or OS/2 command is disabled because you do not have sufficient NetWare rights to use it. You may not have the right to delete files in a particular directory, in which case the ERASE command does not work. Or you may not be permitted to create directories on a certain volume, causing the MD command to return the error message Unable to create directory.

With few exceptions, and with the skillful use of the MAP command, you can make a NetWare server's disk look just like a DOS or OS/2 volume.

Chapter Summary

In this chapter, you learned that understanding how NetWare organizes data on its servers is an important first step toward using your network effectively. You must be familiar with how NetWare identifies files and directories because this information is required to skillfully use MAP and a number of other NetWare commands. You will put this knowledge to good use as you learn how to add users and give them access to the directories and files on your servers.

10

Adding Users

Very few networks are set up for the sole use of the network installer or supervisor. At some point, other users need to be given login names so they can access the files that are stored on network servers. In this chapter, you will learn about using the SYSCON utility to give login names to users. SYSCON is the network supervisor's primary tool for managing user access. In upcoming chapters, you will see how to use it to manage security, accounting, and login scripts.

NetWare lets the network supervisor control access to servers and their files in four ways: login control, user rights, directory rights, and file attribute control. In this chapter, you will look at the first element—login control. In the next chapter ("Understanding NetWare Rights"), you will study user and directory rights. Next, you will look at file attribute control in the chapter called "Managing Files." You will discover how to combine all four elements in the chapter titled "Establishing Real-World Security."

The Purpose of a Login Name

Unless you have a login name on a server, you have absolutely no access to the files it stores. You become a server user when a login name is created for you. This enables you to use the LOGIN and ATTACH commands to gain access to the server.

Whether or not you have a login name determines whether you can access a server. In a multiserver network, some users have login names on some servers and no login name on others. Only the network supervisor has the ability to add a user by giving him or her a login name.

Different Categories of Users

NetWare 286 offers two categories of users. A user can be a server *supervisor*, meaning that he or she has unlimited access to the server's files and directories. Server supervisors also can add and delete users. Users who are not supervisors have only the access privileges assigned to them by a server supervisor.

With NetWare 386, this distinction becomes less rigid. A third category of user exists, called a *workgroup manager*, which is somewhere between a complete supervisor and a normal user. Workgroup managers can control particular lists of users and can add new users as well. They only can give those users access to certain directories on the server, as determined by a server supervisor.

A normal user also can be designated by his or her workgroup manager or a server supervisor to *manage* other users. In this capacity, the manager user can give his or her managed users access to a certain list of directories (as determined by his or her workgroup manager or the server supervisor) and even delete a managed user.

Now that you understand the importance of login names and the various categories of users available with NetWare 286 and 386, you're ready to use SYSCON to add users and manage user accounts.

Introducing SYSCON

SYSCON is short for System Configuration. Most network supervisors use it as their primary tool for managing file server security and configuration. Although SYSCON is normally used by the network supervisor or workgroup managers, other users can also use it to make changes to their individual "accounts" on a file server. Even if you are not the network supervisor, for example, you can still use SYSCON to change your password or view your access rights. However, the ability to use SYSCON to manage the accounts of other users and make changes to the file server configuration require that you have the access level of a network supervisor.

The exercises in this chapter require that you be a network supervisor or workgroup manager. If you want to try them as you read, first log in to a file server where you have supervisor or workgroup manager access. At the DOS prompt, type

SYSCON

and press Enter. SYSCON is stored in the SYS:PUBLIC directory of every file server. Because NetWare makes SYS:PUBLIC a search drive by default, you don't have to worry about it being the default directory when you start SYSCON.

SYSCON greets you with the main menu shown in figure 10.1.

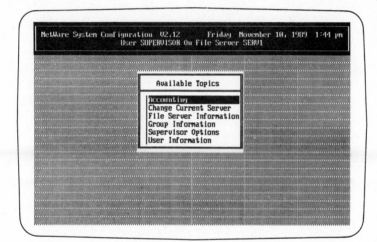

Fig. 10.1.
The SYSCON utility's main menu.

SYSCON is typical of all NetWare menu utilities. It uses pop-up boxes (fondly referred to as the "exploding window look" by some) to show menus and submenus, and it uses a standard set of keys to perform various actions. Notice that the name of the utility (NetWare System Configuration) is shown in the upper left corner. Your login name and the name of the server you are using are shown in the upper center portion of the screen.

Managing Login Names

You can use the process of adding user login names to learn how the menus for a NetWare utility work. You will see that certain keys on the keyboard have special functions. These special keys and their functions are shown in table 10.1.

Table 10.1
Special Keys and Their Functions
for NetWare Menu Utilities

Key Description	Keyboard Keys To Press	Key Function
Escape	Esc	Move back to the preceding menu or level
Exit	Alt-F10	Exit the utility from any screen
Cancel	F7	Cancel changes without saving them
Backspace	Backspace	Delete the character to the left of the cursor
Insert	Ins	Insert a new item
Delete	Del	Delete an item
Modify	F3	Rename/modify/edit an item
Select	Enter	Accept information entered or select an item
Help	F1	Access help screens
Mark	F5	Mark an unmarked item or unmark a marked item
Cycle	Tab	Cycle through menus or screens
Mode	F9	Change modes
Up	↑	Move up one line
Down	↓	Move down one line
Left	←	Move left one position
Right	→	Move right one position
Special Up	Ctrl-PgUp	Move to the very beginning

Table 10.1—continued

Key Description	Keyboard Keys To Press	Key Function
Special Down	Ctrl-PgDn	Move to the very end
Special Left	Home	Move to the left-most position on the line
Special Right	End	Move to the right-most position on the line
Page Up	PgUp	Move up one page
Page Down	PgDn	Move down one page
Field Left	Ctrl-←	Move left one field or word
Field Right	Ctrl-→	Move right one field or word

Notice that the options in SYSCON's main menu are displayed in alphabetical order. You want to select the option called User Information. To select a menu option, you can use the up- or down-arrow keys to highlight an item, or you can press the first letter of the menu choice and it is highlighted automatically. (If two menu choices start with the same letter, the highlight moves to the first; pressing the second letter of the desired option moves the highlight again to the option you want to choose.) Use either method to highlight User Information, and press Enter. (After an item is highlighted, pressing Enter selects that menu option and takes you to the appropriate submenu.)

A new box opens that displays a list of existing users. At this point, you can perform four operations: add a new user, delete a user, work with the account of a user, or rename a user. To add a user, press the Ins key on your keyboard. A small box opens and you are prompted to type the new user's login name. Notice that the Ins key is used in NetWare utilities any time you need to add an item (in this case, a login ID) to a list. Type the name you want to add and press Enter. The new name is added to the list.

You can change an existing login name by highlighting it and pressing the F3 key. A small box opens, and you are prompted to enter the new login name you want to use. Typing that name and pressing Enter completes the change.

Deleting a login name is a similar process. Highlight a name you want to delete and press the Del key. You are asked to confirm your choice. After you do so, the login name is deleted. Use the Del key in NetWare utilities to remove an item from a list.

If you need to delete more than one name, you can highlight each and mark it with the F5 key. You can then delete all marked login names by pressing the Del key. With all NetWare menu utilities, you can work with multiple items from a list by marking them first with the use of the F5 key.

When you are finished working with login names, you can press Esc to close the box listing the login names. You are returned to the main menu. Use the Esc key in NetWare utilities to return to the preceding menu. You can press Esc from SYSCON's main menu if you want to exit the program.

Adding, Deleting, or Renaming a User with SYSCON

1. Start SYSCON and select User Information from its main menu. A list of existing user login names appears.

2. To add a new login name, press Ins. You see a prompt telling you to enter the user's login name. The new name is added to the login name list.

3. To delete a login name, highlight it and press Del. After confirming that you want to delete the name, it disappears from the list.

4. To change a login name, highlight it and press F3. You are prompted to revise the login name. After revising it, the list is updated to show your change.

Using Special Login Names

When you first install NetWare on a server, two login names are automatically created: SUPERVISOR and GUEST. SUPERVISOR has unlimited access to all server directories and is the login name you use when you are using SYSCON and other NetWare utilities to manage the server. If you want, you can establish other login names with the same access level as SUPERVISOR.

GUEST is almost the opposite of SUPERVISOR. GUEST has limited access to only two directories (SYS:PUBLIC and SYS:LOGIN) and can send jobs to server printers.

Working with a User's Account

After a user has a login name, the next step is to set up his or her account. Your account on a file server is your *profile*, or everything relating to you on that particular server. To begin working with a user account, make sure that you are logged in with supervisory access and start SYSCON by typing the following at the DOS prompt:

SYSCON

Press Enter. When SYSCON's main menu appears, select the User Information option. This option displays a list of login names. Choose the name you want to work with by highlighting it and pressing Enter. The menu shown in figure 10.2 appears.

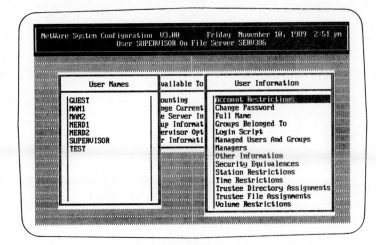

Fig. 10.2.
SYSCON's User Information menu.

The following items make up your server user account:

- ❏ Login name
- ❏ Password
- ❏ Full name
- ❏ Login script
- ❏ Time and station restrictions
- ❏ Trustee rights
- ❏ Groups you belong to
- ❏ Security equivalences
- ❏ The users you manage (NetWare 386 only)
- ❏ The users who manage you (NetWare 386 only)

Each item above plays a part in defining a user's access to the server. Without any trustee rights, for example, the user cannot use any of the files in the directories on the file server. Without a password, there is nothing to prevent anyone who knows a user's login name from logging in and accessing personal files.

If you think that creating a user account can be a detailed process, you're right. However, you don't have to use all the weapons in the SYSCON arsenal when creating a user account. A login name is the minimum required to establish a user account. Passwords, full names, restrictions, groups, security equivalences, and even trustee rights are optional. (Without trustee rights, however, the user cannot use any files on the server disk.) Each of these options is available for a good reason, though, and a network that does not use at least some of them is probably not as secure as it should be.

In the following sections, you will examine each of the previously listed items.

Working with a User's Account

1. Start SYSCON and select User Information from its main menu. A list of existing user login names appears.

2. Highlight the user that you want to work with and press Enter. The User Information menu appears.

3. Select the option that deals with the aspect of the user's account that you want to change. To change the user's password, for example, select Change Password.

Login Names

A login name is used for gaining access to a server. You cannot log into a server without having a login name on that server. As discussed in Chapter 8, the login name is used with NetWare's LOGIN or ATTACH commands to access a server. Login names can be up to 47 characters long and cannot contain spaces. In fact, if you enter a space, SYSCON automatically converts it to an underline (FRANK SMITH becomes FRANK_SMITH, for example).

You have already discovered how to create, delete, and change login names. Next you need to know a method of choosing login names. Not much is said in computer literature about good and bad systems for constructing login names for users. You may be inclined to take the informal approach and give users login names that are similar to what they are called around the office (like BOB, FRED, SALLY, or BUBBA). Although this practice gives your network a personal touch, it causes problems when your network grows and you begin to have more than one user with the same first name. You can also be impersonal to an extreme. On a network used by a financial institution, for example, each user was given a login name that was a random string of letters and numbers chosen by a program written by the security department.

Here are two tips to consider as you design your own login name scheme:

❏ Use login names that are no more than eight characters in length; anything longer is hard to type. You also may want to use the login name as the name of the user's personal subdirectory on the server disk. (PC DOS limits subdirectory name lengths to eight characters.)

❏ Use login names that begin with the users' last names. Because all NetWare utilities that list login names do so alphabetically, your login names are automatically alphabetized by last name.

One popular method is to use the first six characters of the last name followed by the first and second initial. With this method, a user named James E. Carpenter can have the login name CARPENJE.

Passwords

You can designate a password to make a login name more secure. When you log in or attach to a server using a particular login name, you are prompted to enter the correct password. If you know a login name but don't know its corresponding password, you are not able to gain access to the server.

Assigning a password is easy. Starting from SYSCON's main menu, select User Information, which lists all login names for the server. Select the login name for which you want to add or change the password and press Enter. This action brings you to the User Information menu. Select the option called Change Password and press Enter. You are prompted to enter the new password. If you have supervisory access, you can change the password of any user on the server. For security reasons, you are not shown the user's old password; you can only enter a new one.

If you do not have supervisory access, you cannot change the passwords of other users. You can change your own, but you must enter your old password before SYSCON accepts the new password in its place.

By default, NetWare makes passwords optional, but most network supervisors agree that all users should use passwords. In the section called "Requiring a Password," you will learn how to require that a user create a password for his account.

Full Names

Your login name may be something cryptic like LAWRENCB or SMITHFD. Your full name can also be listed in your account to document your full name. Because SYSCON lets you store up to 48 characters of information here, you may also want to list other information, such as a phone extension or a mail stop, in addition to the full name. On one large network, the social security number is listed in addition to the full name. The social security number is used for cross-referencing users' names on the network to their login IDs on mainframe and electronic-mail systems in a large security-administration database.

Only users with supervisory access can enter or update the full name information. To do so, select User Information from SYSCON's main menu. Select the login name for which you want to enter or update the full name information. The User Information menu appears. Select the option Full Name and press Enter. A box opens, showing the current full name information, if any. Enter the full name information as you want to list it. If necessary, backspace over the old information first to delete it.

Account, Station, and Time Restrictions

The network supervisor can control many aspects of how a user is allowed to log in. Should the user be required to use a password? Should the user be required to change it at certain intervals? Should the user be limited to using a certain amount of file server disk space? Should the user be allowed to log in at all hours of the day and from any PC he or she chooses? All these and several other conditions can be controlled by using restrictions.

Deciding which restrictions to implement is one of the network supervisor's most important decisions. On some networks, restrictions are not used at all, but on others, restrictions are used very effectively to make the network more secure. The only way you can make an informed decision is to understand what your options are.

You can use three options from SYSCON's User Information menu to implement restrictions. These options are Account Restrictions, Station Restrictions, and Time Restrictions.

Account Restrictions

The SYSCON Account Restrictions option allows the network supervisor to control four aspects of a user account: enabling or disabling the account, controlling password usage, controlling concurrent connections, and limiting disk space.

To get to the Account Restrictions screen from SYSCON's main menu, select User Information. Select the login name for which you want to implement account restrictions and press Enter. You can also mark the login names of multiple users with the F5 key and press Enter if you want to give more than one user the same type of account restrictions. Either method brings you to the User Information menu. Select the Account Restrictions option and press Enter. The Account Restrictions screen appears (see fig. 10.3).

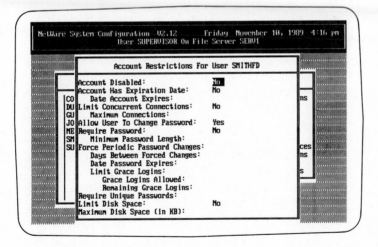

Fig. 10.3.
SYSCON's Account Restrictions screen.

You do not have to implement every option available on the Account Restrictions screen. Any changes you make while at the Account

Restrictions screen are saved when you press Esc to exit. If you make changes and then want to cancel them, press F7.

Next, you will examine the options on this screen.

Disabling an Account

The first two options on the Account Restrictions screen deal with disabling or enabling an account. Disable an account if you need to remove temporarily a user's ability to log in, such as while the user is on vacation. (If you need to remove an account permanently, simply delete the user's login name.) The second option is related to the first; if you need to make sure that an account is automatically disabled at a future date, you can enter the date upon which that account expires. This option is useful if you are setting up accounts for short-term visitors, or in a school environment where student accounts need to expire automatically at the end of a semester.

To disable an account, use the up- or down-arrow keys to move the highlight box to Account Disabled. Press Y and then press Enter so that the box displays Yes. Press Esc to return to the User Information menu.

To set an account expiration date, move the highlight box to Account Has Expiration Date. Press Y and then press Enter to change the box contents from No to Yes. You are prompted to enter the expiration date. Enter the date in one of three formats: 01/15/90, JAN 15, 1990, or JANUARY 15, 1990. If you do not want to add any more account restrictions, press Esc to return to the User Information menu.

Limiting Concurrent Connections

The term *concurrent connection* refers to being logged from more than one PC at the same time using the same login name. For security reasons, you may want to make this connection impossible. If you are the only one who should have access as the network supervisor, for example, you may want to limit concurrent connections to one; that way, if some other user learns your login name and password, the user still will not be able to log in. Similarly, if the user is secretly using your login name and password while you try to log in, you are notified that someone else has your name and password in use.

To limit concurrent connections, move the highlight box to Limit Concurrent Connections. Press Y and then press Enter so that the highlight box shows Yes. The number next to Maximum Connections is set by default to 1, indicating that one concurrent connection is allowed. You can move the highlight to this number and enter any other amount up to 100 if you need to increase the number of allowed concurrent connections. If you do not want to add any other account restrictions, press Esc to return to the User Information menu.

Controlling Passwords

Passwords are useful only as long as they are kept private. Over time, the tendency is for users to learn each others' passwords. This situation is not a problem as long as all network users are honest, but one dishonest or disgruntled user can cause considerable disruption if he or she has learned someone else's password.

For the safety of everyone, users should periodically change their passwords. The old adage "An ounce of prevention is worth a pound of cure" applies, and password maintenance is the ounce of prevention.

The SYSCON Account Restrictions screen offers several ways to control password usage. First, you can control whether users are required to use passwords. You can also set a time period after which each user must change his or her password. You can set a minimum password length to prevent users from picking one- or two-character passwords that are easy to guess. And you can require users to choose unique passwords at each password change so that they don't reuse old ones.

To require the use of a password, move the highlight box to Require Password on the Account Restrictions screen. Press Y and then press Enter to change the highlight box from No to Yes. As soon as you make this change, the other password options, such as the password minimum length and periodic password change, are activated with default settings, as shown in figure 10.4.

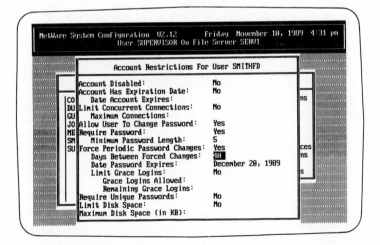

Fig. 10.4.

The password options activated.

The next time the user logs in, he or she is prompted to select a password.

You probably will want to require that passwords be of a minimum length so that users don't choose one- or two-character passwords that are easy to guess. The Account Restrictions screen defaults to a minimum length of 5 characters when you say yes to requiring a password. If you want to change this to another setting, move the highlight box to the minimum password length setting and type a number between 1 and 128.

Perhaps the best method of keeping passwords private is to require that they be changed at regular intervals. When you use SYSCON's Account Restrictions option to require that a user have a password, the user is required automatically to change his or her password every 40 days. You can change this interval by moving the highlight box to Days Between Forced Changes. Enter the number of days (1 to 365) that you want to use as an interval between changes. The new password expiration date changes to match this interval. If you do not want to require periodic password changes, move the highlight box to Force Periodic Password Changes, press N, and then press Enter to change the setting from Yes to No.

If you have required passwords, the Account Restrictions screen lists a number of "grace logins" that are allowed. A *grace login* occurs when you log in with a password that has expired (when you log in after the date of your required password change, for example). You are told that your password has expired and are asked whether you want to change it. If you answer no, you may log in with your old password if you have at least one grace login left.

The SYSCON Account Restrictions option automatically sets the number of grace logins to 6. If you want to change this setting, move the highlight box next to Grace Logins Allowed and enter the number (between 1 and 200) of your choice. The number of remaining grace logins is automatically updated. If you want to allow unlimited grace logins (not a good idea because it eliminates the user's requirement to change his password), move the highlight box next to Limit Grace Logins and press N to change the setting from Yes to No.

You can use another method to ensure password privacy. Require that the user choose a *new* password each time passwords are changed. This policy prevents the user from choosing two similar passwords and using one or the other every time a change must be made.

You can require that the user change to a unique password by moving the highlight box next to Require Unique Passwords and pressing Y to change the box to Yes. The server keeps track of the eight most recently used passwords and does not permit them to be reused. A password must be in use for one day before the server starts to keep track of it; this practice discourages users from changing their passwords eight times in a row to be able to use the original password over again.

In almost all cases, you will want users to be able to change their own passwords. In a few special situations, however, you will want to withhold this ability. An example is with the GUEST login name. On many networks, GUEST gives limited access to a server without a password. This is useful for people who need to log into a server solely to send jobs to its shared printers or to use shared software on a limited basis.

You don't want a person logged in as GUEST to be able to add a password to that login name. To remove the password feature for a particular login name, move the highlight box next to Allow User To Change Password, press N, and then press Enter to change the response from Yes to No.

Limiting User Disk Space

If you are working on a NetWare 286 server, the last option on the Account Restrictions screen allows you to limit the amount of server disk space that a user can have for the storage of files. This option appears only if the Limit Disk Space option was selected when NetWare was installed on the server.

If your server is running NetWare 386, you can limit a user's disk space by using the Volume Restrictions option on the User Information menu. You will learn about this option in the next section.

If you do not limit disk space, a single user has the ability to fill up the entire server disk with his or her own files. Experience on mature networks shows that the ability of some users to accumulate files and consume disk space is amazing.

Preventing this problem is easy. Move the highlight bar to Limit Disk Space, press Y, and then press Enter so that the setting is changed from No to Yes. Move the highlight box to Maximum Disk Space (in KB) and type in the amount of disk space you want to make available to the user. The number you type is the number of kilobytes (thousands of bytes) you are making available to that user; you can enter a number between 0 and 1,073,741,823. After you exit the Account Restrictions screen, the number you enter is rounded up to the next highest multiple of 4 kilobytes, because file server disks store information in increments (disk blocks) of that size.

If the user attempts to exceed the limit established, the user receives the error message Insufficient Disk Space. PC DOS and OS/2 commands (such as DIR) that show available disk space show only the amount available to the user. This option does not limit the user's access to files created by others; it only limits the user to a fixed amount of space to create his own files.

When you are finished assigning account restrictions, press Esc to return to the User Information menu.

Limiting a User's Disk Space with NetWare 386

NetWare 386 makes limiting disk space more flexible by enabling you to limit a user's disk space on a volume-by-volume basis. A user can be limited to using 10M on one volume, 2M on another, and have unlimited use of a third volume.

To limit disk space for the selected user on a NetWare 386 server, select the Volume Restrictions option on the User Information menu. A list of the server's volumes is displayed. Highlight the volume for which you want to limit the user's space and press Enter. The User Disk Volume Restrictions window opens.

To limit the user's disk space on the volume, move the highlight next to Limit Disk Space, press Y, and then press Enter so that the setting is changed from No to Yes. Next, move the highlight box to the Maximum Disk Space (in KB) option and type the amount of disk space you want to make available to the user. The number you type is the number of kilobytes you are making available to that user. You can enter any number between 0 and 2,147,483,647. After you exit the Account Restrictions option, the number you enter is rounded up to the next highest multiple of your disk block size.

Station Restrictions

You may want to limit the use of a login name to a particular PC or group of PCs. For example, you may have established a special login name to use while doing tape backups of a file server. This login name may have been assigned supervisory rights and you want to make sure that it can be used only from the PC where the tape backup unit is actually attached. You can use SYSCON's Station Restrictions option to make sure that this is the case.

You must know two pieces of information about the PC or PCs on which you want to use the Stations Restrictions option: the network and node addresses. You learned about network addresses in Chapter 4. The network address is the number you choose when installing NetWare on your servers. All servers on a single network must use the same network address. If you have multiple networks bridged together, then you also have multiple network addresses.

Node addresses were discussed in Chapter 8. Every node (PC or server) on a network must have a unique node address. This address is set on the network adapter inside the PC. Some types of network adapters are set at the factory; others are set by the installer.

If you followed the advice in Chapter 8 and labeled every PC with its network and node address as you installed it and made a network diagram afterward, you have this information readily available. If you didn't, or if your network installer left town before giving you a network diagram, you can still use an easy way to find the node and network number for each PC.

Go to the PC for which you need to learn the network and node addresses and log into a server. Type the following from the command prompt:

USERLIST/A

Press Enter. You see a list similar to the following:

```
User Information for Server SERV1
Connection      User Name       Network   Node Address   Login Time

     1        * SUPERVISOR      [     1]  [          2]  11-10-1989  4:15 pm
     2          GUEST           [   10A]  [         BD]  11-10-1989  4:14 pm
```

One of the users listed is marked with an asterisk. That is the workstation you are using. The network and node addresses are listed to the right of the login name; both are in hexadecimal notation, which is exactly the way the SYSCON Station Restriction option expects to have them entered.

After you know the network and node addresses of the PC or PCs you plan to restrict a login name to, you're ready to use SYSCON to assign them. Start SYSCON and select User Information from its main menu; it lists all login names for the server. Select the login name for which you want to implement station restrictions and press Enter. You can also mark the login names of multiple users with the F5 key and press Enter if you want to give more than one user the same station restrictions. Either method brings you to the User Information menu. Select Station Restrictions and press Enter. You see the screen shown in figure 10.5, which lists the

Fig. 10.5.

The Station Restrictions screen.

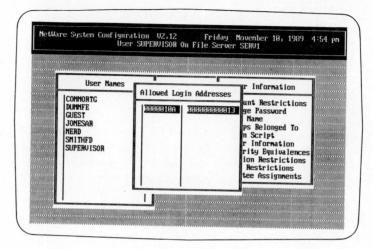

allowed login addresses. If no addresses are listed, the user can log in from any PC.

Press Ins. A box is displayed with the prompt Network Address. Enter the network address of the PC or PCs that are to be assigned as allowed login addresses. Remember to use hexadecimal notation, which is how you entered network addresses at the time of installation and how they are shown when you use USERLIST/A. The network address appears in the left column of the Station Restrictions screen, and the following prompt appears: Allow Login From All Nodes. If you respond with Yes, the user is allowed to log in from all PCs on that network. If you respond with No, the cursor moves to the right column of the Station Restriction screen, where you should type the node address and press Enter. (Again, use hexadecimal notation as displayed when you use USERLIST/A.)

The Station Restriction screen is updated to show the network and node address you have just entered. If this is the only address you need to assign for the login name you selected, you can leave the Station Restriction screen by pressing Esc. If you need to enter additional addresses, press Ins again and repeat the steps in the preceding paragraph.

When you are finished assigning station restrictions, press Esc to return to the User Information menu.

Time Restrictions

The SYSCON Time Restrictions option allows you to designate blocks of time during which users can log in. If your network is not to be used at night, but you leave the servers up to run tape backups, you can prevent users from logging in during those hours.

To restrict a user's login access to certain times of the day, start SYSCON and select User Information from its main menu. Highlight the name you want to restrict and press Enter, or use the F5 key to mark more than one user and press Enter. Select Time Restrictions from the resulting menu and press Enter. A screen showing the allowed login times appears (see fig. 10.6).

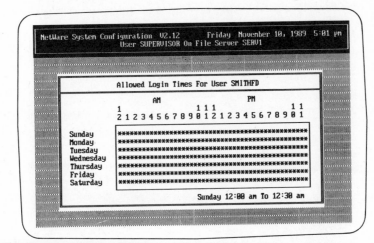

Fig. 10.6.
The SYSCON Time Restrictions screen.

Every half-hour time block in a week is displayed. Each day of the week is represented as a row, and times of day in half-hour increments are represented as columns. The asterisks represent the half-hour time blocks for each day when logins are permitted.

To restrict a user's allowed login times, simply remove the asterisks for the half-hour blocks corresponding to the times you don't want him or her to be able to log in. If you don't want a user to be able to log in on Sunday, for example, move the cursor to the top row of asterisks and delete them.

To delete a single half-hour time block, move the cursor to its asterisk and press the Del key. To reinsert an asterisk (and re-enable login for those time blocks), move the cursor to the appropriate time block and press Ins or the asterisk key. To delete a block of asterisks, move the cursor to the first asterisk in the range you want to delete and press F5. Then use the arrow keys to highlight the entire block and press Del. To insert a range of asterisks, move the cursor to the first time block you want to re-enable and press F5. Use the arrow keys to highlight the range of blocks you want to re-enable and press Ins. The entire range is filled with asterisks.

When you are finished working with the Time Restrictions screen, press Esc to save your settings and return to the SYSCON User Information menu.

Setting Default Account and Time Restrictions

You may think by now that establishing account and time restrictions for each user is a laborious process. It doesn't need to be. If you know that you are going to use the same account and time restrictions for almost all server users, you can set up default settings in advance that are automatically assigned to new users as they are added.

To establish these default settings, start SYSCON and select Supervisor Options from its main menu. The menu shown in figure 10.7 appears.

Fig. 10.7.

The SYSCON Supervisor Options menu.

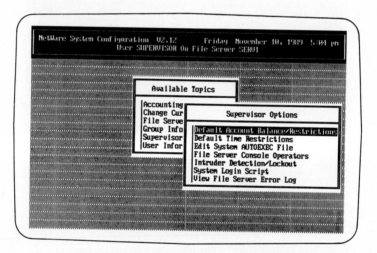

Select Default Account Balance/Restrictions and press Enter. A screen similar to the Account Restrictions screen used for individual users appears. The only difference is a reference to the user's account balance. You will study account balances in detail in Chapter 17; for now, leave this setting as is.

Change each of the account restriction options to match the settings you want to use as defaults. Press Esc when you are finished and these settings are saved.

Setting the default time restrictions is a similar process. From the SYSCON main menu, select Supervisor Options. Select Default Time Restrictions and press Enter. A screen identical to the individual user Time Restrictions screen appears. Set the allowed login times by deleting or inserting asterisks as you did to set individual time restrictions. When you are finished, press Esc and these settings are saved.

After you have established default settings for account and time restrictions, they are applied to all new login accounts added to the server. Already established accounts do not automatically switch to the default settings, although you can change them all at once. From SYSCON's main menu, select User Information and press Enter. Use F5 to mark all existing login names for which you want to use the default settings and then press Enter. From the next menu that appears, select Account Restrictions and press Enter. The Account Restrictions screen appears, showing the default account restriction settings. Press Esc and answer Yes when prompted to confirm that you want to use these settings for all marked login names. Follow the same steps to assign the time restriction default setting to all marked users. Select Time Restrictions from the User Information menu. The Time Restrictions screen appears, showing your default login time settings. Press Esc and answer Yes when prompted to confirm that you want to use these settings for all marked login names.

Press Esc to leave the Supervisor Options menu and return to SYSCON's main menu.

Other User Information

You can look up several items of miscellaneous information about a user from SYSCON's User Information menu. From SYSCON's main menu, select User Information and press Enter. Highlight the name of the user for whom you want to look up the information and press Enter. You are taken to the User Information menu. Select Other Information from this menu and press Enter. The screen shown in figure 10.8 appears.

The first information shown is the most recent login time for the user. Next, you are shown whether the user is a *server console operator*, which refers to whether the user is allowed to use the NetWare FCONSOLE utility to operate the server. You will learn about FCONSOLE in detail in Chapter 18. The maximum disk space the user is allowed to use is listed, along with the disk space the user currently has in use. Finally, the user's ID number is shown. For every login name you establish, a unique ID number is created. This number is used for several purposes, which you

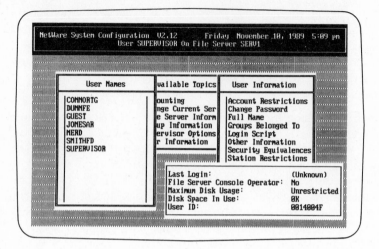

will examine in the chapters on login scripts (Chapter 16) and printing (Chapter 14).

Trustee Assignments, Groups Belonged To, and Security Equivalences

Three options from SYSCON's User Information menu deal with access rights to directories. Because access rights are very important, the entire next chapter is devoted to the subject.

Trustee Assignments

When you are given rights to access a directory or subdirectory on a server, in NetWare terminology you become a trustee of that directory. The level of access you have is controlled by granting or withholding eight rights. You will study these in detail in the next chapter.

Groups Belonged To

Giving directory trustee rights to individual users is a detailed process. If you have a number of users who need the same trustee rights to a certain directory or group of directories, you can save considerable time by creating a group and then giving that group trustee rights to the necessary directories. You then make individual users members of that group. In the next section, you will see how groups are created and assigned members.

Security Equivalence

Security equivalence is similar in concept to a group. If you have one user who needs the same trustee rights as another user, you can make the first user equivalent to the second. The first user will have exactly the same trustee rights as the second.

When you are finished working with a user account, press Esc to leave the User Information menu. The list of login names returns to the screen. Select another name, or press Esc to return to SYSCON's main menu, and press Esc again if you want to exit SYSCON.

Working with Groups of Users

SYSCON enables you to place users into groups and work with those users as a whole instead of as individuals. This approach is used primarily for two purposes: to give groups of users rights to the same directories (which you will learn how to do in the next chapter) or to control users who manage other users (which can be done only with NetWare 386—you will read about this feature in the next section).

A user with supervisory or workgroup-manager access can use SYSCON to work with groups. To start SYSCON, type

SYSCON

and press Enter. From its main menu, select Group Information and press Enter. A list of all currently defined groups on the file server is displayed.

Adding, Deleting, and Renaming Groups

Working with this list of defined groups is like working with the list of login names that appears when you select User Information from SYSCON's main menu. You can add a new group by pressing Ins. A box appears, and you are prompted to enter the name of the group that you want to add.

Press Enter after typing the name, and the new group's name shows up on the list of group names. You can delete a group by highlighting its name and pressing Del. You can delete more than one group by highlighting each one's name, marking it with F5, and then pressing Del. You can change a group's name by highlighting it and pressing F3. A box opens and a message prompts you to enter the new name you want to use. Typing the new name and pressing Enter completes the change.

Creating, Deleting, or Renaming a Group with SYSCON

1. Start SYSCON and select Group Information from its main menu. A list of existing group names appears.

2. To add a new group, press Ins. You are prompted to enter the group's name, which is added to the group list.

3. To delete a group, highlight it's name and press Del. After confirming that you want to delete the name, it disappears from the list.

4. To change a group name, highlight it and press F3. A prompt tells you to revise the group name. After you change the name, the list is updated to show the new name.

Working with a Group Account

To work with a group, highlight that group's name from the Group Names list and press Enter. The Group Information menu is displayed on-screen (see fig. 10.9).

Enter a Full Name for the Group

The first option on the Group Information menu is Full Name. Like the Full Name option for a user account, this option enables you to enter a descriptive name for the group, up to 48 characters in length. For a group of users in the accounting department, a full name might be ACCOUNTING DEPARTMENT EMPLOYEES.

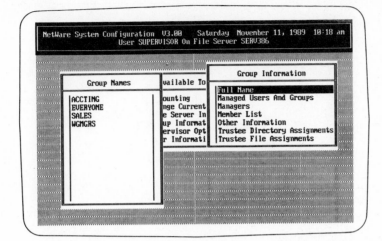

Fig. 10.9.
SYSCON's Group
Information menu.

Adding Users to a Group

To add users to a group, select the Member List option on the Group Information menu. When you choose this option, a list appears that contains all login names for users who are group members. If you want to add more users, press Ins, and a list of all other login names on the server appears. Highlight the name you want to add from this list and press Enter. You can add several users at one time by highlighting each one's login name and marking it with F5. After the names you want to add are all marked, press Enter, and the users you selected are added to the group. Press Esc to save your changes and return to the Group Information menu.

Removing users from the group is a similar process. Select the Member List option from the Group Information menu and press Enter. The list of group members appears. Highlight the name you want to remove and press Del. The name is removed from the list. You can delete multiple users by highlighting each name and marking it with F5. After the names you want to remove are marked, press Del, and the names are removed from the group list. Press Esc to save your changes and return to the Group Information menu.

Adding or Removing Users

1. Start SYSCON and select Group Information from its main menu. A list of groups appears.

2. Select the group to which you want to add users. The Group Information menu appears. Select the Member List option. A list of the group's current members comes on-screen.

3. To add users, press Ins. A list of the server's users appears. Highlight one you want to add and press Enter, or mark multiple users with F5 and press Enter.

4. To remove users, highlight the name you want to remove and press Del, or mark multiple users with F5 and press Del.

Viewing Information about the Group

The next option on the Group Information menu has the nondescript title Other Information. When you select it, you are shown two items of information about the group. This information tells you whether the group members are Server Console Operators. Their status as server console operators determines whether they are allowed to use the NetWare FCONSOLE utility to operate the server. (You will learn about FCONSOLE in detail in Chapter 18.) The group's identification (ID) number is also shown. This number is used by the file server to identify the group.

Working with the Group's Trustee Assignments

The last option on the Group Information menu is Trustee Assignments. In the next chapter, you will learn about assigning groups as trustees to directories and subdirectories on the server.

Another Way To Add a User to a Group

If you are adding a new user to the server and want to make him or her a group member in the same step, the easiest way to do it is from SYSCON's User Information menu, which has a selection called Groups Belonged To. Selecting this option displays a list of all the groups to which the selected user belongs. If you need to add the user to another group, press Ins. A list of all groups appears; highlight a group and press Enter, or mark more than one group with F5 and press enter. The user is added to the group or groups you selected.

The Everyone Group

When you first install NetWare on a server, a group called EVERYONE is created automatically. When you add new users to the server, they automatically are made members of the group EVERYONE.

In the next chapter, you will learn how this group can be used to automatically assign all users rights to certain directories.

When you are finished working with a group account, press Esc to leave the Group Information menu. The list of group names returns to the screen. Select another name, or press Esc to return to SYSCON's main menu, and press Esc again if you want to exit SYSCON.

NetWare 386's Advanced-User and Group-Management Features

As you already have read, NetWare 386 adds several new aspects to managing users and implementing login-control security. Users can be designated as workgroup managers and can create and delete login names and manage the accounts of other users. Users who are not workgroup managers can manage other users, changing various aspects of the managed users' accounts, and can even delete the login names of the users they manage.

Workgroup managers and users who manage other users can grant access only to those directories where they have been given NetWare 386's ACCESS CONTROL or SUPERVISORY right. You will learn about how to grant rights to directories in the next chapter.

Creating Workgroup Managers

The server supervisor can use SYSCON to designate a user or group as a workgroup manager. To perform this task, log in with supervisory access to the server where you want to designate a workgroup manager. Type *syscon* and press Enter. From SYSCON's main menu, select Supervisor Options. From the Supervisor Options menu that appears, select the option called Workgroup Managers. A list of the current workgroup managers appears (if none have been designated, the list is blank). To add a new workgroup manager, press Ins, and a list of all the users and groups on the server is shown. Highlight the user or group that you want to designate and press Enter, or mark multiple users with F5 and press Enter. The workgroup manager list is updated to show your additions.

You can remove a user's workgroup manager status by highlighting his or her name from the workgroup manager list and pressing Del. You can remove multiple users by marking their login names with F5 and pressing Del.

When you are finished working with the list of workgroup managers, press Esc to return to the Supervisor Options menu, and press Esc again to return to SYSCON's main menu.

Assigning Users or Groups To Manage Other Users and Groups

A user with supervisory-level access to a server can assign a user or group to manage the accounts of other users and groups. A workgroup manager similarly can make one of his or her users or groups a manager for another of his or her users or groups. SYSCON is used to make these assignments. Log in with supervisory or workgroup manager access to the server where you want to designate a manager. Start SYSCON by typing *syscon*, then press Enter. From SYSCON's main menu, select User Information (if you want to make a user a manager) or Group Information (if you want to make a group a manager). From the list of names that appears, highlight the one to whom you want to assign management responsibilities for others and press Enter. Next, select Managed Users and Groups and press Enter. A list of the user's or group's currently managed users and groups is shown. To add a user or group to the list, press Ins, and a list of the server's users and groups is displayed. Highlight the user or group that you want to add and press Enter, or mark multiple names with F5 and press Enter. The list is updated to show your selections.

You can remove a name from the selected user's or group's list of managed users and groups by highlighting it and pressing Del. You can delete several names at one time by marking multiple names with F5 and pressing Del.

When you have finished working with the list of managed users and groups, press Esc to return to the User Information menu or Group Information menu. Press Esc to return to the user listing, and press Esc again to return to SYSCON's main menu.

Viewing a User's or Group's Managers

You also can use SYSCON to view a list of the users and groups who are managing a particular user or group. If you are logged in with supervisor-level access, you also can add or remove names from this list. If you are a workgroup manager, you can add and remove names from the list of users and groups for which you are responsible.

From SYSCON's main menu, choose User Information if you want to work with a user, or Group Information if you want to work with a group. A list of the server's users or groups is displayed. Highlight the name whose manager list you want to work with and press Enter. From the menu that results, select Managers. A list of the user's or group's managers is displayed on-screen.

If you are a supervisor or the user's workgroup manager, you can add to this list by pressing Ins and choosing additional names. You also can remove names by highlighting them and pressing Del. When you have finished working with the user's or group's list of managers, press Esc to return to the User Information menu or Group Information menu. Press Esc to return to the user listing and press Esc again to return to SYSCON's main menu.

Other NetWare Utilities and Commands that Control User Accounts

Although SYSCON is your primary tool for working with user accounts and groups, two other utilities play a smaller but nevertheless useful role. SETPASS can by used by a user to change his or her password, and DSPACE is used by a supervisor, workgroup manager, or user manager to restrict a user's disk space.

Changing Your Password with SETPASS

SETPASS provides a quick method of changing your password for all the servers to which you are currently attached. Type *setpass* and press Enter.

First, you are prompted to enter your old password. Enter it, or if you have not yet used a password, simply press Enter by itself. You are then prompted to enter your new password. After you enter the new password, a prompt tells you to retype it to confirm that you typed it correctly the first time. The passwords you type are not shown on-screen so that someone looking over your shoulder cannot learn your password.

If you are attached to multiple servers, you can specify the server on which you want to change your password by typing the server name after SETPASS, such as

    SETPASS SERV2

Next, you press Enter. You are prompted to enter your old and new passwords.

If you are attached to multiple servers using the same login name, SETPASS lists those servers and offers you the opportunity to change your password on them all to the password you just entered. You see the following prompt:

    Synchronize passwords on these file servers?   (Y/N)

If you press Y for yes, your password is changed on the listed servers.

If you have a password restriction of any type in place on one of the servers, the synchronization does not take effect on that server. You must use SYSCON to change it on that particular server.

Using DSPACE To Manage Disk Space Restrictions (NetWare 386 Only)

NetWare 386's DSPACE utility can be used in lieu of SYSCON to limit a user's disk usage to a particular amount of space. Only supervisory-level users can use DSPACE to set another user's maximum disk space. Workgroup managers and normal users can use DSPACE to look up their maximum disk space and current disk usage.

Start DSPACE by typing *dspace*. Press Enter. DSPACE's opening menu offers three options:

    Change File Server
    User Restrictions
    Directory Restrictions

The User Restrictions option enables you to view and update a user's disk space restriction. Select User Restriction and, if you are server supervisor, a list of the server's users is shown. Select the user you want to work with and press Enter. Next, you see a list of the server's volumes. Choose the one for which you want to view or change the user's disk space restriction.

A window opens that shows the user's current maximum disk space, his or her current amount of disk space in use, and a setting that controls whether the user's disk space is restricted. To implement a disk space limitation for a user, move the highlight next to Limit Disk Space, press Y, then press Enter to change its setting from no to yes. Next, move the highlight to Available Space and enter the amount of disk space that you want to allow the user to use.

Press Esc when you are finished working with the user's disk restriction settings. The list of the server's volumes returns to the screen. If you want to restrict the user's disk space on a different volume, choose that volume and repeat the above steps. Otherwise, press Esc to return to the list of server users. You can either select another user to work with or press Esc to return to DSPACE's menu. If you want to exit DSPACE, press Esc one more time.

DSPACE also is used to set the maximum size for a directory. You will learn how to do that in the next chapter.

Chapter Summary

In this chapter, you learned that adding users and working with their accounts is a detailed process and one that you're likely to repeat often as your network grows. You also saw how important it is that you establish the right blend of security tools so that users are assured of private and secure access to your network's servers.

Now that you are familiar with establishing and controlling user and group accounts, you are ready to examine the topic of giving users and groups rights to access directories and files that are stored on servers, the subject of the next chapter.

11

Understanding NetWare Rights

You already have seen scenarios where users need different levels of access to different types of directories. A user should have unlimited access to a personal directory on a file server disk; users should be free to create, delete, and change files just as if they were using the hard disk on their own PCs. Access to a shared copy of 1-2-3 should be different; the user should be able to use the program but not be allowed to delete or change its files in any way. If the company's accounting system is stored on the same disk and the user is not in the accounting department, the user should have no access to the accounting system's files.

How do you give three different levels of access to three different directories on the same disk? You use NetWare rights. In the preceding chapter, you learned the four ways that a network supervisor controls a user's access: login control, user rights, directory rights, and file-attribute control. The second and third elements, user and directory rights, are the main players in controlling what type of access a user has to a particular directory. Because these two methods are closely related, you will look at them together in this chapter.

Learning how to use NetWare rights correctly is not optional for the network supervisor. When you give a user an account on a server, the user's default access is limited. In fact, the user has the same access as the GUEST user; he or she can use shared printers and has limited use of the SYS:PUBLIC and SYS:LOGIN directories. Unless the network supervisor gives the user access to other directories on the server disk, the user can do little useful work.

If the user needs to use the network copy of 1-2-3, you must give him or her rights to the directory that stores the 1-2-3 files. NetWare calls this procedure making the user a *trustee* of that directory. NetWare also gives you a powerful method to fine-tune the user's level of access to that directory. When you make a user a trustee, you give or withhold eight different access rights to that directory. Each right governs a particular aspect of the way the user can work with the files in that directory.

Examining the Eight NetWare Directory Rights

The eight NetWare directory rights are READ, WRITE, OPEN, CREATE, DELETE, PARENTAL, SEARCH, and MODIFY for NetWare 286, and SUPERVISORY, READ, WRITE, CREATE, ERASE, MODIFY, FILE SCAN, and ACCESS CONTROL for NetWare 386. Often these rights are abbreviated by using their initials: RWOCDPSM (NetWare 286) or SRWCEMFA (NetWare 386). Veteran network supervisors can recite these rights and their initials from memory and often communicate with each other using sentences like "I gave them R, O, and S to the dBASE directory" (further arousing well-founded suspicions about the normalcy of network supervisors).

Table 11.1 gives a definition of each right and a short discussion of what each allows a trustee to do.

Table 11.1
NetWare Directory Rights

NetWare 286 Right	NetWare 386 Right	Definition
READ	READ	Enables a directory trustee to read the contents of existing files
		Common operations requiring the READ right: using the OS/2 or PC DOS TYPE command to display the contents of a file, using a database manager to look up information in a database

WRITE	WRITE	Enables a directory trustee to change or add to the contents of existing files
		Common operations requiring the WRITE right: using the PC DOS EDLIN command to edit a text file, using a word processor to make changes to a document
OPEN		Enables a user to open an existing file. You must be able to open a file before you can read it, write to it, or change its name or attributes.
		Common operations requiring the OPEN right: Any of the preceding examples of reading or writing to a file also require the OPEN right because you have to open a file before you can read from it or write to it.
		NetWare 386 does not use OPEN as a separate right. Instead, NetWare 386 gives the OPEN right automatically when you give someone READ and/or WRITE rights to a directory.
CREATE	CREATE	Enables a user to create a new file in the directory. NetWare 386's CREATE right also enables a user to create subdirectories. (NetWare 286 requires that a user have both CREATE and PARENTAL rights to create subdirectories.)
		Common operations requiring the CREATE right: copying files into a directory, saving a worksheet to a file for the first time with a spreadsheet program

Table 11.1—continued

NetWare 286 Right	NetWare 386 Right	Definition
DELETE	ERASE	Enables a user to erase an existing file in the directory.
		Common operations requiring the DELETE or ERASE right: using the PC DOS or OS/2 ERASE and DELETE commands
PARENTAL	ACCESS CONTROL	Enables a user to give other users rights to a directory and to modify the directory's rights mask. NetWare 286's PARENTAL right enables a user to give to and take away from other users any combination of rights. NetWare 386's ACCESS CONTROL right is similar, except that the SUPERVISORY right cannot be given to someone else.
		NetWare 286's PARENTAL right also is required when a user needs to create subdirectories.
		Common operations requiring the PARENTAL or ACCESS CONTROL right: using the GRANT command to give other users rights to the directory. The NetWare 286 PARENTAL right (coupled with the CREATE right) also enables a user to use the PC DOS or OS/2 MD (MAKE DIRECTORY) command to create a subdirectory and the RD (REMOVE DIRECTORY) command to delete a directory (you must have the DELETE right also).
SEARCH	FILE SCAN	Enables a user to list the SCAN files in the directory

		Common operations requiring the SEARCH or FILE SCAN right: using the PC DOS or OS/2 DIR command to see a list of files and subdirectories, using a spreadsheet program to list the worksheet files in a directory
MODIFY	MODIFY	Enables a user to rename a file or subdirectory or change the attributes of a file or subdirectory
		Common operations requiring the MODIFY right: using the PC DOS or OS/2 REN (RENAME) command to change the name of a file, using the PC DOS or OS/2 ATTRIB or NetWare FLAG command to change the attributes of a file, using the NetWare RENDIR command to change the name of a subdirectory (renaming or changing the attributes of a subdirectory requires the PARENTAL right also).
	SUPERVISORY	The SUPERVISORY right is unique to NetWare 386. When a user has this right, he or she has the equivalent of all other rights to the directory and all its subdirectories.
		The SUPERVISORY right also overrides the rights withheld by a directory's inherited rights mask.
		When a user has the SUPERVISORY rights to a directory, no rights can be subtracted from subdirectories below that directory.

Granting Rights to Individual Files

NetWare 386 adds another dimension to directory rights. In NetWare 386, in addition to granting and revoking rights to directories, you can give and withhold the eight rights to individual files. This capability enables you to fine-tune a user's access even further.

When assigned to files, the eight NetWare 386 rights sometimes have purposes slightly different from their purposes when assigned to directories. You may be wondering, for example, what possible purpose the CREATE right can serve when assigned to a file that already exists. So that you are aware of these distinctions, the eight rights and how they work when assigned to files are summarized in table 11.2.

Table 11.2
NetWare 386 File Rights

File Right	Use When Assigned to File
READ	Enables a file trustee to read the contents of the file
WRITE	Enables a file trustee to change or add to the contents of the file
CREATE	Enables a user to use NetWare 386's SALVAGE utility to recover the file after it has been deleted
ERASE	Enables a user to erase the file
ACCESS CONTROL	Enables a user to give other users rights to the file or to modify the file's rights mask. The ACCESS CONTROL right does not enable you to give other users the SUPERVISORY right to the file.
FILE SCAN	Enables a user to list the file even when he or she does not have the FILE SCAN right to the file's directory
MODIFY	Enables a user to rename the file or change its attributes
SUPERVISORY	Gives the user all rights to the file and enables the user to give other users the SUPERVISORY right to the file. The user also can change the file's rights mask.

Combining Directory and File Rights

NetWare 386 lets you combine directory and file rights to fine-tune a user's access. You need to remember two rules when you combine directory and file rights:

❏ File rights always take precedence over directory rights. For example, if you want to give a user the READ, WRITE, CREATE, ERASE, and FILE SCAN rights to most of the files in a directory but no rights to a few of the directory's files, you can give the user READ, WRITE, CREATE, ERASE, and FILE SCAN as directory rights and then remove all rights from the files in the directory that you do not want the user to access.

❏ Users automatically get the same rights to a directory's files as they have to the directory itself *unless* you specifically give or withhold certain file rights. If you want users to have READ and FILE SCAN rights to all the files in a directory, give READ and FILE SCAN rights at the directory level. Users automatically have READ and FILE SCAN rights to the directory's files.

Using the Right Combination of Rights

The key to using rights effectively is knowing how to combine them to achieve exactly the type of access needed to make using a directory easy but safe. In Chapter 3, you learned about a user named Adam and his server access. You were deciding what type of access to the various directories on that server to give Adam. Adam had his own subdirectory under a directory called USERS for personal storage. Another directory, called SOFTWARE, stored network versions of software, such as 1-2-3 and WordPerfect, that Adam and other users shared. A directory called ACCTING stored the company's accounting system. To refresh your memory, look at figure 11.1, which shows a diagram of these directories on the file server's disk.

In his personal subdirectory under USERS (SYS:USERS\Adam), Adam needs unlimited access so that he can create, delete, and modify files as he pleases. What rights should Adam have to this directory? As network supervisor, you probably will give him all eight rights: (NetWare 286)

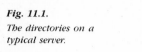

Fig. 11.1.
The directories on a
typical server.

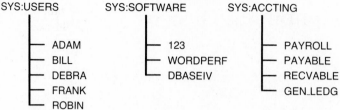

READ, WRITE, OPEN, CREATE, DELETE, PARENTAL, SEARCH, and MODIFY or (NetWare 386) SUPERVISORY, READ, WRITE, CREATE, ERASE, MODIFY, FILE SCAN, and ACCESS CONTROL. You can abbreviate these rights in a way consistent with many NetWare utilities and commands by placing their initials in brackets: [RWOCDPSM] or [SRWCEMFA].

Because Adam is not in the accounting department, he should have no access to the ACCTING directory. A network supervisor would simply withhold all rights to this directory and abbreviate that type of access as [_ _ _ _ _ _ _ _]. (Note: In this chapter, the underscore [_] means a space.)

Adam should have limited access to the SOFTWARE directory, being able to use the files there but not change them. What rights would you give Adam to this directory? You can make this decision by thinking about each right individually:

READ. You must be able to read a file to execute it. **Yes.**

WRITE. Writing to a file means being able to change its contents, and you don't want Adam to change these contents because they are shared by all other network users. **No.**

OPEN (NetWare 286 only). You must be able to open a file to execute it or use it in any way. **Yes.**

CREATE. If Adam can create files, he can copy new files into the directory or save his data files there. **No.**

DELETE or ERASE. This decision is easy. If Adam can delete files, he can accidentally erase some or all of the files in the shared software directory. **No.**

PARENTAL or ACCESS CONTROL. If Adam has the PARENTAL right, he can give himself and other users more rights to this directory. **No.**

SEARCH or FILE SCAN. This choice is not obvious. Adam may or may not need to be able to list the files and subdirectories in this directory. Some shared programs may require him to find a file in order to execute it. At any rate, it probably will not hurt anything if he can list files. **Yes.**

MODIFY. This right enables Adam to change the name and attributes of files—not a desirable situation. **No.**

SUPERVISORY (NetWare 386 only). **No.**

Adam ought to have READ, OPEN, and SEARCH or FILE SCAN rights to this directory. Using NetWare's standard abbreviation, this list is shown as [R_O___S_] or [_R____F_]. (Notice that the rights withheld have their initials replaced by spaces.)

Figure 11.2 shows the type of access that the user named Adam should have to each of the directories on the server disk.

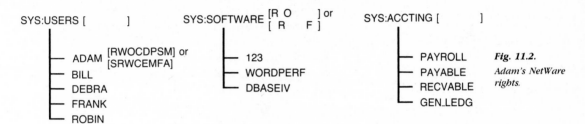

SYS:USERS [   ]

— ADAM   [RWOCDPSM] or [SRWCEMFA]
— BILL
— DEBRA
— FRANK
— ROBIN

SYS:SOFTWARE [R O   ] or [R   F]

— 123
— WORDPERF
— DBASEIV

SYS:ACCTING [   ]

— PAYROLL
— PAYABLE
— RECVABLE
— GEN_LEDG

Fig. 11.2.
Adam's NetWare rights.

To save the network supervisor a great deal of work, NetWare makes an assumption. If you give a user certain rights to a directory, NetWare automatically assigns those same rights to all subdirectories below that directory. In figure 11.2, Adam has READ, OPEN, and SEARCH rights to the SYS:SOFTWARE directory; this assignment automatically gives him READ, OPEN (NetWare 286), and SEARCH or FILE SCAN rights to the 123, WORDPERF, and DBASE subdirectories under SYS:SOFTWARE.

You can override this default by assigning different rights to a particular subdirectory. In figure 11.2, Adam was not given any rights to the SYS:USERS directory because you don't want him to be able to look in the private subdirectories of other users. To give him rights to his personal subdirectory (SYS:USERS\Adam), you assign him all rights to that subdirectory.

Knowing Which Rights To Give

How do you know what rights to give users to the various categories of directories on your servers? Your servers may store shared databases, electronic mail, communication packages, and many other types of software. In some cases, the manuals that come with a program tell you which rights to give and which to withhold. In other cases, you have to experiment with various rights combinations until you find the one that is best.

For safety's sake, give as few rights as possible. Any software package works when the user has all rights to its directory, but you are exposed to the possibility that the software files may be accidentally deleted or modified, or that a program's configuration may be changed so that others can no longer use the package. The wise withholding of rights can prevent these types of problems. If you have to experiment, start by giving the READ, OPEN (NetWare 286), and perhaps SEARCH or FILE SCAN rights. If the program fails to run properly, add other rights as needed. In Chapter 22, "Installing Network Versions of Software," you will walk through the process of choosing the correct rights for four different types of programs.

Using NetWare Commands That Control Trustee Rights

Several NetWare commands and utilities enable you to make users trustees to directories and control the rights they have. To make users trustees and give them rights, you must be the network supervisor or have the PARENTAL right (NetWare 286) or have the ACCESS CONTROL or SUPERVISORY right (NetWare 386) to the directory you are working with. Now you are ready to learn about the commands and utilities that are used to give and withhold rights.

Controlling Rights with SYSCON

SYSCON is the network supervisor's primary tool for controlling user access to servers. You studied SYSCON's use for managing user accounts in the preceding chapter. You also can use SYSCON to give trustee rights to users.

To start SYSCON, log in to a file server as SUPERVISOR (or use a login name that has supervisory access). At the system prompt, type

    SYSCON

and press Enter. SYSCON is stored in the SYS:PUBLIC directory, which is a search directory by default, so you do not have to change to SYS:PUBLIC before starting SYSCON.

Making Users Directory Trustees

From SYSCON's main menu, select User Information and press Enter. This option displays a list of login names for the users who have accounts on the server. Highlight the name of the user to whom you want to give rights and press Enter. This action brings you to SYSCON's User Information menu. Highlight the option called Trustee Assignments or Trustee Directory Assignments. A box showing the user's current trustee directory assignments appears (see fig. 11.3). When you first add a user, he or she is a trustee only to one subdirectory under SYS:MAIL. (Chapters 15 and 16 discuss how this directory is used.)

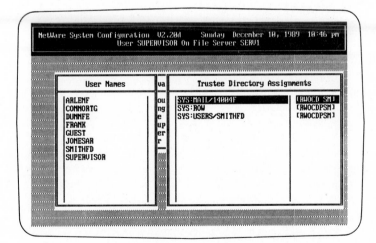

Fig. 11.3.
SYSCON's Trustee Directory Assignments screen.

The left column of the Trustee Assignments window shows the names of directories or subdirectories on the server, listing the volume name followed by a colon and then the name of the directory or subdirectory to which the user has specific rights. The right column shows the rights granted (showing only the initials, as mentioned).

To add the user as a trustee to other directories, press Ins. An entry box opens, prompting you to enter the directory to which the user should be added (see fig. 11.4). Enter the NetWare name of the directory. (See Chapter 9 if you need more information about NetWare names for directories.)

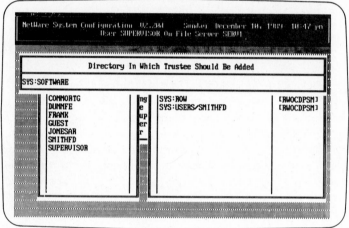

Fig. 11.4.

Adding a trustee to a directory.

If you type the name of a directory that doesn't exist, you are asked whether you want to create it. This capability can be convenient because you may want to create a directory and make the user a trustee in one step (such as when you are adding the user account and creating and giving that user access to his or her private directory in the same step). The prompt also can mean that you misspelled the name of an existing directory.

If you aren't sure of the directory name, you can build it one step at a time. Start by pressing Ins from the entry window; the name of the file server you are working on appears. Press Enter, and the file server name is placed in the entry window. A list of the volumes on that server is displayed in a window called Available Volumes. Select the volume that contains the directory or subdirectory you want to work with and press Enter again. The volume name is added to the directory name in the entry window, and a new window called Network Directories opens, listing the directories on the volume you selected. Highlight the directory you want to work with and press Enter. The directory name is added to your list, and the subdirectories under that directory (if any) are listed in the

Network Directories window. Select the subdirectory you want to work with and press Enter (you may need to continue this process if you need to get through several levels of subdirectories). When the entry window shows the name of the directory or subdirectory you want to work with, press Esc to leave the Network Directories window. When you press Enter, the Trustee Assignment window is updated to list the user as a trustee in the directory you entered.

If you need to remove a directory from the user's trustee assignments, highlight that directory in the Trustee Assignment window and press Del. You are prompted to confirm your choice. After you confirm the deletion, the directory no longer is listed in the user's trustee assignments. You also can delete several directories in one step by highlighting each directory name and marking it with F5. When you press Del, all marked directories are removed.

Using SYSCON To Add a User as a Trustee to a Directory or File

1. Start SYSCON and select User Information from its main menu. A list of existing user login names appears.

2. Select the login name for the user you want to make a trustee. The User Information menu appears.

3. To add the user to a directory, select Trustee Directory Assignments or Trustee Assignments. A list of the user's current directory trustee assignments appears.

4. To add the user to another directory, press Ins. An entry window opens, prompting you to enter the name of the directory to which the user should be added as a trustee. Type the name, or choose the name by pressing Ins to see a list of servers, volumes, and directories available. After you have typed or constructed the correct directory in the entry box, press Enter. The user's directory trustee assignments list is updated to show the new directory.

5. To remove a user as a directory trustee, highlight the directory name on the user's directory trustee list and press Del.

6. See the next sidebar ("Adding or Removing Rights") for details about changing a user's rights to a directory.

When you make a user a trustee in a directory, he or she automatically is given a default set of rights to that directory. Next, you will learn how to change a user's rights to a directory.

Adding or Deleting Directory Rights

From the Trustee Assignments window, highlight the name of the directory for which you want to add or delete rights. When you press Enter, a list called Trustee Rights Granted appears (see fig. 11.5).

Fig. 11.5.

The Trustee Rights Granted window.

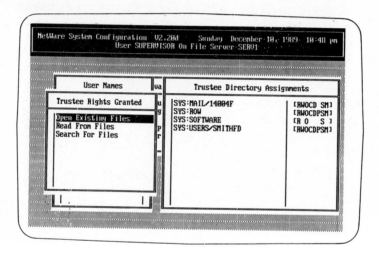

To delete a right, highlight that right and press Del. After you confirm your choice, the right is deleted from the Trustee Rights Granted list. You can delete more than one right at once by highlighting each right and marking it with the F5 key. Press Del and confirm your choice, and all marked rights are removed from the list. Press Esc and your changes are saved, and you are returned to the Trustee Assignments window. The rights shown next to the directory are updated to show your changes.

Adding rights is a similar process. In the Trustee Assignments window, highlight the directory for which you want to change the rights and press Enter. The Trustee Rights Granted list appears, showing the currently assigned rights. Press Ins and a list called (you guessed it) Trustee Rights Not Granted appears (see fig. 11.6).

To add a right, highlight it on the list and press Enter. The Trustee Rights Granted list is updated to show the addition of the new right. You can add more than one right at once by highlighting each and marking it with the

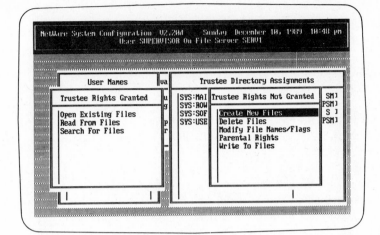

Fig. 11.6.

The Trustee Rights Not Granted window.

F5 key. When you press Enter, all the rights you selected are added to the Trustee Rights Granted list. Press Esc to save your changes and return to the Trustee Assignments window. The rights shown next to the directory are updated to show your changes.

When you have finished working with the user's trustee assignments, press Esc to leave the Trustee Assignments window. If you want to leave SYSCON, press Alt-F7. Press Esc to move to other SYSCON menus.

Making Users File Trustees

As you have read, NetWare 386 enables you to give users rights to individual files as well as to directories. The process for making users file trustees is almost identical to making users directory trustees. Start SYSCON and select User Information from its main menu. A list of user login names appears. Select the login name for the user you want to make a trustee. The User Information menu appears. Select Trustee File Assignments from this menu. The Trustee File Assignments window opens, listing the user's current file trustee assignments.

To add a user as a trustee to a file, press Ins. An entry window opens, prompting you to enter the name of the directory that stores the file to which the user should be added as a trustee. Type the directory name. If you aren't sure of the directory name, you can build it one step at a time. Start by pressing Ins from the entry window, and the name of the file server on which you are working appears. When you press Enter, the file server name is placed in the entry window, and a list of the volumes on

Adding or Removing Rights

1. Start SYSCON and select User Information from its main menu. A list of existing user login names appears. Select the login name for the user you want to make a trustee. The User Information menu appears.

2. Select Trustee Directory Assignments or Trustee Assignments. A list of the user's current directory trustee assignments appears.

3. To give a user more rights to a directory, highlight the directory name on the directory trustee list and press Enter. The Trustee Rights Granted window opens, listing the user's current rights to the directory. Press Ins, and a window opens, showing the rights not granted to the directory. Highlight the right you want to add and press Enter, or mark several rights with F5 and press Enter. The Trustee Rights Granted list is updated to show your additions. Press Esc to save your changes and return to the directory trustee list.

4. To remove certain rights a user has to a directory, highlight the directory name on the directory trustee list and press Enter. The Trustee Rights Granted window opens, listing the user's current rights to the directory. To remove a right, highlight it and press Del, or mark multiple rights with F5 and press Del. The rights you select are removed from the list. Press Esc to save your changes and return to the directory trustee list.

5. When you are finished working with the user's directory trustee list, press Esc to return to the User Information menu, and press Esc again to return to the list of user login names. Select another user to work with, or press Esc to return to SYSCON's main menu.

that server is displayed in a window called Available Volumes. Select the volume that contains the directory or subdirectory with which you want to work and press Enter again. The volume name is added to the directory name in the entry window, and a new window called Network Directories opens, listing the directories on the volume you selected. Highlight the directory with which you want to work and press Enter. The directory name is added to your list, and the subdirectories under that directory (if any) are listed in the Network Directories window. Select the subdirectory with which you want to work and press Enter (you may need to continue this process if you have several levels of subdirectories). When the entry window shows the name of the directory or subdirectory that stores the file you want to work with, press Esc to leave the Network Directories window.

After the correct directory name appears in the entry box, press Enter. Another entry box opens, prompting you to enter the name of the file with which you want to work. Type the file name, or press Ins to list the files in the selected directory. Highlight the file with which you want to work and press Enter. You must enter or select a single file name. Unfortunately, you cannot use wild-card characters and name patterns (such as *.TXT) to select multiple files. You also cannot mark multiple files with F5. You must add files one at a time.

After the correct file name appears in the entry box, press Enter, and the file is added to the user's Trustee File Assignment window.

You can remove a file from the user's file trustee assignments list by highlighting the file name and pressing Del. You also can remove multiple files from the list by marking them with F5 and pressing Del.

When you add a file to the user's list of trustee file assignments, the user automatically is given a default set of rights to the file. You can add or remove rights to or from this default set. You will learn how in the next section.

Adding or Deleting File Rights

Changing the rights a user has to a file is exactly like changing the rights to a directory. From the Trustee File Assignments window, highlight the name of the file for which you want to add or delete rights. Press Enter, and a list called Trustee Rights Granted appears. To delete a right, highlight it and press Del. You are asked to confirm your choice; after you confirm the choice, the right is deleted from the Trustee Rights Granted list. You can delete more than one right at a time by highlighting each right and marking it with the F5 key. Press Del and confirm your choice, and all marked rights are removed from the list. Press Esc to save your changes and return to the Trustee Assignments window. The rights shown next to the directory are updated to show your changes.

Adding rights is a similar process. In the Trustee File Assignments window, highlight the file for which you want to change the rights and press Enter. The Trustee Rights Granted list appears, showing the currently assigned rights. Press Ins, and a list called Trustee Rights Not Granted appears. To add a right, highlight it on the list and press Enter. The Trustee Rights Granted list is updated to show the addition of the new right. You can add more than one right at once by highlighting each right and marking it with the F5 key. Press Enter, and all the rights you selected are added to the Trustee Rights Granted list. Press Esc to save your changes and return to the Trustee File Assignments window. The rights shown next to the file name are updated to show your changes.

When you are finished working with the user's file trustee assignments, press Esc to leave the Trustee File Assignments window and return to the User Information menu. If you want to leave SYSCON, press Alt-F7, or press Esc to move to other SYSCON menus.

Adding Rights to Groups of Users

Controlling trustee assignments and rights is a detailed process. Often, groups of users need to be given the same rights to the same directories. If all 15 members of the accounting department need to be given the same rights to the SYS:ACCTING directory, for example, giving the rights to a group is much easier than updating each user's trustee assignments one at a time.

You learned in the last chapter that SYSCON enables you to place users in groups and give them rights as a whole instead of as individuals. To use SYSCON for this purpose, you must be logged in with supervisory access. To start SYSCON, type the following from the DOS prompt:

SYSCON

Press Enter. From its main menu, select Group Information and press Enter. This option displays a list (called Group Names) of all currently defined groups on the file server.

Working with this list is like working with the list of login names that appears when you select User Information from SYSCON's main menu. You can add a new group by pressing Ins. A box appears, and you are prompted to enter the name of the group you want to add. Press Enter after typing the name, and the new group's name is shown on the list of group names. You can delete a group by highlighting its name and pressing Del. You can delete more than one group by highlighting each group's name, marking it with F5, and then pressing Del to remove all marked group names. You can change a group's name by highlighting it and pressing F3. A box opens, and you are prompted to enter the new name you want to use. Type the new name and press Enter to complete the change.

To work with a group, highlight that group's name from Group Names list and press Enter. The Group Information menu is shown (see fig. 11.7).

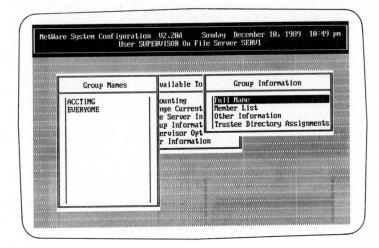

Fig. 11.7.
*The SYSCON Group
Information
window.*

The first option on the Group Information menu is Full Name. Like the Full Name option for a user account, this option enables you to enter a descriptive name of up to 48 characters for the group. For the group of users in the accounting department, you might enter a full name like ACCOUNTING DEPARTMENT EMPLOYEES.

The second option on the menu is Member List. If you select this option and press Enter, a list of all login names for users who are group members appears. If you want to add users, press Ins and a list of all other login names on the server appears. Highlight the name you want to add from this list and press Enter. You can add multiple users by highlighting each login name and marking it with F5. After the names you want to add are all marked, press Enter, and the users you selected are added to the group. Press Esc to save your changes and return to the Group Information menu.

Removing users from the group is a similar process. Select the Member List option from the Group Information menu and press Enter. The list of group members appears. Highlight the name you want to remove and press Del. The name is removed from the list. You can delete multiple users by highlighting each name and marking it with F5. After the names you want to remove are marked, press Del, and the names are removed from the group list. Press Esc to save your changes and return to the Group Information menu.

The next option on the Group Information menu has the nondescript title Other Information. When you select Other Information, you are shown two items of information about the group. You are shown whether the group members are Server Console Operators—whether the group members are allowed to use the NetWare FCONSOLE utility to operate the server. (You will learn about FCONSOLE in detail in Chapter 19.) The group's ID number also is shown. The file server uses this number to identify the group.

The options entitled Trustee Assignments (or Trustee Directory Assignments) and Trustee File Assignments (NetWare 386 only) enable you to assign the group as a trustee to directories, subdirectories, and files on the server (and save you the work of individually assigning each user as a trustee). Select one of these options and press Enter. A Trustee Assignments window is opened.

The left column of this window shows the name of a directory, subdirectory, or file on the server, and the right column shows the rights granted, showing only the initials (as already discussed).

The steps to assigning a group as a trustee to a directory are identical to those you use to assign an individual user. Follow the steps outlined in the sections called "Making Users Directory Trustees" and "Adding or Deleting Directory Rights."

If you are adding a new user to the server and want to make him or her a group member in the same step, the easiest way is from SYSCON's User Information menu, which has an option called Groups Belonged To. Selecting this option shows you a list of all the groups of which the selected user is a member. If you need to add the user to another group, press Ins. A list of all groups appears; highlight a group and press Enter, or mark more than one group with F5 and press Enter. The user is added to the group or groups you selected.

The Everyone Group

When you first install NetWare on a server, a group called EVERYONE is automatically created. When you add new users to the server, they are automatically made members of the group EVERYONE.

This group has READ, OPEN, and SEARCH rights (NetWare 286) or READ and FILE SCAN rights (NetWare 386) to SYS:PUBLIC, which stores all important NetWare commands. If you have other directories that every user on the server should have rights to access, the easiest way to do so is to make the group EVERYONE a trustee to that directory.

Combining Individual and Group Rights

When a user has individual rights to a directory and also has rights to the same directory through group membership, the user's effective rights are the combination of his or her group and individual rights. For example, if a user has READ, OPEN, and SEARCH rights to a directory through the EVERYONE group, and READ, WRITE, OPEN, CREATE, and DELETE rights as individual rights to the same directory, his or her effective rights are READ, WRITE, OPEN, CREATE, DELETE and SEARCH, as illustrated below:

```
GROUP RIGHTS          [R  O    S ]
INDIVIDUAL RIGHTS     [RWOCD   ]

EFFECTIVE RIGHTS      [RWOCD S ]
```

Adding Rights Using Security Equivalence

In addition to assigning rights directly to a user or giving a group of users rights, you can make a user equivalent to another user or group so that he or she inherits the trustee assignments and rights of the other user or group. The most common use of this feature is to give another user the same access level as the SUPERVISOR login name. This feature also helps when one user has to assume the same access rights as another user temporarily, perhaps while one user is covering for another who is on vacation.

In most cases, security equivalence is probably not a good way to give users their permanent trustee rights assignments. Security equivalence makes one user's rights dependent on another user's rights. This situation can get confusing if a user leaves the company and has his or her user account deleted. When security equivalence is extensively used, seeing what trustee rights are assigned on a user-by-user basis is more difficult. Except for temporary situations or cases where you need to make a user equivalent to the supervisor, you should assign rights to a user directly or through a group.

To make one user equivalent to another user or group, select User Information from SYSCON's main menu. A list of all users on the server is displayed. Highlight the name of the user you want to work with and press Enter. The User Information menu is displayed. Select the option called Security Equivalences and press Enter. A list of the users and groups to which this user is equivalent appears. Press Ins to add a new security equivalence. A list of all other users and groups on the server is shown. Highlight the name of a user or group and press Enter, or mark multiple users and groups with F5 and press Enter. You are returned to the Security Equivalences screen, and the list of equivalences is updated to show the users or groups you added.

You can delete an equivalence by highlighting the user or group you want to remove from the equivalence list and pressing Del. You can remove multiple equivalences by marking user or group names on the list with F5 and pressing Del. The list of equivalences is updated to eliminate the names you have removed.

When you have finished working with security equivalences for that user, press Esc to return to the User Information menu. You can then press Esc to move to other SYSCON menus or press Alt-F7 to exit SYSCON.

Controlling Rights with TLIST, GRANT, REVOKE, and REMOVE

SYSCON gives you complete control of trustee assignments and rights, but you have to work with its many layers of menus. Sometimes you need to make small changes to a user's or group's rights, and SYSCON—for all its power and versatility—is overkill. Four commands—TLIST, GRANT, REVOKE, and REMOVE—enable you to control rights from the DOS prompt. You can add users and groups as trustees to directories and fine-tune their rights from the command line.

TLIST

TLIST shows the users and groups that are trustees for a particular directory or file, as well as their rights for that directory or file. Although the SYSCON utility allows you to view trustee rights one user or group at a time, TLIST displays trustee rights for all users and groups at one time. In order to use TLIST, you must be logged into the server that contains the directory you are checking and you must have supervisory access or the PARENTAL right (NetWare 286) or the ACCESS CONTROL or SUPERVISORY right (NetWare 386) to the directory or file you are checking. To use TLIST to show trustee information for your current directory, type the following:

    TLIST

Then press Enter. You see a display similar to the following:

```
SYS:SOFTWARE
User trustees:  TBACK                  [RWOCDPSM]  (Tape Backup ID)
    -----
Group trustees:
    EVERYONE              [R O   S ]  (All users)
    SOFTWRE_MGMT          [RWOCDPSM]  (Shared software admin)
```

The first line shows the volume and directory name. Next the user and group trustees are shown, along with their trustee rights and full names.

To see the trustees for a directory other than the default, type *tlist* followed by the full NetWare name of the directory. For example, type

TLIST SERV1/SYS:ACCTING

and then press Enter. You can shorten the directory name under certain conditions. If SERV1 is the only server you are logged into, for example, you can safely leave its name out of your request and type the following:

TLIST SYS:ACCTING

Press Enter. Similarly, if your current default volume is SYS:, you can leave its name out of the request also. Type the following:

TLIST \ACCTING

Press Enter. If you have drive letter J mapped to SERV1/SYS:ACCTING, you can type the following:

TLIST J:

Press Enter.

With NetWare 386's TLIST, you can check the trustee list for a file. Simply follow TLIST with the name of the file you want to check. For example, to list the trustees for the file JOURNAL.DAT in the SERVI/SYS:ACCTING directory, type

TLIST SERVI/SYS:ACCTING\JOURNAL.DAT

and press Enter. You also can shorten the directory name by using the methods just discussed.

You also can specify whether you want TLIST to list only user trustees or only group trustees. For example, typing

TLIST SERV1/SYS:ACCTING USERS

and then pressing Enter shows only the trustees who are users and does not display groups. Typing

TLIST SERV1/SYS:ACCTING GROUPS

and then pressing Enter shows only groups, not users.

GRANT

The GRANT command enables you to assign users and groups as trustees to a directory or file and give them rights to that directory or file. The command format to grant rights to a user is as follows:

GRANT *rights list* [FOR] *directory/file* TO [USER] *user name*

Press Enter.

Granting rights to a group requires the same format:

GRANT *rights list* [FOR] *directory/file* TO [GROUP] *group name*

Press Enter.

The words in brackets (FOR, USER, and GROUP) are optional but may be helpful in making GRANT's command parameters easier to understand and remember. Do not type the brackets in your command. The word GROUP must be used before a group name if you are giving rights to a group that has the same name as a user.

You can use the following items to make up the rights list part of the GRANT command:

NetWare 286

R	(the READ right)
W	(the WRITE right)
O	(the OPEN right)
C	(the CREATE right)
D	(the DELETE right)
P	(the PARENTAL right)
S	(the SEARCH right)
M	(the MODIFY right)
ALL	(grant all eight rights)
NO RIGHTS	(revoke all rights)
ALL BUT	(grant all rights but the ones listed)
ONLY	(grant only the right or rights listed)

NetWare 386

S	(the SUPERVISORY right)
R	(the READ right)
W	(the WRITE right)
C	(the CREATE right)
E	(the ERASE right)
M	(the MODIFY right)

F	(the FILE SCAN right)
A	(the ACCESS CONTROL right)
ALL	(grant all eight rights)
NO RIGHTS	(revoke all rights)
ALL BUT	(grant all rights but the ones listed)
ONLY	(grant only the right or rights listed)

To grant the READ, WRITE, OPEN, CREATE, DELETE, and SEARCH rights for the SYS:SOFTWARE directory to a user named Adam, type the following:

GRANT RWOCDS FOR SERV1/SYS:SOFTWARE TO USER ADAM

and press Enter.

The GRANT command confirms that the rights have been granted and lists the current rights for the user named Adam.

If a user or group already has rights to a particular directory, the rights you give with the GRANT command are added to the rights the user or group already has, unless you use the ALL BUT or ONLY option. If Adam already has READ, WRITE, OPEN, CREATE, DELETE, and SEARCH rights for the SYS:SOFTWARE directory, for example, and you want to change his rights to just READ and OPEN, you can type

GRANT ONLY RO FOR SERV1/SYS:SOFTWARE TO USER ADAM

and then press Enter. His rights are reduced to READ and OPEN.

The same rules for abbreviating the directory name that apply to TLIST apply to GRANT. If you are granting rights for the default directory, you can leave out the directory name. If you are logged into only one server, you can leave out the server name. If your default volume is the same as the directory you want to revoke rights for, you can leave off the volume name. If the directory you are working with has a drive letter mapped to it, you can refer to the directory by using just the drive letter (*H:*, for example).

REVOKE

The REVOKE command is similar to GRANT. Instead of giving a user or group rights to a directory or file, however, REVOKE removes them. The command format to revoke rights from a user is as follows:

REVOKE *rights list* [FOR] *directory/file* FROM [USER] *user name*

Press Enter.

Revoking rights from a group requires the same format:

REVOKE *rights list* [FOR] *directory/file* FROM [GROUP] *group name*

Press Enter.

The words in brackets (FOR, USER, and GROUP) are optional but may be helpful in making REVOKE's command parameters easier to understand and remember. Do not type the brackets in your command. The word GROUP must be used before a group name if you are removing rights from a group that has the same name as a user.

You can use the following items to make up the rights list part of the REVOKE command:

NetWare 286

R	(the READ right)
W	(the WRITE right)
O	(the OPEN right)
C	(the CREATE right)
D	(the DELETE right)
P	(the PARENTAL right)
S	(the SEARCH right)
M	(the MODIFY right)
ALL	(revoke all eight rights)

NetWare 386

S	(the SUPERVISORY right)
R	(the READ right)
W	(the WRITE right)
C	(the CREATE right)
E	(the ERASE right)
M	(the MODIFY right)
F	(the FILE SCAN right)
A	(the ACCESS CONTROL right)
ALL	(revoke all eight rights)

To revoke the CREATE and DELETE rights for the SYS:ACCTING directory from a user named Adam, type the following:

REVOKE CD FOR SERV1/SYS:SOFTWARE FROM USER ADAM

Press Enter.

This REVOKE command confirms that the rights have been removed and lists the current rights for the user named Adam.

The rights you take away with the REVOKE command are subtracted from the rights the user or group previously had to a particular directory or file.

If Adam has READ, WRITE, OPEN, CREATE, DELETE, and SEARCH rights for the SYS:SOFTWARE directory, for example, and you want to revoke the WRITE, CREATE, and DELETE rights, type the following:

REVOKE WCD FOR SERV1/SYS:SOFTWARE FROM USER ADAM

Press Enter.

Only READ, OPEN, and SEARCH rights remain.

The same rules for abbreviating the directory name that apply to TLIST and GRANT apply to REVOKE. If you are revoking rights for the default directory, you can leave out the directory name. If you are logged into only one server, you can leave out the server name. If your default volume is the same as the directory you want to revoke rights for, you can leave off the volume name. If the directory you are working with has a drive letter mapped to it, you can refer to the directory by using just the drive letter (*H:*, for example).

REMOVE

Even if you remove all rights by using the REVOKE command, the user or group still remains as a trustee to the directory or file. The REMOVE command enables you to remove a user or group as a trustee to a particular directory or file.

When removing a user, follow this format for the REMOVE command:

REMOVE [USER] *user name* [FROM] *directory name/file name*

Press Enter.

When removing a group, follow this format:

REMOVE [GROUP] *group name* [FROM] *directory name*

Press Enter.

The words in brackets (USER, GROUP, and FROM) are optional but can be used to make the command syntax easier to understand and remember. Do not type the brackets. As with GRANT and REVOKE, you must use the word GROUP if you are removing a group that has the same name as a user.

To remove a user named Adam from a directory called SERV1/SYS:ACCTING, type the following:

REMOVE USER ADAM FROM SERV1/SYS:ACCTING

Press Enter.

The same directory naming shortcuts that apply to TLIST, GRANT, and REVOKE apply to REMOVE.

Setting Rights Masks

NetWare provides a second way to control the type of access that users can have to a directory or subdirectory. Each directory can be assigned a *rights mask*, which controls the way trustee rights can be exercised by users when they are working in that directory.

NetWare 286 and NetWare 386 handle the rights mask differently. NetWare 286 calls the rights mask the maximum rights mask. As its name implies, NetWare 286's maximum rights mask determines the maximum rights that can be exercised in the directory. NetWare 386 calls its rights mask the inherited rights mask. By default, the rights that a user has to a directory are transferred to all of that directory's subdirectories. The inherited rights mask enables you to limit the rights a subdirectory can "inherit" from any directory above it.

Setting NetWare 286's Maximum Rights Mask

NetWare 286's maximum rights mask can be used to guarantee that a certain group of rights cannot be exercised in a directory. Simply withhold those rights from the directory's rights mask. For example, if you want to be sure that users cannot delete files in a directory that stores your company's payroll records, simply withhold the DELETE right from that directory's maximum rights mask. Even if a user has DELETE as part of his or her trustee rights to the directory, the user still cannot delete files because DELETE is not in the maximum rights mask.

The rights that can be included in the NetWare 286 maximum rights mask are the same eight rights you can grant to a directory trustee: READ, WRITE, OPEN, CREATE, DELETE, PARENTAL, SEARCH, and MODIFY. Each right serves exactly the same purpose as its trustee right counterpart. Many network supervisors opt not to use directory rights as part of their security plan and do not set up rights masks for directories. Instead, they control access through trustee rights only. Setting maximum rights masks on a directory-by-directory basis can be a cumbersome process, and no directory rights equivalent to a group are available, so each maximum rights mask must be set up one directory at a time. In cases where an extra level of security and control are worth the effort, however, the maximum rights mask is an effective tool.

Setting NetWare 386's Inherited Rights Mask

NetWare 386's inherited rights mask is used to control the way rights given to users at a higher directory level are inherited by the directory's subdirectories. Suppose that users need to be given the ERASE right to the SYS:ACCTING directory, but you want to ensure that those same users do not have the same right in the subdirectory SYS:ACCTING\DATFILES. You can set the inherited rights mask for SYS:ACCTING\DATFILES to exclude the ERASE right so that users cannot inherit the ERASE right from the SYS:ACCTING directory.

The rights that can be included in NetWare 386's inherited rights mask are the same eight rights you can grant to a directory or file trustee: SUPERVISORY, READ, WRITE, CREATE, ERASE, MODIFY, ACCESS CONTROL, and FILE SCAN. They serve exactly the same purpose as their trustee right counterparts.

NetWare 386 enables you to set inherited rights masks for both directories and files. The rights mask for a subdirectory controls how that directory inherits rights from its parent directories. The rights mask for a file controls which rights that file inherits from its directory.

When a directory or file is created, its inherited rights mask is set to include all eight rights by default.

Setting Rights Masks with FILER

The FILER utility is used to control rights masks for directories (NetWare 286 and 386) and files (NetWare 386 only). FILER has a number of other uses, which you read about in the next chapter ("Managing Files").

You must be logged into a FILER server with supervisory access or have the PARENTAL right (NetWare 286) or the ACCESS CONTROL or SUPERVISORY right (NetWare 386) to the directory or file where you want to change a rights mask. From the command prompt, start FILER by typing

FILER

and pressing Enter. As with most NetWare utilities and commands, FILER is stored in the SYS:PUBLIC directory, which becomes a search drive by default, so you do not have to make SYS:PUBLIC your default directory to use FILER.

You must be logged into a file server with supervisory access or have the PARENTAL right to a directory to change its maximum rights mask. At the DOS prompt, start FILER by typing

FILER

Press Enter. As with most NetWare utilities and commands, FILER is stored in the SYS:PUBLIC directory, which becomes a search drive by default, so you do not have to make SYS:PUBLIC your default directory to use FILER. FILER's main menu is shown in figure 11.8.

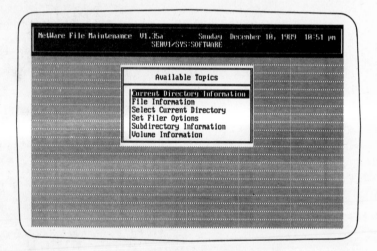

Fig. 11.8.
The FILER main menu.

FILER displays the current directory in the upper center part of the screen. If this directory is not the directory for which you want to change the maximum rights mask, highlight the Select Current Directory option and press Enter. A box called Destination Directory opens, showing the full NetWare name for the current directory (see Chapter 9 for information about full NetWare directory names).

Use the Backspace key to backspace over as much of the name as you need to discard. If the current directory is SERV1/SYS:USERS/ADAM, for example, and you want to switch to SERV1/SYS:SOFTWARE, backspace over USERS/ADAM. You then can type *software* so that the directory name is SERV1/SYS:SOFTWARE.

If you are not sure of the correct directory name, you can build it one part at a time. Backspace over the entire name in the box and press Ins. A list of the servers you are attached to is displayed in a box called File Servers/Local Drives. Select the server that contains the directory you want to work with and press Enter. If the server you need is not on the list, you are not attached to that server. Press Ins and a list of all other servers appears; select the correct one and press Enter. After you enter a login name and password, you are attached to the server, and its name is added to the list of servers in the File Servers/Local Drives box. Highlight that server and press Enter. That server's name is listed in the Destination Directory box.

A list of volumes on the server you selected is displayed. Select the volume containing the directory you plan to work with and press Enter. The name of this volume is added to the Destination Directory box after the server name. You are shown a list of directories on that volume. Choose the directory you want to work with and press Enter, and that directory name is shown in the Destination Directory box. You are shown the subdirectories under that directory (if any). Select the subdirectory you want to work with and press Enter. You may need to repeat this process several times if you need to select a subdirectory that is several levels deep.

After you have selected the correct directory or subdirectory, and the correct name of that directory is shown in the Destination Directory box, press Enter. You are returned to the FILER main menu, and the top of the screen is updated to show the directory you have selected.

Choose the Current Directory Information option and press Enter.

For NetWare 286's FILER, your next step is to select the option called maximum rights mask and press Enter. A list of the currently selected maximum rights appears (see fig. 11.9).

For NetWare 386's FILER, you should highlight the rights mask shown next to inherited rights mask and press Enter. The rights that make up the inherited rights mask are listed.

To remove a right from the rights mask, highlight the right and press Del. To remove more than one right, use F5 to mark the rights you want to remove and press Del. The rights you have selected are removed from the maximum rights mask.

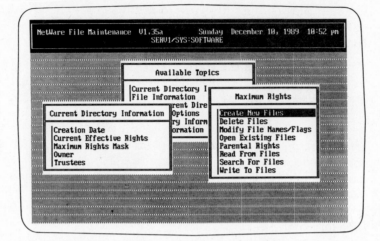

Fig. 11.9.

Setting the Rights Mask.

To add rights that have been previously removed, press Ins. A list titled Other Rights appears. To add one of these rights, highlight the right and press Enter. To add more than one, use F5 to mark the rights you want to add and press Enter. The rights you have selected are added to the rights mask.

When your rights mask contains the rights you want, press Esc to save your changes. Press Esc again to return to the FILER main menu.

If you want to modify the rights mask of subdirectories in the currently selected directory, choose the Subdirectory Information option (NetWare 286) or the Directory Contents option (NetWare 386) from the FILER main menu. You are shown a list of subdirectories. Mark the ones you want to work with by pressing F5 and then press Enter. A menu called Multiple Subdirectory Operations appears. Select the option called Set Maximum Rights (NetWare 286) or Set Inherited Rights (NetWare 386) and press Enter. Remove and add rights by following the same procedure as before.

NetWare 386's FILER also can be used to set the inherited rights mask for files. To modify the inherited rights mask for files in the currently selected directory, choose the Directory Contents Option from the FILER main menu. You are shown a list of the directory's subdirectories and files. Mark the files you want to work with by pressing F5 and then press Enter. A menu called Multiple Files Operations appears. Select the option Set Inherited Rights and press Enter. Remove and add rights by following the same procedure as previously described.

Understanding Effective Rights

Your effective rights in a directory are determined by evaluating both your trustee rights and that directory's rights mask. With NetWare 286, for you to have a particular right as part of your effective rights, it must be allowed as part of both your trustee rights and the directory's maximum rights mask. For example, if your trustee rights for SYS:SOFTWARE are [RWOCD_S_], and the maximum rights mask is [R_O___SM], what are your effective rights?

TRUSTEE RIGHTS	RWOCD_S_
MAXIMUM RIGHTS MASK	R_O___SM
EFFECTIVE RIGHTS	R_O___S_

Your effective rights are [R_O_ _ _S_] because READ, OPEN, and SEARCH are the only rights available in *both* the trustee rights and the NetWare 286 maximum rights mask.

For NetWare 386 rights, you must evaluate five factors:

❏ Your trustee directory rights to the parent directories of your current directory

❏ Your trustee rights to the current directory

❏ Your trustee rights to the current directory's files

❏ The inherited rights mask of the current directory

❏ The inherited rights mask of the current directory's files

Several rules apply as you determine your effective rights. When you have trustee rights to the current directory and the current directory has an inherited rights mask, only your trustee rights apply. For example, if you have READ, WRITE, CREATE, ERASE, and FILE SCAN ([_RWCE_F_]) as trustee rights and the inherited rights mask of current directory includes only READ and FILE SCAN ([_R_____F_]), what are your effective rights? They are [_RWCE___F_] (the same as your trustee rights), because your trustee rights to the current directory override its inherited rights mask.

The second rule is that a file's inherited rights limit its directory's trustee rights. For example, if you have READ, WRITE, CREATE, ERASE, and FILE SCAN ([_RWCE_F_]) rights to a directory, and a file in that directory has an inherited rights mask of READ and FILE SCAN ([_R____F_]), what are your effective rights to that file? They are READ and FILE SCAN (the same as the file's inherited rights mask), because the file's rights mask determines which rights the file inherits from its directory.

If you have trustee rights to a directory and trustee rights to a file in that directory, the trustee rights to the file determine your effective rights to the file. For example, if you have only READ and FILE SCAN rights to a directory, but have READ, WRITE, ERASE, and FILE SCAN rights to a file in that directory, your effective rights to the file are READ, WRITE, ERASE, and FILE SCAN. Similarly, if you have no rights to a directory, but have all rights to a file in the directory, your effective rights to the file are all rights.

Finally, if a file has an inherited rights mask, and you have trustee rights to the file, your effective rights are equal to your trustee rights. Your trustee rights to the file override its inherited rights mask.

You can check your effective rights by using a command called RIGHTS. To check your rights to your default directory, type

RIGHTS

and then press Enter. You are shown a list of your effective rights.

To check your rights for another directory, type *rights* followed by the directory name:

RIGHTS SERV1/SYS:SOFTWARE.

and press Enter.

On a NetWare 386 server, you can use the same method to check your effective rights to a file. Type *rights* followed by the name of the file, such as

RIGHTS SERV1/SYS:ACCTING\JOURNAL.DAT

and press Enter.

The same rules for shortening the directory name that apply with the TLIST, GRANT, REVOKE, and REMOVE commands apply to RIGHTS.

Shortcuts for Adding Users and Granting Rights

Now that you have a good understanding of the steps required to add users to a server and give them rights to directories and files, you may be wondering if any shortcuts exist to reduce the number of steps and keystrokes for adding a user.

Two NetWare utilities, USERDEF and MAKEUSER, are available to help the process of adding and managing users. Because these utilities deal with areas you have not read about yet, such as login scripts and NetWare accounting, the utilities are discussed at the end of this book in Appendix E ("Shortcuts for Managing Users").

Chapter Summary

Using NetWare rights wisely is perhaps the most important part of making your network secure and safe to use. The best way to gain the skill you need is to practice. Test the behavior of familiar programs and DOS commands in directories with various rights enabled and disabled. The experience you gain will be put to good use as your network grows and becomes the host system to a wide variety of software and data.

12

Managing Files

You learned about three elements of NetWare security in Chapters 9 and 10. This chapter examines the fourth element of NetWare security: file control. Login control is the tool you use to select which users can log into a server. After a user logs in, his or her trustee rights and the directory rights for that server determine which directories and subdirectories can be used, and how they can be used.

Sometimes you need to give varying levels of access to the files in a particular directory. For example, if a directory stores a shared-database application, you need users to be able to read and write to the data files, but only read (and not change) the program files. With NetWare 386, you can make this distinction easily by giving users READ and WRITE rights to the data files but only the READ right to program files. NetWare 286 does not enable you to make this distinction. With NetWare 286, you can give users trustee rights only to directories and not to individual files.

File control takes up where NetWare 286's trustee and directory rights leave off. If a directory stores files that you must write to *and* files that you cannot write to, you can protect some files by making them *read-only*. You designate the files that must be written to as *read/write*. Even if you have NetWare privileges to write to or delete files in a particular directory, you cannot exercise those rights on files that are read-only.

Making files read-only is only one use of NetWare file control. You also can control whether two or more users can access a file simultaneously by designating files as *shareable* or *nonshareable*. If you want to permit users to run a program file but not to copy it, you can make the file *execute-only*. If you want to speed up the way that NetWare accesses your very large files, you can designate them as *indexed*.

This chapter discusses every NetWare command and utility that controls server files and directories. Don't be intimidated by the number of commands available. You really only need to know something about the first command discussed in this chapter (FLAG) to implement the basic aspects of NetWare file control. The others are quite useful but not essential.

File Attributes

File attributes are file designations such as READ ONLY and SHAREABLE. You already may be familiar with attributes from working with files using PC DOS or OS/2. An attribute is a characteristic of a file that you can turn on or off. READ ONLY, for example, is an attribute. When READ ONLY is on, the file can be read only; when READ ONLY is off, the file can be read and written to. The four file attributes supported by DOS and OS/2 are READ ONLY, HIDDEN, SYSTEM, and ARCHIVE. You can turn these attributes on or off for files that you store on your PC's local disks and for files you store on a file server. NetWare also makes some special attributes available that can be used only for files that you store on a file server. These attributes are sometimes called *NetWare extended attributes*. For NetWare 286, these additional attributes are SHAREABLE, INDEXED, EXECUTE ONLY, and TRANSACTIONAL. NetWare 386 adds COPY INHIBIT, DELETE INHIBIT, PURGE, RENAME INHIBIT, READ AUDIT, and WRITE AUDIT to NetWare 286's attributes.

Note: If you are thoroughly familiar with the way DOS or OS/2 controls attributes, you know that one byte (8 bits) of the file's directory entry (the file's identification listing on the disk) is used to designate which attributes are turned on. Four bits of this byte are used to determine whether the READ ONLY, HIDDEN, SYSTEM, and ARCHIVE attributes are turned on or off. Two other bits are reserved to identify whether the directory entry refers to a file, a subdirectory, or a volume label. Two bits remain unused. NetWare 286 gives you an additional byte for files stored on servers, and this byte partially has been used to support the extended attributes. NetWare 386 uses two additional bytes to support extended attributes and file rights.

Table 12.1 lists all file attributes and the abbreviations used by NetWare 286 and 386 to show them. The sections following discuss each file attribute and give examples of how that attribute can be used effectively.

Table 12.1
NetWare File Attributes

Attribute Name	Available with These Operating Systems	NetWare 286 Name/ Abbreviation	NetWare 386 Name/ Abbreviation
ARCHIVE	DOS, OS/2 Netware 286, Netware 386	MODIFIED, MODIFIED SINCE LAST BACKUP	ARCHIVE NEEDED, A
COPY INHIBIT	NetWare 386		C
DELETE INHIBIT	NetWare 386		D
EXECUTE ONLY	NetWare 286, NetWare 386		EX
HIDDEN	DOS, OS/2 NetWare 286, NetWare 386	H	H
INDEXED	NetWare 286, NetWare 386	I	I
PURGE	NetWare 386		P
READ AUDIT	NetWare 386		RA
READ ONLY	DOS, OS/2, NetWare 286, NetWare 386	RO	RO
RENAME INHIBIT	NetWare 386		R
SHAREABLE	NetWare 286, NetWare 386	S	S
SYSTEM	DOS, OS/2, NetWare 286, NetWare 386		SY
TRANSACTIONAL	NetWare 286, NetWare 386	T	T
WRITE AUDIT	NetWare 386		WA

NetWare 286 File Attributes

NetWare 286 supports the DOS and OS/2 file attributes and adds four additional ones:

READ ONLY. Making a file read-only means that you cannot write to it, change it, or delete it, even when you have enough trustee rights to do so.

Turn on this attribute to protect a file from being written to or deleted in a directory where you must give the WRITE or DELETE NetWare rights.

HIDDEN. Turning on the HIDDEN attribute makes a file invisible to programs that try to list, copy, or delete files. These commands include the DOS commands DIR, ERASE, COPY, and DEL.

Make a file hidden when it should be used only by programs that are designed to use hidden files. NetWare's own security information files are hidden to protect them.

SYSTEM. The SYSTEM attribute is used for two files created when you make a DOS disk bootable. The SYSTEM attribute has no real purpose for files that you create and use yourself, either on your local disks or on a file server.

ARCHIVE. The ARCHIVE attribute is turned on automatically when a file has been changed by a program or a DOS or OS/2 command.

This attribute is put to good use by backup devices in situations where you want to limit the backup to only those files that have changed since the last backup. The backup program checks to see if the ARCHIVE attribute is turned on; if it is, the backup program backs up the file and then turns off the ARCHIVE attribute. The next time the file is changed, the ARCHIVE attribute is turned on again.

NetWare 286 utilities and commands sometimes call the ARCHIVE attribute MODIFIED or MODIFIED SINCE LAST BACKUP. NetWare 386 utilities call this attribute ARCHIVE NEEDED.

SHAREABLE. Files with the SHAREABLE attribute turned on can be accessed by more than one user at a time.

If you want your tape backup device to be able to back up your word processing documents even while you are using them, designate them SHAREABLE.

Turning on the SHAREABLE attribute is not a guarantee that a file can be shared in all situations. Some programs check to see if a file is open before retrieving it; if the file is open, the retrieval operation stops. Conversely, turning off the SHAREABLE attribute does not guarantee that a file will not be shared. Certain programming techniques (such as using what is called a shared file open) permit a file to be accessed by multiple users even if the SHAREABLE attribute is turned off.

INDEXED. Turning on the INDEXED attribute makes the access to very large files (2M or larger) more efficient. On a NetWare 286 server, the network installer chooses the maximum number of allowable indexed files during the server installation process. This setting can be revised by downing the server and running NETGEN.

On NetWare 386 servers, this attribute is turned on automatically when a file occupies more than 64 disk blocks.

When a file has the INDEXED attribute set, the file server builds an index in its memory of all the disk locations where the file is stored so that individual segments of the file can be accessed quickly.

EXECUTE ONLY. Turning on the EXECUTE ONLY attribute prevents files from being copied. This attribute is available only for executable files (files that have the extension EXE or COM) and you must have SUPERVISOR equivalence to turn it on.

If a user has READ and SEARCH or FILE SCAN access to a directory, he or she can copy its files. Some directories may store executable files that you do not want users to copy, such as the executable files for network-licensed programs. Turning on the EXECUTE ONLY attribute makes these programs uncopyable.

After you have turned on the EXECUTE ONLY attribute, it cannot be removed. The only way to undo the effects of this attribute is to delete or copy over the file that has it turned on. An EXECUTE ONLY file also may prove impossible to back up, so you probably should store a non-EXECUTE ONLY copy in a safe place in case it becomes necessary to replace the file.

TRANSACTIONAL. The TRANSACTIONAL attribute works in conjunction with NetWare's Transaction Tracking System (TTS). The Transaction Tracking System is an option that can be activated if you are using System Fault Tolerant NetWare. The TTS ensures that all file updates to data files with the TRANSACTIONAL attribute turned on are made only as complete transactions. To take advantage of this attribute, you must have an application that is designed to work with NetWare's Transaction Tracking System.

NetWare 386 File Attributes

NetWare 386 supports the same attributes as NetWare 286 and adds six additional ones. The additional attributes are described below:

COPY INHIBIT. This attribute is designed for Macintosh users. When a file has this attribute is turned on, a Macintosh user may not copy it.

This attribute is useful in the same way as the EXECUTE ONLY attribute. Some files may be installed on your server that you do not want users to copy, such as the files for network-licensed programs. Turning on the COPY INHIBIT attribute makes these files uncopyable by Macintosh users.

DELETE INHIBIT. When this attribute is turned on, even users who have the ERASE right cannot delete the file. Turn on this attribute when a file exists that the user must be able to write to, but should not be able to delete.

PURGE. Normally, NetWare 386 retains a deleted file so that it can be salvaged if necessary. When a file has the PURGE attribute turned on, it is purged immediately upon deletion, making the file unsalvageable.

RENAME INHIBIT. A file with this attribute turned on cannot be renamed even if the user has the MODIFY right.

READ AUDIT. This attribute can be turned on but is not used by NetWare 386 Version 3.0. In future releases of NetWare 386, READ AUDIT will provide an audit trail listing users who have read the file.

WRITE AUDIT. Like READ AUDIT, this attribute can be turned on but is not used by NetWare 386 Version 3.0. In future releases of NetWare 386, WRITE AUDIT will provide an audit trail listing users who have written to the file.

Directory Attributes

If you have NetWare 286 Version 2.15 or later, or NetWare 386, you also can change attributes for directories. For NetWare 286, three attributes can be turned on or off for directories: HIDDEN, PRIVATE, and SYSTEM. NetWare 386 does not support the PRIVATE attribute but adds three additional directory attributes: DELETE INHIBIT, PURGE, and RENAME INHIBIT.

The HIDDEN and SYSTEM attributes are identical to the corresponding file attributes. When the HIDDEN or SYSTEM attribute is turned on for a directory, you cannot view the directory with DOS or OS/2 commands that list directories. You still can change to the directory by using the DOS or OS/2 CHANGE DIRECTORY (CD) command, and you also can use NetWare's MAP command to set up a drive letter for the directory.

The PRIVATE attribute is used to prevent users from seeing a directory's subdirectories. With NetWare 286, you can withhold the SEARCH right to prevent users from viewing a directory's files, but you do not prevent them from viewing a directory's subdirectories. When you turn on the PRIVATE attribute for a directory, users who do not have rights to the directory cannot see its subdirectories. NetWare 386 does not need to support the PRIVATE directory attribute because NetWare 386 automatically makes invisible the directories that a user cannot access.

NetWare 386 lets you turn on three additional attributes for directories: DELETE INHIBIT, PURGE, and RENAME INHIBIT. These attributes function exactly as they do when you turn them on for files. When a directory has the DELETE INHIBIT attribute turned on, users cannot remove the directory even if they have the ERASE right. When the PURGE attribute is turned on for a directory, that directory is purged and made unrecoverable as soon as the directory is removed (NetWare 386 normally retains deleted directories and files so that they can be salvaged). When a directory has the RENAME INHIBIT attribute activated, users who have the MODIFY right cannot rename it.

Table 12.2 lists NetWare's directory attributes.

Table 12.2
NetWare's Directory Attributes

Attribute Name	Available with These Operating Systems	NetWare 286 Name/ Abbreviation	Netware 386 Name/ Abbreviation
DELETE INHIBIT	NetWare 386		D
HIDDEN	DOS, OS/2 NetWare 286, NetWare 386	H	H
PRIVATE	NetWare 286	P	
PURGE	NetWare 386		P
RENAME INHIBIT	NetWare 386		R
SYSTEM	NetWare 286, NetWare 386	S	SY

Rules for Using Attributes

You must have the NetWare MODIFY right to a directory in order to change the attributes in its files. When you first create a file, all of its attributes are set to off by default except for ARCHIVE.

File and Directory Information

NetWare stores several useful items of information about every file and directory on the server. PC DOS and OS/2 record only the file name, size, attributes, and creation or modification date, and time. NetWare records four additional items of information—the file owner (usually the user who created the file) and the dates that the file was last modified, accessed, and archived (or more accurately the date that the ARCHIVE attribute was changed from on to off).

PC DOS and OS/2 record only the name and date of creation for directories. NetWare also records the directory owner (usually the user who created the directory), the list of trustees (the users and groups who have rights to the directory), and the maximum rights mask (you will learn about rights masks later in this chapter).

Controlling File Attributes

Three NetWare utilities enable you to change the attributes of server-based files and directories. You use FLAG and FLAGDIR from the command line, but FILER is a utility with menus that enables you to view and change not only attributes, but also file and directory information items.

FLAG

The FLAG command is a command line program that provides a quick way to set file attributes. Because it is simple and direct, Network supervisors report that they use the FLAG command more often than the more powerful and menu-driven FILER utility.

With NetWare 286, FLAG can be used to work with four of NetWare 286's supported attributes: READ ONLY, SHAREABLE, INDEXED, and TRANSACTIONAL. (You can work with all eight NetWare 286 attributes using FILER, which is discussed later in this chapter.)

NetWare 386's FLAG command is more powerful than FILER and can be used to turn on and turn off all of NetWare 386's supported attributes. FLAG also can be used to work with files on both NetWare 286 and 386 servers. If you are working on a network with both types of servers, you may want to copy the NetWare 386 FLAG command to your NetWare 286 servers so that you have one command to learn and remember.

To use FLAG or FILER to turn attributes on or off, you must have MODIFY and SEARCH (NetWare 286) or MODIFY and FILE SCAN (NetWare 386) rights to the directory with which you are working.

Using FLAG To View Attribute Settings

FLAG can view and change the current attribute settings for a file or group of files. To see which attributes are turned on for the files in your current directory, simply type

    FLAG

and press Enter. If you are using NetWare 286's FLAG command, you see a listing similar to the following:

```
DBPROG.EXE          Shareable            Read Only
DBPROG.C            Non-shareable        Read/Write
DBPROG.DAT          Shareable            Read/Write
                                         Transactional Index
```

If you are using NetWare 386's FLAG utility, you should see a list similar to the following:

```
DBPROG.EXE   [ Ro S - - - -- - - -- -- - - - ]   None changed
DBPROG.C     [ Ro S - - - -- - - -- -- - - - ]   None changed
DBPROG.DAT   [ Rw - - I - -- T - -- -- - - - ]   None changed
```

Notice that NetWare 286's FLAG display lists the active attributes as full names, but NetWare 386's FLAG display uses abbreviations (because it works with a longer list of attributes). When a particular attribute is not turned on, NetWare 286's FLAG may display Read/Write or Non-shareable or nothing at all when the TRANSACTIONAL or INDEXED attributes are turned off. NetWare 386's FLAG display indicates the attributes that are turned off by leaving their abbreviations out of the attribute list (except for READ ONLY—NetWare 386's FLAG display shows Rw when this attribute is not turned on).

When you type *flag* without parameters, all files in the directory are listed, as well as their attribute settings. In the example above, the first file (the database program DBPROG.EXE) has the SHAREABLE and READ ONLY attributes on. The second file (DBPROG.C, the source code file for the program) has the SHAREABLE and READ ONLY attributes off, so it is listed as being NON-SHAREABLE READ WRITE. DBPROG.DAT, the data file, has the SHAREABLE attribute on, the READ ONLY attribute off (so it is listed as READ WRITE), and the TRANSACTIONAL and INDEXED attributes on.

The FLAG command also displays the attribute settings of single files or groups of files. If you only want to list the attributes of the DBPROG.DAT file, type

FLAG DBPROG.DAT

and press Enter. Only the information for DBPROG.DAT appears on-screen.

You can use wild-card characters to list groups of files. To see the attribute settings for all the EXE files in a directory, type

FLAG *.EXE

and press Enter. You also can use Flag to view the attribute settings for files in directories other than your current one by entering the name of the directory. To see the attribute settings for all the files in the directory that stores WordPerfect, type

FLAG SERV1/SYS:SOFTWARE\WORDPERF

and press Enter. As with other NetWare commands, (MAP, TLIST, GRANT, and REVOKE), you can shorten the directory name. If you are logged into SERV1 only, you can shorten the directory name to SYS:SOFTWARE/WORDPERF. If SYS: is your default volume, you can shorten the directory name to \SOFTWARE\WORDPERF. If you have assigned a drive letter (for example, J:), to the directory for WordPerfect, type

FLAG J:

and press Enter. The same rules for looking at the attribute settings for individual files or groups of files apply when you specify a directory name. For example, you can list attribute settings for the EXE files in the WordPerfect directory by typing

FLAG SERV1/SYS:SOFTWARE\WORDPERF*.EXE

and pressing Enter.

Viewing Attribute Settings for Files in Subdirectories

If you want to list attribute settings for files in subdirectories under the directory you specify, add the word SUB to the end of your FLAG command. To view the attribute settings for all files in subdirectories under the SYS:SOFTWARE directory, for example, type

FLAG SERV1/SYS:SOFTWARE SUB

and press Enter.

Using FLAG To Change Attribute Settings

You can use FLAG to change attribute settings by stating which attributes you want to turn on when you type the command. The respective FLAG commands for NetWare 286 and 386 handle this process differently, so they will be discussed separately.

NetWare 286 FLAG

With NetWare 286's FLAG, you use the initials listed below to identify each attribute setting:

Initials	Settings
S	SHAREABLE
NS	NON-SHAREABLE
RO	READ ONLY
RW	READ WRITE
T	TRANSACTIONAL
NT	NON-TRANSACTIONAL
I	INDEXED
NI	NOT INDEXED
N	NORMAL (turns all attributes off)

To change the attribute settings for the DBPROG.C file to SHAREABLE, READ ONLY, INDEXED, and TRANSACTIONAL, type

FLAG DBPROG.C S RO I T

and press Enter. The attribute initials are separated by a space, and you can list them in any order. Veteran Flaggers may tell you that you do not need to separate attribute settings by spaces. This is true in most cases, but because the letter N is used alone to turn off all attributes and in combination with other initials to turn off individual attributes, there are a few situations where you will get the wrong results if you omit these spaces.

To change DBPROG.C to be NON-SHAREABLE, READ WRITE, NOT INDEXED, and NON-TRANSACTIONAL, type

    FLAG DBPROG.C NS RW NI NT

and press Enter. Alternatively, you can type

    FLAG DBPROG.C N

and press Enter because the letter N tells FLAG to turn off all attributes and make the file NORMAL (remember that files have no attributes turned on when they are created, except ARCHIVE, so a NORMAL file has none of the attributes that FLAG controls turned on).

By using the proper combinations of initials, you can turn off or on any group of attributes with one FLAG command. You also can change the settings for groups of files by using wild-card characters. To change all the EXE files in your current directory to be SHAREABLE and READ ONLY, for example, type

    FLAG *.EXE S RO

and press Enter. The same rules for working with files in directories other than the default directory apply when changing attributes as when viewing them. For example, to change all the files in the SERV1/SYS:WORDPERF directory to SHAREABLE and READ ONLY, type

    FLAG SERV1/SYS:SOFTWARE\WORDPERF*.* S RO

and press Enter.

You can shorten the directory name using the same guidelines that apply when you use FLAG to view file attributes. You also can end the FLAG command line with SUB to change attributes in the directory you specify as well as those in subdirectories under that directory.

NetWare 386 FLAG

With NetWare 386's FLAG command, you change attributes by using the abbreviations shown below:

Abbreviations	*Settings*
C	COPY INHIBIT
D	DELETE INHIBIT
EX	EXECUTE ONLY
H	HIDDEN
P	PURGE
RA	READ AUDIT
RO	READ ONLY
R	RENAME INHIBIT
S	SHAREABLE
SY	SYSTEM
T	TRANSACTIONAL
WA	WRITE AUDIT
A	ALL (all attributes turned on)
N	NORMAL (turns off all attributes)

(You may have noticed that the ARCHIVE and INDEXED attributes are not listed; these attributes are handled automatically.)

To turn on the EXECUTE ONLY, RENAME INHIBIT, and DELETE INHIBIT attributes for DBPROG.EXE, type

FLAG DBPROG.EXE EX R D

and press Enter. The attribute abbreviations are separated by a space and can be listed in any order. You have the option of preceding each attribute's abbreviation with a plus sign (+), as shown below:

FLAG DBPROG.EXE +EX +R +D

When you want to turn off an attribute, you precede the attribute abbreviation with a minus sign (−). To turn off the EXECUTE ONLY, RENAME INHIBIT, and DELETE INHIBIT attributes for DBPROG.EXE, type

FLAG DBPROG.EXE −EX −R −D

and press Enter.

If you want to turn on certain attributes and turn off others in the same command, you must precede the ones that you want to turn on with the plus sign.

As with NetWare 286's FLAG command, you can use wild-card characters to change the attributes of multiple files. You also can work with files in directories other than your default directory by specifying the directory name along with the file name.

FLAGDIR

The FLAGDIR command is very similar to the FLAG command. FLAG changes the attributes of files; FLAGDIR changes the attributes of directories. With NetWare 286, FLAGDIR is available only with Version 2.15 or later. If you have an earlier release of NetWare, you cannot set directory attributes. FLAGDIR is available with all versions of NetWare 386.

With NetWare 286, directories can have three attribute settings: SYSTEM, HIDDEN, and PRIVATE. NetWare 386 does not support or require the PRIVATE directory attribute, but supports three additional attributes: DELETE INHIBIT, PURGE, and RENAME INHIBIT. If your current directory has the attributes PRIVATE and HIDDEN turned on, you can view these settings by typing

    FLAGDIR

and pressing Enter. You then see a display similar to the following:

```
SERV1/SYS:USERS
         ADAM          PRIVATE HIDDEN
```

Your screen shows only the attributes that are turned on.

You can view the attributes of a directory other than your default by entering its name after the FLAGDIR command. To see the attribute settings for the WordPerfect directory, type

    FLAGDIR SERV1/SYS:WORDPERF

and press Enter.

As you probably have guessed, you can shorten the directory name using the same rules that apply to FLAG.

To change the attribute settings of a directory, type the settings that you want to invoke at the end of the FLAGDIR command. As with the FLAG command, you use the following initials:

Initial	Settings
D	DELETE INHIBIT (NetWare 386 only)
H	HIDDEN
P	PRIVATE (NetWare 286 only)
P	PURGE (NetWare 386 only)
R	RENAME INHIBIT (NetWare 386 only)
S	SYSTEM
N	NORMAL (no attributes turned on)

Suppose, for example, that you want to make the user Adam's personal directory PRIVATE and HIDDEN. Type

FLAGDIR SERV1/SYS:USERS/ADAM P H

and press Enter.

As with FLAG, you list the initials of the settings that you want to activate and separate the initials with spaces.

To turn off all attributes, use N to return the directory to the Normal setting. When you combine N with other attribute initials in one FLAG command, all attributes are turned off except the ones you list. For example, typing

FLAGDIR SERV1/SYS:USERS/ADAM N R D

turns off any previously set attributes and turns on the RENAME INHIBIT and DELETE INHIBIT attributes.

FILER

FILER is NetWare's all-in-one file- and directory-management utility. You can use it to view and change almost every information item or attribute setting for a file or directory. You also can perform other management tasks, such as copying, deleting, or renaming files.

Like SYSCON, FILER is a complex utility that can perform many tasks. You can perform some of these tasks, such as renaming, copying, or deleting files, easily with DOS commands. For others, like setting the rights mask for a directory, it's your only option. For the sake of giving you a complete overview, all of FILER's uses are covered, but feel free to skip over those tasks that you don't need to do or that you have other ways to accomplish.

To use FILER to change file attributes or to rename a file, you must have the MODIFY right to the directory that stores the files. To change information about a file or directory (such as the owner or the creation date) you must have supervisory access.

Log into the server that stores the files and directories with which you want to work. Type

FILER

from the command line and press Enter. (Because it is stored in SYS:PUBLIC, which is by default a search directory, you don't have to worry about moving to the SYS:PUBLIC directory first). FILER's main menu (see fig. 12.1) appears. FILER uses the same function keys as SYSCON and all other NetWare menu utilities.

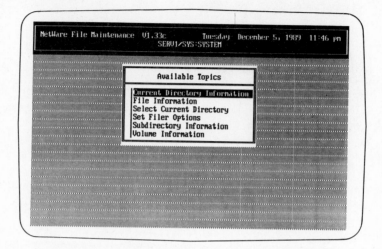

Fig. 12.1.
The FILER main menu.

Selecting the Current Directory

Your first step when using FILER is to choose the directory with which you want to work. To do so, choose Select Current Directory from the FILER main menu and press Enter. An entry box called Destination Directory opens, showing the full NetWare name for the current directory.

Use the Backspace key to backspace over as much of the name as you need to discard and enter the name of the directory you want to make current. For example, if the current directory is SERV1/SYS:SOFTWARE\WORDPERF and you want to switch to SERV1/SYS:SOFTWARE\DBASE, backspace over WORDPERF and type *dbase* so that the directory name is SERV1/SYS:SOFTWARE\DBASE.

If you are not sure of the correct directory name, you can build it one part at a time. Backspace over the entire name in the box and press Ins. A list of the servers you are attached to appears in the File Servers/Local Drives box. Select the server that contains the directory with which you want to work and press Enter. If the server you need is not on the list, you are not attached to it. Press Ins and a list of all other servers appears; select the correct server and press Enter. You are prompted to enter a login name and password. You then are attached to the server, and NetWare adds that name to the list of servers in the File Servers/Local

Drives box. Highlight that server and press Enter. That server's name is listed in the Destination Directory box.

A list of volumes on the server you selected appears on-screen. Select the one containing the directory with which you plan to work and press Enter.

NetWare adds the name of this volume to the Destination Directory box after the server name. A list of directories on that volume appears on-screen. Choose the one you want to work with and press Enter, and its name appears in the Destination Directory box. You also see the subdirectories under that directory (if any). Select a subdirectory and press Enter (you may need to repeat this process several times if you need to select a subdirectory that is several levels deep).

When the correct name of the directory that you want to work with appears in the Destination Directory box, press Enter. You return to the FILER main menu, and the top of the screen is updated to show the directory you have selected.

Setting FILER's Default Options

After you choose the correct current directory, you may want to set options that govern how FILER lists files and directories. For example, if you are working with a directory that has many files, you may want to tell FILER to show only files that match a certain name pattern (for example, *.EXE).

To set this and other Filer defaults, select Set Filer Options from the main menu and press Enter. Note, however, that the changes you make with this command are temporary. They only last as long as your current session. When you run FILER again, the program resets all options to their default settings.

When you choose Set Filer Options, a menu called Filer Options Settings appears with the following selections:

    Confirm Deletions
    Confirm File Copies
    Confirm File Overwrites
    Directories Exclude Pattern
    Directories Include Pattern
    File Exclude Pattern
    File Include Pattern
    File Search Attributes
    Directory Search Attributes (NetWare 386 only)

Setting Confirmation Options

The first three options control how FILER asks you to confirm your choices when you delete, copy, or overwrite files. If you plan to use FILER to mark and delete groups of files, you are normally prompted to confirm your choice only once—just before FILER begins deleting the files you have marked. If you prefer to be prompted for confirmation before each file is deleted, select the Confirm Deletions option and press Y to change the default to yes.

The Confirm File Copies option controls how FILER prompts you for confirmation when you mark multiple files to be copied. Why this option is listed is one of NetWare's great mysteries, because you cannot use FILER to mark and copy multiple files simultaneously.

The Confirm File Overwrites option is a little more useful. When you use FILER to copy a file to another directory, FILER checks to see if a file by the same name exists. If one does exist, a prompt appears asking you to confirm that you want to overwrite that file. If you don't want to be bothered by this confirmation request, select the Confirm File Overwrites option and press N to change its setting to no.

Specifying File and Directory Names To Include and Exclude

When you use FILER to list the files or subdirectories under the current directory, it lists all of them by default. If you want to limit this list to show only directories or files with names that fit a certain pattern, you can use the Directories Exclude Pattern, Directories Include Pattern, File Exclude Pattern, and File Include Pattern options to enter the name patterns to exclude and include.

If you are working in the directory SYS:USERS and want to list only subdirectories whose names start with A, B, C, and D, select the Directories Include Pattern option and press Enter. (For NetWare 286's FILER, you select a menu option; for NetWare 386's FILER, you highlight the words See list, next to Include Directory Patterns, and press Enter. The Include Directory Patterns window appears. It contains one entry that consists of an asterisk (*), indicating that all subdirectories should be listed. Because you don't want to list all subdirectories, you first should delete this entry. Highlight it and press Del to remove it. Next press Ins, and a prompt appears asking you to enter a new pattern. Type *a** and press Enter. Press Ins again and enter *b**, and repeat the process for *c** and *d**.

You also can change a pattern by highlighting it and pressing Enter. A box opens showing the pattern; you can backspace over it and make changes to it. You can delete a pattern by highlighting it and pressing Del, or you can mark more than one pattern with F5, and then press Del to remove them. When the list of patterns is the way you want it, press Esc. That pattern remains in effect until you change it or exit FILER.

The steps to set up an exclude pattern are identical. When an exclude and include pattern overlap, the exclude pattern takes precedence. In the preceding example where you included directories beginning with A, B, C, and D, you could exclude the subdirectories BUBBADOC and BUBBAGAM by entering an exclude pattern of BU*.

Including and Excluding by Attribute

By default, FILER does not show files that have the HIDDEN and SYSTEM attributes turned on. You can specify that it show these files by selecting the File Search Attributes option on the FILER Options Settings menu. An empty box called Search File Attributes appears. Press Ins to list the two attributes that you can add (HIDDEN and SYSTEM). Highlight the one you want to add and press Enter, or mark both of them with F5 and press Enter. NetWare then adds your selection to the list.

To remove an attribute from the list, highlight it and press Del, or mark both (if two are listed) and press Del. NetWare removes your selection from the list. When the list shows the file attributes that you want to include, press Esc. FILER's file listing commands show the files with the attributes you select until you change this setting or exit FILER.

With NetWare 386, the FILER Options Settings menu offers a similar option called Directory Search Attributes to enable you to choose whether to view directories where the HIDDEN and SYSTEM attributes have been turned on. Follow the same steps described for the File Search Attributes option.

Viewing and Changing Current Directory Information

You can use FILER to view and change a number of items for your chosen directory by using the Current Directory Information option. Highlight the Current Directory Information option and press Enter.

The FILER utilities for NetWare 286 and NetWare 386 display the current directory information in differing formats. With NetWare 286's FILER, you choose which information which you want to view from the menu shown in figure 12.2. With NetWare 386's FILER, the information is shown on one screen (see fig. 12.3). The following instructions presume that you are using NetWare 286's FILER. If you are using NetWare 386's FILER, you do not have to choose the menu option to view an information item—it will already be on-screen.

The Current Directory Information menu enables you to work with five items of information about the current directory: the creation date, the current effective rights, the maximum rights mask, the owner, and the directory trustees.

Fig. 12.2.

The FILER Current Directory Information menu.

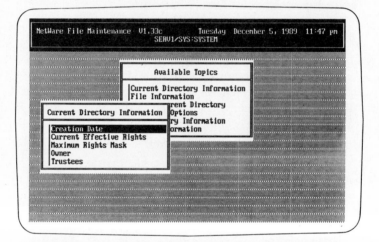

```
NetWare File Maintenance  V1.33c        Tuesday  December 5, 1989  11:47 pm
                         SERV1/SYS:SYSTEM

                              ┌─────────────────────────┐
                              │     Available Topics     │
                              ├─────────────────────────┤
                              │ Current Directory Information
                              │ File Information
                     ┌────────────────────────┤ rent Directory
                     │ Current Directory Information │ Options
                     ├────────────────────────┤ ry Information
                     │ Creation Date          │ ormation
                     │ Current Effective Rights
                     │ Maximum Rights Mask
                     │ Owner
                     │ Trustees
                     └────────────────────────┘
```

Fig. 12.3.

Using the NetWare 386 FILER utilities.

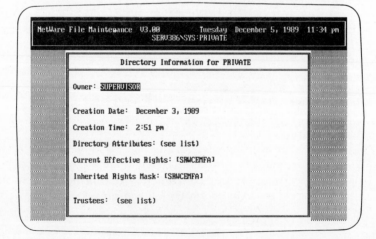

```
NetWare File Maintenance  V3.00         Tuesday  December 5, 1989  11:34 pm
                         SERV386\SYS:PRIVATE

              ┌──────────────────────────────────────────┐
              │     Directory Information for PRIVATE      │
              ├──────────────────────────────────────────┤
              │  Owner:  SUPERVISOR
              │
              │  Creation Date:  December 3, 1989
              │
              │  Creation Time:  2:51 pm
              │
              │  Directory Attributes: (see list)
              │
              │  Current Effective Rights: [SRWCEMFA]
              │
              │  Inherited Rights Mask: [SRWCEMFA]
              │
              │
              │  Trustees:  (see list)
              └──────────────────────────────────────────┘
```

The Creation Date

To see the directory's creation date, highlight Creation Date from this menu and press Enter. A box opens showing the current creation date. There are not many good reasons to change the creation date of a directory, but if you want to do so, you can backspace over the date shown and type the date of your choice. Press Enter to return to the Current Directory Information menu.

Viewing Your Effective Rights

The next menu option is Current Effective Rights. Your effective rights to a directory are the lowest combination of your trustee rights and the directory's rights mask. To view your effective rights for the current directory, highlight Effective Rights and press Enter. After viewing your rights, press Esc to return to the Current Directory Information menu.

You already have learned about the Maximum Rights Mask option in a previous chapter.

Viewing or Changing the Directory's Owner

When you create a directory, NetWare records the login name of the user who created it. If you are the network supervisor and you need to track the person responsible for creating a directory, you can view this information using the Owner option. Highlight this option and press Enter. The login name of the owner is displayed. You can change this information if you need to by pressing Ins. A list of the login names for the server that contains the directory appears on-screen. Select the name you want to use by highlighting it and pressing Enter. The name you selected appears in the box. Press Esc to return to the Current Directory Information menu.

Working with the Directory's Attributes

NetWare 386's FILER adds an additional option: Directory Attributes. Highlight this option and press Enter, and the directory's current attributes are listed. To turn on an additional attribute, press Ins, and you see a list of available attributes. Highlight the one you want to add and press Enter, or mark multiple attributes with F5 and press Enter. The directory's attribute list is updated to show your additions. You can turn off an attribute by highlighting it and pressing Del, or mark multiple attributes with F5 and press Del. When you have finished working with the directory attributes, press Esc to return to the Directory Information screen.

Viewing and Changing the Directory's Trustees

The final option on the Current Directory Information menu is Trustees. You have already learned how to use SYSCON to add a user or group as a trustee to a directory. FILER offers an alternate way to do the same thing (remember that you must have the Parental or Access Control right or be a supervisory-level or workgroup manager user to give other users rights to use a directory). If you need to give a user rights to use the current directory, highlight the Trustees option and press Enter. A list of the current directory trustees appears. Press Ins to display a list of all other users and groups on the server, and highlight the user or group you want to add and press Enter. You can add multiple users or groups by marking them with F5 and pressing Enter. NetWare updates the list of trustees to show the users and groups you have added.

You also can delete users and groups from the trustee list. Highlight the name you want to remove and press Del, or mark more than one name with F5 and press Del. NetWare removes the names you selected.

The rights that a particular user or group has to the directory appear next to the user or group name. To add or remove rights, highlight the user or group's name and press Enter. A box opens showing the rights currently granted. To remove rights from this list, highlight the one you want to remove and press Del, or mark more than one with F5 and press Del. NetWare removes the rights you selected from the list of granted rights. To add rights, press Ins. A list of rights not granted appears on-screen. Highlight the right you want to add and press Enter, or mark more than one right with F5 and press Enter. The right or rights you selected are added to the list of granted rights. When you finish selecting rights to add or remove, press Esc to save your changes and return to the list of directory trustees. When you finish working with this list, press Esc to return to the Current Directory Information menu. Although you can view the Trustee rights of groups and individual users with SYSCON, you must use the Trustee option in FILER to get a list of all users and groups who have rights to a directory.

When you finish working with the Current Directory Information menu, press Esc. You are returned to the FILER main menu.

Working with Files in the Current Directory

FILER enables you to do almost anything with the files in the currently selected directory (provided that you have sufficient rights). If you are using NetWare 286's FILER utility, select File Information from the main menu and press Enter to work with the files in the current directory. An alphabetized list of files in the current directory appears on-screen. If you are using NetWare 386's FILER, select Directory Contents from the main menu. You see a list of the current directory's files and subdirectories.

Working with this list of files is very similar to working with the list of login names using the SYSCON utility. To delete a file, highlight it and press Del. To delete a group of files, mark them with F5 and press Del. You also can rename a file by highlighting it and pressing F3. A box appears showing the file's name. Backspace over the current name and type the name that you want to use. Press Enter, and the file name changes and the file list is updated (remember that you must have the MODIFY right to change the file's name).

To work with a particular file, highlight its name and press Enter. A menu appears (called File Information for NetWare 286's FILER, and File Options for NetWare 386's FILER). The options on these menus enable you to view and change the file's attribute settings, creation and modification dates, and owner name. You also can copy the file to another directory or view its contents. With NetWare 386, you also can modify the file's inherited rights mask.

Working with a File's Attributes

After you have selected a file to work with, you can view and change its attributes. With NetWare 286's FILER utility, select Attributes from the File Information menu, and a box opens showing the attributes that are turned on for the currently selected file. To see the same information with NetWare 386's FILER utility, choose View/Set File Information from the File Options menu, and the File Information window opens (see figure 12.4). The file's attributes (using NetWare 386's attribute abbreviations) are displayed next to Attributes. Highlight this attribute list and press Enter, and a box opens listing the attributes by name.

To turn on additional attributes, press Ins, and a list of attributes that can be added appears on-screen. Highlight the one you want to add to the list, or highlight more than one with F5, and press Enter to update the list of attribute settings with your selections.

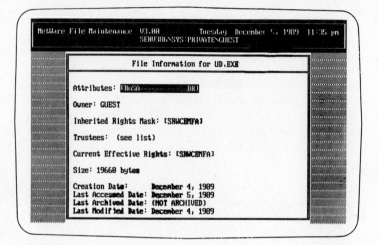

Fig. 12.4.
NetWare 386 FILER's
File Information
window.

You should add certain attributes with caution. If the file you are working with is an executable file (with a COM or EXE extension) and you have supervisory-level access, one of the attributes you can turn on is EXECUTE ONLY. This makes the file impossible to copy. After you set this attribute, you cannot remove it. Your only alternatives are to copy over the file or delete it.

Adding the HIDDEN or SYSTEM file attribute makes the file invisible to most commands and programs. Make sure that the programs that use the file that you hide can still work with it when it is hidden.

Deleting an attribute setting is simply a matter of highlighting it on the File Attribute list and pressing Del. You also can delete multiple attributes simultaneously by marking them with F5 and pressing Del.

When you finish working with the file's attributes, press Esc to return to the File Information screen.

Viewing Information about a File

You can view several items of information about the selected file; if you are logged in with supervisory access, you also can change this information.

With both NetWare 286 and NetWare 386, you can view and change the following file information items:

Creation Date	Date the file was created
Last Accessed Date	Date the file was last used
Last Archived Date	Date the file was last backed up and the ARCHIVE attribute was turned off
Last Modified Date	Date the file was last written to
Owner	Usually the user who created the file
Size	The size of the file in bytes

To view one of these options when using NetWare 286's FILER, highlight it from the File Information menu and press Enter. When using NetWare 386's FILER, choose View/Set File Information from the File Options menu. In either case, you then see the current information on-screen. If you have supervisory access, you can change that information. For the date information items, you simply backspace over the old date and replace it with a new one. To change the owner information, press Ins to see a list of login names on the server. Select the one you want to use and press Enter. NetWare updates the file's owner information with your selection.

You can check the file's size by choosing the Size option. Because this information is taken from the actual byte size of the file, you cannot change it.

Using NetWare 386's FILER To Work with the File's Trustee Rights and Rights Mask

With NetWare 386, you can work with three additional file information items:

Inherited Rights Mask	The rights inherited from the directory's rights mask
Trustees	The users with rights to the file
Current Effective Rights	Your actual access rights to the file (a combination of the trustee rights and the rights mask)

You cannot change the Current Effective Rights setting, but you can modify either the Inherited Rights Mask or Trustees option.

To work with the file's trustees, move highlight to the Trustees option and press Enter. A list of the file's current trustees appears. To add a new trustee, press Ins to display a list of all other users and groups on the server and highlight the user or group you want to add and press Enter. You can add multiple users or groups by marking them with F5 and then pressing Enter. The list of trustees is updated to show the users and groups you have added.

You can delete users and groups from the trustee list by using a similar process. Highlight the name you want to remove and press Del, or mark more than one name with F5 and press Del. The names you selected are removed from the list.

The rights that a particular user or group has to the file are shown next to the user or group name. (For complete information about rights, refer to the preceding chapter). If you want to add or remove rights, highlight the user's or group's name and press Enter. A box opens showing the rights currently granted. To remove rights from this list, highlight the one you want to remove and press Del, or mark more than one with F5 and press Del. To add rights, press Ins. A list of rights not granted appears. Highlight the right you want to add and press Enter, or mark more than one right with F5 and press Enter. When you are finished selecting rights to add or remove, press ESC to save your changes. The list of directory trustees comes back on-screen. When you are finished working with this list, press Esc to return to the Current Directory Information menu.

You learned about changing a file's inherited rights mask in the preceding chapter.

When you have finished working with the file's rights information, press Esc to return to the File Information window. Press Esc again to return to the File Options menu.

NetWare 386's FILER provides one other option for viewing a list of users and groups with rights to the currently selected file. From the File Options menu, select Who Has Rights Here. A list appears showing the users and groups who have rights and the rights they have. This screen enables you only to view this information; you cannot use it to change the list of users and groups or to change any user's or group's rights. Press Esc when you are finished viewing this screen, and the File Options menu returns to the screen.

Viewing a File's Contents

You can view the currently selected file's contents by selecting View File from the File Information menu (NetWare 286) or the File Options menu (NetWare 386). The file is displayed as ASCII text. Program files (files ending in COM and EXE) as well as control characters in word processing, database, and spreadsheet files are not displayed. You can scroll through the file using the arrow keys as well as PgUp or PgDn. With NetWare 286's FILER, you also can move directly to a particular location of the file (if you know the position in bytes) by pressing F3. A prompt asks you to enter the byte number to where you want to go. Enter the correct byte number and press Enter, and that position in the file is displayed. When you finish viewing the file, press Esc to return to the File Information menu or File Options menu.

Copying or Moving a File

You can copy the selected file to another directory by selecting the Copy File option (from the File Information menu for NetWare 286's FILER or the File Options menu for NetWare 386's FILER). Highlight this option and press Enter. A box called Destination Directory appears. If you know the name of the directory to which you want to copy the file, enter it into the entry box. If you aren't sure, you can build the name in the box one step at a time using exactly the same method you used to select the current directory (see the previous section called "Selecting the Current Directory"). After the name is properly listed, press Enter. You see an entry box called Destination File Name listing the current name of the file. If you want to change the name, backspace over it and type the name you want to use and then press Enter. To retain the name, simply press Enter. The file is copied and you again see the File Information menu. You must have enough rights in both the source and destination directories to successfully copy a file.

With NetWare 386, you can move a file by using a similar technique. Moving a file differs from copying a file because when you move the file, the file is deleted from its original location after being placed in its destination directory. To move the currently selected file, select Move File from the File Options menu.

When you finish working with the selected file, press Esc to return to the file list. If you are finished working with files, press Esc again to return to FILER's main menu.

Working with Multiple Files

NetWare 286's FILER enables you to change the attribute settings, date information, and owner for multiple files simultaneously. From FILER's main menu, select File Information. From the list of files that appears, mark the files with which you want to work by pressing F5, and then press Enter. The Multiple File Operations menu appears. Select the operation you want to perform (Set Attributes, Set Creation Date, Set Last Accessed Date, Set Last Modified Date, or Set Owner) and press Enter. If you choose Set Attributes, a prompt appears asking you to select from the available attributes by highlighting or marking them with F5 and pressing Enter. To change one of the date settings, enter the date you want to use at the prompt. To set a new owner, press Ins when prompted to enter the new owner name, and a list of users on the server is displayed. Select the name you want to use and press Enter.

NetWare 386's FILER enables you to perform all the above operations and adds a few additional ones. To work with multiple files when using NetWare 386's FILER, select Directory Contents from FILER's main menu. A list of the currently selected directory's files and subdirectories appears. Use the F5 key to mark the files you want to work with (take care not to mark subdirectories; you must mark only files to perform multiple file operations). Press Enter, and the Multiple File Operations menu appears. In addition to the options available from NetWare 286's FILER described in the preceding paragraph, you also can copy the selected files or set their inherited rights masks. Using these options is just like using their counterparts when you perform the same operation on a single file.

When you are finished working with the Multiple File Operations Menu, press Esc to return to FILER's file or directory contents listing.

Renaming Multiple Files

From the file list, you also can rename a group of files. You can mark each file manually by highlighting each one and pressing F5, or you can press F6 to mark files that fit a certain pattern (such as C*.* or *.BAK). The files that match the pattern you entered are marked. If you know that there are certain files that have been marked that you do not want to rename, you can unmark them manually by highlighting them and pressing F5, or you can unmark files that fit a certain pattern by pressing F8 (you are prompted to enter an Unmark Pattern). The files that match the mark and unmark patterns are then unmarked.

After the appropriate files are marked, you can rename them by pressing F3. A prompt asks you to enter the Original Name Pattern (that is, the pattern to rename from, such as *.BAK or C*.*). Next, a prompt tells you to enter the Rename Pattern (the pattern to change to). The file names change when you type this pattern and press Enter.

Working with Subdirectories

Using FILER to work with subdirectories is similar to working with the current directory information. You can view (and change, if you are the supervisor) information about each subdirectory.

To work with subdirectories with NetWare 286's FILER, select Subdirectory Information from FILER's main menu. A list of all the subdirectories under the current directory appears. With NetWare 386's FILER, select Current Directory Contents from the main menu. A list of the current directory's files and subdirectories appears. From this list you can rename, create, or delete directories in much the same way that you worked with the list of user names in SYSCON. To create a new subdirectory, press Ins; at the prompt that appears, enter the name of the subdirectory you want to create.

Press Enter to create the new subdirectory. To rename a subdirectory, highlight it and press F3. Enter the new name you want to use at the prompt that appears. The directory is now renamed.

Deleting Multiple Subdirectories

An especially handy (although potentially dangerous) feature of FILER is its ability to delete multiple subdirectories in one step. The DOS and OS/2 RD (REMOVE DIRECTORY) commands require you to empty a directory of all its files and subdirectories before you remove it. This can be a tedious process if you are working with a complex directory structure with many layers of subdirectories. FILER makes it easy. To delete a subdirectory as well as all of its files and subdirectories in one operation, highlight its name in the subdirectory list and press Del. A prompt asks you whether you want to delete the entire subdirectory structure (all files, lower subdirectories and the subdirectory itself) or just the files in the subdirectory you have selected. Select the operation you want to perform and press Enter. If you selected the option to delete the entire subdirectory structure, FILER then begins to delete every file and subdirectory under the subdirectory you selected (which can take a few minutes if it contains many files). If FILER encounters a READ ONLY file during the delete operation, it pauses and asks you to confirm that you want to delete it (if you answer yes, the file is deleted). You can perform the same type of deletion operation on multiple subdirectories simultaneously by marking them with F5 and then pressing Del. Use this option carefully; deleting the wrong subdirectory is not a reversible process and results in a test of the integrity of your backup method.

Working with Subdirectory Information

Besides renaming, creating, and deleting subdirectories, NetWare 286's FILER also enables you to work with the subdirectory's rights, owner, and creation date information. Highlight the subdirectory that you want to work with and press Enter. The Subdirectory Information menu appears.

When you select a subdirectory with NetWare 386's FILER, the Subdirectory Options menu appears (see fig. 12.5). To work with the subdirectory's information items, select View/Set Directory Information. A window showing information about the subdirectory appears (see fig. 12.6).

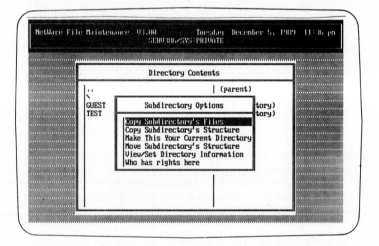

Fig. 12.5.
The Subdirectory Options menu.

The following instructions presume that you are using NetWare 286's FILER, which requires that you select a menu option to view each item. With NetWare 386's FILER, these items are displayed on the window displayed in figure 12.6.

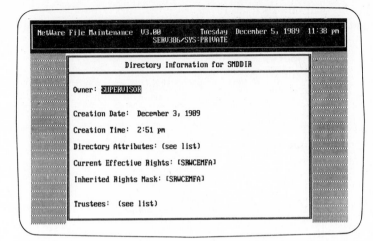

```
NetWare File Maintenance  V3.00        Tuesday  December 5, 1989  11:38 pm
                          SERV386/SYS:PRIVATE

            ┌──────────────────────────────────────────────┐
            │        Directory Information for SMDDIR        │
            │                                                │
            │  Owner: SUPERVISOR                             │
            │                                                │
            │  Creation Date:  December 3, 1989              │
            │                                                │
            │  Creation Time:  2:51 pm                       │
            │  Directory Attributes: (see list)             │
            │  Current Effective Rights: [SRWCEMFA]          │
            │  Inherited Rights Mask: [SRWCEMFA]             │
            │                                                │
            │  Trustees:  (see list)                         │
            │                                                │
            └──────────────────────────────────────────────┘
```

Fig. 12.6.
Viewing subdirectory information.

To view or change the subdirectory's creation date, highlight Creation Date and press Enter to see the current creation date of the directory. If you want to change this date, backspace over the old date and type the date of your choice. The date changes after you press Enter.

The next option on the Subdirectory Information menu is the Rights Mask option.

To find out who is listed as the subdirectory owner, highlight the Owner option and press Enter. The login name of the owner appears on-screen. You can change this information by pressing Ins. A list of the login names for the server that contains the directory is displayed. Highlight the name you want to use and press Enter. The name you selected now appears in the box. Press Esc to return to the Subdirectory Information menu.

Working with the Subdirectory's Trustee List

The last option on the Subdirectory Information menu is Trustees. You already know how to use SYSCON to add a user or group as a trustee to a subdirectory and how to use FILER to add users to the current directory. If you need to give a user rights to use the selected subdirectory, highlight this option and press Enter to see a list of the current subdirectory trustees. Press Ins to display a list of all other users and groups on the server, highlight the user or group you want to add and press Enter. You can add multiple users or groups by marking them with F5 and pressing Enter. The list of trustees is updated to show the users and groups that you added.

You can delete users and groups from the trustee list using a similar process. Highlight the name you want to remove and press Del, or mark more than one name with F5 and press Del. NetWare removes the names you select.

The rights that a particular user or group has to the directory appear next to the user or group name. If you want to add or remove rights, highlight the user's or group's name and press Enter. A box opens showing the rights currently granted. To remove rights from this list, highlight the one you want to remove and press Del, or mark more than one with F5 and press Del. NetWare removes the rights you selected from the list of granted rights. To add rights, press Ins. A list of rights not granted appears. Highlight the right you want to add and press Enter, or mark more than one right with F5 and press Enter. NetWare adds the right or rights you selected to the list of granted rights. When you finish selecting rights to add or remove, press Esc to save your changes. You are then returned to the list of directory trustees. When you finish working with this list, press Esc to return to the Current Directory Information menu.

Viewing the list of directory trustees is especially important for systems managers. Although SYSCON enables you to view the rights of one group or user at a time, you cannot view the profile of access rights of all users and groups to a particular directory.

By viewing the trustee rights of a directory in FILER, the system manager can see the complete picture of access rights to any directory, with the following important exception: users and groups who have access rights to a parent directory have by default the same rights to all subdirectories of the parent directory. For example, if you have R O S rights to the PROGRAMS directory, then you also have R O S rights to subdirectories of PROGRAMS, such as \PROGRAMS\WP and \PROGRAMS\EXCEL, unless more restrictive rights have been set up explicitly for those subdirectories. When looking at the trustee rights of a directory in FILER, the system manager does not see the names of users and groups who have not been given explicit rights to that directory but who nevertheless have access rights because of their rights in a parent directory.

The NetWare 386 FILER provides one other option for viewing a list of users and groups who have rights to the currently selected subdirectory. From the Directory Options menu select Who Has Rights Here. A list appears showing the users and groups who have rights and the rights they have. This screen enables you only to view this information; you cannot use it to change the list of users and groups or to change any user's or group's rights. Press Esc when you are finished viewing this screen, and the Directory Options menu returns to the screen.

Copying or Moving a Subdirectory with NetWare 386's FILER

NetWare 386's FILER adds a useful feature to its Directory Options menu: the ability to copy or move a subdirectory. To copy the current subdirectory's files into another existing directory, select Copy Subdirectory's Files from the Directory Options menu. A prompt tells you to enter the destination directory for the files. After you enter the destination directory, NetWare copies the files.

You also can copy the subdirectory's structure (all its files, the subdirectories under it, and all the files those subdirectories contain). Select Copy Subdirectory's Structure from the Directory Options menu and a prompt asks you to enter the destination directory for the structure. After you enter the destination directory, NetWare copies the subdirectory, its files, its subdirectories, and the files in those subdirectories.

You also have the option of moving the subdirectory's structure (all its files, the subdirectories under it, and all the files those subdirectories contain). *Moving* a subdirectory structure differs from *copying* a subdirectory's structure in that the subdirectory structure is deleted from its original location after being placed under its destination directory. Select Move Subdirectory's Structure from the Directory Options menu and you are prompted to enter the destination directory for the structure. After you enter the destination directory, NetWare moves the subdirectory and its files, subdirectories, and the files in those subdirectories.

When you finish working with the Subdirectory Information menu (NetWare 286 FILER), or Directory Options (NetWare 386 FILER), press Esc. You then are returned to the list of subdirectories. If you are finished working with subdirectories, press Esc again to return to FILER's main menu.

Working with Multiple Subdirectories

FILER lets you change the creation date, owner information, and rights mask for multiple subdirectories simultaneously. You also can rename subdirectories in groups, and with NetWare 386's FILER, you can copy multiple subdirectories in one step. From FILER's main menu, select Subdirectory Information (NetWare 286 FILER) or Directory Options (NetWare 386 FILER). From the list of subdirectories that appears, mark the ones with which you want to work by pressing F5 and then Enter. The Multiple Subdirectory Operations menu appears. Select the operation you want to perform and press Enter. When you are finished working with the group of subdirectories you have marked, press Esc to return to the subdirectory list. To stop working with the subdirectory list, press Esc again to return to the FILER main menu.

Volume Information

Volume Information is the last option on FILER's main menu. This is an information-only option; you do not use it to modify any file or subdirectory settings. When you select this option and press Enter, you see the Volume Information screen (see fig. 12.7). The screen displays the server and volume name, the volume type (fixed or removable; a *removable* volume is a device that uses interchangeable disk platters), the total capacity of the volume in bytes, the number of bytes still available, the maximum number of directory entries, and the number of available entries.

Fig. 12.7.
The FILER Volume Information screen.

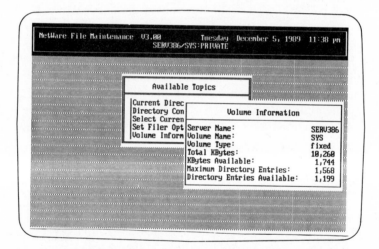

```
NetWare File Maintenance  V3.00          Tuesday  December 5, 1989  11:38 pm
                         SERV386/SYS:PRIVATE

                    ┌─────────────────────────┐
                    │    Available Topics     │
                    ├──────────────┬──────────┴──────────────────────┐
                    │Current Direc │                                  │
                    │Directory Con │      Volume Information          │
                    │Select Curren ├─────────────────────────────────┤
                    │Set Filer Opt │Server Name:              SERV386 │
                    │Volume Inform │Volume Name:              SYS     │
                    │              │Volume Type:              fixed   │
                    │              │Total KBytes:             10,260  │
                    │              │KBytes Available:         1,744   │
                    │              │Maximum Directory Entries: 1,568  │
                    │              │Directory Entries Available: 1,199│
                    └──────────────┴─────────────────────────────────┘
```

File and Directory Commands

Eight other NetWare commands can help you manage files and directories: HIDEFILE, SHOWFILE, DSPACE, PURGE, SALVAGE, NCOPY, NDIR, LISTDIR, and SMODE. With the possible exception of PURGE and SALVAGE, none of these are essential, but all are useful tools that give you more efficiency in managing files and getting information.

HIDEFILE and SHOWFILE (NetWare 286 Only)

As you probably can guess from their names, HIDEFILE and SHOWFILE are NetWare 286 commands that enable you to make files hidden and to list files that are already hidden. They are for the exclusive use of the supervisor, and are stored in the SYS:SYSTEM directory instead of the SYS:PUBLIC directory. HIDEFILE hides files by turning on the HIDDEN and SYSTEM attributes. SHOWFILE lists these files and reverses what HIDEFILE does: it turns off the HIDDEN and SYSTEM attributes.

To use HIDEFILE, log in with supervisory access and make the SYS:SYSTEM directory the default. Then type *hidefile* followed by the complete NetWare name of the file you want to hide. For example, if you need to hide the file PAYROLL.DAT in the accounting directory on the SYS2 volume of SERV1, type

    HIDEFILE SERV1/SYS:ACCTING\PAYROLL.DAT

from the SYS:SYSTEM directory, and press Enter.

You also can use wild-card characters; to hide all the files with the extension DAT, type

    HIDEFILE SERV1/SYS:ACCTING*.DAT

and press Enter. Using SHOWFILE is just like using HIDEFILE. If you want to make the PAYROLL.DAT file visible, type

    SHOWFILE SERV1/SYS:ACCTING\PAYROLL.DAT

and press Enter. You also can use wild-card characters as in HIDEFILE.

The same rules for shortening directory names that were discussed for FLAG earlier in this chapter apply to HIDEFILE and SHOWFILE.

SALVAGE and PURGE

The NetWare 286 and 386 SALVAGE and PURGE commands differ significantly. With NetWare 286, you can use SALVAGE only to recover the most recent file or group of files that you have deleted. After you log out from a server, you cannot salvage any files that you have deleted.

NetWare 386's SALVAGE is not nearly so limited. Because NetWare 386 retains deleted files until the disk space they occupy must be reused, it is possible to use NetWare 386's SALVAGE command to recover files that were deleted in the fairly distant past.

NetWare 286 SALVAGE and PURGE Commands

To use SALVAGE to recover a file that you deleted from the SYS: volume on server SERV1, type

SALVAGE SERV1/SYS:

and press Enter. If SERV1/SYS: is your default volume, you can simply type

SALVAGE

and press Enter. SALVAGE recovers an erased file provided that you have not logged out from the server before trying to recover the file, have not created or deleted any additional files, or have not used the PURGE command. You also must run SALVAGE from the same workstation that you used to erase the file.

PURGE permanently removes any erased files. When you erase files, you may notice that the disk space used by the file is not released. This is because NetWare keeps the file in case you need to recover it. You can be certain that the disk space is released by typing *purge.*

NetWare 386 SALVAGE and PURGE Commands

The NetWare 386 SALVAGE utility can be used to find and recover files that have been deleted previously. NetWare 386 saves a deleted file for as long as the server volume disk space permits or until a user invokes the PURGE command to remove the file permanently. When the space occupied by deleted files is needed to store new and existing files, deleted files are purged automatically on a first-deleted, first-purged basis.

Deleted files are stored invisibly and can be listed only with the SALVAGE utility. A deleted file is stored in its original directory unless the directory itself has been deleted, in which case the file is placed in a directory called DELETED.SAV. The DELETED.SAV directory has the HIDDEN and SYSTEM attributes turned on, and only users with supervisory equivalence have rights to it.

Using SALVAGE To Recover a Deleted File

To recover a file that you have deleted, change to the directory where that file was stored and start SALVAGE by typing *salvage* and then pressing Enter. SALVAGE's menu appears and offers the following options:

Salvage From Deleted Directories
Select Current Directory
Set Salvage Options
View/Recover Deleted Files

Select View/Recover Deleted Files, and you see a list of the deleted files in the current directory (see fig. 12.8). This list displays each file's name, the date and time it was deleted, its size, and its owner.

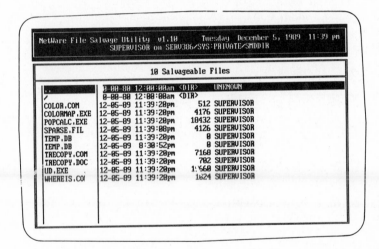

Fig. 12.8.

The NetWare 386 SALVAGE listing of salvageable files.

To recover a file, highlight it and press Enter. You see the date that the file was deleted, the user who deleted it, the date the file was last modified, and the file's owner. The prompt Recover This File appears on-screen. If you respond by selecting yes, the file is recovered.

You can recover multiple files by marking them with F5 and pressing Enter. A prompt tells you to confirm that you want to recover the marked files. If you answer yes, the files are recovered.

While using the file listing screen, you can change the order in which the files are listed. Press F3, and a menu appears offering you the following options:

Sort List by Deletion Date
Sort List by File Size
Sort List by Filename
Sort List by Owner

By selecting one of the options above, you can change the order in which the deleted files are displayed.

Recovering Files from a Deleted Directory

Deleted files normally are stored in the directory in which they originally existed. A special situation arises when a file is erased and then its directory also is deleted. These files are automatically held in a directory called DELETED.SAV on the volume where they originally existed.

Only users with supervisory-level access can recover files from the DELETED.SAV directory. To recover a file that was stored in a deleted directory, select Salvage From Deleted Directories on SALVAGE's main menu. You see a list of the deleted files in the DELETED.SAV directory. This list displays each file's name, the date and time it was deleted, its size, and its owner. To recover a file, highlight it and press Enter. The prompt Recover This File appears on-screen. If you respond by selecting yes, the file is recovered. You can recover multiple files by marking them with F5 and pressing Enter. You can change the sort order for the file list by pressing F3 and selecting a different sort order.

Selecting a Directory To Work with

There are several ways to tell SALVAGE which directory to look in for deleted files. From SALVAGE's main menu, you can choose Select Current Directory, and you are prompted to enter the name of the directory where you want to look for deleted files (as with FILER and SYSCON, you either can type the name, or choose it interactively by pressing the Ins key to first list the available servers, followed by the selected server's volumes, and finally the selected volume's directories).

You also can choose the directory to work with by entering it when you start SALVAGE. For example, to tell SALVAGE to search for deleted files in a directory called SERV2/SYS:OLDFILES, you start SALVAGE by typing

SALVAGE SERV2/SYS:OLDFILES

and pressing Enter. SERV2/SYS:OLDFILES automatically becomes SALVAGE's default directory. The same rules for shortening the directory name apply to SALVAGE as apply to FLAG and MAP.

Changing SALVAGE's Default Listing Order

Normally, SALVAGE lists deleted files in name order. You can change this default by selecting Set Salvage Options from the main menu. You are offered four sorting options: Sort List by Deletion Date, Sort List by File Size, Sort List by Filename, and Sort List by Owner. Choose the option that you want to use, and it remains in effect until you leave SALVAGE or select another sorting option.

When you are finished working with SALVAGE, press Esc to exit.

Using PURGE To Remove a File Permanently

Sometimes you want to make sure that a file is erased permanently. You can use the PURGE command to make deleted files unrecoverable. Unless you have supervisory access, you can purge only files that you own (in other words, you are listed as the file's owner).

To purge a file, type *purge* followed by the file name. For example, to purge a file called EXPIRED.DAT in the OLDFILES directory, type

> PURGE SERV2/SYS:OLDFILES\EXPIRED.DAT

and press Enter. The EXPIRED.DAT file is permanently removed and is not recoverable with SALVAGE.

You can purge all the files in a directory by typing *purge* followed by the directory name. For example, to purge all the deleted files in the OLDFILES directory, type

> PURGE SERV2/SYS:OLDFILES

and press Enter. (To shorten the directory name, use the same rules that apply to MAP and FLAG.)

If you want to purge all the files in a particular directory tree structure, follow PURGE with /ALL. For example, to purge all the files in all the directories and subdirectories in the VOL1 volume, on the SERV1 server, you can type

> PURGE SERV1/VOL1: /ALL

and press Enter. Every deleted file on the VOL1 volume is purged.

Purging Files Automatically

As you have read already, you can turn on the PURGE attribute for a file to guarantee that it is purged automatically as soon as it is erased. You can use FLAG or FILER to turn on this attribute.

You also can give directories the PURGE attribute. When a directory's PURGE attribute is turned on, its files are automatically purged as soon as they are erased. You can use FLAGDIR or FILER to turn on a directory's PURGE attribute.

NCOPY

NCOPY is NetWare's high-speed alternative to the COPY command. It is noticeably faster when you are copying files from one disk location on a server to another.

Similar to the COPY command, you use NCOPY by specifying the source directory and file, followed by the destination directory and file name. For example, to NCOPY all the EXE files from SERV1/SYS:ACCTING to SERV1/SYS2:ACCTBACK, type

>   NCOPY SERV1/SYS:ACCTING*.EXE SERV1/SYS2:ACCTBACK

and press Enter. NCOPY is like other NetWare commands when it comes to shortening directory names. If SERV1/SYS:ACCTING is your default directory, you can leave out its name and type

>   NCOPY *.EXE SERV1/SYS2:ACCTBACK

and press Enter. If SERV1/SYS2:ACCTBACK is mapped to drive G, you can further shorten the command by typing

>   NCOPY *.EXE G:

and press Enter. NCOPY provides one shortcut not supplied by the COPY command. You can copy all the files from the default directory on drive F to the default directory on drive G by typing

>   NCOPY F: G:

and pressing Enter. If you want NCOPY to verify the results of the copy by comparing the copied file to the original, you can type /verify or /v after any NCOPY command, such as

>   NCOPY F: G: /verify

and then press Enter. Unlike the DOS COPY command, in which the /v option can follow the target directory specification without a space (COPY *.* \DATA/v), with NCOPY you must insert a space before the /v option (NCOPY *.* \DATA /v).

Extra Features of NetWare 386's NCOPY

The NetWare 386 NCOPY command adds several useful features. You can copy one entire tree structure of subdirectories and files by using the /S parameter. For example, to copy the files in the SYS:SOFTWARE directory and all its subdirectories and the files they contain to the VOL1:BACKUP directory, you type

    NCOPY SYS:SOFTWARE VOL1:BACKUP /S

and press Enter.

When you use the /S option to copy subdirectories, those subdirectories without files or other subdirectories below them are not copied. You can tell NCOPY to copy empty subdirectories by adding the /E parameter to the /S parameter, as shown below:

    NCOPY SYS:SOFTWARE VOL1:BACKUP /S/E

By default, when files are copied, their attributes are not retained. When the duplicate of the copied file is created, it has no attributes turned on. You can specify that NCOPY override this default and turn on the same attributes on the duplicate file by using the /P (for preserve). For example, to copy all the files from SYS:OLDFILES to VOL1:NEWFILES and to duplicate the attribute settings of the original files in the duplicate files, you use the following command:

    NCOPY SYS:OLDFILES*.* VOL1:NEWFILES /P

followed by Enter.

The NetWare 386 NCOPY command automatically verifies the files it copies, so the /V or /VERIFY option is not supported as it is with NetWare 286's NCOPY.

NCOPY for NetWare 386 has a special parameter to force the creation of what are called *sparse files*. A sparse file has one or more disk blocks that are empty. For efficiency's sake, NetWare normally does not actually write the empty disk blocks for sparse files. However, when you copy a sparse file with NCOPY, you can specify that the empty blocks actually be written by following the NCOPY command with the /F (for Force sparse file) parameter, as shown in the following example:

NCOPY SYS:OLDFILES*.* VOL1:NEWFILES /F

NDIR

NDIR is an extremely flexible file- and directory-listing command that enables you to list information selectively, based on almost every NetWare setting.

NDIR lists the following information about files by default: name, extension, size, last updated date, last accessed date, creation date, attribute settings, and owner name. For subdirectories it lists the name, creation date and time, the maximum rights mask, the user's current effective rights, and the directory owner.

NDIR enables you to sort and list files by all the file information items and attributes listed in the explanation of FILER. The syntax for using NDIR is

NDIR directory\filename options

followed by pressing Enter.

If you simply type

NDIR

and press Enter, you see the list of files and subdirectories in your current directory.

You also can specify a particular directory for which NDIR lists the requested information. As with other NetWare commands, you can list the directory name several ways. For example, if the directory SERV1/ SYS:ACCTING\PAYABLES is mapped to drive H and the SYS: volume is your current default volume, you can use NDIR to list its files and subdirectories using any one of the following methods:

NDIR SERV1/SYS:ACCTING\PAYABLES
NDIR SYS:ACCTING\PAYABLES
NDIR \ACCTING\PAYABLES
NDIR H:

Remember to press Enter after each of these commands. The list of options for NDIR is comprehensive. They fall into seven categories:

❏ Listing files only, directories only, the specified directory only, or its entire tree structure

❏ Listing files by name, extension, or a part of either

❏ Listing files by attributes

❏ Listing files by creation, modification, or last archived date

❏ Listing files by owner

❏ Listing files by size

❏ Sorting files by name, size, owner, or date

When you use any of the above options with NDIR, you must specify the name of the directory, even if it is the default (so that NDIR does not try to interpret your option as a directory name).

Listing Files Only or Directories Only

If you want to limit NDIR's output to listing only the files in the directory SERV1/SYS:ACCTING, type

    NDIR SERV1/SYS:ACCTING FO

where FO stands for files only. Press Enter. You can show only subdirectories (and not list files) by typing

    NDIR SERV1/SYS:ACCTING DO

where DO stands for directories only. Press Enter.

If you want to list information for the entire tree structure of subdirectories (all subdirectories and their subdirectories) you can type

    NDIR SERV1/SYS:ACCTING SUB

where SUB stands for subdirectories. Press Enter.

You also can limit the information about each file and subdirectory to only the name and last modified date by typing

    NDIR SERV1/SYS:ACCTING BR

where BR stands for brief. Press Enter. This results in output similar to the DOS or OS/2 DIR command.

Listing by File Name

NDIR enables you to use wild-card designations to specify which files you want to list, just as you do with the DOS or OS/2 DIR command. To list all files beginning with the letter A, type

    NDIR SERV1/SYS:ACCTING\A*.*

and press Enter.

To list all files with the extension EXE, type

    NDIR SERV1/SYS:ACCTING*.EXE

and press Enter.

You can get the same result by using the FILENAME parameter:

    NDIR SERV1/SYS:ACCTING FILENAME=*.EXE

Press Enter.

This by itself isn't very useful, but when used a different way it enables you to specify which files not to list. You can add the word NOT to the command if you want to see every file except those with the EXE extension:

    NDIR SERV1/SYS:ACCTING FILENAME NOT=*.EXE

Press Enter.

Listing by Attribute

NDIR enables you to see files that have a certain attribute turned on or off.

For example, to see all files in your directory that are READ ONLY, type

    NDIR SERV1/SYS:ACCTING RO

and press Enter. As with the FILENAME option discussed in the preceding section, you also can put the word NOT to good use when listing files by attribute. If you want to see all files that do not have the SHAREABLE attribute turned on, type

    NDIR SERV1/SYS:ACCTING NOT SHA

and press Enter.

You can use the following abbreviations to specify file attributes:

NetWare 286		NetWare 386	
H	HIDDEN	H	HIDDEN
M	MODIFIED (ARCHIVED)	A	ARCHIVE NEEDED
EO	EXECUTE ONLY	EX	EXECUTE ONLY
SHA	SHAREABLE	S	SHAREABLE
SY	SYSTEM	SY	SYSTEM
RO	READ ONLY	RO	READ ONLY
RW	READ WRITE	RA	READ AUDIT
I	INDEXED	I	INDEXED
T	TRANSACTIONAL	T	TRANSACTIONAL
		P	PURGE
		WA	WRITE AUDIT

Listing by Date

If you have read this far, you are an expert on the subject of NetWare file dates, and you know that NetWare tracks four dates for each file: the creation date, the date the file was last modified, the date the file was last archived, and the date the file was last accessed. NDIR enables you to view files by three of these dates: the creation date, the last modified date, and the last accessed date.

If you want to see all files accessed on the date 4/15/90, for example, type

    NDIR SERV1/SYS:ACCTING ACCESS = 04-15-90

and press Enter. You also can view all files that have dates before a certain date. To see all files created before 4/15/90, type

    NDIR SERV1/SYS:ACCTING CREATE BEF 04-15-90

and press Enter.

To look at all files created after 4/15/90, type

    NDIR SERV1/SYS:ACCTING CREATE AFT 04-15-90

and press Enter.

You can combine these parameters with the word NOT to view files in a certain date range. For example, if you want to see all files modified during the week from 4/21/90 to 4/28/90, type

NDIR SERV1/SYS:ACCTING UPDATE NOT BEF 04-21-90 NOT AFT 04-28-90

and press Enter.

You can use the following words to build NDIR commands that list files by date:

ACCESS	Specifies last accessed date
CREATE	Specifies creation date
UPDATE	Specifies last modified date
AFT	Lists files *after* a certain date
BEF	Lists files *before* a certain date
=	Lists files with dates equal to a certain date
NOT	Views files in a certain date range. Use with AFT, BEF, or =

Listing by Owner

To list files that have the user Adam as their owner, type

NDIR SERV1/SYS:ACCTING OWNER=ADAM

and press Enter.

You can also use NOT to list all files not owned by a certain user by typing

NDIR SERV1/SYS:ACCTING OWNER NOT=ADAM

and pressing Enter.

Listing by Size

You can use NDIR to list files according to their sizes. For example, to list all files bigger than 1,000,000 bytes, type

NDIR SERV1/SYS:ACCTING SIZE GR 1000000

and press Enter, where GR stands for greater than.

You also can use K for kilobytes or M for megabytes, so you can specify the size in the preceding command as 1M or 1000K.

You also can list files less than a certain size by using LE (for less than), or equal to a certain size by using =. As with most NDIR options, you also can use the word NOT to list files not greater than, not less than, or not equal to the specified size.

Sorting with NDIR

You can tell NDIR to list file information in order by size, name, creation date, last accessed date, or last modified date. You also can specify whether the list should be in ascending or descending order.

To list files in order by name, type

    NDIR SERV1/SYS:ACCTING SORT FILENAME

and press Enter.

To list files in order by size, type

    NDIR SERV1/SYS:ACCTING SORT SIZE

and press Enter.

To list files in order by owner, type

    NDIR SERV1/SYS:ACCTING SORT OWNER

and press Enter.

You can sort by the same three date types that you can list by: the creation date, the last modified date, or the last accessed date. To list files sorted in creation date order, type

    NDIR SERV1/SYS:ACCTING SORT CREATE

and press Enter.

You can use the word ACCESS instead of CREATE to sort by the last accessed date, or, you can use UPDATE to sort by the last modified date.

All sort options list files in ascending order (in alphabetical order for FILENAME and OWNER, earliest to latest for date options, and smallest to largest for SIZE). You can change to descending order by using the word REVERSE. For example, to show files in descending order by size, type

    NDIR SERV1/SYS:ACCTING REVERSE SORT SIZE

and press Enter.

Combining Options

You can combine many of NDIR's options. For example, if you want to search the entire disk volume for files owned by Adam and list them in descending order by size, type

> NDIR SERV1/SYS: OWNER = ADAM REVERSE SORT SIZE SUB

and press Enter.

There are many useful combinations available from NDIR's options.

Printing Results or Sending Results to a File

You can use DOS redirection to send the results of your NDIR request to a file or to a printer. For example, to send output normally shown on the screen to a file named FILEINFO.TXT, type

> NDIR SERV1/SYS:ACCTING SORT FILENAME > FILEINFO.TXT

and press Enter.

To send the output to a printer, type

> NDIR SERV1/SYS:ACCTING SORT FILENAME > PRN

and press Enter.

Getting NDIR Help

Most people have trouble remembering NDIR's options. You can get quick assistance by typing

> NDIR HELP

and pressing Enter.

The help provided is quite brief, but may jog your memory enough to be useful.

NetWare 386 NDIR Menu

With NetWare 386, a menu has been added to NDIR that enables you to choose easily from NDIR's many options. When you type *ndir* without any parameters and press Enter, the menu shown in figure 12.9 appears. Use the up and down arrows to select from the menu's five categories of options: SORT BY, RESTRICTIONS, PATH/FILE, SCREEN FORMAT, and DIRECTORIES. When a particular option is selected, it blinks. You then can use the right and left arrows to choose the setting for that option. After you make a selection for the last option (DIRECTORIES), the NDIR command is executed.

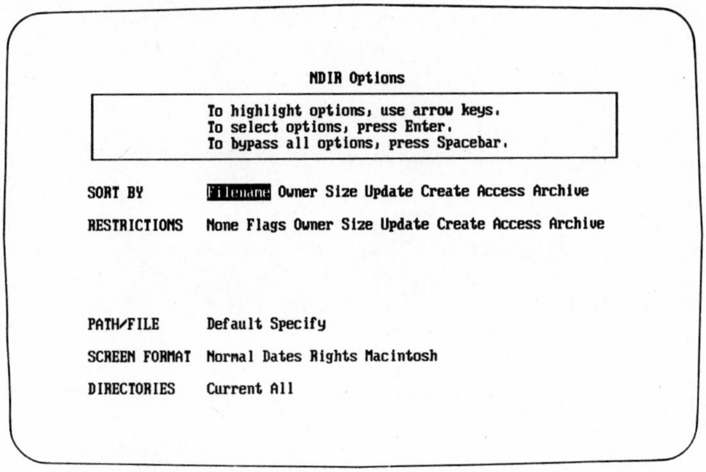

```
                          NDIR Options

              ┌──────────────────────────────────────────┐
              │     To highlight options, use arrow keys. │
              │     To select options, press Enter.       │
              │     To bypass all options, press Spacebar.│
              └──────────────────────────────────────────┘

     SORT BY        Filename Owner Size Update Create Access Archive

     RESTRICTIONS   None Flags Owner Size Update Create Access Archive



     PATH/FILE      Default Specify

     SCREEN FORMAT  Normal Dates Rights Macintosh

     DIRECTORIES    Current All
```

Fig. 12.9.
NetWare 386's NDIR menu.

LISTDIR

LISTDIR shows information about directories and subdirectories. To show the names of all subdirectories in your current directory, type

LISTDIR

and press Enter. You then see an output similar to the following:

```
The sub-directory structure of SERV1/SYS:SOFTWARE/123
   WORDPERF
      PRINT
      MACROS
      GRAPHICS
   DBASE
      TUTORIAL
7 sub-directories found
```

If you want to list the subdirectories under a directory other than the default directory, you can specify it with the LISTDIR command:

LISTDIR SERV1/SYS:ACCTING

Press Enter after typing the command. The normal rules for shortening directory names apply.

Like NDIR, you can use LISTDIR to show additional information about directories and subdirectories. You can use the following parameters with LISTDIR:

/S (Subdirectories)	Lists the entire tree structure (all levels of subdirectories), starting from the current or specified directory; similar to the NDIR's SUB parameter
/R (Rights)	Shows the rights mask for each subdirectory
/D (Date)	Shows the creation date for each subdirectory
/T (Time)	Shows the creation time for each subdirectory
/E (Effective Rights)	For NetWare 386 only; shows your effective rights for each subdirectory (see the preceding chapter for details about effective rights)
/A (All)	Shows the combined information for the preceding parameters

You can use these parameters separately or in combination to list the information desired. For example, to list the maximum rights mask for the entire tree structure under SERV1/SYS:ACCTING, type

LISTDIR SERV1/SYS:ACCTING /S/R

and press Enter.

DSPACE (NetWare 386 Only)

If you have read Chapter 10, you already have learned about using NetWare 386's DSPACE utility to assign a particular user a maximum

amount of disk space on a server (DSPACE is not available with
NetWare 286).

You also can use DSPACE to set a directory's maximum size. This tool is
useful when you need to control the amount of disk space that a particular
application or file library should use. To set a directory's maximum size,
you must have supervisory equivalence.

Start DSPACE by typing *dspace* and pressing Enter. A menu appears with
the following three options:

Change File Server
User Restrictions
Directory Restrictions

Select Directory Restrictions. An entry box opens prompting you to enter
the name of the directory where you want to limit disk space. Your
current directory is shown by default. Press Enter to work with this
directory, or backspace over it and enter the appropriate directory name
(as with FILER and SYSCON, you can either type the name or choose it
interactively by pressing the Ins key first to list the available servers,
followed by the selected server's volumes, and then the selected volume's
directories).

After the correct directory name is shown in the entry box, press Enter.
A window appears (see fig. 12.10).

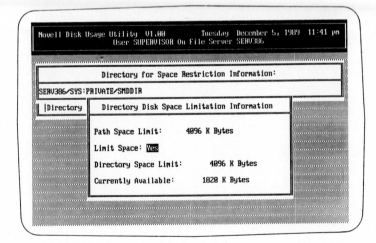

Fig. 12.10.

*The DSPACE disk
space limitation
window.*

If a number is shown next to Path Space Limit, it indicates that a directory above the current one has a disk space limitation. If that is the case, you cannot enter a maximum size greater than this limit.

To set a size limit for the current directory, move the highlight to Limit Space and press Y to change its setting to yes. Next, move the highlight to Directory Space Limit and enter the number of kilobytes that you want to set as the directory's maximum size.

The number next to Currently Available is updated to show the remaining available space in the directory.

When you are finished setting the maximum directory size, press Esc, or press F7 to cancel your changes. An entry box returns to the screen, prompting you to enter the directory you want to work with. Enter another directory name, or press Esc to return to the DSPACE menu. Press Esc to leave DSPACE.

SMODE

SMODE is a specialized NetWare command that is very similar to OS/2's DPATH command. It assigns a search mode to an executable file (executable files end with the EXE or COM extension).

With SMODE, you can control the way that an executable file searches for its data files. To use it effectively, you need to know how the executable file attempts to access its data files. You probably will use it in cases where you are working with the programmer who created the executable file or if you have a detailed knowledge of how the executable file accesses its data files. Table 12.3 shows the search modes you can specify with SMODE.

To use SMODE to view the current search mode of a file, type *smode* followed by the complete file name. For example, type

    SMODE SERV1/SYS:ACCTING\DBPROG.EXE

and press Enter.

You can list the search modes of all executable files in a directory by typing *smode* and the directory name. For example, type

    SMODE SERV1/SYS:ACCTING

and press Enter.

The usual rules for shortening or eliminating directory names apply.

Table 12.3
The SMODE Search Modes

Search Mode	Explanation
0	Use the search mode specified in the SHELL.CFG file (see Chapter 8, "Activating Workstations" for details about SHELL.CFG).
1	If the executable file explicitly searches for the file using a specific directory, it searches that directory only. If no directory is specified, the default is searched first, followed by all search drives.
2	The executable file searches the default directory only.
3	If the executable file explicitly searches for the file using a specific directory, it searches that directory only. If no directory is specified and the executable file opens the data file in READ ONLY mode, the default directory is searched first, followed by all search drives.
4	This number is not used.
5	The executable file searches the default directory and then all search drives regardless of whether a specific directory is specified as the location of the data file.
6	This number is not used.
7	If the executable file opens the data file in READ ONLY, the default directory is searched first, followed by all search drives.

To change the search mode of a file, type *smode* followed by its name and the search mode number you want to use:

SMODE SERV1/SYS:ACCTING\DBPROG.EXE 5

Press Enter.

To set the search mode for all executable files in a directory, use the wild card *.* as shown in the following command:

SMODE SERV1/SYS:ACCTING*.* 5

Press Enter.

Chapter Summary

In this chapter, you learned that NetWare's file-management tools are many and varied. You probably will not use all of them on a regular basis, especially because you also can use almost all the DOS and OS/2 commands to work with server-based files. Although most of NetWare's file-management commands do not represent the only way to accomplish a particular task, they can be useful resources that expand your ability to get information or to work with files and directories quickly and efficiently.

13

Establishing Real-World Security

You have learned about the individual elements of NetWare security (login control, trustee rights, directory rights, and file attributes). You also have learned about NetWare directory structures and the utilities you can use to manage files and directories. Intelligently combining these elements to achieve the right result is the key to building a secure and easy-to-use network.

You must balance two interests:

❏ The needs of the users to access the files on your servers

❏ The need to protect those files from being changed or deleted in the wrong way by the wrong person at the wrong time

Although malicious sabotage is always a possibility, the experience of most network supervisors indicates that when damage occurs, it generally is not because the user intended harm. Instead, the user had more access than he or she should have had and did something wrong through ignorance. When you have done a good job using NetWare's security tools, the user has just the right level of access—no more or no less than needed.

This chapter begins with three real-life situations that illustrate how NetWare's directory and security elements can be combined for just the right level of access. The chapter ends with an inside look at the structure of NetWare's security system and examines several NetWare utilities that work with NetWare's security files.

Using Security in Real Situations

Many network supervisors face the three situations examined in this section. First, you will set up personal directories for your network users. You also will set up a file-sharing pool where word processing users can retrieve documents on a read-only basis. Finally, you will set up the correct type of access for a shared-database application.

Setting Up Personal Directories

On most networks, users are given personal storage areas to use as they please. Users may have workstations that don't have hard disks, so their personal storage areas are the only places available for storing personal files. Even if each user has a hard disk in his or her PC, the personal storage area on the network may still be useful. It may be a convenient place to store files that need to be backed up on a regular basis, because backing up one server disk is much easier than moving a tape unit to each user's PC for a backup.

Naming Each Directory

You need to decide what to name the user directory areas. Your first inclination may be to use a directory name that readily identifies it—JOESDIR or MARYDIR, for example. This method works, but a better way is available. In Chapter 10, "Adding Users," you received the suggestion to give each user a login name beginning with the first six letters of his or her last name and ending with his or her initials. With this system, a user named Frank J. Henderson will have the login name HENDERFJ. Because most NetWare utilities list items such as login names and subdirectories in alphabetical order, when you list login names, they will be alphabetized by last name.

Using the same method to name each user's directory makes sense. When you use FILER to list users' subdirectories, they also will be alphabetized by last name. In Chapter 16, "Creating Login Scripts," you will see how naming each user's personal directory with his or her login name saves you several steps when creating his or her NetWare environment.

Designing the Right Directory Structure

Next, you need to decide how to structure your user directories. Your first inclination may be to create each user directory one level under the root directory. This method results in a directory structure similar to that shown in figure 13.1.

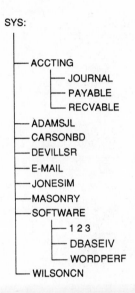

```
SYS:


       ACCTING
              JOURNAL
              PAYABLE
              RECVABLE
       ADAMSJL
       CARSONBD
       DEVILLSR
       E-MAIL
       JONESIM
       MASONRY
       SOFTWARE
              1 2 3
              DBASEIV
              WORDPERF
       WILSONCN
```

Fig. 13.1.

Creating each user directory one level under the root directory.

Structuring your user directories in this way has several disadvantages. First, as you add users and subdirectories to your server, the directory structure becomes cluttered with numerous private directories just under the root. Even more importantly, if you need to run a special tape backup of just the users' personal storage areas, you will have a hard time doing so. Consider figure 13.1. When your tape backup software asks you to specify which directories to back up, you need to enter

\ADAMSJL
\CARSONBD
\DEVILLSR
\JONESIM
\MASONRY
\WILSONCN

and so on. This method works fine if you have only 10 users, but if your list of users grows to 50 or 75, you will find this a cumbersome task.

A better method is to create one directory under the root called \PRIVATE or \USERS and then give each user a personal subdirectory under it. This method results in a structure similar to that shown in figure 13.2. You will be able to back up this area easily by setting your tape backup unit to back up all subdirectories under \PRIVATE, for example.

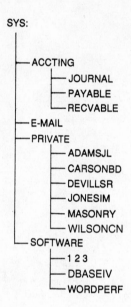

```
SYS:
  |
  |— ACCTING
  |      |— JOURNAL
  |      |— PAYABLE
  |      └— RECVABLE
  |— E-MAIL
  |— PRIVATE
  |      |— ADAMSJL
  |      |— CARSONBD
  |      |— DEVILLSR
  |      |— JONESIM
  |      |— MASONRY
  |      └— WILSONCN
  └— SOFTWARE
         |— 1 2 3
         |— DBASEIV
         └— WORDPERF
```

Fig. 13.2.

Creating one directory under the root and then giving each user a personal subdirectory under that directory.

Assigning Rights

You probably want to give each user all rights to his or her personal directory. Doing so enables the user to use the area as if it were his or her own hard disk. The user can create and delete subdirectories and add, delete, and change files as needed, just as with a personal hard disk.

You do not want to give users rights to each other's directories. If you give NetWare 286's PARENTAL right or NetWare 386's ACCESS CONTROL right, the user actually can give other users access to his or her personal directory if desired.

Restrictions

One danger exists when you give each user his or her own directory on a server disk. Some users may view it as an unlimited storage area where they can dump files without restraint. Before you know it, your file server disk will be full and you will be faced with the unpleasant task of persuading (or ordering) users to delete files. Be prepared to hear some interesting excuses.

An ounce of prevention is worth a pound of cure. To keep users from overrunning your server disk with files, you should use SYSCON to activate the Limit Disk Space account restriction (see the section called "Account Restrictions" in Chapter 10). This practice effectively limits users to the amount of space you decide is best.

You can activate the capacity to limit disk space during the server installation. If it was not activated and you want to activate it retroactively, see Chapter 6.

The strategy for establishing personal storage areas for each user involves choosing a directory-naming method, developing an easy-to-use directory structure, and then assigning the correct rights and account restrictions. When you give a new user a login name by using SYSCON, you can create his or her private directory and give the user all rights to it at the same time. You also can limit the user's disk space in the same step.

Setting Up a File-Sharing Pool

One of the biggest benefits of connecting PCs together in a network is the ability to share access to disk space. Because many users can access the same files, creating systems that share data (such as multiuser database applications, electronic mail, or groupware packages) is possible. Also possible are some simpler types of information sharing that do not require the purchase of specialized software.

The ability to share files can add new power to already useful stand-alone PC applications. Word processing is an important function in most companies. Often one of the best uses of a network is to give a group of PCs the same capability as a powerful (and expensive) multiterminal, dedicated word processing system.

In many businesses, certain types of documents are created over and over again. In a law office, for example, a particular type of contract may be generated on a frequent basis, and the typist simply "fills in the blanks" or adds a few unique paragraphs to each contract, with most of the information remaining the same. An efficient typist will start with a *boilerplate* version of the original document and customize only those parts of the document requiring it.

With a network, you can create a pool of boilerplate documents and make these documents available to many users. This idea isn't limited to a word processing context. Users of spreadsheet programs can work well with a shared pool of templates containing formulas and macros but no data. A user can retrieve a template from the pool, plug in his or her own numbers, and save the results to a new file in the user's personal storage area. The original template file remains in the pool unchanged and ready for the next user.

You can use NetWare's security tools to protect the files in the pool from modification or deletion, and you can give access to only those users who should be able to use the files. You can give increased access to one or two trusted users so that they can add new files or delete from the pool files that are no longer needed.

Creating and Mapping to the Directory

To create a pool of shared files, you first need to create a directory for the pool. The name you decide to use for the directory will depend on what types of files it is storing. You may choose to create a directory and several subdirectories if the categories of files you are storing lend themselves to that scheme. For example, a file pool of contract boilerplate documents may have the directory name CONTRACT with the subdirectories WILLS, DEEDS, INCORP, and so on.

After the directory has been created, users can use the MAP command to assign the directory a drive letter. Suppose, for example, that a user wants to make the directory SYS:CONTRACTS\WILLS his drive G before starting his word processor. The user types

    MAP G: = SERV1/SYS:CONTRACTS\WILLS

and then press Enter. (For complete information about the MAP command, see Chapter 9, "Organizing Information with NetWare.") The user then can start his or her word processor and access the boilerplate files relating to wills by referring to drive G.

Assigning Rights

Choose carefully the rights you give users to a shared file pool. Your objective is to give users the ability to retrieve the files but not change or delete them. You also want the users to be able to use their DOS and OS/2 commands and word processing and spreadsheet programs to list the files in the directory so that they can choose the ones they need to work with. You want to prevent the users from accidentally saving their completed documents or spreadsheets in the shared-file-pool directory so that it doesn't become cluttered with unneeded files.

Can you use NetWare rights to do all of this? Consider the rights and decide which ones to give or withhold:

NetWare 386	NetWare 286	Grant?
READ	READ	Yes

You must be able to read the file so that your word processor or spreadsheet can retrieve it.

WRITE	WRITE	No

Being able to write to a file means that you can change its contents.

	OPEN	Yes

You also must be able to open a file so that your word processor or spreadsheet can retrieve it.

CREATE	CREATE	No

Being able to create files means that you can copy new files into the shared-file pool or use your word processor or spreadsheet program to save files there.

ERASE	DELETE	No

You do not want users to be able to delete files from the shared-file-pool.

ACCESS	PARENTAL	No

This right lets you control other users' rights or give yourself more rights to the directory. This right also lets you create subdirectories.

FILE SCAN	SEARCH	Yes

You must have this right to be able to list the files in the shared-file pool directory.

MODIFY	MODIFY	No

The MODIFY right lets you rename a file or change its attributes, both of which are undesirable for a shared-file pool.

SUPERVISORY		No

The SUPERVISOR right gives you all rights to the shared file pool.

For NetWare 286 in this example, you have given only READ, OPEN, and SEARCH rights. For NetWare 386 in this example, you have given only READ and FILE SCAN rights (unlike NetWare 286, the READ right for NetWare 386 also gives you the ability to open a file).

What is the best way to give users the preceding rights? You can give each user these rights one user at a time, or you can create a group and give it the proper rights to the shared-file pool. Creating a group is probably less work. You can add or remove individual users to and from the group as needed. You can use SYSCON, FILER, or GRANT to give users or groups rights, but only SYSCON lets you manage groups, so it is probably the best choice for this job.

Managing the Shared-File Pool

At least one user has to be given the ability to maintain the shared-file pool. New files will need to be added, and files that are no longer needed will have to be removed. On a small network, the network supervisor may be the best choice for this task. On a larger or very busy network, the job would best be given to one or two well-trained users. These users would need to have increased access to enable them to add new files, change existing ones, and delete old ones.

Looking at the previous list of rights, can you decide which additional rights should be given? You would certainly need to give the CREATE, WRITE, and DELETE or ERASE rights. PARENTAL or ACCESS CONTROL depends on whether you wanted the pool manager to be able to grant access to other users or change the directory structure in any way. MODIFY depends on whether you need the pool manager to change the name or attributes of files.

Using File Attributes

As the last step in protecting the files in the shared pool, you should use file-attribute control. Although NetWare rights are effective in protecting the files, you can use attributes to make the files shareable. You also can use file attributes to protect the files while users who are pool managers (and have increased access rights) access them. Consider the list of file attributes and decide which ones would be useful in this situation:

File Attribute	Turn On?
READ ONLY	Yes

Turning on this attribute means the file cannot be changed or deleted. This is a good extra layer of protection, particularly when the users with increased rights are working with the files.

HIDDEN	No

No reason exists for hiding the files.

SYSTEM	No

No reason exists for designating the files as system files.

ARCHIVE	No

This attribute will be turned on and off automatically when the file is changed and backed up.

SHAREABLE	Yes

More than likely, two users will attempt to use a particular file at the same time.

INDEXED	No

This attribute will not help you in the typical word processing or spreadsheet-file-pool situation. With NetWare 386, the INDEXED attribute is not set by the user but is handled automatically if the file is large enough to require it.

EXECUTE ONLY	No

This attribute only applies to executable files. Shared-pool files are typically data files.

TRANSACTIONAL	No

The TRANSACTIONAL attribute is only useful for shared database applications.

In this example, two attributes have been turned on: READ ONLY and SHAREABLE. The SHAREABLE attribute enables multiple users to access the file at the same time. (Note that not all word processors and spreadsheet programs will cooperate; you should test the software to see how the package you are using behaves when two users simultaneously attempt to access a SHAREABLE file.) The READ ONLY attribute protects the file from being deleted or changed even if the user has rights to do so. This attribute prevents the pool manager or supervisor from accidentally deleting a file. The supervisor first must turn off the attribute before making the change.

Shared-file pools are one of many ways that creative network supervisors and users can effectively use their networks. The proper use of NetWare security tools makes file sharing safe.

Setting Up a Shared Database

The ability to run a multiuser application such as an accounting system or an order-processing and inventory-control application gives a network the same capability as its mainframe and minicomputer cousins. Some networks are installed solely for the purpose of running such systems. With others, multiuser applications are added as an afterthought.

The most common type of multiuser application is the shared database. If your company's inventory is stored in a database, it is likely that several users will need to look at the database at the same time. The sales department will need to check stock levels to quote delivery times to customers. The shipping and receiving department will need to change the database to reflect newly received items or items that have been shipped out. The purchasing department will need to generate reports to list out-of-stock items that need to be reordered.

Shared databases can be built in several ways. You can use an off-the-shelf database manager such as dBASE or Paradox to create the application. You also can program it from scratch by using C or Pascal. Some applications can be purchased ready-made from a vendor.

If you use an off-the-shelf product or buy the shared-database application ready-made, there should be instructions concerning the types of access that need to be given to users. Sometimes these instructions are designed to accommodate all types of network operating systems, so you will not find specific instructions for NetWare.

Consider the general rules that apply to installing shared databases. Although specific situations you encounter may prove to be different in some respects, this exercise should help you make the right choices in those cases where the instructions you have to follow are less than complete.

Which Files Go Where

A shared-database application uses several categories of files, and you treat each category differently when you are making decisions about rights, directories, and file attributes.

Program files contain the instructions that your PC follows when it runs the database application. Program files generally consist of executable files with the EXE or COM extension. You also may find other types of files containing information used in execution of the program, including overlay files (which sometimes have the extension OVL) and help files (which contain the information contained in help screens that users access while running the program).

Program files generally are not changed by the user while the program is running. Program files are sometimes modified by the program installer when he or she is configuring the program. Because program files are not changed or written to, you can give users limited access to them.

Data files differ in that they are written to and changed frequently. In a database application, there may be multiple database and index files. If a user is only looking up information (such as when the sales department checks stock levels to quote times), the user needs only limited access. Other users may need to make changes to the file (such as when a shipping and receiving clerk changes the stock level information to reflect newly received items). This type of user needs a higher level of access.

Finally, a small group of users may need the rights to change both program files and data files in major ways. For example, someone may need to reindex all the databases, which means that all index files are deleted and recreated. Or someone may need to update the program files to make improvements or install a new version of the application.

As you can see, a shared database can involve a potpourri of access. Database access is considered further in the following sections.

Access to Program Files

We have established that most users need only limited access to the program files of a shared-database application. If your application permits it, you may want to store your program files in a directory separate from the data files. For an inventory-control database, you may want to set up a directory structure similar to that shown in figure 13.3.

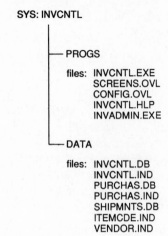

SYS: INVCNTL

─── PROGS

files: INVCNTL.EXE
SCREENS.OVL
CONFIG.OVL
INVCNTL.HLP
INVADMIN.EXE

─── DATA

files: INVCNTL.DB
INVCNTL.IND
PURCHAS.DB
PURCHAS.IND
SHIPMNTS.DB
ITEMCDE.IND
VENDOR.IND

Fig. 13.3.
The directory
structure for a
shared database.

What rights would you give users to the directory that stores the programs? You probably will want to give them READ and OPEN rights (for NetWare 286). The SEARCH right also will be required if files are in a search directory. For example, if the executable files are in a search path and the program is "run" from a data directory, the user needs to have search rights to look for the executable files in the search directory.

READ ONLY and SHAREABLE are the file attributes that you will want to turn on for each program file. You also may want to make the EXE files EXECUTE ONLY so that users cannot copy the executable program files to their personal directories.

The user who maintains the shared-database programs needs to be given other rights to the directory so that he or she can make changes to the program files. This person may be the network supervisor or some other knowledgeable and trusted user.

Access Rights to Data Files

Deciding what type of access to give to the files in the data directory is more complicated. Some users only need to read from the files, and others need to read and update them.

Consider the users who need to read and update the files; examine each right individually and determine which will be granted and which will be withheld:

NetWare 386	NetWare 286	Grant?
READ	READ	Yes

You must be able to read the file to see the information it contains.

WRITE	WRITE	Yes

You must be able to write to a file to update its contents.

	OPEN	Yes

With NetWare 286, you also must be able to open a file to read from it or write to it.

CREATE	CREATE	No

Being able to create files means that users can copy new files into the data directory or copy a new file over one of its existing files.

ERASE	DELETE	No

You do not want users to be able to delete files from the data directory.

ACCESS	PARENTAL	No

This right lets you control other users' rights or give yourself more rights to the directory. It also lets you create subdirectories.

FILE SCAN	SEARCH	No

The users do not need to list files in the data directory (unless the file is in a search directory that the user will access from another directory).

MODIFY	MODIFY	No

The MODIFY right lets a user rename a file or change its attributes, both of which are undesirable for the data directory.

SUPERVISOR		No

The SUPERVISOR right gives the user all rights to the data directory.

For NetWare 286 in this example, you are giving only READ, WRITE, and OPEN rights. For NetWare 386, the rights to be granted are READ and WRITE.

Some users only need to read from the shared-data files. You may assume that you would withhold the WRITE right from those users. This may work, but in reality most shared-database applications control what the user is doing to the file within their programs. If a user is only supposed to read from the file, the program he or she is using never attempts to write to the file.

File Attributes for Data Files

You also need to determine which file attributes will be turned on. Again, consider the options individually:

File Attribute	Turn On?
READ ONLY	No

Turning on this attribute means that the data files cannot be updated.

HIDDEN	No

No reason exists for hiding the files.

SYSTEM	No

No reason exists for designating the files as system files.

ARCHIVE	No

This attribute is turned on and off automatically when the file is changed and backed up.

SHAREABLE	Yes

Because the data is being shared, multiple users will need to access the files at the same time.

INDEXED	Maybe

This attribute is useful if your program is written to take advantage of it, and the file is several megabytes in size or larger. With NetWare 386, the INDEXED attribute is not set by the user but is handled automatically if the file is large enough to require it.

EXECUTE ONLY	No

This attribute only applies to executable files, not to data files.

TRANSACTIONAL	Maybe

The TRANSACTIONAL attribute is useful if your application is written to use NetWare's Transaction Tracking System (TTS) and TTS has been activated on your server.

In this example, the SHAREABLE attribute has been turned on. Two other attributes, INDEXED and TRANSACTIONAL, would be turned on if your application specifically has been written to work with them.

Figure 13.4 shows the rights and attributes used for the shared-database program and data files.

SYS: INVCNTL

```
├─ PROGS [READ, OPEN]
│
│   files:  INVCNTL.EXE   SHAREABLE, READ ONLY, EXECUTE ONLY
│           SCREENS.OVL  SHAREABLE, READ ONLY
│           CONFIG.OVL    SHAREABLE, READ ONLY
│           INVCNTL.HLP  SHAREABLE, READ ONLY
│           INVADMIN.EXE SHAREABLE, READ ONLY, EXECUTE ONLY
│
└─ DATA [READ, WRITE, OPEN]
```

Fig. 13.4.

The rights and attributes used to control access to a database application.

```
    files:  INVCNTL. DB   SHAREABLE
            INVCNTL.IND   SHAREABLE
            PURCHAS.DB   SHAREABLE
            PURCHAS.IND   SHAREABLE
            SHIPMNTS.DB  SHAREABLE
            ITEMCDE.IND   SHAREABLE
            VENDOR.IND    SHAREABLE
```

Deciding which rights and attributes to use to control access requires careful analysis of how the directories and files will be used. If you are not sure about which rights and attributes to use, start with the most restrictive settings and let trial and error show which additional rights need to be granted. In Chapter 22, "Installing Network Versions of Software," rights and attributes are suggested for several popular software packages designed for network use.

Examining NetWare Security from the Inside

Like many computer aficionados, you may be the type who not only wants to know how to use something but also how it works. NetWare security has been discussed in the last few chapters; now you will take an inside look at how security works.

You now know that NetWare security consists of the following elements: login control, trustee directory rights, trustee file rights (for 386 only), directory rights masks, and file attributes. In this section, you will learn the mechanics of how NetWare implements these controls.

Login control consists of user names, groups, passwords, account restrictions, and other similar items. On a NetWare server, this information is stored in hidden files in the SYS:SYSTEM directory. These files collectively are called the Bindery. NetWare 286 has two Bindery files: NET$BIND.SYS and NET$BVAL.SYS; NetWare 386 has three: NET$OBJ.SYS, NET$PROP.SYS, and NET$VAL.SYS. "NetWare-aware" backup devices must know to back up these files. If you ever have to use a backup to recreate a server and do not restore the Bindery files, all your login names, passwords, groups, and account restrictions are lost.

Two utilities are stored in the SYS:SYSTEM directory that work directly on the Bindery files: BINDFIX and BINDREST. BINDFIX diagnoses and fixes the Bindery files if they ever become partially damaged. To run BINDFIX, make the SYS:SYSTEM directory the default, type *bindfix*, and press Enter. BINDFIX first renames and makes visible the existing Bindery files. It then creates new Bindery files.

If for some reason you need to revert to the old Bindery files after BINDFIX attempts to rebuild them, you can type *bindrest*, press Enter, and the original files are restored.

Fortunately, needing to use BINDFIX is a rare event. If the server loses power or stops operating at the precise moment that you are updating or adding user or group information, the Bindery files could possibly become partially damaged. Disk failure is another possible source of Bindery problems.

The SECURITY utility stored in the SYS:SYSTEM directory checks the Bindery files and shows security weaknesses that the network supervisor may elect to correct. It lists the following information:

- ❏ Users without passwords
- ❏ Users with passwords identical to their login names
- ❏ Users with passwords of less than five characters
- ❏ Users who are not required to change their passwords every 60 days
- ❏ Users with unlimited grace logins
- ❏ Users who are not required to use a unique password at every password change

❑ Users who are equivalent to the supervisor

❑ Users who have trustee rights to the root directory of a server volume

❑ Users who have more than the default rights to NetWare's standard directories (SYS:SYSTEM, SYS:PUBLIC, SYS:LOGIN, and SYS:MAIL)

❑ Users who have no login script (login scripts are discussed in detail in Chapter 16)

To run the SECURITY utility, make the SYS:SYSTEM directory the default, type *security*, and press Enter.

The information items discussed previously are shown. You may want to capture this information in a file you can print or display with a text editor. You can capture this information with DOS or OS/2 redirection by typing

SECURITY > FILENAME.EXT

and pressing Enter (replace FILENAME.EXT with the file name of your choice).

Trustee directory rights and directory rights masks are stored as part of the directory information. Within each directory, a list of trustees and their rights is stored. As with the Bindery files, a NetWare-aware backup device must know to back up this information. You also must perform backups by using a login name that has supervisory equivalence in order to have access to the trustee rights information. The consequence of restoring data from a backup that does not have this information is having to rebuild manually all directory rights information. With NetWare 386, each file can have a list of trustees also. This information is stored with the file.

File attribute settings are stored as part of the file's directory entry. File attributes are stored as part of a 2-byte (NetWare 286) or 4-byte (NetWare 386) field.

Chapter Summary

In this chapter, you learned that creating a secure and safe network is perhaps the network supervisor's most important job. NetWare gives you abundant tools to do this effectively, but it is up to you to combine them intelligently to achieve the desired result. It is easy to underestimate the need to be diligent in this area and to give users more access to sensitive or shared files than they should have. Don't make this mistake; losing files because of a user's act of ignorance or maliciousness is a bad way to find out that your security planning has been inadequate.

14

Implementing Shared Printing

A network is a system designed to provide services and benefits to its users. One of the easiest to use and most practical services it provides is access to shared network printers. Just as a printer is the first peripheral you buy when you purchase a PC, a printer is probably the first shared peripheral you will install when you set up a network.

Shared printing has some compelling benefits. Instead of providing each user with a personal printer, you can consolidate your expenditure and provide a few high-quality printers instead. A network can make it economically feasible to install a high-speed laser printer because the cost of that printer can be spread over many users.

Because printers can be shared, LAN users can have access to a wider variety of them. If you need to print a spreadsheet that is more than 80 characters wide, you're in luck as long as there is a shared wide-carriage printer on your LAN.

With NetWare, sharing printers is easy. Simply connecting a printer to the parallel or serial port of a server makes it possible for all LAN users to access it. NetWare 386 also enables you to share printers connected to workstations.

In this chapter, you will learn how to implement shared printing on your servers. The terminology and mechanics of NetWare's printer sharing are discussed first. Next, you will learn how to create and configure print queues on your servers. You will also find out how to configure and bring up print servers for use with NetWare 386.

Setting up and configuring shared printers is only half the task. In Chapter 15, you will learn how to use and manage NetWare's printer-sharing features. Before learning about these individual steps, however, you need to understand the printer-sharing process as a whole.

The Shared-Printing Process

The purpose of the shared-printing process is simple: a print request from a user's workstation must travel to a shared printer. During this journey, the print request passes through several stages that you should understand. The next sections follow a typical print request through the printing process.

Step One: Redirecting Printer Output

Print requests start at user workstations. Usually, print jobs consist of the output from programs such as word processors, spreadsheets, databases, and graphics packages. These programs usually are not aware of network printing; they only send requests to a printer port on a local PC.

When you decide to use a network printer, you execute a NetWare command called CAPTURE. It tells the NetWare shell to "capture" the output that would normally go to a local printer and redirect it to the network printer that you select. The software doing the printing is unaware of this redirection and sends its output normally; the software is fooled into thinking a real printer is attached to your PC.

In addition to enabling you to redirect output to a printer, NetWare also enables you to control the printer in certain ways. Printer sharing can introduce some unique technical and human-relations challenges. Suppose that one of your shared printers is a laser printer that is capable of printing vertically (portrait) or horizontally (landscape) on the page. If you send a job to be printed in landscape mode but do not send a command to reset the printer to portrait mode after your print job, the print job after yours will be in landscape orientation also, to the surprise of the person who requested the second print job. You can eliminate this possibility by configuring NetWare to automatically send a reset command to the printer before every job.

Step Two: Waiting in a Print Queue

When the NetWare shell redirects your printer output, it must have a place to send it. It cannot safely send the print request directly to the printer itself, because the printer might be busy with another user's job, or off-line, or out of paper. Instead, your job is sent to a *print queue*. A print queue is a holding area on a file server disk where print requests are stored. The print requests wait in line (queue) for the printer to become available.

When print requests are redirected, they are routed to the file server on which the print queue resides. As the print output from a workstation is received, it is converted to a file on the server disk. When the print job is completed, this file is closed and takes its place in line in the print queue. If no jobs are in the queue ahead of it, the file is sent to the printer immediately. This process is diagrammed in figure 14.1.

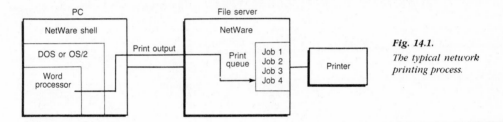

Fig. 14.1.
The typical network printing process.

NetWare provides you with a wide variety of queue-management and configuration options. Jobs that are in a queue waiting to be printed can be moved up in line, deleted, or even partially rerun or restarted to correct for paper jams and so on. If you have a lengthy job that you want to print after hours, you can specify that it be held in the queue until a certain time.

Step Three: Moving from the Queue to the Printer

The last step in your print request's journey is its movement from the print queue to the printer itself. In most cases, this movement involves going from the queue on the server disk to a printer attached to a port on the server. As you might suspect, NetWare enables you to make this process more sophisticated (and complicated). For a particularly busy office, you can arrange for more than one printer to accept print jobs from the same queue (see fig. 14.2). You also can go the other way—multiple print queues, each with different configuration options, serviced by one printer (see fig. 14.3). You can make one of the queues a high-priority queue, so that its jobs are always printed as soon as the printer becomes available (even if jobs from other queues were in line first).

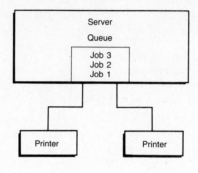

Fig. 14.2.

A single print queue can be serviced by multiple printers.

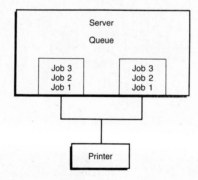

Fig. 14.3.

Multiple print queues can be serviced by a single printer.

NetWare 386 uses a more flexible but more complicated method for routing jobs from print queues to printers. Its print server module (which runs as a NetWare Loadable Module, or NLM, on a server or on a dedicated workstation) can route jobs to server-connected printers or printers connected to workstations (see fig. 14.4). It may not be convenient to connect printers to servers. You may have decided to keep your network's servers in a centralized and secure location. Thanks to NetWare 386's print server module, workstations can be configured to service queues in the same way that file server-connected printers do. If you want this capability with NetWare 286, you need to purchase a third-party product, such as Network Assistant (3rd Planet Software), LanSpool (Lan Systems) or QueueIt! (Brightwork Software).

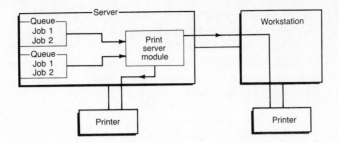

Fig. 14.4.
NetWare 386 uses its
print server module
to direct print jobs.

Setting Up Shared Printing

Your first step to implementing printer sharing on your network is to set up print queues on certain file servers to receive print jobs. You use the NetWare command PCONSOLE to perform this task. After setting up the print queues, you need to assign those queues to be serviced by printers, either printers connected to servers (with NetWare 286 or 386) or printers connected to workstations (NetWare 386). With NetWare 286, you use commands from the server console to assign queues to printers. With NetWare 386, you need to activate the print server module (PSERVER) and use PCONSOLE to assign queues to printers.

After printers are in place to receive print jobs, you need to learn how to use the CAPTURE command to redirect printer output to the appropriate print queue. After you have mastered CAPTURE, you can use PRINTDEF and PRINTCON to improve your control over shared printers by building job profiles that control printer operation.

Finally, you need to learn how to manage print jobs while they are waiting to be printed. PCONSOLE and server console commands are your main tools for this task.

The following sections describe in detail how to set up shared printing. Setting up print queues is the first step and is described next.

Creating Print Queues

As already defined, a print queue is a holding area on a server disk that stores print request files that are ready to be printed.

Your main tool for working with print queues is the PCONSOLE utility. It enables you to create new queues or delete or rename existing ones. To create and configure queues, you need to be logged in with supervisory rights to the server where you want to work with queues. You can then start PCONSOLE by typing *pconsole* and pressing Enter. (PCONSOLE is stored in the PUBLIC directory, which is automatically mapped as a search drive.)

PCONSOLE's opening menu offers the following three options:

Change Current File Server
Print Queue Information
Print Server Information

Begin by selecting Print Queue Information. A list of the current print queues is displayed. If you started PCONSOLE from a server running NetWare 286, you may see queues on the list already, even if you have never created any. If printer ports were designated for spooled printers when NetWare 286 was installed on the server, a print queue was automatically created for each one. The queues that are set up automatically are PRINTQ_0 for printer 0, PRINTQ_1 for printer 1, and so on. With NetWare 386, no queues are created automatically.

To create a new print queue, select Insert from PCONSOLE's Print Queues list. You are prompted to enter a print queue name. The queue names should be brief and descriptive, such as ACCT-LJ (for accounting department LaserJet) or SALES-132 (for a 132-column wide printer in the sales department). Type the name of your choice and press Enter. The print queue list is updated to show your entry.

You also can delete or rename queues that are shown in the Print Queues list. To rename a queue, highlight its name and press F3. You are prompted to type the new name. To delete a queue, highlight it and press the Del key, or mark multiple queues with F5 and press the Del key. The selected queues are deleted.

Creating, Deleting, and Renaming Print Queues

1. Start PCONSOLE and select Print Queue Information from its main menu. A list of existing print queues appears.

2. To create a new queue, press Ins. A prompt tells you to enter the new queue's name. When you do so, the new queue is added to the list.

3. To delete a queue, highlight it and press Del. After confirming that you want to delete it, the queue is removed from the list.

4. To change a queue name, highlight it and press F3. You are prompted to revise the queue name. After revising the name, the list is updated to show your change.

Adding Queue Operators and Users

Your main task when configuring a queue is to choose its operators and users. Queue operators are permitted to control the flow of print requests through the queue. They can delete individual jobs, change the order of jobs, start or stop the queue, prevent new jobs from being placed in the queue, and stop jobs from being sent to printers. Queue users are allowed to place jobs in the queue.

When you create a new queue, the user SUPERVISOR is the only user designated as a queue operator. The group EVERYONE is designated as a queue user (because all users are members of the group EVERYONE by default, all users are queue users). If you are creating a queue that is to be used only by a particular department, rather than all server users, you need to make only the users from that department queue users, and perhaps a select few queue operators.

To configure a queue, highlight its name from PCONSOLE'S queue list and press Enter. The Print Queue Information menu is displayed (see fig. 14.5). To change the list of queue operators, select Queue Operators. You see a list of the current queue operators. To add a new operator, press the Ins key. A list of all server users and groups appears. Highlight the user you want to add and press Enter, or mark multiple users and groups with F5 and press Enter. The queue operator list returns, updated to show your additions. To delete a queue operator, highlight the name from the queue operator list and press the Del key (delete multiple users by marking their names with F5 and pressing Del). When your updates are complete, press Esc to return to the Print Queue Information menu.

You can follow similar steps to update the list of queue users. Select Queue Users from the Print Queue Information menu and a list of queue users is displayed. The group EVERYONE is listed as the sole queue user. If you want to limit the queue users, you first need to remove EVERYONE from the list, so highlight it and press the Del key. Press the Ins key and,

Fig. 14.5.

The Print Queue Information menu.

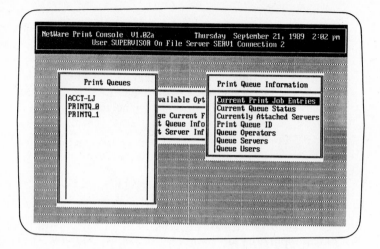

from the resulting list of user and group names, select the users you want to make queue users. When you have finished, press Esc to return to the Print Queue Information menu.

Configuring a Print Queue

1. Start PCONSOLE and select Print Queue Information from its main menu. A list of existing print queues appears.

2. Highlight the queue that you want to work with and press Enter. The Print Queue Information menu appears.

3. Select the queue operators. Choose Queue Operators to list the current queue operators. To add a queue operator, press Ins to list all other users and groups, and highlight the name you want to add and press Enter.

   To remove a queue operator, highlight the name from the Queue Operator list and press Del.

4. Select the queue users. Choose Queue Users to list the current queue users. To add a queue user, press Ins to list all other users and groups, highlight the name that you want to add, and press Enter.

   To remove a queue user, highlight the name from the Queue Users list and press Del.

5. Select the queue servers. Choose Queue Servers to list the servers whose attached printers are allowed to service the queue. To add a server, press Ins to list all other available servers, highlight the server you want to add, and press Enter. (When using NetWare 386, if you have not yet defined any print servers, you need to do so before being able to add a queue server to the list—come back to this step after you have defined a print server). To remove a queue server, highlight its name from the Queue Server list and press Del.

6. Assign printers to the queue. If you have NetWare 286, use the PRINTER command from the file server console. If you are using NetWare 386, you perform this step when you configure a print server.

Other options on the Print Queue Information menu control the operation of the queue. You will learn how to use some of these options later, but first you need to learn about assigning a printer or print server to a queue.

Assigning Queues to Printers

When you assign a queue to a printer, you cause print jobs in that queue to be routed there. NetWare lets you dynamically match and unmatch queues to printers. With a single command, you can assign a queue to be serviced by a particular printer. Later, with another command, you can reassign that queue to a different printer. If a particular printer fails, for example, you can reassign its queue (or queues, if it is servicing more than one) to another printer until the nonworking printer can be repaired. With NetWare 286, queue assignments are made from the server console. With NetWare 386, they are made by using the PCONSOLE command.

Assigning Queues with NetWare 286

When you install NetWare 286, you designate which printer ports in your server PC are to be used by shared printers. NetWare automatically creates a queue for each printer port you designate as shared, and that queue is assigned to its printer. You and other users then can send jobs to that printer without queue configuration being done.

If you are like most network supervisors, you probably will add additional queues. When you do, you need to assign those queues to one of your server printer ports. With NetWare 286, this can only be done from the server console.

The server console prompt is a colon (:), and from that prompt you can enter NetWare console commands (you will learn about other console commands in Chapter 18). The following console command assigns a queue named ACCT-LJ to printer 0:

    Printer 0 ADD queue ACCT-LJ

(You should replace the printer number and queue name with the number and name of your printer and queue.)

Abbreviations enable you to shorten this command. The uppercase letters are the only ones that are required. In the rest of this chapter, whenever a NetWare console command is shown, the optional parts of the command are shown in lowercase letters, and the essential ones in uppercase. The preceding command could be shortened to

    P 0 ADD ACCT-LJ

You should select carefully the queue that you assign to printer 0. Printer 0 is the default printer that print requests are routed to when users run NetWare commands to redirect output to a shared printer.

Queue and Printer Priorities

You also can establish a priority level for a queue and printer relationship. If a printer is servicing multiple queues, it accepts requests from them in priority order. If a printer is servicing a queue with a priority level of 1 that is holding three jobs, and another queue with a priority level of 3 is holding two jobs, the three jobs in the priority 1 queue are printed before the two jobs in the priority 3 queue.

To add a priority level when you assign a queue to a printer, type the following command:

    Printer 0 ADD queue ACCT-LJ at priority 3

and press Enter. (You should substitute your own printer number, queue name, and priority number for those shown in this example.)

You probably will want your printer and queue assignments to be made automatically when you start your file server. You can create them automatically by placing the appropriate console commands in your server's AUTOEXEC.SYS file. See Chapter 19 for details about creating this file.

After you have added queues and assigned them to printers, you are ready to send print requests to them.

Creating a NetWare 386 Print Server

1. Start PCONSOLE and select Print Server Information from its main menu. A list of existing print servers appears.

2. To create a new print server, press Ins. A prompt tells you to enter the new print server's name. When you enter it, the new print server is added to the list.

3. To delete a print server, highlight it and press Del. After confirming that you want to delete it, it is removed from the list.

4. To change a print server name, highlight it and press F3. You are prompted to revise the print server name. After changing the name, the list is updated to show your change.

Assigning Queues with NetWare 386's Print Server Module

NetWare 386 uses a more sophisticated and flexible method of routing jobs from queues to printers. Its print server module (called PSERVER) acts as the routing agent, managing up to 16 printers that can be connected to the server or workstations. PSERVER can run as an NLM or on a dedicated PC.

If you are not using NetWare 386, you can skip this section and proceed to the section called "Sending Print Jobs to Shared Printers."

Defining a Print Server

Before starting PSERVER, you need to define at least one print server. Each print server definition includes the print server name, password, the queues it services, and up to 16 printers to which it can route jobs.

PCONSOLE is the utility used to define print servers. With supervisory access, start PCONSOLE by logging into the server that will run the print server. Type *pconsole* and press Enter.

From PCONSOLE's main menu, select Print Server Information. A list of all currently defined print servers is displayed (the list is empty if you are running PCONSOLE for the first time). To create a new definition, press Ins, and you are prompted to enter the name of your print server. The name you choose should be brief and easy to remember, because you need to specify it every time you start the PSERVER print server module. After you have entered the name, the print server list is updated to include it.

The next step in the process of setting up shared printing is configuring the print server. Highlight its name on the print server list and press Enter. The Print Server Information menu is displayed (see fig. 14.6).

Fig. 14.6.

The Print Server Information menu.

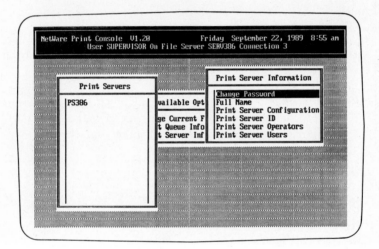

Configuring a NetWare 386 Print Server

1. Start PCONSOLE and select Print Server Information from its main menu. A list of existing print servers appears.

2. Highlight the server that you want to work with and press Enter. The Print Server Information menu appears.

3. Select the print server password. Select Change Password and then enter a password.

4. Select the print server full name. Select Full Name and enter a full name.

5. Select the print server operators. Choose Print Server Operators to list the current print server operators. To add an operator,

press Ins to list all other users and groups, highlight the name you want to add, and press Enter. To remove an operator, highlight the name from the Print Server Operator list and press Del.

6. Select the print server users. Choose Print Server Users to list the current print server users. To add a user, press Ins to list all other users and groups, highlight the name that you want to add, and press Enter.

   To remove a user, highlight the name from the Print Server Users list and press Del.

7. Specify the file servers whose queues the print server will work with. Choose Print Server Configuration, and from the resulting Print Server Configuration menu, choose File Servers Serviced. A list of the file servers whose queues the print server can service is displayed. To add a server, press Ins and select a file server name from the resulting list.

   To remove a file server, highlight its name and press Del.

   The queues on the file server on which you have defined the print server are automatically serviceable, so don't worry that this file server is not listed.

8. Configure the print server printers. From the Print Server Configuration menu, choose Printer Configuration. A list of the 16 available printer assignments is shown on-screen, numbered from 0 to 15. Highlight the printer number that you want to configure and press Enter. A window opens prompting you to enter the printer name, port type (such as Parallel LPT1, Serial COM2, Remote Parallel LPT1, or Remote Serial COM3), and other parameters. Press Esc when you are finished to save your changes and return to the printer number list. Configure other printers as needed. Press Esc until you return to the Printer Configuration Menu.

9. Match printers to queues. From the Printer Configuration Menu, choose Queues Serviced by Printers. The printers you defined in the previous step are listed. Select one and a list of the queues it services is displayed. Press Ins to list file servers and queues from which you can pick a queue to place on the list. A prompt

tells you to assign a priority level from 1 to 10 to the queue/printer match.

Remove a queue from the printer's list by highlighting it and pressing Del.

Press Esc to return to the printer list. You can match other printers to queues or press Esc to return to the Printer Configuration menu.

10. Select a notification list for the printer. From the Printer Configuration Menu, choose Notify List for Printer. The printers you have previously defined are listed. Select one, and a list of the users it currently notifies when it needs attention is displayed. Press Ins to list additional users and groups from which you can pick a new name. You are prompted to specify notification intervals in seconds. Remove a user or group from the printer's notification list by highlighting it and pressing Del.

    Press Esc to return to the printer list. You can set up notification lists for other printers, or press Esc to return to the Printer Configuration menu. Press Esc until you return to PCONSOLE's main menu.

11. Don't forget that if you are configuring a new print server, you need to add it to the queue server list for each queue that it services.

The first option available on the Print Server Information menu enables you to change the print server's password. When you select this option, you are prompted to enter a new password for the print server. Adding a password to a print server means that you will be prompted to enter it every time you start the PSERVER print server module to run your print server definition. It's a good idea to add a password to prevent users from accidentally or maliciously starting the print server from their own workstations.

The next option enables you to add a full name to the print server's definition. This option is very similar to adding a full name to a user account with SYSCON—it is useful for descriptive purposes. Select this option and you are prompted to enter a full name for the print server.

Before configuring a print server's printers, you need to select which users will be print server operators and which will be print server users. Operators can start and stop the print server and control its printers. They can perform all print server and printer configuration tasks except changing the list of users and operators. Users can use PCONSOLE to monitor the status of the print server and its printers. You don't have to be a print server user to use one of its printers. All that is required is that you are a queue user for one of the queues being serviced by the print server.

When you create a new print server, the user SUPERVISOR is the only one designated as a print server operator. The group EVERYONE is designated as a print server user (because all users are members of the group EVERYONE by default, all users are print server users). If you are creating a print server to control the printers used by a particular department and not by all server users, you should make only the users from that department print server users, and perhaps a select few print server operators.

To change the list of print server operators, select Print Server Operators from the Print Server Information menu. A list of the current print server operators is displayed on-screen. To add a new operator, press Ins. A list of all eligible users and groups appears. Highlight the user you want to add and press Enter, or mark multiple users and groups with F5 and press Enter. The print server operator list returns to the screen, updated to show your additions. To delete a print server operator, highlight his or her name from the print server operator list and press Del (you delete multiple users by marking their names with F5 and pressing Del). When your updates are complete, press Esc to return to the Print Server Information menu.

You can follow similar steps to update the list of print server users. Select Print Server Users from the Print Server Information menu and a list of print server users is displayed. The group EVERYONE is listed as the sole print server user. If you want to limit the print server users, you first need to remove EVERYONE from the list, so highlight it and press Del. Next, press Ins, and from the resulting list of user and group names, select the users you want to make print server users. When you have finished, press Esc to return to the Print Server Information menu.

The Configure Print Server option from the Print Server Information menu is where the real work of defining a print server is done. When you select it, a menu with the following options appears:

File Servers Serviced
Notify List for Printer
Printer Configuration
Queues Serviced by Printer

The first option, File Servers Serviced, enables you to choose up to seven additional file servers whose queues can be serviced by the print station. (If you want your print server to work only with queues on your current file server, you don't need to select this option because the current server is included automatically). To add file servers to your list, select this option, and a list of the file servers being serviced is displayed. To add a server to the list, press Ins and a list of all the servers currently running on your network comes on-screen. Highlight the server you want to add and press Enter. When you are finished adding to the list, press Esc to return to the Configuration menu.

The next option you need to select is Printer Configuration. With this option, you specify up to 16 printers to which the print station can route jobs. When you select Printer Configuration, a list of 16 printers is displayed, and if you have not configured any of them, they all show the message Not installed. Highlight the printer number you want to configure and press Enter; a window opens that prompts you through the process of configuring the printer (fig. 14.7).

Fig. 14.7.

The Printer Configuration screen.

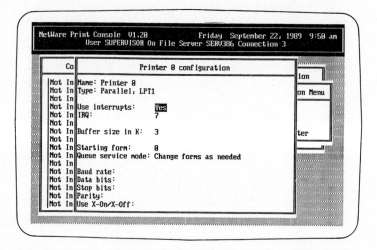

The first option you configure is the printer Name. By default, the printer number is used as the name (such as Printer 0), but you may want to use a name that is more descriptive, such as *Third Floor Laser* or *Warehouse Dot-Matrix*. Type the name of your choice. After entering the name, you are prompted to choose the printer Type. Move the highlight to Type: and press Enter. A list of printer types is displayed (see fig. 14.8). Printers that are connected directly to the server or to the dedicated PC (running the PSERVER print server module) can be identified by using one of the descriptions that start with Parallel or Serial. Printers that are connected to workstations are identified with a description starting with Remote. Choose the port description that matches your printer port. You also are prompted to specify whether your printer port uses interrupts and which interrupt is used. If the printer you specify is serial, you need to enter its communication parameters at the bottom of the window.

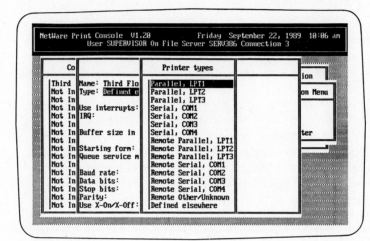

Fig. 14.8.
List of printer types.

Another prompt tells you to enter the printer's Buffer Size. The print server module maintains a memory buffer to hold information to feed to the printer. A default size of 3K is shown, but you can enter a buffer size from 1K to 20K. If you notice that the printer often starts and stops while printing jobs, you may want to increase the size of its buffer. If you are concerned about the print server module's memory consumption on the server, you can decrease each printer's buffer size.

Finally, you are asked to specify how the printer should handle forms. When users send requests to a printer, they can specify a form type. For example, if the printer normally has plain paper loaded and your job needs to be printed on your company's letterhead, you can specify the form type Letterhead when you send the job to the queue. When your job is ready to print, the printer stops, and the print server shows that a different form needs to be loaded. Each form you create is assigned a number (defining forms is described later in this chapter).

You can specify two options concerning forms. First, you can designate the Starting Form number. From that point forward, the print server assumes that this form type is loaded by default and only stops printing when a different form number is called for. Second, you can specify how the print server handles form changes by moving the highlight to Queue Service

Mode and pressing Enter. A window with the following choices is displayed:

Change forms as needed
Minimize form changes across queues
Minimize form changes within queues
Service only currently mounted form

The default mode is Change Forms As Needed, which means that the print server stops printing and prompts for a form change every time a job with a different form number is ready to print. If you select one of the options starting with Minimize Form Changes..., then the print server prints all jobs with the currently loaded form type before requesting a change. (Minimizing changes *across queues* means it prints all jobs from all queues that call for the current form type. Minimizing changes *within queues* means that jobs within the highest priority queue with the same form type are all printed before a job requesting a form change is printed, regardless of which job was first in line.) Service Only Currently Mounted Form instructs the print server to print all jobs that call for the current form type, but not print jobs that call for another form type. Printing does not stop and you do not receive a prompt.

After you have defined the printer, press Esc to save your definition. The printer list returns to the screen. Repeat the above steps for every printer you need to define. If you need to delete a defined printer, highlight it and press Del. When you are finished working with the printer list, press Esc to return to the Print Server Configuration menu.

If you want someone to be notified automatically if the printer needs attention (such as when it is out of paper or needs a form change) you should select the Notify List for Printer option from the Print Server Configuration menu. A list of the defined printers appears. Select the one for which you want to create a notification list. A blank list is displayed. To add a user to the list, press Ins, and a list of all users and groups is shown on-screen. Select the user or group you want to add. You are prompted to specify how quickly, in seconds, the user should be notified when there is a problem, and how frequently thereafter. Implement this feature with caution—having your work interrupted by a printer attention notice every minute or so can become like the infamous Chinese water torture. As a general rule, users go to the printer to check on their jobs shortly after sending them, so problems are quickly identified without notification.

The final step in configuring the print server is deciding which queues are to be serviced by each printer. As previously discussed, one queue can be serviced by multiple printers, or one printer can service multiple queues. To assign a printer to a queue, select Queues Serviced by Printer from the

Print Server Configuration menu. A list of the print server's printers is displayed on-screen. Select the printer you want to assign to a queue; a list of the queues that the printer is currently servicing (if any) appears. To add a queue, press Ins, and you see a list of queues. Highlight the queue you want to add and press Enter. You are prompted to assign a priority to that queue. This priority determines how the printer services this queue in relation to how it services other queues. Print requests in queues with a higher priority are printed first. Enter a number between 1 and 10 (the default priority for all queue/printer relationships is 1). The queue is updated to show the queue you have added.

Repeat this process if you want to assign this printer to other queues. Otherwise, press Esc to save your changes and to return to the list of print server printers. If you need to assign queues to another printer, highlight that printer, press Enter, and repeat the preceding steps to select a queue.

When you have finished assigning printers to queues, press Esc to return to the printer list, and press Esc again to return to the Print Server Configuration menu. At this point, you should be finished configuring your print server, so press Esc one more time to return to the Print Server Information menu.

One important option on the Print Server Information menu has not yet been described. The Print Server Status/Control selection enables you to control the operation of the print server and its printers. This selection is described later in this chapter. For now, one final step in the print server and queue configuration process must be described: designating your newly created print server as a queue server for the queues you have assigned to printers. This step is easily missed but must be done before print requests in the queue can be serviced by an assigned printer.

Return to the PCONSOLE Available Topics main menu and select Print Queue Information. You see a list of queues displayed on-screen; select the one to which you want to assign a print server. The Print Queue Information menu is displayed. Select the Queue Servers option, and you see a list of currently assigned print servers. To add your newly created print server to the list, press Ins. A list of your current file server's defined print servers comes on-screen. Highlight your print server and press Enter. The queue server list is updated to show your addition. Press Esc to leave the list and to return to the Print Queue Information menu.

You have now completely defined a print server, and it is ready to manage printers and send them print requests from queues. In the next section, you will learn about starting the print server module and sending print requests to it.

Starting a NetWare 386 Print Server

After you have set up a print server definition, you are ready to use it with the PSERVER program. PSERVER can be run as an NLM from the server console or on a dedicated workstation. While PSERVER is running with your print server definition, it continuously checks the queues assigned to your print server's printers for new print requests. When a new request appears, it is directed to the appropriate printer. Whenever you add a new printer or queue to the print server definition, you need to stop PSERVER and restart it in order for the new information to become effective.

Starting PSERVER at the Server Console

To start PSERVER with your print server definition from the server console, you need to be at the server colon prompt. Type

    LOAD PSERVER PSNAME

(Substitute the name of your print server for PSNAME.) The Print Server Status screen shown in figure 14.9 is displayed. The name and current status of each printer is shown, and you can toggle between the displays for printers 0-7 and 8-15 by pressing Esc.

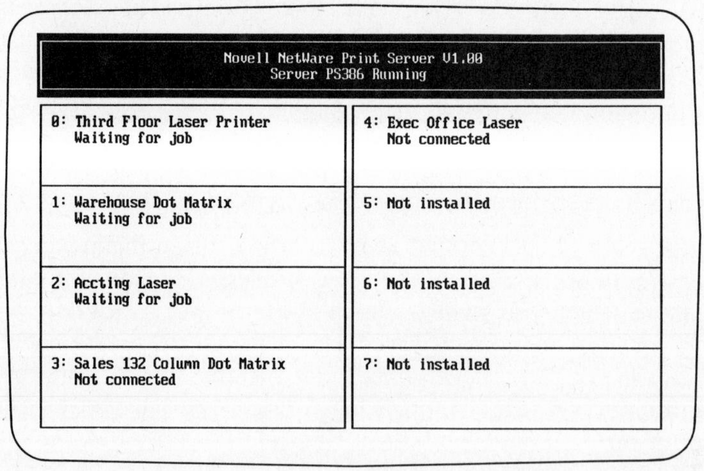

Fig. 14.9.

The Print Server Status screen.

```
              Novell NetWare Print Server V1.00
                    Server PS386 Running
┌─────────────────────────────┬─────────────────────────────┐
│ 0: Third Floor Laser Printer │ 4: Exec Office Laser         │
│    Waiting for Job           │    Not connected             │
├─────────────────────────────┼─────────────────────────────┤
│ 1: Warehouse Dot Matrix      │ 5: Not installed             │
│    Waiting for Job           │                              │
├─────────────────────────────┼─────────────────────────────┤
│ 2: Accting Laser             │ 6: Not installed             │
│    Waiting for Job           │                              │
├─────────────────────────────┼─────────────────────────────┤
│ 3: Sales 132 Column Dot Matrix │ 7: Not installed           │
│    Not connected             │                              │
└─────────────────────────────┴─────────────────────────────┘
```

You probably will want the print server to start automatically when you start the file server. You can ensure that automatic start-up takes place by adding the preceding command to your server's AUTOEXEC.NCF file. The easiest way to do this is to load the INSTALL NLM by typing *load install* and pressing Enter from the server console's colon prompt. From its main menu, select System Options, and from the resulting menu select the Edit AUTOEXEC.NCF File option.

Starting PSERVER on a Dedicated PC

You also can run PSERVER on a dedicated PC. When a PC is running PSERVER, it can be used for no other purpose while PSERVER is active. Before running the program, you need to increase the PC's number of SPX connections, which you can do by customizing its NetWare shell. In the directory where you start the NetWare shell, create an ASCII text file called SHELL.CFG with the following line in it:

    SPX CONNECTIONS = 50

If you already have added a SHELL.CFG file to the shell directory, then add the preceding information to it. Reboot the workstation and reload the NetWare shell.

Log into the server where you defined your print server and type

    PSERVER PSNAME

(Substitute the name of your print server for PSNAME.) The Print Server Status screen is displayed. The name and current status of each printer is shown and you can toggle between the displays for printers 0-7 and 8-15 by pressing Esc.

Starting a Workstation-Based Shared Printer

If one or more of the printers defined in your print server definition is a remote printer, you can activate it by using NetWare 386's RPRINTER command. RPRINTER runs as a memory-resident program on a workstation. It allows the printer or printers connected to the workstation to be shared. Even with RPRINTER running, you can continue to use the workstation as you normally would.

As with PSERVER on a workstation, you need to customize the NetWare shell to increase the number of SPX connections. In the directory where you start the NetWare shell, create an ASCII text file called SHELL.CFG with the following line in it:

    SPX CONNECTIONS = 50

If you already have added a SHELL.CFG file to the shell directory, then add the preceding information to it. Reboot the workstation and reload the NetWare shell.

Make sure that the print server where you have defined remote printers is active. Log into the NetWare 386 server where your print server is defined, type *rprinter*, and press Enter. A menu is displayed that prompts you to choose the print server and the remote printer you want to activate. After it is activated, the remote printer can be used as a shared printer by users who have been assigned the right to put jobs in a queue that the printer services.

If you want to activate the printer automatically without using menus (for example, to activate it from a batch file) you can type

RPRINTER PSNAME 3

and press Enter. (Substitute the name of your print server for PSNAME and the printer number you are activating for 3.)

RPRINTER is a memory-resident program that manages the remote printer's communication with the print server. You can run multiple shared printers on one workstation by executing the RPRINTER command for each one. Each printer you activate uses approximately 8K of memory.

To deactivate a shared printer, type the following command:

RPRINTER PSNAME 3 -R

and press Enter. (As before, substitute the name of your print server for PSNAME and the printer number that you are deactivating for 3.) The 8K of memory occupied by RPRINTER for that printer is freed. You must be careful to ensure that no other memory-resident programs that were loaded after RPRINTER are still loaded when you remove RPRINTER.

Designating a Default Queue

You can perform one final, optional step to configure the shared printing for NetWare 386. To accommodate users who want simple access to a shared printer, you can define a default printer for users who use the NetWare CAPTURE command to redirect their printer output but do not use its parameters to specify a queue. From the server console colon prompt, type the following:

SPOOL 0 TO ACCT-LJ

and press Enter. (Substitute your queue name for ACCT-LJ.) This enables users to redirect printed output to the ACCT-LJ queue without knowing how to specify the queue name.

You probably will want to set this default automatically when you start the file server. You can ensure that this default is set by adding the preceding command to your server's AUTOEXEC.NCF file. The easiest way to add it is to load the INSTALL NLM by typing *load install* and pressing Enter from the server console's colon prompt. From INSTALL's main menu, select System Options, and from the resulting menu select the Edit AUTOEXEC.NCF File option.

Chapter Summary

In this chapter, you learned how to create and configure queues and
activate print stations and printers, so now you are ready to learn how to
use them. In the next chapter, you will learn how to send print requests to
the queues and shared printers that you have activated and how to manage
them along the way.

15

Using
Shared Printers

Managing the shared printing process is a large part of the network supervisor's job when a well-implemented assortment of shared printers is heavily used. In this chapter, you will learn how to use and manage shared printers. You first learn how to send print jobs to the printers, and then you learn about advanced configuration options, which enable you to minimize some of the inconveniences of printer sharing. (Because printers are highly configurable devices, you may need to take steps to ensure that the configuration loaded by one user's print request doesn't stay behind and disrupt the next user's job.) Finally, you learn how to control the flow of print requests through the shared-printing process and how to control the operation of the printers themselves.

Sending Print Requests
to Shared Printers

The command most frequently used to send jobs to a shared printer is CAPTURE. The CAPTURE command tells the NetWare shell to redirect any output targeted for a printer port on your computer to a print queue on a server. You normally designate to which queue the output should be routed when you use CAPTURE (although default print queues can be established, as discussed in the preceding chapter).

When you execute CAPTURE, a "pipeline" is opened between your PC and the print queue. As soon as print output comes down this pipeline, a file is opened on the server to receive it. This file remains open until the server receives a signal from the PC that this job has no more print output. At that point, the file is closed and placed in the print queue. As soon as a printer is available, the file is printed (see fig. 15.1).

Fig. 15.1.

The three steps of print output redirection.

Step 1: CAPTURE has been executed and print output is being redirected to a file on the server.

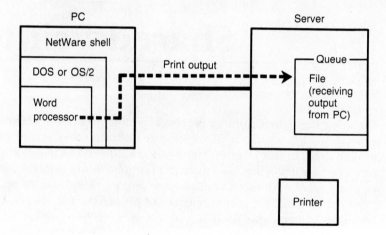

Step 2: Print output has stopped, but ENDCAP has not been executed, so the file is still waiting for more print output from the PC.

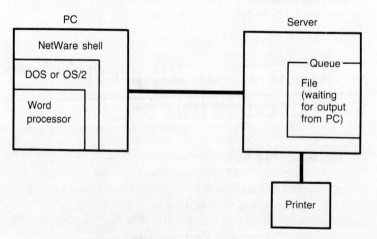

Step 3: ENDCAP has been executed. The file is placed in the print
        queue as a print job and is ready to print.

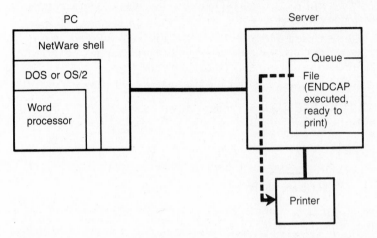

This end-of-job signal can be sent in several different ways. You can
execute the NetWare command ENDCAP, which stops the redirection of
your print output to the server and causes the server to close your print
request file and place it in the queue for printing. Or you can execute the
CAPTURE command again, which also sends an end-of-job signal and re-
establishes redirection of print output to the server. The application you
are printing from also can send an end-of-job signal (by explicitly closing
the DOS device PRN), and many network-aware programs use this
technique. With some network-*una*ware programs, you can get the same
result by exiting the program or temporarily exiting to DOS. Finally, you
can specify that if the server receives no print output for a certain number
of seconds, the server should assume that the print job is complete and
close the print request file and place it in the queue for printing. This
method is called setting a time-out value.

The bottom line is that the server must receive an explicit signal that the
print job is complete. If the program you are printing from doesn't send
this signal, you must take other steps. You must execute the ENDCAP
command, reexecute the CAPTURE command, or set a time-out value.

When you execute CAPTURE, status information is shown on your screen,
indicating where your output is being redirected. The following is a typical
status message from CAPTURE:

```
Device LPT1: re-routed to queue ACCT-LJ on server SERV1
```

The CAPTURE command offers more than 20 parameters you can use to customize the way you redirect your printed output. Using several of these parameters in the same CAPTURE command is not unusual. You can type each parameter's complete name or use its abbreviation (usually its first letter or first two letters). When you use CAPTURE with multiple parameters, you can separate the parameters with spaces or with forward slashes (/). The following sample CAPTURE command uses multiple parameters separated by spaces, with each parameter's full name:

CAPTURE QUEUE = PRINTQ_0 SERVER = SERV1 BANNER = BILL TIMEOUT = 10

Following is the same command using slashes to separate the abbreviated parameters:

CAPTURE/Q = PRINTQ_0/S = SERV1/B = BILL/TI = 10

A complete list of CAPTURE parameters is found in table 15.1. The use of each is described in the following sections.

Table 15.1
CAPTURE/NPRINT Parameters

Parameter	Abbr.	Formats	Comments
AUTOENDCAP	AU	CAPTURE AU CAPTURE AUTOENDCAP	Not used with NPRINT
BANNER	B	CAPTURE BANNER = ROOM_112 CAPTURE B = ROOM_112	
COPIES	C	CAPTURE COPIES = 3 CAPTURE C = 3	
CREATE	CR	CAPTURE CREATE = path\filename.ext CAPTURE CR = path\filename.ext	Not used with NPRINT
DELETE	D	NPRINT path\filename.ext DELETE NPRINT path\filename.ext D	Not used with CAPTURE
FORM	F	CAPTURE FORM = 1 CAPTURE FORM = LETTERHEAD CAPTURE F = 1 CAPTURE F = LETTERHEAD	
FORMFEED	FF	CAPTURE FORMFEED CAPTURE FF	
JOB	J	CAPTURE JOB = COMPPRINT CAPTURE J = COMPPRINT	

Parameter	Abbr.	Formats	Comments
LOCAL	L	CAPTURE LOCAL = 3 CAPTURE L = 3	Not used with NPRINT
KEEP	K	CAPTURE KEEP CAPTURE K	Not used with NPRINT
NAME	NAM	CAPTURE NAME = SMITHFD CAPTURE NAM = SMITHFD	
NOAUTOENDCAP	NA	CAPTURE NOAUTOENDCAP CAPTURE NA	Not used with NPRINT
NOBANNER	NB	CAPTURE NOBANNER CAPTURE NB	
NOFORMFEED	NFF	CAPTURE NOFORMFEED CAPTURE NFF	
NONOTIFY	NNOTI	CAPTURE NONOTIFY CAPTURE NNOTI	NetWare 386 only
NOTABS	NT	CAPTURE NOTABS CAPTURE NT	
NOTIFY	NOTI	CAPTURE NOTIFY CAPTURE NOTI	NetWare 386 only
PRINTER	P	CAPTURE PRINTER = 1 CAPTURE P = 1	NetWare 286 only
QUEUE	Q	CAPTURE QUEUE = ACCT-LJ CAPTURE Q = ACCT-LJ	
SERVER	S	CAPTURE SERVER = SERV1 CAPTURE S = SERV1	
SHOW	SH	CAPTURE SHOW CAPTURE SH	
TABS	T	CAPTURE TABS = 5 CAPTURE T = 5	
TIMEOUT	TI	CAPTURE TIMEOUT = 10 CAPTURE TI = 10	Not used with NPRINT

Using CAPTURE without Parameters

When you use the CAPTURE command without specifying any command-line parameters, your print output is automatically redirected to the queue serviced by the default printer (if you specified one).

Choosing How Your Output Should Be Redirected

The following options let you choose where and how your output should be redirected.

QUEUE

The QUEUE option lets you choose which queue your output will be directed to.

>Sample usage: CAPTURE QUEUE = ACCT-LJ
>Abbreviated: CAPTURE Q = ACCT-LJ

SERVER

The SERVER option lets you choose which server your output will be directed to. You should use SERVER when you are attached to multiple servers that have queues with the same name.

>Sample usage: CAPTURE SERVER = SERV1 QUEUE = ACCT-LJ
>Abbreviated: CAPTURE S = SERV1 Q = ACCT-LJ

LOCAL

Use the LOCAL option to specify which LPT port to capture from. By default, output to LPT1 is captured. If you enter LOCAL = 1, you specify LPT1, LOCAL = 2 specifies LPT2, and LOCAL = 3 specifies LPT3.

>Sample usage: CAPTURE LOCAL = 3
>Abbreviated: CAPTURE L = 3

KEEP

The KEEP parameter specifies that a partial print request be kept and printed in the event that your workstation abruptly loses power or "hangs" while a print job is being captured. Normally, a partial print job is discarded. Use this option if you are leaving your workstation unattended (perhaps while it is printing an overnight report).

Sample usage: CAPTURE KEEP

Abbreviated: CAPTURE K

PRINTER

The PRINTER option is available for NetWare 286 servers only. If you used a console command to assign printer numbers to queues, you can use the PRINTER parameter to direct jobs to a printer number.

Sample usage: CAPTURE PRINTER = 1

Abbreviated: CAPTURE P = 1

CREATE

Use the CREATE parameter to print output to a file instead of to a printer. The file destination you specify must be on a server where you are logged in, and you must have rights to create the file in the directory that you designate.

Sample usage: CAPTURE CREATE = SERV1/SYS:PRIVATE
                \SMITHFD\PRINFILE

Abbreviated: CAPTURE CR = SERV1/SYS:PRIVATE\SMITHFD\PRINFILE

Setting Output and Format Options

You can set a number of output and format options when you are starting CAPTURE. You can designate the number of copies of the print request to be printed, you can specify that a page-eject command be sent to the printer after every job, and you can specify how tabs should be handled.

More sophisticated formatting can be set up by specifying that a job configuration be used. A job configuration can send printer setup commands before the job and can specify how other CAPTURE parameters are handled.

COPIES

Use the COPIES parameter to specify a certain number of copies of a request to be printed. The default setting is 1, and the range allowed is 0 to 256.

Sample usage: CAPTURE COPIES = 3

Abbreviated: CAPTURE C = 3

FORMFEED

Use the FORMFEED parameter to specify that a page eject or form feed be sent to the printer after your print job. By default, this option is enabled so that the next print request after yours will not start on the same page as yours. Many applications send form feeds after they print. If the CAPTURE command sends one also, a blank page is printed after the job.

Sample usage: CAPTURE FORMFEED
Abbreviated: CAPTURE FF

NOFORMFEED

NOFORMFEED is the opposite of the FORMFEED option. When you use this parameter, no form feed is sent to your printer after a job.

Sample usage: CAPTURE NOFORMFEED
Abbreviated: CAPTURE NFF

FORM

Use the FORM option to specify that a new form or paper type be put in the printer before the job is printed. For example, if the printer is normally loaded with plain paper and you need to print a particular job on letterhead, you can use the FORM option to call for a form change. The printer stops printing so that you can change paper before the job and then start the printer. If the following job is to be printed on plain paper, the printer stops again, and you can reload the plain paper and restart the printer.

When you define forms you assign each form a name and number. If no form is specified, a default form number of 0 is assumed. When the printer is stopped for a form change, you are prompted to load the appropriate form number. You will learn how to define forms in the next section.

Sample usage: CAPTURE FORM = 1
                 CAPTURE FORM = LETTERHEAD
Abbreviated: CAPTURE F = 1
                 CAPTURE F = LETTERHEAD

JOB

The JOB parameter is used to designate which job configuration should be used to format your print request. You can define job configurations that specify a number of options, such as the setup codes that are sent to the printer before the job or the way the end-of-job signal is sent. The capability to create print request configurations is a powerful but optional feature. The best use of print request configurations is to ensure that the printer is reset to its default state before every request. Print request configurations also can be used to put the printer into a particular mode, such as compressed print or landscape.

Each job configuration is given a name. That name is specified with the JOB parameter as follows:

Sample usage: CAPTURE JOB = COMPPRINT
Abbreviated: CAPTURE J = COMPPRINT

TABS

TABS is a seldom-used option that specifies whether tab characters embedded in print jobs should be replaced with spaces. You specify the number of spaces to be used to replace the tab characters.

Sample usage: CAPTURE TABS = 5
Abbreviated: CAPTURE T = 5

NOTABS

NOTABS is used to specify that tab characters should not be replaced with spaces. You also should use this parameter when printing graphics.

Sample usage: CAPTURE NOTABS
Abbreviated: CAPTURE NT

Using Banner Options

A shared printer prints a banner page before each job to identify the job and to separate jobs from each other. The banner shows the user's name, the date and time of the job, and other pertinent information. A sample banner is shown in figure 15.2. Several options control the information shown in the banner and whether or not it is printed.

```
****************************************************************
* User Name:   SMITHFD (5)          Queue:   SERV1/ACCT-LJ    *
* File Name:                        Server   PS386            *
* Directory:                                                  *
* Description: LPT1 Catch                                     *
*             September 24, 89                     7:00am     *
****************************************************************
*                                                            *
*          SSS   M   M  III  TTTTT H   H FFFFF DDDD           *
*         S   S  MM MM   I     T   H   H F     D   D          *
*         S      M M M   I     T   H   H F     D    D         *
*          SSS   M M M   I     T   HHHHH FFFF  D    D         *
*            S   M   M   I     T   H   H F     D   D          *
*         S   S  M   M   I     T   H   H F     D   D          *
*          SSS   M   M  III    T   H   H F     DDDD           *
*                                                            *
****************************************************************
*                 JJJJJ  000  BBBB                           *
*                   J   0   0 B   B                          *
*                   J   0   0 B   B                          *
*                   J   0   0 BBBB                           *
*                   J   0   0 B   B                          *
*                 J J   0   0 B   B                          *
*                  J     000  BBBB                           *
****************************************************************
```

Fig. 15.2.
A sample banner.

NAME

The NAME parameter enables you to specify the name that appears in the upper panel of the banner. By default, the user's login name is used.

Sample usage: CAPTURE NAME = SMITHFD
Abbreviated: CAPTURE NAM = SMITHFD

BANNER

Use the BANNER option to specify up to 12 characters of identifying information to be shown in the lower panel of your banner page.

Sample usage: CAPTURE BANNER = ROOM_112
Abbreviated: CAPTURE B = ROOM_112

NOBANNER

Use the NOBANNER option to turn off the printing of the banner page.

Sample usage: CAPTURE NOBANNER
Abbreviated: CAPTURE NB

Using End-of-Job Options

CAPTURE provides a number of options that control how and when your print request file is closed and placed in a queue for printing. The AUTOENDCAP option is the default. With AUTOENDCAP, your print request file is not closed until the application you are printing from closes the DOS PRN device or until PRN is closed after you exit the application. You can override this default by using the NOAUTOENDCAP option, which specifies that your print request file is not closed until you execute the ENDCAP command or rerun the CAPTURE command. The TIMEOUT parameter allows you to use a third method. You can specify that if the server receives no print output for a certain number of seconds, the server should assume that the print job is complete, close the print request file, and place it in the queue for printing.

AUTOENDCAP

With the AUTOENDCAP option, your print request file is not closed and placed in the queue until the application from which you are printing closes the DOS PRN device. By default, the AUTOENDCAP option is enabled.

Sample usage: CAPTURE AUTOENDCAP
Abbreviated: CAPTURE AU

NOAUTOENDCAP

With the NOAUTOENDCAP option, your print request file is not closed until you run the ENDCAP program or rerun the CAPTURE program.

    Sample usage: CAPTURE NOAUTOENDCAP
    Abbreviated: CAPTURE NA

TIMEOUT

The TIMEOUT option enables you to specify that if the server receives no print output for a certain number of seconds, the server should assume that the print job is complete, close the print request file, and place it in the queue for printing. You designate how many seconds (from 1 to 1,000) the server should wait before closing the print request file. Using a TIMEOUT value of 0 results in the TIMEOUT feature being disabled.

    Sample usage: CAPTURE TIMEOUT = 10
    Abbreviated: CAPTURE TI = 10

Using Notification Options (NetWare 386 Only)

With NetWare 386 only, you can designate that a notification message be sent to you when your print request has been printed. When you use the NOTIFY option, you receive a message similar to LPT1 Catch printed on Third Floor Laser Printer. By default, no notification is sent.

NOTIFY

Use the NOTIFY parameter to activate the notification option.

    Sample usage: CAPTURE NOTIFY
    Abbreviated: CAPTURE NOTI

NONOTIFY

Use the NONOTIFY parameter to disable the notification option.

    Sample usage: CAPTURE NONOTIFY
    Abbreviated: CAPTURE NNOTI

Showing CAPTURE's Current Status

With CAPTURE's wide array of options, being able to see which options are active is useful. CAPTURE's SHOW parameter shows the current

CAPTURE status for each LPT port and the CAPTURE options that have been invoked. SHOW does not start or stop printed output redirection or change any of its options.

Sample usage: CAPTURE SHOW
Abbreviated: CAPTURE SH

The following is typical output when you use CAPTURE SHOW:

```
LPT1:  Capturing data to server SERV386 queue ACCT-LJ. User
       will not be notified after the files are printed.
       Capture Defaults:Enabled    Automatic Endcap:Enabled
       Banner :LST:                Form Feed       :Yes
       Copies :1                   Tabs            :Converted to 8 spaces
       Form   :0                   Timeout Count  :Disabled


LPT2:  Capturing Is Not Currently Active.


LPT3:  Capturing Is Not Currently Active.
```

With a mastery of CAPTURE, you can take full advantage of shared-network printing. One other method of printing to a shared printer is available; this method is discussed next.

Printing Files with NPRINT

From time to time, you may need to send a file to a shared printer instead of capturing output from an application. Perhaps you have a text file that needs to be printed or a file in a format that can be copied directly to a particular type of printer. The NPRINT command is designed to handle this type of situation.

To use NPRINT, specify the name of the file you want to print and the shared printing options you want to enable. NPRINT's parameters are similar to those for CAPTURE.

If you have established a default printer, you can use NPRINT with no parameters except the file path and name. The file is sent to the default printer. For example, to print the AUTOEXEC.BAT file in the C:\ directory, type

NPRINT C:\AUTOEXEC.BAT

and press Enter. (See Chapter 14 for details about establishing a default printer.)

If you are printing a file stored on a server volume, you can use the same rules for naming the file as the rules for other NetWare commands. You can use the complete NetWare identification for the file or shorten the identification, based on rules that are discussed with the MAP command in Chapter 9. For example, if you are printing a file called PRINFILE.TXT, which is stored on a server called SERV1 on the VOL1 volume in a directory called OUTPUT, you can use the following command to print the file:

NPRINT SERV1/VOL1:OUTPUT\PRINFILE.TXT

As with CAPTURE, you can add a number of parameters to control many aspects of how the file is printed. For example, to print five copies of the file without a banner page, type,

NPRINT SERV1/VOL1:OUTPUT\PRINFILE.TXT COPIES=5 NOBANNER

and press Enter.

The following CAPTURE parameters do not work with NPRINT:

SHOW
TIMEOUT
AUTOENDCAP
NOAUTOENDCAP
LOCAL
CREATE
KEEP

All other parameters work exactly as they do with CAPTURE.

NPRINT adds one parameter option of its own. The DELETE parameter enables you automatically to delete a file after it has been printed. To use this option, type

NPRINT SERV1/VOL1:OUTPUT\PRINFILE.TXT DELETE

and press Enter.

You can abbreviate the parameter as follows:

NPRINT SERV1/VOL1:OUTPUT\PRINFILE.TXT D

Next, you will learn about the advanced printer control and formatting options provided by creating custom job profiles and form types.

Using Advanced Printer Configuration Options

A basic mastery of working with queues, printers, print servers, and the CAPTURE command is all you need to be able to use and manage shared printing on your network. Some advanced capabilities, however, offer you greater control over the behavior of your shared printers.

Printer sharing has one potential inconvenience. Printers are highly configurable devices, allowing you to frequently change typefaces, fonts, pitches, and the like. A shared printer can change configurations with every job. Shared printers receive output from a wide variety of programs and from users of varying skill levels. Not all programs and users are well-behaved enough to clean up after themselves, so you can never be guaranteed that the printer to which you are sending a job is configured as you expect.

NetWare's advanced printer control features enable you to make a shared printer's configuration more predictable. You can specify a certain configuration to be set up at the beginning of every print job, thereby guaranteeing each user a predictable starting point when using a shared printer.

You use two NetWare utilities to implement these controls. The first, PRINTDEF, enables you to define printer functions, modes, devices, and forms. A *function* is a single printer setup command that sets a specific printer configuration attribute. A *mode* is a collection of functions that together make a complete printer configuration. A *device* is a grouping of modes and functions that apply to a particular type of printer. The relationship between devices, modes, and functions is shown in figure 15.3. A *form* is a definition that describes a paper type that can be used (such as envelope, letterhead, or invoice).

Suppose that you need to send a report to your LAN's shared laser printer and you need it to print sideways in compressed print. You easily can create a mode that automatically sets up the printer in this way. You simply combine three printer functions: one function sends a command to the printer to switch to compressed print, another sets the printer to the landscape orientation, and the third sets the page length to 45 lines.

After you have used PRINTDEF to configure and create printer devices, modes, functions, and forms, you can use PRINTCON to create printer job definitions. A *job definition* specifies the same options that can be

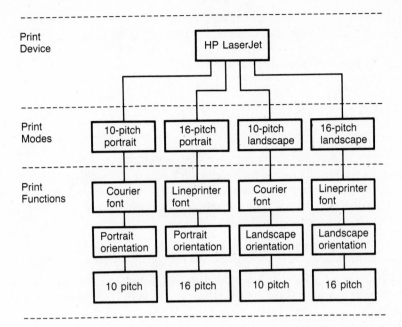

Print Device

HP LaserJet

Print Modes

| 10-pitch portrait | 16-pitch portrait | 10-pitch landscape | 16-pitch landscape |

Print Functions

Courier font	Lineprinter font	Courier font	Lineprinter font
Portrait orientation	Portrait orientation	Landscape orientation	Landscape orientation
10 pitch	16 pitch	10 pitch	16 pitch

Fig. 15.3.

Defining print devices with PRINTDEF.

designated with command-line parameters used with CAPTURE. For example, a job definition can be created to specify the queue the print job goes to, the banner information, the number of copies to be printed, the print mode to be used, and choices of end-of-job options such as a TIMEOUT, COUNT, or AUTOENDCAP.

Job definitions can be used as an alternative to teaching users the intricacies of understanding queues and working with CAPTURE's many command-line parameters. If you need to make sending jobs to various network printers easy for users, you can create for each printer a job definition that specifies the queue and sends the appropriate setup commands to configure the printer. For example, you can create a job definition called LASER for your network's shared laser printer. Users can direct jobs to that printer by typing

CAPTURE JOB = LASER

Using that job definition is much easier than using CAPTURE's many command-line options.

Each user can be given a default job definition. Then, if you know that a user almost always sends his or her jobs to the same printer, he or she can direct print jobs to it simply by typing *capture* and pressing Enter. All the options specified by the default job definition are used automatically.

Next, you will learn the mechanics of setting up devices, modes, functions, forms, and job definitions. You begin by using the PRINTDEF utility to edit and create printer device information. You then use this information to create job definitions with PRINTCON.

Using PRINTDEF

PRINTDEF is used to edit and create printer device definitions, modes, functions, and forms. Only a user with supervisory access (or workgroup-manager access with NetWare 386) can use PRINTDEF to create and edit printer configuration information. Other users may use PRINTDEF to view this information, but they cannot make any changes.

To start PRINTDEF, log in with supervisory or workgroup-manager access to the file server from which your users run CAPTURE and NPRINT. Type *printdef* and press Enter. PRINTDEF is stored in the PUBLIC directory, which is mapped as a search drive by default. A menu appears with the following options:

Print
Devices
Forms

Your first task is to work with print devices.

Working with Print Devices

A print device is associated with the printer or other output device to which print jobs are sent. The print device is made up of the functions and modes that have been defined for the printer (again see fig. 15.3). NetWare comes with a number of predefined print devices, and you probably can find device definitions that match all your shared network printers. In this case, you probably can work with the print device as it is. You don't have to create your own modes and functions.

If you have an unusual type of printer for which no predefined device is supplied, you can create a print device. Your first step is to check this list of predefined devices to see whether it contains a close match for each of your network printers.

Importing Predefined Print Devices

To work with NetWare's list of predefined print devices, select Print Devices from the PRINTDEF main menu. A menu with the following three options is displayed:

Edit Print Devices
Import Print Devices
Export Print Devices

Select Import Print Devices. An entry window opens, prompting you to select the directory from which a print device definition should be imported. Print devices exist as files with the extension PDF and are stored in the SYS:PUBLIC directory of a NetWare server. The entry window shows the NetWare name for the current directory (see Chapter 8 for information about full NetWare directory names).

Use the Backspace key to backspace over as much of the directory name as you need to discard, and enter the name of the SYS:PUBLIC directory. For example, if the current directory is SERV1/SYS:SYSTEM, backspace over SYSTEM and type *public* so that the directory name is SERV1/SYS:PUBLIC.

After you select SYS:PUBLIC as your source directory, press Enter. A window called Available .PDFs appears. This window contains a list of the PDF files in the SYS:PUBLIC directory; each file is named for its printer device. (For example HPLASER.PDF is for Hewlett-Packard LaserJets, and IBMPRO2.PDF is for the IBM ProPrinter.) Select the definition that most closely matches your printer. This definition is imported and its functions and modes made available for your use while you are configuring printers with PRINTDEF. Repeat the import process to find print device definitions for all the shared printers on your network. After print devices are imported, you can work with them to create and configure modes and functions to meet your needs.

Editing Print Devices

You can edit the print devices you have imported to customize them to meet your needs. Select Edit Print Devices from PRINTDEF's Print Device Options menu, and a list of the current print devices comes on-screen. Highlight the name of the print device you want to work with and press Enter. You then see the Edit Device Options menu, which offers two selections:

Device Modes
Device Functions

Remember that a mode is a specific configuration or setup (such as compressed printing in a sideways orientation) that you want to activate on a shared printer. A particular mode may require multiple printer commands to activate. These individual commands are called functions. Because functions are required to build modes, they are described first.

Select Device Functions from PRINTDEF's Edit Device Options menu. A list of currently defined functions is displayed. You can perform three tasks while working with this list: you can add a new function, delete a function, or modify an existing function.

Functions consist of individual printer commands. For example, the command to reset a Hewlett-Packard LaserJet is ESCAPE E. A function called RESET in the HPLASER.PDF device definition sends the ESCAPE E command to the printer.

To add a new function, choose Insert from the function list. A Function Definition Form box is shown on-screen (see fig. 15.4). A prompt instructs you to type a function name and the escape sequence that the function should execute. (Printer commands often start with ESCAPE and so are sometimes called escape sequences.) Type the name you want to give the function, and then type the printer command. Press Esc to save your new function. After you confirm that you want to save the new function, you are returned to the function list.

Fig. 15.4.

The Function Definition Form box.

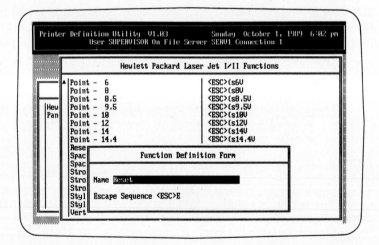

A few rules exist for listing printer commands. If you are familiar with the various ways to represent individual characters in printer commands, you know that a character can be represented by its character, its ASCII value, or its hexadecimal value. For example, the letter E can be represented as itself (E), its ASCII value (69), or its hexadecimal value (45). When you build a printer command using numbers, you must enclose the number in greater-than and less-than signs (such as <69>) or precede the number with a backslash (such as \69). If you decide to show the number in hexadecimal format, you must precede the number with 0x and enclose the number and its prefix in greater-than and less-than signs (such as <0x45>) or precede the number with a backslash (\0x45).

Special characters with ASCII values of less than 33 are often used in printer commands. These characters can be used as shown in table 15.2. The most common of these is ESCAPE (ASCII value 27). You can include ESCAPE in a printer command by listing it as <ESC>.

With the various options for listing the characters used in printer commands, the LaserJet RESET command can be shown as any of the following:

```
<ESC>E
<27><69>
\0x1B\0x45
```

Use the method that is the easiest for you and your coworkers to understand.

In addition to creating a new function, you also can modify an existing one. Highlight the function you want to change and press F3. The function definition window is displayed. You can change a function's listed name or escape sequence. After making the required changes, press Esc to exit. After you confirm that you want to save your modifications, the function list returns to the screen.

You also can delete a function. Highlight the function you want to delete and press the Del key. You are prompted to confirm that you want to delete the function; press Y to answer yes, and the function is deleted. You can delete multiple functions by marking them with F5 and then pressing the Del key.

After you have prepared your printer functions, you are ready to group them into modes.

A print mode is a collection of functions that are sent to the printer in a predefined order at the beginning of a print job. To create and edit modes, select Print Devices from the PRINTDEF main menu. Select Edit Print Devices, and a list of defined print devices is displayed. Highlight the name of the print device you want to work with and press Enter. From the next menu, select Device Modes. A list of the currently defined modes for your printer is shown. From this list, you can create a new mode or edit or delete an existing one.

Table 15.2
Special PRINTDEF Characters

When the following special characters are used in PRINTDEF function print commands, they may be included in the command as shown:

ASCII	Character Description	Use in PRINTDEF Command Value
0	Null	<NUL>
1	Start of header	<SOH>
2	Start of text	<STX>
3	End of text	<ETX>
4	End of transmission	<EOT>
5	Enquire	<ENQ>
6	Acknowledge	<ACK>
7	Bell	<BEL>
8	Backspace	<BS>
9	Horizontal tab	<TAB>
10	Line feed	<LF>
11	Vertical tab	<VT>
12	Form feed	<FF>
13	Carriage return	<CR>
14	Shift out	<SO>
15	Shift in	<SI>
16	Data link escape	<DLE>
17	Device control 1	<DC1>
18	Device control 2	<DC2>
19	Device control 3	<DC3>
20	Device control 4	<DC4>
21	Negative acknowledge	<NAK>
22	Synchronous	<SYN>
23	End of transmission block	<ETB>
24	Cancel	<CAN>
25	End of medium	<EM>
26	Substitute	<SUB>
27	Escape	<ESC>
28	File separator	<FS>
29	Group separator	<GS>
30	Record separator	<RS>
31	Unit separator	<US>
32	Space	<SP>
127	Delete	<DEL>

To create a new mode, press the Ins key. The program prompts you to enter the name for your new mode. Type the name you want to use and press Enter. You see an empty window, in which you list the functions that make up your mode.

In many cases, the order in which print commands are sent to the printer is important. For example, if you send a RESET escape code as your first command to a LaserJet, the command resets the printer to its default state and gives you a predictable starting point for issuing more commands. If the RESET code is sent at the end of your mode list, however, all the previous commands sent by your mode are overridden.

To choose the first function whose command should be sent to the printer, press the Ins key. All the defined functions are listed on-screen. Highlight the function you want to select and press Enter. You see your mode's list of functions, and the one you selected is included. To add your second command, press Ins again, and you again see the list of functions. Select the function you want to use for your second command. Repeat this process until you have selected all the functions you want to include in your mode definition. When you have completed your selections, press Esc to leave the function list. You are returned to the mode list for your print device.

You may want to modify a particular mode's list of functions. Highlight the mode you want to work with and press Enter. You see a list of the functions that make up the mode; functions are listed in the order in which they will be sent to the printer. You can remove a function from the list by highlighting it and pressing the Del key. You can add a function by highlighting the function you want to have your new function precede and marking it by pressing F5. Press the Ins key and a list of your printer's functions is shown. Highlight the one you want to insert and press Enter; the new function is added to the function list just before the function you marked with F5. If you do not mark a function before inserting another, the function you insert is placed at the end of the function list.

When you have finished editing the function list, press Esc to leave it. The mode list for your printer returns to the screen. If you are finished working with modes, press Esc two more times to return to the list of print devices and press Esc again to return to the PRINTDEF main menu.

Properly configuring the functions and modes for a particular print device is the first step to skillful management of the behavior of your shared network printers. You will soon learn how to put these tools to work when you define print job configurations using PRINTCON. You can define one last element with PRINTDEF: forms.

Defining Forms

One of the challenges of sharing a printer is managing the way various types of paper and forms are handled. If you send a 50-page report to a shared printer, you will be frustrated to discover that the report has been printed on invoice forms instead of plain paper because the last user changed the paper type to invoices.

NetWare uses form types to control this situation. With any print job, you can specify a form type on which the job should be printed. When you first activate the shared printer, NetWare operates on the assumption that the default form or paper type is in place. If a job that specifies a different form is placed in the printer's queue, NetWare stops the printer and prompts for the requested form to be loaded. The printer operator can load the right form type, use certain commands to confirm that the form has been loaded, and then restart the printer. The next job that requires a different form goes through the same process.

By default, no form types are defined. On networks that have no need to use diverse paper types, form types are left undefined. If you want to use this feature to manage changing paper types, you must use PRINTDEF to create form definitions. Up to 256 distinct types can be specified.

To create a form type, select Forms from the PRINTDEF main menu. A list of the current forms is displayed. (The list is blank if you are defining a form for the first time.) Press the Ins key and a Forms Definition Form window opens (see fig. 15.5). The prompt instructs you to enter the name of the form, its number, its length, and its width. Enter a name that describes the form (such as LETTERHEAD, INVOICES, or GREENBAR132). Your form name cannot begin with a number and cannot be more than 12 characters in length. The form number can be any number from 0 to 255. You should reserve 0 for your most commonly used form, because that is the default when no form is specified. Finally, for documentation purposes, you are prompted to enter the form length (or the number of lines per page) and the form width (characters per line). These settings have no bearing on the operation of the printer; they are merely for informational purposes. After your settings are entered, press the Esc key to save them. Your newly defined form is added to the forms list.

If you want to edit an existing form, highlight it on the forms list, and press the Enter key. The Forms Definition Form window is displayed, and you can change the form's name, number, or length and width. Press the Esc key to save your changes.

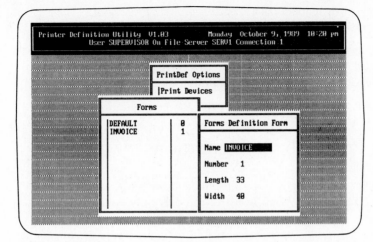

Fig. 15.5.

The Forms Definition Form window.

You can delete a form from the list by highlighting it and pressing the Del key. You can remove several forms at a time by marking each one with F5 and pressing the Del key.

When you are finished working with forms and are ready to leave PRINTDEF, press the Esc key to leave the forms list and return to the PRINTDEF main menu. Next, press the Esc key to exit PRINTDEF. When you exit, you need to confirm that you want to save your updates to the server printer database. Unless you were just practicing, you press Y to respond yes. A file called NET$PRN.DAT in the SYS:PUBLIC directory stores the configuration information you create with PRINTDEF.

You are now ready to use the device, mode, and form definitions to build print job configurations. The PRINTCON utility is used for this task.

Using PRINTCON

PRINTCON is used to create print job definitions. As already discussed, a print job definition can do much of the same work that can be done with skillful use of CAPTURE's command-line parameters. Each user is free to use PRINTCON to create his or her own print job definitions, or a supervisory-level user or workgroup manager can create them and copy them to the print job configuration file of other users.

To start PRINTCON, log into the server from which you run CAPTURE or NPRINT, type *printcon*, and press Enter. PRINTCON is stored in

SYS:PUBLIC, which is mapped as a search directory by default.
PRINTCON's opening menu offers the following options:

Edit Print Job Configurations
Select Default Print Job Configuration
Supervisor - Copy Print Job Configurations

Your first step is to create at least one print job configuration.

Creating Print Job Configurations

To create a print job configuration, select Edit Print Job Configurations
from the PRINTCON main menu. A list of the currently defined
configurations assigned to your user name is shown on-screen. (The list is
empty if no configurations have been created for you.) Press the Ins key to
add a new configuration to the list. You are prompted to enter a print job
configuration name. Enter a name that is brief and meaningful (up to 31
characters in length); it should describe the type of printer the
configuration is to be used with and how the job configures that printer.
For example, a print job configuration that sets a LaserJet printer to 10-
pitch print in the portrait orientation using the Courier font can be called
LJ_COUR_10_PORT. Type a suitable name and press Enter.

The Print Job Configuration screen is displayed (see fig. 15.6). A number
of configuration options are shown. The configuration options are
described one at a time.

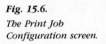

Fig. 15.6.

*The Print Job
Configuration screen.*

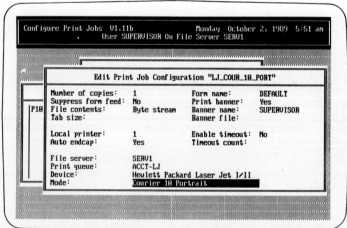

The Number of Copies option determines the number of copies to be printed and performs the same function as CAPTURE's COPIES parameter. Normally, this option is left at its default setting of 1. To change the setting, move the highlight next to the number of copies you want to print and press Enter. You then can enter any number from 0 to 65000. If you choose a number at the higher end of this range, make sure that the people you share the printer with are understanding and patient.

The Suppress Form Feed option controls whether or not a page eject or form feed command is sent to the printer after each job. (When this option is set to no, a page eject command is sent after each job.) This setting performs the same function as CAPTURE's FORMFEED parameter. You normally want to eject a page from the printer after each job to prevent two print jobs from sharing the same page. (Your word processor may also send a page eject command for the same reason; if it does, an extra blank page is printed between print jobs.) To toggle this setting, move the highlight to it and press Y to change it to yes and N to change it to no.

Use the File Contents option to designate what type job you are sending to the printer. You can specify that the job be byte stream or text. If you are printing from a program, such as a word processor or spreadsheet, choose the byte stream setting. In this mode, the print job is passed to the printer exactly as is, with no formatting done while the job is in the print queue. When you choose text (instead of byte stream), tabs are converted to spaces and end-of-file markers are observed. In almost every case, you should choose byte stream because this mode causes your print job to be passed to the printer as is.

You use the text option only when you are copying to the printer ASCII files containing tab characters that must be converted to spaces. If you select text as the File Contents setting, the program prompts you to enter the number of spaces that should be used to replace each tab character in a print job. The number you enter as the Tab Size setting is the number of spaces that replaces each tab (the default is eight spaces).

Next, you are prompted to enter the Form Name you want to use. If you used PRINTDEF to define form types, you can choose one of them here. (Remember that form types are used to stop a shared printer and to prompt for a paper change.) Move the highlight to the Form Name setting and press Enter; a list of the defined forms is shown. Select the form you want to use from the list.

The next three options have to do with the banner page printed before the print job. The Print Banner setting determines whether the banner page is printed. To change this setting, move the highlight to Print Banner and press Y for yes or N for no. The Banner Name option controls the information printed in the top panel of the banner (again see fig. 15.2 for a sample banner). By default, NetWare prints the name of the user who sent the print job; but when you highlight this option and press Enter, you can type any identifying information you want to use (up to 12 characters in length).

The Banner File option is used to specify what information should be shown in the lower panel of the banner page. This option is equivalent to using CAPTURE's BANNER parameter. You can enter any information up to 12 characters in length. If you leave this setting blank, when you copy or NPRINT a file to a print queue, the name of the file is printed.

The Local Printer setting designates which LPT port is captured or redirected to the print queue. This option is the same as CAPTURE's LOCAL parameter. You can set this option to 1 to redirect output from LPT1, 2 to redirect from LPT2, or 3 to redirect from LPT3.

The next three options are used to specify how the server is notified when the print job is complete. (The server waits until the job is complete before queuing it for printing.) When the AUTOENDCAP option is set to yes, the end-of-job signal is sent when the program from which you are printing closes the DOS PRN device. Some applications send this signal automatically; with others you have to exit the application for the signal to be sent. When this option is set to no, the end-of-job signal is not sent until you run the ENDCAP command or rerun CAPTURE. This option accomplishes the same results as CAPTURE's AUTOENDCAP and NOAUTOENDCAP options.

The Enable Timeout setting controls whether an end-of-job signal is sent after a certain amount of time has passed during which the server has received no output to be printed. This setting can be an effective alternative to leaving your application, as may be required when you use the AUTOENDCAP option alone. This option is identical to using CAPTURE's TIMEOUT parameter. When you set the Enable Timeout option to yes, you are prompted to enter a value for the Timeout Count setting. This setting determines the number of seconds that must pass with no print job output before the end-of-job signal is sent. Make sure that you enter a number that grants enough time to allow for periods during which no output is sent (such as when you are printing a report and the printer pauses while your PC processes information). You can enter a value from 1 to 1,000 seconds. (1,000 seconds is 16 minutes and 40 seconds.)

With the next two options, you choose the file server and queue to which your print job should be sent. If you move the highlight to File Server and press Enter, a list of servers to which you can send jobs is shown on-screen. Select the server that contains the queue you want to use. You are then prompted to make a Print Queue selection. With the highlight at Print Queue, press Enter; a list of queues on the selected server is displayed. Select the queue you want to use, keeping in mind the printer or printers that service that queue.

The final two options control the setup and configuration commands that are sent to the printer before your print job. When you highlight Device and press Enter, a list of the devices you defined or imported using PRINTDEF is displayed. A device is a collection of printer modes and functions that contain configuration commands relating to a particular type of printer. Choose the device that includes the print mode you need to use to configure the printer before it receives your job. You have the option of choosing None if you want no printer commands to be sent. After choosing a device, you are prompted to make a selection for the Mode option. When you move the highlight to Mode and press Enter, the modes for the selected print device are displayed. Choose the mode that contains the printer commands you want to send to the printer before your job.

You have chosen the settings required to create a print job configuration. Press the Esc key to exit the Print Job Configuration editing screen. A message on-screen prompts you to confirm that you want to save the configuration. After you save the configuration, the print job configuration list is displayed. You can create an additional configuration by pressing the Ins key, or you can edit an existing one by highlighting the one you want to edit and pressing Enter. You can delete a print job configuration by highlighting it and pressing the Del key, or you can mark multiple configurations with F5 and delete them all by pressing the Del key. When you are finished working with print job configurations, press the Esc key to return to the PRINTCON main menu.

Choosing a Default Print Job Configuration

A default print job configuration is used automatically if you don't specify one. If you create only one print job configuration for yourself, it automatically becomes the default. If you have created more than one, you need to choose the default.

To choose a default configuration, choose Select Default Print Job Configuration from the PRINTCON main menu. A list of your print job configurations is displayed. Highlight the one you want as your default and press Enter. The list is updated to show your choice. Press the Esc key to return to the PRINTCON main menu. Your default print job configuration cannot be deleted.

Sending Print Job Configurations to Other Users

When you create a print job configuration, you are the only one who can use it. Ideally, all network users should learn how to use PRINTDEF and PRINTCON to configure their network printing. Unless all your network users are adept at changing program settings, this situation is not likely to occur. Fortunately, the network supervisor (or a workgroup manager with NetWare 386) can create print job configurations and make them available to all users. If you have a large number of users, you may find this task to be tedious, and it becomes another step you must go through every time you add a user to your network. Later in this section, you will learn about an alternative method that may be easier.

When you move print job configurations, you copy one user's printer configuration to another. You do not copy just a single job configuration; you copy all job configurations. Before copying the job configurations, make sure that the user to whom you are copying a configuration can use it exactly as the original user does, or be prepared to use the original configuration as a basis on which another one can be customized.

To use PRINTCON to move a print job configuration from one user to another, choose Supervisor - Copy Print Job Configurations from the main menu. (This selection is available only if you are logged in with supervisor equivalence or as a workgroup manager.) You are prompted to enter the name of the Source User, the user whose configuration you are copying. Enter the user's login name exactly as it appears in SYSCON. Unfortunately, you cannot press the Ins key to see a list of users from which to choose; you must know the user's name. After entering the source user's name, you are prompted to enter the name of the Target User (the user who is to receive the configuration). Again, you must enter the user's login name. You cannot enter the name of a group; you must move configurations one user at a time.

This method is slow and tedious. The next section discusses how printer configurations are stored. If you are a clever user of DOS, you can perform the same task without using PRINTCON.

Storing Printer Configurations

Each user's printer configuration information is stored in a file called PRINTCON.DAT in a special private subdirectory under the SYS:MAIL directory. Each user is given a subdirectory under SYS:MAIL when his or her identification number is created. The subdirectory name is a number and is the same as the user ID number NetWare assigns to a user when he or she is added to the network.

If you are a supervisor or workgroup manager, you can look up a user's ID number by using SYSCON. From the SYSCON main menu, select User Information. This option lists the users on the server. Highlight the user whose number you want to look up and press Enter. The User Information menu is then displayed. If you select Other Information, a box opens showing the user's ID number. For example, a user with an ID number of 20007 has a personal mail directory called SYS:MAIL\20007.

You can duplicate printer configurations by directly copying one PRINTCON.DAT file into all subdirectories under SYS:MAIL. This method is a quick alternative to using PRINTCON to move the configurations one at a time.

You have learned how to create and configure queues and assign shared printers to queues. You also have learned how to direct print jobs to those queues and how to take advantage of the special formatting options offered by PRINTDEF and PRINTCON. In short, you have learned how to implement and use shared printing. After you have reached this point, another important skill is required: the ability to manage shared printing. You will learn about shared printing in the next section.

Managing Shared Printing

One of the network supervisor's most frequently recurring jobs is to manage shared printing (unless he or she wisely delegates this task to a few knowledgeable users or assistants). Requests such as "I sent my job to the printer 20 minutes ago, and it still hasn't printed" or "I get an error message every time I try to use CAPTURE" must be dealt with, as well as more mundane tasks like deleting jobs or fine-tuning print job configurations to get the right results.

NetWare gives you and other network users a powerful array of printer- and queue-management capabilities. You can delete a job that is waiting to be printed or rearrange the order of jobs in a queue. You can put a job on hold to prevent it from printing until you take it off hold. You can restart a job whose pages have been damaged by a printer jam. You can stop a queue by temporarily making it unable to receive new jobs, or you can stop a printer to facilitate a ribbon or toner cartridge change.

With NetWare 286, you use the PCONSOLE utility and server console commands to manage shared printing. With NetWare 386, you use PCONSOLE and the PSC command. PCONSOLE is described next.

Using PCONSOLE To Manage Shared Printing

You already have used PCONSOLE extensively to configure print queues and to match them to printers. If you are using NetWare 386, you have used PCONSOLE extensively to create and configure print server definitions. To use PCONSOLE to manage shared printing, you must be designated as a queue operator. Queue users can use PCONSOLE to view the status of a print job. (To learn about queue operators and users, see the section in the preceding chapter called "Adding Queue Operators and Users.") With NetWare 386, you must be a print server operator to use PCONSOLE to control a print server; you must be a print server user to use PCONSOLE to view the printer server status.

To start PCONSOLE, log into the server that has the queues or the definition for the print server you want to manage, type *pconsole*, and press Enter. The PCONSOLE main menu shows the following three options:

    Change Current File Server
    Print Queue Information
    Print Server Information

You use PCONSOLE to perform three categories of shared-printer management: managing individual print jobs in queues, managing queues, and managing print servers (for NetWare 386 only). The next sections describe these tasks.

Managing Queued Print Jobs

A print request travels to a shared printer via a print queue on a server. As you have learned, the queue is a holding area where jobs wait for the printer to become available. While these jobs are waiting in line, a number of management operations can be performed. For example, a high-priority job can be moved up in line so that it is printed next. A job sent in error can be deleted, or one that will take a long time to print can be put on hold until after hours. Many of the options set with CAPTURE parameters or with the job profile can be changed.

To use PCONSOLE to manage queued jobs, select Print Queue Information from the PCONSOLE main menu. A list of the queues on the current server is displayed. Highlight the queue whose jobs you want to work with and press Enter. The Print Queue Information menu is displayed. Select Current Print Job Entries. A screen is displayed that shows a list of the current jobs waiting in the queue (see fig. 15.7).

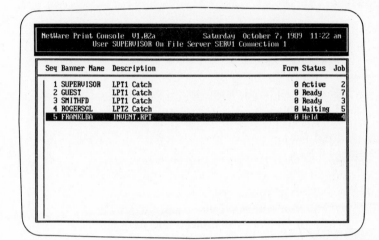

Fig. 15.7.
Jobs waiting in queue.

This screen shows six columns of useful information about the queued print jobs. The numbers in the first column (which is headed Seq for Sequence) show the order in which the jobs will be printed. The second column (headed Banner Name) displays the information that should appear in the upper panel of the banner. By default, this information is the login name of the user who sent the job to the queue. The Description column displays the type of job. If the job has a description of LPT1 Catch, it was sent to the queue by means of the CAPTURE command (which redirected output originally meant for LPT1). The description also can be a file name, meaning that the job was placed in the queue by means of the NPRINT command.

The Form column shows the form number requested by the job. The Status column shows each job's status, which can be one of five possibilities: Active, Ready, Adding, Waiting, or Held. A job showing the Active status is being printed. The Ready status indicates that a job is ready to print but is waiting for an available printer. When a job shows the Adding status, print output is still being received by the queue, and the end-of-job signal has not been received. Two less common status settings are Held and Waiting. A job with the status Held has been placed on hold by a queue operator or by the user who put it in the queue. The Waiting status indicates that the job has been placed in the queue to be printed at a future time specified by the user or queue operator.

From the queue job list screen, you can select individual jobs to work with, or you can add and remove jobs from the queue. These options are described after you learn about removing a print job from the queue.

Removing Jobs from the Queue

Removing a job from the queue is easy. Use the up- or down-arrow key to highlight the job you want to remove and press the Del key. You are prompted to confirm that you really want to delete the job. After you confirm the deletion, the job is removed from the list.

Queue operators can remove any job from the queue. Queue users can delete only their own jobs.

Working with Queued Jobs

After a job is in the queue, you can work with it in several ways. You can change its order in the queue and move it to the front of the line so that the job is printed as soon as possible. You also can put the job on hold so that it is not printed until you take it off hold. You can change many of the options set by CAPTURE or NPRINT's command-line parameters, such as the banner information and the form type to use. You also can defer the print job—you can set a future time at which the job will be printed.

To work with a job, use the up- or down-arrow key to highlight the job and press Enter. The Print Queue Entry Information screen is displayed (see fig. 15.8). You can customize most of the settings on this screen.

Fig. 15.8.

The Print Queue Entry Information screen.

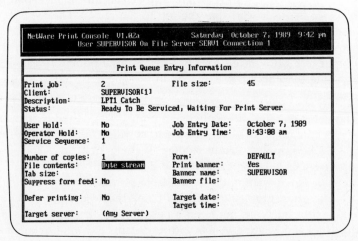

Several items on this screen are for information only and cannot be changed. The print job number, the print job file size, the print job status, the client (the user who placed the job in the queue), and the job entry date and time show information you cannot modify.

The first option you can change is the print job description. This information is the same information shown in the Description column of the queue job list screen and usually identifies whether the job is an LPT catch or a file. You seldom have a reason to change this information, but if you want to, move the highlight to it and press Enter. Backspace over the existing information and enter the description of your choice.

The next option you can change is the User Hold setting. If you are the user who placed the job in the queue, you can change this setting to yes to put the print job on hold. It will not print until you change the User Hold setting to no. The Operator Hold option is similar, except that it can be used by a queue operator only. Both options are useful when a job temporarily has to be prevented from printing.

The Service Sequence setting is used to control the job's order in the queue. Service Sequence shows the job's current place in line in the queue. Only the queue operator can change the order of print jobs. If you need to move a job up in the queue so that it prints sooner, change the job's service sequence setting to a lower number. Similarly, if you want a job to print later, change the service sequence to a higher number.

You can set the number of copies of the job to print with the Number of Copies option. The default is one copy, but you can increase the setting to any number up to 65000.

The File Contents option reflects what type of job you are sending to the printer. You can specify that the job is a byte stream or text. If you are printing from a program, such as a word processor or spreadsheet, you should choose the byte stream setting. In this mode, the print job is passed to the printer exactly as it is, with no formatting done while the job is in the print queue.

You should choose the text option when you are copying ASCII files to the printer. Tabs are converted to spaces, and end-of-file markers are observed in this mode. If you select text as the File Contents setting, you can enter the number of spaces to be used to replace each tab character in the print job. The number you enter as the Tab Size setting is the number of spaces that replaces each tab.

The Suppress Form Feed option controls whether a page-eject or form-feed command is sent to the printer after the job. (When this option is set to no, a page eject command is sent.) You normally will want to eject a page from the printer after each job to prevent two print jobs from sharing the same page. (Your word processor may also send a page-eject command for the same reason; if it does, an extra blank page is printed between print jobs.) To toggle this setting, move the highlight to it, and press Y to change the setting to yes or N to change it to no.

You can use the Form Name option to specify the form type the job should use. If you used PRINTDEF to define form types, you can choose one of them here. (Remember that form types are used to stop a shared printer and to prompt for a paper change.) Move the highlight to the Form Name setting, press Enter, and a list of the defined forms is displayed. From the list, select the form you want to use.

Three options determine the banner page, which is printed before the print job. The Print Banner setting determines whether the banner page is printed. To change this setting, move the highlight to Print Banner and press Y to make the setting yes or N to make it no. The Banner Name option controls the information that is printed in the top panel of the banner. (Figure 15.2, earlier in this chapter, shows a sample banner.) By default, the name of the user who sent the print job is printed, but when you highlight the Banner Name option and press Enter, you can type any identifying information (up to 12 characters in length).

The Banner File option is used to specify what information should be shown in the lower panel of the banner page and is equivalent to using CAPTURE's BANNER parameter. You can enter any information up to 12 characters in length. If you leave this setting blank, when you copy or NPRINT a file to a print queue, the name of the file is shown.

Occasionally, you may want to place a print request in the queue but designate that the job not be printed until a later time. The Defer Printing option allows you to delay printing. Move the highlight to this option and press Y to change its setting to yes or N to change it to no. When you set Defer Printing to yes, you are prompted to enter the Target Date and Target Time, which are, respectively, the date and time you want the job to be made available for printing. Enter the date in one of four formats: 01/15/90; JAN 15, 1990; JANUARY 15, 1990; or 15 JAN 90. Enter the time in one of four formats: 02:30 p.m., 14:30, 02.30 p.m., or 14.30. When you defer a job's print time, its status on the queue job list screen's Status column changes to Waiting.

The final option you can change is the Target Server. Highlight this option and press Enter. A list of the servers that service this queue is displayed. Select the server you want to service the job. If you don't care which server services the job, leave the target server setting as Any Server.

After you have set the queue job options as you want them to be, press Esc to leave the Print Queue Entry Information screen and to return to the queue job list.

Adding Jobs to the Queue

PCONSOLE can be used to place files in the queue for printing. (Using PCONSOLE is just like using NPRINT to send a file to a shared printer.) To place a file in the queue for printing, press the Ins key from the queue job list screen. A window opens, prompting you to choose the directory in which the file exists, and your current default directory is shown. Press Enter if the default directory is the directory you want to use, or backspace over the directory name and replace it with the one in which the file you want to print is stored. (As with other NetWare utilities, like FILER, that prompt for a directory name, you can build this list by pressing the Ins key to list all servers. Select a server, then all volumes, then all directories, then all subdirectories, and so on, until you have selected the appropriate directory.) Press Enter when the correct directory is displayed, and a list of files in that directory is shown on-screen. Use the up- and down-arrow keys to move the highlight to the correct file, and press Enter; or mark several files with the F5 key, and press Enter.

Next, you are prompted to choose the print job configuration. If you defined any print job configurations with PRINTCON, they are listed, along with an option called Pconsole Defaults. Highlight the configuration you want to use and press Enter. A screen similar to the one shown in figure 15.8 is displayed. Set any options you want to change, as described in the section "Working with Queued Jobs". Press Esc to leave this screen. A message prompts you to confirm that you want to save your changes; after you confirm the save, your new print job is added to the queue. The queue job list returns to the screen.

When you are finished working with the queue job list, press Esc to return to the PCONSOLE Print Queue Information menu. You are now ready to learn about using PCONSOLE to control the status of the print queue.

Controlling Print Queues

In addition to being able to control individual print jobs in a queue, queue operators also can control several aspects of the way the queue as a whole operates. To control a queue, start PCONSOLE and select Print Queue Information from its main menu. You see a list of the server's queues; highlight the queue you want to control and press Enter. The Print Queue

Information menu is displayed. Select Current Queue Status from this menu, and the Current Queue Status screen comes on-screen (see fig. 15.9).

Fig. 15.9.

The Current Queue Status screen.

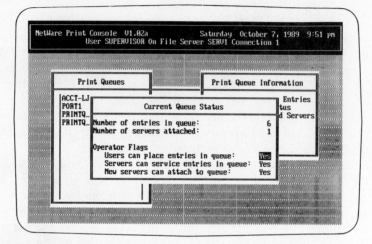

From this screen, you can control the queue in three ways. You can specify whether users can add new jobs to the queue by changing the Users Can Place Entries in the Queue setting to yes or no. When this option is set to no, users cannot use CAPTURE or NPRINT to send print jobs to the queue.

You also can control whether printers attached to servers can service the jobs in the queue by changing the Servers Can Service Entries in Queue setting to yes or no. When this option is set to no, no jobs in the queue are printed because server-attached printers are not permitted to service the queue.

Finally, you can control whether new servers can be attached to the queue so that additional printers can service the queue by changing the New Servers Can Attach to Queue setting to yes or no.

Managing queued print jobs and controlling queues are the main printing management tasks you perform with PCONSOLE. With NetWare 386, you also can use PCONSOLE to view the status of a print server and stop it or control its printers. You will learn how to do these tasks in the next section.

Using PCONSOLE To Control Printers (NetWare 386 Only)

With NetWare 286, most printer control functions take place at the file server console. You use console commands to start and stop the printer and to issue other operating instructions. You will learn about these commands in the section called "Using Console Commands To Manage Shared Printing," later in this chapter.

NetWare 386 enables you to use PCONSOLE to control shared printers from a workstation. You can start and stop printers, record the fact that a new form type is loaded, restart the current print job to correct for paper jams, or use commands that help you align the printer paper. To perform these tasks, you must be logged in with a user name that has print-server operator status. (As previously discussed, a print server is a NetWare 386 software module that controls the movement of print jobs from queues to printers.)

To use PCONSOLE to control a shared printer, log into the NetWare 386 server running the print server that manages the shared printer. If you are working with a print server running on a dedicated workstation, log into the server that stores the workstation's print server definition. Make sure that the login name you use has print-server operator status. Start PCONSOLE by typing *pconsole* and pressing Enter.

From the PCONSOLE main menu, select Print Server Information. A list of the currently defined print servers is displayed; highlight the server that is managing the printer you want to work with and press Enter. The Print Server Information menu comes on-screen. Select the Print Server Status/ Control option. (If this option is not displayed on the menu, the print server you chose to work with is not running.)

From the resulting Print Server Status and Control menu, select Printer Status. A list of the print server's currently active printers appears. Highlight the printer you want to work with and press Enter. You see the printer status screen, showing useful information about the printer's current status (see fig. 15.10).

The bottom part of the screen shows information about the job the printer is currently handling. The file server and queue from which the job originates are displayed, as well as the job's number, description, and requested form type. The number of copies requested, the size of one copy (in bytes), and the completion percentage, and status of the job are shown also.

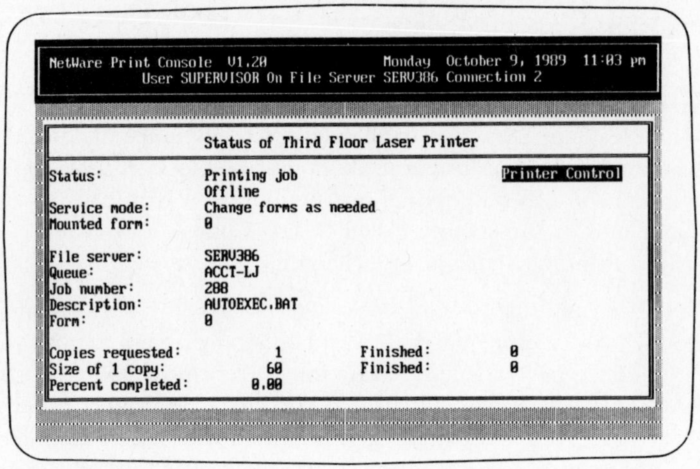

Fig. 15.10.

The Printer Status screen.

```
NetWare Print Console  V1.20          Monday  October 9, 1989  11:03 pm
            User SUPERVISOR On File Server SERV386 Connection 2


                    Status of Third Floor Laser Printer

Status:             Printing job                      Printer Control
                    Offline
Service mode:       Change forms as needed
Mounted form:       0

File server:        SERV386
Queue:              ACCT-LJ
Job number:         288
Description:        AUTOEXEC.BAT
Form:               0

Copies requested:          1         Finished:          0
Size of 1 copy:           60         Finished:          0
Percent completed:      0.00
```

The upper half of the screen consists of settings you can control. The Service Mode setting allows you to determine how the printer handles form changes. You worked with this option when you configured the printer for the first time. If you want to read about your choices for this setting, return to the preceding chapter.

If the print server module has stopped sending jobs to the printer and is requesting that a new form be loaded, you can use PCONSOLE to take care of the form change. First, load the correct type of paper in the printer. Next, move the highlight to the Mounted Form option and press Enter. Type the form number that matches the paper type that is loaded in the printer, and press Enter to save your change. The job waiting for the form change starts to print, and the status message changes from Waiting for Form to Be Mounted to Printing Job. When you select the Printer Control option in the upper right corner of the status screen, you can issue printer commands to start and stop the printer or align the paper. When you highlight Printer Control and press Enter, a menu with the following options is displayed:

Abort print job
Form Feed
Mark top of form
Pause printer
Rewind printer
Start printer
Stop printer

The Abort Print Job option enables you to abort the current job. The remaining part of the job is not printed, and the print job is removed from the queue.

The Form Feed selection sends a page-eject command to the printer. The Mark Top of Form option prints a line of asterisks at the printer's current top-of-form position. You can use this option to check the printer's paper alignment.

The Pause Printer option is used to pause a print job at its current position. When you restart the printer, it resumes printing exactly where it left off. The Stop Printer option is slightly different. When printing resumes after issuing this command, printing starts at the beginning of the print job, not where the printer left off. When you use the Pause Printer or Stop Printer option, the printer usually does not stop immediately because it continues to print whatever is stored in its internal buffer. The Start Printer option is used to restart the printer after you have issued the Stop Printer or Pause Printer command.

The Rewind Printer option offers some time-saving capabilities. If a job is printing when the printer jams, runs out of toner, or has a ribbon problem, several pages of the job may be unusable. The Rewind Printer option enables you to specify that a certain number of pages of the print job be re-sent to the printer. This option works only if the job you are printing is in ASCII format and has page breaks between pages.

To rewind the printer, select Rewind Printer; you are prompted to enter the number of pages to rewind, or you can enter the page number to which you want to rewind. If you enter 0 as the number of pages to rewind, the printer rewinds to the top of the current page. If you enter a number greater than the number of pages already printed, the printer rewinds to the beginning of the job. After entering your rewind instructions, press Esc to return to the Printer Control menu.

After you have finished working with the printer control commands, press Esc to return to the Printer Status screen. You can press Esc again to leave the Printer Status screen and return to the Print Server Status and Control menu. You can continue to press Esc if you want to move to other PCONSOLE menus or leave PCONSOLE altogether.

Controlling NetWare 386 Print Servers

As previously discussed, NetWare 386's print server module runs on a server or on a dedicated workstation and controls the movement of print jobs from queues to printers.

A user who is a print-server operator can use PCONSOLE to view the status of a print server and stop it if necessary. Log into the NetWare 386 server that is running the print server you want to work with. If you are working with a print server running on a dedicated workstation, log into the server that stores the workstation's print server definition. Make sure that the login name you use has print-server operator status. Start PCONSOLE by typing *pconsole* and pressing Enter.

From the PCONSOLE main menu, select Print Server Information. A list of the currently defined print servers is displayed; highlight the server you want to work with and press Enter. You see the Print Server Information menu. Select the Print Server Status/Control option. (If this option is not displayed on the menu, the print server you chose to work with is not running.)

From the Print Server Status/Control menu, select the Server Info option. The Print Server Info/Status window is shown (see fig. 15.11). The window shows the number of active printers being managed by the print server and shows the print server's current status as Running. If you press Enter, two options for stopping the print server are displayed. Selecting the Down option stops the print server immediately, and selecting the Going Down after Current Jobs option stops the print server after all jobs have finished. Select the appropriate option, and the print server stops running. Press Esc to leave the status screen and return to the Print Server Status and Control menu. You can continue to press Esc if you want to move to other PCONSOLE menus or leave PCONSOLE altogether.

Fig. 15.11.
The Print Server Info/Status window.

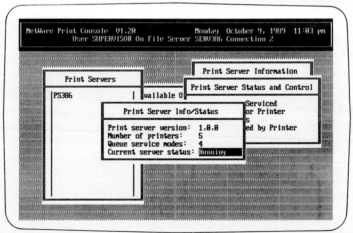

Using NetWare 386's PSC Command To Manage Printing

NetWare 386's PSC command is a command line alternative to using PCONSOLE to control print servers and printers. PSC stands for Print Server Command. To use PSC to control a printer or print server, you must be a queue operator. Users who are not queue operators can use PSC to view the status of a printer.

Like the CAPTURE command, PSC is used with an extensive list of command-line parameters. After you master this list of options, you may find using PSC to be quicker than negotiating PCONSOLE's many layers of menus. PSC also can be used when printer control commands need to be embedded in batch files or menus.

You must be logged into a NetWare 386 server to run PSC. PSC usually requires three parameters: the print server name, the printer number on the print server you want to work with, and the action you want to take. For example, if you want to check the status of printer number 3 on a print server named PS386, you use the following PSC command:

PSC PS = PS386 P = 3 STATUS

Notice that PSC is followed by three parameters. The print server name is the first and is preceded by PS = . The printer number is second, preceded by P = . The action you want to take is the third parameter and in the preceding example is STATUS.

You always must have a print server name parameter and an action parameter. If you omit the printer number, PSC works on the assumption that you want to take the requested action for all printers on the print server.

If you always are going to use PSC to work with the same print server, you can use the DOS SET command to create an environment variable that PSC can use to get the print server name. Using this command saves you the trouble of specifying the print server name every time you use PSC. If your print server is named PS386, you can create this DOS environment variable by typing the following *from the DOS prompt*:

SET PSC = PS386

You can use the same technique to eliminate the need to type a printer number. If you are usually going to use PSC to check on one particular printer, use the SET command to create a DOS environment variable to tell

PSC to check that printer automatically. To include a default printer number when you set PSC defaults, type the following *at the DOS prompt*:

SET PSC = PS386 p1

(Substitute your print server name for PS386, and your printer number for 1.) With these defaults set, you can override them by typing a different print server name and printer number when you type a PSC command.

Now that you know the basics of using PSC, the next section describes how to use each action parameter.

Starting and Stopping a Printer

Several PSC action parameters enable you start and stop a printer. When you use one of the following commands to stop the printer, printing does not stop immediately because the printer continues to print whatever remains in its internal buffer.

Note: In the following examples, the abbreviated version of the command assumes that the DOS SET command has been used to establish a default print server and printer number.

PAUSE

The PAUSE parameter is used to pause a print job at its current position. When you restart the printer, it resumes printing exactly where it left off.

Sample usage: PSC PS = PS386 P = 0 PAUSE
Abbreviated: PSC PAU

STOP

The STOP option differs slightly from PAUSE. STOP also causes printing to cease, but by default STOP deletes the job currently being printed. If you specify the KEEP option, however, when printing resumes, the job starts at the beginning again.

Sample usage: PSC PS = PS386 P = 0 STOP
                         PSC PS = PS386 P = 0 STOP KEEP
Abbreviated: PSC STO
                         PSC STO K

START

Use the START option to restart the printer after you have issued the STOP printer or PAUSE printer commands.

Sample usage: PSC PS = PS386 P = 0 START
Abbreviated: PSC START

ABORT

The ABORT parameter enables you to abort the current job. The remaining part of the job is not printed, and the job is removed from its queue.

Sample usage: PSC PS = PS386 P = 0 ABORT
Abbreviated: PSC AB

Controlling Paper Type and Alignment

Three parameters help you work with the printer's paper so that you can do form alignment, eject a page, or specify that a particular form type be loaded.

FORMFEED

The FORMFEED parameter sends a page-eject command to the printer.

Sample usage: PSC PS = PS386 P = 0 FORMFEED
Abbreviated: PSC FF

MARK

Use the MARK parameter to print a line of characters at the printer's current top-of-form position. You can use this option to check the printer's paper alignment. By default, the asterisk character is used, although you can specify a different character by typing it after the MARK parameter.

Sample usage: PSC PS = PS386 P = 0 MARK
                    PSC PS = PS386 P = 0 MARK !
Abbreviated: PSC MA
                    PSC MA !

MOUNT FORM

The MOUNT FORM parameter can be used to specify that a particular form be loaded. As you have learned, NetWare uses form numbers to enable you to stop a shared printer when a different type of paper is needed to run a job.

Sample usage: PSC PS = PS386 P = 0 MOUNT FORM = 1
Abbreviated: PSC MO 1

Controlling or Showing Print Server Status

Several parameters enable you to work with the print server, stop it from going down, or view the status of its printers.

STATUS

The STATUS parameter lets you view the status of a particular printer or all the printers on the specified print server. If you run PSC and do not specify a printer, STATUS shows you the status of all printers; otherwise, STATUS shows you the status of the printer that you specify.

> Sample usage: PSC PS=PS386 P=0 STATUS
> Abbreviated: PSC ST

When you use the STATUS parameter, you are shown information similar to the following about the print server's printers:

```
Printer 0: Third Floor Laser Printer
Mount form 1


Printer 1: Warehouse Dot Matrix
Printing job


Printer 2: Accting Laser
Printing job
Off-line


Printer 3: Sales 132 Column Dot Matrix
Waiting for job


Printer 4: Exec Office Laser
Not connected
```

CANCELDOWN

The CANCELDOWN parameter can be used to cancel a request issued from PCONSOLE to down the print server after it has finished printing its remaining jobs.

> Sample usage: PSC PS=PS386 CANCELDOWN
> Abbreviated: PSC CD

Making Remote Printers Private or Shared

Two PSC parameters enable you to control whether a shared remote printer temporarily should cease to be shared. In the preceding chapter, you learned the use of the RPRINTER command to make a workstation-based printer shared. A PSC parameter enables you to make that printer temporarily private so that it is available for the exclusive use of the person who uses the workstation to which the printer is connected.

PRIVATE

The PRIVATE parameter is used to make a shared remote printer temporarily private. When you use PSC with this parameter, the print server status screen is updated to show the status message In Private Mode for the printer you are working with.

    Sample usage: PSC PS = PS386 P = 4 PRIVATE
    Abbreviated: PSC PRI

SHARED

The SHARED parameter is used to reverse the effects of the PRIVATE parameter so that the remote printer is again available to all users.

    Sample usage: PSC PS = PS386 P = 4 SHARED
    Abbreviated: PSC SH

Only one more method of controlling printers remains to be learned. A group of commands can be used only from the server console. With NetWare 286, they can be used to perform many of the same functions that PSC performs for NetWare 386.

Using Console Commands To Manage Shared Printing

NetWare 286 is designed to use console commands to control printers. Console commands are issued from the server itself. If you created new queues on your NetWare 286 server, you used console commands to match the new queue to a printer.

A console command is typed on the server keyboard at the NetWare server's colon prompt (:). Console commands also are used to start and stop a server and to monitor its workload and performance. These other uses are discussed in Chapter 19.

Most console commands have both a standard and an abbreviated format. For example, the following two commands accomplish an identical result: both result in a queue's being serviced by a printer at a certain priority level. The first example is the standard form, and the second is the abbreviated form.

Printer 2 ADD queue **ACCT-LJ** at priority **3**
P 2 ADD ACCT-LJ 3

In this chapter, console commands are shown with the essential letters and numbers in boldface. Characters shown in lowercase roman may be omitted.

With NetWare 286, console commands are used to control printers and queues. Starting and stopping a printer and assigning it queues to service are handled with console commands. You also can use console commands to manage queued print jobs (although you may find PCONSOLE to be a more friendly and efficient way to do the same thing).

The following sections describe NetWare 286's printer and queue-management console commands.

Controlling Printers with NetWare 286 Console Commands

At times, shared printers must be stopped and started so that new paper types can be put in or problems corrected. Printers also need to be assigned to queues so that the printers can receive the jobs those queues store. NetWare 286 uses the PRINTER console command to accomplish these tasks. The command-line parameters you use with PRINTER determine what actions the command takes and which printer it works with.

Using PRINTER by Itself

You can use the PRINTER command by itself to show the status of the shared printers connected to your server. Type

   Printer

and press Enter. You can abbreviate this command by pressing P and then Enter.

When you enter the PRINTER console command, information similar to the following is displayed:

```
Printer 0:  Running  On-Line  Form 0 mounted  Servicing 2 Queues.
Printer 1:  Running  On-Line  Form 1 mounted  Servicing 1 Queues.
```

You are shown whether each printer is on-line, which form type is mounted, and how many queues each printer is servicing. Each printer is identified by a printer number, starting with printer 0. These numbers were assigned when you used NETGEN to install NetWare 286.

Stopping a Printer

Sometimes you need to stop a shared printer because of a paper jam or to change a toner cartridge or ribbon. To use PRINTER to stop a shared printer, type

> Printer **2 STOP**

and press Enter. (Substitute the number of the printer you want to stop for 2.) The printer may not stop immediately because it continues to print the contents of its internal buffer.

Starting a Printer

After you have used PRINTER to stop a shared printer, you need to use the START command to restart the printer. To restart a printer, type

> Printer **2 START**

and press Enter. (Substitute your printer number for 2.) If you are starting the printer after stopping it with PRINTER's STOP parameter, printing resumes exactly where it left off.

Rewinding a Printer

The REWIND parameter can be used with PRINTER to stop a job and go back a certain number of pages. This feature is useful if you have a paper jam or other printer problem that makes several pages of a job unusable. The job you are printing must be an ASCII file with embedded page breaks. If the job is not an ASCII file, using the REWIND option results in the job's rewinding to the beginning.

To rewind the printer, type the following command

> Printer **1 REWIND 5** pages

and press Enter. (Substitute your printer number for 1, and the number of pages you want to rewind for 5.) If you omit the number of pages, the job automatically rewinds to the beginning.

After you have used the REWIND option, you need to use the START parameter to restart the printer.

Marking the Top of the Form

Use PRINTER's MARK parameter to print a line of characters at the printer's current top-of-form position. You can use this option to check the printer's paper alignment. Type the following command

Printer 0 MARK top of form

and press Enter. (Substitute your printer number for 0.)

Issuing a Form Feed

The FORM FEED option ejects a page from the printer. The command format is **Printer 2 FORM FEED**, followed by Enter.

You also can abbreviate FORM FEED as FF:

Printer 2 FF

(Substitute your printer number for 2.)

Mounting a New Form Type

The FORM or MOUNT parameter can be used to specify that a particular form be loaded. As you have learned, NetWare uses form numbers to stop a shared printer when a different type of paper is needed to run a job. When a printer has form 0 mounted and the next job requires form 1, the printer stops, and you are prompted at the server console to load form 1. Use the FORM parameter as follows to specify that a particular form has been loaded

Printer 2 FORM mount **1**

and press Enter.

You also can use MOUNT to specify that a particular form has been loaded

Printer 2 MOUNT form **1**

and press Enter. (In both the preceding examples, replace 2 with your printer number and 1 with your form number).

After you have specified that the form is loaded, use the START parameter to restart the printer.

Adding or Deleting Queues from the Printer's Service List

To print jobs, a shared printer must be assigned to service at least one queue. With NetWare 286, console commands are used to make and change these assignments. In the preceding chapter, you learned how to use the ADD parameter to assign queues to printers. The next section describes the ADD parameter more fully.

The ADD parameter is used to add a queue to a printer's list of serviced queues. To assign a printer to service a queue, use the following command

Printer 2 ADD queue **ACCT-LJ**

and press Enter. (Replace 2 with the number of your printer and ACCT-LJ with your queue name.) When a queue is added to a printer's service list, a priority level is assigned to the queue-printer relationship. When you do not specify a priority level with your PRINTER command, a level of 1 is automatically assigned. To assign a specific level, use the following command

Printer 2 ADD queue **ACCT-LJ** at priority 4

Press Enter. (Substitute the priority level you want for the 4—it can be any number from 1 to 10).

The DELETE parameter is used to remove a queue from the printer's list of serviced queues. Use the following command to remove a queue from a printer

Printer 2 DELete queue **ACCT-LJ**

Press Enter. (Use your printer number in place of 2 and your queue name in place of ACCT-LJ.)

The QUEUES parameter is used to show the printer's list of assigned queues. To display this list, type

Printer 2 Queues

and press Enter. (Replace 2 with your actual printer number.) You see a list similar to the following:

```
Printer 2:  Running On-Line Form 1 mounted Servicing 2 Queues.

Servicing ACCT-LJ                           at priority 1
Servicing PRINTQ_2                          at priority 4
```

Controlling Queues with NetWare 286 Console Commands

Although managing printers is the most frequent use of NetWare 286 console commands, you also can create and delete queues and work with their print jobs. Most network supervisors report that they prefer to use PCONSOLE for these tasks, but console commands exist to do the same things.

The QUEUE command is used to work with queues from the server console. The parameters you use with QUEUE dictate what actions are taken.

Showing a List of the Server's Queues

When you use QUEUE by itself (or Q, its abbreviation), the program lists each queue and its status. When you type the following command

Queues

and press Enter, you see a display similar to the following on the server screen:

```
SERV1 Print Queues:

ACCT-LJ        5 queue jobs    serviced by 2 printers
EXECS-DM       2 queue jobs    serviced by 1 printers
PRINTQ_0       0 queue jobs    serviced by 1 printers
PRINTQ_1       0 queue jobs    serviced by 1 printers
PRINTQ_2       3 queue jobs    serviced by 1 printers
SALES          0 queue jobs    serviced by 1 printers
```

Each queue is listed, along with the jobs it currently contains and the number of printers servicing that queue.

Listing a Queue's Jobs

You can list the jobs in a queue with the JOBS parameter. Use the following command

Queue ACCT-LJ jobs

and press Enter. (Replace ACCT-LJ with your queue name). You see a display similar to the following:

```
Jobs currently in Print Queue ACCT-LJ:
Priority  User            File           Job      Copies

1         SUPERVISOR                     2        1
2         GUEST                          3        1
3         SMITHFD                        5        2
4         ROGERSGL        REPORT.TXT     6        1
```

Moving a Job in the Queue

You can use the CHANGE parameter to move a job in the queue priority list. For example, if you want to move the job that belongs to ROGERSGL in the preceding list so that it becomes the next job printed (meaning it will have a priority level of 1), use the following command

Queue **ACCT-LJ** Change job **6** to priority **1**

and press Enter. Notice that you specify the job's number, which is displayed in the next-to-last column (in this case, 6). Mistakenly listing the job's current priority number is easy.

Deleting Queued Jobs

You can use the DELETE parameter to delete a job in a queue. As when you use the CHANGE parameter, the job is identified by its job number (listed in the next-to-last column of the queue status display). For example, to delete SMITHFD's job (which is job number 5) from the ACCT-LJ queue, type

Queue **ACCT-LJ** Delete job **5**

and press Enter. If you enter an asterisk (*) for the job number, all jobs in the queue are deleted.

Creating a Queue

The CREATE parameter lets you create a new queue. To create a queue named SALES-LASER, use the following command

Queue **SALES-LASER CREATE**

and press Enter.

Deleting a Queue

The ominous sounding DESTROY parameter is used to delete a queue. To delete the queue called SALES-LASER, type

Queue **SALES-LASER DESTROY**

and press Enter.

Assigning Printer Numbers to Queues

You have not yet learned about an obscure console command called SPOOL. It is used when you want to use the CAPTURE command in a special way. If printer ports were designated as spooled printers when NetWare 286 was installed on the server, a print queue was automatically created and assigned to each printer port. The queues that are set up automatically are called PRINTQ_0 for printer 0, PRINTQ_1 for printer 1, and so on. You can send jobs to these queues by using CAPTURE's PRINTER parameter. For example, if you want to send a job to PRINTQ_0, you use CAPTURE as follows

CAPTURE PRINTER = 0

and press Enter.

In earlier versions of NetWare, printer numbers were used instead of queues, so this option was carried over for the sake of applications and users who were used to it. Note that NetWare 386 does not support this capability.

If you want to enable other queues to be addressed with printer numbers, you can use the SPOOL console command. For example, to make the queue ACCT-LJ addressable as PRINTER 1, use the following console command

Spool **1** to **ACCT-LJ**

and press Enter.

To view the current printer number assignments, use SPOOL by itself

Spool

and press Enter.

Chapter Summary

You now have learned about implementing, using, and managing shared printing on your LAN. Shared printing probably will become one of your network's busiest resources, and the busier it becomes, the more likely you will be called on to manage the process. Careful configuration and implementation in the beginning ensures that steadily increasing use of your LAN's shared printers does not result in steadily increasing headaches for you.

16

Creating Login Scripts

If you have dutifully read the last 15 chapters (or have gained the equivalent learning from other sources), you have an impressive level of NetWare knowledge. You know how to log in and attach to servers, create drive letters for server volumes, manage files, add user accounts, grant and revoke rights, and use and control networked printers. You now know how to navigate NetWare's complex waters.

When you come to work in the morning and turn on your networked PC to prepare for a day's work, you put a lot of this knowledge to use. First, you log in and attach to the servers that you plan to use. Next, you map drives and search drives to some server directories. You might connect to a networked printer so that your printed output will go to the right place. You create a network environment that suits your needs.

If you go through more or less the same steps every day, it makes sense to create this network environment automatically. Attaching and running five or six MAP commands plus a CAPTURE command is a lot of typing. You have the know-how to do this, but what about users who don't have the level of expertise that you have? Does every network user have to be a NetWare expert to effectively use network resources?

NetWare login scripts enable you to perform repetitive login functions automatically. If you use an AUTOEXEC.BAT file on your PC's boot up disk, you already understand the concept behind login scripts. Both contain a set of instructions that execute automatically. Your AUTOEXEC.BAT file's instructions execute as soon as you boot your PC. Similarly your login script's instructions execute as soon as you log into your server.

Your login script is a predefined list of commands that are executed when you log into the server where your script is stored. You can create a login

413

script that maps drive letters to directories, attaches you to other servers, and directs your printed output to a networked printer.

The network supervisor can create login scripts for users who have little PC or network knowledge. A user doesn't have to know the intricacies of mapping and attaching. All he or she has to know is how to log into the correct server, and the login script can create the necessary network environment automatically.

Login scripts are used first and foremost to create drive letters automatically for users when they log in. You need only master the use of the MAP command to create powerful login scripts that create drive letter and search drive assignments. Although login scripts can do many other things, this is their most important task.

The Two Types of Login Scripts

When you log in, actually two login scripts are executed, one after the other. Consider how both are used.

The System Login Script

The System Login Script, the first to execute, is created and maintained by the network supervisor and is run automatically by every user when he or she logs in. Individual users cannot change or even look at the System Login Script.

The System Login Script is optional. When you install a server, no System Login Script exists. The network supervisor must create it.

If you want all users to map certain drives in exactly the same way, it might be best to place those drive-mapping commands in the System Login Script. There are other advanced uses of the System Login Script that will be discussed with login script commands later in this chapter.

The User Login Script

The User Login Script executes immediately after the System Login Script. Each user can create and change his or her User Login Script as necessary.

The User Login Script is a good place to put commands that may not be the same for all users.

The Default User Login Script

When you create a user account on a server, that user is given a default User Login Script. NetWare uses the following login script as the default when a user account is created. As soon as you add a login script for that user account, this one is no longer used:

```
WRITE "Good %GREETING_Time, %LOGIN_Name."
MAP DISPLAY OFF
MAP ERRORS OFF
MAP *1: = SYS:
MAP *1: = SYS:%LOGIN_NAME
IF "%1" = "SUPERVISOR" THEN MAP *1: = SYS:SYSTEM
MAP S1: = SYS:PUBLIC
MAP S2: = S1:%MACHINE/%OS/%OS_VERSION
MAP DISPLAY ON
MAP
```

This default login script does the following:

❏ Greets the user by name with a "Good Morning," "Good Afternoon," or "Good Evening"

❏ Maps the first available drive letter to the SYS: volume root directory or to a directory with the same name as the user's login name, if such a directory exists. If the login name is SUPERVISOR, then the drive is mapped to SYS:SYSTEM.

❏ Maps the first search directory to the SYS:PUBLIC directory (which stores the important NetWare commands needed by all users) and the second search directory to a directory storing the DOS files that match those for the user's PC, if that directory exists

❏ Displays all the current drive mappings

Don't worry if you find the contents of the preceding default script a bit confusing. It will make more sense after you read this chapter. For now, notice that the login script is nothing more that a series of commands. Each command occupies one line. The MAP command is used in some new ways that were not discussed in Chapter 9. The default login script creates a basic network environment. It creates a search drive for SYS:PUBLIC so that important NetWare commands can execute without making SYS:PUBLIC the default directory. It makes the first nonlocal drive letter a drive on volume SYS:. This will usually be drive F, because DOS Versions 3.0 and later reserve letters A through E for local use.

This login script may be too basic or it may not fit your strategy for creating a NetWare environment. In fact, it may cause some problems. If you remember how NetWare search drives created by the MAP command work with the DOS and OS/2 PATH commands, you know that typing the command

MAP S1:=SYS:PUBLIC

makes SYS:PUBLIC the first directory to be searched when you execute a command file that is not found in your default directory. It also will cancel the first search paths that you have set up using the DOS or OS/2 PATH commands. If you want to preserve DOS or OS/2 search paths, use the following MAP command instead:

MAP INSERT S1:=SYS:PUBLIC

In most situations, you ought to create your own login script. As soon as you do so, the default login script will no longer be used.

Working with Login Scripts

Login scripts can be created and maintained by using SYSCON. The network supervisor or a user with supervisory equivalence can create and manage scripts for all users. With NetWare 386, users with workgroup manager or manager status can create and manage login scripts for the users they manage. Individual users can create and manage their own login scripts.

Creating Login Scripts

As a minimum, every user should have a simple login script that maps a search drive to SYS:PUBLIC and preserves any previously established DOS search paths. A login script that does this need only consist of one line, as follows:

MAP INSERT S1:=SYS:PUBLIC

Log into a server. Use your own login name if you plan to create this login script for yourself, or, with supervisory or workgroup manager status, to create it for someone else. Start SYSCON by typing *syscon* and pressing Enter. From SYSCON's main menu, select User Information to see a list of the user login names for your server. Select the name of the user whose login script you are going to create and press Enter. The User Information menu appears. Select Login Script and press Enter.

If you are a supervisor or workgroup manager, an entry box opens that asks which user's login script you want to read and show in SYSCON's login script editor. It shows the name of the user you selected as the default. Sometimes it is helpful to use another user's login script as a model to customize; backspace over the user's name shown in the box and enter the name of the user whose script you want to use, or press Ins to see a list of users from which to select. Highlight the name of the appropriate user and press Enter. Either method takes you to SYSCON's login script editor.

Using SYSCON's Login Script Editor

Using SYSCON'S login script editor to create or modify a login script is just like using a word processor. You simply type the login script one line at a time. Figure 16.1 shows the screen as it appears at the beginning of the editing process.

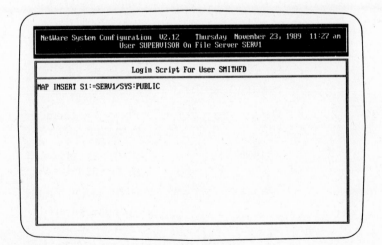

```
NetWare System Configuration  V2.12   Thursday  November 23, 1989  11:27 am
                 User SUPERVISOR On File Server SERV1

                     Login Script For User SMITHFD

MAP INSERT S1:=SERV1/SYS:PUBLIC
```

Fig. 16.1.
*SYSCON's Login
Script Editor.*

Table 16.1 shows the editing keys that you can use to work with login scripts.

Table 16.1
Keys for Editing Login Scripts

Function	Key(s) Used	Description
Escape	Esc	Exits the login script editor and saves your changes
Exit	Alt-F10	Exits the login script editor and saves your changes
Backspace	Backspace	Deletes the character to the left of the cursor
Insert	Ins	Inserts the contents of the paste buffer
Delete	Del	Deletes a character or a group of marked characters and places them in the paste buffer
Help	F1	Gives login script help
Mark	F5	Marks a series of characters
Up	Up arrow	Moves up one line
Down	Down arrow	Moves down one line
Left	Left arrow	Moves one character to the left
Right	Right arrow	Moves one character to the right
Special up	Ctrl-PgUp	Moves to the beginning of the login script
Special down	Ctrl-PgDn	Moves to the end of the login script

Special left	Home	Moves to the extreme left position on the line
Special right	End	Moves to the extreme right position on-screen
Page up	PgUp	Moves up one page
Page down	PgDn	Moves down one page
Field left	Ctrl-left arrow	Moves one word to the left
Field right	Ctrl-right arrow	Moves one word to the right

When you finish typing the script, press Esc to save your changes and to exit the script editor.

Most of the keys and editing functions that you use in SYSCON's login script editor are typical of many word processors, and require little explanation. However, the process of marking, deleting, copying, or moving blocks of text within a login script does require some comment. To mark a block of text, move the cursor to the beginning of the block and press the F5 key. Use the arrow keys to move the cursor over the text that you want to mark. The text is highlighted as you move the cursor. After you mark a block, you can do one of the following two things:

❏ *Place in the Cut and Paste Buffer.* Pressing Del removes the marked text from the screen and moves it into the login script editor's cut and paste buffer.

❏ *Retrieve from the Cut and Paste Buffer.* Pressing Ins retrieves whatever text is stored in the cut and paste buffer and places it where the cursor is positioned.

With careful use of the above options, you can copy, move, or delete blocks of text. For example, to copy a block of text, mark it using F5 and highlight it with the arrow keys. Then press Del to place it in the cut and paste buffer. This removes the text from the screen, so you must press Ins immediately to replace the original text. Next, move the cursor to the location where you want to move the copied text and press Ins again. Another copy of the marked text is placed at the cursor position.

You can move text in a similar fashion. Mark it with the F5 and arrow keys, and then press Del to place the text in the cut and paste buffer. Move the cursor key to the location where you want to move the text and press Ins. The text appears on-screen.

Deleting a block of text is simply a matter of marking it with the F5 and arrow keys and pressing Del to remove the text.

Any time you mark text and place it in the text buffer, you must be careful about using the Ins key, because it automatically retrieves the contents of the text buffer. Anything stored in the text buffer stays there until you replace it with something else.

SYSCON's login script editor handles cutting and pasting text a bit unusually. Fortunately, most login scripts are not complex, and do not require sophisticated text editing features to create.

Creating a System Login Script

The steps for creating a System Login Script are similar to those for creating a script for an individual user. Log in with supervisory equivalence to the server where you want to create the script. Start SYSCON by typing *syscon* and pressing Enter. From SYSCON's main menu, select Supervisor Options, and the Supervisor Options menu appears. Select System Login Script from this menu. You will enter the System Login Script editor, which functions identically to the regular login script editor discussed in the previous section. You can use the editing keys shown in table 16.1 and cut and paste blocks of text. When you finish creating the script, press Esc to save it and leave the editor. You are then returned to the Supervisor Options menu.

Login Script Commands

Table 16.2 lists commands available for your use when you create a login script. These commands are listed in order of importance. You will probably not find uses for every command; in fact, a handful of four or five may be all that you use on a regular basis.

Table 16.2
Login Script Commands by Category

Category	Command
Control drive letters	MAP
	DRIVE
Show information	WRITE
	DISPLAY
	FDISPLAY
Execute external programs	#
	EXIT
Attach user to another server	ATTACH
Control PC DOS functions	DOS BREAK
	DOS SET
	DOS VERIFY
	COMSPEC
Control login script's flow of execution	BREAK
	IF
	THEN
	PAUSE
	WAIT
Specify information about workstation	MACHINE NAME
	PCCOMPATIBLE
Tell login script to look to an external file to run login script commands	INCLUDE
Comment in login script	REMARK
	;
	*
Make noise	FIRE PHASERS
Shift position of command line variables (NetWare 386 only)	SHIFT

Table 16.3 lists the login script commands alphabetically, and gives a brief summary of each:

Table 16.3
Login Script Command Summary

Command	Function	Example
#	Executes an external executable command (EXE or COM file)	#command
ATTACH	Attaches user to another server	ATTACH server /user_name;PSswrd (server, user name may be omitted; user will be prompted for information not entered)
BREAK	Enables or disables the use of Ctrl-Break to halt a login script	BREAK ON BREAK OFF
COMSPEC	Sets DOS COMSPEC environment variable to designate alternate command processor	COMSPEC d:file (replace d: with drive specification, file with file name)
DISPLAY	Displays the contents of an ASCII file	DISPLAY path\file
DOS VERIFY	Turns DOS read-after-write verification on or off	DOS VERIFY ON DOS VERIFY OFF
DOS BREAK	Turns DOS BREAK status on or off	DOS BREAK ON DOS BREAK OFF
DOS SET	Enables you to place variables in the DOS environment	DOS SET varname = "Varinfo"
DRIVE	Establishes the drive that will be the default after the login script is executed	DRIVE d: (replace d with a drive identifier)

EXIT	Halts execution of the login script and executes a comma upon exiting	EXIT "command"
FDISPLAY	Displays the contents of a text file and filters out format characters	FDISPLAY path\file
FIRE PHASERS	Makes a phaser-like sound	FIRE PHASERS n TIMES (replace n with a numeral between 1 and 9)
IF/THEN	Executes a command or series of commands based on a condition or series of conditions	IF condition THEN command IF cond1, cond2 THEN... IF cond1 and cond2 THEN... IF condition(s) THEN BEGIN command 1 command 2 END
INCLUDE	Executes login script commands stored in an external ASCII file	INCLUDE path\ file
MACHINE NAME	Sets the MACHINE NAME to a new setting	MACHINE NAME = "name"
MAP	1. Creates a drive letter	MAP d: = server /volume:directory
	2. Displays currently mapped drives	MAP
	3. Turns information resulting from MAP commands on or off	MAP DISPLAY ON MAP DISPLAY OFF

Table 16.3—continued

Command	Function	Example
	4. Turns information resulting from MAP errors on or off	MAP ERRORS ON MAP ERRORS OFF
PAUSE	Halts login script execution until the user strikes a key	PAUSE
PCCOMPATIBLE	Enables workstations with a customized long machine name to use the EXIT login script command	PCCOMPATIBLE
REMARK * :	Enables comments and noncommand information to be inserted in scripts	REMARK comment text REM comment text * comment text ; comment text
SHIFT	Shifts the position of the login command line parameters	SHIFT 2
WAIT	Halts login script execution until the user strikes a key	WAIT
WRITE	Displays text on-screen	WRITE "message"

MAP

The most important use of the login script is to create drive letter assignments for users when they log in. You use the MAP command to do this. (If you are unfamiliar with MAP, review Chapter 9.) You can use MAP commands in your login script in exactly the same way that you use MAP from the command line. For example, Script 16.1 is a login script for a user named Frank Smith whose login name is SMITHFD. It assigns drive letters to his personal network storage area and the directories that store WordPerfect and Lotus 1-2-3.

MAP F: = SERV1/SYS:USERS\SMITHFD
MAP G: = SERV1/SYS:SOFTWARE\WORDPERF   Script 16.1.
MAP H: = SERV1/SYS:SOFTWARE\123

This script automatically makes Frank's personal storage area drive F and creates a drive G and a drive H, which point to WordPerfect and Lotus 1-2-3, respectively.

To make life easier for Frank, you will also need to make SYS:PUBLIC a search drive. SYS:PUBLIC contains all important NetWare commands; making SYS:PUBLIC a search drive means that you can use these commands to make SYS:PUBLIC the default. You can map a search drive by adding another line to Frank's login script as Script 16.2 shows.

MAP F: = SERV1/SYS:USERS\SMITHFD
MAP G: = SERV1/SYS:SOFTWARE\WORDPERF
MAP H: = SERV1/SYS:SOFTWARE\123   Script 16.2.
MAP INSERT S1: = SERV1/SYS:PUBLIC

Because any MAP statement that is legal to execute from a command prompt can also be placed in a login script, you can use all the variations for the MAP command described in Chapter 9. There are also some interesting additional purposes for MAP when you are using it in a login script. For example, you can assign the first available network drive letter to a directory by using MAP in the following way in a login script.

MAP *1: = SERV1/SYS:SOFTWARE\DBASE

If Frank happened to use drive letters A through J as local drives (as can be the case when you use the DOS or OS/2 ASSIGN command or place a LASTDRIVE = statement in your CONFIG.SYS file), his login script would use drive K for his personal storage. Script 16.3 shows his login script modified to map the first three available drives.

MAP *1: = SERV1/SYS:USERS\SMITHFD
MAP *2: = SERV1/SYS:SOFTWARE\WORDPERF
MAP *3: = SERV1/SYS:SOFTWARE\123   Script 16.3.
MAP INSERT S1: = SERV1/SYS:PUBLIC

Script 16.3. shows the advantages and disadvantages of using this approach. Mapping to the first available drive makes it possible for users to define their local drives as they want. However, everyone agreeing to standardize on a certain pattern of drive letters creates a much more manageable situation. For example, with a particular software package, everyone may need to agree to use the same drive letter for its directory so that a batch file can be written to start it. If everyone standardizes on drive F for a personal storage area, you will be able to configure network spreadsheets, word processors, and databases to use drive F as the default location to store data files. You will explore this concept in more detail in Chapter 22, "Installing Network Versions of Software." You can also control whether the user sees a list of his drive letter assignments when he logs in. By default, as a user's login script maps a drive letter to a directory, the user sees that the drive letter has been assigned. For example, Script 16.3's MAP commands would display the following information:

```
Drive F: = SERV1/SYS:USERS\SMITHFD
Drive G: = SERV1/SYS:SOFTWARE\WORDPERF
Drive H: = SERV1/SYS:SOFTWARE\123
SEARCH1: = Z:. [SERV1/SYS:PUBLIC]
```

You might want to control whether this list is displayed. You can turn it off by including the following statement in your login script:

MAP DISPLAY OFF

You can turn it back on by including this statement:

MAP DISPLAY ON

Suppose that you do not want a particular user to know that you are assigning the SYS:PUBLIC directory to a search drive. Script 16.4 shows how to use MAP DISPLAY OFF and MAP DISPLAY ON for this purpose.

Script 16.4.

```
MAP DISPLAY OFF
MAP INSERT S1:=SERV1/SYS:PUBLIC
MAP DISPLAY ON
MAP F:=SERV1/SYS:USERS\SMITHFD
MAP G:=SERV1/SYS:SOFTWARE\WORDPERF
MAP H:=SERV1/SYS:SOFTWARE\123
```

You can also hide errors that the MAP command might generate by placing

MAP ERRORS OFF

in a login script. This is useful if you need to map a drive to a directory that you are not always sure exists. For example, with the benevolence typical of network supervisors, you offer to map a search drive to a subdirectory in each user's personal storage area where each user can place executable files of his choosing that he can run regardless of what directory is his default. You instruct your users to call this subdirectory

PSEARCH. In Frank's case, this directory would have the full NetWare name of SERV1/SYS:USERS\SMITHFD\PSEARCH. To MAP this directory as a search drive, place the following statement in Frank's login script:

MAP INSERT S2:=SERV1/SYS:USERS\SMITHFD\PSEARCH

What if Frank decided to delete this directory? The next time he logged in, his login script would reward him with an error message.

You could prevent the display of this error message by using the MAP ERRORS OFF statement. In Script 16.5, it has been used to suppress an error message that results if the PSEARCH subdirectory does not exist. MAP ERRORS ON has also been used to turn error messages back on if they occur for subsequent MAP commands in the login script.

```
MAP DISPLAY OFF
MAP INSERT S1:=SERV1/SYS:PUBLIC
MAP DISPLAY ON
MAP ERRORS OFF
MAP INSERT S2:=SERV1/SYS:USERS\SMITHFD\PSEARCH            Script 16.5.
MAP ERRORS ON
MAP F:=SERV1/SYS:USERS\SMITHFD
MAP G:=SERV1/SYS:SOFTWARE\WORDPERF
MAP H:=SERV1/SYS:SOFTWARE\123
```

You also can use the MAP command to display a comprehensive list of all drive letter assignments on local and network disks. Place the MAP command in a login script to produce a display similar to the following:

```
Drive  A:    maps to a local disk
Drive  B:    maps to a local disk
Drive  C:    maps to a local disk
Drive  F:  = SERV1/SYS:USERS\SMITHFD
Drive  G:  = SERV1/SYS:SOFTWARE\WORDPERF
Drive  H:  = SERV1/SYS:SOFTWARE\123
           ————
SEARCH1:   = Z:. [SERV1/SYS:PUBLIC]
SEARCH2:   = Y:. [SERV1/SYS:USERS\SMITHFD\PSEARCH]
```

If you use this option, you also may use MAP DISPLAY OFF to stop each individual MAP statement from displaying its own information (or your users will think they are seeing double). Login Script 16.6 uses MAP to display a complete list of drive letter assignments. Notice that MAP DISPLAY OFF is used at the beginning of the script. Then MAP statements assign drive letters and search drives. Finally, MAP DISPLAY ON is used to reverse MAP DISPLAY OFF, and the MAP command is used by itself to generate the drive assignment display.

Script 16.6.

```
MAP DISPLAY OFF
MAP INSERT S1: = SERV1/SYS:PUBLIC
MAP ERRORS OFF
MAP INSERT S2: = SERV1/SYS:USERS\SMITHFD\PSEARCH
MAP ERRORS ON
MAP F: = SERV1/SYS:USERS\SMITHFD
MAP G: = SERV1/SYS:SOFTWARE\WORDPERF
MAP H: = SERV1/SYS:SOFTWARE\123
MAP DISPLAY ON
MAP
```

Using MAP With Variables

Often you need to plug in information that may vary depending on changing factors such as the day of the week, the user who is running the login script, or the type of his or her workstation. NetWare handles this by making available 25 login script variables that you can use with certain login script commands.

Take a case in point. You have decided to make the login script shown in Script 16.6 the one to be used by all network users. You want to do this by placing the commands shown in Script 16.6 in the System Login Script. (Remember that the System Login Script is executed by all users, but User Login Scripts are executed only by the individual user for whom the script was created.)

Can you see a problem with this? The MAP commands that assign drive F and search drive 2 are specific to SMITHFD (also known as Frank). Fortunately, using variables permits you to achieve the same result. If you replace

    MAP F: = SERV1/SYS:USERS\SMITHFD

with

    MAP F: = SERV1/SYS:USERS\%LOGIN_NAME

you will get exactly the same result. You have simply replaced Frank's specific login name (SMITHFD) with a variable (%LOGIN_NAME). Script 16.7 is generic. Its references to Frank's login name have been replaced by the %LOGIN_NAME variable.

There are two rules for using variables with MAP. You must always precede variables with the percent sign (%), and you must always enter the variables in capital letters.

```
MAP DISPLAY OFF
MAP INSERT S1: = SERV1/SYS:PUBLIC
MAP ERRORS OFF
MAP INSERT S2: = SERV1/SYS:USERS\%LOGIN_NAME\PSEARCH
MAP ERRORS ON
MAP F: = SERV1/SYS:USERS\%LOGIN_NAME
MAP G: = SERV1/SYS:SOFTWARE\WORDPERF
MAP H: = SERV1/SYS:SOFTWARE\123
MAP DISPLAY ON
MAP
```

Script 16.7.

In cases where each user has a personal directory with the same name as his login name, you can effectively use the %LOGIN_NAME variable as a tool to map to that directory.

Table 16.4 lists the 25 login script variables. You can incorporate several of these into MAP commands. For example, if you have users who have varying DOS versions and you want to create a search drive to a network-based copy of that specific version, you can include

MAP S3: = SERV1/SYS:%OS\%OS_VERSION

in your login script. Users with MS-DOS Version 3.2 are mapped to a directory called SERV1/SYS:MSDOS\V3.2, and users with PC DOS Version 4.0 are mapped to SERV1/SYS:PCDOS\V4.0.

Table 16.4
Login Script Variable Summary

Variable	Information Returned	Source of Variable Data
AM_PM	Returns am or pm based on the current time	Workstation time
	Sample Usage:	WRITE "It is %HOUR:%MINUTE AM_PM"
	Displays:	It is 06:30 am

Table 16.4—continued

Variable	Information Returned	Source of Variable Data
DAY	Returns a number from 01 to 31 based on the current day	Workstation date
	Sample Usage:	WRITE "It is %MONTH-%DAY-%YEAR"
	Displays:	It is 04-12-90
DAY_OF_WEEK	Returns the current day (Monday, Tuesday, Wednesday, and so on)	Workstation date
	Sample Usage:	WRITE "Today is %DAY_OF_WEEK"
	Displays:	Today is WEDNESDAY
ERROR_LEVEL	Returns the error level set by the last command; executed by using EXECUTE (#) as a 0 or nonzero number	Workstation operating system error level
	Sample Usage:	#SERV1\SYS: PUBLIC\CAPTURE IF ERROR_LEVEL != "0" THEN BEGIN WRITE "CAPTURE COMMAND FAILED!" WRITE "ERROR LEVEL IS %ERROR_LEVEL" END
FILE_SERVER	Returns the server name	NetWare server
	Sample Usage:	WRITE "You are connected to %FILE_SERVER"
	Displays:	You are connected to SERV386
FULL_NAME	Returns the user's full name	User's full name as entered in SYSCON
	Sample Usage:	WRITE "Hello, %FULL_NAME"
	Displays:	Hello, FRANK SMITH

GREETING_TIME	Returns morning, afternoon, or evening	Workstation time
	Sample Usage:	WRITE "Good %GREETING_TIME!"
	Displays:	Good AFTERNOON!
HOUR	Returns a number between 1 and 12 based on the current hour	Workstation time
	Sample Usage:	WRITE "It is %HOUR:%MINUTE AM_PM"
	Displays:	It is 10:20 pm
HOUR24	Returns a number between 00 and 23 based on the current hour	Workstation time
	Sample Usage:	WRITE "It is %HOUR24:%MINUTE"
	Displays:	It is 22:20
LOGIN_NAME	Returns the user's login name	User's login name
	Sample Usage:	MAP F:=SERV1/ SYS:USERS\%LOGIN_NAME
	(assigns F: to SERV1/ SYS:USERS \SMITHFD)	
MACHINE	Returns the long machine name stored by the NetWare workstation shell (IBM_PC or a customized name)	NetWare workstation
	Sample Usage:	IF MACHINE != "IBM_PC" THEN PCCOMPATIBLE

Table 16.4—continued

Variable	Information Returned	Source of Variable Data
MEMBER	Provides checking for membership in a group	Group membership as established using SYSCON
	Sample Usage:	IF MEMBER OF "ACCT" THEN MAP I:=SERV1/SYS:ACCT
MINUTE	Returns a number from 00 to 59 based on the current time	Workstation time
	Sample Usage:	WRITE "It is %HOUR:%MINUTE AM_PM"
	Displays:	It is 06:30 am
MONTH	Returns a number from 01 to 12 based on the current month	Workstation date
	Sample Usage:	WRITE "It is %MONTH-%DAY-%SYEAR"
	Displays:	It is 04-12-90
MONTH_NAME	Returns the current month (January, February, March, etc.)	Workstation date
	Sample Usage:	WRITE "It is %MONTH_NAME %DAY, %YEAR"
	Displays:	It is MAY 12, 1990
NDAY_OF_WEEK	Returns the number of the current day of the week from 1 to 7 (1 = Monday)	Workstation date
	Sample Usage:	WRITE "It's day %NDAY_OF_WEEK of a long week!"
	Displays:	It's day 2 of a long week!

NETWORK_ADDRESS*	Returns the internal IPX number of the default NetWare 386 server	NetWare 386 server

Sample Usage: WRITE "Your server's number is %NETWORK_ADDRESS"

Displays: Your server's number is 10A

NEW_MAIL	Returns yes or no based on whether you have new mail messages (this works only for Novell's old mail system, which is not shipped with current versions of NetWare)	NetWare mail

Sample Usage: IF NEW_MAIL = "YES" THEN WRITE "You have mail"

OS	Returns the operating system used to boot the user's workstation	Workstation operating system

Sample Usage: MAP INSERT S2:=SERV1/ SYS:OS\OS_VERSION (assigns the second search drive to SERV1/SYS:MSDOS)

OS_VERSION	Returns the version number of the operating system used to boot the user's workstation (such as (V2.11 or V3.3)	Workstation operating systems

Sample Usage: MAP INSERT S2:=SERV1/ SYS:OS\OS_VERSION (assigns the second search drive to SERV1/SYS:PCDOS\V3.3)

Table 16.4—continued

Variable	Information Returned	Source of Variable Data
P_STATION	Returns the node number of network board inside the workstation as a hexadecimal number	Workstation network adapter

	Sample Usage:	WRITE "You are logging in from node %PSTATION"
	Displays:	You are logging in from node 2B

Variable	Information Returned	Source of Variable Data
SECOND	Returns a number from 00 to 59 based on the current time	Workstation time

	Sample Usage:	WRITE "It is exactly %HOUR24:%MINUTE:%SECOND"
	Displays:	It is exactly 12:31:17

Variable	Information Returned	Source of Variable Data
SHELL_TYPE	Returns the shell type number	NetWare workstation shell

	Sample Usage:	IF SHELL_TYPE != 0 THEN BEGIN WRITE "Your shell type is incorrect!" WRITE "Please see the net super for upgrade."

Variable	Information Returned	Source of Variable Data
SHORT_YEAR	Returns a number from 00 to 99 based on the current year	Workstation date

	Sample Usage:	WRITE "It is %MONTH-%DAY-%SYEAR"
	Displays:	It is 04-12-90

SMACHINE	Returns the four character short machine name stored by the NetWare workstation shell (IBM or a customized name)	NetWare workstation shell
	Sample Usage:	WRITE "Your machine type is %SMACHINE"
	Displays:	Your machine type is IBM
STATION	Returns a decimal number that is the user's connection number	NetWare server
	Sample Usage:	WRITE "Your connection number is %STATION"
	Displays:	Your connection number is 27
USER_ID*	Returns the number assigned to the user by NetWare	NetWare user information
	Sample Usage:	WRITE "Your user id number is %USER_ID"
	Displays:	Your user id number is 1007A
YEAR	Returns the year (i.e., 1990, 2001, etc.)	Workstation date
	Sample Usage:	WRITE "It is %MONTH_NAME %DAY, %YEAR"
	Displays:	It is MAY 12, 1990
0, 1, 2, etc.	Returns the command line parameter that corresponds to the number (%0 returns the command)	Login command parameters
	Sample Usage:	WRITE "You typed %1, %2 and %3 after LOGIN"
	Displays:	You typed SMITHFD, HI and HELLO after LOGIN

* These variables can be used only with login scripts on NetWare 386 servers.

Table 16.5 shows the same variables organized by category.

Table 16.5
Login Script Variables
Listed by Category

Category	Variables
Time Variables	HOUR
	HOUR24
	MINUTE
	SECOND
	AM_PM
	GREETING_TIME
Date Variables	MONTH
	MONTH_NAME
	DAY
	YEAR
	SHORT_YEAR
	DAY_OF_WEEK
	NDAY_OF_WEEK
User Information	LOGIN_NAME
	FULL_NAME
	MEMBER
	* USER_ID
Workstation Information	MACHINE
	SMACHINE
	STATION
	PSTATION
	OS
	OS_VERSION
	SHELL_TYPE
File Server Information	* FILE_SERVER
	* NETWORK_ADDRESS
Results of Executed Commands	ERROR_LEVEL
Login Command Line Parameters	0, 1, 2, etc.
Checks to see if there is new mail	NEW_MAIL

*These commands can only be used in login scripts on NetWare 386 servers.

Setting a Default Drive with the Drive Command

After you log in and your login script executes, you must "land" at a particular drive letter and directory. By default, you are placed on the first network drive. In Script 16.6, Frank would arrive at drive F after his login script executes.

There might be cases where you want to set a different drive letter as the default. For example, if a particular user only logs into the network to do word processing, you might want to make drive G (which points to the WordPerfect directory) his default so that he can immediately start the word processing program and get to work. If a user has a personal hard disk called drive C, you might want to make it the default drive after he logs in.

You can place the DRIVE command in a login script to set a user's default after he logs in. Script 16.8 shows how the DRIVE command can be used to establish drive C as the default.

```
MAP DISPLAY OFF
MAP INSERT S1:=SERV1/SYS:PUBLIC
MAP DISPLAY ON
MAP ERRORS OFF
MAP INSERT S2:=SERV1/SYS:USERS\%LOGIN_NAME\PSEARCH        Script 16.8.
MAP ERRORS ON
MAP F:=SERV1/SYS:USERS\%LOGIN_NAME
MAP G:=SERV1/SYS:SOFTWARE\WORDPERF
MAP H:=SERV1/SYS:SOFTWARE\123
DRIVE C:
```

As with the MAP command, you can use DRIVE to assign the default drive relative to a local drive. For example, if you want to assign the second network drive as the default and you are not sure which actual letter that will be (because users can use various DOS and OS/2 commands to change the number of local drives that they have), you can place the following statement in the login script:

DRIVE *2:

Script 16.9 shows how you use this method to make sure that a user's default directory stores WordPerfect.

Script 16.9.

```
MAP *1:=SERV1/SYS:USERS\SMITHFD
MAP *2:=SERV1/SYS:SOFTWARE\WORDPERF
MAP *3:=SERV1/SYS:SOFTWARE\123
MAP INSERT S1:=SERV1/SYS:PUBLIC
DRIVE *2:
```

You should always place the DRIVE command after all of the MAP commands in your login script. Placing the DRIVE command before the MAP command that creates the drive letter you are setting as the default will not work.

Login Script Commands that Display Information

You can make your login scripts more interesting by using them to display information for your users when they log in. This can be anything from a friendly greeting such as "GOOD MORNING, FRANK SMITH," to a meeting notice such as "THERE WILL BE AN EMPLOYEE MEETING AT 4:00 IN THE LUNCHROOM."

Three login script commands can be used for this purpose: WRITE, DISPLAY, and FDISPLAY. You often will use WRITE with login script variables to produce specific results.

WRITE

The WRITE command is the most common way to display information in a login script. Place

WRITE "Welcome to the Network"

in a login script to issue a warm welcome to users that have just logged in. You can be even more personal by adding the following variable

WRITE "Welcome to the Network, %FULL_NAME"

which results in Frank seeing the following friendly greeting:

```
Welcome to the Network, FRANK SMITH
```

There are only two rules for using the WRITE command. You must enclose the text that you want to display in quotation marks and, if the text you want to display is too long to fit on one line (longer than 80 characters), you must use multiple WRITE commands. For example, to display the following message,

```
THE PLANT WILL BE CLOSING EARLY ON NEW YEAR'S EVE. EMPLOYEES
MAY LEAVE AT 2 P.M. THE MANAGEMENT WISHES TO THANK EVERYONE
FOR A VERY PRODUCTIVE YEAR AND WISHES ALL A HAPPY HOLIDAY.
```

you need to use three WRITE commands:

WRITE "THE PLANT WILL BE CLOSING EARLY ON NEW YEAR'S EVE. EMPLOYEES"
WRITE "MAY LEAVE AT 2 P.M. THE MANAGEMENT WISHES TO THANK EVERYONE"
WRITE "FOR A VERY PRODUCTIVE YEAR AND WISHES ALL A HAPPY HOLIDAY."

Normally each new WRITE command displays its text on a new line. You can cause multiple WRITE commands to display on the same line by following each command with a semicolon (;). This enables you to write part of a line and then finish that line with another WRITE command. You can use another login script command combination, IF/THEN, with this as follows:

WRITE "It's %HOUR:%MINUTE AM_PM";
IF HOUR >= TO "08" AND MINUTE > "00" THEN BEGIN
   WRITE "—YOU'RE LATE!"
END
IF HOUR < "08" THEN BEGIN
   WRITE "—THE EARLY BIRD CATCHES THE WORM!"
END

This produces the following output if the user logged in at 8:05 am:

```
IT IS 8:05 AM—YOU'RE LATE!
```

and this if the user logged in at 7:59:

```
IT IS 7:59 AM—THE EARLY BIRD CATCHES THE WORM!
```

You will learn how to use the IF/THEN command to produce other results that resemble artificial intelligence later in this chapter.

There are also four special character combinations that you can place within the text of a WRITE command to get special results. They are the following:

❏ \r produces a carriage return

❏ \n produces a line feed

❑ \" must be used to display quotation marks

❑ \7 produces a beep on your PC's speaker

You can use \r and \n together to produce a new line within one WRITE command. You can use \n by itself to produce a new line without returning to the left edge of the screen. For example,

WRITE "Santa says\n \"Merry Christmas to all!\"\7"

produces the following output:

```
Santa says
    "Merry Christmas to all!" (beep)
```

whereas

WRITE "Santa says\n\r \"Merry Christmas to all!\"\7"

produces

```
Santa says
"Merry Christmas to all!" (beep)
```

Using Variables with WRITE

You can use almost all of the login script variables with the WRITE command in ways that are limited only by your creativity. The following series of WRITE commands uses 16 out of the 25 available variables:

```
WRITE "Good GREETING_TIME, %FULL_NAME—you have logged in as"
WRITE "%LOGIN_NAME on %DAY_OF_WEEK, %MONTH_NAME %DAY, %YEAR at"
WRITE "%HOUR:%MINUTE:%SECOND %AM_PM from node %P_STATION which"
WRITE "was assigned to connection %STATION
WRITE "and you are using an "%MACHINE running
WRITE "%OS version %OS_VERSION."
```

These lines produce the following run on sentence:

```
Good MORNING, FRANK SMITH—you have logged in as
SMITHFD on Monday, APRIL 20, 1990 at
08:05:17 AM from node 37 which
was assigned to connection 15
and you are using an IBM_PC running
PCDOS version 3.3.
```

You probably wouldn't want to use the above sentence in a real login script, but it would be nice to display a greeting and show some useful information to users as they log in. For this growing sample login script, use two WRITE commands to greet the user by name, and display the date, time and connection number (see Script 16.10).

```
WRITE "GOOD %GREETING_TIME %FULL_NAME. IT IS %HOUR:%MINUTE%AM_PM"
WRITE "AND YOU ARE HAVE BEEN ASSIGNED CONNECTION%STATION."
MAP DISPLAY OFF
MAP INSERT S1: = SERV1/SYS:PUBLIC
MAP DISPLAY ON
MAP ERRORS OFF
MAP INSERT S2: = SERV1/SYS:USERS\%LOGIN_NAME\PSEARCH
MAP ERRORS ON
MAP F: = SERV1/SYS:USERS\%LOGIN_NAME
MAP G: = SERV1/SYS:SOFTWARE\WORDPERF
MAP H: = SERV1/SYS:SOFTWARE\123
DRIVE C:
```

Script 16.10.

Although using the WRITE command in combination with variables is hardly as essential to the successful use of the network as mapping drives, it enables you to personalize login scripts and communicate useful information. Later in this chapter, you will see how you can combine variables with the IF/THEN commands.

DISPLAY and FDISPLAY

You use the DISPLAY and FDISPLAY login script commands to display information during the execution of a login script. Both commands show the contents of a text file. They are similar to the DOS or OS/2 TYPE command.

You should use DISPLAY with true ASCII text files that contain no printer or formatting codes. FDISPLAY attempts to filter out these codes and displays only the text information from a file. For the most reliable results, create the file you want to display as an ASCII file and use the DISPLAY command.

To display the contents of a file during login script execution, include the following line in a login script:

```
DISPLAY SERV1/SYS:MESSAGES\MESSAGE.TXT
```

The most common use of DISPLAY is to display a special and lengthy notice to users as they log in. If this notice changes frequently, you only need to change the file that DISPLAY calls; you do not have to modify the login script.

The DISPLAY command is often used with the login script commands PAUSE and WAIT. These commands stop the execution of the login script and display the message "Strike a key when ready. . . ." This gives the user time to read the message that DISPLAY is showing. Execution of the login script continues after the user presses a key.

You need to make sure that the user has READ and OPEN rights to the directory that contains the file you want to display. You also must be sure that the file you specify is no longer than 25 lines of text, or it will not fit on-screen when you display it. If you need to display more than 25 lines of information, you can use two sets of DISPLAY and PAUSE commands.

Script 16.11 shows the sample login script with a DISPLAY and PAUSE command added to show the contents of a file.

Script 16.11.

```
DISPLAY SERV1/SYS:MESSAGES\MESSAGE.TXT
PAUSE
WRITE "GOOD %GREETING_TIME %FULL_NAME. IT IS %HOUR:%MINUTE %AM_PM"
WRITE "AND YOU ARE HAVE BEEN ASSIGNED CONNECTION %STATION."
MAP DISPLAY OFF
MAP INSERT S1:=SERV1/SYS:PUBLIC
MAP DISPLAY ON
MAP ERRORS OFF
MAP INSERT S2:=SERV1/SYS:USERS\%LOGIN_NAME\PSEARCH
MAP ERRORS ON
MAP F:=SERV1/SYS:USERS\%LOGIN_NAME
MAP G:=SERV1/SYS:SOFTWARE\WORDPERF
MAP H:=SERV1/SYS:SOFTWARE\123
DRIVE C:
```

Commands that Control Login Script Flow

Several login script commands enable you to pause, stop, or vary the flow of command execution in a login script. You have already seen how the

PAUSE command stops login script execution until the user presses a key. Another command, called BREAK, controls whether the user can abort the login script using Ctrl-Break. You can use the IF and THEN commands to execute other script commands based on whether a certain condition is true.

IF and THEN

Normally a login script's commands execute from the top to the bottom. Starting with the first command, each command executes until the last one is reached. With most programming or macro languages, you can execute a command conditionally; the login script language is no exception. The classic way to do this is to use the IF/THEN algorithm: IF a certain condition is true, THEN perform a certain action.

You can perform this kind of conditional command execution using the IF and THEN login script commands. IF and THEN are always used with login script variables. For example, the following command uses the variable MEMBER to check whether a user is a member of the group ACCTING, and maps drive I to the SYS:ACCTING directory if the user is a member.

```
IF MEMBER OF "ACCTING" THEN MAP I:=SERV1/SYS:ACCTING
```

This command consists of two parts. The first is the IF statement, which contains a condition (Is the user a member of the group named ACCTING?). If this statement is true, the THEN side of the command executes (assign drive letter I to the ACCTING directory). This two-part pattern is consistent in all IF/THEN login script commands.

Compound Conditions

You can make IF/THEN statements more complex by adding more conditions on the IF side or adding more actions on the THEN side. Consider how to create a statement with a *compound condition:* more than one condition on the IF side of the IF/THEN statement. Suppose that you take the electronic mail on your network out of service every Monday morning between 2:00 a.m. and 3:00 a.m. to perform maintenance on its files. You can advise users who are crazy enough to log in at this hour that E-mail is unavailable by using the following login script command:

IF DAY_OF_WEEK = "MONDAY" AND HOUR = "02" THEN WRITE
"E-MAIL IS OUT OF SERVICE UNTIL 3:00 AM"

This command appears on two lines so that it will fit on the page. In actual practice, it needs to be on one line.

Multiple Commands

Just as you can establish a series of conditions on the IF side of an IF/THEN command, you can also execute a series of commands from the THEN side. You might need to establish a special login name to use when you are running tape backups (TAPEBACK, for example). When the user logs in, you need to assign a drive letter to a special directory that stores the tape backup software and makes that drive the default. The following IF/THEN command accomplishes this:

```
IF LOGIN_NAME = "TAPEBACK" THEN BEGIN
    MAP J: = SERV1/SYS:TAPESOFT
    DRIVE J:
    WRITE "TYPE NBACKUP TO START A BACKUP."
    END
```

When you execute a series of commands, you follow the word THEN with the word BEGIN. You can then list your commands on subsequent lines. You must follow this series of commands with the word END on a line by itself.

Rules for Comparing Variables to Literal Values

You may have noticed that with most IF/THEN commands discussed so far, the IF side of the statement consists of a variable, such as LOGIN_NAME, that is compared to a literal, such as "TAPEBACK." You have seen the use of variables with the MAP and WRITE commands. All of the same variables and more can be used with IF/THEN commands. There is a subtle and easy-to-forget difference between the way variables are used with IF/THEN versus MAP and WRITE. When you use variables with MAP and WRITE, you must precede the variable name with a percent sign (%). With IF/THEN commands, you use the variable name without a percent sign. For WRITE and MAP, the percent sign is required to distinguish the variable name from regular text or a directory name, which is not necessary with an IF/THEN statement.

When comparing variables to literals, there are six possible comparisons:

❏ EQUALS

❏ NOT EQUAL TO

❏ GREATER THAN

❏ LESS THAN

❏ GREATER THAN OR EQUAL TO

❏ LESS THAN OR EQUAL TO

Each of these can be represented several ways.

The EQUALS comparison can be written four ways as illustrated by the following IF statements:

```
IF LOGIN_NAME IS "SUPERVISOR"
IF LOGIN_NAME EQUALS "SUPERVISOR"
IF LOGIN_NAME = = "SUPERVISOR"
IF LOGIN_NAME = "SUPERVISOR"
```

All the preceding statements work equally well. NOT EQUAL TO can be represented in the six following ways:

❏ IF LOGIN_NAME IS NOT "SUPERVISOR"

❏ IF LOGIN_NAME DOES NOT EQUAL "SUPERVISOR"

❏ IF LOGIN_NAME NOT EQUAL TO "SUPERVISOR"

❏ IF LOGIN_NAME != "SUPERVISOR"

❏ IF LOGIN_NAME <> "SUPERVISOR"

❏ IF LOGIN_NAME # "SUPERVISOR"

GREATER THAN and LESS THAN can each be represented in only two ways as follows:

```
IF HOUR IS GREATER THAN "02"
IF HOUR › "02"
```

or

```
IF HOUR IS LESS THAN "03"
IF HOUR ‹ "03"
```

GREATER THAN OR EQUAL TO and LESS THAN OR EQUAL TO each have two representations:

```
IF HOUR IS GREATER THAN OR EQUAL TO "02"
IF HOUR › = "02"
```

or

```
IF HOUR IS LESS THAN OR EQUAL TO "03"
IF HOUR ‹ = "03"
```

The many options available for writing comparisons provide you with yet another outlet for expressing your individuality. Pick the approach that works best for you.

Rules for Building Compound Conditional Statements

You have already considered building an IF/THEN statement that evaluates more than one condition as it decides whether to perform the actions in the THEN part of the statement. You can divide compound conditions by the word AND or by using commas. The following two IF statements work the same way:

IF YEAR = "2076" AND MONTH_NAME = "JULY" AND DAY = "04" THEN WRITE "IT'S THE USA'S TRICENTENNIAL!"

IF YEAR = "2076", MONTH_NAME = "JULY", DAY = "04", THEN WRITE "IT'S THE USA'S TRICENTENNIAL!"

Once again this should be one single line in a real login script. It has been shown here as two so that it fits on the page.

If you are familiar with other programming or macro languages, you may be wondering whether you can create OR conditions such as IF LOGIN_NAME = "SMITHFD" OR LOGIN_NAME = "JONESRH". You cannot do this, but you can get the same result by using two IF/THEN statements: one that evaluates the first condition and one that evaluates the second. You also cannot use nested IF statements or ELSE-type syntax. Again, your only recourse is to use multiple IF/THEN statements.

Despite these limitations, the IF/THEN command combination is the most flexible and powerful member of the login script command family. You can use it to control the execution of almost all other login script commands. Network supervisors have found many clever and useful applications of IF/THEN.

BREAK

You can use the BREAK command to control whether a user can stop the execution of a login script by pressing Ctrl-Break or Ctrl-C. By default, a user cannot halt his login script, but if you place

BREAK ON

in his login script, he will be able to halt his script. You can reverse this setting by placing

BREAK OFF

in the script.

PAUSE and WAIT

You have already examined PAUSE and WAIT with the DISPLAY command. You can use PAUSE or WAIT to halt execution of a login script. You typically use these commands after you have used WRITE or DISPLAY to show some information on-screen that you want the user to read. For example, if you want to notify users that your network will be out of service, you might use the following commands:

WRITE "The SERV1 server will be down between 4p.m. and 6p.m. on"
WRITE "Friday. During that time a second disk volume will be"
WRITE "added.\n\r"
PAUSE

When a user logs in, he or she see the following message:

```
The SERV1 server will be down between 4pm and 6pm on
Friday. During that timea second disk volume will be
added.

Strike a key when ready...
```

PAUSE and WAIT can be used interchangeably.

Commands that Execute External Programs

It is often useful to run programs from within your login script. Two login script commands, # (also called EXECUTE) and EXIT, enable you to do just that.

EXECUTE

The command that enables you to run external programs from a login script is called EXECUTE, but is entered in your login script as a pound sign (#). EXECUTE runs an external program and, when that program finishes running, control returns to the login script, which then finishes executing.

Running external programs from a login script has many uses. You may want to direct your printed output to a network printer automatically every time you log in, which requires you to run NetWare's CAPTURE command. You can do so by entering the following line in your login script:

    #SERV1\SYS:PUBLIC\CAPTURE B=%LOGIN_NAME

Notice that the complete path for the command is listed. Even though the file to be executed may be in a search drive, if that search drive is established by the login script, it will not be in effect until after the login script finishes executing. Also notice that the CAPTURE command is followed by a parameter (B=%LOGIN_NAME). B= is used with CAPTURE to specify what information appears on the banner pages that precede each print job. You can take advantage of a login script variable (%LOGIN_NAME) and set the banner information to show automatically the user's login name. (For complete information on the CAPTURE command, see Chapter 15.)

You may also want to use the EXECUTE command to create a "turn-key" environment for a network user. If you have a user who only logs into a server to use the network version of a word processor, it makes sense to start the word processing program automatically from the user's login script. That user's login script would probably look like the one shown in Script 16.12.

Script 16.12.

    MAP F:=SERV1/SYS:USERS\%LOGIN_NAME
    MAP G:=SERV1/SYS:SOFTWARE\WORDPERF
    MAP INSERT S1:=SERV1/SYS:PUBLIC
    DRIVE G: #SERV1/SYS:PUBLIC\CAPTURE B=%LOGIN_NAME
    #WP #SERV1/SYS:PUBLIC\LOGOUT

This script starts by doing several familiar things. First, it assigns drive F to the user's personal storage area. Then it assigns drive G to a directory that stores WordPerfect. It makes SYS:PUBLIC a search drive and then makes drive G (the WordPerfect directory) the default.

After mapping the correct directories and setting the default drive, you are ready to use the EXECUTE command. First, the login script executes the CAPTURE command to redirect printed output to the server-connected printer. Next, the word processing program executes. After the user exits the word processor, the login script takes over and executes the LOGOUT command. The login script controls everything the user does while he or she is logged into the server.

Rules for Using EXECUTE

The EXECUTE command can only be used to run executable files with the extensions EXE or COM. If a DOS or OS/2 path is established to the directory containing the file you want to execute prior to running the login script, or if the file is in the default directory, you can simply specify the file name in your login script, such as

#SYSTIME

SYSTIME is a NetWare command that shows the server's current date and time (see Chapter 18). However, if no search path exists to the file, or if you are creating a search path in the login script, you must specify the complete directory path to the file in order to execute it:

#SERV1/SYS:PUBLIC\SYSTIME

Running batch files or DOS internal commands using the EXECUTE command requires a special technique. You actually run the command processor (COMMAND.COM) with the /C parameter and then run your batch file or internal command as a parameter. For example, to run the DIR command to show a directory list from a login script, use the following:

#COMMAND /C DIR C:

Running a batch file requires the same approach. To run a file called LOG.BAT, you place the following line in your login script:

#COMMAND /C SERV1/SYS:PUBLIC\LOG.BAT

There is one type of executable file that you should not run from a login script using the EXECUTE command. Terminate and stay resident (TSR) programs (for example, SideKick, which remains in memory after it is run) lose additional memory; the memory used by the login command as it runs the login is not freed because the TSR program is loaded after it.

EXIT

The EXIT command has two uses:

❏ To halt the execution of a login script

❏ To leave a login script and run another command

If you use EXIT without a parameter in a login script, it causes the script to stop executing at that point. This can be used effectively in an IF/THEN statement. For example, if you need to copy a certain group of files from one network directory to another every Friday, you could use the following login script commands:

```
IF DAY_OF_WEEK NOT EQUAL TO "FRIDAY" THEN EXIT
WRITE "It's Friday—files are being copied to SYS:BACKCOPY"
#SERV1/SYS:PUBLIC\NCOPY SERV1/SYS:ACCTING SERV1/SYS:BACKCOPY
```

The first statement uses EXIT with IF/THEN to halt the login script if it is not Friday. On Fridays only, the last two lines execute, copying the files in SYS:ACCTING to SYS:BACKCOPY.

You can also use EXIT to execute a file as soon as the login script stops. For example, if you want to run a command that starts a menu program, place the following command on the last line of your login script:

```
EXIT "MENU"
```

Notice that the command must be enclosed in quotation marks.

Unlike the EXECUTE command, you can locate commands run with EXIT by using the search paths that you created in the login script. If you make SYS:PUBLIC a search drive in your login script, then you can run a command stored there without listing the entire directory name, such as

```
EXIT "SYSTIME"
```

The EXIT command will not accept a command name of more than 14 characters, which is just enough for an eight-character file name, a three-character extension, and the period that separates them.

You can use EXIT to run batch files or DOS internal commands without calling the command processor first.

EXIT and EXECUTE have similar functions. If your command can be run as the last statement of the login script, use EXIT. Otherwise you must use EXECUTE.

Attaching to Other Servers from a Login Script

To attach to another server automatically, use the ATTACH command in your login script. You have already examined the process of attaching to servers. You use LOGIN to your first server, and ATTACH to subsequent ones. When you use LOGIN or ATTACH, you supply the server name, your login name on that server, and your password (see Chapter 8 for details about LOGIN and ATTACH).

You have several options when you use ATTACH in a login script. For example, if you simply place the command by itself in a script

ATTACH

your login script executes and you receive the following prompt:

```
Enter the server name:
```

Suppose that you enter SERV2 as the response. You then receive this prompt:

```
Enter login name for server SERV2:
```

If you enter a login name that requires a password, you are prompted to enter it:

```
Enter password for server SERV2:
```

If you don't want to respond to this many prompts, you can specify some or all of the information in the login script itself. For example, you can specify the file server name with ATTACH by typing

ATTACH SERV2

and you will be prompted to give only your login name and password. You can go a step further and specify your login name as well by typing

ATTACH SERV2/SMITHFD

and you will be prompted for just your password. If you want to eliminate all prompts, you can also specify your password:

ATTACH SERV2/SMITHFD; CALISTO

You must separate your password from the login name with a semicolon (;). There are several potential problems with placing your password in your login script. First, any other user with supervisory rights to the server that stores your login script can view your password on the server to which you attach. Also, you must remember to modify your login script if you change your password.

You have another alternative to placing your password in your login script. If you use the same login name and password on both the server on which you log in and the server to which you attach, you can place only the server name in your login script by typing *attach*. The ATTACH command in your login script attaches you automatically to that server using your same login name and password. Suppose that you need to ATTACH to SERV2 to use a printer that is connected to it. You can place the following two lines in your login script so that you are attached automatically to SERV2, and your printed output is redirected to it as soon as you log in:

```
ATTACH SERV2
#SERV1/SYS:PUBLIC\CAPTURE S=SERV2 P=0 B=%LOGIN_NAME
```

The first line attaches you to SERV2. If your login name and password are the same as on SERV1, you are attached without having to enter your login name and password. The second line runs the CAPTURE command to redirect your printed output to printer 0 on SERV2 and uses your login name for the banner.

Using Commands from an External File

The most direct way to build a login script is to type it using SYSCON's login script editor. This works, but can result in a great deal of typing if you need to create login scripts for a network of 50 users. The typing is multiplied if you need to make changes or additions to login scripts later.

A far more manageable situation is to create one login script that will work for all users and can be stored in one place so that it is easy to maintain. If you use login script variables to make your scripts generic, you can make one script work for everyone. The INCLUDE login script command enables you to store that script in one place.

If you want to make all or part of your login script an external file, use your favorite text editor or word processor to type your login script and then save it as an ASCII file. Store that file in a directory where all users have READ and OPEN access (SYS:LOGIN or SYS:PUBLIC are good choices). Place the following command in your login script using SYSCON'S login script editor:

INCLUDE SERV1/SYS:PUBLIC\SCRIPT.LOG

(Replace SERV1/SYS:PUBLIC\SCRIPT.LOG with the actual directory and file name.)

For networks with many users, this is the best way to go. If you have to change the login script later, you only have to edit one file.

Special-Purpose Login Script Commands

The commands discussed so far are the ones you are the most likely to use on a regular basis. As with most macro or programming languages, there are some commands that are seldom used, designed perhaps to handle unusual situations. The commands discussed in the rest of this section are in this category. However, you may find some of them useful. For example, the FIRE PHASERS command is perfect for network supervisors who like to get attention. You can use four commands, DOS SET, DOS VERIFY, DOS BREAK and COMSPEC, to control certain DOS settings when you log in. They are similar to their DOS counterparts SET, BREAK, VERIFY, and COMSPEC. DOS SET enables you to use login script variables to store network information in the DOS environment. DOS VERIFY, DOS BREAK, and COMSPEC are not widely used.

DOS SET

The SET command enables you to place variables in the DOS environment. If you want to see current variables, type *set* and press Enter from the command line. You will see a listing of your current environment variables. Certain DOS commands such as PATH and PROMPT place information in an area of memory called the DOS environment. You can also use SET to place information of your choosing there. For example, if you type

SET MYNAME = BILL

then a variable called MYNAME is created and its setting is BILL.

Programs and batch files can be designed to use this information. For example, a batch file called PATTACH.BAT to attach users to SERV2 and redirect their printed output to its printer consists of the following two lines:

```
ATTACH SERV2/GUEST
CAPTURE S = SERV2 P = 0
```

You can modify this batch file to use the DOS environment to supply a banner name by changing the second line to the following:

```
CAPTURE S = SERV2 P = 0 B = %MYNAME%
```

%MYNAME% is replaced by whatever is listed in the DOS environment as the MYNAME variable.

Sometimes it is useful to place variables in the DOS environment while executing your login script. You can use the DOS SET login script command to do this. For example, the following login script command creates an environment variable called MYNAME and places the user's login name there:

```
DOS SET MYNAME = "%LOGIN_NAME"
```

DOS SET in a login script differs slightly from using SET from the command line. With DOS SET, you enclose the variable information in quotation marks.

With 25 different login script variables available, you may find some useful information that you can place in the DOS environment by using DOS SET. For example, you may want to place every user's login name in his or her environment so that server-based batch files can make use of them.

The amount of memory space in the DOS environment is not unlimited, so choose carefully the information that you want to store there! For more information about environment variables, the SET command, and controlling the amount of memory used by the DOS environment, consult your DOS manual.

DOS VERIFY

Like DOS SET, DOS VERIFY is similar to a corresponding command that you can use at the DOS prompt. When you type

```
VERIFY ON
```

and press Enter, DOS verifies all information written to your PC's disks by reading the information after it is written. This decreases performance slightly, but the loss of speed may be worth it when you are dealing with important data.

To turn verification off, type

    VERIFY OFF

and press Enter. You can see the current setting by typing

    VERIFY

and pressing Enter.

The default setting is no verification.

You can turn verification on or off from a login script. If you place the line

    DOS VERIFY ON

in your script, then verification is turned on. Similarly, the line

    DOS VERIFY OFF

turns verification off.

DOS BREAK

Like DOS VERIFY and DOS SET, DOS BREAK enables you to invoke a setting from within a login script that is identical to one that you can set using a command.

DOS commands and certain other programs let you stop their execution by pressing Ctrl-Break. Normally, you can interrupt them while they are communicating with the screen, printer, and keyboard but not while they are writing to or reading from a disk. You can control whether you can interrupt these programs during disk operations. The COPY command is a good example. When you type

    BREAK ON

and press Enter, you can halt the copying of a file in midstream. When you type

    BREAK OFF

and press Enter you cannot interrupt the COPY command until it finishes copying the file on which it is working.

You can see the current BREAK setting by typing *break* and pressing Enter.

The default condition is BREAK OFF.

You can change this setting from within a login script. Placing the command

DOS BREAK ON

in your login script is the same as typing *break on* from your command prompt. The command

DOS BREAK OFF

is the same as typing the BREAK OFF command from your command prompt.

COMSPEC

In DOS, COMSPEC is a variable in your environment that controls where your PC searches to access its command processor. By default, it sets this variable equal to the COMMAND.COM file found in the root directory of the disk drive from which you boot. You can vary this default by changing the COMSPEC variable setting to another drive and file name.

You can do this from within your login script by using the COMSPEC login script command. If you want your system to use a file called COMMAND.COM in a directory that you have mapped to drive H, you place the following command in your script:

COMSPEC = H:COMMAND.COM

You can use the same methods to identify the drive letter that you use with the MAP command. For example, *3: can be used to specify the third network drive and S4: the fourth search drive.

Workstation Information Commands

Perhaps the most obscure login script commands are MACHINE NAME and PCCOMPATIBLE. They had their origin in the time that IBM semicompatibles such as the Victor 9000 and the TI Professional Computer were a significant part of the computer market. To enable users of these machines to share login scripts with users of true IBM compatibles, the LOGIN program checked the machine name information stored in the workstation network shell. If the machine was not a true IBM compatible, then the EXIT command (which enables you to execute an external program after leaving the login script) was ignored so that programs written for IBM compatibles did not be run on incompatible machines.

As you saw in Chapter 8, you can use the SHELL.CFG file to customize the long machine name of your PC as it is stored by the network shell. The login script variable %MACHINE uses this name. Unless you customize it, the long machine name will be IBM_PC. Customizing this name might yield several advantages.

Suppose that the workstations on your network have a democratic mix of monitor types. You need to map each machine to the directory of Lotus 1-2-3 that contains the configuration files that match its screen type. You can do this simply by customizing the SHELL.CFG file for each workstation to specify a long machine name that identifies its monitor type. For example, PCs with EGA monitors can have machine names of IBM_EGA, and PCs with monochrome displays can be called IBM_MONO. You can designate names for PCs with VGA, CGA, and Hercules screens as well. Build directories that match each of these machine type names, such as SERV1/SYS:123\IBM_EGA and SERV1/SYS:IBM_MONO. Next, place the following line in your login scripts:

    MAP J: = SERV1/SYS:123\%MACHINE

Each machine is mapped automatically to the directory that stores the Lotus 1-2-3 configuration that matches its screen type.

There is one problem with this approach. If your login script contains the EXIT command, the LOGIN program checks the machine name in your workstation shell. If it is something other than IBM_PC, then the EXIT command is skipped. You can get around this in two ways. You can use the MACHINE NAME command to change the machine name just before running EXIT, or you can use the PCCOMPATIBLE command prior to the EXIT command. If you opt to use the MACHINE NAME command, your script will include the following lines:

    MAP J: = SERV1/SYS:123\%MACHINE
    MACHINE NAME = "IBM_PC"
    DRIVE J:EXIT "LOTUS"

If you decide to use PCCOMPATIBLE to do the job, your script will include the following:

    MAP J: = SERV1/SYS:123\%MACHINE
    DRIVE J: PCCOMPATIBLE

    EXIT "LOTUS"

Either script does the same job.

Placing Comments in Your Login Scripts

Sometimes you may want to put text in your login script other than commands that are executed. It may be useful to place remarks or comments in your scripts so that others can understand and fully appreciate the brilliance of your work. Remarks also have a more humble purpose. Sometimes you may want to temporarily prevent a few commands from executing, but you do not want to delete them because you want to reactivate them later. Turning those commands into remarks lets you keep the commands in the script but causes them not to be executed.

There are two simple rules to follow if you want text in your login script to be treated as a remark:

❑ You must precede the text with REMARK, REM, an asterisk (*), or a semicolon (;).

❑ The remark must be the only entry on the line.

Script 16.13 is liberally sprinkled with remarks.

Script 16.13

```
* Login script created by ADAM ADAMS, 4/15/90
* Modified by Joe Jones, 6/4/90
; Display general interest messages
DISPLAY SERV1/SYS:MESSAGES\MESSAGE.TXT
PAUSE
REM Greet the user by name, show the time and connection number
WRITE "GOOD %GREETING_TIME %FULL_NAME. IT IS %HOUR:%MINUTE %AM_PM"
WRITE "AND YOU HAVE BEEN ASSIGNED CONNECTION %STATION."
REMARK Map the first search drive to the PUBLIC directory
MAP DISPLAY OFF
MAP INSERT S1:=SERV1/SYS:PUBLIC
MAP DISPLAY ON
* If the user has a personal search area, map it as search drive 2
MAP ERRORS OFF
MAP INSERT S2:=SERV1/SYS:USERS\%LOGIN_NAME\PSEARCH
MAP ERRORS ON
; Map drive F: to the user's personal storage area
MAP F:=SERV1/SYS:USERS\%LOGIN_NAME
REM Map G: and H: to WordPerfect and Lotus
MAP G:=SERV1/SYS:SOFTWARE\WORDPERF
MAP H:=SERV1/SYS:SOFTWARE\123
```

```
REMARK Map I: to ACCTING if the user is in the Accounting Dept.
IF MEMBER OF "ACCTING" THEN MAP I: = SERV1/SYS:ACCTING
; Attach to SERV2 and direct printing to its printer
ATTACH SERV2 #SERV1/SYS:PUBLIC\CAPTURE S = SERV2 P = 0 B = %LOGIN_NAME
* Make C: the default drive
DRIVE C:
REMARK Start the menu program
EXIT "MENU"
```

Rather than use all four options for remarking (REMARK, REM, ;, or *), you probably will want to assert your personal style and stick with one as a favorite.

An alternative use for remarks is to deactivate login script commands until they are needed. In Script 16.13, the first two commands display a message file. There may not be a message file every day, and you need to deactivate these commands when there is no message. You can do so by turning them into remarks as follows:

```
REM DISPLAY SERV1/SYS:MESSAGES\MESSAGE.TXT
REM PAUSE
```

You can easily reactivate these command lines by deleting the words REM from each.

Working with Login Command Line Parameters

Your login script can work with the command line parameters that a user types after the LOGIN command. These seldom-used variables are identified by using numbers. When you place a variable identified as %1 in a login script, it returns the first command line parameter that the user entered after typing *login*, and %2 returns the second parameter, %3 the third, and so on.

Network supervisors report that they occasionally use this feature to enable users to specify certain options while logging in. For example, if the user named SMITHFD wants to specify that his printer output be redirected to a particular server and queue by using LOGIN command line parameters, he can type

```
LOGIN SERV1/SMITHFD SERV2 ACCT-LJ
```

The following line in his login script will read these parameters and use them to direct his printing to the ACCT-LJ queue on the server named SERV2:

#SERV1/SYS:PUBLIC\CAPTURE SERVER=%1 QUEUE=%2

NetWare 386 has an additional login script command called SHIFT that enables you to vary the numbering of LOGIN command line parameters. If you place the command

SHIFT 1

in a script, the command line parameter numbering shifts one position to the right (the first parameter is referred to as %0, the second as %1, the third as %2, and so on). If you follow SHIFT with a negative number, all command line parameter positioning shifts to the left. Most network supervisors report that they are at a loss as to how to use this feature, but its comforting to know it is available.

A Command that Makes Noise

The most entertaining login script command has been saved for last. The FIRE PHASERS command enables you to make a sound like the weapon on a ship. To fire five phaser blasts, place the following line in your script:

FIRE PHASERS 5 TIMES

You can replace 5 with any number between 1 and 9.

Whereas the FIRE PHASERS command offers the network supervisor many opportunities for mischief, it also has several legitimate uses. In Script 16.3, the first two lines display a message file. You have already seen that these lines turn into remarks when there is no message to display. On those days when there is a message, you can be sure you get the user's attention by including a little phrase such as the following:

FIRE PHASERS 6 TIMES
DISPLAY SERV1/SYS:MESSAGES\MESSAGE.TXT
PAUSE

Your message will be hard to ignore. The uses for phaser fire are only limited by your imagination. The following login script section uses IF/THEN, FIRE PHASERS, and WRITE to remind users in the group ACCTING of their weekly department meeting:

```
IF MEMBER = "ACCTING" AND DAY_OF_WEEK = "FRIDAY" THEN BEGIN
   FIRE PHASERS 3 TIMES
   WRITE "THE ACCOUNTING DEPARTMENT WILL MEET TODAY AT 4:30"
   PAUSE
END
```

NetWare's login script language is flexible enough to meet the needs of any situation. A creative network supervisor can build scripts to handle a variety of circumstances.

Managing Login Scripts

On a network with a large number of users, it is important to minimize the effort required to manage and change login scripts. You want the process to be simple enough so that changes can be made easily and quickly, and on a daily basis if necessary.

You have already considered the benefits of developing one login script that works for everyone and is customized using variables. Several techniques make this possible. If you give each user a personal directory that has the same name as his login name, you can map to that directory using the %LOGIN_NAME variable:

MAP F:=SERV1/SYS:USERS\%LOGIN_NAME

You can also use IF/THEN to handle the needs of some users. For example, to map a drive just for ACCTING group members, you use the following command:

IF MEMBER OF "ACCTING" THEN MAP I:=SERV1/SYS:ACCTING

You can attempt to match a search drive for the users who have a personal search area, and use MAP ERRORS OFF so that no error message shows if the login script is run for a user who has not created a personal search area:

MAP ERRORS OFF
MAP INSERT S2:=SERV1/SYS:USERS\%LOGIN_NAME\PSEARCH
MAP ERRORS ON

If there are login script commands that you know must be run for all users who log into a server, then you can place them in the System login script. Place all other commands in each user's individual script.

You should seriously consider using the INCLUDE login script command to place every user's login script in an external file. If you use this method, then every user's login script can be one line:

INCLUDE SERV1/SYS:PUBLIC\SCRIPT.LOG

The contents of SCRIPT.LOG consists of the complete login script, such as the script shown in Script 16.13.

Distributing the Same Script to Multiple Users

If you are the network supervisor or a workgroup manager, you can use SYSCON to give one user the same script as another. Log into a server. Start SYSCON by typing *syscon* and pressing Enter. From SYSCON's main menu, select User Information. This lists the user login names for your server. Select the name of the user whose login script you are going to create and press Enter. The User Information menu appears. Select Login Script and press Enter.

An entry box opens that asks which user's login script you want to read and show in SYSCON's login script editor. It shows the name of the user you selected as the default. Backspace over the user's name that appears in the box and enter the name of the user whose script you want to use, or press Ins to see a list of users from which to select. Highlight the name of the appropriate user and press Enter. Either method takes you to SYSCON's login script editor, and the script of the user you choose appears. To save this script for the original user, press Esc. You are returned to the User Information menu. Press Esc again to see a list of the server's users and select another user name to repeat the process, or press Esc to return to SYSCON's main menu. Press Esc once more to exit SYSCON.

Using the LOGIN Command To Control Login Script Execution

With NetWare 386 and NetWare 286 Version 2.15C, you can use command line parameters with the LOGIN command to control whether the system and personal login scripts are executed when you log in. If you follow the LOGIN command with the /Sfilename parameter and replace "filename" with the name of an alternative script file, your system and personal login script is not executed, and the designated script file is executed instead. For example, to log in and execute a script called ALTSCR.TXT on drive C, you type

> LOGIN SERV386/SMITHFD /SALTSCR.TXT

and press Enter. Your script file should be a text file that contains login script commands (it is the same type of file that you can include as part of your login script by using the INCLUDE login script command).

You also can specify that your login scripts be reexecuted without having to log in again. If you follow the LOGIN command with the parameter /NA (for NO ATTACH), your login scripts are reexecuted but you are not logged into the server again. You type

> LOGIN /NA

and press Enter to use this option.

How Netware Stores Login Scripts

NetWare stores login scripts as ASCII text files. With supervisory access, you can manipulate these files directly, using your favorite text editor or a word processor that can work with ASCII files.

The System Login Script is stored in the SYS:PUBLIC directory and is named NET$LOG.DAT. Each user's login script is stored in a file called LOGIN in his or her mail subdirectory. This is the same directory where the user's printer configuration file is stored. A user's mail subdirectory is located under a directory called SYS:MAIL. The subdirectory name is a number and is the same as the user ID number that NetWare assigns to a user when he or she is added to the network. If you are a supervisor or workgroup manager, you can look up a user's ID number using SYSCON. From SYSCON's main menu, select User Information. This lists the users on the server. Highlight the user whose number you want to look up and press Enter. This brings you to the User Information menu. Select Other Information and a box appears with the user's ID number. A user with an ID number of 20007 would have a personal mail directory called SYS:MAIL\20007.

Chapter Summary

In this chapter, you learned that the login script is the most important tool for customizing the LAN environment. It enables you to automatically create drive mappings, run programs, display useful information, and perform other useful tasks. With a little study and experimentation, you can design login scripts that meet the needs of your users very effectively.

17

Implementing NetWare Accounting

In many large companies, users of mainframe-based systems are charged for system access. For example, if the accounting department uses the company's mainframe computers to store the company payroll and payable and receivable records, the data processing department may charge the accounting department a fee. This fee may be based on the amount of disk space occupied by the accounting department's data files, or the amount of time that members of the accounting department are logged into the system, or an amount per year for each login ID that they use.

A similar situation exists when you use your PC and modem to access a commercial bulletin board (such as CompuServe) or a public electronic mail system (such as MCI Mail). You are usually charged for your "connect time" or the number of messages that you send.

Your company's philosophy concerning computer usage may dictate that you charge users for network access. Even if you aren't required to charge, you may be asked to supply network usage statistics to your management on a periodic basis. NetWare's accounting features can help you satisfy this requirement.

NetWare's accounting enables you to track the following information about how your file servers are used:

❏ The amount of time that users are logged in

❏ The amount of information that each user reads from file server disks

❏ The amount of information that each user writes to file server disks

❏ The amount of information that each user stores on file server disks

❏ The number of service requests that are made to the file server

You can also charge users based on any grouping of the above criteria.

You may have purchased or developed a special server such as a communications gateway or a facsimile server that is designed to charge for its services or track its usage with NetWare's accounting features. This special server may enable you to charge for or to track certain aspects of how it is used, such as the number of facsimile transmissions sent or received.

The accounting feature also adds to the server's workload. Depending on what server resources are being tracked, the server processor updates accounting files for each user and for each transaction that is being measured. On a busy server, the enabling of the accounting feature can slow throughput for all users as dozens of transactions per minute are recorded in accounting files.

NetWare accounting is an optional feature that you do not have to implement; in fact, most network supervisors report that they do not use it. Maintaining and updating account balances for each user can be a lot of work, and the benefits may not be worth the effort. If you see no immediate need for the capability that NetWare accounting offers, you can safely skip this chapter for now. Unlike login names and trustee and login scripts, accounting does not have to be implemented when you begin to configure your file server; you can add it at any time.

Accounting Strategy

You can use NetWare's accounting in two ways:

❏ To track the usage of the file server (recording disk usage and the amount of time that users are logged in)

❏ To charge users a certain amount for being logged into the server or using its disks

If you plan to use NetWare accounting only to track server usage statistics, then you only need to choose which server resources you want to track. If you decide to charge users for using the file server, you must also assign each user a starting balance and decide how much credit each user gets.

NetWare accounting has some frustrating limitations. You must charge all users the same rate for each service. For example, if you decide to charge a dollar a day for each unit of disk storage used, that rate applies to all users. Fortunately, you can give each user an individual account balance and credit limit.

User account balances are only updated when the user logs in or logs out. This means that a user who stays logged in for a long period can "overdraw" his account by a significant amount without being notified.

Installing NetWare Accounting

NetWare accounting is activated one server at a time and is managed using SYSCON. To install accounting on a file server, log into it with supervisory-level access and start SYSCON by typing

SYSCON

at the command prompt. Press Enter. From SYSCON's main menu select the option called Accounting and press Enter. A box appears with the prompt Install Accounting. Select yes in response to this prompt, and NetWare accounting is installed. SYSCON's Accounting menu (see fig. 17.1) now appears.

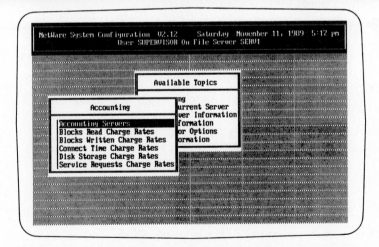

Fig. 17.1.
SYSCON's Accounting menu.

After you install accounting, NetWare automatically creates a log file and tracks each user's login and logout from the server. You will learn how to view and work with this file later in this chapter.

Selecting Accounting Servers

The first option on SYSCON's Accounting menu is Accounting Servers. This option is used to list all servers that charge for their services using NetWare accounting. You do not need to use this option unless you have installed a special server (other than a normal NetWare file server) that is designed to use NetWare accounting to charge for its services. The most common example is the printer server module that comes with NetWare 386. If you have implemented a NetWare 386 print server and you want to use NetWare accounting to charge users for using it, you use the Accounting Servers menu option to add it to the list of accounting servers. You may have purchased and installed a third-party device such as a communication server that is designed to use NetWare accounting to charge for its services. If this is the case, you also can add it to the list of accounting servers. If you have no servers of this type, or if you do not want to use them in conjunction with NetWare accounting, then skip to the next section.

When you select Accounting Servers from SYSCON's Accounting menu, a list of servers is displayed. The file server on which you used SYSCON to install accounting is automatically the first server on the list of accounting servers, and it is the only file server that will be listed. The rest of the list is reserved for print servers and similar specialized servers, as previously discussed. Each file server on which you have installed NetWare accounting maintains its own list of accounting servers.

To add a server to the list of accounting servers, select the Accounting Servers option and press Enter. A list of the current accounting servers is shown (see fig. 17.2)—unless you have installed other servers, only the current file server is shown.

Press Ins and a list of other available types appears (such as print servers). Select the appropriate type for the server you want to add and press Enter. A list of servers matching the type you selected appears. Highlight the server you want to add and press Enter. The server is added to the list of accounting servers. You can add multiple servers by marking each with the F5 key and pressing Enter.

You can remove a server from the list of accounting servers by highlighting its name on the accounting server list and pressing Del. You can remove multiple servers by marking each with the F5 key and then pressing Del.

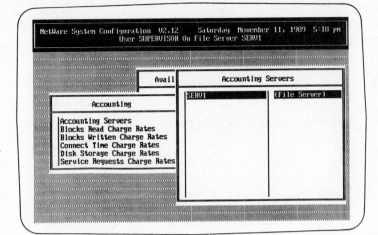

NetWare System Configuration V2.12   Saturday November 11, 1989 5:18 pm
User SUPERVISOR On File Server SERV1

Avail   Accounting Servers

Accounting

Accounting Servers
Blocks Read Charge Rates
Blocks Written Charge Rates
Connect Time Charge Rates
Disk Storage Charge Rates
Service Requests Charge Rates

SERV1   (File Server)

Fig. 17.2.
The Accounting
Servers option
display.

Setting Up Server Charge Rates

NetWare's accounting tracks a particular usage statistic as soon as you
assign a *charge rate* to that item. A charge rate is the amount of money
you want to charge for a particular interval of time for a particular service.
Even if you plan to use NetWare accounting only to track usage statistics,
you still need to set up charge rates for the items you want to track.

There are five items for which you can establish charge rates: *Blocks Read*,
Blocks Written, *Connect Time*, *Disk Storage*, and *Service Requests*. Three of
the items have to do with disk blocks, so you need to learn what disk
blocks are and how they are used.

Understanding Disk Blocks

NetWare reads and writes to file server disks in units called blocks. For
NetWare 286, the disk block is set automatically to 4,096 bytes, or four
kilobytes. For NetWare 386, the disk block size is set when you install the
disk volume, and can range from 4 to 64 kilobytes. When you store a file
on a NetWare disk, a sufficient number of disk blocks are allocated to store
it. For example, if you store a file that is 18,000 bytes in size, it is stored
in five disk blocks (presuming that your block size is 4,096 bytes). Because
five disk blocks of 4,096 bytes occupy just over 20,000 bytes, about 2,000

bytes worth of space in the fifth disk block is wasted. This inefficiency is the price paid for achieving good disk performance. DOS and OS/2 also use the disk block method to store data on your PC's local hard disk.

Chargeable Items

NetWare accounting has five items for which you can establish charge rates:

❑ *Disk Blocks Read*. You can establish a charge rate for each disk block read. You can set up variable charge rates based on the time of day or day of the week. For example, you might want to charge less for disk blocks read during nonbusy times, such as after hours or on the weekend.

Many operations that you perform with files on a server disk involve reading disk blocks. For example, if you execute the ATTACH command, which is approximately 27,000 bytes in size, the disk blocks that contain the ATTACH.EXE file are all read. If your server disk block size is 4,096 bytes, you will read seven disk blocks when executing this command. If you are being charged for reading disk blocks, you will be charged for reading seven blocks.

You also read disk blocks when you retrieve a document with your word processor or a data file with your database manager.

❑ *Disk Blocks Written*. Charging for the writing of disk blocks is similar to charging for the reading of disk blocks. You can establish one charge rate for all hours of the week or vary the charge rate for certain hours of the day or days of the week.

Anytime you create a new file or write new information to an existing file, you are writing disk blocks. When you copy a file to a server disk, use your spreadsheet to save a file to a server directory, or update a shared data file, you are writing disk blocks. Anytime you write to a file, the information is written in units of disk blocks.

❑ *Disk Storage*. NetWare accounting lets you charge each user for the number of blocks of disk storage used. Users are charged on a daily basis.

When you park your car at the airport while you are away on a three-day business trip, you are charged for using a parking space for three days. Similarly, when you store a file that occupies five disk blocks for three days and then erase it, you are charged for occupying five disk blocks for three days.

The network supervisor establishes a rate per block per day. NetWare's accounting keeps track of the number of blocks each user is storing and charges the user at the daily rate. You can vary the daily rate if you want to charge more on some days of the week and less on others.

❑ *Connect Time*. You can charge users for the number of minutes that they are logged into a server. You can also set variable charge rates, charging more for one time of day or one day of the week versus another.

Charging for connect time is similar to the type of charge you receive when you use public bulletin boards like CompuServe or The Source. You are generally billed at a certain rate for each minute that you are connected.

❑ *Service Requests*. Charging for service requests is probably a less useful option than charging for disk usage or connect time. Anytime you perform any task on a file server, such as using the DIR command to list the files on a server directory, or using MAP to show the current drive letter assignments, service requests are generated. A user's service requests are a very comprehensive gauge of his or her file server usage, but they do not show what specific resources he or she is using. You probably will find it more helpful to track disk usage and connect time.

Understanding Charge Rates

When you decide upon a charge rate for one of the previously discussed resources, you are specifying how much money to charge for one unit of that resource. For example, if you are setting a connect time charge rate, you must decide how much to charge for every *minute* that a user is logged in. If you are setting a rate for disk blocks read or written, you are deciding how much to charge for each *block* read or written. When you set a charge rate for disk storage, you are determining how much to charge for each *block-day*. You are charging the user per day for each block of disk space being used. If you charge for service requests, then you decide how much to charge for each *service request* generated.

NetWare provides you with a clever way to fix charge rates and to make them any increment of your currency that you want. When you set up a charge rate, you create a simple fraction that is the proportion of your currency that you want to use. For example, if your currency is the dollar, and you want to charge two dollars for every disk block written (and thereby get rich quick), your charge rate is 2/1. If you want to charge only one half of a dollar (50 cents) for each disk block read, your charge rate is 1/2.

When you use SYSCON to establish charge rates, the top number is called the *multiplier*, and the bottom number is called the *divisor*. The resulting fraction represents the proportion of your currency that you want to charge for each unit of the resource.

An example will clarify this. You want to charge users for connect time and decide upon a rate of five-hundredths of your currency per minute. Using dollars, this would be five cents. Your charge rate is 5/100, which can be reduced to 1/20; you can use 1/20 and get the same result. If a user is logged in for 35 minutes, what would the total charge be? Simply multiply the charge rate by the number of minutes used:

$$35 \times \$.05 = \$1.75$$

Assigning Charge Rates with SYSCON

As you prepare to set charge rates for any or all of the five items for which you can charge, you need to know two things:

❑ The charge rates that you want to use (expressed as a multiplier over a divisor)

❑ The times during the week that you want to use those rates. For example, you might want to have the following charge schedule for connect times:

Monday-Friday	7:00 a.m.-5:59 p.m.	5/100 per minute
Monday-Friday	6:00 p.m.-6:59 a.m.	2/100 per minute
Saturday-Sunday	all times	no charge

You can use SYSCON to implement these charge rates. Log into the appropriate server with supervisory access and type

    SYSCON

at the command prompt. Press Enter. From SYSCON's Available Topics main menu, select Accounting and press Enter. You are taken to SYSCON's Accounting menu. If you are going to set charge rates for connect time, select Connect Time Charge Rates and press Enter. The Connect Time Charge Rates screen shown in figure 17.3 appears. On the right half of this screen, a grid is displayed that divides every day of the week into half-hour increments. Each increment has a number in it corresponding to the charge rate shown in the lower corner of the screen. By default, every half hour is set to charge rate number 1, which is the no-charge rate. Only the times 8:00 a.m. and 4:30 p.m. show on the screen. You can use the up and down arrows and the PgUp and PgDn keys to scroll the screen up or down to show other times.

```
NetWare System Configuration  V2.12    Saturday  November 11, 1989  5:18 pm
                   User SUPERVISOR On File Server SERV1

                                     Sun  Mon  Tue  Wed  Thu  Fri  Sat
       Connect Time Charge Rates   8:00am  1    1    1    1    1    1    1
                                   8:30am  1    1    1    1    1    1    1
                                   9:00am  1    1    1    1    1    1    1
   Sunday                          9:30am  1    1    1    1    1    1    1
   8:00 am To 8:29 am             10:00am  1    1    1    1    1    1    1
                                  10:30am  1    1    1    1    1    1    1
   Rate  Charge    Rate   Charge  11:00am  1    1    1    1    1    1    1
    1   No Charge   11             11:30am  1    1    1    1    1    1    1
    2                12            12:00pm  1    1    1    1    1    1    1
    3                13            12:30pm  1    1    1    1    1    1    1
    4                14             1:00pm  1    1    1    1    1    1    1
    5                15             1:30pm  1    1    1    1    1    1    1
    6                16             2:00pm  1    1    1    1    1    1    1
    7                17             2:30pm  1    1    1    1    1    1    1
    8                18             3:00pm  1    1    1    1    1    1    1
    9                19             3:30pm  1    1    1    1    1    1    1
   10                20             4:00pm  1    1    1    1    1    1    1
       (Charge is per minute)       4:30pm  1    1    1    1    1    1    1
```

Fig. 17.3.
The Connect Time Charge Rates screen.

Assume that you want to set 7:00 a.m. through 5:59 p.m., Monday through Friday to a charge rate of 5/100. The first step is to highlight this block of time. Use the cursor arrows to move to the 7:00 a.m. time block for Monday and press the F5 key. Use the right- and down-arrow keys to position the lower right corner of your highlight box at Friday at 5:30 p.m. You will have highlighted all time increments between Monday at 7:00 a.m. and Friday at 5:59 p.m., as figure 17.4 shows.

The upper left corner of the screen displays the time range that you have highlighted and should read

    Monday to Friday 7:00 a.m. to 5:59 p.m.

Press Enter, and a box opens prompting you to choose between setting the selected time range to a no-charge rate or to another rate. Select Other Charge Rate and press Enter. A box opens as shown in figure 17.5, which prompts you to enter the multiplier and divisor that become the charge rate. Enter 5 for the multiplier and 100 for the divisor. Press Esc to save your entries.

Fig. 17.4.

Setting a charge rate.

Fig. 17.5.

Entering a charge rate.

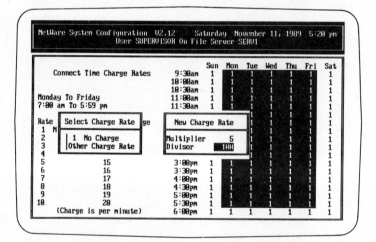

The charge rate entries in the highlighted time range change from the number 1 to 2, and the new charge rate of 5/100 is entered as charge rate number 2 in the Rate Charge section in the lower left corner of the screen, as shown in figure 17.6.

You can change charge rates for other time ranges using the same procedure as described in the preceding paragraphs. You also can delete a charge rate by highlighting its time range and then selecting a time rate of no charge. When you are finished establishing charge rates for all time ranges, press Esc to exit and save your changes. If you want to cancel your changes, press F7.

```
NetWare System Configuration  V2.12     Saturday  November 11, 1989  5:21 pm
                     User SUPERVISOR On File Server SERV1

                                        Sun  Mon  Tue  Wed  Thu  Fri  Sat
        Connect Time Charge Rates   9:30am   1    2    2    2    2    2    1
                                   10:00am   1    2    2    2    2    2    1
                                   10:30am   1    2    2    2    2    2    1
Friday                             11:00am   1    2    2    2    2    2    1
5:30 pm To 5:59 pm                 11:30am   1    2    2    2    2    2    1
                                   12:00pm   1    2    2    2    2    2    1
Rate  Charge      Rate  Charge     12:30pm   1    2    2    2    2    2    1
  1  No Charge     11               1:00pm   1    2    2    2    2    2    1
  2  5/100         12               1:30pm   1    2    2    2    2    2    1
  3                13               2:00pm   1    2    2    2    2    2    1
  4                14               2:30pm   1    2    2    2    2    2    1
  5                15               3:00pm   1    2    2    2    2    2    1
  6                16               3:30pm   1    2    2    2    2    2    1
  7                17               4:00pm   1    2    2    2    2    2    1
  8                18               4:30pm   1    2    2    2    2    2    1
  9                19               5:00pm   1    2    2    2    2    2    1
 10                20               5:30pm   1    2    2    2    2    2    1
        (Charge is per minute)      6:00pm   1    1    1    1    1    1    1
```

Fig. 17.6.

The Connect Time Charge Rates screen set.

In this example, set the charge rates for connect time, the time that a user is logged into the server. You will be glad to know that the procedure for setting charge rates for Blocks Read, Blocks Written, and Service Requests is identical. When you select Blocks Read Charge Rates, Blocks Written Charge Rates, Connect Time Charge Rates, or Service Requests Charge Rates, you are presented with virtually the same charge rate selection screen. The only difference is the resource for which you are charging. With Blocks Read and Blocks Written, you are charging for disk blocks used; with Connect Time you are charging for minutes of login time, and with Service Requests you are charging for each service request.

Setting the Charge Rate for Disk Storage

The Disk Storage Charge Rate option uses a slightly different method of establishing charge rates. Disk storage is charged according to the number of disk blocks used per day. Unlike the other options, where you can set charge rates for half-hour blocks of time, there is no charge other than once a day, because charges are based on a full day of use. When preparing to establish charge rates for disk storage, select a time of day at which you want the file server to assess disk storage charges.

Suppose that you want to establish charge rates of 1/2, one-half of a unit of your currency. You might want to use 50/100 if your currency is the dollar. You want the file server to assess charges at 12 midnight every day.

Log into the appropriate server with supervisory access and type

SYSCON

at the command prompt. Press Enter. From SYSCON's Available Topics main menu, select Accounting and press Enter. You see SYSCON's Accounting menu (see fig. 17.1).

To set rates for disk storage, select Disk Storage Charge Rates and press Enter. Figure 17.7 shows the menu that appears.

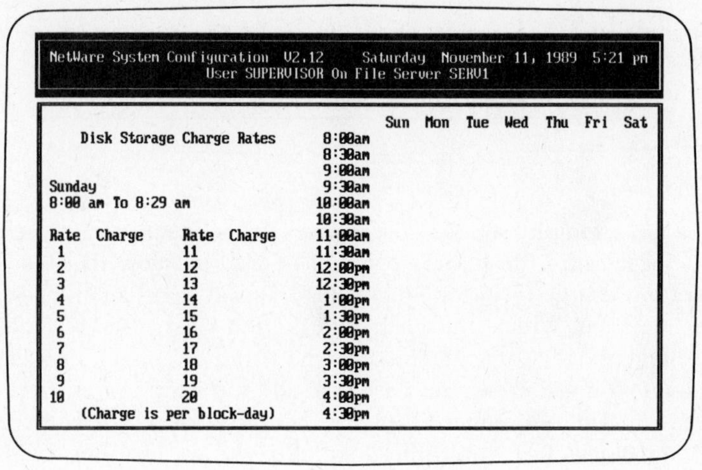

Fig. 17.7.

The Disk Storage Charge Rates screen.

```
NetWare System Configuration  V2.12    Saturday  November 11, 1989  5:21 pm
                    User SUPERVISOR On File Server SERV1

                                         Sun  Mon  Tue  Wed  Thu  Fri  Sat
         Disk Storage Charge Rates    8:00am
                                      8:30am
                                      9:00am
Sunday                                9:30am
8:00 am To 8:29 am                   10:00am
                                     10:30am
Rate  Charge    Rate  Charge        11:00am
 1              11                   11:30am
 2              12                   12:00pm
 3              13                   12:30pm
 4              14                    1:00pm
 5              15                    1:30pm
 6              16                    2:00pm
 7              17                    2:30pm
 8              18                    3:00pm
 9              19                    3:30pm
10              20                    4:00pm
      (Charge is per block-day)       4:30pm
```

Use the down-arrow key to move the cursor to the time block for Sunday at 12:00 midnight. Press F5 and use the right-arrow key to highlight the 12:00 midnight time block for each day of the week, ending with the Saturday 12:00 midnight position. Press Enter, and an entry box called New Charge Rate appears, as figure 17.8 shows.

As with other charge rates, you are prompted to enter the rate as a multiplier and a divisor, which become the proportion of your currency that is charged for each disk block-day used. You want to establish a charge rate of 50/100, or 1/2, so enter 1 for the multiplier and 2 for the divisor. Press Esc to save your entries.

A charge rate of 1 appears in each of the highlighted time blocks and the new charge rate of 1/2 is entered as charge rate number 1 in the Rate Charge section in the lower left corner on-screen, as shown in figure 17.9. Press Esc to save your changes and exit, or press F7 to cancel your changes.

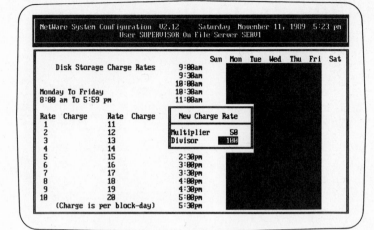

Fig. 17.8.
Entering a Disk Storage Charge rate.

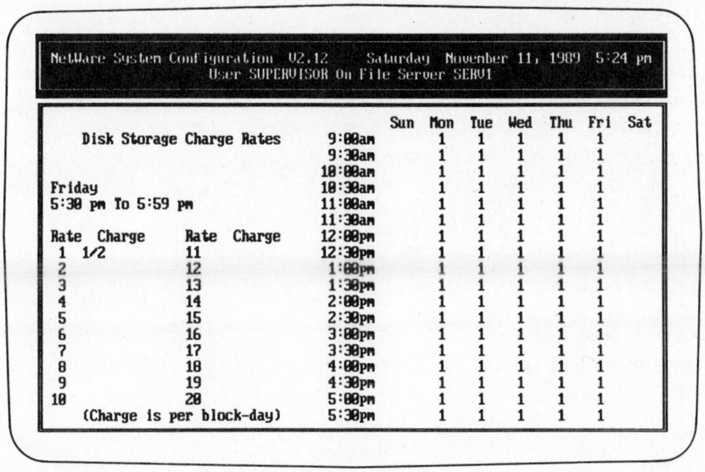

Fig. 17.9.
The Disk Storage Charge Rates screen set.

If you plan to use NetWare accounting to generate server statistics only, then there is one last bit of setup work that you must do. Every user must be given unlimited credit so that the charges assessed by NetWare accounting do not prevent him or her from using the server as he or she normally would. Refer to the section "Giving Unlimited Credit to All Users" (later in this chapter), and immediately give all users credit so that they can continue to use resources for which they are being charged. If you are actually going to charge individual users for using server resources, then you need to give each user an account balance and a credit status. The next section discusses these steps.

Establishing Account Balances and Credit Status

After you establish charge rates for any or all of the five chargeable server resources, you need to give users some "spending money" so that they can buy the services that you are offering.

This spending money comes in two parts. You can give each user an account balance that he can spend on server resources. You can also give each user credit that he can draw upon when his account balance reaches zero.

By default, users have an account balance of zero and no credit. If you have established charge rates for server resources, you *must* immediately give all users an account balance or credit, or they will be unable to use the resources for which they are being charged.

For NetWare 286, only a user with supervisory equivalence can set account balances and credit limits. For NetWare 386, workgroup managers can set account balances and credit limits for the users they manage.

Setting Account Balances for Individual Users

SYSCON gives a user an account balance and a credit limit. Log into the appropriate server and type

SYSCON

from the command line. Press Enter. From SYSCON's Available Topics main menu, select User Information and press Enter. You see a list of users; highlight the user with whom you want to work and press Enter. You see the User Information menu. Select the first option on this menu, Account Balance, and press Enter. You see a screen similar to the one shown in figure 17.10.

To assign a user an account balance, simply fill in a number up to 99,999,999 next to Account Balance. If you decide to give the user unlimited credit, highlight the box next to Allow Unlimited Credit and press Y to change the setting from no to yes. Allow unlimited credit in those cases where you do not want to disable a user's access to a resource

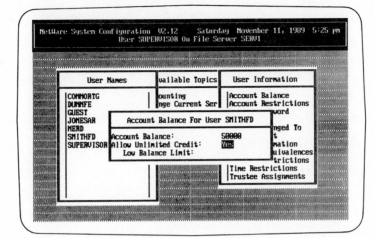

Fig. 17.10.

The Account Balance window from SYSCON's User Information menu.

under any circumstances, even if the user hasn't paid the bill. If you are using NetWare accounting only to track server-usage statistics, give all users unlimited credit so that they can have uninterrupted access to all server resources.

The last step is to assign a low balance limit. This sets the point at which the user can no longer use charged server resources. If you set a limit as a negative number, such as −$1,000, the user is allowed to "overdraw" the account balance. If you make the low balance limit a positive number, the user cannot go below that amount. To assign a low balance limit, move the highlight to Low Balance Limit and enter the amount you want to set as the user's low balance limit.

Press Esc to save your changes and return to the User Information menu. Press F7 if you want to cancel your changes. Press Esc again to return to the list of users. At this point, you can select another user to work with or press Esc again to go back to SYSCON's main menu.

Setting Account Balances for Multiple Users

Assigning account balances to many users individually can be a tedious process. If you want to assign many users the same account balance and low balance limit, you can do so. From SYSCON's Available Topics main menu, select User Information. You see a list of all users on the server.

Mark the users whose balances you want to set with F5. When all the appropriate users are highlighted, press Enter. The User Information menu then appears. Select Account Balance from this menu and press Enter. You see the same window as shown in figure 17.10. Enter the desired account balance and low balance limit settings, and set Allow Unlimited Credit to yes or no. Press Esc to exit and save your settings, or F7 to cancel them.

Default Account Balances for Future Users

To save having to set up account balance information for new users, you can establish a default account balance, credit status, and low balance limit. These defaults are given automatically to newly added users.

From SYSCON's Available Topics main menu, select Supervisor Options. From the Supervisor Options menu, select Default Account Balance/ Restrictions and press Enter. Figure 17.11 shows the screen that is then displayed. Move the highlight to Account Balance and enter a default balance figure (between 99,999,999 and −99,999,999). Next, move the highlight to Allow Unlimited Credit and enter Y (for yes) if you want to allow unlimited credit by default, or N (for no) if you don't. Finally, move the highlight to Low Balance Limit and enter the default low balance limit. When you finish entering the default settings, press Esc to save them and exit, or press F7 to cancel your changes. The Supervisor Options menu returns to the screen. Press Esc once to go back to SYSCON's main menu.

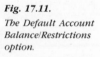

Fig. 17.11.

The Default Account Balance/Restrictions option.

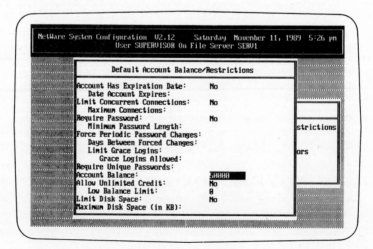

Giving Unlimited Credit to All Users

If you are using NetWare's accounting to track server usage but not to actually charge users for accessing server resources, you need to give all users unlimited credit so that they are not prevented from using the server due to lack of "spending money" in their accounts. You can use SYSCON to give all users unlimited credit quickly.

Log into the appropriate server with supervisory access and start SYSCON by typing

SYSCON

at the command line. Press Enter. From SYSCON's Available Topics main menu, select User Information. You are shown a list of all users on the server. Mark all user names with F5. When all users are highlighted, press Enter, and the User Information menu appears. Select Account Balance from this menu and press Enter. You see the window shown in figure 17.10. Move the highlight to Allow Unlimited Credit and press Y to change its setting to yes. Press Esc to exit and save your settings. Press Esc again to return to SYSCON's main menu.

It is a good idea to set the default credit status to allow unlimited credit for all newly added users. Follow the instructions detailed in the previous section, "Setting Account Balances for Individual Users."

Managing NetWare Accounting

After you establish all charge rates and user balances, you need to monitor account balances frequently and get the information necessary to perform billings. On a large network, this is not an easy task.

You already have learned how to use SYSCON to see and change the account balances for users. You can use this method periodically to look up each user's account balance and bill. Two other utilities are available to help you view charge information. PAUDIT is a command that lists all accounting charges chronologically for all users. ATOTAL displays a summary report of the accounting resources that have been used.

PAUDIT and ATOTAL read accounting information written by the file server to the accounting log file. This file is named NET$ACCT.DAT and is stored in the SYS:SYSTEM directory. On a busy server this file can grow to be very large. You should use PAUDIT and ATOTAL regularly to draw information from the log file's contents and then delete it so that it does not grow too large and unmanageable.

Next, you will examine how to use PAUDIT and ATOTAL to display accounting information.

PAUDIT

PAUDIT is a command that enables the network supervisor to view a list of all user logins and accounting charges. It is stored in the SYS:SYSTEM directory. To use PAUDIT, make SYS:SYSTEM your default directory and type

    AUDIT

Press Enter. You should see output similar to that shown in figure 17.12.

Fig. 17.12.

Sample output from the PAUDIT command.

```
7/8/90 12:57:51  File Server SERV1
    NOTE: about User SUPERVISOR during File Server services.
    Login from address 00000001:00000000003C.
7/8/90 13:03:37  File Server SERV1
    CHARGE: 113 to User SUPERVISOR for File Server services.
    Connected 6 min.; 5116 requests; 000000053E5Ch bytes read; 000000000000h
    bytes written.
7/8/90 13:03:37  File Server SERV1
    NOTE: about User SUPERVISOR during File Server services.
    Logout from address 00000001:00000000003C.
7/8/90 13:03:37  File Server SERV1
    NOTE: about User SMITHFD during File Server services.
    Login from address 00000001:00000000004A.
7/8/90 13:06:07  File Server SERV1
    CHARGE: 1350 to User SMITHFD for File Server services.
    Connected 3 min.; 6935 requests; 0000001F57BEh bytes read; 0000001A16B7h
    bytes written.
7/8/90 13:06:07  File Server SERV1
    NOTE: about User SMITHFD during File Server services.
    Logout from address 00000001:00000000004A.
```

If you examine the output from PAUDIT closely, you should notice several things. First, each entry consists of two or three lines, and all entries are listed in chronological order. The first line of every entry shows the date, time, and server. The second line begins with the word *NOTE* or *CHARGE*. Lines that begin with *NOTE* record a user login or logout. The user name and network and node address are shown also (the addresses are displayed in hexadecimal notation).

Lines that begin with *CHARGE* show the total amount charged to the user during the time he or she has been logged in. The amount charged appears after the word *CHARGE*. The next line shows how long the user was connected in minutes, followed by the number of bytes read and written (again in hexadecimal), and the number of server requests.

On even moderately busy file servers, the output from PAUDIT can be many screens long. You probably will want to use redirection to send PAUDIT's contents to a file. You can do so by typing

  PAUDIT > file name

and pressing Enter. Replace *file name* with the name of the file you want to use. If you experiment with your word processor or a programming language, you might be able to reformat the output file from PAUDIT into a useful report.

You can also send PAUDIT's output directly to a printer by typing

  PAUDIT > PRN

ATOTAL

ATOTAL is very useful if you want to use NetWare accounting to generate server-usage statistics. It produces a summary report showing accounting charges for the preceding day and a total for the preceding week.

Like PAUDIT, ATOTAL is located in the SYS:SYSTEM directory and can only be used by someone with supervisor equivalence. To use ATOTAL, make SYS:SYSTEM your default directory and type

  ATOTAL

Press Enter. You see output similar to that shown in figure 17.13. ATOTAL's output is easy to read; all numbers are displayed in decimal notation, and each is explained.

```
07/08/1989:
    Connect time:      9010    Server requests:   103447
    Blocks read:      50108    Blocks written:     23890
    Blocks days:     145980

Totals for week:
    Connect time:    103420    Server requests:   842787
    Blocks read:     395670    Blocks written:    145327
    Blocks days:     924376
```

Fig. 17.13.

Sample from the ATOTAL command.

You can use the same techniques described for PAUDIT to send ATOTAL's output to a file or printer (see the preceding section).

Removing NetWare Accounting

If you want to remove NetWare accounting from a server, you have two options. If you want to stop all user charges only, you can enter the Charge Rate screen for each charge option and set the charge rate for all time increments to no charge, as described in the section called "Setting Up Server Charge Rates." Accounting is still installed on the server, and user logins and logouts are still logged to the NET$ACCT.DAT file.

If you want to remove accounting completely, select Accounting from SYSCON's Available Topics main menu. From the Accounting menu that is displayed, select Accounting Servers, which lists all accounting servers. Your file server is all that is listed, unless you have installed specialized servers as previously discussed. Mark each server with F5, and with all servers highlighted, press the Del key. After you have deleted all the desired servers from the list, press Esc to leave the Accounting Servers screen. A prompt box opens asking if you want to remove accounting. Answer yes, and accounting is removed.

Chapter Summary

In this chapter, you learned that NetWare accounting is a powerful and complex option that may be very useful to you. If you implement it to charge for network services, it requires continual maintenance as you monitor and update account balances. If you use it merely to track server usage, the burden is much lighter, and you can gather much valuable information about how your server is used. such as user login and logout times, the disk blocks read and written, and the amount of information being stored on the server disks.

Part IV

Managing
Your Network

Includes

Management Utilities
Server Console Commands
Establishing a Network-Management Plan

18

Using NetWare's Network-Management Commands

You have probably invested a tremendous amount of time and energy in properly designing, installing, and configuring the LAN. After it's up, you need to keep your finger on its pulse to make sure that it continues to operate as you designed it to: responsively and reliably. Fortunately, NetWare has a number of tools to help you know how well the network is behaving.

A network supervisor is like the captain of a large passenger ship. A good captain does not spring into action only when the ship is dangerously close to rocks or shallow waters. Rather, the captain keeps the ship in safe, open waters. NetWare has a number of commands and utilities that help you "navigate" and keep abreast of the LAN's status.

As a network supervisor, you are called upon to manage various aspects of the network. You need to monitor the condition of the LAN's servers to make sure that they are up and running and are not overloaded with users. You need to be able to check the status of the users logged into each server. Server disk use must be monitored to ensure that enough disk space is available to satisfy user and application needs.

You are also called upon to solve problems. For example, if a multiuser application stops working, you need to check the status of its files, perhaps to see if errant file or record locks are the cause of the problem. If users report that they are unable to log into a particular server, you need to use NetWare utilities to see if the server is up or down.

An assortment of NetWare commands and utilities enables you to learn the status of the LAN and its servers and to take action to correct problems. The commands and utilities that you use from the PC workstation are discussed in this chapter. Commands that you use from the server console are discussed in the next chapter.

NetWare's network-management utilities let you control or monitor the following aspects of the LAN:

- ❏ Server availability and information
- ❏ User connections to servers
- ❏ Disk space
- ❏ File use and record locking
- ❏ Server performance information
- ❏ User-to-user communication
- ❏ Personal network session

NetWare also has a number of commands to enable you to manage shared printers. These commands are discussed in detail in Chapters 14 and 15.

Of the many NetWare management commands and utilities, one stands out as being the most comprehensive and powerful: FCONSOLE. It is referred to throughout this chapter because it enables you to work with all aspects of the network.

Introducing FCONSOLE

FCONSOLE is to network management what SYSCON is to network security. FCONSOLE stands for File Server Console; it can be used to view and control a wide variety of server functions.

Starting FCONSOLE

To start FCONSOLE, log into the server whose operations you want to manage or observe, type *fconsole*, and press Enter. (FCONSOLE is stored in SYS:PUBLIC, so if you are making that directory a search drive in the login script, you don't have to worry about making SYS:PUBLIC the default.) FCONSOLE's main menu appears (see fig. 18.1).

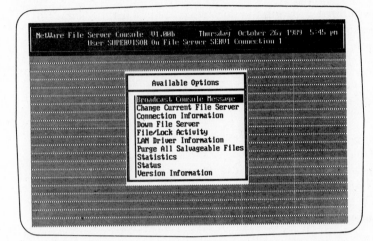

Fig. 18.1.
FCONSOLE's main menu.

If you are logged as SUPERVISOR or with supervisory equivalence, you can use all of SYSCON's menu selections. If you do not have supervisory access, you can use only four options (Change Current File Server, Connection Information, LAN Driver Information, and Version Information).

Users who do not have supervisory access can be given the ability to use most of FCONSOLE's menu options when they become console operators.

Creating Console Operators

Users who become console operators can use all of FCONSOLE's options except Down File Server and Delete Current Connections (which require supervisory access). Someone with supervisory access can use SYSCON to make users and groups console operators.

Log into the server whose users you want to make console operators. Start SYSCON by typing *syscon* and pressing Enter. From its main menu, select Supervisor Options. From the resulting Supervisor Options menu, choose File Server Console Operators. A list of the current console operators is shown. Press Ins to add a new user, and a list of all of the server's users and groups is displayed. Highlight the user or group you want to add and press Enter, or mark multiple names with F5 and press Enter.

To remove a user or group's console operator status, highlight the user or group name on the console operators' list and press Del, or mark multiple names with F5 and press Del.

When you have finished updating the console operator's list, press Esc to return to the Supervisor Options menu, and press Esc again to go to SYSCON's main menu. Press Esc again to exit SYSCON.

FCONSOLE and NetWare 386

As of this writing, you cannot use FCONSOLE fully with NetWare 386 Version 3.0. Four of its options (File/Lock Activity, LAN Driver Information, Purge All Salvageable Files, and Statistics) do not work. You can perform equivalent functions using NetWare 386's MONITOR NetWare Loadable Module, which is run from the server console. You will learn about MONITOR in the next chapter.

Choosing the Server To Work With

Like most NetWare utilities, FCONSOLE has a Change Current File Server option to enable you to move among multiple servers without exiting the utility. The top panel of FCONSOLE shows the name of the the current default server and the login name on that server. To use FCONSOLE to work with a server other than the one used to start the utility, select Change Current File Server from FCONSOLE's menu. A list of the servers to which you are currently attached appears. To choose a server from this list, highlight its name and press Enter. To attach to a new server, press Ins, and a list of all remaining servers on the LAN appears. Select one from the list, and you are returned to the server list, which is updated to show the addition of the new server. Press Esc to return to FCONSOLE's main menu.

Now that you are familiar with starting FCONSOLE, you are ready to learn about the commands that control various aspects of the network that NetWare helps you manage.

Managing Server Availability and Information

Several commands show different types of information about the servers on the LAN. FCONSOLE can be used to view this information and can control whether the server can be accessed.

Listing All Servers with SLIST

The most basic command and the one you use to see the status of the servers is SLIST. When you type *slist* and press Enter, you are shown a list of servers currently available on the network. The display is similar to the following:

```
Known NetWare File Servers     Network      Node Address
ACCTING                      [      3]    [        15]
EMAIL                        [      1]    [        44]
SERV1                        [      1]    [         1] Default
SERV2                        [      2]    [         A]
Total of 4 file servers found
```

You see several items of information about each server. The file server's name is displayed, as well as the server's network address and node address.

Both the node and network addresses are shown in hexadecimal notation. The node address listing is the address of the network adapter installed for LAN A. The network number is the physical network number that the file server's LAN A network adapter is attached to. For NetWare 386 servers, the internal IPX number that was chosen for the server at installation time is shown.

SLIST is a valuable tool for quickly checking server availability. If you receive a call from a user who reports trouble logging into a server, you can quickly run SLIST to see if the server is up.

SLIST is stored in both SYS:PUBLIC and SYS:LOGIN. When you load the NetWare workstation shell, SYS:LOGIN becomes the first nonlocal drive (usually drive F). Because it is stored in that directory, SLIST can be run from SYS:LOGIN after you load the NetWare shell and before you log into a particular server. After you have logged in, you can run SLIST from SYS:PUBLIC.

Displaying File Server Information with SYSCON

You already know the SYSCON utility from adding users and granting them rights to use server directories and files. You can also use it to view detailed NetWare information about every file server on the network. Log into any server on the network and start SYSCON by typing *syscon* and pressing Enter. Select File Server Information from the main menu. A list of all active file servers appears. Highlight the server for which you want to view information and press Enter. A window displays a number of items about the file server (see fig. 18.2). The server name, NetWare version, and revision are shown, as well as the System Fault Tolerance level and whether Transaction Tracking is activated. The number of connections supported and the number of connections actually in use are also displayed. In NetWare terms, a connection is a user login or attachment. Certain special programs that run on the server, such as database servers, can also use connections. Below the connection information, the number of volumes that can be supported by the version of NetWare running on the server is shown.

Fig. 18.2.

SYSCON's File Server Information window.

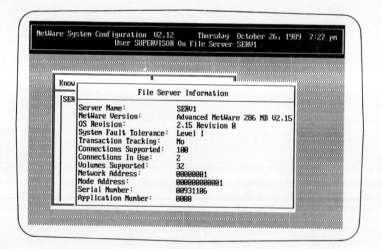

Like SLIST, SYSCON's File Server Information window displays the server's network address and the node address of the network adapter for LAN A, both in hexadecimal format. For NetWare 386 servers, the network number corresponds to the server's internal IPX number. If you are logged in with supervisory access, NetWare's serial number and application number are shown. The NetWare software on each server must have a unique serial number, so you must take care not to install the same NetWare software on two servers. If you do, a message is broadcast to all users on both servers every other minute stating that a copyright violation has occurred. Save yourself some embarrassment and don't make this mistake.

When you have finished viewing the NetWare information, press Esc to close the window and return to the list of servers. Press Esc again to go back to SYSCON's main menu, and again to exit SYSCON altogether.

Displaying File Server Information with NVER

The NVER command can be used to display NetWare version information for the file servers you are currently attached to. It also displays information about the NetWare workstation shell, the NetBIOS emulator (if you have loaded it), and the DOS version.

When you type *nver* and press Enter, information similar to the following is displayed:

```
The NetWare NetBIOS module is not loaded,
unable to provide version information.

IPX Version: 2.15
SPX Version: 2.15

LAN Driver:  Standard Microsystems ARCNET/Pure Data
             V1.00 (881010) V1.00
             IRQ = 2, I/O Base = 2E0h, RAM Buffer at D000:0

Shell:       V2.15 Rev. A
DOS:         MSDOS V3.10 on IBM_PC

FileServer:  SERV386
    Novell  NetWare 386 V3.00 Rev. A Rev. A  8/17/89
    Serial Number: 1810350   Application Number : 349
```

NetWare 386's NVER shows the serial and application numbers of the servers you check as well as their NetWare versions; NetWare 286's NVER shows only the NetWare version number.

Viewing and Controlling Server Status with FCONSOLE

FCONSOLE is NetWare's most versatile management utility. This section shows you how to use it to monitor and control the status of a server. Log in with supervisory equivalence to the server that you want to control and start FCONSOLE by typing *fconsole* and pressing Enter. FCONSOLE's main menu appears. From this menu you can select options that let you view a number of information items about the server's configuration, control whether users can log in, set the server date and time, and even down the server. FCONSOLE can be used to perform a number of other tasks, which you will learn about later in this chapter.

Downing the File Server

The first server management option on FCONSOLE's menu is Down File Server. In NetWare terms, "downing" the server means making it inactive. Any users who are attached are logged out, and any files that they are using are closed. Downing the server is FCONSOLE's most powerful and final server control task; obviously you should down a server only after warning its users (you will read about several methods of warning users later in the chapter).

Downing a server is necessary before turning off the server PC. When you need to stop the server, its easy to assume that turning off the power switch is all you need to do. Nothing could be further from the truth. Because NetWare uses server memory to cache file writes for as long as several seconds, a file that has not yet been written to disk may still be in server memory. Turning the server off at the wrong moment can result in the loss of those files.

To down a server, select Down File Server from FCONSOLE's main menu. You are prompted to confirm that you do indeed want to down the server. If you answer yes, FCONSOLE checks to see if any of the server's users have any files currently open (an open file is one currently in use and open for reading or writing). If FCONSOLE finds any open files, you receive the message Server Has Open Files, Force Down Server and you are asked to reconfirm that you still want to down the server. If you answer yes, the server is downed.

Don't down a server with open files if you can avoid it. A better alternative is to use some of FCONSOLE's other features to determine which users have files open and contact them so they can close all files in a normal way. You will learn how to see who has open files later in this chapter in the section called "Using FCONSOLE To Manage User Connections."

Controlling User Access to the Server

You can use FCONSOLE to control whether users can attach or log into the server. At times you may have to prevent users from accessing the server, perhaps while you are performing maintenance on a server database application.

You can use the Status option from FCONSOLE's main menu to prevent users from accessing a server. Highlight Status and press Enter, and the File Server Status window opens. Use the arrow keys to move the highlight to Allow New Users To Login, and press N to change the setting from yes to no. Users then will not be able to log into the server, although users who are already logged in will not be affected. You will learn how to remove the connections of currently attached users in the section in this chapter called "Using FCONSOLE To Manage User Connections."

To allow users to log in again, return the Allow New Users To Login setting to yes. After you have finished working with this setting, press Esc to close the window and return to FCONSOLE's main menu.

Setting the Server's Date and Time

The same option that enables you to control whether users can log in also can be used to set the server's date and time. When you boot a server, the time and date that it maintains are taken from the hardware setting of the server PC. If you need to change that setting (to accommodate a change to daylight savings time, for example) you can use FCONSOLE's Status option. It updates the time kept by the server's "software clock," but does not change the time stored in the server's hardware.

To change the server's date and time, select Status from FCONSOLE's menu. To change the date setting, highlight the server's current date and press Enter. Backspace over the old information and type the new date in one of these formats: 01/13/91, January 13, 1991, or 13 January 1991. Press Enter to save the new setting.

Setting the time is a similar process. Highlight the current setting and press Enter. Backspace over the time information and type the desired time. You can enter the time in 12-hour increments with the designation AM or PM

(1:35:00 PM) or in 24-hour increments (13:35:00). After you have updated the server date and time, press Esc to leave the File Server Status window and return to FCONSOLE's main menu.

Viewing the Server's LAN Driver Information

You can use FCONSOLE, like SYSCON and SLIST, to view the settings for the network adapters in the server and the network numbers to which they are attached. SYSCON and SLIST have a frustrating limitation if you have more than one network adapter in the server: they show you only the settings for the adapter that is configured for LAN A. FCONSOLE displays this information for all network adapters.

To view the configuration information for the server's network adapters, select LAN Driver Information from FCONSOLE's main menu. If you have more than one network adapter in the server, you are shown a list of them (the first is called LAN A Configuration, the second LAN B Configuration, and so on). Choose the network configuration that you want to view and press Enter. A window displays the network and node addresses for the network adapter (as usual, in hexadecimal format), the network adapter type, its interrupt, I/O and ROM buffer addresses, and its configuration number (you chose a configuration for the network adapter while you were generating NetWare).

When you have finished viewing the network adapter configuration information, press Esc to return to the list of configurations, and Esc again to return to FCONSOLE's main menu.

Unfortunately, you cannot use the LAN Driver Information option if the server you are working with is running NetWare 386. You can, however, use a utility called MONITOR to view the same information. MONITOR is run from the server console, and you will learn about it in the next chapter.

Viewing the Server's NetWare Version Information

You can also use FCONSOLE to view the NetWare version information for the server you are working with. Select Version Information from FCONSOLE's main menu, and a window shows the version of NetWare running on the server. Press Esc to return to the main menu.

Managing the Server's Disk Space

One of your most important tasks is managing server disk space. Disk space is the network's primary commodity; virtually every service provided by the network depends on it. Network disks store the files for network-based programs and applications. Network disks also make it possible to queue print jobs as files and place them in line for the next available network printer. Users are probably storing important personal files on network disks, such as word processing documents and spreadsheets.

Disk space should be available whenever required for legitimate uses. You can use a number of NetWare commands to monitor disk space.

In Chapter 10 you learned how to use SYSCON or DSPACE to limit the amount of disk space that a particular user could use on a server. In Chapter 12, you learned how to use DSPACE to control how much space a particular directory can occupy on a NetWare 386 server (DSPACE is a NetWare 386 command; it is not available with NetWare 286). Hopefully, you have implemented these controls.

You can use VOLINFO and CHKVOL to check on how disk space is being used on the servers.

Checking Disk Space Usage on All Volumes with VOLINFO

VOLINFO is the most comprehensive command to use when you need to see the status of the server's disk volumes. Log into the server that you want to check, type *volinfo*, and press Enter. A screen similar to that shown in figure 18.3 appears.

Each box on the screen shows the total amount of space available on the volume and the amount of free space. Every five seconds, VOLINFO updates this information to reflect any changes in available disk space. VOLINFO also shows the maximum number of directory entries that each volume can accommodate and the number of entries that remain available.

VOLINFO's display for NetWare 286 is different in some ways from the display for NetWare 386. With NetWare 386's VOLINFO, you can press F2 to toggle the display between showing the amount of free disk space in

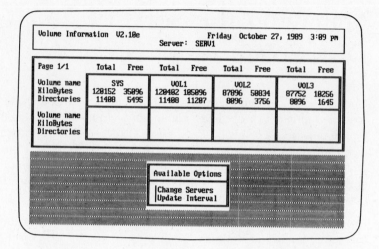

Fig. 18.3.
VOLINFO's volume
information display.

kilobytes or megabytes. NetWare 386 shows information for the first six volumes on the screen, and NetWare 286 shows information for the first eight (because NetWare 386's volumes can be much larger in size, more display space is needed for each volume). With both, you can view subsequent screens of volume information, if necessary, by pressing PgDn.

VOLINFO also shows the maximum and available numbers of directory entries. In NetWare terms, a directory entry is a file, directory, or subdirectory. With NetWare 286, you established the maximum number of directory entries for a volume during installation, and you can modify this maximum by downing the server and running NETGEN (you can increase the setting to a maximum of 32,000 entries per volume). NetWare 386 allocates directory entries as required, up to a maximum of more than two million entries per volume.

VOLINFO's menu is displayed at the bottom of the screen. You can use the Change Servers option to view the volume information on another server. Highlight this option and press Enter, and a list of the servers to which you are currently attached appears. To choose a server from this list, highlight its name and press Enter. To attach to a new server, press Ins, and a list of all remaining servers on the LAN appears. Select one from the list, and you are returned to the server list, which is updated to show the addition of the new server. Press Esc to return to VOLINFO's menu. The Update Interval option lets you control how often VOLINFO checks the server volumes and updates its display. When you select this option, you are prompted to enter a new time interval in seconds (the default is 5).

After you have typed the new interval, press Enter to return to the VOLINFO display.

After you are finished working with VOLINFO, press Esc to exit.

Checking Disk Space Usage with CHKVOL

CHKVOL is similar to VOLINFO. It also shows the amount of available disk space for a disk volume but, unlike VOLINFO, does not stay running and continue to update the information.

To use CHKVOL, log into a server, type *chkvol*, and press Enter. For NetWare 286, a display similar to the following appears:

```
Statistics for fixed volume SERV1/SYS:
179345098  bytes total volume space.
134232074  bytes in 2905 files.
 45113024  bytes remaining on volume.
 45113024  bytes available to user SMITHFD.
     7155  directories available.
```

With NetWare 386's CHKVOL, the display shows some additional information about space used by deleted files:

```
Statistics for fixed volume SERV386/SYS:
Total volume space:                 179345 K Bytes
Space used by files:                134232 K Bytes
Space in use by deleted files:         294 K Bytes
Space available from deleted files:    294 K Bytes
Space remaining on volume:           45113 K Bytes
Space available to SUPERVISOR:       45113 K Bytes
```

With both NetWare 286 and NetWare 386, you are shown the total volume space and the space in use. You are also shown the amount of space available to you. If you have been restricted to a certain amount of disk space, the space available is the amount of space you were allocated less the amount you have already used.

NetWare 286 shows the number of directory entries used and available on the volume. Because NetWare 386 doesn't limit directory entries, it does not show this information.

NetWare 386 shows the amount of space used by deleted files. When you delete a file on a NetWare 386 server, it is kept on the disk so that you can use the SALVAGE command to recover it. It is deleted when the disk space it occupies is needed for new files or when someone uses the PURGE command (for more information about SALVAGE and PURGE, see Chapter 12).

When you use CHKVOL with no parameters, it displays information for the default volume. If you follow it with a volume name, (such as CHKVOL VOL1) it displays information for the volume you specify. If you are attached to multiple servers, you can follow CHKVOL with both the server name and the volume name (such as CHKVOL SERV2/VOL1). You can also follow CHKVOL with multiple volume names if you want it to display information for more than one (i.e., CHKVOL SERV1/SYS SERV2/SYS). You can also use the disk drive letter assigned to the volume you want to check (i.e., CHKVOL F:).

Wild-card characters can also be used. If you type *chkvol* * and press Enter, all volumes on the default server are checked. If you type *chkvol* */* and press Enter, all volumes on all servers that you are attached to are checked. If you type *chkvol ?* and press Enter, all volumes assigned drive letters are checked.

Checking Directory Sizes with CHKDIR

CHKDIR, a NetWare 386 command, displays the disk space used by a particular directory. To view the space used by the default directory, type *chkdir* and press Enter. You see a display similar to the following:

```
Maximum        In Use         Available
179,345 K      134,232 K      45,113 K       Volume Size
               5,904 K        45,113 K       \PUBLIC
```

Notice that the disk space used by the volume is shown on the first line, and the disk space used by the particular directory is shown on the second.

To check a directory other than the default, specify it after you type *chkdir*. For example, to check the size of a directory named EMAIL on the VOL1 volume of the SERV1 server, type *chkdir serv1/vol1:email* and press Enter. You can shorten the name of the directory by using the same rules that apply to abbreviating directory names when using NetWare commands like MAP.

Checking a User's Disk Space Usage with DSPACE

In Chapter 10, you learned about using NetWare 386's DSPACE utility to assign a particular user a maximum amount of disk space on a server (DSPACE is not available with NetWare 286).

You can also use DSPACE to determine the amount of space in use by a particular user. To learn how much space a user is using, you must be logged in as his or her workgroup manager or with supervisory equivalence. Start DSPACE by typing *dspace* and pressing Enter. A menu appears with the following three options:

    Change File Server
    User Restrictions
    Directory Restrictions

Select User Restrictions. A list of all users appears if you have supervisory access. If you are a work group manager, the users that you manage are shown. Select the user whose disk usage you want to see. A window opens, and the number next to In Use shows the user's disk usage in kilobytes. Press Esc to leave this window and return to the list of users. When you have finished checking disk usage, press Esc to return to DSPACE's menu, and press Esc to exit.

Checking a User's Disk Space Usage with SYSCON

You can also use SYSCON to check a user's disk space usage. If you are logged in with supervisory access, you can check disk space usage for all users. If you are a work group manager, you can check disk usage for the users you manage.

Start SYSCON by typing *syscon* and pressing Enter. From its main menu, select User Information. A list of the server's users appears. Highlight the name of the user you want to work with and press Enter. From the User Information menu that appears, select Other Information. A window opens containing several items of information about the user. Next to Disk Space In Use the user's disk space usage is shown in kilobytes.

When you have finished viewing the disk space usage information, press Esc to return to the User Information menu. Press Esc again to return to the list of users. Select another user to work with, or press Esc to return to SYSCON's main menu, and press Esc again to exit SYSCON.

Managing User Connections

One of the most important aspects of knowing how the network servers are being used is monitoring how many users are logged in. Although a single gauge cannot tell you how busy a file server is, the number of user connections a server is handling is an important indicator of activity.

From time to time, you may also need to look up the connections of individual users. A particular user may take a long lunch, leaving his PC logged in with an important file open that someone else needs to use. FCONSOLE gives you the ability to view the connection information for an individual user and clear a connection if necessary.

Listing User Connections with USERLIST

The USERLIST command enables you to list all the connections on a server. A connection is usually occupied by a user who is logged in or attached to a server, but it can also be used by a program running on the server. A NetWare 286 server supports 100 connections; a NetWare 386 server supports 250.

To see a list of the users on a server, log into that server, type *userlist*, and press Enter. You see a display similar to the following:

```
User Information for Server SERV1

 Connection   User Name     Login Time
───────────────────────────────────────────────
      1          SMITHFD       10-28-1989 11:15 am
      2        * SUPERVISOR    10-28-1989 11:39 am
      3          JONESBR       10-28-1989 07:29 am
      7          ARRENSJW      10-28-1989 08:25 am
      9          GUEST         10-28-1989 09:42 am
     18          JENSONCR      10-28-1989 02:19 pm
```

Notice that you are shown the user's name, login date, and login time. Each connection has a number. Your connection is marked with an asterisk.

You also can use USERLIST to see the network and node address for each user by using the /A parameter. When you type *userlist/a* and press Enter, the display you see is similar to the following:

```
User Information for Server SERV1
Connection  User Name        Network    Node Address   Login Time
----------  --------------   --------   ------------   -------------------
    1       SMITHFD          [     1] [           A]   10-28-1989 11:15 am
    2     * SUPERVISOR       [     2] [           3]   10-28-1989 11:39 am
    3       JONESBR          [     1] [          BC]   10-28-1989 07:29 am
    7       ARRENSJW         [     2] [          15]   10-28-1989 08:25 am
    9       GUEST            [     1] [          1F]   10-28-1989 09:42 am
   18       JENSONCR         [     1] [           9]   10-28-1989 02:19 pm
```

Notice that each user's network and node address are listed (in hexadecimal format).

NetWare 386's USERLIST makes an additional parameter available: /O for OBJECT TYPE. Because not all connections are necessarily users, /O can be used to distinguish human users from programs that use connections.

If you are logged into multiple servers, you can specify which server's connection information USERLIST displays by following the command with the name of the server followed by a slash (/). For example, to list the connection information for server SERV2, you type *userlist serv2/* and press Enter.

USERLIST displays information for every connection by default. If you need only to view the information for one user, specify that name by typing the user name after the USERLIST command. For example, to see only information about a user named SMITHFD, you type *userlist smithfd*.

You can combine these parameters. For example, to look for SMITHFD on SERV2 you type *userlist serv2/smithfd*. You also can have multiple parameter combinations, such as USERLIST SERV2/SMITHFD SERV1/ JONESBR /A. You can use the asterisk (*) as a wild-card character. For example, to see all users on all servers, you type *userlist */*.

The USERLIST display shows one screen's worth of information at a time and prompts you to press a key to see the next screen. You can use the /C parameter to specify a continuous display.

Managing User Connections with FCONSOLE

FCONSOLE not only lets you list connections, but also allows you to see a number of information items about each one. You can see what files the user connection is using, whether those files are locked, and the number of disk bytes that the user has read and written. You also can send a message to the user, and even clear or remove his or her connection.

To view this information about a user requires that you be logged in with supervisory access or as a user with file server console operator status. Log into the server whose connections you plan to work with and start FCONSOLE by typing *fconsole* and pressing Enter. From its main menu, select Connection Information. A list of the server's connections is displayed in order by connection number. Highlight the connection that you want to work with and press Enter. The Connection Information menu appears on the screen (see fig. 18.4).

Fig. 18.4.

FCONSOLE's Connection Information menu.

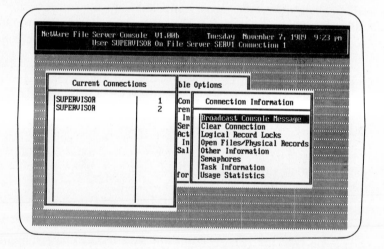

```
NetWare File Server Console  V1.00b        Tuesday November 7, 1989  9:23 pm
                 User SUPERVISOR On File Server SERV1 Connection 1


      ┌────── Current Connections ──────┐   ble Options
      │                                 │
      │ SUPERVISOR            1         │ Con ┌─── Connection Information ───┐
      │ SUPERVISOR            2         │ ren │ Broadcast Console Message    │
      │                                 │ In  │ Clear Connection             │
      │                                 │ Ser │ Logical Record Locks         │
      │                                 │ Act │ Open Files/Physical Records  │
      │                                 │ In  │ Other Information            │
      │                                 │ Sal │ Semaphores                   │
      │                                 │     │ Task Information             │
      │                                 │ for │ Usage Statistics             │
      │                                 │     └──────────────────────────────┘
      └─────────────────────────────────┘
```

Sending Messages to the User Connection

The Connection Information menu offers you a number of options for working with the selected connection. The first, Broadcast Console Message, lets you send a message to the user. This message interrupts whatever the user is doing and appears on the bottom line of his or her screen. This is a good method of sending a user a message in an emergency (such as when the server is about to go down).

To send a message to the selected user connection, highlight Broadcast Console Message and press Enter. A box opens that prompts you to type the message that you want to send. Type a message up to 55 characters long and press Enter. The message is sent to the user.

You should use this feature cautiously. Users who are displaying graphics information on their screens do not see the message that you have sent. A few interrupt driven programs (such as pop-up applications and memory-resident terminal emulators) may conflict with NetWare's messages, causing the workstation to lock up when a message is received.

Broadcasting Messages to Multiple Users

FCONSOLE also can be used to broadcast the same message to multiple users. From FCONSOLE's main menu, select Connection Information, and the list of connections appears. Highlight with F5 the connections you want send to and press Enter. From the menu that appears, select Broadcast Console Message. A box opens that prompts you to type the message you want to send. Type a message up to 55 characters in length and press Enter. NetWare sends the message to the selected users.

Clearing a Connection

You also can use FCONSOLE to clear or remove a user's connection. When you clear a user's connection, he or she is no longer logged into the server, and any files that he or she had open are closed. You should exercise this option with extreme caution, because being suddenly and unexpectedly logged out from a server is disruptive and can result in lost data. You should use this procedure only when you have to remove all users from the server for a good reason, or when a user has left his or her PC unattended for an extended period and has left a file or record lock in place.

To clear the connection you are working with, highlight Clear Connection and press Enter. You are prompted to confirm that you want to clear the connection; answer yes and the connection is cleared. Only a user with supervisory equivalence can clear a connection.

Clearing Multiple Connections

FCONSOLE can be used to remove multiple connections in the same operation. From FCONSOLE's main menu, select Connection Information, and the list of connections appears. Highlight with F5 the connections you want to clear and press Enter. From the resulting menu, select Clear Connection. A prompt asks you to confirm that you want to clear the connections; answer yes and the connections are cleared.

Viewing a Connection's Open Files, Locks, and Semaphores

Three options on FCONSOLE's Connection Information menu enable you to see the files, record locks, and semaphores that a connection has in use. If a user is having difficulty using a network-based program or application, you can use FCONSOLE to monitor the way files are being used as he or she tries to use the application.

To see a connection's open files, select Open Files/Physical Records from FCONSOLE's Connection Information menu. A list of the files that the user has open is displayed. You can see more information about how a particular file is being used by highlighting it and pressing Enter. A small menu appears offering two options:

> File Status
> Physical Record Locks

When you select the File Status option, a window shows you information about how the file has been opened. When a program opens a file, it specifies how the file is used. Messages like File is open in share mode, open for read and write, locked by file lock, and others are shown to describe how the file was opened and how it is being used. This information may be useful in understanding how the applications you are using on the network are functioning. When you have finished viewing the File Status window, you can press Esc to leave it.

The other option, Physical Record Locks, can be used to see if any physical areas of the file you have selected have been locked by the user connection. A window opens displaying any physical locks in use by the connection. For each lock, the beginning and ending addresses of the lock are displayed, as well as the lock type. As with the information shown in the File Status window, the lock information can be useful in debugging problems with a network-based application. When you have finished viewing the Physical Record status window, press Esc to return to the File/Physical Records Information menu, and press Esc again to return to the connection's list of open files. At this point you can choose another file to work with, or press Esc to return to FCONSOLE's Connection Information menu.

The Logical Record Locks option displays information about a different and less common type of record lock. A physical record lock locks a particular physical area of the file; a logical lock locks a record by a name that the program has assigned to a data area. You can display any logical record locks by selecting Logical Record Locks. A window opens displaying both the lock and the lock status. When you have finished viewing this information, press Esc to return to FCONSOLE's Connection Information menu.

The Semaphores option displays information about semaphores in use by the connection. *Semaphores* are used to arbitrate access to a shared resource. For example, if you have a network-licensed copy of a software package that allows only a certain number of users to access it at the same time, it may use semaphores to control the access process. Each user who accesses the package activates a semaphore. When a new user attempts to access the program, the semaphores are checked. If they indicate that no free copies are available, the user is not allowed to use the program.

To view the semaphore information for a workstation, highlight Semaphores from the Connection Information menu and press Enter. A window displays the name of the semaphore and its open count and value. The open count shows the number of users who have the semaphore open. The value shows the remaining available opens (that is, the number of additional users who will be allowed to open the semaphore). When you have finished viewing the semaphore information for a connection, press Esc to return to the Connection Information menu.

Viewing Assorted Information about the Connection

Three options from the Connection Information menu show information about the connection you are working with. When you select Other Information, a window opens showing four information items about the connection. The Object Name is the login name of the user who has the connection. The Object Type is the number assigned by NetWare to the object that has the connection. Type 1 is reserved for users. Other items that use connections, such as a program that runs on the server or a print server, use other object type numbers. The Login Time shows the date and time that the user logged in. The Network Address shows the network address and node address of the workstation using the connection. Press Esc to leave the Other Information window.

The Task Information option shows two items of information about the connection. When you select Task Information, two windows open. The top one is called Connection Status and shows whether the connection is waiting to lock a file or record or waiting for a semaphore or logical lock. Most applications that use locks or semaphores continue trying to invoke the lock or semaphore if it is busy on the first attempt. The bottom window is called Active Tasks and shows whether transactions or shared file-set locks are in progress. Transactions are managed by NetWare's Transaction Tracking System (TTS). File-set locks are multiple-record locks that must be invoked simultaneously to perform an update. When you have finished viewing the task information, press Esc to return to the Connection Information menu.

The final option on the Connection Information menu is Usage Statistics. When you select this option, a window opens showing four information items about the connection's network usage. Connection Time shows the total time the user has been logged into the server. Requests Received show the number of incoming network request packets that have been received from the connection. Disk Bytes Read and Disk Bytes Written show how many bytes have been read and written to the server since the connection was made. When you have finished viewing the connection's usage statistics, press Esc to return to the Connection Information menu.

Managing File Usage and Record Locking

In Chapter 12 ("Managing Files"), you learned how to manage the storage of files on the servers and how to control the way users access those files. In this section, you will learn about a different type of file management: monitoring the ways that files are used. You will learn how to check to see if a file is open. A program *opens* a file to read and write its contents. You also will learn how to find out if a file is locked. *File locks* and *record locks* are used to ensure that changes made to shared files are handled in an orderly fashion. When a file is locked, it cannot be written to by any user except the one who has the lock in place. Similarly, if a record from a file is locked, that record can be updated only by the user who has the lock.

The following scenarios, based on real occurrences reported by network supervisors, illustrate the importance of this type of file management.

A network user comes to you complaining that when he tries to access a particular spreadsheet file, he gets the message File in use, and he has been trying for a number of hours. You use FCONSOLE to determine who has the file open and find that it is one of the user's coworkers. Armed with the information you have given him, the user contacts his coworker and resolves the situation.

In another situation, users of a multiuser database call you and report that every time they try to add a new record to the database, the application generates an error message stating that it is unable to lock the database record. You use FCONSOLE to view the physical record locks on the database file and find that a user has the record locked and has not released it for several minutes. You visit the user's PC and find that at the moment the record was locked, he activated a pop-up program that put the database application's record lock on hold. You advise the user to deactivate the pop-up program for a moment and to return to the database program. He does so, the lock is released, and other users are again able to add new records.

Using FCONSOLE To View File and Record Lock Information

The File/Lock Activity option from FCONSOLE's main menu gives you the ability to view the status of files and record locks so that you can take the action needed to deal with situations similar to those discussed above. With supervisory equivalence, log into the server with whose files you want to work. Start FCONSOLE by typing *fconsole* and pressing Enter. From FCONSOLE's main menu, select File/Lock Activity.

The File/Lock Activity submenu appears and offers the following three options:

File/Physical Records Information
Logical Lock Information
Semaphore Information

Viewing File and Physical Record Lock Information

The option you will use most often is File/Physical Records Information. It prompts you to specify a file and then enables you to view a list of users who have it open, and also to see if any physical record locks are in place for the file.

Highlight File/Physical Records Information and press Enter. An entry window opens at the top of the screen prompting you to enter the directory path containing the file. You should enter the directory only, not the file name. The entry window shows the name of the default server. Type the rest of the full NetWare name of the file, such as *serv1/sys:software\dbase* and press Enter (for more information about complete NetWare directory names, see Chapter 9). You also can press Ins to pick the file's directory from a list of options. When you press Ins, a list of the server's volumes are displayed. Highlight the volume that stores the file you want to work with and press Enter. You are shown a list of directories on that volume. Select the one that stores the file. You are shown a list of that directory's subdirectories and files. Continue selecting subdirectories if necessary to get to the one storing the file.

After the correct directory is displayed in the entry box, press Enter. You are prompted to enter the name of the file you want to check. Type the name and press Enter. Two windows displaying the file status open (see fig. 18.5).

Fig. 18.5.

File status information displayed by FCONSOLE.

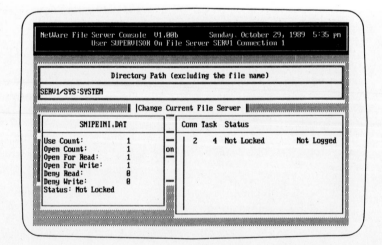

The left window displays seven information items about the file. The Use Count shows the number of connections that have the file in use. The Open Count shows the number of connections that have the file open. Open for Read and Open for Write show the number of connections whose programs have opened the file for reading or writing respectively. If a connection's program has opened the file for both reading and writing, each count reflects it. Deny Read shows the number of connections that have opened the file with exclusive reading privileges (in other words, no other connection can read the file while this connection has the file open). Deny Write is similar to Deny Read; it shows the number of connections that have opened the file with exclusive writing privileges (so that no other connection can write to the file while this connection has it open). Status shows whether the file is locked. Its three possible settings are Not Locked (meaning the file is not locked), Locked By File Lock (the file is locked), or Locked By Share File Set Transaction (the file is locked with a group of related files).

The right window lists the connections that have the file in use. Each connection's number and the status of the file are shown. The status shows whether the file is locked or logged. When a file is logged, it means that a program is waiting to lock it, but has to lock the file at the same time it locks several others. The file is logged while the program checks the other files to see if they can be locked.

If the file is locked, the lock type is shown. The three possible lock types are Exclusive (meaning the file is locked so that no other user can read or write to it), Shareable (meaning other users can read the file), and TTS Holding Lock (the record lock has been released by the application but the Transaction Tracking System is holding it until the transaction is completely written).

When you have finished viewing the status of a file, press Esc to return to the File/Physical Records Information submenu.

The second option, Physical Record Locks, can be used to see if any physical areas of the file you have selected are locked. For each lock, the beginning and ending addresses of the lock are displayed, as well as the lock type and connection number. For example, the screen may show Locked Exclusive by Connection 3, meaning that the user who has connection 3 has locked the file. As with the information shown in the File Status window, the lock information can be useful in solving problems with multiuser programs that are reporting locking errors. When you have finished viewing the Physical Record status window, press Esc to return to the File/Physical Records Information submenu, and press Esc again to return to the file-name window. At this point you can enter another file name to work with or press Esc to return to the directory-name entry window. If you have finished viewing file-status information, press Esc until you return to FCONSOLE's main menu.

Viewing Logical Lock Information

FCONSOLE also enables you to view information about logical record locks. To look at the status of a logical lock, you must be familiar with the application making the lock and you must know the name of the lock that it uses.

You can display logical-record-lock status by selecting File/Lock Activity from FCONSOLE's main menu. From the resulting submenu, choose Logical Record Locks. A window opens prompting you to enter the name of the logical record lock that you want to view. Type the name of the lock and press Enter. Two windows open. The left window displays three information items about the lock. The Use Count shows the number of users who have the logical record in use. The Share Count shows the number of connections that have the logical record locked in shared mode. The Status shows whether the logical record is locked. Its three possible settings are Not Locked, Locked Exclusive (meaning no other connection can read or write the record), or Locked Shareable (the record can be read by other connections).

The right window lists the connections that have the logical record in use. Each connection's number and the status of the logical record are shown. If the record is locked, the lock type is shown. The three possible lock types are Exclusive (meaning the record is locked so that no other user can read or write to it), Shareable (meaning other users can read the record), and TTS Holding Lock (the record lock has been released by the application but the Transaction Tracking System is holding it until the transaction is completely written).

When you have finished viewing the status of a record, press Esc to return to the record-name-entry window. You can either enter another record name to view or press Esc until you have returned to the FCONSOLE main menu.

Viewing Information about Semaphores

Semaphores are used to arbitrate access to a shared resource. If you are running a network-licensed copy of a program that allows only a certain number of users to access it at the same time, it may use semaphores to control the access process. Each user that runs the program activates a semaphore. When a new user attempts to access the program, the semaphores are checked. If they indicate that no free copies are available, the user is not allowed to use the program. To view information about a semaphore, you must know its name.

To view information about a semaphore, select File/Lock Activity from FCONSOLE's main menu. From the resulting submenu, select Semaphore Information. An entry window opens prompting you to enter the name of the semaphore that you want to work with. After you enter the name, two windows open. The left one displays the semaphore's open count and value. The open count shows the number of users that have the semaphore open. The value shows the number of remaining usages for the semaphore. The right window shows the connection numbers that have the semaphore open. Press Esc when you have finished viewing the semaphore information and you are returned to the semaphore-name-entry window. You can enter the name of another semaphore or press Esc until you return to FCONSOLE's main menu.

If you do not know the name of a semaphore, use FCONSOLE's Connection Information option to select a user you think may be using the semaphore. From the Connection Information menu, select Semaphores to display the name of any semaphores in use by that user.

Using FCONSOLE To Purge Files

FCONSOLE performs one additional file-management function. From its main menu you can purge all files that have been deleted but are still recoverable with the SALVAGE command. This option is identical to running the PURGE command that you learned about in Chapter 12.

To purge all recoverable files, select Purge All Salvageable Files from FCONSOLE's main menu. You are prompted to confirm that you want to perform this task. Answer yes and all files are purged and you are returned to FCONSOLE's main menu.

Viewing Advanced File-Server Performance and Configuration Statistics with FCONSOLE

Experienced network supervisors find one feature of FCONSOLE especially useful: the Statistics option. More than any other NetWare utility, it gives you a window into the in-depth operations of the servers. As your knowledge of NetWare grows, you will find this type of information to be very helpful.

FCONSOLE's Statistics option gives you an inside look at how each server is using its resources. You can see detailed information about the server's memory, disks, and network adapters. Rather than guessing whether a particular server needs an additional memory board, or whether a particular network adapter's physical network is overloaded, you can use FCONSOLE to view information that enables you to make intelligent decisions.

The information displayed by FCONSOLE's Statistics option is advanced. Some of it requires a good understanding of disk and memory technology. You do not have to be conversant with FCONSOLE's advanced statistical information to use NetWare effectively, but you may want to begin studying it and mastering it a little at a time.

Unfortunately, as of this writing, these powerful features are not available with NetWare 386 Version 3.0. Future versions probably will support them. You can find equivalent information using the MONITOR NLM from the server's console (you will learn how to use NetWare 386's MONITOR in the next chapter).

To use FCONSOLE's Statistics option on a NetWare 286 server, you need to be logged in with supervisory access or be using a login name with console operator status. Start FCONSOLE by typing *fconsole* and pressing Enter. From FCONSOLE's main menu, select Statistics. The File Server Statistics menu appears (see fig. 18.6).

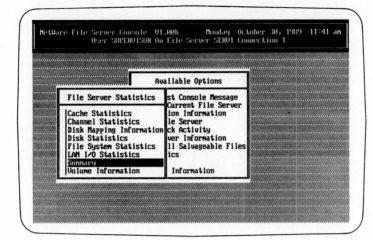

Fig. 18.6.
*FCONSOLE's File
Server Statistics
menu.*

Viewing a Summary of Server Statistics

The best starting point when you are learning to use advanced file server statistics is to select the Summary option. Highlight this option and press Enter. A screen similar to the one shown in figure 18.7 appears.

Fig. 18.7.
*The File Server
Statistics Summary
from FCONSOLE.*

The Statistics Summary screen is divided into two halves. The top half shows 11 items of information about the server. File Server Up Time shows the total time that the file server has been active. The Number Of File

Service Processes displays the total number of service processes available on the server. A service process manages a particular task being performed on a server by a workstation, such as copying a server-based file or executing a server-based program file. The number of service processes is a measure of how many simultaneous tasks can be performed by the server. The number is fixed for NetWare 286 servers but is set dynamically for NetWare 386. The number of available service processes on a NetWare 286 server depends on a number of factors, including the number of network adapters installed in the server, the number and size of its disk drives, and the number of programs running on the server. (Programs that run on a NetWare 286 server are called VAPs, for value-added processes.

Current Server Utilization is a measure of the percentage of time that the file server CPU was busy with NetWare activity during the last second, a gauge of how busy the file server is from a processing standpoint.

Disk Requests Serviced From Cache is an important statistic that shows the percentage of disk read and write requests taken care of using NetWare's file-caching feature. When you are working with a server-based file, NetWare attempts to store intelligently the parts of the file that you are working with in the server's memory. Because retrieving from memory is much faster than retrieving from disk, file caching gives server performance a significant boost. Ideally, the Disk Requests Serviced From Cache statistic should show that 90% or more of the disk requests are handled using NetWare file caching. A lower figure is an indicator that more memory may be required for the server.

The next three statistics have to do with packets. Packets are the units of information sent by the network adapters on the network. Each packet contains information about its destination and source addresses, as well as data. The size of the packet and the number of bytes of data it contains vary according to the type of network adapter you are using.

Packets Routed shows the number of network packets received by the server for rerouting to another physical network. If the server is a bridge, it routes packets of information from one physical network to another, and the count of those packets is shown by Packets Routed.

The Total Packets Received figure shows the total number of packets received by the server through its network adapters. File Service Packets shows only packets that have to do with transmitting actual file data to and from the server.

The Total Number Of Cache Buffers shows the number of 4,096-byte memory buffers available for file caching. When NetWare 286 allocates memory, it first takes whatever memory is needed to load the operating system file (NET$OS.EXE) and to perform basic operating system functions. All remaining memory becomes file-cache buffers. You can increase the cache buffers by adding memory to the server PC. The Dirty Cache Buffers count shows the number of cache buffers containing file information that has been changed and must be written to disk. When you write to a server file that is cached in memory, you write to cache buffers first, and then NetWare takes care of writing the contents of those buffers to disk. NetWare 286 does not allow cache buffers to remain "dirty" for more than a few seconds.

The Total Server Memory figure displays the total amount of memory available to NetWare. Unused Server Memory is the amount of memory that NetWare cannot use. Because NetWare allocates memory in round numbers (often in multiples of 4,096 bytes or more), it's possible that small amounts of memory are left over.

The bottom half of the File Server Statistics Summary screen shows nine statistics about the server you are working with. For each statistic, it shows three columns of information: Maximum, Peak Used, and Currently In Use. The Maximum column shows the uppermost limit of the statistic you are viewing. Peak Used shows the highest figure that the particular statistic has reached since the file server has been running. Currently In Use shows the current value of the statistic. In every case, you should compare the Currently In Use and Peak Used figures with the Maximum setting. If the current and peak statistics are far below the maximum, you may want to use NETGEN to lower the maximum setting. If the peak and current listings are close to the maximum, you should increase the maximum, if possible.

Routing Buffers are memory buffers used to store incoming packets waiting to be handled by a file-service process. They also store packets being sent out by the server. The maximum number of routing buffers is set when the server is installed. If the numbers under the Peak Used and Currently In Use columns are far below the maximum setting, you should consider rerunning NETGEN to lower the routing buffer setting and conserve memory. Conversely, if the peak and current settings are too near the maximum, then the setting should be increased.

Open Files displays the number of files in use by all server connections. The maximum setting is established during installation. If the peak and current figures are far below the maximum, you should consider lowering it. If the peak and current figures are at or near the maximum, you should increase it. You must down the server and run NETGEN to change the maximum.

Indexed Files shows information about the files that have the INDEXED attribute turned on (see Chapter 12 for information about the INDEXED attribute). The number of allowed INDEXED files is set during installation.

Transactions lists the number of transactions managed by NetWare's Transaction Tracking System. The maximum number of simultaneous transactions is set during installation and can be modified by downing the server and running NETGEN.

Bindery Objects are entries in the server's security database (which NetWare calls the Bindery). User names, group names, other file servers, and print queues are all bindery objects. If you activated the Limit Disk Space option during installation, you were prompted to select a maximum number of bindery objects. You can rerun NETGEN and modify this setting if required.

Connections are users, programs, or devices that log in or attach to the server. Unfortunately, the maximum setting is fixed at 100 for NetWare 286. If the peak and current listings are near this limit, the only alternative is to get a new server or upgrade the existing one to run NetWare 386 (which supports 250 connections).

The final three listings show information about dynamic memory pools. These are memory areas that grow or shrink to meet the current needs of the server. They cannot grow beyond their maximum size, however, and the maximum cannot be increased. Dynamic Memory 1 shows memory used for the first pool, which is used for mapping directories and file-service-request processing. If the peak and current listings for this figure are approaching the maximum, see if the number of mapped drives used by the server's users can be decreased. Make sure that the users' login scripts map no more drives than are really necessary (mapped drives are discussed in Chapter 9; login scripts are discussed in Chapter 16). Dynamic Memory 2 shows memory used for the second pool. It is used to keep track of open files and file and record locks. Its size is based on the Maximum Number of Open Files setting that is configured when you run NETGEN. Dynamic Memory 3 shows memory used for the third pool, which is used to track information about other file servers, bridges, and routes to other physical networks. The maximum size of this pool cannot be changed, but it should be adequate even if the network is extremely large.

When you have finished working with the File Server Statistics Summary, press Esc to return to the File Server Statistics submenu. The File Server Statistics Summary screen is probably the most often used source of information for in-depth server operating and performance information.

You will learn about a number of other useful options from the File Server Statistics submenu discussed in the following sections.

Viewing Cache Statistics

The Cache Statistics option from FCONSOLE's File Server Statistics menu displays in-depth performance information about NetWare file caching in the server you are working with. Highlight this option and press Enter, and the Cache Statistics window is displayed (see fig. 18.8). The window begins with the File Server Up Time, which shows the time that has elapsed since the file server was started.

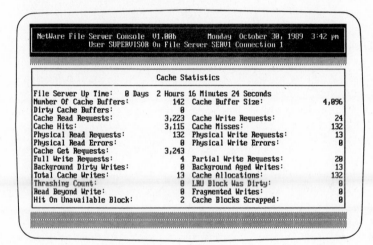

Fig. 18.8.
The Cache Statistics window from FCONSOLE.

Some of the statistics shown are the same as those shown on the File Server Statistics Summary screen. The Number Of Cache Buffers shows the total number of 4,096-byte memory buffers available for file caching. The Cache Buffer Size shows NetWare 286's standard cache-buffer size (4,096 bytes). Dirty Cache Buffers shows the number of cache buffers containing file information that has been changed and must be written to disk.

Cache Read Requests and Cache Write Requests show the number of file-read and file-write requests that have occurred since the server was brought up. Cache Hits shows the number of times the read or write request was handled from a memory cache, and Cache Misses lists the times that the disk had to be accessed to fulfill the request. Ideally, hits should far outnumber misses; if this is not the case, it could be an indicator that the server PC needs more memory so that it can allocate more cache buffers.

Physical Read Requests and Physical Write Requests show the number of times that NetWare's file-caching system wrote or read information to and from server disks in order to prepare for read and write requests from users. Physical Read Errors and Physical Write Errors each show the number of times a physical read or write request resulted in a disk error. These numbers should be zero or very low. A large number of read or write errors could be an indicator of impending disk failure.

Cache Get Requests is the total number of requests for information that has been made to NetWare's file-caching system. Full Write Requests shows the number requests to write from cache to disk that filled complete disk sectors. This means that the NetWare file-caching system was able to write the complete sectors to the disk (a disk sector is 512 bytes). On the other hand, Partial Write Requests shows the number of requests to write partial disk sectors. Disks can only accept writes in units of 512 byte sectors, which results in the caching system reading the existing disk sector so that the new information can be added to it. The complete information is then rewritten as a complete sector.

Background Dirty Writes totals the number of times that the caching system wrote cache buffers to disk because they were full. Background Aged Writes totals the number of times that the caching system wrote less than full cache buffers to disk because the time limit to keep them in memory (three seconds) had been reached. Total Cache Writes totals the number of cache blocks that have been written to disk.

Cache Allocations shows the number of times a new cache buffer has been allocated. This happens when a user connection requests to read or write a block that is not already in a cache buffer. The Thrashing Count shows the number of times that a cache block was requested but was not available because all existing blocks were in use. This has serious consequences for server performance and is a definite indicator that the server needs more memory or a reduced workload. LRU Block Was Dirty records the number of times that the requested cache block was dirty. The block's contents had to be written to disk before it could be reused.

Read Beyond Write shows the number of times that a connection asks to read information that is being copied from disk into a cache block. The requested information is not yet in the cache block and has to be retrieved directly from disk. Fragmented Writes records the number of times that the contents of a cache buffer had to be written to disk in more than one write operation because part of the cache buffer consisted of complete disk sectors but one part consisted of a partial sector.

Hit On Unavailable Block displays the number of times that a read or write request attempted to access a cache buffer that was being updated from disk or having its contents written to disk. Cache Blocks Scrapped records an event that can occur when two read or write requests are made for the same information. The first attempts to allocate a cache block for the request. While waiting for the cache block to become available, another cache block that contains the same information is allocated by the second request. Because the cache block allocated by the second request also can be used by the first, the original cache block allocation request is canceled or "scrapped."

When you have finished viewing the Cache Statistics information, press Esc to return to FCONSOLE's File Server Statistics menu.

Viewing Disk Statistics

Three options on FCONSOLE's File Server Statistics menu deal with server-disk information. The first, Channel Statistics, shows information about the disk channel use in the server. The second, Disk Mapping Information, shows information about disk mirroring and duplexing. The third, Disk Statistics, shows information about individual disks.

Each disk interface card in the server PC occupies a disk channel. An AT-compatible or ESDI controller occupies channel 0. Novell Disk Coprocessor boards can use channels 1 through 4 (for more information about disk controllers, see Chapter 4). To view information about the disk channels in the server, select Channel Statistics from the File Server Statistics submenu. If the server is using multiple disk channels, you are asked to choose which channel you want to work with. After you choose a channel, an information window appears. This window displays configuration information about the disk channel, including the NetWare disk driver and version that it uses, and the I/O address, memory address, interrupts, and DMA channels used by the disk interface board. Particularly useful is the information next to the word Status. Under normal circumstances the message Channel is running should appear there. If the information instead says that the channel is stopped or nonfunctional, the disks or disk interface board on the channel have failed in some way and should be checked. The Synchronization entry shows the activity of the disk channel if it is being shared between NetWare and DOS (as is the case on a nondedicated server with a DOS partition on the server disk). When you have finished viewing the Channel Information window, press Esc to return to the File Server Statistics submenu.

The Disk Mapping Information option shows information about the number of disks attached to the server and how they are being used. Select Disk Mapping Information and press Enter, and the Disk Mapping Information window opens. It displays the SFT Support Level (I for no disk mirroring or II for disk mirroring—see Chapter 4 for information about different NetWare versions) and the Pending I/O Commands (the number of disk reads or writes waiting to be processed). It also shows both the Physical Disk Count, which is the actual number of disks attached to the server, and Logical Disk Count. When two disks are designated as a mirrored or duplexed pair during installation, they are counted as one logical disk. A status for each disk channel is displayed; the ones marked Active are in use, the ones marked Unused are not installed, and the ones marked Failed require attention and are not usable. The Disk Mapping Information window also shows each logical disk and lists whether it consists of two mirrored disks. Beside each logical disk number is the physical disk number or numbers that it consists of. When you have finished viewing the Disk Mapping Information window, press Esc to return to the File Server Statistics submenu.

The Disk Statistics option enables you to see information about each physical disk on the file server. Select this option and, if you have more than one disk in the server, you are shown a list of physical disks. Select the one you want to work with and the Physical Disk window opens. It displays the disk type as well as the disk channel and controller number that the disk is attached to. The disk size and its number of heads and cylinders are also displayed. The number of disk errors that have occurred since the server was brought up are listed. (If this number is increasing rapidly, the disk is failing.) The size and status of the disk's Hot Fix table are also shown. When you have finished working with the Physical Disk window, press Esc to return to the File Server Statistics submenu.

Viewing File System Statistics

The File System Statistics option displays information about how files are being used on the server. Choose this option to open the File System Statistics window.

This window displays 15 items of information about file usage. The Configured Max Open Files shows the maximum number of concurrently open files that the server can support. Peak Files Open shows the most files that have been open concurrently since the server has been brought up. If this number is far below the maximum setting, you may want to consider lowering the maximum setting to save memory. Conversely, if the peak number is close to the maximum, you should down the server and use NETGEN to increase the number of maximum open files.

Open Requests shows the cumulative number of file opens that have been performed since the server was started. Currently Open Files shows the number of files currently open. Read Requests and Write Requests show the cumulative number of file read and write requests that have been issued since the server was started.

Five items deal with the server's File Allocation Table (FAT). The FAT is a list of all the server's files and their locations. NetWare reads the FAT every time a request to read from or write to a file is received. The FAT is cached in memory to speed up FAT reads and writes. When the FAT changes, the change must be written to the copies of the FAT stored on the server disk (two copies are stored for safety's sake).

FAT Sector Writes records the number of times that a sector containing FAT information has been written to the server disk. Dirty FAT Sectors displays the number of FAT sectors that have changed and need to be written to disk. NetWare writes dirty sectors to the disk within three seconds.

FAT Write Errors displays the number of times that an error occurred while trying to write a FAT sector. This is a serious problem, but because two copies of the FAT are maintained, the good copy can be used if you encounter this error. Fatal FAT Write Errors shows the number of times that NetWare could not write an entry to either copy of the FAT table. This is a very serious problem and requires careful action. The error is recorded in the file SYS$LOG.ERR in the SYS:SYSTEM directory, and shows the name of the server volume for which the FAT entry was to be written. The FAT stored in memory is accurate and enables you to back up the files from the affected volume before downing the server. After backing up the files, you can down the server, correct the disk problem, and restore the volume.

FAT Scan Errors displays the number of times that the information in the FAT was found to be inaccurate when compared to the actual information on a server disk.

The Configured Max Index Files shows the maximum number of files that can exist with the INDEXED attribute turned on. This limit is set during installation and can be modified using NETGEN. The Peak Indexed Files Open shows the highest number of INDEXED files that have been open at any one time since the server was started. Active Indexed Files shows the number of currently open INDEXED files, and Attached Indexed Files shows the number of INDEXED files that exist and have been used in the past.

When you have finished viewing the file system information, you can press Esc to leave the File System Statistics window and return to the File Server Statistics menu.

Viewing LAN I/O Statistics

Perhaps the most complex information provided by FCONSOLE's Statistics option is its LAN I/O Statistics. A staggering 23 separate statistics are available with this option, and some of them will not be clear to you unless you are thoroughly familiar with the way network communication systems handle data packets and the way NetWare processes service requests.

When a workstation sends a data packet to a NetWare server, that packet is assigned to a service-request process. The service-request process then manages all subsequent incoming and outgoing packets relating to the workstation's original operation. For example, if a workstation is copying a file from the server disk to its own C drive, a service-request process coordinates the movement of all packets from the server to the workstation. The file is divided into multiple packets as it is copied. When the file copy is complete, the service process is released until another request comes requiring its attention. The LAN I/O Statistics option displays information relating to this complex interaction between the server, data packets, and service-request processes.

When you select LAN I/O Statistics from FCONSOLE's File Server Statistics menu, you see the window shown in figure 18.9. The Total Packets Received is a count of all the packets received by the file server; the Packets Routed is the total number of packets received by the server and directed or routed to a different physical network (this occurs when the server is a bridge). File Service Packets totals only the packets that were received related to accessing server-based files. NetBIOS Broadcasts indicates the number of packets received by the server that require support for the NetBIOS protocol. The server must retransmit these packets to every NetBIOS device on the network.

The next several statistics cover obscure and fairly rare occurrences. Packets With Invalid Slot totals the number of packets received stating that they have a connection number that does not exist on the server (such as connection 105 on NetWare 286, which supports only 100 connections).

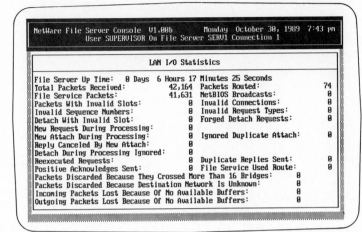

```
NetWare File Server Console V1.00b        Monday October 30, 1989  7:43 pm
              User SUPERVISOR On File Server SERV1 Connection 1

┌──────────────────────────── LAN I/O Statistics ────────────────────────────┐
│ File Server Up Time:    0 Days  6 Hours 17 Minutes 25 Seconds               │
│ Total Packets Received:        42,164  Packets Routed:              74      │
│ File Service Packets:          41,631  NetBIOS Broadcasts:           0      │
│ Packets With Invalid Slots:         0  Invalid Connections:          0      │
│ Invalid Sequence Numbers:           0  Invalid Request Types:        0      │
│ Detach With Invalid Slot:           0  Forged Detach Requests:       0      │
│ New Request During Processing:      0                                       │
│ New Attach During Processing:       0  Ignored Duplicate Attach:     0      │
│ Reply Canceled By New Attach:       0                                       │
│ Detach During Processing Ignored:   0                                       │
│ Reexecuted Requests:                0  Duplicate Replies Sent:       0      │
│ Positive Acknowledges Sent:         0  File Service Used Route:      0      │
│ Packets Discarded Because They Crossed More Than 16 Bridges:      0         │
│ Packets Discarded Because Destination Network Is Unknown:         0         │
│ Incoming Packets Lost Because Of No Available Buffers:            0         │
│ Outgoing Packets Lost Because Of No Available Buffers:            0         │
└────────────────────────────────────────────────────────────────────────────┘
```

Fig. 18.9.

The LAN I/O Statistics window from FCONSOLE.

Invalid Connections is similar; it records the number of packets showing a connection number that is not active or does not match the source workstation's node and network address. This can happen when the workstation is cleared from the server but continues to send packets. Each count in the Invalid Sequence Number listing indicates that one packet in a series received from a workstation (all related to a particular task being handled by a service process) has arrived in the wrong order. If this error occurs often, it indicates that the network communication system is not stable. Invalid Request Types reports the number of packets received by the server with a request type unknown to the server.

Detach With Invalid Slot and Forged Detach Requests both indicate that the server has received a request to detach a workstation from a connection but could not process it. Detach With Invalid Slot is issued when the connection is no longer active (indicating that the workstation has already been cleared). Forged Detach Requests is issued when the workstation's node and network address do not match what the server shows for the connection (indicating that the workstation has been cleared and another has already taken its connection).

New Request During Processing, New Attach During Processing, Ignored Duplicate Attach, Reply Canceled During Attach, and Detach During Processing Ignored all deal with the server receiving a second request from a workstation interrupting an existing request. A request to attach is a request for a server connection, probably indicating that the workstation has been rebooted and is sending a new request to attach. A request to detach is a request to give up a connection.

Reexecuted Request and Duplicate Replies Sent both show cases where the file server has had to respond to a request for a second time, probably because the first response was lost by the network communication system. In the first case the request is reprocessed; in the second case the request result still exists in server memory and is sent again. If either (or both) of these statistics is steadily rising, it could indicate that the file server is overloaded or the network communication system is generating errors.

Positive Acknowledges Sent indicates the number of times that the server has received a request a second time and has acknowledged that it received the first request and is still working on it. An acknowledgment is sent so the workstation knows the request was received.

File Service Used Route is a count of the times that an incoming request packet had to be stored in a routing buffer while waiting for a service process to become available.

Packets Discarded Because They Crossed More Than 16 Bridges shows the number of packets received that have already been rerouted by a bridge 16 times. NetWare does not allow a packet to be rerouted more than 16 times. When this extensive rerouting occurs, it probably indicates that the packet's address information has been corrupted in some way. Packets Discarded Because Destination Network Is Unknown indicates that a network to which packets are being routed has suddenly become unavailable. This can occur when a link between networks fails suddenly while a workstation is sending a series of packets from one network to another.

Incoming Packets Lost Because Of No Available Buffers and Outgoing Packets Lost Because Of No Available Buffers both mean that insufficient routing buffers were available to handle the number of incoming or outgoing packets. If the count next to these statistics indicates that this is a frequent problem, you should use NETGEN to reconfigure the server to have more routing buffers (communications buffers).

When you have finished viewing the LAN I/O Statistics window, press Esc to return to FCONSOLE's File Server Statistics menu.

Viewing Transaction Tracking Statistics

If you are using FCONSOLE to work with a server that has NetWare's Transaction Tracking System running, you will see an option on the File Server Statistics menu called Transaction Tracking Statistics. When you select this option, a window shows 13 information items about TTS.

The first item, Transaction Tracking Status, shows whether TTS is enabled. You decide whether the server runs TTS when you generate NetWare 286 using NETGEN. Transaction Tracking Volume shows the volume that TTS is using to store the files it creates while protecting transactions.

Configured Max Transactions displays the maximum number of simultaneous transactions that TTS can manage. This figure is set when you run NETGEN to install NetWare. Peak Transactions shows the maximum number of simultaneous transactions that have been managed since the server was booted. Current Transactions shows the number of transactions currently being managed by TTS. Transactions Performed is the total number of transactions that TTS has managed since the server was brought up.

Transactions Written totals the number of transactions that actually resulted in data being written to a file. In such cases, TTS has to be prepared to "back out" or undo the transaction in case it is aborted. Requested Backouts records the number of times that TTS actually had to back out a transaction that was not completed. Unfilled Backout Requests shows the number of times that TTS could not successfully back out a transaction, perhaps because TTS was disabled, or the volume that TTS was using was full or not available.

Current Used Disk Space shows the amount of disk space in bytes that TTS is using to store transaction backout information. Total File Extensions records the number of times that a file tracked by TTS has grown in size and required a new disk block. If the transaction that caused the file to grow has to be backed out, TTS must be prepared to deallocate that disk block. Total File Size Changes shows the number of times that files managed by TTS have increased or decreased in size. Total File Truncations shows the number of times that a TTS-managed file has decreased in size. If the transaction that caused the file to shrink has to be backed out, TTS must be prepared to restore the old information.

When you have finished viewing the Transaction Tracking Statistics window, press Esc to return to the File Server Statistics window.

Viewing Volume Information

The last item on the File Server Statistics menu is Volume Information. When you select this option, a list of volumes on the selected server is displayed (if the server has more than one volume). Choose the volume about which you want to view information and the Volume Information window opens showing 17 information items.

Volume Name shows the name of the volume. Volume Number shows the number of the volume. Volumes are numbered according to the order in which the server mounts them. Volume Mounted shows whether the volume is mounted and active. With NetWare 286, only volumes on removable disks can be mounted and dismounted. Volume Removable shows whether the volume is on a removable disk.

Volume Hashed shows whether the volume uses NetWare's hashing feature. Hashing is an efficient method that NetWare uses to find a particular file in its directory listing and is implemented automatically unless the server is critically low on memory. Volume Cached shows whether NetWare directory caching is active on the volume. Directory caching stores the volume's directory list in memory, resulting in greater efficiency as the server reads its directories to perform various tasks. You specify whether directory caching is active on a volume when you install NetWare. Directory caching is turned off automatically if the server has insufficient memory to support it.

Block Size shows the size of a disk block in bytes. A disk block is the unit in which NetWare reads and writes disk information, and is always 4,096 bytes for NetWare 286. Starting Block shows the disk block on which the volume starts. Total Blocks shows the size of the volume in blocks, and Free Blocks shows the number of blocks unused and available to store information.

Maximum Directory Entries displays the maximum number of files, directories, and subdirectories that the volume can store. This figure is set during installation and can be modified using NETGEN. Peak Directory Entries Used is slightly misleading. Directory entries are numbered, and this figure shows the highest number that has been assigned. As files and directories are deleted, lower directory entry numbers are freed and reused. Thus the highest directory entry number is not necessarily a reflection of the peak number of directory entries that have been used. Current Free Directory Entries shows the number of currently available directory entries.

Logical Drive Number shows the number of the logical drive that stores the volume. The count of logical disks is based on the total number of disks that exist when mirrored or duplexed disk pairs are counted as one drive. Volume Mirrored shows whether the volume is on a disk that is part of a mirrored or duplexed pair. Primary Disk Number shows the number of the primary disk that contains the volume; Mirror Disk Number shows the number of the disk drive that mirrors it (if there is one).

When you have finished viewing the Volume Information window, press Esc to return to the list of disk volumes. You can select another volume to view information about, or press Esc again to return to FCONSOLE's File Server Statistics window. To return to FCONSOLE's main menu, press Esc one more time.

You have now learned about all of FCONSOLE's features and menu options. To leave FCONSOLE, press Esc and confirm that you want to exit.

Communicating with Other Workstations

NetWare's SEND command enables you to send messages to other users who are logged into the server. The CASTOFF command enables you to block messages addressed to you from other users. CASTON is used to reverse the effects of CASTOFF.

The message that you send or receive appears along the bottom line of the screen and causes the recipient's PC to beep. The user can clear the message by pressing Ctrl-Enter. If the user has his or her workstation screen in graphics mode (that is, the screen is displaying graphics instead of text), the message does not appear, but the PC still beeps.

You should use this message-sending feature cautiously. A few interrupt-driven programs (such as pop-up applications and memory-resident terminal emulators) may conflict with NetWare's messages, causing the workstation to lock up when a message is received. You probably should use the CASTOFF command to block messages on workstations that run programs that conflict with NetWare's message feature. You also should block messages on workstations that run long tasks and run unattended, such as tape backup workstations and communication gateways.

Using SEND

SEND lets you send a message to any user who is logged into a server that you are also logged into. To send a message, type *send,* the message you want to send in quotes, and the login name of the intended recipient. The message can be up to 45 characters in length, less the number of characters in the login name. For example, to send a user named SMITHFD a message inviting him to lunch, type the following:

SEND "How about lunch today, Smitty?" TO USER SMITHFD

and press Enter. SMITHFD is pleasantly surprised with the following message across the bottom of his screen:

```
>> From JONESJS[3]: How about lunch today, Smitty?
(Ctrl-Enter to clear)
```

Notice that the message shows your name and connection number. SMITHFD can make the message disappear by pressing Ctrl-Enter. You see a message confirming that the message has been sent to SMITHFD.

You can shorten the SEND command shown in the above example by leaving out the optional words TO and USER.

SEND also can be used to send messages to group names. If a group called ACCTING is on the server, you can send every group member who is logged in a message using the following command:

SEND "The Accounting Dept meeting is at 2" TO GROUP ACCTING

and press Enter.

You can shorten the command by leaving out the optional words TO and GROUP.

You can send to multiple users and groups by listing each name in the SEND command, as in the following example:

SEND "Come to my office" TO SMITHFD ACCTING JONESJS

Press Enter.

If you are logged into multiple servers, you can specify the server and user or group name to send to by preceding the user or group name with the server name followed by a slash (/), as shown in this example:

SEND "Paychecks are ready" TO SERV1/SMITHFD SERV2/ACCTING SERV1/JONESJS

Press Enter.

Blocking Messages with CASTOFF

You can use the CASTOFF command to stop your PC from receiving messages from other users. You already have read about the difficulty that can arise if you receive a message while you are running certain pop-up or terminal emulation packages. To block incoming messages, type *castoff* and press Enter. You will not receive messages, and any user who attempts to send to you will be notified that you did not receive the message.

CASTOFF does not block messages from the server console unless you use its ALL parameter. To stop messages sent from the server console, type *castoff all* and press Enter.

Unblocking Messages with CASTON

The CASTON command reverses the effects of CASTOFF, letting you receive messages again. To use the command, type *caston* and press Enter.

Managing Your Personal Session

The SESSION command enables you to manage your personal network connection and gives you a menu-driven way to send messages to users and groups and map disk drives. To start SESSION, log into a server, type *session*, and press Enter. The menu shown in figure 18.10 appears.

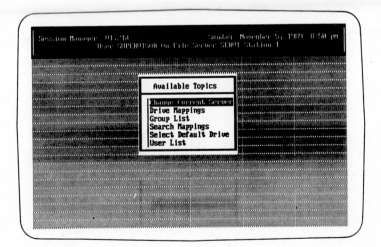

Fig. 18.10. SESSION's main menu.

Sending Messages

You can choose from two options to send messages to users and groups. To send a message to a user or multiple users, select User List from SESSION's main menu. A list of the users logged into the server appears. Highlight the user to whom you want to send a message and press Enter. A small menu appears, offering you the option to Display User Info or Send Message. Choose Send Message and an entry window opens prompting you to enter the text of the message. Type the message and press Enter, and the message is sent. You are returned to the small menu. Press Esc to leave it and return to the list of users.

You can send a message to multiple users from this list by highlighting each user name with F5 and then pressing Enter. The message entry window appears; type the message and press Enter, and the message is sent.

When you have finished sending messages to users, press Esc to return to SESSION's main menu.

You can use similar methods to send messages to groups. Select Group List from SESSION's main menu. A list of the groups defined on the server appears. Highlight the group that you want to send to and press Enter, or mark multiple groups with F5 and press Enter.

The message-entry window appears; type the message and press Enter. The message is sent to all members of the group who are currently logged in.

When you have finished sending messages to groups, press Esc to return to SESSION's main menu.

Viewing User Information

You can also use SESSION's User List menu selection to view information about a particular user. Highlight User List and press Enter, and a list of the server's users appears. Highlight the name of the user you want to learn more about and press Enter. From the small menu that appears, select Display User Info. A window opens showing the user's full name, object type, login time, network address, and node address.

When you have finished viewing this information, press Esc to return to the User List menu, and press Esc again to return to the user list itself. Select another user to work with, or press Esc to go back to SESSION's main menu.

Working with Drive Mappings

Three of SESSION's options let you work with the disk-drive mappings. To see and work with the regular drive mappings, choose Drive Mappings. A list of the current drive mappings appears.

You can add new drive mappings to this list by pressing Ins. You are prompted to enter the drive letter that you want to use. After you choose a letter, an entry window prompts you to enter the name of the directory that you want to map to. Type the name of your choice, or press Ins to pick a directory name from a list of options. When you press Ins, a list of the servers you are logged into appears. Highlight the server you want to map to and press Enter, and the entry window is updated to show your choice. Next, the server's volumes are displayed. Highlight the volume that stores the directory you want to map to and press Enter. You are shown a list of directories on that volume. Select the appropriate one. You are shown a list of that directory's subdirectories. Continue selecting subdirectories until the complete directory name that you want to map to is shown, and then press Esc. Press Enter to map the directory name you selected to the previously selected drive letter.

To delete a drive mapping, highlight it on the list and press Del. After you confirm that you want to delete the drive mapping, it is removed from the list. (SESSION does not permit you to delete the drive letter that is your default.)

To view the NetWare effective rights to a network directory, highlight it on the mapped drive list and press Enter. A window lists the effective rights to the directory. Press Esc when you have finished viewing the rights information.

When you have finished working with the drive list, press Esc to return to SESSION's main menu.

You can use similar techniques to work with the list of search drives. Select Search Mappings from SESSION's main menu, and a list of the current search drives is displayed. You can add a new search drive to this list by pressing Ins. You are prompted to enter the number in the search order that the new drive occupies, and by default the number one greater than the last search drive is shown, making the new drive last in the search order. You can enter a smaller number to give the new drive a higher priority in the search order.

After you select a search-order number, a window prompts you to enter the directory to which the search mapping points. You can type a name or press Ins to choose the name interactively, as discussed above. After you type or select the directory name, press Enter, and the search drive list is updated to show the new search drive.

To delete a search drive mapping, highlight it on the list and press Del. After you confirm that you want to delete the drive mapping, it is removed from the list.

To view the NetWare effective rights to a network search directory, highlight the directory on the mapped drive list and press Enter. A window lists the effective rights to the directory. Press Esc when you have finished viewing the rights information.

When you have finished working with the search mapping list, press Esc to return to SESSION's main menu.

You also can use SESSION to choose the current default directory. Highlight Select Default Drive from SESSION's main menu and press Enter. A list of the currently mapped disk drives is displayed. Highlight the drive that you want to make the default and press Enter. You are returned to SESSION's main menu.

When you have finished using SESSION, press Esc to leave it.

Chapter Summary

As you saw in this chapter, the amount of information that NetWare puts at your finger tips is amazing. Rather than feeling overwhelmed by the sheer volume of data and statistics that it presents, think in terms of the management tasks that you need to perform on a regular basis. Seek out the commands and options that supply you with the information required to do those tasks. Learn how to check on server availability and how to list a server's users and check its available disk space. After you master the basics, you can move on to viewing file and record lock information and analyzing advanced server performance statistics. Before you know it, you will be using NetWare's management commands and utilities like an expert.

19

Server Console Commands and Loadable Modules

NetWare is designed so that you do not have to enter commands often from your file server's keyboard. For the sake of security, you may have decided to place your network's servers in a locked room or closet, or some other place with limited access; using the server frequently is inconvenient.

As you learned in the last chapter, virtually all server-management tasks can be performed from a network workstation. Utilities like FCONSOLE enable you to control the server almost completely without ever having to visit it.

A number of useful commands can be executed from the server, and a few of these commands are the only way to perform a particular task. Commands that you enter from the server's keyboard are called console commands. They are used for a variety of purposes, including managing its printers, displaying or changing its configuration, and controlling whether users can access the server.

Many of the server console commands are the same for NetWare 286 and NetWare 386, but some key differences still exist. Both versions of NetWare provide single-purpose console commands, but NetWare 386 enables you to run NetWare Loadable Modules (NLMs), which are multipurpose utilities (as are SYSCON and FCONSOLE). If you installed

NetWare 386, you are already familiar with an NLM called INSTALL that is used to install and configure the server.

In this chapter, you will learn how to use NetWare 286's and NetWare 386's console commands, and NetWare 386's NLMs. They are discussed based on the type of tasks they are used to perform, starting with simple console commands and followed by NLMs. You also will learn about a special NetWare 286 software module called the Value Added Process (VAP), a forerunner to the NLM.

Two groups of console commands have been omitted because they are discussed in other chapters. Console commands that are used to configure and manage shared printers are discussed in detail in Chapters 14 and 15. Console commands and NLMs used to install NetWare 386 are covered in Chapter 7.

Executing console commands and NLMs in general will be described first, followed by a discussion of individual commands.

Running Console Commands and NLMs

Console commands and NLMs are executed from the server's keyboard and display their output on the server screen. When you start a server, it initializes its network adapters and print queues, and mounts its disk volumes. After these tasks have been completed, the server screen displays a colon and a flashing cursor (called the *colon prompt*) that is similar to DOS or OS/2 command prompts. Like DOS or OS/2 commands, console commands are executed by typing the command name and then pressing the Enter key.

NetWare 286's colon prompt is like the DOS prompt in another respect. With DOS, you can run only one program at a time. When that program is finished you can start another. NetWare 286's console is like DOS—it can run only one command at a time.

NetWare 386 is more like OS/2 in that you can have multiple commands and NLMs active at the same time. OS/2 calls each running task a *session*, but NetWare 386 calls each task a *screen*. With OS/2 and NetWare 386's console, you can move from one session or screen to another by holding down the Alt key and pressing the Esc key (Alt-Esc). If you want to see a menu showing the currently active screens, type Ctrl-Esc. A menu prompting you to choose the screen you want to switch to is displayed. NetWare 386 also lets you use the up-arrow key to recall the last 10 console commands you have typed. When you press the up-arrow key, the command you just entered is displayed. If you press the up-arrow key again, the command you entered before that is displayed. You can scroll backward through your previous 10 commands by successively pressing the up-arrow key. You can scroll forward through these commands by pressing the down-arrow key.

NetWare 386's server screen clears the screen automatically and displays character patterns if you have not typed on the server keyboard for several minutes. You can clear this pattern and return to the server console prompt by pressing any key.

Getting to the Console on a Nondedicated Server

When you are working on a nondedicated NetWare 286 server (where the PC can run DOS programs as well as operate as a server), you can get to the server console by typing *console* and pressing Enter from the DOS prompt while you are logged into the server, or from the LOGIN directory (usually on drive F), if you are not logged in.

After you are in the console screen, you can return to the DOS prompt by typing *dos* and pressing Enter from the server console.

Now you are ready to learn some console commands. Commands that display server information are described first.

Console Commands that Display Server Information

One of the most common uses of the server screen is to display server status information. The seven commands discussed in this section are used for this purpose. NetWare 386 also offers an NLM called MONITOR to display server information. You will learn about MONITOR later in this chapter in the section called "Working with NetWare Loadable Modules."

NAME (NetWare 286 and 386)

The NAME console command displays the most basic item of information about the server—its name. Type *name* and press Enter from the server colon prompt, and information similar to the following is displayed:

```
This is server SERV1
```

This information remains on the screen until another console command causes it to scroll off.

CONFIG (NetWare 286 and 386)

The CONFIG command shows several items of useful information about the file server. When you type *config* and press Enter from the colon prompt, the server's name, network addresses, and network adapter information are displayed. For NetWare 286, the type and node address for each network adapter is displayed. On a NetWare 386 server, the LAN protocol bound to each network adapter is displayed.

TRACK (NetWare 286 and 386)

The TRACK console command is used to display the information received from servers and other network devices that "advertise" their availability more than the network. Servers, gateways, bridges, and certain other devices broadcast their names and network addresses to other servers at regular intervals (usually once per minute). These broadcasts let all devices on the network know what servers are up or down and what bridges can be used to move information from one physical network to another.

To turn on the TRACK display, type *track on* and press Enter. To stop the display, type *track off* and press Enter. A typical NetWare 386 TRACK display is shown below:

```
OUT [00000001:FFFFFFFFFFFF] 7:06:44p.m. SERV1
IN [00000001:000000000002] 7:07:01p.m. Get Nearest Server
OUT [00000001:000000000002] 7:07:01p.m. Give Nearest Server SERV1
IN [00000001:000000000001] 7:07:01p.m. SERV2
OUT [00000001:FFFFFFFFFFFF] 7:07:44p.m. SERV1
IN [00000001:000000000001] 7:08:01p.m. SERV2
```

Notice that each line of the display starts with IN or OUT. Lines that begin with OUT display a broadcast made by the server you are using. Lines that begin with IN record a broadcast made by another device and received by your server. After the IN or OUT are two numbers within brackets and separated by a colon. The first number is the physical network number where the broadcast originated. The second is a code that denotes the type of broadcast sent or received. The time of the broadcast is shown next, followed by information about the broadcasting device. If the broadcast shows only the server name, the broadcast is an advertisement that the server is up. Other types of messages include Get Nearest Server, which indicates that a workstation has just loaded the NetWare shell and is broadcasting a request to attach to a server. The server responds with a Give Nearest Server broadcast. Route Request indicates that information is being routed through a bridge from one physical network to another.

NetWare 286's TRACK display does not show the time or the physical network number. Instead, the TRACK display shows the letter number of the network from which or to which the broadcast is made, such as A:.

DISPLAY SERVERS (NetWare 286 and 386)

The DISPLAY SERVERS command lists the currently known servers on the server display. To use this command, type *display servers* and press Enter.

DISPLAY NETWORKS (NetWare 286 and 386)

The DISPLAY NETWORKS command is similar to DISPLAY SERVERS. It lists the currently known physical networks on the server display (it shows the network numbers in hexadecimal format). To use this command, type *display networks* and press Enter.

TIME (NetWare 286 and 386)

The TIME console command shows the current server date and time. Type *time* and press Enter to display this information. This command does not continue to update the display with the current date and time; it merely shows that information at the moment you execute the command.

Later in this chapter you will learn to use the SET TIME command to change the server date and time.

VERSION (NetWare 286 and 386)

This console command displays the version and revision level of NetWare currently running on the server. Execute the command by typing *version* and pressing Enter.

MONITOR (NetWare 286)

The NetWare 286 MONITOR console command displays server utilization statistics and information about each connection to the file server (each user who logs in or attaches to a server uses a connection, and each connection is numbered). When you type *monitor* and press Enter, a screen similar to the one shown in figure 19.1 is shown.

```
┌─Advanced NetWare 286 MD V2.15─Utilization (%) =  35─┬─Disk I/O Pending =  5─┐
│Stn  1: Read File        │Stn  2:               │Stn  3: Clr Phy Rec      │
│                         │                      │                         │
│File            Stat     │File            Stat  │File            Stat     │
│                         │                      │                         │
│Z:SYS$HELP.DAT    7   RP │                      │R:BUDGET.WK1     5  PRPW  │
│Z:SYSCON.HLP      7   RP │                      │R:123.DLD        5  RP    │
│Z:SYS$ERR.DAT     7   RP │                      │R:123.CMP        5  R     │
│Z:SYS$MSG.DAT     7   RP │                      │                         │
│                         │                      │                         │
│Stn  4:                  │Stn  5: Lock Phy Rec  │Stn  6: End of Job       │
│                         │                      │                         │
│File            Stat     │File            Stat  │File            Stat     │
│                         │                      │                         │
│                         │F:SRU00093       4 R W│                         │
│                         │F:LANMDATA       4 R W│                         │
│                         │F:LANCDATA       4 R W│                         │
│                         │                      │                         │
│                         │                      │                         │
└─────────────────────────┴──────────────────────┴─────────────────────────┘
```

Fig. 19.1.

Using the MONITOR command.

Server Utilization Statistics

Several items of information are shown on the top line of the MONITOR screen. The version of NetWare the server is running is shown in the upper left corner. In the center, the percentage of the file server's CPU utilization required for server requests is shown. This is a gauge of how busy the file server is from a processing standpoint. In the upper right corner, the number of 4096-byte disk cache buffers that are waiting to be written to disk is shown. This is a gauge of the server's disk writing backlog.

Connection Information

Below the top line, the display is divided into six sections; each shows information about a single server connection. In the upper left of each section is the station or connection number. Next to that number is the area used to show the type of server request the workstation is making. Typical examples are Read File or Log Out. A complete list of server request status messages is shown in table 19.1. Just below the request type information is a message showing the status of file-sharing transactions. If you do not have any applications using NetWare's Transaction Tracking System, this area remains blank.

The bottom two-thirds of each section is used to show the files the workstation has open and the way they are being used. Beneath the heading File, the name of each file is displayed; under the heading Stat is information about how each file is being used. One of seven status codes is shown:

R	Stands for Read. Indicates that the file is open for reading.
W	Stands for Write. Indicates that the file is open for writing.
P	Stands for Private. The P precedes R and/or W and indicates that the file is being read and/or written exclusively and cannot be read and/or written by another workstation.
LOCK	Shows that the file is locked. The file cannot be written to by another station until the lock is released.
PERS	Shows that the file is logged to be locked. Sometimes a multiuser application "logs" several files that it must lock at the same time. A file that is logged is locked as soon as all logged files are available for locking.

T   Stands for Transactional. The file is open and is
                  flagged as Transactional.

H   Stands for Hold. The H always follows T and shows
                  that the file is on hold until the current transaction
                  is completed.

Table 19.1
NetWare 286 MONITOR Server Request Status Messages

Message	Meaning
Alloc Resource	Allocate a resource
Begin Trans	Begin a transaction
Clear File	Clear or release a file lock
Clear File Set	Clear or release a set of file locks
Clear Record Set	Clear or release a set of record locks
Close File	Close a file
Clr Phy Rec	Clear a physical record lock
Clr Phy Rec Set	Clear a set of physical record locks
Copy File	Copy a file
Create File	Create a file
Dir Search	Search a directory
End of Job	End of a service request
End Trans	End of a transaction
Erase File	Erase a file
Floppy Config	Floppy configuration
Get File Size	Get a file's size
Lock File	Lock a file
Lock Phy Rec Set	Lock a set of physical records
Lock Record	Lock a record
Log Out	Log out from the server
Log Pers File	Log a file to be locked
Log Phy Rec	Log a physical record to be locked

Log Record	Log a record to be locked
Open File	Open a file
Pass File	Pass a file
Read File	Read a file
Rel Phy Rec	Release a physical record
Rel Phy Rec Set	Release a physical record set
Rel Record Set	Release a record set
Rel Resource	Release a resource
Release File	Release a file
Release File Set	Release a set of files
Release Record	Release a record
Rename File	Rename a file
Search Next	Search for the next file in a directory
Semaphore	Activate a semaphore
Set File Atts	Set a file's attributes
Start Search	Start a directory search
Sys Log	Log into the server
Unlock Record	Unlock a record
Win Format	Window format
Win Read	Window read
Win Write	Window write
Write File	Write to a file

Looking at Different Connections

By default, MONITOR shows you only the first six connections. To look at another group of six connections, type *monitor* followed by the number of the connection you want to view, such as

MONITOR 14

Because connections are displayed in consecutive groups of six, typing *monitor 14* results in the screen displaying information about connections 13 through 18. NetWare 286 permits a maximum of 100 connections.

SPEED (NetWare 386)

The SPEED console command displays NetWare 386's calculation of your processor speed. To see your server's speed rating, type *speed* and press Enter. Check the result as an indicator that your server PC may not be set to its maximum operating speed. A server PC running at 16 MHz with an 80386 processor should have a speed rating of approximately 120. An 80386SX processor produces a speed rating of approximately 95. A 25 MHz 80386 processor should have a rating of 150 or greater. If the speed rating shown is significantly lower than these numbers, check to make sure that your server PC is configured to operate at its maximum speed.

PROTOCOL (NetWare 386)

The PROTOCOL console command displays the list of NetWare 386 registered communication protocols. The command also registers new protocols that become available after you purchased NetWare 386.

Controlling Access to the Server

Two console commands control whether or not new users can log in or attach to the server. A third lets you remove the connection of an existing user.

DISABLE LOGIN (NetWare 286 and 386)

The DISABLE LOGIN console command is used to prevent new users from logging in or attaching to the server. Type *disable login* and press Enter to prevent new users from accessing the server.

ENABLE LOGIN (NetWare 286 and 386)

ENABLE LOGIN reverses the effect of DISABLE LOGIN. When a server is first started, log in is enabled by default, so you only have to use ENABLE LOGIN if you have previously used DISABLE LOGIN. Type *enable login* and press Enter to enable users to log in.

CLEAR STATION

CLEAR STATION is used to remove a user from the server. To clear a user, you must first know his or her connection number and then type *clear station* followed by that number. For example, if the user you want to remove is on connection 7, type

    CLEAR STATION 7

and press Enter. Of course, you should use this command with care. Clearing the wrong user at the wrong time is a proven way to make an enemy.

Sending Messages to Users

Sometimes you need to send a message to some or all of the users who are logged in or attached to the server. Two NetWare commands enable you to do this. Each command sends a message that appears along the bottom line of the screen and causes the user's PC to beep. The user can clear the message by pressing Ctrl-Enter. If the user has his workstation screen in graphics mode (displaying graphics instead of text), the message does not appear, but the computer still beeps.

BROADCAST (NetWare 286 and 386)

To use BROADCAST in its simplest form, type *broadcast* followed by the message (up to 55 characters long) you want to send. For example, to notify all users that the SERV1 server is going down in five minutes, type the following:

BROADCAST SERV1 GOING DOWN IN 5 MIN, PLS LOGOFF NOW

and press Enter. The message, SERV1 GOING DOWN IN 5 MIN, PLS LOGOFF NOW, is sent to every user connected to the server.

You also can use BROADCAST to send messages to a specific list of users. With NetWare 286, you must identify all users by their connection number. When you use this method, you must enclose the text of the message in quotation marks ("). For example, you can send a message to the users on connections 5 and 17 by using the following command:

BROADCAST "YOUR PRINT JOB IS READY" TO 5, 17

(you can omit the word TO if you like). Notice that the connection numbers are separated by commas.

With NetWare 386, you can identify users by their login names and you can mix login names with connection numbers. You can use the following command to broadcast a message to four individual users:

BROADCAST "OUR MEETING IS AT 2" TO SMITHFD, ADAMSJF, 5, 13

Users can prevent BROADCAST messages from being received at their workstations by using the CASTOFF ALL command (see the preceding chapter for information about CASTOFF ALL).

SEND (NetWare 286 and 386)

SEND is used almost exactly like BROADCAST. The only difference is that users can prevent messages sent with SEND by using the CASTOFF command, but BROADCAST requires the CASTOFF ALL command (the preceding chapter has complete details about using CASTOFF and CASTOFF ALL).

To use SEND in its simplest form, type *send* followed by the message (up to 55 characters long) you want to send. For example, to notify all users that a network printer will be unavailable, type the following:

SEND THE NETWORK LASER PRINTER IS BEING REPAIRED TODAY

and press Enter. The message, THE NETWORK PRINTER IS BEING REPAIRED TODAY, is sent to every user connected to the server.

Like BROADCAST, you can use SEND to send messages to a specific list of users. With NetWare 286, you must identify all users by their connection number. When you use this method, you must also enclose the text of the message in quotation marks ("). You can send a message to the users on connections 6 and 13 by using the following command:

SEND "YOUR PAYCHECKS ARE READY" TO 6, 13

(you can omit the word TO if you like). Notice that the connection numbers are separated by commas.

With NetWare 386, you also can identify users by their login names, and you can mix login names with connection numbers. You can use the following command to broadcast a message to four individual users:

SEND "OUR MEETING IS AT 2" TO SMITHFD, ADAMSJF, 5, 13

Stopping the Server

When you need to stop the server, you may assume that turning off its power switch is all you need to do. Nothing can be further from the truth. Because NetWare uses server memory to cache file writes for as long as several seconds, a file that has not yet been written to disk may remain in server memory. Turning the server off at the wrong moment can result in those files being lost. The console command that stops the server "flushes" the memory buffers to disk first, and then stops the server.

DOWN (NetWare 286 and 386)

The DOWN command is the proper way to stop a server. Before stopping the server, it completes any file writes that are stored in memory, and clears all connections. To stop the server, type *down* and press Enter. The server stops, and a message is sent to all attached users that the server is down. You then can turn off the server.

EXIT (NetWare 386)

After you have downed a NetWare 386 server, you can use the EXIT command to return to the DOS prompt of the server PC. Type *exit* and press Enter to leave the colon prompt and go to the DOS prompt.

Controlling the Console Display

Several commands are used to manage the console display. Sometimes you may want to clear the console screen. Another command is used to clear a message sent to the server console from a workstation.

OFF (NetWare 286 and 386)

The OFF command clears the console screen and places the colon prompt at the top line. To clear the screen, type *off* and press Enter.

CLS (NetWare 386)

The CLS command is a duplicate of the OFF command but works in NetWare 386 only. To clear the NetWare 386 console, type *cls* and press Enter.

CLEAR MESSAGE (NetWare 286)

The CLEAR MESSAGE command can be used to remove a message sent to the console by a user, or to clear any other information displayed on the bottom line of the NetWare 286 MONITOR display. To clear this screen area, type *clear message* and press Enter.

Controlling Disks

Several console commands enable you to work with server disks. With NetWare 286, you can use console commands to view the status of disks, to mount and dismount removable disks, and to control the mirroring of duplexed or mirrored disks. With NetWare 386, you can activate and deactivate volumes. NetWare 386 also enables you to work with disks using its INSTALL NLM. You will learn about the INSTALL NLM later in this chapter, in the section called "Working with Netware Loadable Modules."

DISK (NetWare 286)

The DISK command is used to display information about file server disks. You can check the status of your drives in conjunction with NetWare's fault tolerance features—Hot Fix and disk mirroring and duplexing (see Chapter 4 for details about these features).

When you type *disk* and press Enter, a screen similar to that in figure 19.2 is displayed. This screen shows some valuable information arranged in columns. The first column shows the disk number assigned to the drive by NetWare. The second column (headed with cha) shows the disk channel.

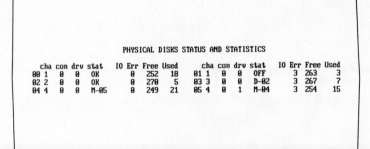

```
                    PHYSICAL DISKS STATUS AND STATISTICS

        cha con drv stat    IO Err Free Used      cha con drv stat    IO Err Free Used
        00 1   0   0  OK      0   252  18          01 1   0   0  OFF     3  263   3
        02 2   0   0  OK      0   270   5          03 3   0   0  D-02    3  267   7
        04 4   0   0  M-05    0   249  21          05 4   0   1  M-04    3  254  15
```

Fig. 19.2.
Using the DISK command.

The third (headed with con) shows the controller number, and the fourth (headed with drv) displays the drive number assigned to the disk by its controller. The fifth column (headed with stat) shows the current status of the disk, listing one of five possible options:

OK	The drive is operating normally and is not mirrored or duplexed to another drive.
OFF	The drive is not operating (this can be an indicator that the drive has failed).
NO HOT	The drive is operating, but NetWare's Hot Fix feature is not functioning. The disk should be checked for excessive bad blocks or other problems.

M-01   M indicates that the disk is part of a mirrored disk
                        pair. The number after the M shows the NetWare
                        number of the disk this disk is paired to.

D-03   D stands for dead and indicates that the disk is part
                        of a mirrored disk pair but is no longer operating.
                        The number after the D shows the NetWare number
                        of the disk that this disk is paired to.

The column headed with IO Err shows the number of disk write errors
that have occurred since the drive was initialized with the Hot Fix feature.
Each of these errors results in the disk using a block from its Hot Fix
redirection area (when you installed NetWare on your server, you
established these areas when you configured your server disks). The
number of disk blocks available in the Hot Fix redirection area is shown in
the column labeled Free. The number of bad blocks on the disk is shown
in the column labeled Used.

Periodically check the bad blocks for an unusually large increase in the
number of I/O errors. This can indicate that the disk is failing.

When you type *disk* * and press Enter, all server volumes are listed with
the physical drives where they reside. The display is similar to the
following:

```
                            FILE SERVER VOLUMES
Volume Name    Phy Drv    Mir Drv    Volume Name    Phy Drv    Mir Drv
SYS              00                     VOL2           01
VOL3             02         03          VOL4           04         05
```

Typing *disk* followed by a particular volume name shows similar
information about that volume's disks. For example, if you type *disk vol3*
and press Enter, the following is displayed:

```
Information for Volume VOL3
Physical drive number : 04
Physical drive type : Maxtor-1140
IO errors on this drive : 0
Redirection blocks available: 241
Redirection blocks used : 21

Mirror physical drive number: 05
Mirror physical drive type : Maxtor-1140
IO errors on this drive : 03
Redirection blocks available: 254
Redirection blocks used : 15

Other volumes sharing these physical drive(s) : none
```

UNMIRROR and REMIRROR (NetWare 286)

With NetWare 286, you can use the UNMIRROR and REMIRROR commands to manage mirrored or duplexed disk pairs. When NetWare was installed on your server, you had the option of mirroring or duplexing disk pairs to guard against data loss resulting from disk failure.

If you need to remove a disk from a mirrored pair, type *unmirror* followed by the drive number (the DISK command can be used to find the disk number). For example, to unmirror drive 3, type *unmirror 03* and press Enter. If you need to remirror a drive (such as when you replace a failed drive), type *remirror* followed by the drive number, such as *remirror 04*.

MOUNT and DISMOUNT (NetWare 286)

If your server uses disk drives with removable platters or packs, you can use the MOUNT and DISMOUNT commands to change them.

The first step to changing removable disks is to remove the currently loaded platter or pack. Using the DISMOUNT command closes all the files open on the removable disk and writes all cache buffers to it. Type *dismount* followed by the number assigned by NetWare to the removable disk (you can find the disk number by using the DISK console command). For example, to dismount disk number 4, type *dismount 4* and press Enter.

If your removable disk drive uses a disk pack, you may need to use the PACK parameter with DISMOUNT. Type the command *dismount pack 4* and press Enter (check the manufacturer's instructions to determine if this option applies to you).

After the drive has been dismounted, you can remove its disk or platter and insert another one. Mount the new platter or pack by typing *mount 4* and pressing Enter (substitute the actual number of your disk for *4*).

If your removable disk drive uses a disk pack, you may need to use the PACK parameter with MOUNT. If this is the case, use the command, *mount pack 4* (check the manufacturer's instructions to determine if this option applies to your removable disk drive).

MOUNT and DISMOUNT (NetWare 386)

The MOUNT and DISMOUNT commands for NetWare 386 are slightly different from their counterparts in NetWare 286. As you have learned in Chapter 7 ("Installing NetWare 386"), NetWare 386's MOUNT and DISMOUNT commands are used for all disk volumes, not just those on removable disk platters.

When you use MOUNT to mount a NetWare 386 volume, the mount becomes available to server users. To mount a specific volume, type *mount* followed by the volume name, such as *mount data3*. You can mount all server volumes by typing *mount all*.

DISMOUNT makes a volume unavailable. It takes a volume off line so that you can perform maintenance or change its configuration. To dismount a volume, type *dismount* followed by the volume name, such as *dismount data3*.

VOLUME (NetWare 386)

NetWare 386's VOLUME console command shows a list of the currently mounted volumes. To view the list, type *volume* and press Enter.

Reconfiguring the Server

NetWare 386 enables you to change a number of the server's configuration options using console commands. NetWare 286 provides limited server reconfiguration options from the console.

SET (NetWare 386)

NetWare 386's SET command is its most versatile and powerful server configuration tool. You can use the SET command to modify an extensive array of server operating settings. Fortunately, most of these operating system parameters are set to defaults that are probably the best in almost every case.

When you type *set* (without any parameters), the following menu of nine categories of configuration parameters you can work with is displayed:

```
Setable configuration parameter categories

    1.  File caching
    2.  Directory caching
    3.  File system
    4.  Communications
    5.  Memory
    6.  Locks
    7.  Transaction tracking
    8.  Disk
    9.  Miscellaneous

Which category do you want to view:
```

You are prompted to select one of the categories. Enter the number of your choice. For each option you select, you are asked to choose whether you want to view the advanced configuration parameters. Press Y to see a complete list of the parameters.

A list of the configuration parameters for the category you chose and its current setting is displayed. The highest and lowest possible settings for each option, as well as a brief description of each option's purpose, is also displayed.

These options are used to fine tune various aspects of the file server's operation and performance. To intelligently change some of the advanced parameters requires a systems level understanding of NetWare beyond what is required to use and configure it in most situations. You should change the default settings of most of these parameters only if you are sure that you have a good reason to do so. Tables 19.2 through 19.10 list each of these options. For a detailed discussion of each, you should refer to NetWare 386's System Administration manual.

Table 19.2
Commands that Control File Caching

Command	Default Setting	Allowed Range
SET MAXIMUM CONCURRENT DISK CACHE WRITES = 50	50	10 to 100

Controls the maximum number of concurrent writes of dirty cache buffers (a buffer containing something) that can be made to the disk

Command	Default Setting	Allowed Range
SET DIRTY DISK CACHE DELAY TIME = 3.3	3.3 sec	.1 to 10 sec

Sets the minimum time delay before writing a dirty cache buffer to disk

Command	Default Setting	Allowed Range
SET MINIMUM FILE CACHE REPORT THRESHOLD = 20	20	0 to 1000

Sets the level at which a warning will be issued that the minimum number of file cache buffers has almost been reached

Command	Default Setting	Allowed Range
SET MINIMUM FILE CACHE BUFFERS = 20	20	20 to 1000

Sets the minimum number of file cache buffers that the server will maintain

Table 19.3
Commands that Control Directory Caching

Command	Default Setting	Allowed Range
SET DIRTY DIRECTORY CACHE DELAY TIME = 0.5	.5 sec	0 to 10 sec

Sets the minimum time delay before writing a dirty directory cache buffer to disk

SET MAXIMUM CONCURRENT DIRECTORY CACHE WRITES = 10	10	5 to 50

Controls the maximum number of concurrent writes of dirty directory cache buffers that can be made to the disk

SET DIRECTORY CACHE ALLOCATION WAIT TIME = 2.2 sec	2.2 sec	.5 sec to 2 min

Sets the minimum time to wait between new directory cache buffer allocations

SET DIRECTORY CACHE BUFFER NONREFERENCED DELAY = 5.5 sec	5.5 sec	1 sec to 5 min

Sets the time to wait after the last reading of a directory cache buffer before reusing it

SET MAXIMUM DIRECTORY CACHE BUFFERS = 500	500	20 to 4000

Sets the maximum number of directory cache buffers that can be allocated

SET MINIMUM DIRECTORY CACHE BUFFERS = 20	20	10 to 2000

Sets the minimum number of directory cache buffers that can be allocated

Table 19.4
Commands that Control the NetWare 386 File System

Command	Default Setting	Allowed Range
SET IMMEDIATE PURGE OF DELETED FILES = OFF	OFF	OFF or ON

Determines whether deleted files are immediately purged

Table 19.4—continued

Command	Default Setting	Allowed Range
SET MAXIMUM SUBDIRECTORY TREE DEPTH = 25	25	10 to 100

Sets the maximum depth of subdirectories allowed (must be set in STARTUP.NCF)

Command	Default Setting	Allowed Range
SET VOLUME LOW WARN ALL USERS = ON	ON	ON or OFF

Determines whether all users receive a "volume low on available space" warning

Command	Default Setting	Allowed Range
SET VOLUME LOW WARNING RESET THRESHOLD = 256	256	0 to 100000 blocks

Sets the level above the low volume warning level to which the volume's free disk space must rise before users are eligible to receive another warning when the low volume threshold is again reached

Command	Default Setting	Allowed Range
SET VOLUME LOW WARNING THRESHOLD = 256	256	0 to 100000 blocks

Sets the number of available blocks level at which users will receive a low disk space warning

Command	Default Setting	Allowed Range
SET TURBO FAT RE-USE WAIT TIME = 5 minutes 29.6 seconds	5 min 29.6 sec	.3 sec to 1 hr 5 min 29.6 sec

Sets the minimum time before reusing a closed Turbo FAT

Command	Default Setting	Allowed Range
SET MINIMUM FILE DELETE WAIT TIME = 5 minutes 29.6 seconds	5 min. 29.6 sec	0 sec to 7 days

Sets the minimum wait time after a file is deleted before it is purged

Command	Default Setting	Allowed Range
SET FILE DELETE WAIT TIME = 5 minutes 29.6 seconds	5 min 29.6 sec	0 sec to 7 days

Sets the standard time to wait after a file is deleted before it is purged

Table 19.5
Commands that Control the NetWare Communications

Command	Default Setting	Allowed Range
SET CONSOLE DISPLAY WATCHDOG LOGOUTS = OFF	OFF	OFF or ON

Determines whether the console shows a status message when a station is cleared for an inactive connection

Command	Default Setting	Allowed Range
SET MAXIMUM PHYSICAL RECORD RECEIVE PACKET SIZE = 1130	1130	618 to 4202

Sets the largest packet size that can be received on any of the server's network adapters (must be set in STARTUP.NCF)

Command	Default Setting	Allowed Range
SET NEW PACKET RECEIVE BUFFER WAIT TIME = 0.1	.1 sec	.1 to 20 sec

Sets the minimum time to wait before allocating a new packet receive buffer

Command	Default Setting	Allowed Range
SET MAXIMUM PACKET RECEIVE BUFFERS = 100	100	50 to 2000

Sets the maximum number of packet receive buffers that can be allocated

Command	Default Setting	Allowed Range
SET MINIMUM PACKET RECEIVE BUFFERS = 10	10	10 to 1000

Sets the minimum number of packet receive buffers that can be allocated

Table 19.6
Commands that Control Memory Usage

Command	Default Setting	Allowed Range
SET CACHE BUFFER SIZE = 4096	4096 bytes	4096 to 16384 bytes
Sets the size of the cache buffer (must be set in STARTUP.NCF)		
SET MAXIMUM DYNAMIC MEMORY = 1048576	1048576 bytes	50000 to 16777216 bytes
Sets the maximum amount of memory that can be used as dynamic memory		

Table 19.7
Commands that Control Locks

Command	Default Setting	Allowed Range
SET MAXIMUM RECORD LOCKS PER CONNECTION = 500	500	10 to 10000
Sets the maximum number of record locks and semaphores allowed per connection		
SET MAXIMUM FILE LOCKS PER CONNECTION = 250	250	10 to 1000
Sets the maximum number of open files and file locks per connection		
SET MAXIMUM RECORD LOCKS = 2000	20000	100 to 200000
Sets the maximum record locks allowed on the server		
SET MAXIMUM FILE LOCKS = 10000	10000	100 to 100000
Sets the maximum file locks allowed on the server		

Table 19.8
Commands that Control the Transaction Tracking System (TTS)

Command	Default Setting	Allowed Range
SET AUTO TTS BACKOUT FLAG = ON	ON	ON or OFF

Determines whether or not TTS backouts are done automatically upon restarting the server (must be set in STARTUP.NCF)

Command	Default Setting	Allowed Range
SET TTS ABORT DUMP FLAG = OFF	OFF	OFF or ON

Determines whether or not data from aborted transactions is written to a log file

Command	Default Setting	Allowed Range
SET MAXIMUM TRANSACTIONS = 10000	10000	100 to 10000

Sets the maximum number of concurrent transactions for the server

Command	Default Setting	Allowed Range
SET TTS UNWRITTEN CACHE WAIT TIME = 1 minute 5.9 seconds	1 min 5.9 sec	11 sec to 10 min 59.1 sec

Sets the maximum time a cache buffer write to disk can be delayed by a TTS hold

Command	Default Setting	Allowed Range
SET TTS BACKOUT FILE TRUNCATION WAIT TIME = 59 minutes 19.2 seconds	59 min 19.2 sec	1 min 5.9 sec to 1 day 2 hrs 21 min 51.3 sec

Sets the minimum time to wait before freeing blocks allocated to the TTS backout file but not used

Table 19.9
Command To Control Server Disks

Command	Default Setting	Allowed Range
SET DISK READ AFTER WRITE VERIFY = ON	ON	ON or OFF
Determines whether or not the Hot Fix read after write verify is active		

Table 19.10
Miscellaneous Set Commands

Command	Default Setting	Allowed Range
SET MAXIMUM OUTSTANDING NCP SEARCHES = 51	51	10 to 1000
Sets the number of concurrent NCP (NetWare Core Protocol) searches per connection		
SET ALLOW UNENCRYPTED PASSWORDS = OFF	OFF	ON or OFF
Determines whether or not unencrypted passwords can be used (the NetWare 2.1x workstation shell can only send unencrypted passwords)		
SET NEW SERVICE PROCESS WAIT TIME = 2.2	2.2 sec	.3 to 20 sec
Sets the minimum time to wait before creating additional service processes		
SET MAXIMUM SERVICE PROCESSES = 20	20	5 to 40
Sets the maximum number of service processes		

To learn how to use SET, follow the procedure of looking up and changing a current file server configuration setting. For this example, you change the setting that controls how much memory the server can devote to keeping its directory (the list of files that it stores) in memory. When most or all of the directory is in memory, the time necessary to retrieve and work with a file is decreased because the server does not have to read its hard disk to find the file. Your first step is to use SET from the NetWare 386 console to look up the current setting. Type *set* and press Enter from the server console. Select option 2, Directory Caching, from the list of options that is displayed. Select the option to view the advanced configuration parameters. A list of parameter settings is displayed. Look for one with the heading Maximum Directory Cache Buffer. Information similar to the following is displayed:

```
Maximum Directory Cache Buffers: 500
    Limits: 20 to 4000
    Description: maximum number of directory cache buffers that
        can be allocated by the system.
```

Notice that the current cache buffer setting is 500 buffers (the default size for a cache buffer for NetWare 386 is 4096 bytes, although you can use the SET command to change it). This means that up to 500 memory cache buffers (2M of memory if the cache buffer size is 4096 bytes) can be used by the server to store the directory list.

You can use the information in the SET display to build a SET command to change the parameter you are viewing. For example, if you want to increase the number of buffers that can be used for directory caching, you use the following SET command:

SET MAXIMUM DIRECTORY CACHE BUFFERS = 750

Notice that the parameter setting's name (MAXIMUM DIRECTORY CACHE BUFFERS) is preceded by the command SET and followed by an equal sign and the new setting you want to use (= 750). You can use this method to build SET commands for any of the parameter settings listed when you use SET without parameters.

In actual practice, you probably do not need to increase the Maximum Directory Cache Buffers setting unless you have an unusually large number of files stored on the server. First, use NetWare 386's MONITOR NLM to view the actual memory used by the directory caching before deciding to increase the maximum setting (you will learn how to use the MONITOR NLM later in this chapter).

SET is the primary console command used to control NetWare 386's server configuration. It can be used to change a wide variety of server parameters.

SET TIME (NetWare 286 and 386)

SET TIME is used to update the server's date and time settings. It resets the server's software clock but does not change the time stored in the server's hardware setup. If the server PC's hardware time is wrong, you can set the time the server keeps by using SET TIME. If you reboot the server and don't correct the server PC's hardware time, you have to use SET TIME again to set the time because the server's time is taken from the server PC's hardware time setting at boot up.

To change the date and/or time, type *set time* followed by the date and/or time, as shown in the following example:

SET TIME 01/13/91 12:35:00

If you need to set only the time, you can omit the date. Conversely, if you need to set only the date, you can omit the time. The time information can be listed in either 12-hour increments with the designation a.m. or p.m. (1:35:00 p.m.) or in 24-hour increments (13:35:00). The date can be listed in one of three formats: 01/13/91; January 13, 1991; or 13 January 1991.

RESET ROUTER (NetWare 286 and 386)

Every NetWare server maintains a router table that tracks the availability of other servers and bridges. This table is updated every two minutes. If servers or bridges go down unexpectedly (without the benefit of the DOWN command), the remaining servers' router tables are inaccurate until they update themselves. You can use the RESET ROUTER command to initiate manually the update process on a particular server. To update the router table on a server, type *reset router* and press Enter.

DISABLE TTS (NetWare 386)

The DISABLE TTS command is used to deactivate NetWare 386's Transaction Tracking System. TTS can be used by database application developers to protect their data files from corruption resulting from an incomplete update transaction. In the course of developing an application that uses TTS, you may have to deactivate TTS for testing purposes. To deactivate TTS, type *disable tts* and press Enter.

Under normal circumstances, you should leave TTS enabled because NetWare 386 uses it to protect its own security files from corruption.

ENABLE TTS (NetWare 386)

ENABLE TTS reverses the effect of DISABLE TTS. It can be used to reactivate TTS if you have previously used DISABLE TTS to deactivate it. Type *enable tts* and press Enter to reenable transaction tracking.

ADD NAME SPACE (NetWare 386)

The ADD NAME SPACE console command is used to permit non-DOS files to be stored on a server volume. Before you can use ADD NAME SPACE, you must load the matching Name Space NetWare Loadable Module.

To use ADD NAME SPACE to enable the storage of Macintosh files on the server volume called VOL1, type

ADD NAME SPACE MAC to volume VOL1

and press Enter. (You can omit *to volume* if you want.) Using the preceding command presumes that you already have loaded the MAC.NAM NLM.

If you plan to store non-DOS files on a particular volume, you should add the console commands that load the file protocol's NLM and add its name space to your server's AUTOEXEC.NCF file. You will learn how to do that in the final section of this chapter.

BIND and UNBIND (NetWare 386)

If you have installed NetWare 386 or read the chapter about how to install it, you already are familiar with the BIND command. The BIND command is used to match a communication protocol to each of your server's network adapters. Because NetWare 386 can support a variety of communication protocols (unlike NetWare 286, which only supports NetWare's native IPX protocol), you need to specify which protocol each network adapter uses. When you use BIND, you specify the protocol name followed by the name of the LAN driver that matches your network adapter. For example, to assign the IPX protocol to a Token Ring board, type

BIND IPX TO TOKEN

and press Enter. (Substitute the protocol you are actually using for IPX, and the network adapter driver you are actually using for TOKEN.) Before you can use BIND, you must have loaded the appropriate LAN driver NLM for the network adapter you are working with.

In most cases, you place a BIND command in your server's AUTOEXEC.NCF file so that the protocol match happens when you start your server.

The UNBIND command is used to unlink a communication protocol from a network adapter so that the adapter is free to be matched to another protocol. To unlink the IPX protocol from a Token Ring adapter, you type

UNBIND IPX FROM TOKEN

and press Enter.

You have now learned how to use NetWare's console commands. If you are using NetWare 386, you should read the next section and learn about using NetWare Loadable Modules. If you are using only NetWare 286, you can skip the following section and proceed to the section called "Working with NetWare 286 VAPs".

Working with NetWare 386 NetWare Loadable Modules

NetWare 386 permits you to run NetWare Loadable Modules (NLMs). NLMs are usually hardware drivers or multipurpose utilities that use menus. If you installed NetWare 386, you are already familiar with the INSTALL NLM that is used to install and configure the server.

Most of the console commands you have studied so far are single-purpose programs that perform one function and then stop running. NLMs are more sophisticated programs that continue running until you stop them. They may have extensive interactive menu interfaces.

NetWare comes with a number of NLMs. Each falls into one of three categories. An NLM can be a driver that works in conjunction with a particular hardware device (such as a hard disk, network adapter, or uninterruptible power supply), a utility (usually a menu-driven program that enables you to configure, control, or monitor the server in some way), or a name space that allows you to store and work with non-DOS files on your server volumes.

You may have NLMs from third parties that perform different tasks from those just described. In certain situations, running a program from the server instead of a workstation has compelling advantages. Programs that run on a NetWare 386 server use the full capabilities of the 80386 processor, not the 8086 mode used by DOS or the 80286 mode used by OS/2. An emerging category of software that benefits from running on the server is the database server (sometimes called a database "engine"). A database server receives requests for data from workstations, and then does the required processing and file retrieval within the server itself, cutting down on the network communications necessary to satisfy the request.

Loading an NLM

The LOAD console command is used to start an NLM. Type *load* followed by the name of the NLM you want to activate. For example, to load the INSTALL NLM, type *load install* and press Enter. By default, LOAD looks to the SYS:SYSTEM directory to locate the NLM file. You can tell LOAD to look elsewhere to find the file by preceding the NLM name by its location. Any legal NetWare or DOS directory name on the server PC can be used. For example, to load INSTALL from a directory called NET386 on the server PC's DOS partition, type *load c:\net386\install* and press Enter. Similarly, to load INSTALL from a server directory called MODULES on a volume called VOL1, type *load vol1:modules\install* and press Enter. When you load an NLM, it is placed in the memory of your server and continues to run until you unload it.

Later in this section, you will learn about a command called SEARCH that lets you establish a list of locations where LOAD searches for NLM files.

Unloading an NLM

You can stop an NLM and remove it from memory by using the UNLOAD command. To unload an NLM you have previously loaded, type *unload* followed by the name of the NLM you want to remove. For example, to stop the INSTALL NLM and remove it from memory, type *unload install*.

Some NLMs unload themselves automatically. For example, the INSTALL NLM module unloads itself when you select the Exit option from its main menu.

Now that you know the basics of starting and stopping an NLM, you are ready to learn how to use one that you may use frequently.

Using the MONITOR NLM

The MONITOR NLM is used to monitor your server's performance and to view the status of many of its important elements. You can use MONITOR to work with the connections of your server's users or to see the status of your server's disks and network adapters. MONITOR also lists the NLMs that are loaded and displays their memory usage. You also can use MONITOR to view the status of any file stored on a server volume, to list the processes and tasks that are using server memory, and to check on how much memory each is using.

MONITOR can be used to lock and password-protect the server keyboard to prevent unauthorized users from entering console commands or loading NLMs.

Some of the information MONITOR displays, such as its statistics on memory usage, presumes an advanced understanding of NetWare 386. You do not have to understand all of the information shown by MONITOR to use it effectively.

Starting MONITOR

To start MONITOR, type *load monitor* and press Enter from the server console. The screen shown in figure 19.3 is displayed. This screen is in two sections. The bottom half offers a number of menu options you can select; the top half displays information about the current status of the server.

The first information item displayed at the top of the screen, File Server Up Time, shows the total elapsed time since the server was started. The number next to the item labeled Utilization is the percentage of the server's CPU utilization required to handle server requests. This number is a gauge of how busy the file server is from a processing standpoint. The Original Cache Buffer count shows the amount of memory devoted to the cache buffer pool when the server was first started. When a server is booted, all unused memory is made available for caching. As other

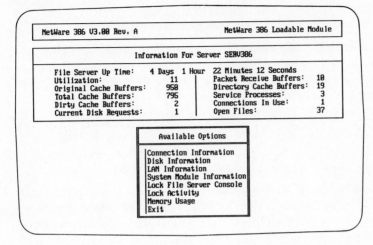

Fig. 19.3.
Starting MONITOR.

requirements for memory arise, memory is taken from the cache buffer pool. The Total Cache Buffers count shows the current number of available cache buffers. The Dirty Cache Buffers count shows the number of cache buffers that contain file information that has been changed and must be written to disk.

Current Disk Requests shows the number of disk read and write requests that are waiting to be handled. This number is a gauge of the server's disk I/O backlog. The Packet Receive Buffers count shows the number of memory buffers that are available to receive incoming packets from workstations. Similarly, the Directory Cache Buffers count shows the number of buffers devoted to storing the server's file listing in memory.

Service Processes shows the number of NetWare service processes that have been allocated. A service process manages a particular task being performed on a server by a workstation, such as copying a server-based file or executing a server-based program file. The number of service processes allocated is a good gauge of how busy the server is.

The Connections In Use count shows the number of logins or attachments to the server. The Open Files count tells how many files are currently open on the server.

The bottom half of the display is MONITOR's main menu. Its options are described in the following sections.

Working with Server Connections

When you select the Connection Information option from MONITOR's main menu, a list of the current server connections is displayed. The connection number and login name for each connection are shown. From this list you can do one of two things: select a connection for viewing information or remove a connection from the server.

To remove a connection, highlight it and press the Del key, or mark multiple connections with the F5 key and press Del. After confirming that you want to clear the selected connections, they are removed.

To view more information about a connection, highlight it and press Enter. The information screen shown in figure 19.4 is displayed. Like MONITOR's opening screen, the connection information screen is shown in two halves. The upper half displays statistics about the selected connection. The Connection Time shows how long the user has been logged into or attached to the server. The Network Address shows the physical network number and node address of the network adapter in the user's workstation, as well as the socket number assigned to the connection. Socket numbers are used to accommodate operating systems, such as OS/2, that enable a workstation to have multiple connections from the same physical network and node address.

Fig. 19.4.

Getting information about a connection.

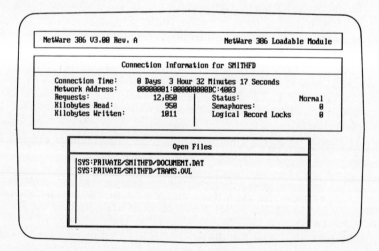

Requests shows the number of requests made by the connection to the server. Kilobytes Read and Kilobytes Written show the number of kilobytes read and written to the server, respectively. The Status setting displays one of three messages: Normal (meaning the connection is logged in and operating normally), Waiting (the connection is waiting for a file to be unlocked so it can lock the file), or Not-Logged-In (the workstation has attached to the server with the NetWare workstation shell, but the user has not logged in).

The Semaphores count shows the number of semaphores the connection has in use. Certain programs use semaphores to control access to a certain resource, such as a shared data file or program. Logical record locks are similar. The Logical Record Lock setting shows the number of logical record locks in use.

The bottom half of the Connection Information screen lists the files that the workstation currently has open. You can view the record locks in use in a particular file by highlighting the file and pressing Enter. A window opens and, under the headings Start and End, the beginning and ending locations (or offsets) of the locked record are displayed. Under the heading Record Lock Status, the record lock type and whether or not the file is logged is displayed. Four record locks types exist: Locked Exclusive (meaning the record is locked so that no other user can read or write to it), Locked Shareable (the record can be read by other stations but not written to), Locked (the record has been logged for a lock pending the capability to lock other files or records) and TTS Holding Lock (the record lock has been released by the application but the Transaction Tracking System is holding it until the transaction is completely written).

The Record Lock Status column also can show whether or not the record is logged for future locks. Some applications require that multiple records be locked before a transaction can occur. In such cases, a lock is logged or reserved first while other records are checked. After all records are logged and ready to lock, the locks are made.

To leave the Record Lock Status screen, press Esc. To leave the Connection Information Screen, press Esc, and you are returned to MONITOR's main menu.

Viewing Disk Information

To view information about the server's disks, select Disk Information from MONITOR's main menu. A list of the currently active disks is displayed. Select the one to view, and a two-part display screen is shown.

The top part of the screen shows 10 items of information about the selected disk. The Driver setting shows the name of the NLM driver that controls the disk. Disk Size shows the size of the selected disk in megabytes. Partitions shows the number of partitions that exist on the disk (including NetWare and non-NetWare partitions).

The Mirror Status setting shows whether or not the drive is mirrored or duplexed so that all information written to it is duplicated on another disk. This setting shows Mirrored, Not Mirrored, or Remirroring (remirroring indicates that a mirrored pair is in the process of being created). For more information about disk mirroring and duplexing, see Chapter 4.

Hot Fix Status shows the status of NetWare's Hot Fix feature. Hot Fix checks each disk block as it is written to; if the information written to a block of the disk cannot be read, then the information is rewritten to a disk block in the Hot Fix redirection area. The Hot Fix Status setting should be Normal. If it shows Not-hot-fixed instead, the disk should be checked for excessive bad blocks or other failure. For more information about NetWare's Hot Fix feature, see Chapter 4.

The remaining five items show information about how the disk blocks are allocated. The Partition Blocks setting shows the total number of blocks in the NetWare 386 partition on the disk. Data Blocks shows the number of blocks available for general use by server users. Redirection Blocks shows the number of blocks reserved for use by the Hot Fix feature. This pool of blocks is used to replace blocks that fail the read-after-write test previously discussed. The Redirected Blocks count shows the number of blocks already used from the pool of redirection blocks. Reserved Blocks lists the number of blocks used to store operating system information, such as the redirection table.

The bottom half of the disk information screen lists the volume segments on the selected disk. The number of megabytes for each segment and the name of the volume to which the segment belongs are shown.

To leave the disk information screen, press Esc. You are returned to the list of disk drivers. Press Esc again to return to MONITOR's main menu.

Viewing LAN Information

The LAN Information option enables you to view the network address and protocol information for each of the network adapters that are active in your server. You also can view a number of statistics about the usage of the selected network adapter, including the number of data packets sent and received.

Highlight LAN Information from MONITOR's main menu and press Enter. A list of the loaded LAN driver NLMs that are controlling network adapters is displayed. Select the one that matches the card you want to work with. A window is displayed showing a list of statistics about the selected network adapter. You can scroll through this window using the up and down arrows or the PgUp and PgDn keys.

Of the most interest in this list of information are the Total Packets Sent and Total Packets Received counts. These counts show the outgoing and incoming number of packets for the network adapter and are an accurate gauge of the activity of that particular network. Most of the other listed statistics are counts of error conditions (which should be very low on a healthy network). One statistic to watch closely is the No ECB Available Count. This count is the number of times that a data packet was received by the network adapter but for which the server did not have an available receive buffer. If this number is high, you can use the SET command to increase the maximum number of receive buffers.

To leave the LAN driver information screen, press Esc. You are returned to the list of loaded LAN drivers. Press Esc again to return to the MONITOR main menu.

Viewing the List of Loaded NLMs

Selecting the System Module Information option displays a list of the currently loaded NLMs. If you highlight one of the listed NLMs and press Enter, that module's memory size, the amount of server short-term memory it is using at the moment, and the name of the NLM file is displayed.

Press Esc to leave this window and return to the list of NLMs; press Esc again to return to MONITOR's main menu.

Locking and Unlocking the Server Console Keyboard

Given the power of NLMs and the significant amount of server reconfiguration that can be performed from the server console, you may want to password protect access to the server keyboard. Select the Lock File Server Console option from MONITOR's main menu to protect access to the server keyboard. You are prompted to enter a password that must be entered to unlock the keyboard. Type the password carefully and press Enter; you are not given an opportunity to retype or confirm it.

After you have locked the server console, you can use the server supervisor's password or the password you typed to unlock the keyboard.

If the server screen is displaying patterns instead of the MONITOR password lock screen, press any key and then press Enter to clear any keystrokes entered by others. Type the correct password and press Enter. You are returned to the MONITOR main menu.

Viewing File Status Information

You can use MONITOR to view the status of any file stored on a server volume. Select Lock Activity from MONITOR's main menu. A list of the server's volumes is displayed. Highlight the volume that stores the file you want to work with and press Enter. A list of directories on that volume is displayed. Select the one that stores your file. A list of that directory's subdirectories and files is displayed. Continue selecting subdirectories if necessary to get to the one storing your file, and then select the file itself.

After your file is selected, two side-by-side windows are displayed, each with information about the file. The left window displays seven items of information about the file's usage. Use Count shows the number of users or connections that have the file open or logged. Open Count shows the number of connections that have the file open. Open For Read displays the number of connections that have opened the file in read-only mode. Open For Write shows the number of connections that have the file open for writing. Deny Read displays the number of connections that have opened the file in a mode that denies other connections the capability to read the file. Deny Write shows the number of connections that have opened the file in a way that denies other connections the capability to write to the file.

The right window lists the connections that have the file open and whether or not they have the file locked. The column headed Conn shows each connection number that has the file in use. The Lock Status column shows whether or not the file is locked. Three lock types exist: Exclusive (meaning the file is locked so that no other user can read or write to it), Shareable (meaning other users can read the file), and TTS Holding Lock (the record lock has been released by the application but the Transaction Tracking System holds the record lock until the transaction is completely written).

The Lock Status column also can show whether or not the file is logged for future locks. Some applications require that multiple files be locked before a transaction can occur. In such cases, a lock is logged or reserved first while the other files that need to be locked are being logged.

After viewing the status of a particular file, press Esc to return to the file listing window. Press Esc again to return to MONITOR's main menu.

Viewing Memory Usage Information

One of MONITOR's most useful options is Memory Usage, which enables you to track in precise detail how the server memory is being used. When you select Memory Usage, a two-part memory screen similar to the one shown in figure 19.5 is displayed.

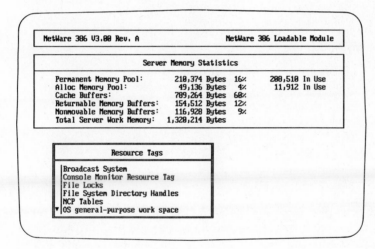

Fig. 19.5.
The Memory Usage screen.

The top part of the screen lists six server memory usage statistics. For each item, the number of bytes allocated and their percentage of the whole are shown. Permanent Memory Pool shows memory that is permanently allocated for use in directory caching or for packet receive buffers. The Alloc Memory Pool setting shows the memory available for short-term usage by NLMs. Memory is drawn from the cache buffer pool to be placed in the Alloc Memory Pool and is not returned. Cache Buffers displays the memory available for file caching. This is the memory pool from which all other pools draw when a need arises. If the Cache Buffer pool consistently falls to a low percentage of the whole, you should add more memory to the server. Returnable Memory Buffers and Nonmovable Memory Buffers are memory pools that are used temporarily by certain server tasks and then returned to the cache buffer pool. The Total Server Work Memory number shows the entire amount of working memory in the server. The Total Server Work Memory is not the same as the total amount of memory installed in the server because the amount of memory required to load the SERVER file into memory is not included (SERVER is the NetWare 386 operating system file—see Chapter 7 for details about how it is loaded).

The bottom half of the Memory Usage screen displays resource tags. Resource tags are various operating system functions, such as record locking, print job queuing, and router and server tracking, that use memory in proportion to how heavily that function is being used. When you select a particular resource tag from the list, several items of information about it are displayed. Next to Module, you are shown whether the resource tag is part of the operating system or a particular NLM. Resource shows which memory pool the resource tag is drawing from, and In Use shows the amount of memory being used.

To return to the list of resource tags, press Esc. Press Esc again to return to MONITOR's main menu.

To leave MONITOR altogether, select Exit from its main menu. The MONITOR NLM is unloaded from memory and you are returned to the colon prompt.

NLMs Discussed in Other Chapters

Because a number of NLMs are used when installing and booting NetWare 386, they have been discussed in Chapter 7, "Installing NetWare 386." The INSTALL NLM is used to install NetWare 386 and to add new disks or to modify its STARTUP.NCF and AUTOEXEC.NCF files. Loading LAN and disk driver NLMs as well as loading non-DOS file protocols are also discussed in Chapter 7.

PSERVER is an NLM used to control shared network printers. PSERVER is discussed in Chapter 14, "Implementing Shared Printing."

Managing NLMs

Several NetWare 386 console commands are available to enable you to manage the way NLMs are used. One command displays a list of currently loaded NLMs. Two other commands restrict the directories from which NLMs can be loaded, and a fourth enables you to establish a search path that the LOAD command can use to find the NLM file you want to load.

MODULES

The MODULES console command lists the NLMs that are currently active on the server. To display this list, type *monitor* and press Enter. Each NLM's file name and description are shown.

SEARCH

SEARCH can be used to tell the LOAD command where to look for NLM files. By default, LOAD searches the SYS:SYSTEM directory for an NLM file and reports that it is unable to find the file if your NLM is not stored in SYS:SYSTEM.

To view your current list of searched directories, type *search* and press Enter. A message similar to the following is displayed:

```
Search 1: [Server Path] SYS:SYSTEM\
```

To add a search area, use the ADD parameter. For example, to add the directory called \NET386, on the server PC's C drive, type

```
SEARCH ADD C:\NET386
```

and press Enter. C:\NET386 is added as the second NLM search path. You can control the order in which the areas are searched by specifying a number when you add a search area. Suppose that you already have two search areas (SYS:SYSTEM and C:\NET386), and you want to add SYS:NLM to the list and make SYS.NLM the first area searched. From the server console, type

```
SEARCH ADD 1 SYS:NLM
```

and press Enter. SYS:NLM becomes the first area searched, and SYS:SYSTEM and C:\NET386 the second and third, respectively.

You can remove a search area using the DEL parameter. To remove a search path, you must know its number. If you want to remove C:\NET386 from the search list, first type *search* to see the following list:

```
Search 1: [Server Path] SYS:NLM\
Search 2: [Server Path] SYS:SYSTEM\
Search 3: [DOS Path] C:\NET386\
```

which confirms that C:\NET386 is search area 3. You then remove it from the list by typing

```
SEARCH DEL 3
```

and pressing Enter. Any DOS drive and directory on the server PC, as well as any directory on a server volume, can be inserted in the search list. For security reasons, you may want to inhibit the capability to load NLMs from the server's DOS drives. You can do that by using the command discussed next.

SECURE CONSOLE

The capability to load NLM files stored on the server PC's DOS drives or any directory on a server volume opens up some disturbing security risks. A user who has access to the server console can load an NLM of his own design from the server PC's drive A or from his personal directory on a server volume. This NLM can crash the server or damage its files. NLMs automatically have supervisory access to all the server's resources, so you must exercise caution to prevent unauthorized NLMs from running on your server.

The SECURE CONSOLE command prevents NLMs from being loaded from a DOS drive on the server PC or from any server directory besides SYS:SYSTEM. SECURE CONSOLE also prevents users from changing the server time using FCONSOLE, and requires all time changes to be made from the server console instead.

SECURE CONSOLE prevents the loading of NLMs from the server PC's DOS drives by removing the DOS COMMAND.COM file from the server's memory (which happens to result in a small memory savings for the server). You cannot use the EXIT command to return to the DOS prompt after you down the server. You must reboot instead. You can provide an extra measure of security to your server PC by giving it a power-up password if the server PC supports that feature. This password prevents someone from rebooting your server and then using a DOS-based utility to damage the server's files.

To activate these measures, type *secure console* and press Enter. You may want to add the SECURE CONSOLE command to your AUTOEXEC.NCF files so that the command is executed when the server starts.

REMOVE DOS

REMOVE DOS performs some of the same functions as SECURE CONSOLE. After typing *remove dos* and pressing Enter, you can no longer load NLMs from the server PC's DOS drives. You also cannot use the EXIT command to return to the server PC's DOS prompt after downing the server.

NetWare 286 VAPs— A Special Situation

Netware 286 does not support the use of NLMs but does provide a forerunner of the NLM called a Value Added Process, or VAP. NetWare 286 comes with two VAPs: the BSERVER VAP, which supports the Btrieve file manager, and LOCK, which enables you to lock the server console keyboard. A number of third-party VAPs that perform various functions are available.

VAPs usually are provided with installation instructions. To activate a VAP, copy the VAP file into the SYS:SYSTEM directory of a server. The VAP file must end with the extension VAP. When the server is started, you see the following prompt:

```
Value Added Processes have been defined. Do you want to load them?
```

If you press Y for yes, the VAP is loaded.

If you want to eliminate the requirement to respond to the prompt described above every time the server is booted, you can specify that all VAPs be loaded automatically. To make them load automatically, create a text file in the SYS:SYSTEM directory called SERVER.CFG. Place the following line in this file:

VAP WAIT 10

where 10 specifies that the server will wait 10 seconds after booting to load the VAP (you can replace 10 with any number from 10 to 360). During the specified waiting period, the following prompt appears:

```
To Abort Loading of VAPs, Press Any Key
Time Left to Abort: 10 seconds
```

The display counts down the number of seconds. A user can interrupt the loading of VAPs by pressing a key at the server keyboard while this prompt is displayed.

Running Console Commands Automatically

You now have learned how to use NetWare's extensive array of console commands and NLMs. You have the option of running console commands or loading NLMs automatically by placing commands to start them in your server's AUTOEXEC file. A server's AUTOEXEC file performs exactly the same function as the AUTOEXEC.BAT file on a DOS PC. Each runs a series of commands automatically when the PC starts.

NetWare's server AUTOEXEC file is stored in the SYS:SYSTEM directory of the server. The AUTOEXEC file for NetWare 286 is named AUTOEXEC.SYS, and the AUTOEXEC file for NetWare 386 is AUTOEXEC.NCF. BOTH files are in ASCII format and can be edited with any word processor or text editor that can save files in ASCII format.

If you have learned how to install NetWare 386, you are already familiar with creating and editing its AUTOEXEC.NCF file. Any of the NetWare 386 console commands you learned about in this chapter can be executed automatically by adding them as command statements to your AUTOEXEC.NCF file. You can edit AUTOEXEC.NCF with the INSTALL NLM (see chapter 7).

NetWare 286's AUTOEXEC.SYS file can be created and edited by using SYSCON as long as you are logged in with supervisory rights. Start SYSCON by typing *syscon* followed by pressing Enter. Select Supervisor Options from SYSCON's main menu. From the resulting Supervisor Options menu, select Edit System AUTOEXEC File. An editing screen is displayed, and you can type your AUTOEXEC.SYS file one line at a time. When you are finished, press Esc to save the file. Press Esc again to leave the Supervisor Options menu and return to SYSCON's main menu. Press Esc again to leave SYSCON.

One precaution must be exercised when you create an AUTOEXEC.SYS file for a NetWare 286 server. When a NetWare 286 server has no AUTOEXEC.SYS file, it automatically assigns printer numbers to queues with names such as PRINTQ—0, PRINTQ—1, and so on. But after an AUTOEXEC.SYS file exists, these assignments are no longer automatically made. You must put the appropriate console command in the AUTOEXEC.SYS file to create these assignments.

An additional option exists for NetWare 286 servers. As mentioned in the preceding section, you can create a text file called SERVER.CFG and place it in the SYS:SYSTEM directory. The SERVER.CFG file enables you to load server VAPs automatically, specify certain operating parameters for the Transaction Tracking System, and configure your server to monitor the status of the Uninterruptible Power Supply (UPS) it is connected to. Refer to your NetWare 286 documentation and UPS instructions for complete details.

Special Server-Management Situations

Several console commands are available to handle special server configuration situations. NetWare 386 and NetWare 286 have console commands that enable you to implement *UPS monitoring*. You may have connected your server to an uninterruptible power supply that can signal the server in the event of a power failure. When the server receives this signal, you can specify that the server shut itself down after a certain time interval. Refer to your UPS documentation and NetWare manuals for instructions specific to your UPS type.

NetWare 386 and NetWare 286 provide a utility called VREPAIR that can be used to attempt to recover information from a damaged disk volume. With NetWare 386, VREPAIR is an NLM, but with NetWare 286, it is a utility that is run while the server is down. VREPAIR is not a substitute for a network backup plan, but can be tried in cases where disk failure is not extensive. As one network supervisor said, "VREPAIR should be tried when you have nothing else to lose." Refer to your NetWare documentation for complete instructions.

Chapter Summary

In this chapter, you learned that NetWare's console commands and NLMs provide useful information about your server and enable you to control many of its operations. Most of NetWare 286's console command functions can be duplicated with workstation commands such as FCONSOLE. On the other hand, certain of NetWare 386's NLMs are not optional. A thorough knowledge of NetWare's console commands is helpful as you manage your servers on a day-to-day basis.

20

Establishing a
Network-Management
Plan

When you first activate your network, its users are likely to be enthusiastic about being able to share data and programs and use network disks and printers. If you take care to install useful software (such as an appealing electronic-mail program, network-licensed word processors, spreadsheets, databases, and graphics software, and perhaps an interesting groupware package), you are likely to experience a rising tide of enthusiasm as users discover the benefits of these new resources.

Before long, however, the novelty will fade, and users will begin to judge your network by a new standard. As users come to depend on the network to do their jobs, reliability becomes your LAN's most important asset. Is the network available when needed? Is it fast? Is an adequate amount of disk space always available? Are users notified in advance if the network is going to be down for maintenance? Are requests for new login IDs handled promptly and correctly? Can users be certain that files stored on server disks are safe? If a file is lost or accidentally deleted, does a backup copy exist?

If your company already has a computer system, such as a mainframe or a minicomputer, then a standard exists by which your network will be judged. With an effective network-management plan in place, your LAN can be at least as reliable and responsive (if not more so) as any other computer system in use at your company.

581

If your LAN is small, you may have to serve as the network designer, installer, operator, security administrator, and customer-support representative. A good plan of operation ensures that the time you invest is well spent.

If your LAN is larger and you delegate many of the network management tasks to others, a detailed plan of operation is also essential. You must analyze the tasks that need to be performed daily, weekly, and monthly and then divide them among your coworkers.

What Should a Network-Management Plan Accomplish?

A network-management plan must accomplish two things: the plan should prevent network problems where possible, and it should prepare for those problems that inevitably occur. Because no two networks are exactly alike, no two network-management plans can be the same.

In most cases, a network-management plan should address the following areas:

❏ Monitoring and controlling hard disk space usage

❏ Monitoring file-server workload and performance

❏ Adding and maintaining user login IDs and workstation information

❏ Checking and resetting network devices on a regular basis

❏ Performing regular maintenance on databases and other software stored on network servers

❏ Making regular backups of files stored on server disks

If your plan is effective in each of these areas, you avoid many typical problems and are prepared for those that cannot be avoided. Each of these areas is discussed individually in this chapter so that you can see how to integrate them into a comprehensive management plan.

Monitoring and Controlling Hard Disk Space Usage

Hard disk space is your network's primary commodity. Almost every service that your network provides uses disk space. The files for network-based programs and applications are stored on server hard disks. Print jobs that are sent to network printers are saved on server disks. If each network user has a personal directory, then server disk space is used for storing these personal files.

Imagine the inconvenience that results when a server disk suddenly fills up. A user who spent several hours working on a word processing document is unable to save it. Print jobs cannot be sent to the network printer because no disk space is available to hold them. A data-entry clerk using a network database application cannot add new records. In fact, database files may be damaged. Enough disk space may be available to update the data file but not its indexes, for example, or a partial update may be written to the file, making it unusable.

Disk space must be available on demand for legitimate uses. Monitoring disk usage as part of your network-management plan ensures that sufficient disk space is available to serve users' needs.

The first step to managing disk space is an easy one: check your available disk space daily. Two NetWare commands that make this possible, CHKVOL and VOLINFO, are discussed in Chapter 17. Briefly, CHKVOL shows the available disk space on a specific server volume. VOLINFO shows the available disk space on all volumes on a particular server. Use one of these utilities daily to check your available disk space on each server volume. You also should record the amount of available space. You may find that the space available on a particular volume is steadily declining, perhaps because that volume is used for storing a database application in which the files are gradually increasing in size. If you record daily the amount of available space, you can review past figures to note trends and use them to predict when the volume will be full.

You also should use NetWare's growth-control tools. Both NetWare 286 and 386 allow you to restrict the amount of disk space available to each user (see Chapter 10). Using this feature to set reasonable limits prevents a single user with pack-rat tendencies from using an inordinate amount of disk space.

Limiting individual disk space usage does not help in cases where the files taking up the disk space are part of a shared application, such as an electronic-mail system or a database. NetWare 386 enables you to set a limit on the amount of space that a particular directory structure can use (see Chapter 12). With this tool, you can set a growth cap on the size of a particular shared application in your network.

Even with all these controls in place, the available space on a particular disk may still fall below a safe level. What should you do then? First, determine which users or applications are the primary culprits. If you need to see how much disk space is occupied by a particular user's files, you can use SYSCON. Log into the appropriate server with supervisory access, type *syscon*, and press Enter. Select User Information from SYSCON's Available Topics menu. Select the name of a user from the list displayed and press Enter. The User Information menu appears, from which you should select Other Information. The resulting window shows the amount of disk space occupied by that user's files (see fig. 20.1).

Fig. 20.1.
Using the User
Information menu.

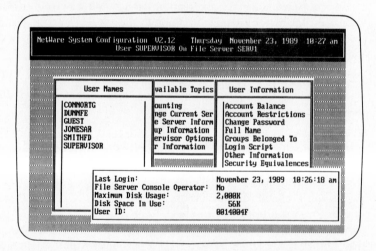

If your LAN has many users, this process is tedious. Unfortunately, no other tools are available within NetWare to make this process any quicker. The NDIR command can list all files and their sizes for a particular directory tree structure, and produces totals or subtotals of those sizes. If you find that you need to get directory size information often, a third-party disk-management product, such as XTreeNet, can analyze volume information and show you a directory-by-directory size listing.

After you identify the primary consumers of disk space in your network, you need to work with these users to determine whether their disk space use is justified. Users often accumulate more files than they actually use.

With a little cleanup, unneeded files can be deleted, freeing valuable disk space. However, you may determine that the user legitimately requires additional disk space. In this case, another disk volume may need to be added. If you monitor disk space daily, this additional capacity can be added in a planned and orderly manner instead of at the last minute or during an emergency.

Besides controlling hard disk space usage, you need to monitor two other aspects of your server disks. For NetWare 286 servers, you need to monitor the number of directory entries. In NetWare terms, a directory entry is a file, directory, or subdirectory. With NetWare 286, you established the maximum number of directory entries for a volume during installation, and you can modify this maximum by downing the server and running NETGEN. NetWare 386 allocates directory entries as required, so there is no maximum. On NetWare 286 servers, you can use VOLINFO or FCONSOLE to view the number of remaining directory entries on your server volumes. If a volume is approaching its upper limit for directory entries, you need to decrease the number of files it stores, or down the server and run NETGEN to increase the limit. (See Chapter 18 for details concerning VOLINFO and FCONSOLE, and Chapters 5 and 6 to learn about NETGEN.)

You also need to check periodically to see if any of your server disks are experiencing an unusual number of disk I/O errors. On a NetWare 286 server, FCONSOLE and the DISK console command are your best methods for viewing this information (see Chapter 18 for information about FCONSOLE, and Chapter 19 for instructions on using the DISK console command). On a NetWare 386 server, you should use the MONITOR NLM (see Chapter 19). If a disk shows a steadily increasing number of I/O errors, it's an indication that the disk is failing.

Monitoring Server Performance

Although disk space is your network's primary commodity, the performance of your LAN's servers determines how quickly and responsively that commodity is delivered to your users. You need to keep your finger on the pulse of your servers to make sure that they are performing at peak efficiency.

You should check several operating factors regularly for each of your servers. The first operating factor is the number of connections the server is supporting. As you already have learned, connections are users, programs, or devices that log in or attach to the server. A NetWare 286 server supports a maximum of 100 connections, and a NetWare 386 server supports a total of 250. If a server shows that its peak and average number of connections are dangerously near its maximum limits, you may need to consider adding a server to take part of its load.

You also need to make sure that your server is able to use memory efficiently. A NetWare server uses memory as a highly intelligent disk buffer. This buffer cannot function if there is not enough memory to provide caching for the number of files stored on the server disks. The most effective way to check this memory usage on a NetWare 286 server is to use FCONSOLE's Statistics Summary screen. This screen shows the single most telling memory statistic: the percentage of disk requests serviced from memory cache. More detailed and in-depth information is available from other FCONSOLE statistics options.

Unfortunately, NetWare 386 does not have a comparable memory statistic screen. You can get some information about memory usage from its MONITOR NLM, but there is not a statistic showing the percentage of disk requests serviced from memory cache.

Finally, for your NetWare 286 servers, you need to view the FCONSOLE Statistics Summary screen regularly to make sure that none of the factors it tracks are approaching NetWare 286's maximum settings. Skilled network supervisors use FCONSOLE's Statistics Summary screen like airline pilots use the instrument panels on their airliners—to avoid the unexpected.

Maintaining User Login IDs and Workstation Information

When you first install your network and begin to add users, you're likely to overlook recording user and workstation information that could be useful later. If your LAN will never grow beyond 10 or 15 users, you may never have a need for such information. Most successful networks have a way of growing beyond even the most optimistic expectations of their designers, however, so you should seriously consider how you will manage user and workstation information.

You first need to decide what information you will "capture" about each user when you give him or her a login name. You probably will want to get the user's first and last name, telephone number, mailing location, supervisor, and department. If your company uses an identification number, such as an employee badge number or social security number, you may want to include it also. If you have an electronic-mail system in your company, you may want to record the user's ID as well.

If your LAN has multiple servers and some employees have login names on more than one server, you also should record the servers where each particular user has a login name. You also may want to record what NetWare groups the user belongs to.

Another type of information that is important to document is the user's node address and network address (if your LAN consists of multiple physical networks). If the type of network adapter you are using requires that you set the node address with switches, no two users on the same network can have the same setting. By keeping a record of each address used, you ensure that no address is duplicated. You also may want to record the type of workstation each user has.

All this information can be stored in a database. A network-licensed database manager such as dBASE, R:BASE, or Paradox can be used for creating a user information database. Figure 20.2 shows an example of a typical record from such a database.

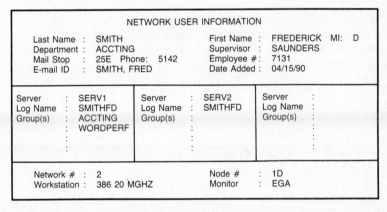

```
                    NETWORK USER INFORMATION

    Last Name  :   SMITH              First Name  :   FREDERICK   MI:   D
    Department :   ACCTING            Supervisor  :   SAUNDERS
    Mail Stop  :   25E  Phone:  5142  Employee #  :   7131
    E-mail ID  :   SMITH, FRED        Date Added  :   04/15/90

    Server     :   SERV1      Server     :   SERV2      Server     :
    Log Name   :   SMITHFD    Log Name   :   SMITHFD    Log Name   :
    Group(s)   :   ACCTING    Group(s)   :              Group(s)   :
               :   WORDPERF              :                         :
               :                         :                         :
               :                         :                         :

    Network #   :   2                  Node #    :   1D
    Workstation :   386 20 MGHZ        Monitor   :   EGA
```

Fig. 20.2.

A data-entry screen for a network-management database.

In addition to the user information database, you also may want to document other useful information. For example, if your network cable system is such that all cables to workstations come together in a communication closet, you should label each cable with enough information to identify it (such as the node and network numbers). This information is invaluable if you have to troubleshoot a network problem and need to isolate the source of the trouble by disconnecting cables inside the communication closet. If one connection is causing the problem, you can identify it and go right to the offending PC to make the appropriate repairs.

You also may find it useful to place a label on each network workstation, showing its network and node numbers. If the network adapter has to be replaced, the new one can be set to the same address settings.

The final item of network user and workstation information that you may want to add to your information arsenal is a network diagram. Ideally, this diagram should show all servers, the location and addresses of all workstations, and enough cabling information to allow you to correct any problems that may arise when a particular workstation fails and needs to be disconnected and repaired.

Maintaining user and workstation information takes diligent effort. Although gathering detailed information about a user may be tedious, you can simplify the process by using a database manager. The results are worth the effort when users need changes made to their login accounts or when problems with workstations arise.

Checking and Resetting Network Devices

Your network may consist of a variety of shared devices that require regular attention. Some types of devices may be more reliable if they are reset (restarted) on a regular basis. Others may need some sort of periodic check or maintenance.

As you know, the most common shared device on a network is a file server. File servers require little or no regular maintenance and don't have to be restarted unless something unusual happens. Even though servers normally do not need to be reset, you may want to start each day by clearing users who remain logged in from the previous day. (A user may make the mistake of remaining logged in from the previous day, an unsafe practice because anyone with access to that PC could access the user's personal storage area and delete his or her files.) Clearing all connections every morning ensures that connections are not used by unmanned PCs. If your network is used around the clock, or if no network operators come in before the majority of your users, this practice may not be feasible.

Other kinds of network devices may need more frequent attention. For example, if you have a communications device that automatically routes electronic-mail messages from one electronic-mail system to another on an unattended basis, you may want to check it hourly, or at least several times a day, to make sure that the communications device is running properly.

You also may have devices that need to be reset daily. Some communication gateways need to be reset to clear all sessions with their host systems or to clear connections left from the previous day. This task, like clearing server connections, is best performed at a regularly scheduled time very early in the day.

Certain devices may require periodic maintenance. For example, your network tape backup unit may need its read/write head cleaned regularly.

To make sure that your network devices receive the kind of attention they need, make up a precise schedule of tasks that need to be done. If you are delegating some network-management tasks to others, a schedule of tasks is a necessity. Figure 20.3 shows a typical day's schedule.

6:00 am	Clear all connections from servers Reset host gateways Check E-mail routing PCs
8:00 am	Check E-mail routing PCs Check all servers for disk free space
10:00 am	Check E-mail routing PCs Check number of users on servers Check number of users on gateways
12:00 noon	Check E-mail routing PCs
2:00 pm	Check E-mail routing PCs
4:00 pm	Check E-mail routing PCs
6:00 pm	Check E-mail routing PCs Start nightly backups

Fig. 20.3.

A daily network-management schedule.

Maintaining Network Databases and Other Software

Database applications usually need periodic maintenance to rebuild files and reclaim the space left when records are deleted (a practice called *repacking*). Indexes may have to be rebuilt as part of the same operation. Your electronic-mail system, which you can think of as a database of messages, may also require this type of periodic maintenance.

Because every database and electronic-mail system has its own way of handling the maintenance process, specific instructions cannot be given here. If you are responsible for performing this type of maintenance, your network-management plan needs to include the details. Ideally, this type of operation should be performed during off-hours so that users can have continuous access to the databases and electronic-mail system during normal work hours. If your schedule or budget does not permit such an arrangement, however, repacking must be done during regular work hours. If this is the case for your network, try to schedule the operation at the same time each day so that users expect the interruption and plan their work around it. You may want to use some of the methods described in Chapter 16 ("Creating Login Scripts") to notify users as they log in of the pending unavailability of a system on your LAN.

Other types of software maintenance also might need to be performed on a regular basis. If NetWare accounting is installed on any of your file servers, then a log file called NET$ACCT.DAT in SYS:SYSTEM is continually growing as it regularly receives information. Over time, this file grows quite large and consumes needed disk space. Periodically delete this file (after you have used it to generate needed reports and accounting information, as discussed in Chapter 17). You also may want to consider archiving the file to floppy disks or tape prior to deleting it, just in case a future need for its information arises. The NetWare accounting system recreates a new file and continues the logging process after you delete the old file.

Other applications or systems you have may generate log files of some sort. These files also should be checked and deleted periodically.

Making Regular Backups

A network user's biggest fear is a server hard disk failure. Whenever a piece of network server hardware fails, you lose access to the server while you replace the failed component. Perhaps more important, you also lose your data.

The only way to guard against the disaster of losing the files on a server disk is to make sure that another copy of these files exists elsewhere. This additional copy is called a backup. Many devices are available to assist you in making backup copies of data. The most commonly used kind of backup device for LANs is a tape backup system.

Tape backups offer several advantages. Tape reels or cartridges are relatively inexpensive and can hold great amounts of data, anywhere from 40M to 2,200M. Tapes can be overwritten, so the same tape can be used many times. Tape has some disadvantages, however. Writing to a tape is a slow process. Network supervisors report speeds of 1M to 3M copied per minute when using tape devices to make backups.

Choosing a Backup Device

The device that you use to back up your server disks has to meet several criteria. Above all, the device must be reliable, because you will depend on it to restore files in the event of a disk failure or accidental deletion of files. Network supervisors report that some tape devices are notorious for creating backup tapes that cannot be used to restore files because they do not detect flaws in the tape itself (which becomes a bigger problem when tapes are reused a number of times). To avoid this problem, purchase a tape unit that verifies that a tape is readable after it makes a backup copy.

NetWare compatibility is also important. In the preceding chapters, NetWare's special security files, trustee rights, and extended file attributes were discussed. A backup device should be designed to capture this extended information during a backup session. NetWare 286 and 386 differ in these areas in subtle ways. If your network consists of only one type of NetWare, make sure that your backup device is compatible with your version. If you have both versions, your backup device must be compatible with both.

Check to see if the device you select is capable of backing up open files. This feature is a real time-saver because you can make backups while users continue to have access to the files you are backing up. This process will be discussed in detail later in this chapter.

The speed and capacity of your backup device are also important considerations. If you have a large number of server volumes to back up, the backup device should have the speed and capacity to back them all up quickly. Your backup requirements will increase as your LAN grows in popularity and as you add more disk space to accommodate the increased demand.

Implementing a Backup Strategy

Developing a backup strategy consists of deciding what files to back up and how often to repeat the process. If your server disk space is small, you may be able to back up all server files daily. If you have too much disk space to back them all up in one day or night, you need to decide how to limit what you back up while maintaining maximum protection.

The safest strategy to adopt is to back up all files daily. If you have only one or two servers, you may be able to start a backup session as you leave for the night and have it run to completion on an unattended basis. If you have too much disk space to back up daily, you need to run frequent partial backups, interspersed with periodic full-system backups. Most tape devices are capable of determining whether a particular file has changed since you made your last backup. These devices determine if changes have been made by checking to see if the ARCHIVE attribute is on (NetWare turns on this attribute every time a file is changed) or by checking NetWare's last modification date. For complete information about attributes and file dates, see Chapter 12. If you perform one complete backup, then a series of incremental backups of files that have changed since the previous backup, you can restore all files to their current state. Figure 20.4 shows how this practice works.

Fig. 20.4.

A typical backup schedule for one server.

MONDAY	TUESDAY	WEDNESDAY	THURSDAY	FRIDAY
Full backup (all files)	Incremental backup (files changed since Monday)	Incremental backup (files changed since Tuesday)	Incremental backup (files changed since Wednesday)	Incremental backup (files changed since Thursday)

Based on the schedule in figure 20.4, if your hard disk failed on Thursday, you would install a new disk and restore the full backup performed on Monday. Next, you would restore the backup made on Tuesday to add the files that were changed from Monday to Tuesday. You then would use the backup made on Wednesday to restore the files changed from Tuesday to Wednesday. Finally, you would restore Thursday's backup to add the files changed from Wednesday to Thursday.

If you have five servers to back up and only have time each day to perform one full backup and an incremental backup, you could arrange your backup schedule as shown in figure 20.5. Based on this schedule, can you tell which tapes you would restore if SERV5's hard disk failed on Wednesday? You first would restore SERV5's backup tape from the previous Friday, followed by its incremental tapes from Monday and Tuesday.

For peace of mind, keep backup tapes as long as possible. The more iterations of your backups that are available, the more protected you are from the effects of the occasional tape that cannot be restored. Backups are required not only in case of hard disk failure, but also in case of user or software error. Suppose that a software bug or a workstation crash causes a shared data file to be partially damaged, but the problem goes unnoticed for several weeks. If you have one or two month's worth of tapes, you can restore a copy of the file made before the damage was done and use it as the basis for performing a file repair.

MONDAY	TUESDAY	WEDNESDAY	THURSDAY	FRIDAY	
Full backup SERV1 (all files)	Full backup SERV2 (all files)	Full backup SERV3 (all files)	Full backup SERV4 (all files)	Full backup SERV5 (all files)	*Fig. 20.5.* *A typical backup schedule for multiple servers.*
Incremental backup all servers (files changed since Friday)	Incremental backup all servers (files changed since Monday)	Incremental backup all servers (files changed since Tuesday)	Incremental backup all servers (files changed since Wednesday)	Incremental backup all servers (files changed since Thursday)	

Consider storing some of your tapes in a location other than the building that houses your network. If your building and your tapes were to burn or be destroyed in some other way, you would have nothing with which to rebuild your network. On one large network, tapes are moved to a remote storage facility once a week and are returned when they are ready to be reused.

Backing Up Open Files

On some 24-hour networks, certain important files are like convenience stores: they are always open. If you turn on the SHAREABLE attribute for these files, your backup device may be able to back them up even though they are in use. Users do not have to stop using the files while you back them up, so you can perform backups during regular working hours.

If you decide to back up open files, exercise caution. Even though your file can be backed up and restored successfully, the file may still be unusable because changes were being made to the file while it was being backed up. Test this method thoroughly before depending on it. A good test technique is to back up the file while it is in use, then restore it to another disk area, checking to see if it is usable.

Netware's Backup Utilities

NetWare 286 and 386 each include backup utilities that enable you to back up server files to a local hard disk or server volume. These utilities are notoriously slow, and although they may be useful in short-term situations or in cases where you need to perform small-scale backups, they should not be relied upon in your long-term backup strategy.

If you already have a backup device and don't anticipate using these utilities, you may want to skip the next section.

LARCHIVE and NARCHIVE

Netware 286 has two backup utilities. LARCHIVE (for local archive) is a utility that backs up data from file server disks to any DOS-formatted local disk (that is, a local hard disk or floppy disks). NARCHIVE (for network archive) backs up data from one file server volume to another. NARCHIVE can back up only to a volume on the same server, not to a volume on a different server.

You have two options for starting LARCHIVE and NARCHIVE. One backs up only the files in one directory or tree structure, the other backs up all files in all directories on all server volumes. You must have supervisory equivalence to back up all directories. All NetWare rights and security information are automatically backed up as well. If you do not have supervisory equivalence, LARCHIVE and NARCHIVE only back up files in directories where you have READ, OPEN, SEARCH, and MODIFY rights.

To start LARCHIVE or NARCHIVE to back up from all server directories, make any server directory your default and type:

    LARCHIVE SYSTEM

Press Enter to start LARCHIVE.

To start NARCHIVE, type

    NARCHIVE SYSTEM

Press Enter. You are prompted to select each volume that you want to back up, starting with SYS. Press Y for each volume that you want to back up, and N for each that you don't.

If you're using LARCHIVE, you then are prompted to enter the letter of the drive of the local disk to which you want to back up your files. Type the appropriate drive letter (A, B, C, and so on) and press Enter. The files are written to the current default directory of the drive you chose.

If you're using NARCHIVE, you are asked to enter the volume name and directory to which you want to back up files (such as DISK2:BACKUP).

Next, NetWare asks whether you want to print a log report of the backup session. This report is created as a text file named ARCHIVE.LOG in the backup destination directory. If you opt to print the report, you are asked to choose between a local and network printer and to specify the number of copies to print.

The following prompt appears next:

```
SELECT SPECIFIC DIRECTORIES TO BE BACKED UP? (N = BACK
UP ALL DIRECTORIES)
```

If you press N, the program scans and backs up files from all directories automatically. If you press Y, all directories are scanned and you are prompted to reply Y or N to each one. (This means you have to be standing by to answer for each directory—bring something interesting to read!)

If you opted to back up files from all directories, you are presented with the following three options:

1) BACK UP ALL QUALIFIED FILES IN EACH DIRECTORY.

2) BACK UP ONLY QUALIFIED FILES THAT HAVE BEEN MODIFIED SINCE LAST BACKUP.

3) CHOOSE SPECIFIC FILES TO BE BACKED UP.

Select option 1 to back up every file on the server, option 2 to do an incremental backup of changed files, or option 3 to enter a file include and exclude pattern (such as *.TXT or NET*.DAT).

If you opt to select particular directories to back up, you are asked this same question about every directory that you choose to back up.

After all of these questions are answered, you are prompted to strike a key to start the backup session.

With one subtle change, you can direct LARCHIVE and NARCHIVE to back up a particular directory tree structure. Simply make the top of the directory tree the default and type *larchive* or *narchive* and press Enter. You also can pass the name of the directory as a parameter, as in LARCHIVE SYS:SYSTEM, or, if SYS:SYSTEM is the default on drive G, LARCHIVE G:. You are asked the same questions as before, with one addition. Because you are not backing up the entire server, you are asked the following:

DO YOU WANT TO SAVE DIRECTORY RIGHTS AND TRUSTEE LISTS?

If you answer yes, the directory rights and trustee lists are backed up with each directory that you back up in the tree structure that LARCHIVE or NARCHIVE is working with. You also are asked the following:

DO YOU WANT TO ARCHIVE THE SYSTEM'S USER AND GROUP DEFINITIONS?

If you answer yes, the two files that NetWare 286 uses to store security information, NET$BVAL.SYS and NET$BIND.SYS in SYS:SYSTEM, are backed up.

Compared to most commercially available backup systems, LARCHIVE and NARCHIVE are cumbersome and slow. But they do work, and you can be assured that they are compatible with NetWare 286!

LRESTORE and NRESTORE

You can use the LRESTORE and NRESTORE commands to restore files backed up with LARCHIVE and NARCHIVE. To restore using one of these commands, log into the file server to which you want to restore files. Make a directory on that server your default and type *lrestore* or *nrestore*, as appropriate, then press Enter.

If you're using LRESTORE, a prompt tells you to enter the drive letter of the local disk from which you want to restore files. Type the appropriate drive letter (A, B, C, and so forth) and press Enter. The current default directory of the drive you choose must contain the files that you want to restore.

If you're using NRESTORE, you are asked to enter the volume name and directory from which you want to restore backup files (such as DISK2:BACKUP).

You also are asked whether you want to restore security information with each directory that you restore. Answer yes only if you have supervisory equivalence and you plan to restore NET$BIND.SYS and NET$BVAL.SYS to the SYS:SYSTEM directory. Restoring these files overwrites the current security information completely and changes all login names, passwords, and account restrictions to those contained in the files you are restoring.

Next, you see the following prompt:

```
SELECT SPECIFIC DIRECTORIES TO BE CONSIDERED FOR
RESTORATION? (N = CONSIDER ALL ARCHIVED DIRECTORIES).
```

If you press N, the program scans and restores files to all directories automatically. If you press Y, you are prompted to enter the names of all directories to be restored. To select a directory and all its subdirectories, simply enter that directory name, such as SYS:USERS. To select only the subdirectories in a certain directory, enter the name followed by a slash (/), such as SYS:USERS/. To select a directory and none of its subdirectories, enter

=SYS:USERS.

You see the following prompt:

```
SPECIFY FILES TO RESTORE TO EACH SELECTED DIRECTORY? (Y/N)
(N = RESTORE ALL SELECTED DIRECTORIES).
```

If you want to be asked individually whether or not to restore each file, press Y. Otherwise, press N to restore all files automatically.

After the preceding questions are answered, you are asked to press a key to start the restore session. During the session, if you attempt to restore a file that already exists, you are asked to confirm that you want to recreate this file.

NBACKUP

NBACKUP is NetWare 386's server backup utility. It is considerably more friendly to use than LARCHIVE and NARCHIVE, and you can use it to back up both NetWare 386 and NetWare 286 servers. NBACKUP can back up files to local or network disks, or to any device that appears as a DOS volume. It also works with some types of tape drives (check with your NetWare supplier for a current list).

To back up a complete server with all its security information, you must be logged into that server with supervisory equivalence. You can back up selected directories to which you have READ, OPEN, and SEARCH rights (NetWare 286), or READ and FILE SCAN rights (NetWare 386).

Log into a server that stores the NBACKUP utility, type *nbackup*, and press Enter. The opening menu displays a list of the devices that can be used with NBACKUP. If you are backing up to a local or server disk, select DOS Devices. Otherwise, choose the name of the device you are using from NBACKUP's list of choices.

The next menu that appears offers the following three choices:

Change Current Server
Backup Options
Restore Options

Use the Change Current Server to change to the server that you are going to back up. Highlight this option and press Enter. A list of the servers to which you are currently attached appears. Select the one you want to work with. To attach to an additional server, press Ins. The remaining servers on your LAN are shown. Select the one you want to attach to, and you are prompted to enter a login name and password to attach. After attaching to the server, the server list returns to the screen. Press Esc to return to the NBACKUP menu.

Backup Options

To back up data from the current server, select Backup Options from NBACKUP's menu. The menu shown in figure 20.6 appears. You first need to select a *working directory* for your backup. The working directory stores backup and error logs for the backup session. The working directory can be on any DOS volume except the one that will be removed during the backup session (such as a floppy drive).

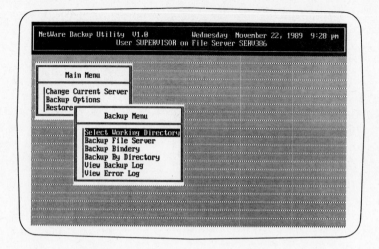

Fig. 20.6.
NBACKUP's Backup
Menu.

The files stored in the working directory during the backup session must be kept with the backed-up data itself. Without these files, you cannot perform a restore.

To choose a working directory, select Working Directory from the NBACKUP Backup Menu. A prompt tells you to enter the working directory. Type your directory choice and press Enter.

After you have chosen a working directory, you have three options for performing a backup: Backup File Server, Backup Bindery, and Backup By Directory. Choose Backup File Server when you want to back up the entire server. Use Backup Bindery when you need to back up the security files stored in SYS:SYSTEM, which store network security and user information. Select Backup By Directory when you want to back up selected directories and files.

Backing Up a Complete Server

When you choose Backup File Server, the menu shown in figure 20.7 appears. You are first prompted to enter a Session Description. You need to enter a descriptive title for the backup because this title will be used to identify the backup if you should ever need to work with the it later (to do a restore, for example). Type a session description and press Enter. Next, you are prompted to choose a whether or not to Backup Trustees. When this is set to yes, all user trustee rights to files and directories are backed up. Highlight this option and press Y to set it to yes or N to set it to no.

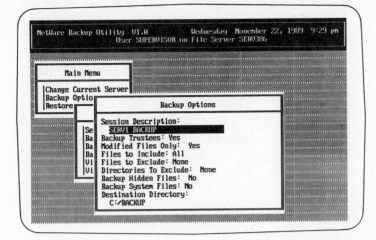

Fig. 20.7.
NBACKUP's Backup File Server window.

Next, you must choose whether to back up Modified Files Only. When this option is set to yes, the only files backed up are those with the ARCHIVE attribute turned on. When this option is set to no, all files are backed up. The ARCHIVE attribute is turned on whenever a file is changed, and it is turned off by NBACKUP and other backup programs when the file is backed up. Selecting the Modified Files Only option backs up only those files changed since the last backup.

The next two options, Files To Include and Files To Exclude, enable you to choose files to include in and exclude from the backup. Use these options to enter a file list or wild-card pattern to exclude or include files. Select the desired option and you are shown a list of the currently included or excluded file names or patterns. Press Ins to add to the list. You can remove names or patterns from the list by highlighting them and pressing Del, or by marking multiple items with F5 and pressing Del.

The Directories To Exclude option is similar to the preceding two options. It enables you to list directories that you want to exclude.

The Backup Hidden Files and Backup System Files options control whether or not files with the SYSTEM and HIDDEN attributes turned on will be included in the backup. Highlight the box next to either option and press Y to set it to yes or N to set it to no.

The final selection, Destination Directory, is where you specify the drive and directory to which NBACKUP should copy the files that it backs up. Enter the drive letter and directory that you want to back up to. After entering this information, you are prompted to specify whether or not the drive you entered is a removable volume. When you back up to removable volumes, NBACKUP prompts you to enter a new disk when the current one is full.

After entering your backup specifications, press Esc. You are prompted to confirm that you want to save your changes. Answer yes and a prompt asks you to confirm that you want to start the backup. Answer yes, and the backup begins. A status screen is displayed that lists the backup's progress and the current directory and file that is being archived. The backup will run to completion unless you interrupt it by pressing ESC.

Backing Up the Bindery

The Backup Bindery option is a quick way to back up a server's security and user information. Select this option from NBACKUP's backup menu, and you see the window that prompts you to enter two items: the Session Description and the Destination Directory. Move the cursor to Session Description and enter a descriptive title for the backup. Next, move the cursor to Destination Directory and enter the drive and directory to which you want to copy the bindery files. After entering this information, you are prompted to specify whether the drive you entered is a removable volume. When you back up to removable volumes, NBACKUP prompts you to enter a new disk when the current one is full.

After entering your backup specifications, press Esc. You are prompted to confirm that you want to save your changes. Answer yes and you then are prompted to confirm that you want to start the backup. Answer yes, and the backup begins. A status screen displays the progress of the backup and the current directory and file being archived. The backup runs to completion unless you interrupt it by pressing ESC.

Backing Up Selected Directories

When you need to back up only certain files and directories from your server, choose the Backup By Directory option. When you select this option, the entry window shown in figure 20.8 appears. The first prompt asks you to enter a Session Description. Type a session description and press Enter. The next option prompts you to choose whether to Backup Subdirectories. When this is set to yes, all subdirectories under the directories that are listed to be backed up also will be backed up. When this option is set to no, only the selected directories themselves are backed up.

The next prompt asks you to choose a whether to Backup Trustees. When this is set to yes, all user trustee rights to files and directories are backed up. Highlight this option and press Y to set it to yes or N to set it to no. Next, you must choose whether to backup Modified Files Only. When this option is set to yes, only those files with the ARCHIVE attribute turned on are backed up. When this option is set to no, all files are backed up. The ARCHIVE attribute is turned on whenever a file is changed, and it is turned

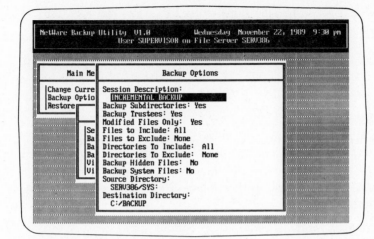

Fig. 20.8.
NBACKUP's Backup
By Directory
window.

off by NBACKUP and other backup programs as the file is backed up. Selecting the Modified Files Only option backs up only those files changed since the last backup.

The next two options, Files To Include and Files To Exclude, enable you to choose files to include in and exclude from the backup process. Use these options to enter a file list or wild-card pattern to exclude or include files. Select the desired option, and you see a list of the currently included or excluded file names or patterns. Press Ins to add to the list. You can remove names or patterns from the list by highlighting them and pressing Del, or by marking multiple items with F5 and pressing Del.

The Directories To Include and Directories To Exclude options are similar to the preceding two options. They enable you to list directories that you want to include and exclude.

The Backup Hidden Files and Backup System Files options control whether or not files with the SYSTEM and HIDDEN attributes turned on will be included in the backup. Highlight the box next to either option and press Y to set it to yes or N to set it to no.

The Source Directory specifies the top of the tree structure that you are backing up. Enter the server, volume, and directory of your choice.

The final selection, Destination Directory, is where you specify the drive and directory to which NBACKUP will copy the files that it backs up. Enter the drive letter and directory that you want to back up to. After entering this information, you are prompted to specify whether the drive you entered is a removable volume. When you back up to removable volumes, NBACKUP prompts you to enter a new disk when the current one is full.

After entering your backup specifications, press Esc. A prompt asks you to confirm that you want to save your changes. Answer yes and you are prompted to confirm that you want to start the backup. Answer yes, and the backup begins. A status screen then displays the progress of the backup and the current directory and file that is being archived. The backup runs to completion unless you interrupt it by pressing ESC.

Viewing Log Information

After you have performed a backup, you can view the backup log or error log for that backup session. When you select either View Backup Log or View Error Log from NBACKUP's backup menu, you are shown a list of the backup sessions that used the selected working directory. Choose a session, and its log information is displayed.

When you are finished working with backup options, press Esc to return to NBACKUP's main menu.

Restore Options

When you need to restore data from a backup that you have made with NBACKUP, select Restore Options from NBACKUP's main menu. The Restore Menu appears and offers the following options:

Select Working Directory
Restore Session
View Backup Log
View Error Log

Your first step when performing a restore is to use the Select Working Directory option to choose the directory that contains the backup session files. Highlight this option and press Enter, and you are prompted to enter the name of the appropriate working directory.

Next, choose Restore Session. A list of the backup sessions whose files are contained in the working directory is displayed. Highlight the one you want to restore from and press Enter. The Restore Options window appears on-screen (see fig. 20.9).

The first setting in this window prompts you to choose what should happen when NBACKUP attempts to restore a file that already exists. The default setting for this option causes the existing file to be overwritten by the backup copy. If you highlight this setting and press Enter, a submenu appears offering the following alternatives: Do Not Overwrite (leave the existing file intact), Interactive (prompt for user input about each existing

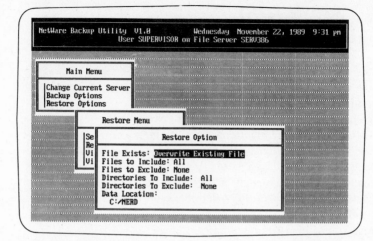

Fig. 20.9.
NBACKUP's Restore
Options window.

file encountered), Overwrite Existing File, Rename Existing File (and restore the backup copy to the original name), and Rename Restored File (and restore the backup copy to another name). Choose one of these options.

The next two options, Files To Include and Files To Exclude, enable you to choose files to include in and exclude from the backup process. Use these options to enter a file list or wild-card pattern to exclude or include files. Select the desired option, and you see a list of the currently included or excluded file names or patterns. Press Ins to add to the list. You can remove names or patterns from the list by highlighting them and pressing Del, or by marking multiple items with F5 and pressing Del.

The Directories To Include and Directories To Exclude options are similar to the preceding two options. They enable you to list directories that you want to include and exclude.

The final item that you specify is the Data Location. Enter the location of the data files from the backup session (do not confuse this location directory with the working directory).

After entering your restore specifications, press Esc. A prompt asks you to confirm that you want to save your changes. Answer yes and you are prompted to confirm that you want to start the restore. Answer yes, and the restore begins. A status screen displays the progress of the restore and the current directory and file being restored. The restore runs to completion unless you interrupt it by pressing ESC.

When you are finished working with the Restore Menu, press Esc to return to NBACKUP's main menu. Press Esc once more to leave NBACKUP.

Chapter Summary

This chapter discussed the six essential considerations that make up your management strategy. These considerations include controlling hard disk space usage, monitoring file-server performance, maintenance and workstation information, checking and resetting network devices on a regular basis, performing regular maintenance on network databases and other software, and making regular backups of files stored on server disks. You are encouraged to develop a daily or weekly schedule of operation for your network that specifies when each of these tasks should be carried out. If you delegate these tasks to others, require each person to submit a written or electronic-mail sign-off sheet to confirm that his or her part of the network-management plan has been carried out.

Although these recommendations may seem needlessly formal, remember that the integrity and reliability of your LAN is at stake. As users begin to trust the integrity of your network, you, the network supervisor, become their partner. You have an obligation to see that their trust is not misplaced.

Part V

Advanced Topics

Includes

Building Menus
Installing Network Versions of Software

21

Building Menus

Your network probably offers its users a wide variety of services. Shared software, communication gateways, electronic mail, and network printers are some of the resources available to the users of a well-designed LAN.

You need a way to make each resource easy to use. A user-friendly menu system is probably the best way to accomplish this goal. Users who are not knowledgeable about NetWare, DOS, or OS/2 will have a hard time learning and remembering a long list of commands, one for each of the services they plan to use. A well-designed menu system helps them access these resources with ease and gives your network an organized appearance.

If you like the "exploding window" look of NetWare's utilities and want to design your own menus with the same appearance, you should consider using NetWare's menu builder. It enables you to create menus with the same look as SYSCON, FILER, and NetWare's other utilities.

NetWare's menu builder is surprisingly easy to use and yields very professional-looking results. You create an ASCII file (with your word processor or favorite text editor) that contains the instructions the MENU command follows when it executes your menus.

You can probably identify several aspects of your network that a menu can make easier to use. You might want to create one menu system that helps users connect to the network printer of their choice and another to help them start and use network software packages. When you become skilled at creating menus, you will be able to add a professional-looking menu interface to any network resource.

Preparing To Use NetWare's Menu Builder

The commands used to run the menus you create are stored in SYS:PUBLIC. Users who run your menus must start the menu program from a network directory in which they have the ability to read, write, open, create, delete, and search for files. For NetWare 286, the required trustee rights are READ, WRITE, OPEN, CREATE, DELETE, and SEARCH. For NetWare 386, the required rights are READ, WRITE, CREATE, ERASE, and FILE SCAN.

The menu program also can be adapted for use on local hard disks. You will learn how to adapt the menu program later in this chapter.

Designing Your Menus

Before you start creating the ASCII file that serves as the instructions for NetWare's MENU command, you must develop a menu design. As you create this design, you decide what selections your main menu will contain and what actions these selections will initiate. For example, you may want your main menu to have these selections:

NETWORK MENU

NETWORK SOFTWARE PACKAGES

PRINTER SELECTIONS

ELECTRONIC MAIL

COMMUNICATION GATEWAYS

NETWORK INFORMATION

LOGOUT

You then need to decide what should happen when a user selects each of these options. As an example, consider the Printer Selections option. Perhaps you have three types of network output devices: laser printers, dot-matrix printers, and plotters. You decide to have the Printer Selections option from your menu show a submenu that lists these three choices:

PRINTER SELECTIONS

LASER PRINTERS

DOT-MATRIX PRINTERS

PLOTTERS

You next must decide what actions each of the submenu selections initiates. Consider the Laser Printers selection. Perhaps you have three laser printers: one in the accounting department, one in the sales department, and one in the warehouse. When Laser Printers is selected, you want the menu to show a list of these printers:

LASER PRINTERS

ACCTING DEPT LASER

SALES DEPT LASER

WAREHOUSE LASER

Finally, when a specific laser printer is selected, the CAPTURE command is executed with the appropriate parameters to connect the user to the selected printer.

To build a complete menu system involves going through the above process for each of your menu options. You define the successive submenus and the command for each menu selection.

Fortunately, you can begin with a single menu and build your menu system gradually. To expand an existing menu system, you need only add more options to the ASCII file that contains its definition. Figure 21.1 is a diagram showing the complete design for a typical network menu system.

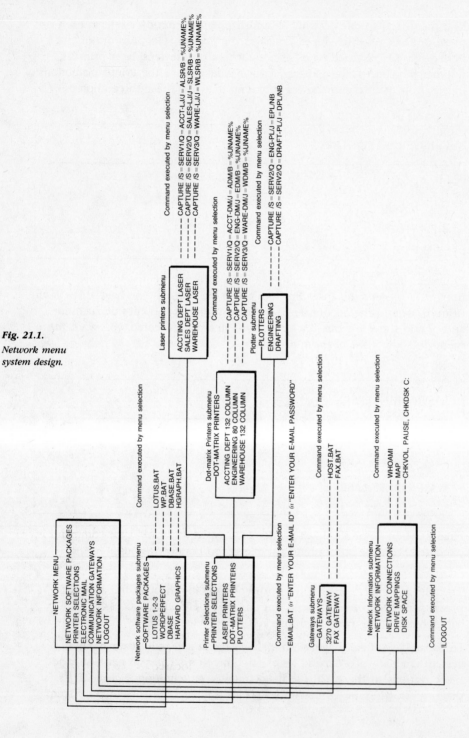

Fig. 21.1.
*Network menu
system design.*

Creating and Running Your First Menu

The menu script is the set of instructions the MENU command follows to build and operate your menus. The menu script is an ASCII file (your word processor may use the term "text file" or "DOS text file") entered in a certain pattern that the MENU command can interpret. A simple menu and its script are examined here to help you understand this pattern.

Suppose that you want to design a menu that does three things:

- ❏ Shows available disk space (using the CHKVOL command)

- ❏ Shows drive mappings (using the MAP command)

- ❏ Shows network connection information (using the WHOAMI command)

To create this menu, type the following information with your word processor and save it as an ASCII text file, with the name NETINFO.MNU:

```
%NETWORK INFORMATION
Disk Information
    CHKVOL
Drive Mappings
    MAP
Network Connection Information
    WHOAMI
```

Running A Script

You can run your newly-created menu by using the following command (be sure your default directory contains NETINFO.MNU):

    MENU NETINFO

You see a menu like that shown in figure 21.2.

When you use the MENU command, follow it with the name of the script file. If the script file has the extension MNU, you do not have to type in the extension. If the script file is in the default directory, you do not have to type its complete network location. If it is located in another directory, enter its location and name, such as

    MENU F:\USERS\SMITHFD\MENUSCRP.ASC

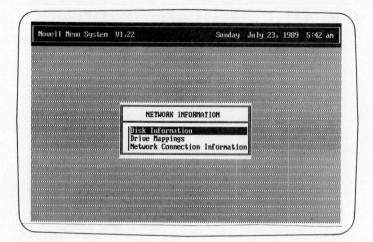

Fig. 21.2.
The Network
Information menu.

MENU is stored in SYS:PUBLIC, so it can be accessed from any directory as long as you have mapped a search drive to SYS:PUBLIC. Sometimes users have programs on their own local disks that have the name MENU. If a user has a search path established to the directory containing another menu command, and that directory is earlier in the search order than SYS:PUBLIC, NetWare's MENU does not work properly. Network supervisors get around this by renaming NetWare's MENU command to another less common name, such as NETMENU. You can use FILER or the DOS or OS/2 REN (rename) command to do this. You must temporarily remove MENU's READ ONLY attribute to rename it (for information about attributes and the FILER utility, see Chapter 12).

Examining Script File Structure

Consider the script file structure. The first line (%NETWORK INFORMATION) is the menu title. Menu titles are always preceded by a percent sign (%). The second line (Disk Information) is a menu option. Notice that it is not indented but is aligned on the left margin of the script file. The third line is the command that is executed when you select the menu option immediately preceding it. These three types of items (menu titles, menu options, and commands) plus a fourth (a submenu) are the building blocks for a menu script file. Figure 21.3 points out each type of item in the script file just created.

```
%NETWORK INFORMATION    ◄────────Menu title (always precede with %)
Disk Information         ◄────────Menu option 1 (do not indent a menu option)
    CHKVOL              ◄────────Command for option 1 (commands must be indented)
Drive Mappings          ◄────────Menu option 2
    MAP                 ◄────────Command for option 2
Network Connection Information ◄──Menu option 3
    WHOAMI              ◄────────Command for option 3
```

Fig. 21.3.
A script file.

You are allowed to have multiple commands for each menu option. For example, if you want to list disk information for both the network volume and the local hard disk (C:), you can modify the Disk Information option to show the following:

```
Disk Information
    CHKVOL
    PAUSE
    CHKDSK C:
    PAUSE
```

This menu selection now shows the disk information for the network volume (using CHKVOL), then executes the DOS command PAUSE (which stops and prompts the user to Strike a key when ready...), and then shows disk information for drive C (using the CHKDSK command).

Instead of listing multiple items on a command line, you have the option of combining them into a batch file and listing only the batch file name as the command. This method has two advantages. First, your menu file is less cluttered and shorter, so it can be run more efficiently by the MENU program. Second, you have to change your menu file less often, because you can change the actions started by a menu selection by changing an external batch file instead of the script file itself. Because the menu script file is open whenever your menu is in use, you must ask users to stop using it before you can edit the script (most word processors do not let you edit and save a file that is in use at another workstation). It is best not to have to change the script file often.

Creating Submenus

You probably need to build more complicated menus than the one you just created. For example, you may want to create submenus that are activated when you select a menu option. In the example below, a submenu has been added to the Network Information menu that lets you list the users logged into your server and list all other servers on the network. In the following script file, this option is called List Users and Servers:

```
%NETWORK INFORMATION
Disk Information
    CHKVOL
    PAUSE
    CHKDSK C:
Drive Mappings
    MAP
List Users and Servers
    %Users and Servers
Network Connection Information
    WHOAMI
%Users and Servers
List Users
    USERLIST/A
List Servers
    SLIST
```

The option line List Users and Servers has been added. Unlike the first three option lines, this one is not followed by a line with a command. Instead, the next line (which is indented) is another menu (%Users and Servers). Like our first menu title, it begins with a percent sign. This line tells the MENU command to start a submenu when the List Users and Servers option is selected.

When you insert a menu option that starts a submenu, you must define the submenu in the script file after the lines that contain the main menu's definition. In the list above, the definition for the Users and Servers submenu appears in the script file after the main menu has been defined. If you have a menu design with a number of submenus, they all must be defined at the end of the script file.

You also may have submenus that call their own submenus (nested submenus). For example, if you build a print menu according to the design discussed at the beginning of this chapter, it will have two levels of submenus, as shown in figure 21.4.

How does NetWare's MENU program expect you to handle this? Submenu 2 must be defined within Submenu 1, as shown in figure 21.5.

If a submenu starts other submenus, the submenus that are started should be defined in the script file immediately after the submenu doing the starting.

There are two other rules for using submenus. First, you cannot mix commands and submenus together on the indented lines after each menu option. For example, you cannot have

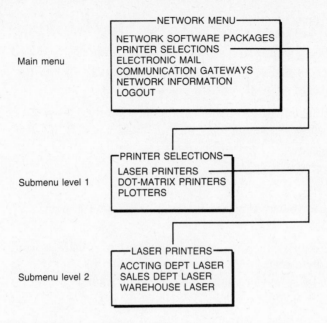

Fig. 21.4.
A print menu with two levels of submenus.

```
┌────────────NETWORK MENU─────────────┐
│ NETWORK SOFTWARE PACKAGES           │
│ PRINTER SELECTIONS ─────────────┐   │
│ ELECTRONIC MAIL                 │   │
│ COMMUNICATION GATEWAYS          │   │
│ NETWORK INFORMATION             │   │
│ LOGOUT                          │   │
└─────────────────────────────────┼───┘
                                  │
Main menu

      ┌──PRINTER SELECTIONS──┐
      │ LASER PRINTERS ───┐  │
      │ DOT-MATRIX PRINTERS │ │
      │ PLOTTERS          │  │
      └───────────────────┼──┘

Submenu level 1

      ┌──LASER PRINTERS──┐
      │ ACCTING DEPT LASER │
      │ SALES DEPT LASER   │
      │ WAREHOUSE LASER    │
      └────────────────────┘

Submenu level 2
```

Fig. 21.5.
Defining the second submenu within the first submenu.

```
┌─%NETWORK MENU──────────────────────────────┐
│ Network Software Packages                  │
│    %Software packages                      │
│ Printer Selections                         │
│    %Printer menu                           │
│ Electronic Mail              Main Menu     │
│    EMAIL                                    │
│ Communication Gateways                     │
│    %Gateways                               │
│ Network Information                        │
│    %Network info                           │
│                                            │
│                                            │
│   ┌─%Printer Menu──────────────────────┐   │
│   │ Laser Printers                     │   │
│   │    %Laser printer                  │   │
│   │ Dot-Matrix Printers                │   │
│   │    %Dot-matrix                     │   │
│   │ Plotters                           │   │
│   │    %Plotters                       │   │
│   ┌─%Laser Printers ───────────────────┐   │
│   │ Accting Dept Laser                 │   │
│   │   CAPTURE /S=SERV1/Q=ACCT-LJ/J=ALSR/B=%UNAME% │
│   │ Sales Dept Laser                   │   │
│   │   CAPTURE /S=SERV2/Q=SALES-LJ/J=SLSR/B=%UNAME% │
│   │ Warehouse Laser                    │   │
│   │   CAPTURE /S=SERV3/Q=WARE-LJ/J=WLSR/B=%UNAME% │
│   └────────────────────────────────────┘   │
└────────────────────────────────────────────┘
```

Start Electronic Mail
MAP G: = SERV1/SYS:EMAIL
%EMAIL MENU

in your script because it mixes a command (MAP G: = SERV1/SYS:EMAIL) with a submenu request (%EMAIL MENU).

You also cannot have more than one submenu request on the indented lines after a menu option. For example,

Start Electronic Mail
%SERVER SELECTION MENU
%EMAIL MENU

does not work because you have two submenu requests after a menu option.

As with all NetWare utilities, the menu option titles that you place in your script are automatically alphabetized. You cannot override this, but there is a way to work around it. You can control the order by beginning your menu option titles with numbers or letters as shown below:

A-NETWORK SOFTWARE PACKAGES
B-PRINTER SELECTIONS
C-ELECTRONIC MAIL
D-COMMUNICATION GATEWAYS
E-NETWORK INFORMATION
F-LOGOUT

Prompting for User Input

A particularly useful feature is the ability to prompt users to type input during menu execution. For example, if you have a menu option that connects to a network printer, you may want to prompt users to enter a banner name and the number of copies to print. Your menu script contains the following to do this:

Accounting Laser
CAPTURE /P1/S = SERV1/Q = ACCT-LJ/B = @"Enter the banner info: "
@"Enter the number of copies: "

(The CAPTURE command above should be all on one line, but cannot be shown that way in this book.)

When the user selects this option from the menu, he sees the prompt shown in figure 21.6. A prompt is always displayed along the bottom of the screen. Your prompt text can be up to 40 characters long.

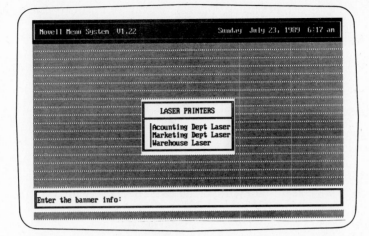

Fig. 21.6.
The Menu prompt.

Notice that menu options that are to be input are preceded by the "at" symbol: @. The prompt text is enclosed in quotes. The actual information the user enters is placed in the command at the same position where the @ appears.

If you need to use the user-entered information more than once, you can do so within the same series of commands for one option. You need to modify the script by giving each user input item a number that follows the @. For example, you can "reuse" what the user entered by doing the following:

    Accounting Laser
        CAPTURE /P1/S = SERV1/Q = ACCT-LJ/B = @1"Enter the banner info: "
            @2"Enter the number of copies: "
        ECHO The banner will be @1.
        ECHO The number of copies is set to @2.

(Put the CAPTURE command on one line.)

Controlling Menu Window Position

If you test any of the above examples in which a submenu is defined and used, you notice that both the main menu and submenu windows open in the center of the screen. This means that the submenu window covers up the main menu window while it is open. You may want to change the position of the submenu so that it opens in a different position, allowing you to see both levels of menus at the same time.

With a small change to the definition line of the submenu, you can specify where on the screen it is placed. In the original example, the submenu definition begins with the line

%List Users and Servers

If this line is changed to

%List Users and Servers,20,15

the submenu is centered at a position 20 lines down from the top of the menu screen, and 15 columns from the left.

If you want to position a menu window somewhere other than the center of the menu screen, you need to follow the menu definition line with a comma, followed by the menu's line position (between 1 and 24) and its column position (between 1 and 80). You are specifying the line and column position where the menu window should be centered.

If you enter numbers that are too high, the MENU program places the menu as far as possible in the direction you specified. For example,

%List Users and Servers,30,85

places the submenu window in the lower right corner.

Entering a value of 0 for the line or column position centers the menu on the screen as if you entered no number at all. If you want a menu to be centered vertically but want it to be centered on column 20 horizontally, enter

%List Users and Servers,0,20

Determining Menu Width and Height

Knowing a menu window's width and height helps you decide where to place it on the screen. The menu width is determined automatically by the widest item in the menu definition. For example, if you have a menu with a title of Printer Selections (which is 18 characters long) and two options, Ink Jet Printers (16 characters long) and Laser Printers (14 characters long), the menu is 22 characters across (18 characters to accommodate the longest item, plus four characters for borders). If you add an item called Dot-Matrix Printers (19 characters), the width increases to accommodate it.

The menu height also is determined automatically based on the number of items in the menu. The Laser Printers submenu shown in figure 21.6 has three options. Its total height is 7 lines (3 for the menu options plus 4 to accommodate the menu title and borders).

You may need to build menu windows with many options. If the number of options exceeds 18, the MENU program shows the first 18 options and a down-arrow indicator to prompt the user to scroll through the rest of the entries.

Changing Menu Colors

By default, the menus you design have the same colors as NetWare utilities like SYSCON and FILER. You may want to liven things up a bit by varying your colors. The MENU command enables you to specify which color palette is used by each submenu. A color palette is a color combination defining the foreground and background colors that can be used by a menu window. Figure 21.7 shows the color palette menu screen.

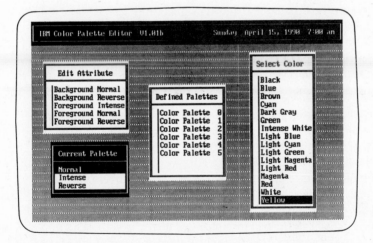

Fig. 21.7.
The Color Palette menu screen.

When NetWare is first installed, five color palettes numbered 0 through 4 are available. You can specify which palette number to use on the menu definition line as follows:

    %List Users and Servers,20,15,1

where the color palette is the third parameter (after the line and column position numbers). When you specify no number, color palette 0 is used.

Using COLORPAL To Create Your Own Palettes

NetWare supplies a utility called COLORPAL to create and control color palettes. To add new color palettes to the existing list, you must be logged in with supervisory equivalence. You also must turn off the READ ONLY attribute of a file in SYS:PUBLIC called IBM$RUN.OVL, because it stores the color palette definitions (you cannot change a file that is READ ONLY). Use the FLAG command or FILER utility to change this attribute setting (for complete information about attributes and FLAG and FILER, see Chapter 12). After making the necessary change, type

COLORPAL

and press Enter.

You see a menu listing the current color palettes (0 through 4). These five palettes are used by all NetWare utilities. Palette 0 controls regular menus, lists, and displays. Palette 1 controls the headers at the top of the screen and the screen background. Palette 2 is used for help screens, palette 3 for error messages, and palette 4 for exit and alert windows.

It is probably best to leave palettes 0 through 4 alone. These default colors are appealing and hard to improve upon. You can add your own palettes that can be used for your own menus, so you still have ample outlet for your creativity. A few types of PCs, such as certain COMPAQ models with monochrome screens, require special settings, but these can be made without changing the colors for others, as discussed in the next section.

To add another color palette, press Ins. A new color palette number is added and its listing is highlighted. Press Enter to work with the new palette. You see a menu listing the five settings that you can change (Background Normal, Background Reverse, Foreground Intense, Foreground Normal, Foreground Reverse) and a screen showing the current palette settings. To change a setting, highlight it and press Enter, and a list of the colors you can change to appears. Highlight the color you want to use and press Enter; the Current Palette window changes to show your selection. By trial and error, you can arrive at a color combination that is pleasing. When you are finished defining the palette, press Esc to return to the main menu.

You can add more palettes (up to a total of 100) by repeating the above process. You also can delete a palette by highlighting it and pressing Del. You can delete multiple palettes by marking each one with the F5 key and pressing Del.

When you are finished making your palette modifications, press Esc and confirm that you want to save your changes and exit.

Handling Special Color Configurations

A few PCs have special displays that enable them to emulate full-color screens by using varying shades of green or amber. Certain color palette combinations are unreadable on these types of displays. These PCs need to use a color definition file called CMPQ$RUN.OVL instead of the standard IBM$RUN.OVL (CMPQ stands for COMPAQ). If you modify the SHELL.CFG file on that PC's boot disk to change the short machine name to CMPQ, it uses the CMPQ$RUN.OVL file automatically.

You also can create custom color palette definition files that are only used by certain computers. In the next section, using MENU and COLORPAL on a stand-alone PC is discussed. If you use COLORPAL on your local disk to create a custom IBM$RUN.OVL file, and then copy that file to SYS:PUBLIC using a new name such as CSTM$RUN.OVL, PCs that have a short machine name of CSTM as defined in their SHELL.CFG files will use CSTM$RUN.OVL instead of IBM$RUN.OVL.

Running The Menu Utility without a Network

When you become skilled at writing menu scripts, you may want to build local PC menus in addition to network-based ones. To build local PC menus, create a directory on your disk and copy the following files there from SYS:PUBLIC:

    IBM$RUN.OVL
    MENU.EXE
    MENUPARZ.EXE
    MENUPARZ.HLP
    SYS$ERR.DAT
    SYS$HELP.DAT
    SYS$MSG.DAT

Rename IBM$RUN.OVL to $RUN.OVL when you run MENU locally. You also must execute MENU from the directory where the above files are stored (creating a search path to that directory is not sufficient).

When you have copied these files to the menu, you also can copy and run COLORPAL there. The following files need to be present for COLORPAL:

COLORPAL.EXE
COLORPAL.HLP
IBM$RUN.OVL

When running COLORPAL, a file named IBM$RUN.OVL must be in its default directory; it records all color palette definitions to that file. When you have set up your palettes, you can copy IBM$RUN.OVL to the name $RUN.OVL to make the changes effective for your local menus.

Handling Special Situations

The MENU command is flexible and can be used to start a variety of commands, programs, and batch files. It can run internal DOS commands such as COPY and DIR. When a command is finished executing, control is returned to the MENU command and your menu reappears.

Your menus should not be used to start memory-resident programs (such as SideKick). When you stop using the menu, the memory it uses cannot be released because of the memory-resident program loaded beneath it.

When you use the menu to log off the network, use the special option shown below:

Logout
   !LOGOUT

The !LOGOUT command closes all the files the menu program uses and stops the menu automatically. If you use the regular LOGOUT command, the menu system's temporary files are not properly deleted and the user receives error messages.

As you create and test your menu scripts, error messages appear if the MENU program encounters an error in your script. Usually, these errors concern menu-definition lines that are not preceded with the percent sign (%), command lines that are not indented, or submenus whose definitions are incorrectly placed or left out. The text of the error message assists you in determining the nature of the problem.

Figure 21.8 is the script for the menu design shown earlier in the chapter. It uses all the techniques discussed in this chapter, and you may want to refer to it as a model as you create your own scripts.

```
%NETWORK MENU,12,0
Network Software Packages
  %Software Packages
Printer Selections
  %Printer Menu
Electronic Mail
  EMAIL @"ENTER YOUR E-MAIL ID" @"ENTER YOUR E-MAIL PASSWORD"
Communication Gateways
  %Gateways
Network Information
  %Network Information
Logout
  !LOGOUT
%Software Packages,20,15
Lotus 1-2-3
  LOTUS
WordPerfect
  WP
dBASE
  DBASE
Harvard Graphics
  HGRAPH
%Printer Menu,20,15
Laser Printers
  %Laser Printers
Dot Matrix Printers
  %Dot Matrix Printers
Plotters
  %Plotters
%Laser Printers,20,65,5
Acctng Dept Laser
  CAPTURE /S = SERV1/Q = ACCT-LJ/J = ALSR/B = %UNAME%
Sales Dept Laser
  CAPTURE /S = SERV4/Q = SALES-LJ/J = SLSR/B = %UNAME%
Warehouse Laser
  CAPTURE /S = SERV3/Q = WARE-LJ/J = WLSR/B = %UNAME%
%Dot Matrix Printers,20,65,5
Accting Dept 132 Column
  CAPTURE /S = SERV1/Q = ACCT-DM/J = ADM/B = %UNAME%
Engineering 80 Column
  CAPTURE /S = SERV2/Q = ENG-DM/J = EDM/B = %UNAME%
Warehouse 132 Column
  CAPTURE /S = SERV3/Q = WARE-DM/J = WDM/B = %UNAME%
%Plotters,20,65,5
Engineering
  CAPTURE /S = SERV2/Q = ENG-PL/J = EPL/NB
Drafting
  CAPTURE /S = SERV2/Q = DRAFT-PL/J = DPL/NB
%Gateways,20,15
3270 Gateway
  HOST.BAT
FAX Gateway
  FAX.BAT
%Network Information,20,15
Network Connections
  WHOAMI
Drive Mappings
  MAP
Disk Space
  CHKVOL
  PAUSE
  CHKDSK C:
%Logout,20,15
  !LOGOUT
```

Fig. 21.8.
The menu script for the Chapter 21 menu design.

Chapter Summary

You learned in this chapter how NetWare's MENU builder lets you create flexible, powerful, and attractive menus quickly. Menu scripts are easy to write and can be added to and changed as your menu requirements grow. NetWare's menu builder is a strategic tool that can help make your network's resources easy to use.

22

Installing Network
Versions of Software

People buy personal computers to run programs. PCs would be of little or
no value without the word processors, spreadsheets, database managers,
graphics packages, and other types of software that enable people to use
computers to do work.

Because PCs exist to run programs and LANs exist to enhance the
usefulness of PCs, understanding the role that a LAN can play to enhance a
PC's capability to run software is important. Most of today's popular PC
applications are available in network versions, enabling you to install one
copy of a program that can be shared by all your network users.

In this chapter, you will learn the benefits of using LAN-based software
packages and the techniques that experienced network supervisors have
developed to install LANs. You will learn several strategies for making
accessing LAN-based applications easy for users of the LAN. Finally, the
chapter will discuss several popular network-based programs in order to
give you a taste of what you will experience as you install typical LAN
software packages.

The Benefits of LAN-Based Software

Many good reasons for using LAN-based software exist. If you carefully and aggressively choose the right packages to install, your LAN can enable a PC user to access a wide variety of programs. Your network can become a "software library," where users can access an interesting and useful variety of programs that help them be more productive.

Network-based programs are infinitely more convenient to manage and make available than are individual copies of software. If your company has 50 nonnetworked PCs (a horrible thought), buying and installing 50 copies of every software package someone at the company may some day want or need is a headache. The problem is aggravated when a new version of a widely used package is released. You have to do a tremendous amount of administration and leg work to purchase and install 50 upgrades.

If those 50 PCs are connected to a LAN, you can consolidate these tasks by purchasing and using network versions of software. Installation is a one-time process, and when an upgrade becomes available, you simply purchase it and install it one time.

Using network-based software has several other advantages. Many of today's full-featured programs use large amounts of disk space. (Requirements of three to four megabytes per program are not uncommon.) A user who installs even a handful of these programs on his or her hard disk can be faced with a significant shortage of disk space. On the other hand, when the same user accesses the same programs on a network server, his or her own storage needs are minimized.

Using network-based software also enables you to share "home-grown" enhancements to off-the-shelf programs. Perhaps someone in your company has developed a special word processing macro that can benefit others. You can add this macro file to your installation so that all network users can access it.

Similarly, when your software is network-based, you can create standard printer and screen configurations for each package so that less skilled users do not have to become experts at configuring the programs they use.

A few risks arise when your users depend on network-based software. Your LAN must be reliable and up almost all the time, because users cannot run programs without it. Your LAN's performance must be such that loading a network-based program compares favorably to loading it from a local hard disk.

Some LAN-based programs use *counters* to govern the number of users who can access the program at the same time. You buy not only the network version of the program but also a *use-count program* that controls the number of users who can use the package simultaneously. You must remember to monitor the program's counter to make sure that you have enough copies of the program available to satisfy the needs of your users.

Installation Strategies for Network Software

You must make several decisions about installation of shared software packages on your network. First, you need to determine on what server and in what type of directory structure you will store shared programs. You also need to decide how you will give rights to the users who want to access the program.

Choosing the Servers on Which To Store Shared Programs

If your network consists of multiple servers, you must decide which ones you will use to store shared programs. (If your network consists of one server, your decision is easy.)

You need to consider several factors as you make this decision. Suppose that your LAN has three file servers; the first is used by the accounting department, the second by the sales department, and the third by engineering. Each department has about 60 users. You want to install network versions of several programs for all three departments to use.

You have several strategies available for installing these programs. You can purchase three server copies for each program and install one copy on each server (see fig. 22.1). You can buy and install one copy of each on the accounting department server and have users from the other two servers attach to that server when they need to use the program (see fig. 22.2). Or you can set up a special server for running shared applications and have users from all three servers attach to it when they need to run a shared program (see fig. 22.3).

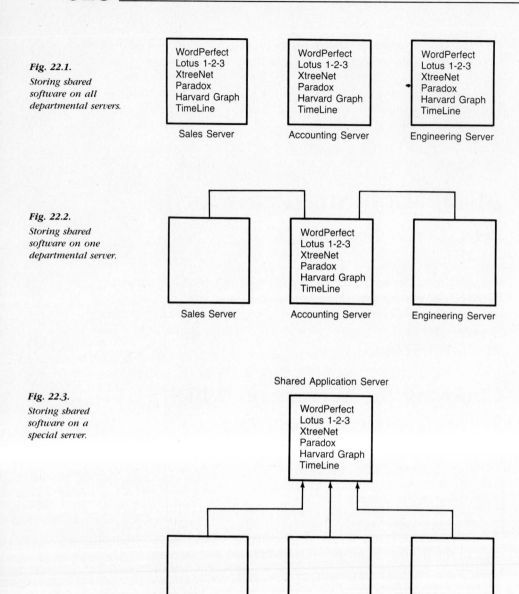

Fig. 22.1.

Storing shared software on all departmental servers.

| WordPerfect
Lotus 1-2-3
XtreeNet
Paradox
Harvard Graph
TimeLine | WordPerfect
Lotus 1-2-3
XtreeNet
Paradox
Harvard Graph
TimeLine | WordPerfect
Lotus 1-2-3
XtreeNet
Paradox
Harvard Graph
TimeLine |
| Sales Server | Accounting Server | Engineering Server |

Fig. 22.2.

Storing shared software on one departmental server.

Sales Server — Accounting Server (WordPerfect, Lotus 1-2-3, XtreeNet, Paradox, Harvard Graph, TimeLine) — Engineering Server

Fig. 22.3.

Storing shared software on a special server.

Shared Application Server (WordPerfect, Lotus 1-2-3, XtreeNet, Paradox, Harvard Graph, TimeLine)

Sales Server — Accounting Server — Engineering Server

Each of the three approaches has pros and cons. Installing a separate copy of each program on each department's server means that you must purchase three separate copies of the server copy of the program (again see fig. 22.1). Depending on how the software companies charge for a network license, this purchase may result in an extra expense. Using this method also means that you have to install, configure, and maintain three separate copies of the program.

Installing the programs only on the accounting server means that you have to buy and install only one copy of each. However, having users from the other two servers attach to the accounting server to use the shared programs may put undue stress on the accounting server. NetWare 286 servers can handle up to 100 users, but performance diminishes as you approach that limit. If the server already is busy running several accounting applications, you may not want to tax it further.

Setting up a special server just for shared software is an elegant solution if you can afford it. When a user needs to use a shared program, he or she attaches to this server. You do not have to buy and maintain multiple copies of the program, and departmental servers are not loaded with additional tasks. You must carefully predict the number of users who will be logging into the server that stores shared programs to make sure that you have enough connections to handle the load. (NetWare 286 can accommodate up to 100 users, and NetWare 386 has a limit of 250 users per server.)

If you cannot justify a shared server, you may want to spread your shared software among your departmental servers (see fig. 22.4). You need to purchase only one server copy of each package, and the extra load created by each package is spread evenly among your departmental servers.

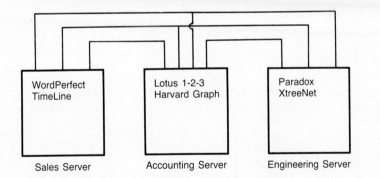

Fig. 22.4.
Spreading shared software over all departmental servers.

Choosing a Directory Structure for Shared Programs

Next, you need to decide how to structure the directories that store your shared software. Your first inclination may be to create each program's directory one level under the root directory.

This structure works but has several disadvantages. First, as you add more shared programs to your server, the directory structure becomes cluttered with numerous software directories just under the root. Even more important, you may have difficulty running a special tape backup of just the shared-software storage areas. When your tape backup software asks you to specify the directories to back up, you must enter each program's directory individually.

A better method is to create one directory under the root. Call this directory SOFTWARE or PROGRAMS; then under it create a separate subdirectory for each program. You can back up this area easily by telling your tape backup unit to back up all subdirectories under SOFTWARE.

Figure 22.5 shows both methods of creating a directory structure for shared software. The preferred method is shown on the right.

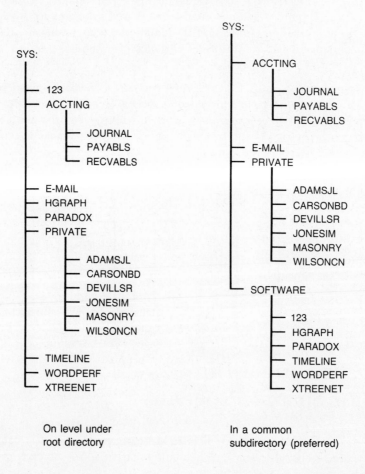

Fig. 22.5.

Two methods of storing shared software.

Installing Your Program

After you create a directory to store a shared program, you must install it. Read the instructions for installing the shared program's files on your server disk. Before installation, you probably need to map a drive letter to the program's directory, because most programs need a drive letter to reference during the installation process.

Controlling Access to Shared Programs

Installing and configuring a shared program puts to use a number of your NetWare skills. You need to use several of NetWare's tools to make sure that users can run shared programs with just the right level of access. Users should be able to use shared programs almost as if they were using a personal copy of the same program. They should be able to modify their individual configurations (such as printer and monitor settings) and create and store personal data files. On the other hand, users should not have the freedom to delete the shared program's files or alter the configurations of other users.

You must decide what trustee rights to give to the shared program's users and whether to give those rights to users individually or to organize users into groups. You also need to decide what attributes (such as SHAREABLE and READ ONLY) to turn on for each program file. (For a complete explanation of NetWare rights, see Chapter 11; see Chapter 12 for a complete discussion of NetWare file attributes.)

Fortunately, most network versions of programs come with detailed and NetWare-specific instructions for installation. In most cases, a shared program's documentation tells you exactly which rights to give and which file attributes to turn on. Some packages, however, have woefully deficient manuals, and you are left to use your best judgment and trial and error to determine which NetWare rights and file attributes to use.

Choosing Which Netware Rights To Grant

Hopefully, every shared software package you install comes with detailed documentation, which specifies exactly the NetWare rights to give to the program's users. Otherwise, you must make your own decisions about what rights to give.

Your goal is to enable a user to run the program but not allow that user to change or delete its files. If the documentation for the program you are working with provides no guidance as to what specific rights to grant, your best bet is to use the SYS:PUBLIC directory on a NetWare server as a model. Like the directory that stores your shared program, SYS:PUBLIC contains program files that users must be able to run but not change.

By default, all users have READ, OPEN, and SEARCH rights to the SYS:PUBLIC directory on a NetWare 286 server, and READ and FILE SCAN rights on a NetWare 386 server. In cases where your shared program's manuals offer no guidance, grant these rights to users who need to access the shared program. Next, test the program to make sure that it can be used successfully with these rights. You should grant additional rights with caution and only after your testing has determined that a right is absolutely necessary.

Granting Rights to Groups instead of Individuals

In Chapters 10 and 11, you learned about giving users rights collectively by making users members of groups. This method is particularly suited to granting users rights to access shared programs.

Perhaps you have decided that every user on your network should be given access to every shared program. In this case, you can give the group EVERYONE the necessary access rights to each shared program. As the group's name indicates, every user is made a member of the EVERYONE group, so all rights given to this group are available to all users.

You may need to be more selective about who can and cannot use a particular program. For example, the accounting department may have funded the purchase of your LAN's copy of Lotus 1-2-3 and ask you to ensure that only accounting department members use it. Similarly, the marketing department may have purchased a network copy of Harvard Graphics and give you a list of a select group of users in that department who should have access to Harvard Graphics.

In cases like the two just described, the sensible approach is to create a group for each program for which you need to control access. Give each group rights to its respective program, and then place the appropriate users in each program's group.

Setting the Program File Attributes

The documentation for your shared software packages may or may not mention turning on certain attributes for your shared program's files (file attributes are discussed in detail in Chapter 12). As a general rule, you should make the program's files shareable and read-only. Making the files shareable ensures that multiple users can access them at the same time and may enable you to back up those files even while other users have them in use. Making a program's files read-only protects them from accidental erasure or modification, even by users who have enough NetWare rights to do so (such as the network supervisor).

You should read a shared program's documentation carefully to find the recommended file attribute settings. If no recommendation is made, you should try turning on the SHAREABLE and READ ONLY attributes and testing the program to make sure that it runs properly.

NetWare's EXECUTE ONLY attribute can be turned on for a program's executable files in order to prevent them from being copied. Turning on this attribute eliminates the possibility that a user will illegally copy a shared program to his or her own drive and directory.

Making Shared Programs Easy To Use

Your shared software installation and configuration efforts are wasted if the programs on your network are difficult to access and run. Starting and using a network-based program usually consists of the following steps:

1. Attach to the server that stores the shared program.

2. Map a drive letter to the directory where the program is stored.

3. Type the command used to start the program.

4. Use the program, and exit it when you are finished.

5. Delete your mapped drive letter to the program directory.

6. Log out from the server that stores the shared program.

These six steps are cumbersome to perform manually, especially if the program is one that you use often. Attaching to servers and mapping drive letters may be difficult for the users on your LAN, who are not familiar with NetWare commands.

Starting Shared Programs with Batch Files

You can dramatically simplify the preceding steps by creating batch files to start shared programs. A *batch file* is a DOS or OS/2 file that executes a series of commands. A batch file is simply an ASCII file consisting of a series of commands to be executed automatically. Each command occupies one line of the file. The most common batch file is the AUTOEXEC.BAT file, which is run automatically as soon as you start your computer. You easily can create batch files to perform the steps to start a shared program. If you do not know how to create and use batch files, study your DOS or OS/2 manual for more information.

A batch file to start a network copy of WordPerfect might consist of the following lines:

```
ATTACH SERV2/GUEST
MAP G: = SERV2/SYS:SOFTWARE \ WORDPERF
G:
WP
LOGOUT SERV2
```

This batch file is designed for situations in which shared programs are stored on a special server to which users must attach when they want to run a shared program. The first line attaches the user to the special server (named SERV2 in this example). Next, the file maps drive G to the directory that stores WordPerfect, makes drive G the default, and runs the command to start the program (WP). After WordPerfect is exited, the LOGOUT command is executed to log out from the server storing WordPerfect (logging out automatically deletes the mapping of drive G).

This batch file is simple, and many network supervisors create considerably more sophisticated batch files. Notice, for example, that the user is attached to SERV2 using the login name of GUEST. GUEST is usually a general-purpose login name that has no password and is useful for attaching to servers where only limited access is required. If you want to refrain from using a generic login name and use an individual login name for each user instead, you can replace the line that attaches the user to SERV2 with the following:

ATTACH SERV2/

This change results in the user's being prompted to enter his or her login name. If you elect to use the DOS SET command in every user's login script to create each user's login name as an environment variable named UNAME (see Chapter 16 for information about login scripts and the DOS SET command), you can supply the login name automatically by using the following command:

ATTACH SERV2/%UNAME%

(Within a batch file, when the name of an environment variable is surrounded by percent signs, the value for that variable replaces the variable itself when the batch command is executed.) Consult your DOS or OS/2 manual for complete information about environment variables.

Sometimes, displaying prompt information in the batch file is useful to help a user understand how to use a program. For example, the following lines in a batch file advise a user that the network version of WordPerfect will ask him or her to enter a three-letter identification code every time the program is started:

ECHO Notice for first time users! You will be prompted to
ECHO select a 1- to 3-character identification code to
ECHO access WordPerfect. Remember this code and enter it
ECHO every time you use WordPerfect.

(The ECHO command in a batch file displays the information listed after the word ECHO.)

The batch files you create to start shared programs should be stored in the SYS:PUBLIC directory or in a directory that is similarly available to all users and is always mapped as a search drive. A user then can start a shared program simply by typing the name of its batch file from the command prompt. For example, if the name of the batch file to start the network copy of Lotus 1-2-3 is NET123, a user can start the program by typing *net123* and then pressing Enter from the command prompt of the PC.

Starting Shared Programs from a Menu

Although starting programs with batch files shields users from having to know the intricacies of mapping drives and attaching to servers, using menus to access shared programs is even more convenient, particularly for users who have limited PC experience.

With NetWare's menu builder (see Chapter 21) or with most commercially available menu-building programs, the batch files you create can be started from the menu program. When your batch file has finished running, the menu automatically returns to the screen. Menu-controlled access to your shared programs can be added with little extra work after batch files have been created for each program.

Installing Shared Software— Three Case Studies

Perhaps the best way to gain an insight into what you encounter when you install shared software is to examine how the network versions of three popular software packages work. In this section, you will compare the network versions of WordPerfect, Lotus 1-2-3, and Paradox. You will learn about the network-specific features each package offers and the methods the programs use to control the number of users who can use the package at the same time.

This section is not meant to replace the installation manuals that come with these software packages. Rather, this material is intended to give you a comparative overview of the three. Even if your company uses different software packages for its word processing, spreadsheet, and database-management needs, those packages most likely use network installation and configuration techniques similar to the techniques of these three programs.

WordPerfect

WordPerfect is one of the leading word processors for IBM PCs and compatibles. This program is highly regarded for its comprehensive array of features and its flexibility. WordPerfect's network version offers some useful network-specific features.

The documentation for network installation consists of a booklet called the *Network Installation Guide*. Clear instructions are provided, including a section specifically dealing with installation on NetWare servers.

Buying a WordPerfect Network License

WordPerfect's network license is relatively uncomplicated. You purchase a special copy of WordPerfect that entitles you to one installation on a server. For each user who will access the program, you purchase a network station copy, which is a complete set of documentation without software. Users who have been issued the network station are legally entitled to use the program installed on a server. Unlike many network versions of programs, WordPerfect does not use a counter program to enforce its license arrangement by limiting the number of users who can use the program at the same time. The publishers of WordPerfect trust you to abide by the license agreement.

WordPerfect's Network-Specific Features

The network version of WordPerfect has three useful network-specific features. First, you can define network printers by server name and queue so that you do not have to remember to run CAPTURE before starting the program. The network version of WordPerfect also automatically locks document files you retrieve from a network disk. While you have a document file in use, other users may only read it. They may retrieve the file but cannot save it to the same file name while you have the file open.

Document files also may be password protected. If you give a document a password, only users who know that password may use WordPerfect to retrieve the document file.

Creating a Directory for WordPerfect

According to WordPerfect's *Network Installation Guide*, your first step in installing the network version of WordPerfect is to create a subdirectory on a server volume for WordPerfect's files. You already have read that probably the best approach is to group all your shared software under a common directory, such as \SOFTWARE or \PROGRAMS. Assuming that you want this structure, you probably will create a subdirectory so that you have a directory structure like the following:

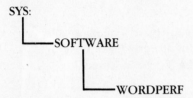

```
SYS:
   └──SOFTWARE
            └──WORDPERF
```

After the subdirectory is created, all the WordPerfect program files should be copied into it. WordPerfect has a number of supplemental files, such as its printer definitions, spell checker and thesaurus, graphics files, screen fonts, and tutorial files. Rather than lump these into one directory, most network supervisors place them in separate subdirectories under the main program directory. Some supervisors also create a subdirectory to store shared macros. If you use this approach, you end up with a directory structure similar to the following:

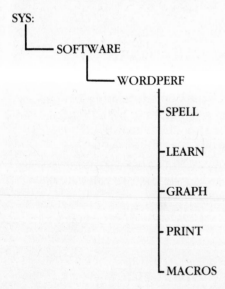

```
SYS:
   └── SOFTWARE
            └── WORDPERF
                      ├─SPELL
                      ├─LEARN
                      ├─GRAPH
                      ├─ PRINT
                      └─MACROS
```

The appropriate files need to be copied from WordPerfect's program disks to the subdirectories.

Turning On File Attributes

WordPerfect's *Network Installation Guide* provides you with a list of the files for which you should turn on the SHAREABLE and READ ONLY attributes. You can use the FLAG command or the FILER utility to perform this task (see Chapter 12 for details about using FLAG and FILER).

Giving Users Rights to the WordPerfect Directories

WordPerfect's documentation provides no guidance as to what rights to directories to give users. You should give users READ, OPEN, and SEARCH rights for NetWare 286, and READ and FILE SCAN rights for NetWare 386.

Configuring WordPerfect

After WordPerfect's files are installed on a server disk, you need to choose a default configuration that users will receive when they first use the program. Users are free to customize this configuration, but you have the responsibility to create a set of useful default values.

When you start WordPerfect to configure it, you are first prompted to enter the network type you are using. Of course, you should answer this question by selecting the option named Novell NetWare. Next, you are prompted to enter a three-letter identification code. WordPerfect enables each user to have a unique configuration, which is tied to this identification code. The first time you enter the program, and every other time when you enter it to configure its default settings, you should respond with {wp and press Enter.

WordPerfect's *Network Installation Guide* tells you how to create two configuration files that are stored in the WordPerfect program directory. The first file is called WP{WP}.ENV and specifies the type of network you are using. This file also can be used to specify the drive and directory where each user's configuration files will be stored. The second file is called WP{WP}.SET, and it contains the default configuration information that users receive the first time they start WordPerfect.

As you begin to configure WordPerfect, you need to specify the drive letter and directory where WordPerfect will locate its various files (such as its spell checker, thesaurus, and printer definitions). At this point, you probably should establish two standard drive-letter mappings that all users

must use when they start WordPerfect. Establish a drive letter for
WordPerfect's program directory and supplemental files and a drive letter
for documents and individual configuration files. For example, as you
configure WordPerfect, you must specify where WordPerfect can find its
spell checker files. If you enter *y:\software\wordperf\spell*, you are
assuming that all users will map drive Y to the volume where WordPerfect
is stored when they start the program. If an independent-minded user maps
to drive H instead, he or she gets an error message when the spelling
checker is invoked.

As you configure WordPerfect, you can establish default settings for a
number of items. At a minimum, you probably will want to create default
settings for

❏ Printer selections

❏ Locations of auxiliary files

You have the option of changing the default values for screen colors,
keyboard mappings, margins, and virtually every configurable option in
WordPerfect.

Storing and Updating Individual Configuration Files

One option you set when you create the WP{WP}.ENV file is where
WordPerfect will store individual configuration files. As you already have
read, when you start WordPerfect, you are prompted to enter a three-
character identification code. The first time a user starts WordPerfect, he
or she enters this code for the first time. If a user enters the code BIL, a
file is created with the name WPBIL}.SET; this file stores his or her
configuration information.

As the network supervisor, you tell WordPerfect where to place this file.
The choice you make has implications later on, when you need to revise
the configuration information for all WordPerfect users. You can specify
that this file be placed in one of two areas: in a private directory to which
only the individual user has access (such as a local disk drive or a private
directory on a server) or in a centralized shared location (such as a special
subdirectory beneath the WordPerfect program directory). If you place this
file in a centralized and shared directory, you can use a special
WordPerfect utility called NWPSETUP to do blanket updates and changes
to user configuration files. However, you must give all users the right to
read, create, open, search for, and write to files in this common directory.
Nothing prevents two users from picking the same three-letter code so that
they use the same configuration file.

Starting WordPerfect

After you have configured WordPerfect, you need to provide a method to enable users to start the program easily. WordPerfect's documentation suggests that every user's login script contain a MAP command to make the WordPerfect program directory a search drive. In this case, users can start WordPerfect simply by typing *wp* and pressing Enter.

Most Network supervisors do not find this method satisfactory. Rather, they opt to use a batch file that creates the search directory just before you start WordPerfect. (Search drives use environment memory space on the workstation and should only be used as needed—for details about search drives, see Chapter 9.) The batch file can provide other useful features, such as warning first-time users about the need to enter a unique three-letter identification or setting a default directory in which WordPerfect will store and look for the user's document files.

The following batch file is typical:

```
ECHO OFF
REM make the c: drive the default
C:
REM make a document directory
MD \WPDOC
REM make the \WPDOC directory the default
CD\WPDOC
REM notify users about the WordPerfect id code
CLS
ECHO----------------------------------------------------------------
ECHO.
ECHO                Notice for first-time users!
ECHO You will be prompted to select a 1- to 3-character
ECHO identification code for WordPerfect. Remember
ECHO this code and enter it every time you use Word
ECHO Perfect.
ECHO.
ECHO----------------------------------------------------------------
PAUSE
ECHO.
ECHO.
ECHO LOADING WordPerfect
ECHO.
ECHO.
REM attach to the server that stores WordPerfect
ATTACH SERV2/GUEST
```

```
REM map a search drive to the WordPerfect directory
MAP INS S2:=SERV2/SYS:SOFTWARE/WORDPERF
REM start WordPerfect
WP
ECHO.
ECHO.
ECHO EXITING WordPerfect AND RETURNING TO SYSTEM
C:
REM log out from the server that stores WordPerfect
LOGOUT SERV2
```

If your network offers its users a menu system, you easily can use a batch file similar to this one to start WordPerfect.

Lotus 1-2-3

Lotus 1-2-3 is the leading spreadsheet for IBM PCs and compatibles. Many PC users are familiar with 1-2-3 and use it extensively. A number of third-party supporting products are available to make 1-2-3 even more versatile and useful. Like WordPerfect, 1-2-3's network version is thoroughly documented and offers several useful network-specific features.

Two versions of 1-2-3 are available. Release 3 is the more powerful version of the program and requires a 286 or 386 computer with at least 1M of RAM. Release 3 can be run with PC DOS or OS/2. Release 2.2 can run on any PC-compatible computer running PC DOS. Network versions of both programs are available.

Buying a Network License for 1-2-3

As with WordPerfect, with 1-2-3 you purchase a server edition of the program and install it on a server volume. You also purchase user licenses, which consist of the documentation for 1-2-3 but no software. With the count program, which is provided, you enter the number of user licenses you have purchased. This count program ensures that no more than this number of users can use 1-2-3 at the same time.

1-2-3's Network-Specific Features

1-2-3 provides several useful network-specific features. The network supervisor can use the count program to view the number of users who are running 1-2-3 at any time. Using this count program is an excellent way to see how actively 1-2-3 is used on your network. Users also can control the way 1-2-3 locks its worksheet files. Users can open a file with a *reservation*, meaning that the file is locked and cannot be written to by any other user until the reservation is released. When you have opened a file with a reservation, other users can read the file but cannot save it unless they save it to another name.

1-2-3 also lets you save a file with a password. If you give a worksheet file a password, only users who know that password may use 1-2-3 to retrieve the worksheet.

Creating Directories for 1-2-3

The instructions for installing and configuring the 1-2-3 are contained in a booklet called the *LAN Administrator's Guide*.

You need to create two directories for 1-2-3. The first directory is used to store the program files, and the second directory stores the license or use-count program. 1-2-3's manuals suggest that you name the program directory 123RXX (replace XX with the version of 1-2-3 you are using); name the use-count directory LOTSHARE\123.VXX (again, replace XX with the 1-2-3 version number you are installing). You probably will want to create a directory structure similar to the following:

SYS:

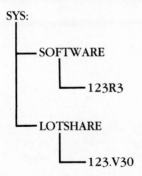

SOFTWARE

123R3

LOTSHARE

123.V30

If you are running both Release 3 and Release 2.2, you probably will want to have a directory structure resembling the following:

The use-count directory (\LOTSHARE) must be just under the root directory, as described in the *LAN Administrator's Guide*.

SYS:

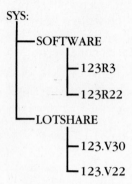

SOFTWARE

123R3

123R22

LOTSHARE

123.V30

123.V22

Giving Users Rights to 1-2-3's Directories

1-2-3's *LAN Administrator's Guide* states that you should give users READ, OPEN, and SEARCH rights to the program directory. (To give equivalent rights with NetWare 386, grant the READ and FILE SCAN rights.) The guide suggests giving all rights to the license-count directory, although you are better advised to give all rights but PARENTAL for NetWare 286 and all rights except ACCESS CONTROL and SUPERVISORY for NetWare 386.

In order to view the license-count information or to update it with additional counts, you must have all rights to the license-count directory.

Installing the Program Files and Configuring the License Count

After you have created the necessary directories, you can run 1-2-3's INSTALL program, which automatically copies all the necessary files to the directories you specify. After installing the program files, you should start the COUNT program to set the number of licenses to match the number you have purchased.

Setting File Attributes

1-2-3's documentation provides no recommendation concerning how to set file attributes. You should set all files in the program directory to be READ ONLY and SHAREABLE.

Starting 1-2-3

After you have configured 1-2-3, you need to provide a method to enable users to start 1-2-3 easily. 1-2-3's documentation suggests that each user create a search path to the 1-2-3 directory and then start 1-2-3 from the directory where he or she plans to store configuration and worksheet files. You can consolidate these steps into a batch file to minimize the keystrokes and NetWare knowledge required to use the program. You also can use a batch file with your network's menu system.

Establishing a Default Configuration

Unlike WordPerfect, 1-2-3 does not enable you to establish a default configuration for your users. Every user is expected to run the install program the first time he or she uses 1-2-3. Some clever network supervisors have gotten around this requirement by installing 1-2-3 for themselves and then copying the configuration files they need to the directory from which the user starts 1-2-3. The exact files to be copied depend on which version of 1-2-3 you are working with. The easiest way to create these files is to start the network version of 1-2-3 in an empty default directory. Run the installation program, creating the configuration you want to use as a default. The files that are created in the directory are those you need to copy to each user's default directory to transfer this configuration to your users. This procedure eliminates the need for inexperienced users to learn how to use 1-2-3's INSTALL program.

The following batch file uses several advanced batch-file techniques to check to see whether the user is using 1-2-3 for the first time. If he or she is a first-time user, the configuration files are automatically copied to the user's 1-2-3 start-up directory.

```
ECHO OFF
C:
CD\
REM check to see whether 1-2-3's configuration file exists
IF EXIST C:\NET123\123.CNF GOTO SKIP1
CLS
ECHO.
ECHO                    Notice for first time users!
ECHO.
ECHO Before you can use Lotus 1-2-3 from the network, setup
ECHO files must be installed on your C: drive. If you do not
ECHO want to install setup files for Lotus 1-2-3, press Ctrl-
```

```
ECHO Break. Otherwise, press any key to continue.
ECHO.
PAUSE
REM create a directory for 1-2-3 config and data files
MD \NET123
REM make that directory the default
CD\NET123
REM attach to the server that stores 1-2-3
ATTACH SERV2/GUEST
REM copy configuration files to user's private directory
NCOPY SERV2/SYS:SOFTWARE\LOTUS\SETFILES\:*.* C:
CLS
ECHO.
ECHO LOADING LOTUS 1-2-3
ECHO.
ECHO ALL DATA FILES ARE STORED BY DEFAULT IN C:\NET123
ECHO.
PAUSE
GOTO SKIP2
:SKIP1
REM non-first-time users skip to here
CLS
ECHO.
ECHO.
ECHO LOADING LOTUS 1-2-3
ECHO.
ECHO ALL DATA FILES ARE STORED BY DEFAULT IN C:\NET123
ECHO.
PAUSE
ATTACH SERV2/GUEST
:SKIP2
REM first-time users skip to here
REM make the 1-2-3 directory a search drive
MAP INSERT S2:=SERV2/SYS:SOFTWARE\LOTUS\123R3
REM check to see whether the user has requested a custom .set file
IF %1A == A GOTO STD
REM start 1-2-3 with a custom .set file
LOTUS C:\NET123\%1.SET
GOTO SKIP3
:STD
REM users who didn't request a custom .set file start with this line
LOTUS C:\NET123\123.SET
:SKIP3
```

```
ECHO.
ECHO.
ECHO EXITING LOTUS 1-2-3 AND RETURNING TO SYSTEM
REM log out from server
LOGOUT SERV2
cd \
```

Paradox

Paradox is a widely used database manager. Highly regarded for its rare combination of power and ease of use, Paradox is also designed with network use in mind.

Paradox has a host of network-specific features. Paradox enables users to share access to data tables freely so that multiuser database applications can be built. Paradox also enables you to view the names of other users who are accessing your files.

Paradox's network documentation is called the *Network Administrator's Guide*. It is very thorough, and has a section devoted to NetWare.

Buying a Network License for Paradox

Your first step in installing Paradox on your LAN is to buy a regular single copy of the program. This purchase entitles one user to access the program. To add more users, you buy Paradox's LAN Pack, which enables five additional users to run Paradox. For every five concurrent users you want to allow, you must buy a LAN Pack.

Creating Directories To Store Paradox's Files

Paradox's manual recommends that you create one directory to store its program files and a second directory to store shared data tables. In addition, Paradox's separate modules, such as its application generator and programming toolkits, are stored in separate subdirectories beneath the program subdirectory. Your directory structure for Paradox probably will be similar to the following:

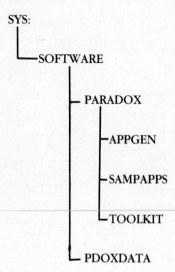

SYS:

SOFTWARE

PARADOX

APPGEN

SAMPAPPS

TOOLKIT

PDOXDATA

Granting Rights to Users

Paradox's *Network Administrator's Guide* recommends that you give users
READ, OPEN, and SEARCH rights to the program directory (to give
equivalent rights with NetWare 386, use the READ and FILE SCAN rights).
All users also must be given access to the directory you designate for
storing shared data. Paradox uses this directory to keep its license-counter
information to ensure that no more than the licensed number of users can
use Paradox at the same time. Give users these rights to this directory:
READ, WRITE, OPEN, CREATE, DELETE, SEARCH, and MODIFY for
NetWare 286, and READ, WRITE, CREATE, ERASE, FILE SCAN, and
MODIFY for NetWare 386.

Setting File Attributes

Paradox's *Network Administrator's Guide* specifically states that you do
not need to turn on any file attributes for Paradox's program files.
Nevertheless, your tape backup unit may require that the SHAREABLE
attribute be turned on so that files can be backed up while Paradox is
in use.

Configuring Paradox

Users can customize their own Paradox configurations and store that configuration information in private directories. For first-time users, the network supervisor can create a default Paradox configuration, which is used until the user creates his or her custom configuration.

Starting Paradox

As with WordPerfect and Lotus 1-2-3, when you start Paradox, you need to map a search drive to the Paradox program directory and then run the program from the directory you want to be your default for data. You also need to make sure that the directory you specified for shared-data storage is mapped to the letter you entered when you installed Paradox. You can easily automate these steps with a batch file and call that batch file from your network's menu system. For example, if you want to use C:\PARADOX as the default directory for storing data, and G:\SOFTWARE\PDOXDATA as the shared-data area, you can start Paradox with the following batch file:

```
ECHO OFF
REM make the c: drive the default
C:
REM make a data directory
MD \PARADOX
REM make the \PARADOX directory the default
CD \PARADOX
ECHO.
ECHO LOADING PARADOX
ECHO.
ECHO.
REM attach to the server that stores Paradox
ATTACH SERV2/GUEST
REM map a search drive to the Paradox directory
MAP INS S2:=SERV2/SYS:SOFTWARE\PARADOX
REM map drive g: to the shared-data directory
MAP G:=SERV2/SYS:SOFTWARE\PDOXDATA
REM start Paradox
PARADOX3
ECHO.
ECHO.
ECHO EXITING PARADOX AND RETURNING TO SYSTEM
C:
REM log out from the server that stores Paradox
LOGOUT SERV2
```

Chapter Summary

You can find many good reasons for using LAN-based software. Your LAN can enable a PC user to access a wider variety of programs. Your LAN can become a software library, where users can access an interesting and useful variety of programs that will help them be more productive. In this chapter, you learned about three of the most popular network versions of software: WordPerfect, 1-2-3, and Paradox.

Network-based programs centralize the task of installing, managing, and upgrading software. They also save disk space, because multiple copies of the same program do not have to be stored on individual PC hard disks. If you are careful to install and configure the shared software on your network servers, your users can run network-based programs with the same freedom and convenience as running software installed on their personal hard disks.

NetWare Attributes Summary

NetWare 286 and NetWare 386 have a wealth of commands, rights, and attributes that you can apply to make your network powerful, efficient, and secure. This appendix summarizes these features of NetWare.

NetWare Commands

The following table displays the NetWare commands discussed in this book. For each command, the NetWare version or versions that support it are indicated (NetWare 286 and NetWare 386). The table also gives the command type and the chapters or appendix where the command is discussed. Commands fall into one of the following four categories:

COMMAND	A single-purpose command used from a workstation
CONSOLE	A single-purpose command used from the server console
NLM	A NetWare Loadable Module (used from the NetWare 386 server console)
UTILITY	A multipurpose program with menus run from a workstation

Command	286	386	Type	Chapter	Purpose
ADD NAME SPACE		X	Console	7, 19	Enables the storage of non-DOS files on a server volume
ALLOW		X	Command	11	Works with a directory's or file's inherited rights mask
ATOTAL	X	X	Command	17	Produces a summary of resource usage on a server
ATTACH	X	X	Command	8	Attaches to another server
BIND		X	Console	7, 19	Links a LAN driver to a particular protocol
BINDFIX	X	X	Command	13	Repairs damaged bindery files
BINDREST	X	X	Command	13	Restores bindery files copied prior to running BINDFIX
BROADCAST	X	X	Console	19	Sends messages from the server console
CAPTURE	X	X	Command	15	Redirects printer output to a shared printer

Command	286	386	Type	Chapter	Purpose
CASTOFF	X	X	Command	18	Blocks the receipt of messages sent by other users
CASTON	X	X	Command	18	Enables the receipt of messages sent by other users
CHKDIR		X	Command	18	Displays the size and maximum space limitation of a directory
CHKVOL	X	X	Command	18	Displays information about a volume
CLEAR MESSAGE	X		Console	19	Clears the message area of the server display
CLEAR STATION	X	X	Console	19	Removes a station's connection from a server
CLS		X	Console	19	Clears the server display
COLORPAL	X	X	Utility	21	Controls the colors of NetWare menu utilities
CONFIG	X	X	Console	19	Displays a server's configuration

Command	286	386	Type	Chapter	Purpose
CONSOLE	X		Command	19	Moves from workstation to server console mode on a nondedicated server PC
DISABLE LOGIN	X	X	Console	19	Prevents users from logging into a server
DISABLE TTS		X	Console	19	Disables the Transaction Tracking System
DISK	X		Console	19	Displays server disk information
DISKSET	X		Utility	6	Configures a Novell Disk Coprocessor Board
DISKSET		X	NLM	7	Configures a Novell Disk Coprocessor Board
DISMOUNT		X	Console	7, 19	Deactivates a volume
DISMOUNT	X		Console	19	Deactivates a removable volume
DISPLAY NETWORKS	X	X	Console	19	Displays all physical networks known to the server

Command	286	386	Type	Chapter	Purpose
DISPLAY SERVERS	X	X	Console	19	Displays all other servers known to the server
DOS	X		Console	19	Moves from server console mode to workstation mode on a nondedicated server
DOWN	X	X	Console	6, 7, 19	Stops the server
DSPACE		X	Utility	10, 18	Limits a user's or directory's disk space
ENABLE LOGIN	X	X	Console	19	Reenables users to log in
ENABLE TTS		X	Console	19	Reenables the Transaction Tracking System
ENDCAP	X	X	Command	15	Ends the redirection of printed output to a network printer
EXIT		X	Console	19	Returns to the DOS prompt after the server has been downed
FCONSOLE	X	X	Utility	18	Manages servers and monitors their performance
FILER	X	X	Utility	12	Manages files and directories

Command	286	386	Type	Chapter	Purpose
FLAG	X	X	Command	12	Sets file attributes
FLAGDIR	X	X	Command	12	Sets directory attributes
GRANT	X	X	Command	11	Gives users and groups rights to directories and files
HELP	X	X	Utility	18	Accesses NetWare's help system
HIDEFILE	X		Command	12	Hides a file by turning on its SYSTEM and HIDDEN attributes
INSTALL		X	NLM	7, 19	Used to configure the server
LARCHIVE	X		Utility	20	Archives server files to a local disk
LISTDIR	X	X	Command	12	Lists all subdirectories below the current directory
LOAD		X	Console	7, 19	Loads a NetWare Loadable Module
LOGIN	X	X	Command	8	Logs into a server
LOGOUT	X	X	Command	8	Logs out from a server

Command	286	386	Type	Chapter	Purpose
LRESTORE	X		Utility	20	Restores server files from a local disk
MAKEUSER	X	X	Utility	E	Adds users and gives them rights
MAP	X	X	Command	9	Assigns drive letters to volumes and directories
MENU	X	X	Command	21	Runs menu script files
MODULES		X	Console	19	Displays the loaded NLMs
MONITOR	X		Console	19	Displays server usage information and statistics
MONITOR		X	NLM	19	Displays server usage information and statistics
MOUNT	X		Console	19	Mounts a removable volume
MOUNT		X	Console	7, 19	Mounts server volumes
NAME	X	X	Console	19	Displays the server name
NARCHIVE	X		Utility	20	Archives server files to another volume on the same server
NBACKUP		X	Utility	20	Backs up server files
NCOPY	X	X	Command	12	Copies files

Command	286	386	Type	Chapter	Purpose
NDIR	X	X	Command	12	Lists information about files and directories
NPRINT	X	X	Command	15	Prints files on shared network printers
NRESTORE	X		Utility	20	Restores server files from another volume on the same server
NVER	X	X	Command	18	Lists version information about NetWare shell and operating system
OFF	X	X	Console	19	Clears the server display
PAUDIT	X	X	Command	17	Displays server accounting log
PCONSOLE	X	X	Utility	14, 15	Configures and manages shared printers and queues
PRINTCON	X	X	Utility	15	Creates print job configurations
PRINTDEF	X	X	Utility	15	Configures printer definitions, functions, and modes

Command	286	386	Type	Chapter	Purpose
PRINTER	X		Console	14, 15	Used to manage server-connected printers
PROTOCOL		X	Console	19	Displays protocol numbers
PSC		X	Command	15	Manages shared printers
PSERVER		X	NLM	14	Operates shared printers
PURGE	X	X	Command	12	Permanently removes erased files from server volumes
QUEUE	X		Console	14, 15	Manages queues
REMIRROR	X		Console	19	Remirrors a matched pair of mirrored or duplexed server disks
REMOVE	X	X	Command	11	Removes a user or group as directory or file trustee
REMOVE DOS		X	Console	19	Disables access to DOS drives from the server's console prompt; also removes COM-MAND.COM from server memory
RENDIR	X	X	Command	12	Renames a directory

Command	286	386	Type	Chapter	Purpose
RESET ROUTER	X	X	Console	19	Causes the server to relearn the list of other servers and bridges
REVOKE	X	X	Command	11	Removes certain directory or file rights from a user or a group
RIGHTS	X	X	Command	11	Displays rights to a file or directory
RPRINTER		X	Command	14	Operates a workstation-based shared printer
SALVAGE	X		Command	12	Recovers deleted files
SALVAGE		X	Utility	12	Recovers deleted files
SEARCH		X	Console	19	Establishes a search order for the LOAD command when it seeks NLMs
SECURE CONSOLE		X	Console	19	Prevents the loading of NLMs from directories other than SYS:SYSTEM
SECURITY	X	X	Command	13	Shows security weaknesses

Command	286	386	Type	Chapter	Purpose
SEND	X	X	Command	18	Sends a message to another user
SEND	X	X	Console	19	Sends messages from the server console
SESSION	X	X	Utility	18	Used to manage drive mappings and send messages
SET		X	Console	7, 19	Sets server configuration options
SET TIME	X	X	Console	19	Sets the server date and time
SETPASS	X	X	Command	10	Changes passwords
SHOWFILE	X		Command	12	Removes the HIDDEN and SYSTEM attributes from a file
SLIST	X	X	Command	18	Lists the network's servers
SMODE	X	X	Command	12	Sets the search mode of an executable file
SPEED		X	Console	7, 19	Displays speed information about the server's processor

Command	286	386	Type	Chapter	Purpose
SPOOL	X	X	Console	14	Maps queues to printer numbers (NetWare 286) or establishes a default queue (NetWare 386)
SYSCON	X	X	Utility	10, 11,16, 17,18	Manages login names, user accounts, rights, login scripts, and accounting
SYSTIME	X	X	Command	18	Displays server time and sets workstation time to match
TIME	X	X	Console	19	Displays server date and time
TLIST	X	X	Command	11	Displays a directory's trustees
TRACK OFF	X	X	Console	19	Turns off server tracking
TRACK ON	X	X	Console	19	Displays server availability broadcasts and workstation ATTACH requests
UNMIRROR	X		Console	19	Unmirrors a previously matched pair of server disks

Command	286	386	Type	Chapter	Purpose
UNBIND		X	Console	19	Unbinds a protocol from a network adapter driver
UNLOAD		X	Console	19	Removes an NLM from server memory
UPS	X	X	Console, NLM	19	Monitors the operation of a server-connected uninterruptible power supply
USERDEF	X	X	Utility	E	Adds users to a server
USERLIST	X	X	Command	18	Lists users logged into a server
VAP	X		Console	19	Displays a list of the server's loaded VAPs
VERSION	X	X	Console	19	Displays the NetWare version running on the server
VOLINFO	X	X	Utility	18	Displays disk space utilization information about the server's volumes
VOLUMES	X	X	Console	19	Displays information about the server's volumes

Command	286	386	Type	Chapter	Purpose
VREPAIR	X	X	Command	18	Used to repair a damaged server volume
WHOAMI	X	X	Command	18	Displays information about your connection

NetWare Rights

NetWare 286 and NetWare 386 enable you to give or withhold a combination of eight rights. NetWare 286's rights can be granted at the directory level only. NetWare 386's rights can be granted at both the directory level and the individual file level.

NetWare 386 Right	NetWare 286 Right	Purpose
READ	READ	Enables a user to read the contents of existing files.
WRITE	WRITE	Enables a user to change or add to the contents of existing files.
	OPEN	Enables a user to open an existing file. You must be able to open a file before you can read it, write to it, or change its name or attributes.
CREATE	CREATE	Lets a user create a new file in the directory. NetWare 386 only—enables the user to make subdirectories within the directory.
ERASE	DELETE	Lets a user erase an existing file in the directory.
	PARENTAL	Enables a user to make or remove subdirectories under the directory and give other users rights to that directory.

NetWare 386 Right	NetWare 286 Right	Purpose
ACCESS CONTROL		Enables a user to grant other users rights to the directory.
FILE SCAN	SEARCH	Lets a user list the files in the directory.
MODIFY	MODIFY	Lets a user rename or change the attributes of a file or subdirectory.
SUPERVISORY		Gives the user all rights to the directory and its subdirectories. Rights cannot be withheld from subdirectories beneath a directory where a user has the SUPERVISORY right, and the SUPERVISORY right overrides rights withheld by the inherited rights mask.

File and Directory Attributes

You can give attributes to files and directories in NetWare 286 and NetWare 386. The following paragraphs specify those attributes and their functions.

NetWare 286 File Attributes

NetWare 286 supports the DOS and OS/2 file attributes and adds four others:

READ ONLY	Making a file READ ONLY means that it cannot be written to, changed, or deleted, even when you have enough trustee rights to do so.
HIDDEN	Turning on the HIDDEN attribute makes a file invisible to commands and programs that try to list, copy, or delete files. These commands include the DOS commands DIR, ERASE, COPY, and DEL.
SYSTEM	The SYSTEM attribute makes files invisible and indicates that the file is reserved for system use.

ARCHIVE

The ARCHIVE attribute is turned on automatically when a file has been changed by a program or a DOS or OS/2 command. NetWare 286 calls this attribute MODIFIED, and NetWare 386 calls it ARCHIVE NEEDED.

SHAREABLE

Files that have the SHAREABLE attribute turned on can be accessed by more than one user at a time.

INDEXED

Turning on the INDEXED attribute makes the access to very large files (2M or larger) more efficient.

For NetWare 286, the program that creates the files must turn on the INDEXED attribute so that an index of disk blocks can be created as the file is built.

On NetWare 386 servers, this attribute is turned on automatically when a file occupies more than 64 disk blocks.

EXECUTE ONLY

Turning on the EXECUTE ONLY attribute prevents files from being copied. This attribute is only available for executable files (files that have the extension EXE or COM) and you must have supervisory equivalence to turn it on.

After you have turned on the EXECUTE ONLY attribute, it cannot be removed. The only way to undo the effects of this attribute is to delete or copy over the file that has it turned on.

TRANSACTIONAL

The TRANSACTIONAL attribute works in conjunction with NetWare's Transaction Tracking System (TTS). TTS is an option that can be activated if you are using System Fault Tolerant NetWare. TTS ensures that all file updates to data files with the TRANSACTIONAL attribute turned on are made only as complete transactions.

To take advantage of this attribute, you must have an application that is designed to work with NetWare's Transaction Tracking System.

NetWare 386 File Attributes

NetWare 386 supports the same attributes as NetWare 286 and adds six others:

COPY INHIBIT | This attribute is designed for Macintosh users. When a file has this attribute turned on, a Macintosh user may not copy it.

DELETE INHIBIT | When this attribute is turned on, even users who have the ERASE right cannot delete the file.

PURGE | Normally, NetWare 386 saves a deleted file so that it can be salvaged if necessary. When a file has the PURGE attribute turned on, it is purged immediately upon deletion so that it cannot be salvaged.

RENAME INHIBIT | A file that has this attribute turned on cannot be renamed even if the user has the MODIFY right.

READ AUDIT | This attribute can be turned on but is not used by NetWare 386 Version 3.0. In future releases of NetWare 386, it will provide an audit trail listing users who have read the file.

WRITE AUDIT | Like READ AUDIT, this attribute can be turned on but is not used by NetWare 386 Version 3.0. In future releases of NetWare 386, it will provide an audit trail listing users who have written to the file.

Directory Attributes

NetWare 286 Version 2.15 and NetWare 386 enable you to turn on attributes for directories. For NetWare 286, three attributes can be turned on or off for directories:

HIDDEN | Makes the directory invisible

SYSTEM | Makes the directory invisible and designates that the directory is for system use

PRIVATE | Used to prevent users from seeing a directory's subdirectories

NetWare 386 does not require the PRIVATE attribute because it makes a directory private by default unless the user has rights to it. NetWare 386 lets you turn on three additional attributes for directories:

DELETE INHIBIT	When this attribute is turned on, even users who have the ERASE right cannot delete the directory.
PURGE	When a directory has the PURGE attribute turned on, its files are purged immediately upon deletion so that they cannot be salvaged.
RENAME INHIBIT	A directory that has this attribute turned on cannot be renamed even if the user has the MODIFY right.

B

Special Keys for Menued Utility Commands

Function	Key To Use	Description
ESCAPE	Esc	Move back to the previous menu or level
EXIT	Alt-F10	Exit the utility from any screen
CANCEL	F7	Cancel changes without saving them
BACKSPACE	Backspace	Delete the character to the left of the cursor
INSERT	Ins	Insert a new item
DELETE	Del	Delete an item
MODIFY	F3	Rename/modify/edit the item
SELECT	Enter	Accept information entered or select the item
HELP	F1	Access help screens
MARK	F5	Mark an unmarked item or unmark a marked item

Function	Key To Use	Description
CYCLE	Tab	Cycle through menus or screens
MODE	F9	Change Modes
UP	↑	Move up one line
DOWN	↓	Move down one line
LEFT	←	Move left one space
RIGHT	→	Move right one space
SPECIAL UP	Ctrl-PgUp	Move to the very beginning
SPECIAL DOWN	Ctrl-PgDn	Move to the very end
SPECIAL LEFT	Home	Move to the far-left position on the line
SPECIAL RIGHT	End	Move to the far-right position on the line
PAGE UP	PgUp	Move up one page
PAGE DOWN	PgDn	Move down one page
FIELD LEFT	Ctrl-←	Move left one field or word
FIELD RIGHT	Ctrl-→	Move right one field or word

Important NetWare Files and Directories

The following directories and subdirectories are automatically created on the SYS volume when you install NetWare. During the installation and configuration process, NetWare's important files are placed in these subdirectories as shown in the diagram on the following page.

```
SYS:
  ├──SYSTEM   Operating system files
  │           Bindery files (NetWare 386: NET$OBJ.SYS, NET$PROP.SYS
  │                                         NET$VAL.SYS)
  │
  │                         (NetWare 286: NET$BIND.SYS, NET$BVAL.SYS)
  │
  │           NLMs (NetWare 386)
  │           VAPs (NetWare 286)
  │           Accounting data file: NET$ACCT.DAT
  │               Supervisor and accounting commands
  │               Server AUTOEXEC file
  │               Server configuration file (SERVER.CFG—NetWare 286)
  │
  │      ├──09001B (queue subdirectory)
  │      │     print job files
  │      │
  │      └──160069 (queue subdirectory)
  │            print job files
  │
  ├──MAIL Each user has a personal subdirectory name that matches the
  │       user's id number
  │
  │      ├──1
  │      │
  │      ├──20007
  │      │
  │      └──11003B
  │           Each user's subdirectory may contain:
  │               LOGIN (personal login script file)
  │                   PRINTCON.DAT (personal printer configuration file)
  │
  ├──LOGIN
  │     LOGIN.EXE
  │     SLIST.EXE
  │
  └──PUBLIC
        NetWare user commands and utilities
        NET$LOG.DAT (System login script file)
        Printer definition files
```

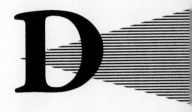

Network Node Address Reference Chart

Use this chart to look up node addresses for network adapters where the node address is established by setting dip switches. The first column shows the regular decimal number. The second shows the same number in hexadecimal format (as it appears when displayed by USERLIST/A, FCONSOLE, and other NetWare utilities). The binary columns show the same number as set by using eight-position dip switches. Most dip switches start with the lowest switch (or least significant bit) to the left. Switch settings for this type of switch are shown in the first binary column. With some network adapter dip switches, the highest numbered switch (or most significant bit) is on the left. The second binary column displays the switch settings for this type of adapter. Compare this chart to the manual for your network adapter to determine which number (0 or 1) corresponds to the address switch's ON position.

Decimal	Hex	Binary	
		Least to Highest	*Highest to Least*
1	1	10000000	00000001
2	2	01000000	00000010
3	3	11000000	00000011
4	4	00100000	00000100
5	5	10100000	00000101
6	6	01100000	00000110
7	7	11100000	00000111
8	8	00010000	00001000
9	9	10010000	00001001

Decimal	Hex	Binary	
		Least to Highest	*Highest to Least*
10	A	01010000	00001010
11	B	11010000	00001011
12	C	00110000	00001100
13	D	10110000	00001101
14	E	01110000	00001110
15	F	11110000	00001111
16	10	00001000	00010000
17	11	10001000	00010001
18	12	01001000	00010010
19	13	11001000	00010011
20	14	00101000	00010100
21	15	10101000	00010101
22	16	01101000	00010110
23	17	11101000	00010111
24	18	00011000	00011000
25	19	10011000	00011001
26	1A	01011000	00011010
27	1B	11011000	00011011
28	1C	00111000	00011100
29	1D	10111000	00011101
30	1E	01111000	00011110
31	1F	11111000	00011111
32	20	00000100	00100000
33	21	10000100	00100001
34	22	01000100	00100010
35	23	11000100	00100011
36	24	00100100	00100100
37	25	10100100	00100101
38	26	01100100	00100110
39	27	11100100	00100111
40	28	00010100	00101000
41	29	10010100	00101001
42	2A	01010100	00101010
43	2B	11010100	00101011
44	2C	00110100	00101100
45	2D	10110100	00101101
46	2E	01110100	00101110
47	2F	11110100	00101111
48	30	00001100	00110000
49	31	10001100	00110001

Decimal	Hex	Binary	
		Least to Highest	Highest to Least
50	32	01001100	00110010
51	33	11001100	00110011
52	34	00101100	00110100
53	35	10101100	00110101
54	36	01101100	00110110
55	37	11101100	00110111
56	38	00011100	00111000
57	39	10011100	00111001
58	3A	01011100	00111010
59	3B	11011100	00111011
60	3C	00111100	00111100
61	3D	10111100	00111101
62	3E	01111100	00111110
63	3F	11111100	00111111
64	40	00000010	01000000
65	41	10000010	01000001
66	42	01000010	01000010
67	43	11000010	01000011
68	44	00100010	01000100
69	45	10100010	01000101
70	46	01100010	01000110
71	47	11100010	01000111
72	48	00010010	01001000
73	49	10010010	01001001
74	4A	01010010	01001010
75	4B	11010010	01001011
76	4C	00110010	01001100
77	4D	10110010	01001101
78	4E	01110010	01001110
79	4F	11110010	01001111
80	50	00001010	01010000
81	51	10001010	01010001
82	52	01001010	01010010
83	53	11001010	01010011
84	54	00101010	01010100
85	55	10101010	01010101
86	56	01101010	01010110
87	57	11101010	01010111
88	58	00011010	01011000
89	59	10011010	01011001
90	5A	01011010	01011010
91	5B	11011010	01011011
92	5C	00111010	01011100

Decimal	Hex	Binary	
		Least to Highest	*Highest to Least*
93	5D	10111010	01011101
94	5E	01111010	01011110
95	5F	11111010	01011111
96	60	00000110	01100000
97	61	10000110	01100001
98	62	01000110	01100010
99	63	11000110	01100011
100	64	00100110	01100100
101	65	10100110	01100101
102	66	01100110	01100110
103	67	11100110	01100111
104	68	00010110	01101000
105	69	10010110	01101001
106	6A	01010110	01101010
107	6B	11010110	01101011
108	6C	00110110	01101100
109	6D	10110110	01101101
110	6E	01110110	01101110
111	6F	11110110	01101111
112	70	00001110	01110000
113	71	10001110	01110001
114	72	01001110	01110010
115	73	11001110	01110011
116	74	00101110	01110100
117	75	10101110	01110101
118	76	01101110	01110110
119	77	11101110	01110111
120	78	00011110	01111000
121	79	10011110	01111001
122	7A	01011110	01111010
123	7B	11011110	01111011
124	7C	00111110	01111100
125	7D	10111110	01111101
126	7E	01111110	01111110
127	7F	11111110	01111111
128	80	00000001	10000000
129	81	10000001	10000001
130	82	01000001	10000010
131	83	11000001	10000011
132	84	00100001	10000100

Decimal	Hex	Binary	
		Least to Highest	Highest to Least
133	85	10100001	10000101
134	86	01100001	10000110
135	87	11100001	10000111
136	88	00010001	10001000
137	89	10010001	10001001
138	8A	01010001	10001010
139	8B	11010001	10001011
140	8C	00110001	10001100
141	8D	10110001	10001101
142	8E	01110001	10001110
143	8F	11110001	10001111
144	90	00001001	10010000
145	91	10001001	10010001
146	92	01001001	10010010
147	93	11001001	10010011
148	94	00101001	10010100
149	95	10101001	10010101
150	96	01101001	10010110
151	97	11101001	10010111
152	98	00011001	10011000
153	99	10011001	10011001
154	9A	01011001	10011010
155	9B	11011001	10011011
156	9C	00111001	10011100
157	9D	10111001	10011101
158	9E	01111001	10011110
159	9F	11111001	10011111
160	A0	00000101	10100000
161	A1	10000101	10100001
162	A2	01000101	10100010
163	A3	11000101	10100011
164	A4	00100101	10100100
165	A5	10100101	10100101
166	A6	01100101	10100110
167	A7	11100101	10100111
168	A8	00010101	10101000
169	A9	10010101	10101001
170	AA	01010101	10101010
171	AB	11010101	10101011
172	AC	00110101	10101100
173	AD	10110101	10101101
174	AE	01110101	10101110
175	AF	11110101	10101111

Decimal	Hex	Binary	
		Least to Highest	*Highest to Least*
176	B0	00001101	10110000
177	B1	10001101	10110001
178	B2	01001101	10110010
179	B3	11001101	10110011
180	B4	00101101	10110100
181	B5	10101101	10110101
182	B6	01101101	10110110
183	B7	11101101	10110111
184	B8	00011101	10111000
185	B9	10011101	10111001
186	BA	01011101	10111010
187	BB	11011101	10111011
188	BC	00111101	10111100
189	BD	10111101	10111101
190	BE	01111101	10111110
191	BF	11111101	10111111
192	C0	00000011	11000000
193	C1	10000011	11000001
194	C2	01000011	11000010
195	C3	11000011	11000011
196	C4	00100011	11000100
197	C5	10100011	11000101
198	C6	01100011	11000110
199	C7	11100011	11000111
200	C8	00010011	11001000
201	C9	10010011	11001001
202	CA	01010011	11001010
203	CB	11010011	11001011
204	CC	00110011	11001100
205	CD	10110011	11001101
206	CE	01110011	11001110
207	CF	11110011	11001111
208	D0	00001011	11010000
209	D1	10001011	11010001
210	D2	01001011	11010010
211	D3	11001011	11010011
212	D4	00101011	11010100
213	D5	10101011	11010101
214	D6	01101011	11010110
215	D7	11101011	11010111

Decimal	Hex	Binary	
		Least to Highest	Highest to Least
216	D8	00011011	11011000
217	D9	10011011	11011001
218	DA	01011011	11011010
219	DB	11011011	11011011
220	DC	00111011	11011100
221	DD	10111011	11011101
222	DE	01111011	11011110
223	DF	11111011	11011111
224	E0	00000111	11100000
225	E1	10000111	11100001
226	E2	01000111	11100010
227	E3	11000111	11100011
228	E4	00100111	11100100
229	E5	10100111	11100101
230	E6	01100111	11100110
231	E7	11100111	11100111
232	E8	00010111	11101000
233	E9	10010111	11101001
234	EA	01010111	11101010
235	EB	11010111	11101011
236	EC	00110111	11101100
237	ED	10110111	11101101
238	EE	01110111	11101110
239	EF	11110111	11101111
240	F0	00001111	11110000
241	F1	10001111	11110001
242	F2	01001111	11110010
243	F3	11001111	11110011
244	F4	00101111	11110100
245	F5	10101111	11110101
246	F6	01101111	11110110
247	F7	11101111	11110111
248	F8	00011111	11111000
249	F9	10011111	11111001
250	FA	01011111	11111010
251	FB	11011111	11111011
252	FC	00111111	11111100
253	FD	10111111	11111101
254	FE	01111111	11111110
255	FF	11111111	11111111

Shortcuts for Managing Users

Two NetWare utilities, USERDEF and MAKEUSER, enable you to make the process of adding users more automatic. If the users that you add fall into similar patterns when it comes to login scripts, group memberships, account restrictions, and so on, these utilities may save you time or enable you to automate the process so that you can hand off to an assistant the task of adding users.

MAKEUSER is not easy to learn, but it is powerful and flexible. You use it by creating a script file that contains instructions for adding users and configuring their accounts. not many network supervisors use it regularly, but some supervisors say that it is useful when they need to add or delete a large number of new users. A few of these supervisors have written programs to create the instruction files used by MAKEUSER.

USERDEF is actually a friendly "front end" for MAKEUSER. USERDEF prompts you to create templates that define the account restrictions, group memberships, login scripts, printer configuration, and accounting information for your users. After you configure USERDEF's templates, you can use it to create script files for MAKEUSER and to run the MAKEUSER program behind the scenes to process those scripts and add users.

USERDEF and MAKEUSER operate on the assumption that you already have configured your server and that the groups, shared printers, accounting definitions (if you have decided to implement NetWare accounting), and application directories already exist.

Using USERDEF

You should be logged in with supervisory rights to use USERDEF. Start USERDEF by typing *userdef* from the command prompt and pressing Enter.

Some versions of USERDEF start by asking if you want to load the DOS command files to the server, which seems to be the case because USERDEF's default login script attempts to map a search drive to a server-based DOS directory. If you do not want to store DOS on the server, answer no to this prompt. If you answer yes, you are prompted to insert your DOS disks one at a time in your PC's floppy drive, and the files are copied to the server in a subdirectory under the SYS:PUBLIC directory. The default version of the login script that USERDEF creates for the users it adds maps a search drive to this DOS directory. You are free to create your own default login script that doesn't perform this mapping.

After responding to the prompt discussed in the preceding paragraph, USERDEF brings you to its main menu, which offers two options:

Add Users
Edit Template

These options are discussed in the following sections.

Creating a Template

Select Edit Template to display a list of the currently defined templates. If you are running USERDEF for the first time, the only template listed is DEFAULT. This template cannot be modified, and serves as the model from which you can build a custom template.

To create your own template, press Ins. You are prompted to enter the name of the template that you want to create. Choose a name that will identify the template according to its use. For example, if you are creating a template to add users from the accounting department, you might name your template ACCTING.

After you enter a template name, the Template menu appears (see fig. E.1). This menu offers you two options: Edit Login Script and Edit Parameters.

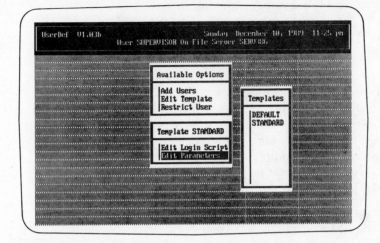

Fig. E.1.
USERDEF's Template menu.

Editing the Template's Parameters

Select the Edit Parameters option from the Template menu. The template parameters window opens, and you are prompted to set the parameters for a variety of items (see fig. E.2).

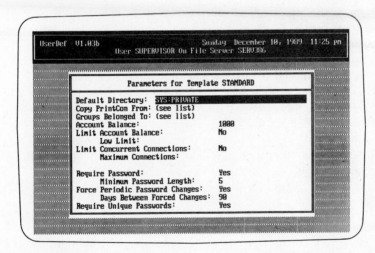

Fig. E.2.
USERDEF's template parameters window.

The first template item you are prompted to enter is the default directory. Enter a directory to serve as the parent directory for each user's personal subdirectory. USERDEF creates a subdirectory named with the user's login name under this default directory. For example, if you enter a default directory name of SYS:PRIVATE, when a user named SMITHFD is created, the directory SYS:PRIVATE\SMITHFD is created, and SMITHFD is given all rights to it. Type the default directory name of your choice and press Enter.

Next, you are prompted to choose a user with the set of print job definitions that you want to copy. With the highlight next to Copy Printcon From, press Enter. You see a list of all users who have print jobs defined. Highlight the user with the print job definitions you want to copy to new users you are adding and press Enter. You have the option of selecting none if you do not want to copy any print job definitions. After you select a user, you return to the template parameters window.

Next, you must specify which groups the new user should be added to. Move the highlight to Groups Belonged To and press Enter. A Groups Belonged To window opens showing only the EVERYONE group. To select additional groups, press Ins. A list of all the groups on the server appears. Highlight the one you want to add and press Enter, or mark multiple groups with F5 and press Enter. The Groups Belonged To window is updated to show your additions. To remove a group from the list, highlight the group and press Del, or mark multiple groups with F5 and press Del. After you select the groups to which new users will be added, press Esc to return to the template parameters window.

The next two items in the template parameters window have an effect only if you have implemented NetWare accounting (see Chapter 17). To set a starting account balance, move the highlight to Account Balance and press Enter. Backspace over the default setting and enter your desired balance. Next, you are prompted to specify whether to limit the user's account balance. Leaving this setting at no means that the user can continue to use server resources even when his account balance falls below zero. If you change the setting to yes, you are prompted on the next line to set a *low limit*, which is used as the user's minimum account balance allowed. Enter your desired minimum account balance. You should set the Limit Account Balance to yes only if you have activated NetWare accounting. Otherwise, you get an error when you try to add users with the template.

Next, you are prompted to choose whether to limit concurrent connections. A *concurrent connection* is a situation where two or more workstations using the same login name are logged into the server. If you want to limit a user's concurrent connections, change this setting from no to yes. You are then prompted to enter a number for Allowed Maximum

Connections. Enter the number of concurrent connections that you want to permit (see Chapter 10).

The next several items deal with passwords (see Chapter 10 for information on password control options). The Require Password setting specifies whether the user is required to use a password. By default, this is set at yes. Choose no if you do not want to require a password.

If you require a password, you must set a minimum password length. The default setting is five characters; move the highlight to this option and enter a new setting if you want to change it. Next, you are prompted to specify whether you want to force periodic password changes. The default setting is yes; you may highlight this setting and press N to change it to no if you prefer. If you require periodic password changes, you must select a number for the Days Between Forced Changes field. The default setting is 90 days. Highlight the setting and enter the number of days of your choice.

Next, you must set the Require Unique Passwords field. By default, this setting is yes, which means that users will not be able to reuse old passwords when they make password changes. Move the highlight to this setting and press N to change it to no if you do not want to require unique passwords.

On NetWare 286 servers, you must set the Limit Disk Space option. Answering yes to this option limits the user's maximum disk space. The default setting is no; highlight the setting and press Y to change it to yes if you want to limit disk space. If you select yes, you are prompted to enter the amount of disk space in kilobytes to which you want to limit the user. Highlight this setting and enter the number of your choice.

NetWare 386's USERDEF does not enable you to assign a disk space limitation to a user with a template. Instead, a third option is included on USERDEF's main menu called Restrict User. This option functions identically to the DSPACE utility (see Chapter 10 for details concerning limiting disk space with DSPACE).

After you set the parameters for your template, press Esc to leave the template parameters window and save your changes. You then return to the Template menu.

Editing the Template's Login Script

The next option that you should select from the Template menu is Edit Login Script. When you select this option, you are taken to a login script editing window, and the default login script is shown. Change this login script to meet your specifications. After you create your script, press Esc to save it and to return to the Template menu. (For complete details about login scripts, see Chapter 16).

Your template is now complete and ready to be used to add new users. Press Esc to save your template definition. You are returned to the Template list. Press Ins to define another template, or press Esc to return to USERDEF's main menu.

Adding Users with USERDEF

After you have defined at least one template, you are ready to use USERDEF to add new users to your server. From USERDEF's main menu, select Add Users. A list of the defined templates appears. Highlight the template that should be used for the user you are adding and press Enter. A list of the server's existing users appears. Press Ins to add a new user.

You are prompted to enter the full name (not the login name) of the new user. Type the appropriate full name and press Enter. Next, you are prompted to enter a login name; the user's first name is offered as a default. To add the new name backspace over the default and type the name of your choice. Press Enter, and the list of users is updated to show the name you have added. That name is designated as (new) to show that it has been added but not processed.

Repeat the procedure if you have more users to add using the selected template. After you enter all new user names, press Esc to leave the user list. Answer yes at the prompt to confirm that you want to create the new users. A status screen appears to confirm that the users have been added. Press Esc to return to USERDEF's list of users. Press Esc twice to return to the main menu, and press Esc again to exit USERDEF.

Using MAKEUSER

Skillful use of the USERDEF utility may be all you need to handle adding new users. If you need to customize the process beyond what USERDEF provides, consider using MAKEUSER.

MAKEUSER requires that you create a text file script containing key words that indicate what actions MAKEUSER will take. Script files can be designed not only to add users, but also to delete them. You also can implement account restrictions that USERDEF does not support, including station and time restrictions. Also, you can use MAKEUSER to give users rights to any existing directory (unlike USERDEF, which only can give the user rights to his or her home directory).

Consult your NetWare manuals for complete details about MAKEUSER's script key words and how to process script files.

Working with ELS NetWare

ELS stands for Entry-Level Solution. ELS NetWare is a special version of NetWare designed for small networks. It provides many of the same features as NetWare 286 and 386 but limits the number of users who can connect to the server to either four or eight.

ELS NetWare Level I is for networks of no more than four users, and is priced with the budget-conscious buyer in mind. Like Advanced NetWare, it requires at least an 80286-based file server, and enables you to run the file server as a nondedicated PC (as a server and workstation simultaneously).

ELS NetWare Level I is an older release level of NetWare (Version 2.0) and does not have some of the features and commands described in this book. Level I is lacking chiefly in network-management utilities, which is probably not a major concern when your maximum network size is four users. It also requires that you use different commands for printing than those that are discussed in this book.

ELS NetWare Level II is current with the latest NetWare 286 release level (2.1x). It includes all the features and commands of Advanced NetWare, and permits a maximum of eight users at a time. When running ELS NetWare Lavel II, you can operate the server as a dedicated or nondedicated file server.

This appendix gives you an overview of ELS NetWare and points out areas where you encounter functions and features different from those described in this book.

Designing an ELS NetWare Network

The main factor to keep in mind when you design a LAN that will use an ELS NetWare server is that the number of users and file servers is limited. With ELS NetWare Level I, you are limited to one of three types of network adapters (EtherNet, ARCNet, IBM PC Network).

Design Considerations with ELS NetWare Level I

ELS NetWare Level I limits the maximum number of file server connections to four at one time. You may connect more than four workstations to the network, but only four can use the server simultaneously.

You can use ELS NetWare Level I with only three types of network adapters: EtherNet, ARCNet, or IBM's PC Network adapter (not to be confused with IBM's Token Ring network adapter). Make sure that you can meet the cable requirements for one of these three types of adapters before making ELS NetWare Level I your final choice.

Like ELS NetWare Level II, ELS NetWare Level I limits you to one file server per network, and that file server is limited to two hard disks connected to an ST506 or ESDI controller (for details about controllers, see Chapter 4). If you need more disk space or file servers, you should use a version of NetWare other than ELS.

ELS NetWare Level I automatically makes the file server nondedicated. It requires that your server be an 80286, 80386, or 80486 PC, and that it have a minimum of 1.2M of RAM. Your server PC should be certified by Novell for use as a nondedicated server (check with your NetWare vendor to ensure that your server PC is usable as a nondedicated file server).

Design Considerations with ELS NetWare Level II

ELS NetWare Level II limits the maximum number of file server connections to eight at one time. You may connect more than eight workstations to the network, but only eight can use the server simultaneously.

ELS NetWare also limits you to one file server per network, and that file server is limited to two hard disks connected to either an ST506 or ESDI controller (for details about controllers, see Chapter 4). If your requirements are such that more disk space or file servers are needed, then you should use a version of NetWare other than ELS.

If your file server is dedicated (the server PC is used exclusively as a server, and not as a server and workstation), it can be an XT-compatible (using an 8088 or 8086 processor), an AT-compatible (using an 80286 processor), or an 80386 PC. Note: ELS NetWare Level II Version 2.15 *cannot* run on an XT-compatible computer. The server PC also must have at least 640K of RAM. If your server is nondedicated (used as a server and workstation at the same time), it must be an 80286, 80386, or 80486 PC with at least 2M of RAM, and should be certified by Novell for use as a nondedicated server. Check with your NetWare vendor to make sure that your server PC is usable as a nondedicated file server.

Installing ELS NetWare

The installation procedures for ELS NetWare differ from those for other NetWare versions. ELS Level II's installation is very similar to that for NetWare 286 Version 2.1 (see Chapters 5 and 6). ELS Level I uses a very simple and unique installation procedure.

Tips for Installing ELS NetWare Level I

ELS NetWare Level I's installation process is completely automatic. It starts by performing a COMPSURF check on the file server disk and then copies all of NetWare's files to the server volumes.

NetWare's Hot Fix feature, which performs read-after-write verification on all disk writes (see Chapter 4), is automatically activated on the first hard disk drive. You active Hot Fix on the second hard disk drive by running the PREPARE utility after you install NetWare on the server. It's easy to miss this step because it is not discussed in the installation documentation, but in an appendix instead.

After NetWare is fully installed on the server, prepare a server-boot disk to match the type of network adapter that you are using.

You do not have to generate a NetWare workstation shell. ELS NetWare Level I comes with this already created. You simply copy the NetWare shell to each workstation's boot disk.

Tips for Installing ELS NetWare Level II

Generating and installing ELS NetWare is very similar to performing the same functions for Advanced NetWare 286. Although Advanced and SFT NetWare 286 use a utility called NETGEN for these tasks, ELS NetWare Level II uses a utility called ELSGEN. Generating ELS NetWare Level II using ELSGEN is very similar to using the custom level of NETGEN (generating NetWare with NETGEN is discussed in Chapter 5). Installing with ELSGEN is almost identical to using NETGEN, and ELSGEN offers a default and custom level.

As with NetWare 286, you can install and configure ELS NetWare Level II's files from working copies of floppies or from a hard disk or network drive. If possible, use the hard disk or network drive method to avoid an excessive amount of disk-swapping and to have your configuration files readily available for future use.

You should use ELSGEN's COMPSURF utility to check the server disks for bad blocks prior to installation.

Generating workstation shells for ELS NetWare Level II is identical to performing the same task with NetWare 286. The same SHGEN utility is supplied with ELS NetWare Level II (see Chapter 8 for instructions on using SHGEN).

Examining the Differences Between ELS NetWare and NetWare 286 Version 2.1

Most of the commands and utilities discussed in this book are available with ELS NetWare. In fact, virtually all of them are available with ELS NetWare Level II. ELS NetWare Level I, however, has a few key differences.

The biggest difference is in the area of shared printing. Although NetWare 286 enables you to create queues and assign them to printers, ELS NetWare Level I automatically creates one queue per printer. All users have the right to use shared printers, and you cannot set priorities or printer notification options as you can with NetWare 286 and 386. You direct output to the printer by using a command called SPOOL (instead of CAPTURE). Instead of using a utility called PCONSOLE to view and control queued print jobs, you use a utility called QUEUE.

ELS NetWare Level I does not support account restrictions. You cannot force users to use passwords or restrict their access based on time or station addresses. NetWare's accounting also is not supported.

You also cannot control the server from a workstation as you can with NetWare 286. ELS NetWare Level I does not support the FCONSOLE utility.

ELS NetWare provides a low-cost method of bringing the benefits of networking to an office that has only a few PCs. ELS NetWare can be a cost-effective way to begin a network. If your office grows beyond its capabilities, you can easily upgrade to Advanced NetWare 286 or SFT NetWare 286.

NetWare and OS/2

Considerable confusion surrounds OS/2 and networking, including confusion about whether NetWare is OS/2 compatible. In this appendix, you will learn how NetWare coexists with OS/2 and how both can be used on the same network.

OS/2 is a PC operating system that removes two of the most frustrating constraints of PC DOS: the maximum memory limitation of 640K and the inability to run more than one program at a time. OS/2 is capable of using up to 16M of memory.

OS/2 is designed to be multitasking, which enables it to run multiple programs at the same time. You can operate multiple OS/2 sessions, each of which is capable of running a program.

You can use OS/2 as part of a network in three ways. First, a file server can be OS/2-based. File server operating systems such as IBM's LAN Server or 3COM's 3 Plus Open are examples of how OS/2 can serve as the platform upon which a file server operating system can be built. OS/2-based file servers use OS/2's file system, memory management, and multitasking abilities as the basis for file serving. Because NetWare existed before OS/2, NetWare does not require a separate platform to build upon. NetWare's own file system, memory management, and multitasking abilities are highly developed and widely respected.

Second, OS/2 can be used to operate networked workstations. Workstations running OS/2, like their DOS counterparts, can access NetWare servers and use server disks to store and retrieve files. OS/2 workstations also can send print jobs to shared printers. DOS workstations use the NetWare Workstation Shell, but OS/2 workstations use the NetWare OS/2 Requester. The OS/2 Requester will be discussed in the next section.

A third method of incorporating OS/2-based devices into your network exists. OS/2 is sometimes used to turn a PC into a specialized server that can be accessed by other workstations. The most common example is the database server. Workstations send requests for database records to the database server. The database server in turn processes the requests by searching its databases for the records and then returns the result to the workstation.

The NetWare OS/2 Requester

To enable an OS/2 workstation to access NetWare file servers, you need to use the NetWare OS/2 Requester. The OS/2 Requester consists of a two parts: the files used to enable the workstation to access the server and the OS/2 versions of NetWare commands.

The NetWare OS/2 Requester does not work with all types of network adapters. Consult the documentation that comes with your NetWare Requester, or check with your NetWare vendor to make sure that the network adapter you plan to use is supported by the NetWare OS/2 Requester.

Installing the OS/2 Requester is a two-part process. You first copy the OS/2 versions of NetWare commands to the file servers to which OS/2 workstations will log in. You then copy to each OS/2 workstation's boot disk the files used to enable the workstation to connect to the server. You also modify the CONFIG.SYS file on the OS/2 workstation so that the drivers and programs required to use NetWare file servers are activated.

Installing OS/2 Versions of NetWare Commands

OS/2 workstations cannot run programs designed to be run on DOS workstations. For this reason, OS/2 versions of popular NetWare commands are provided, and they must be placed on the servers to be used by OS/2 workstations.

You need to create two directories for these commands. The documentation for the OS/2 Requester suggests that you create a subdirectory under SYS:PUBLIC called OS2, and another subdirectory under

SYS:LOGIN also called OS2. You can use NetWare's FILER or the DOS MD command to perform this task. (Chapter 12 provides details for using FILER.)

After you have created these directories, use the NetWare MAP command to assign drive letters to the two new directories (see Chapter 9 for details about using MAP). For example, you might want to assign drive letter G to SYS:LOGIN\OS2 and H to SYS:PUBLIC\OS2.

After drive letters have been assigned, place the disk labeled PUBLIC/OS2 (1 of ...) into your PC's floppy drive. Make your floppy drive the current drive and type

SERVINST A G H

and press Enter (replace A with the drive letter of your floppy drive, G with the drive letter of the SYS:LOGIN\OS2 directory, and H with the drive letter of the SYS:PUBLIC\OS2 directory. The OS/2 NetWare command files are copied into the correct directories.

After the command files have been placed in the appropriate directories, use the FLAG command or the FILER utility to turn on the SHAREABLE and READ ONLY attributes for all the files in the SYS:LOGIN\OS2 and SYS:PUBLIC\OS2 directories (see Chapter 12 for information about FLAG and FILER). Next, use SYSCON or GRANT to give OS/2 workstation users READ, OPEN, and SEARCH rights (NetWare 286) or READ and FILE SCAN rights (NetWare 386) to the directories discussed in the preceding paragraph.

Activating OS/2 Workstations

After you have installed the OS/2 versions of the NetWare commands on the server, you are ready to connect OS/2 workstations to your network. Each OS/2 workstation must have the NetWare OS/2 Requester files copied to its disk, and the CONFIG.SYS file for each workstation must be modified to include commands for activating the NetWare Requester.

Boot the OS/2 workstation on which you want to install the NetWare Requester and move to the OS/2 command prompt. Place the disk labeled Requester in a floppy drive of the workstation, make that floppy drive the default, type *install*, and press Enter. The installation program prompts you to select the directories where you want to copy the NetWare Requester's files. Your configuration job will be easier if you copy the Requester's Dynamic Link Library files (the files with the extension DLL) into a directory where other OS/2 DLL files are stored. If you copy them to a directory that is not already used to store other DLL files, you will need to add the name of the new directory to the SET LIBPATH = statement in the workstation's CONFIG.SYS file. Device drivers and programs should be copied to a directory called \NETWARE.

After you have copied the files to the appropriate directories, you need to update the workstation's CONFIG.SYS file to include the statements that will activate the NetWare Requester. A file called CONFIG.PST is provided to guide you. Use your word processor or favorite text editor to append the CONFIG.PST file to the workstation's CONFIG.SYS file.

Every statement in the CONFIG.PST file is preceded by the word REM, which means it is treated as a comment when you boot the PC and OS/2 reads the CONFIG.SYS file. Instructions are embedded in the CONFIG.PST file that prompt you to remove the REM statement from the appropriate statements. Removing the REM statement causes those lines to be treated as commands and no longer as comments.

You need to remove the word REM from the statement that loads the OS/2 driver that activates your PC's network adapter. You also have the option of activating the SPX and NETBIOS protocols. If the PC is going to run any applications that use Named Pipes (a special OS/2 protocol for creating shared applications), you also need to remove REM from the appropriate statements to activate Named Pipes support and then follow the instructions for providing a unique Named Pipes server name. If the workstation needs to use shared printers, remove the word REM from the command that runs the NetWare Requester Spooler.

After you have successfully modified the CONFIG.SYS file, you are ready to boot the workstation. The NetWare Requester is activated, and you can log into file servers and use them.

NetWare'S OS/2-Specific Features

The OS/2 versions of NetWare's commands and utilities provide some interesting additional capabilities that maximize the usefulness of OS/2's multisession environment. OS/2 enables you to operate multiple sessions, and each can be running a different program or performing a different task. Several OS/2 versions of NetWare commands take advantage of this capability.

Running Commands in Global or Private Mode

With several of NetWare's commands, you can determine whether the command takes effect for the current OS/2 session only or for all OS/2 sessions running on the workstation. When you designate that the command is to take effect only in the current session, you are running the command in *private* mode. If you designate that the command take effect in all sessions, you are running it in *global* mode.

The following commands can be run in global or private mode:

    ATTACH
    CAPTURE
    ENDCAP
    LOGIN
    LOGOUT
    MAP

By default, each of these commands runs in global mode. To cause the command to run in private mode, follow the command with the /P parameter, as shown in the following examples:

    ATTACH /P SERV1/SMITHFD
    CAPTURE S=SERV1 Q=ACCT-LJ B=SMITTY /P
    ENDCAP /P
    LOGIN /P SERV1/SMITHFD
    LOGOUT SERV1/P
    MAP G:=SERV1/SYS:PRIVATE/SMITHFD /P

When you log in or attach to a server in private mode and then attach to the same server globally, the global attachment is added to the private login or attachment. The global attachment does not cancel or override the previous private login or attachment. If you want to log out of a private attachment, you must do so from the session where you logged in or attached to the server with the private option, and you must use the /P option with the LOGOUT command. You can logout from both global and private connections by following the LOGOUT command with the /S (for System) parameter.

Special Rules for Running NetWare OS/2 Commands

A few special rules apply when you use OS/2 versions of NETWARE's MAP and CAPTURE commands. On an OS/2 workstation, you cannot use MAP to create search drives. You should use OS/2's PATH command instead to place a network drive on the search list (see Chapter 9 for information about using MAP to create search drives).

As of this writing, the OS/2 version of the CAPTURE command does not permit you to use the TIMEOUT, NOAUTOENDCAP, JOB, or CREATE options. Certain other NetWare printer-management utilities also are not available, including PRINTCON, PRINTDEF, and PCONSOLE.

OS/2 is a recently introduced and rapidly changing operating system. The NetWare Requester also is a recently released product and is changing to match OS/2 as new developments occur. You should read your NetWare Requester documentation carefully to see which features and commands have been added.

NetWare for Macintosh—An Overview

The Apple Macintosh has become a widely used computer. In many organizations, Macintoshes are as common as IBM-compatible PCs. The same benefits that inspire organizations with multiple IBM-compatible PCs to network also have compelled Macintosh users to "get connected." Several products are available that enable Macintoshes to be networked with each other, but few products have enabled both Macintoshes and IBM-compatible PCs to be linked in such a way as to enable them to share files, printers, and other network resources.

NetWare for Macintosh enables Macintoshes and IBM-compatible PCs to share access to NetWare file servers and to share printers by using Appletalk (a Macintosh cannot print to standard printers on the servers serial and parallel ports). In addition to the economy and efficiency resulting from not having to provide equivalent but separate hard disks and printers, PC and Macintosh users can share files and electronic mail. In time, applications will become available that enable PC and Macintosh users to share resources with each other in many other ways.

How NetWare for Macintosh Works

Macintosh computers create and manage files in a format and protocol referred to as the Apple File Protocol (AFP). NetWare's equivalent to AFP is called the NetWare Core Protocol (NCP). For a Macintosh to use a NetWare file server, a method must exist to translate Macintosh AFP transactions into a format compatible with NCP and vice versa.

NetWare for Macintosh uses a program running on a server or external bridge called a VAP (Value Added Process) to accomplish this translation (VAPs are discussed in Chapter 19). This VAP runs in the server that contains the network adapter and that is connected to the Macintosh network. The VAP is called the Service Protocol Gateway. (In Chapter 2 you read that a gateway enables users connected to one type of system to communicate with another type of system by performing connection and translation services between the two dissimilar environments.)

A second VAP is provided with NetWare for Macintosh that permits Macintoshes to use NetWare print queues and to share Apple LaserWriter, or compatible ImageWriter, printers. This VAP can run in the same server as the Service Protocol Gateway VAP, or can be run in a separate server. Network supervisors who have used NetWare for Macintosh report that the Service Protocol Gateway VAP significantly increases the server's workload. If the server is already busy, you may want to place the Service Protocol Gateway VAP and printer VAP on separate servers or bridges.

After the Service Protocol Gateway VAP is running on a server in the network, connected Macintoshes may store and retrieve files from any NetWare server. NetWare 386 servers must load the name space for Macintosh files (see Chapter 7 for information about loading name space for file protocols on a NetWare 386 server).

Hardware and Software Requirements

The NetWare for Macintosh VAPs can be installed on a server or external bridge running NetWare 286 Version 2.15C or greater. Any server or bridge running a NetWare for Macintosh VAP must have a network adapter that is connected to the installed Macintosh network. Not all types of network adapters can be used for this purpose; you should check with your NetWare vendor for a current list of supported adapters.

Backing up server-based files stored by Macintosh users may require special handling. Not all backup devices can back up Macintosh files; you should check with your backup device vendor to see if your backup device is capable of this task. NetWare's NBACKUP utility safely backs up Macintosh files (see Chapter 20 for details about running NBACKUP).

Special Instructions

As of this writing, NetWare for Macintosh is shipped with an important supplement to its installation documentation. This supplement contains instructions concerning loading the Server Protocol Gateway VAP and replacing certain NetWare utilities. The instructions must be followed exactly to install and use NetWare for Macintosh. This installation supplement is easy to miss because it is packaged separately and the regular documentation does not refer to it. Make sure that you locate this supplement and read it thoroughly.

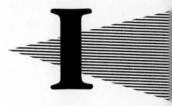

Winning at Network Snipes

No book about NetWare would be complete without a discussion of its most unusual facet: Network Snipes, or NSNIPES for short. NSNIPES is a game. You guide your on-screen player through an endless maze in which you encounter an ever-increasing number of pernicious network snipes. Your mission is simple—destroy the snipes before they destroy you.

NSNIPES is available with all versions of NetWare 286, but as of this writing the game is mysteriously missing from NetWare 386 (an omission sure to bring howls of protest from NetWare 386 buyers). NSNIPES can be played by one user, or becomes a multiuser contest if two to five users start the game together from the same default directory.

Starting NSNIPES

To start NSNIPES, log into a server running NetWare 286. Switch to a network directory in which you have READ, WRITE, OPEN, CREATE, and SEARCH rights. Type

   NSNIPES

and press Enter if you have a monochrome screen. Or, type

   NCSNIPES

and press Enter if you have a color screen. The game maze shown in figure I.1 appears.

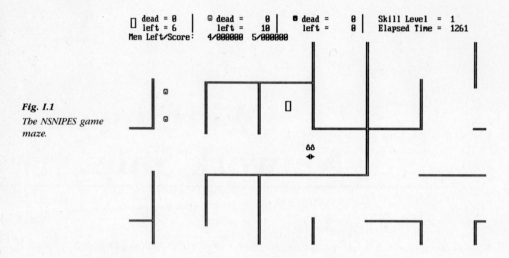

Fig. I.1

The NSNIPES game maze.

Notice that your player appears in the center of the screen. The snipes are small oval-shaped faces that are capable of shooting at and destroying your player. Snipes come from rectangular boxes that some NSNIPES experts have dubbed "mother ships."

The game begins with a certain number of mother ships and each mother ship begins producing snipes as the game progresses.

Starting Multiuser Snipes

The same commands discussed above can be used to start a multiuser NSNIPES game. All players (as many as five) should make the same network directory their default directory. All players must have READ, WRITE, OPEN, CREATE, and SEARCH rights to the directory. The first player should execute the NSNIPES (or NCSNIPES) command. The following prompt appears:

```
Hit ENTER to start the game.
Stations in the game
```

At this point, other users can execute the start-up command. As they do, their connection numbers appear under the above prompt. When all the users have executed the command, the first user can press Enter and the game begins.

The Rules of the Game

You win an NSNIPES game by destroying all snipes and mother ships. You start the game with a certain number of "lives" (in other words, you can be destroyed by a snipe a certain number of times before you lose the game).

If you are playing NSNIPES with other players, you also must emerge as the last survivor to be declared the winner. To become the last survivor, you must destroy your fellow players if you encounter them in the maze.

A score is kept for each player. You score the following points for each item that you destroy:

SNIPES	10 points
MOTHER SHIPS	500 points
ANOTHER PLAYER	500 points

The number of mother ships, your number of lives, and your score are displayed at the top of the screen.

Shooting

You can shoot at other players by using the following keys:

A	shoots to the left
D	shoots to the right
W	shoots up
X	shoots down

The following are key combinations and both keys should be pressed at the same time:

A and X	shoots diagonally left and down
A and W	shoots diagonally left and up

D and X   shoots diagonally right and down

D and W   shoots diagonally right and up

Your player is equipped with unlimited ammunition.

Moving Your Player

Your player can be moved by using the arrow keys. You can move and shoot at the same time by pressing an arrow key and a shooting key together. If you press an arrow key and the space bar at the same time, your player moves at high speed.

Playing at Higher Levels

Becoming proficient at the default level is easy. Ten levels of NSNIPES are available, however, and advanced players find the higher levels very challenging even after years of playing experience.

To start NSNIPES at a higher level, follow the command NSNIPES or NCSNIPES with the number of the level at which you want to play. For example, to play NSNIPES at its eighth level, type

    NSNIPES 8

and press Enter.

As the playing level increases, so does the viciousness of the snipes. At higher levels, they shoot at you with increasing frequency and ferocity. The mother ships also become more prolific, spewing out new snipes at an increasing rate. The number of lives that you have and the number of mother ships vary according to the level.

Advanced Features

At higher levels, several advanced features are activated. These features include "electric walls," ricochet shooting, and ghosts. These advanced features are described in the following paragraphs.

Electric Walls

Electric walls first appear in level six. From that level on, your player cannot run into a maze wall without being destroyed.

Ghosts

Ghosts also first appear at level six. When you shoot a snipe, you destroy it, but it is replaced by a "snipe ghost" that cannot shoot but can destroy your player by colliding with it. You can destroy a ghost by shooting it, for which you receive ten points.

Ricochet Shooting

Starting with level four, your diagonal shots ricochet through the maze. You can use this feature to great advantage, enabling you to shoot around corners. However, you must be careful not to destroy your own player with a ricochet shot.

Information about the features available at each level is shown in table I.1

Table I.1
NSNIPES Level Comparison

Level:	1	2	3	4	5	6	7	8	9	10
Number of lives	5	5	5	5	5	5	5	5	4	3
Number of mother ships per player	3	4	4	4	4	4	4	5	5	5
Electric walls						x	x	x	x	x
Ghosts						x	x	x	x	x
Ricochet shooting				x	x	x	x	x	x	x

Stopping NSNIPES

To stop playing NSNIPES, press Ctrl-Break. You may have to press Ctrl-Break more than once to interrupt the game. On color screens, leaving NSNIPES causes the cursor to disappear. You can make it reappear by rebooting your PC or by running a program that restores the cursor (any NetWare menu utility restores the cursor automatically).

Erasing the NSNIPES Data Files

Whenever you have played NSNIPES, two data files are left behind (SNIPEINI.DAT and SNIPESYN.DAT). These files are affectionately called "snipe droppings" by some experienced players. You should erase these files if you plan to play multiuser NSNIPES again using the same default directory.

Removing NSNIPES from a Server

Some organizations prohibit the use of recreational software. To remove NSNIPES from your network, remove the following files from each server's SYS:PUBLIC directory:

NSNIPES.EXE
NCSNIPES.EXE

You need to use the FLAG command or FILER utility to turn off the READ ONLY attribute before the files can be erased.

Index

A

ACCESS CONTROL, 665
  directory rights, 230, 232, 236-237
  file rights, 234
access
  rights, 26
  speed, 42
  to shared programs, 631-633
    controlling, 631-633
    other computer systems, local area
    network (LAN), 8
account restrictions, 206-212
  defaults, 216-217
accounting, 465-466
  account balances, 478-481
  charge rates, 469-481
    assigning, 472-477
    disk storage, 475-477
    time connected, 473-477
    user, 203-204
    chargeable items, 470-472
    credit status, 478-481
    default account balances, 480

installing, 467-468, 477-481
  multiple user accounts, 479-481
  network management, 481-484
  removing, 484
  servers, 468-481
  unlimited credit, 481
accounts
  disabling, 208
  group, 220
activating
  network adapters, 136-138
  server disks, 135-136
ADD NAME SPACE console command,
  563, 652
address reference chart, 673-679
addresses, node, 212-214
Advanced NetWare, 35-36, 38
ALLOW command, 652
Apple Macintosh NetWare, 701-703
ARCHIVE file attribute, 267-268, 666
ARCnet networks, 47
assigning
  charge rates, SYSCON command,
  472-476
  disk space, 315

drive letters, 189-191
trustees, 239-241
ATOTAL command, 483-484, 652
ATTACH command, 197, 204, 451-452, 652
attaching, 22-26
servers, 178-179
attributes
directory, 270-271
file, 266-270
AUTOEXEC.BAT file, 133-134, 179
AUTOEXEC.NCF file, 150-151
AUXGEN
disk, 55
file, 81-82

B

backing up
file servers, 590-603
open files, 593
schedule, 592-593
utilities, 593-603
Backspace key, 669
banner options, shared printing, 369-370
batch files, 634-636
BIND console command, 563-564, 652
Bindery, 112
BINDFIX command, 652
BINDREST command, 652
blocks, 469-471
booting the file server, 120-125, 130-133
BREAK command, 446, 455-456
bridges
external, 18, 49-52
internal, 18, 49-52, 63-64
BROADCAST command, 545-546, 652
broadcasting messages to users, 506-508
BRUTILS disks, 61
bugs, installing NetWare, 101-102
bus
data, 39-43
hardware, 45-46

C

cables
coaxial, 47
fiber-optic, 47

shielded twisted-pair, 47
unshielded twisted-pair, 47
caching
cache statistics, FCONSOLE command, 519-521
directory, 44-45
file, 44-45
CAPTURE command, 28, 338, 341, 361-372, 652
parameters, 364-365
CASTOFF command, 530-531, 653
CASTON command, 531, 653
central processing unit *see* CPU
channel
configuration, 85-86
numbers, 85-86
charge rates, 470-471
assigning, 472-477
chargeable items, 470-472
checking network devices, 588-589
CHKDIR command, 500, 653
CHKVOL command, 499-500, 653
CLEAR MESSAGE console command, 548, 653
CLEAR STATION command, 545, 653
clearing user connections, 505-508
clock speed, 40-43
CLS console command, 548, 653
COLORPAL
command, 620-621, 653
utility, 653
combining file and directory rights, 235-237
commands
ADD NAME SPACE, 563, 652
ALLOW, 652
ATOTAL, 483-484, 652
ATTACH, 197, 204, 451-452, 652
BIND, 563-564, 652
BINDFIX, 652
BINDREST, 652
BREAK, 446, 455-456
BROADCAST, 545-546, 652
CAPTURE, 28, 338, 341, 361-372, 652
CASTOFF, 530-531, 653
CASTON, 531, 653
CHKDIR, 500, 653
CHKVOL, 499-500, 653
CLEAR MESSAGE, 548, 653
CLEAR STATION, 545, 653
CLS, 548, 653

COLORPAL, 620-621
COMSPEC, 456
CONFIG, 538, 653
DISABLE LOGIN, 544, 654
DISABLE TTS, 562, 654
DISK, 549-550, 654
DISKCOPY (DOS), 55
DISKSET, 654
DISMOUNT, 551-552, 654
DISPLAY, 441-442
DISPLAY NETWORKS, 539, 654
DISPLAY SERVERS, 539, 655
DOS, 655
DOS SET, 453-454
DOWN, 547, 655
DRIVE, 437
DSPACE, 298, 314-315, 501
ENABLE LOGIN, 545, 655
ENABLE TTS, 563, 655
ENDCAP, 362-363, 655
EXECUTE, 448-449
EXIT, 450, 547, 655
FCONSOLE, 488-528
FDISK (DOS), 132
FDISPLAY, 441-442
FIRE PHASERS, 460-461
FLAGDIR, 272-279, 656
FORMAT (DOS), 132
GRANT, 656
GRANT (DOS), 250-253
HIDEFILE, 298-299, 656
IF/THEN, 443-446
INSTALL, 656
LARCHIVE, 594-595, 656
LISTDIR, 298, 313-314, 656
LOAD, 656
LOGIN, 197, 204, 459, 656
LOGOUT, 656
LRESTORE, 596, 657
MACHINE NAME, 456-457
MAKEUSER, 657
MAP, 27, 188-194, 424-436, 657
MENU, 611, 622, 657
MODULES, 657
MONITOR, 540-543, 657
MOUNT, 551-552, 657
NAME, 538, 657
NARCHIVE, 594-595
NBACKUP, 597-603
NCOPY, 298, 304-306, 657
NDIR, 298, 306-314, 658

NPRINT, 364-365, 372-373, 658
NRESTORE, 596
NVER, 493, 658
OFF, 548, 658
PAUDIT, 482-483, 658
PAUSE, 447
PCCOMPATIBLE, 456-457
PCONSOLE, 341-343, 390-400
PRINTER, 659
PROTOCOL, 544, 659
PSC, 401-405, 659
PSERVER, 347-358
PURGE, 298-304, 659
QUEUE, 659
REMIRROR, 551, 659
REMOVE, 659
REMOVE (DOS), 250, 255-256, 659
RENDIR, 659
RESET ROUTER, 562, 660
REVOKE, 660
REVOKE (DOS), 250, 253-256
RIGHTS, 660
RPRINTER, 660
SALVAGE, 298, 300-303, 660
SEARCH, 660
SECURE CONSOLE, 660
SECURITY, 660
SEND, 529-531, 546-547, 661
SESSION, 532-534
SET, 552-561, 661
SET TIME, 562, 661
SETPASS, 661
SHOWFILE, 298-299, 661
SLIST, 661
SMODE, 298, 316-317, 661
SPEED, 544, 661
SPOOL, 662
SYSCON, 492-493, 501-502
SYSTIME, 662
TIME, 539-540, 662
TLIST, 662
TLIST (DOS), 250-251
TRACK, 538-539
TRACK OFF, 662
TRACK ON, 662
UNBIND, 563-564, 663
UNLOAD, 663
UNMIRROR, 551, 662
UPS, 663
USERLIST, 502-503, 663
VAP, 663

VERIFY, 454-455
VERSION, 540, 663
VOLINFO, 497-499
VOLUME, 552, 663
VREPAIR, 664
WAIT, 447
WHOAMI, 664
WRITE, 438-441
comments, login scripts, 458-459
COMPSURF (COMPrehensive SURFace analysis) utility, 54, 84-93, 105, 142-143
COMSPEC command, 456
concurrent connections, 208-209
CONFIG command, 538, 653
CONFIG.SYS file, 81-82
configuration files, 61
configuring
    drivers, 72-73
    file servers, 109-112, 552-564
    LAN drivers, 73, 167-168
    resource sets, 72-74, 167-168
    server hardware, 54
    servers, 62-63, 98-99
    system, 116-117
connection information, MONITOR command, 541-543
CONSOLE command, 654
console
    commands, 405, 535-537, 654
    executing, 536, 537
    display, file servers, 548
    operators, 489-490
controlling user access, 238-263, 320
    assigning rights, 322-323
    file servers, FCONSOLE command, 495
    limiting disk space, 323
    passwords, 209-211
    personal directories, 321-323
COPY INHIBIT file attribute, 267-270
copying
    files, 291-292
    subdirectories, 297-298
CPU (central processing unit), 39-43
CREATE, 664
    directory rights, 230-231, 236-237
    file rights, 234
creating
    NetWare shell, 157-180
    partition tables, 105-107
    templates, USERDEF utility, 682-687

custom level, 56-60, 68-71, 82, 102-120, 173-176
customizing the NetWare shell, 179-180

D

data bus, size, 39-46
data packets, 17-18
DCB (disk co-processor board), 42, 84-86, 138, 143-144
dedicated servers, 35-36, 62-63, 120-121
default
    account balances, 480
    account restrictions, 216-217
    FILER utility, 281-283
    level, 56-62, 82, 93-97, 161-170
    time restrictions, 216-217
    user login scripts, 415, 416
defining
    disk volumes, 112-114, 144-149
    network printers, 99-102
DELETE INHIBIT
    directory attribute, 270-271
    file attribute, 267, 270, 668
DELETE NetWare rights, 664
    deleting
    directory rights, 230-232, 236-237, 242-244
    disk volumes, 148
    drive letters, 190-191
    file rights, 245-246
    groups, 219-220
    login names, 201-202
    users/groups, 286
designing
    menus, 608-610
    networks, 48-52
directories, 185-187
    NetWare, 672
    structure, shared programs, 629-630
    SYS:PUBLIC, 199
directory
    attributes, 270-271
        DELETE INHIBIT, 270-271
        HIDDEN, 270-271
        PRIVATE, 270-271
        PURGE, 270-271
        RENAME INHIBIT, 270-271
        SYSTEM, 270-271
    caching, 44-45

hashing, 44-45
hierarchy, 185-187
information, 272-278
changing, 283-288
management, 279-314
map, 191-194
rights, 230-237
adding, 242-244
combining with file rights, 235-237
deleting, 242-244
DISABLE LOGIN command, 544, 654
DISABLE TTS command, 654
console command, 562, 654
disabling accounts, 208
disk blocks, 469-471
disk coprocessor board *see* DCB
DISK console command, 549-550, 654
disks
AUXGEN, 55
boot, server, 131-133
BRGEN-1, 61
BRGEN-2, 61
BRGEN-3, 61
BRUTILS, 61
drives, 184-191
drivers, selecting, 64-65, 71-72
duplexing, 36-37, 95-97, 108-109, 143-144
failure protection, Hot Fix, 35-36, 107-108, 141-143
file servers, 548-552
formatting, 139
GENDATA, 55-56
hard
initializing, 109-114
preparing servers, 83
mirroring, 36-37, 95-97, 108-109, 143-144
NETGEN, 55, 67-77
OSEXE, 115-116
OSEXE-1, 55, 67, 77
OSEXE-2, 55
pair, 95-96
duplexing, 97, 108-109, 143-144
mirroring, 97, 108-109, 143-144
partitioning server, 140-143
PUBLIC-1, 116
PUBLIC-2, 116
PUBLIC-3, 116
SHGEN-1, 61
SHGEN-2, 61

space
assigning, 315
limiting, 211-212
statistics, 521-522
SUPPORT, 55, 67, 77
SYSTEM, 116
UTILEXE, 87
UTILEXE-1, 55, 67, 77, 87
UTILEXE-2, 55, 67, 77
volumes
defining, 112-114, 144-149
deleting, 148
information, 298
mounting, 148-149
naming, 146-147, 186-187
size, 147
DISKCOPY (DOS) command, 55
DISKSET
command, 654
NetWare loadable module, 654
program, 84-86, 138
utility, 654
DISMOUNT command, 551-552, 654
DISPLAY command, 441-442
DISPLAY NETWORKS command, 539, 654
DISPLAY SERVERS command, 539, 655
displaying
drive letters, 189
file
attributes, 273-276
contents, 291
information, 288-289
servers, 491-493
distributed star topology, 47-48
DMA (direct memory access) channel, 57-58
DOS commands, 55, 132, 250-256, 655, 659
file server disk, 195
DOS SET command, 453-454
DOWN console command, 547, 655
downing the server, 125
DRIVE command, 437
drive letters
assigning, 189-191
deleting, 190-191
displaying, 189
drive mappings
SESSION command, 533-534
drivers
configuring, 72-73

disk, 64-65, 71-72
LAN, 64
other, 65-66, 72
selecting, 63
drives
disk, 184-191
search, 191-194
DSPACE (restrict disk space)
command, 298, 314-315, 655
managing disk space, 501
utility, 225-227, 655
duplexing, disk, 36-37, 95-97, 108-109,
143-144

E

editing
print devices, 376-381
resource lists, 74-76
resource sets, 74-76, 169-170
templates, USERDEF utility, 682-687
effective rights, 261-263
EISA (Extended Industry Standard
Architecture) bus, 45-46
ELS (Entry Level Solution) NetWare,
33-35, 38, 689-693
ENABLE LOGIN command, 545, 655
ENABLE TTS console command, 563, 655
encrypted passwords, 149-152
end of job options, 370-371
ENDCAP command, 362-363, 655
Enhanced Small Device Interface *see* ESDI
ERASE, 664
directory rights, 230-232, 236-237
file rights, 234
ESDI (Enhanced Small Device Interface),
42
EtherNet network, 46, 47
EVERYONE group account name, 223,
248-250
EXECUTE command, 448-449
EXECUTE ONLY file attribute, 267-269,
666
executing
console commands, 536-537
NetWare loadable modules, 536-537
EXIT console command, 450, 547 655
expiration date of account, 208-209
Extended Industry Standard Architecture
see EISA
external bridges, 18, 49-52

F

FAT (file allocation table), 44
fax servers, 15
FCONSOLE command, 217-218, 222,
488-490, 655
date and time, setting, 495
file
servers, 490-491
usage, managing, 508-513
purging, 513
statistics, 514-528
stopping file servers, 494
transaction tracking statistics,
526-527
user
access, controlling, 495
connections, 504-508,
messages, sending, 505-508
viewing
file and record locks, 509-512
LAN driver information, 496
user connections, 506-508
FDISK (DOS) command, 132
FDISPLAY command, 441-442
file allocation table *see* FAT, 44
file attributes, 266, 268, 326-327, 334-335,
633
ARCHIVE, 267-268
changing, 276-277, 287-288
COPY INHIBIT, 267, 270
DELETE INHIBIT, 267, 270
displaying, 273-276
EXECUTE ONLY, 267, 269
HIDDEN, 267-268
INDEXED, 267-269
PURGE, 267, 270
READ AUDIT, 267, 270
READ ONLY, 267-268
RENAME INHIBIT, 267, 270
setting, 272-288
SHAREABLE, 267-269
SYSTEM, 267-268
TRANSACTIONAL, 267, 269
WRITE AUDIT, 267, 270
caching, 44-45
contents, displaying, 291
information, displaying, 288-289
management, 299-314
paths, 186-187

recovery, 301-302
rights, 230-234, 236-237, 243-244
adding, 245-246
combining with directory rights,
235-237
deleting, 245-246
file servers, 14-15, 22-28, 39-46, 134, 537
access, controlling, 495
accounting, 486-481
charge rates, 469-477
backing up, 590-603
booting, 120-125, 130-133
changing, 490
configuring, 562-564
console
commands, 535-537
display, 548
date and time setting, 495
disks, 548-552
displaying, 491-493
managing
disk space, 497-499
file usage, 508-513
user connections, 504-508
monitoring, network management,
585-586
naming, 98, 134
purging files, 513
statistics, 465-467, 477, 514-528
stopping, 494, 547
storing shared programs, 627-629
viewing
file and record locks, 509-512
LAN driver information, 496
file-sharing pools, 323-326
assigning rights, 324-326, 329-333
file attributes, 327
managing, 326
shared databases, 328-333
FILER
command, 655
utility, 257-260, 272-273, 280-298, 655
default options, 281-283
files
AUTOEXEC.BAT, 133-134, 179
AUTOEXEC.NCF, 150-151
AUXGEN, 81-82
CONFIG.SYS, 81-82
configuration, uploading, 61
copying, 291-292
installing NetWare, 100-101, 119-120

INT2F.COM, 174
IPX.COM, 174
listing, 307-314
moving, 291-292
NET$OS.EX1, 116
NET$OS.EX2, 116
NET$OS.EXE, 116
NET2.COM, 174
NET3.COM, 174
NET4.COM, 174
NETBIOS.EXE, 174
NetWare, 672
Non-DOS, preparing, 151
organizing, 183-194
renaming, 292-294
searching for, 316-317
SERVER.EXE, 133-134
STARTUP.NCF, 152
SUPPORT, 81-82
FIRE PHASERS command, 460-461
FLAG command, 272-278, 656
FLAGDIR command, 272, 278-279, 656
FORMAT (DOS) command, 132
format options, shared printers, 367-369
formatting disks, 139
full names, 206-207, 220

G

game, Network Snipes (NSNIPES),
705-710
gateways, 8, 15
generating NetWare, 53-65, 69-78
saving selections, 66-68, 76-77
shell, 157-180
GRANT
command, 656
DOS command, 250-253
group account, 220
adding users, 221-222
removing users, 221-222
groups
adding, 219-220
rights, 246-249
belonged to, 218-219
deleting, 219-220
of users, 219-220
renaming, 219-220
groupware, 11
GUEST login name, 202

H

hard disks, 40-42
    controller, 40-42
    initializing, 109-114
    partitioning, 131-133
    preparing servers, 83
    space usage, 583-585
    hardware
    assembling NetWare, 80, 129-130
    bus
        EISA (Extended Industry Standard Architecture), 45-46
        ISA (Industry Standard Architecture), 45-46
        MCA (Micro Channel Architecture), 45-46
        CPU (central processing unit), 39-43
        hard disk, 40-42
        network
        adapter, 16-18
        components, 13-15
        interface board, 16
        RAM (random-access memory), 43-45
        requirements, Apple Macintosh, 702-703
        servers, 14-15
        workstations, 16
hashing, directory, 44-45
HELP
    command, 656
    utility, 656
HIDDEN
    directory attribute, 270-271, 665
    file attribute, 267-268, 667
HIDEFILE command, 298-299, 656
hierarchy, directory, 185-187
Hot Fix disk failure protection, 35-36, 107-108, 141-143

I

I/O ports, 58
IF/THEN command, 443-446
INDEXED file attribute, 267-269, 666
Industry Standard Architecture *see* ISA, 45-46
initializing hard disks, 109-114

INSTALL
    command, 656
    NetWare loadable module, 656
    utility, 138-149
installing
    accounting, 467-468
    ELS (Entry-Level Solution) NetWare, 691-693
    NetWare, 86, 79-125, 127-153
    files, 100-101, 119-120
    network adapters, 173-174
    server hardware, 54
INT2F.COM file, 174
internal bridges, 18, 49-52, 63-64
interrupts, 58
IPX internal numbers, 134-135
IPX.COM file, 174
ISA (Industry Standard Architecture) bus, 45-46

K

keys
Alt-F10 (Exit), 669
    Backspace, 669
    Ctrl-left arrow (field left), 670
    Ctrl-PgDn (special down), 670
    Ctrl-PgUp (special up), 670
    Ctrl-right arrow (field right), 670
    Del (Delete), 669
    down arrow, 670
    editing login scripts, 418-419
    End (Special Right), 670
    Enter (Select), 669
    Esc (Escape), 669
    F1 (Help), 669
    F3 (Modify), 669
    F5 (Mark), 669
    F7 (Cancel), 669
    F9 (Mode), 670
    Home (Special Left), 670
    Ins (Insert), 669
left arrow, 670
    NetWare Menu utilities, 200-201
    PgDn (Page Down), 670
    PgUp (Page Up), 670
    right arrow, 670
    Tab (Cycle), 670
up arrow, 670

L

LAN *see* local area network
LARCHIVE
  command, 594-595, 656
  utility, 656
level of operation
  custom, 56-60, 105-120, 173-174, 176
  default, 56-60, 62, 82, 93-97, 161-170
linear bus topology, 47-48
LISTDIR command, 298, 313-314, 656
listing files, 307-314
LOAD command, 656
loaded item, 63-64, 71
loading
  NetWare Loadable Modules (NLM), 565
  operating system, 115-116
local area network (LAN), 6-11, 14-17, 18
  accessing other computer systems, 8
  drivers
    configuring, 73, 167-168
    selecting, 63-64, 71, 166-167
  purpose, 13
  sharing
    communication devices, 8-10
    data, 10-11
    hardware, 6-7
    software, 9-10, 626-636
local menus, 621
locks
  logical, 512
  physical, 510-511
logging into the server, 22-26, 177-178
logical locks, 512
LOGIN command, 22-26, 197, 204, 459, 656
login
  control, 334-335
  names, 198-199, 204-207
    adding, 200-203
    changing, 201-202
    choosing, 205
    deleting, 201-202
    GUEST, 202
    restricting use, 212-214
    SUPERVISOR, 202
  scripts, 413
    commands, 420-461
    comments, 458-459
    creating, 416-424
    default user, 415-416
    editing keys, 418-419
    network management, 461-463
    system, 414
    user, 414-416
    variables, 428-436
LOGOUT command, 656
Lotus 1-2-3, 642-647
LRESTORE
  command, 596, 657
  utility, 657

M

MACHINE NAME command, 456-457
MAKEUSER
  command, 657
  utility, 262-263, 657, 681
MAP command, 27, 188-194, 424-436, 657
mask rights, 256-260, 289-290
MCA (Micro Channel Architecture) bus, 45-46
megahertz (MHz), 40-42
memory
  address, 57-58
  use, 43-45
MENU command, 611-622, 657
menu scripts
  creating, 611
  executing, 611-612
  structure, 612-613
menu-building utility, 27
menus
  colors, 619-621
  creating, 607
  designing, 608-610
  height, 618-619
  local, 621
  shared programs, 636
  submenus, 613-616
  user input, 616-617
  width, 618-619
  window position, 617-618
messages
  receiving, 530, 531
  sending, 529-531, 545-547
Micro Channel Architecture *see* MCA, 45-46

mirroring
    disk, 36-37, 95-97, 108-109, 143-144
    server, 135
modem servers, 15
modes
    protected, 36-37
    real, 36
MODIFY, 665
    directory rights, 230, 233, 236-237
    file rights, 234
modifying partition tables, 105-107
MODULES command, 657
MONITOR command, 540-543, 657
    connection information, 541-543
    file server utilization statistics, 540-541
MONITOR NetWare loadable module,
    566-574, 657
    file
        server connections, 568-569
        status information, 572-573
        loading, 566-567
        locking console keyboard, 571-572
        memory usage information, 573-574
        viewing
        disk information, 569-570
        LAN information, 570-571
        loaded NLMs, 571
monitoring file servers, 585-586
MOUNT command, 551-552, 657
mounting volume, 148-149
multitasking, 695
multiple
    networks, 49-52
    servers, 49-52

N

NAME command, 538, 657
names
    disk volume, 146-147, 186-187
    file
        attribute, 267-270
        servers, 98, 134
        full, 206-207
NARCHIVE
    command, 594-595, 657
    utility, 657
NBACKUP
    command, 597-603, 657
    utility, 657

NCOPY command, 298, 304-306, 657
NDIR command, 298, 306-314, 658
NET$OS.EX1 file, 116
NET$OS.EX2 file, 116
NET$OS.EXE file, 116
NET2.COM file, 174
NET3.COM file, 174
NET4.COM file, 174
NETBIOS.EXE file, 174
NETGEN
    starting, 77
    disk, 55, 67, 77
    utility, 54-87, 93-120, 158
        level of operation, 56-60, 82, 93-97
NetWare
    Apple MacIntosh, 701-703
        hardware requirements, 702-703
        software requirements, 702-703
        assembling hardware, 80, 129-130
        directories, 672
        ELS (Entry-Level Solution), 689-691
        installing, 691-693
        files, 672
        installing, 115
        memory use, 43-45
        menu utility, 27, 199-201
        network operating system, 6, 15,
        18-19, 21-29
        printing, 28-29
        security, 23-26
        versions, 33-39, 53-153
        rights, 632-633
        ACCESS CONTROL, 665
        CREATE, 664
        DELETE, 664
        ERASE, 664
        FILE SCAN, 665
        groups, 632-633
        MODIFY, 665
        OPEN, 664
        PARENTAL, 664
        READ, 664
        SEARCH, 665
        SUPERVISORY, 665
        WRITE, 664
        shell, 22-23, 27-28, 155-156
        creating, 157-180
        customizing, 179-180
        generating, 157-180
        starting, 83, 84, 85
NetWare 286, 33-37, 53-125, 198, 693

Advanced NetWare, 35-36, 38
directory attributes
  HIDDEN, 667
  PRIVATE, 667
  SYSTEM, 667
  directory rights, 230-233, 236, 237
file attributes
  ARCHIVE, 666
  EXECUTE ONLY, 666
  HIDDEN, 665
  INDEXED, 666
  READ ONLY, 665
  SHAREABLE, 666
  SYSTEM, 665
  TRANSACTIONAL, 666
  generating, 53-78
  installing, 79-100, 103-114, 116-125
  bugs, 101-102
  SFT NetWare, 36-37, 95-99, 108-109,
  111-113
NetWare 386, 33-35, 37, 127-153, 198
  advanced user/group management
  features, 223-227
  directory attributes
    DELETE INHIBIT, 668
    PURGE, 668
    RENAME INHIBIT, 668
    directory rights, 230-233, 236-237
  file attributes
    COPY INHIBIT, 667
    DELETE INHIBIT, 667
    PURGE, 667
    READ AUDIT, 667
    RENAME INHIBIT, 667
    WRITE AUDIT, 667
    file rights, 234
    installing, 127-153
    limiting user disk space, 212
    print servers
      configuring, 348-357
      creating, 347
      defining, 347-348
      starting, 358
    shell generation, 159, 171-180
NetWare loadable modules (NLMs), 37,
535, 564
  AUTOEXEC.NCF, 578
  AUTOEXEC.SYS, 578
  definition, 564-565
  DISKSET, 654
  executing, 536-537

INSTALL, 656
loading, 565
  automatic, 578
  managing, NLM commands, 574-576
  MONITOR, 566-574
  PSERVER, 659
  unloading, 565
  UPS, 663
NETWARE subdirectories, 61, 672
NetWare VMS, 38-39
network
  adapters, 16-18, 57-58
    activating, 136-138
    installing, 173-174
  based software, 626-636
  communication systems, 46-47
  components, 39-46
  hardware, 13-15
  software, 13
  designing, 48-52
  interface board, 16
  management, 581-582
    accounting, 481-484
    backing up, 590-603
    commands, 487-528
    databases, 589-590
    devices, 588-589
    hard disk space usage, 583-585
    login scripts, 461-463
    maintenance schedule, 588-589
    monitoring file servers, 585-586
    node address reference chart,
    673-679
    shared printing, 389-412
    software maintenance, 589-590
    supervisor, 199
    user information, 586-588
Network Snipes (NSNIPES) game,
705-710
  advanced features, 708-709
  erasing, 710
  higher levels, 708
  multiuser, 706
  rules, 707
  single user, 705
  stopping, 710
networks
  multiple, 49-52
  small, 689
    designing, 690-691

NLM *see* NetWare loadable modules
node addresses, 212-214
  reference chart, 673-679
nondedicated servers, 35-36, 38-39,
  62-63, 122-124, 537
NPRINT command, 372-373, 658
  parameters, 364-365
NRESTORE
  command, 596, 658
  utility, 658
NSNIPES (Network Snipes) game,
  705-710
NVER command, 658
  displaying file servers, 493

O

OFF command, 658
  console command, 548
OPEN NetWare directory rights, 230-231,
  236-237, 664
operating system
  loading, 115-116
  setting options, 62-63, 69-71
options
  advanced printer configuration,
  374-375
  banner, 369-370
  end of job, 370-371
  format, 367-369
  notification, 371
  output, 367-369
  PSC command, 402-405
organizing files, 183-194
OS/2
  commands, file server disk, 195
  operating system, 695-700
    activating workstations, 697-698, 700
    NetWare, 695-700
    Requester, 696
other drivers, selecting, 65-66, 72
output options, shared printers, 367-369

P

Paradox, 647-649
PARENTAL, 664
  directory rights, 230, 232, 236-237
partition tables, 104

creating, 105-107
  modifying, 105-107
partitioning
  server disks, 140-143
  hard disks, 131-133
passwords, 198
  assigning, 205-207
  control, 23-26, 209-211
  encryption, 149-152
PAUDIT command, 482-483, 658
PAUSE command, 447
  login scripts, 447
PCCOMPATIBLE command, 456-457
PCONSOLE
  command, 341-343, 390-400, 658
  utility, 658
performance, file servers, 40-46
personal directories
  assigning rights, 322-323
  naming, 320
  structure, 321-323
physical locks, 510-511
Portable NetWare, 38-39
preparing
  Non—DOS files, 151
  server disks, 137-139
    hard disks, 83
print
  devices, 375-383
    editing, 376-381
    importing, 376
  queues, 28-29, 339-340
    assigning printers, 345-347
    configuring, 343-345
    creating, 341-343
    deleting, 342-343
    priorities, 346-347
    renaming, 342-343
    server
      configuring, 348-357
      creating, 347
      defining, 347-348
      starting, 358
PRINTCON
  command, 658
  utility, 383-389, 658
    print job configurations, 384-389
PRINTDEF
  command, 658
  utility, 374-383, 658
    defining forms, 382-383

print devices, 375-381
special characters, 380-381
PRINTER command, 659
printers
defining network, 99-100, 102
maintaining information, 118-119
sharing, 7
printing, 28-29
redirecting printer output, 338
shared, 337-347, 361-375
advanced printer configuration options, 374-375
banner options, 369-370
end of job options, 370-371
format options, 367-369
management, 389-390
console commands, 405-412
PCONSOLE command, 390-400
print queues, 390-396
PSC command, 401-405
notification options, 371
output options, 367-369
print job configurations, 384-389
redirecting output, 366-369
sending requests to printers, 361-371
storing printer configurations, 388-389
PRIVATE directory attribute, 270-271, 667
profile, 203-204
programs
DISKSET, 84-86, 138
shared
batch files, 634-636
case studies, 636-649
controlling access, 631-633
directory structure, 629-630
installing, 637-649
Lotus 1-2-3, 642-647
menus, 636
Paradox, 647-649
storing on file servers, 628-629
WordPerfect, 637-642
SYSCON, 238-250
protected mode, 36-37
PROTOCOL command, 544, 659
PSC command, 401-405, 659
options, 402-405
PSERVER command, 347-358, 659
PURGE
command, 298, 300-304, 659
directory attribute, 270-271, 668
file attribute, 267-270
purging files, 513

Q

QUEUE command, 659

R

RAM (random-access memory), 43-45
random I/O test, 89, 91
READ, 664
directory rights, 230, 236-237
file rights, 234
read after write verification process, 36, 83
READ AUDIT file attribute, 267, 270
READ ONLY file attribute, 267-268, 665
real mode, 36
receiving messages, 530-531
recovering deleted files, 301-302
redirecting printer output, 338
REMIRROR command, 659
console command, 551
REMOVE (DOS) command, 250, 255-256, 659
removing
users from group account, 221-222
workgroup managers, 224
RENAME INHIBIT
directory attribute, 270-271, 668
file attribute, 267, 270
renaming
groups, 219-220
files, 292-294
RENDIR command, 659
RESET ROUTER command, 660
console command, 562
resetting network devices, 588, 589
resource lists, 74-76, 169-170
resource sets, 69-70
configuring, 72-74, 167-168
editing, 74-76, 169-170
selecting, 69-70, 165-166
restrictions
account, 206-212, 216-217
station, 206-207, 212-214
time, 206-207, 214-217

REVOKE (DOS) command, 250, 253-256, 660
RIGHTS command, 660
rights
    changing, 289-290
    directory, 230-237, 242-244
    mask, 256-260, 289-290
    setting, 256-260
ring topology, 47-48
root directory
    mapping, 194
routers, 18
RPRINTER command, 660

S

SALVAGE
    command, 298, 300-303, 660
    utility, 660
saving driver selections, 66-67, 76-77
scripts
    login, 413
        commands, 417-461
        comments, 458-459
        creating, 416-424
        default user, 415-416
        editing keys, 418-419
        network management, 461-463
        system, 414
        user, 414-416
        variables, 428-436
    menu, 611
        creating, 611
        executing, 611-612
        structure, 612-613
SCSI (Small Computer System Interface), 42, 84-86
SEARCH, 665
    command, 660
    directory rights, 230, 232-233, 236-237
search
    drives, 191-194
    mode, setting, 316, 317
searching for files, 316-317
sectors, 89
SECURE CONSOLE command, 660
security, 319
    assigning rights, 324-326
    directory rights masks, 334-335
    equivalence, 218-219, 249-250

file
    attributes, 326-327, 334-335
    sharing pools, 323-326
    assigning rights, 324-333
    databases, 328-333
    managing, 326
    limiting disk space, 323
    login control, 334-335
    managing file servers, 198-199
    personal directories
    assigning rights, 322-323
    naming, 320
    structure, 321-323
    system, 23-26
    trustee rights, 334-335
SECURITY command, 660
selecting
    disk drivers, 64-65, 71-72
    file servers, 39
    LAN drivers, 63-64, 71, 166-167
    other drivers, 65-66, 72
    resource sets, 69-70, 165-166
SEND command, 529-531, 546-547, 661
sending messages
    BROADCAST console command, 545-546
    SEND command, 529-531, 546-547
    SESSION command, 532
    to users, 505
sequential disk test, 89, 91
server disks
    activating, 135-136
    partitioning, 140-143
    preparing, 137-139
    mirroring, 135
    SERVER.EXE file, 133-134
servers, 13-15, 22-26, 28, 197, 204-205, 537
    attaching, 178, 179
    configuring, 54, 62-63, 98-99, 109-112
    console operator, 217-218
    dedicated, 35-36, 62-63, 120-121
    downing, 125
    file, 39-46, 134
    group accounts, 222
    installing, 54
    logging into, 177-178
    multiple, 49-52
    nondedicated, 35-39, 62-63, 122-124
    starting/stopping, 152-153
    supervisor, 198
    see also file servers

SESSION
command, 531, 661
drive mappings, 533-534
sending messages, 532
viewing user information, 532
utility, 661
SET command, 552-561, 661
table, 553-560
SET TIME command, 562, 661
SETPASS
command, 661
utility, 225-226
SFT (System Fault Tolerant) NetWare,
36-37, 95-99, 108-109, 111-113
SHAREABLE file attribute, 267-269, 666
sharing
communication devices, 8-10
data, 10-11
disk space, 6-7
files, 323-326
assigning rights, 324-326, 329-333
databases, 328-333
file attributes, 327
printers, 7
software, 9-10
shell generation
NetWare 286, 158-171
NetWare 386, 159, 171-180
SHGEN utility, 157-180
SHOWFILE command, 298-299, 661
size disk volume, 147
SLIST command, 661
Small Computer System Interface *see* SCSI
small networks, 689
designing, 690-691
SMODE command, 298, 316-317, 661
software
LAN-based, 626-636
maintenance, 589-590
network
based, 626-636
components, 13
operating system, 18-19, 21-29
requirements, 702-703
shared programs
batch files, 634-636
case studies, 636-649
controlling access, 631-633
directory structure, 629-630
installing, 637-649
Lotus 1-2-3, 642-647

menus, 636
Paradox, 647-649
storing on file servers, 628-629
WordPerfect, 637-642
sharing files, 323-326
assigning rights, 324-333
databases, 328-333
file attributes, 327
managing, 326
SPEED command, 544, 661
SPOOL command, 662
spooled, 118-119
starting
NETGEN with custom options, 77-78
NetWare, 83-85
servers, 152-153
STARTUP.NCF file, 152
station restrictions, 206-207, 212-214
statistics, 465-467, 477, 515, 517-518
cache, 519-521
disk, 521-522
file servers, 514-528
LAN I/O, 524-526
system, 522-523
transaction tracking, 526-527
volume information, 527-528
stopping file servers, 494, 547
subdirectories, 185-187
copying, 297-298
maintaining, 293-298
moving, 297-298
NetWare, 61, 672
submenus, creating, 613-616
supervisor
network, 199
server, 198-199
SUPERVISOR login name, 202
SUPERVISORY, 665
directory rights, 230, 233, 236-237
file rights, 234
SUPPORT
disk, 55, 67, 77
file, 81, 82
SYS:PUBLIC directory, 199
SYSCON (system configuration)
assigning charge rates, 472-476
command, 467-468, 662
displaying file servers, 492-493
installing accounting, 467
utility, 197-227
login scripts, 417-424

managing disk space, 501-502
program, 238-250
system configuring, 116-117
SYSTEM
   directory attribute, 270-271, 667
   disk, 116
   file attribute, 267-268, 665
system login scripts, 414
system statistics, file servers, 522-523
SYSTIME command, 662

T

tables, partition, 104-107
templates
   creating, 682-687
   editing, 682-687
terminal emulation, 8
terminate-and-stay-resident (TSR), 157
testing server disks, 139
tests
   disk surface, 142-143
   random I/O (COMPSURF), 89, 91
   sequential disk (COMPSURF), 89, 91
TIME command, 539-540, 662
time restrictions, 206-207, 214-215
   defaults, 216-217
TLIST (DOS) command, 250-251, 662
Token Ring network, 46-47
topologies
   distributed star, 47-48
   linear bus, 47-48
   ring, 47-48
TRACK command, 538-539
TRACK OFF command, 662
TRACK ON command, 662
Transaction Tracing System *see* TTS
transaction tracking statistics, file servers, 526-527
TRANSACTIONAL file attribute, 267, 269, 666
trustee
   assignments, 218, 239-241
      group accounts, 222
      directory rights, 286, 334-335
      file rights, 334-335
      list, 295-297
      changing, 290
      deleting users/groups, 286
   rights, 238-290
   TTS (Transaction Tracking System), 36-37, 98-99, 111-113

U

UNBIND command, 663
   console command, 563-564
unduplexing disk pairs, 97
UNLOAD command, 663
unloading netWare loadable modules, 565
UNMIRROR command, 662
   console command, 551
unmirroring disk pairs, 97
uploading configuration files, 61
UPS command, 663
user
   access, controlling, 238-263, 320
      assigning rights, 322-323
      limiting disk space, 323
      personal directories, 321-323
      account, 203-204
      adding, 682, 686-687
      groups, 246-249
      information, 586-588
      login scripts, 414-416
      statistics, 465-467, 477
USERDEF
   command, 663
   utility, 262-263, 663, 681-687
USERLIST command, 663
   managing user connections, 502-503
utilities
   COLORPAL, 653
   COMPSURF (COMPrehensive SURFace analysis), 84-93, 105, 142-143
   DISKSET, 654
   DSPACE, 655
   DSPACE (restrict disk space), 225-227
   FCONSOLE, 217-218, 222, 655
   FILER, 257-260, 272-273, 280-298, 655
   HELP, 656
   INSTALL, 138-149
   LARCHIVE, 656
   LRESTORE, 657
   MAKEUSER, 262-263, 657, 681
   NARCHIVE, 657
   NBACKUP, 657
   NETGEN, 54-87, 98-120, 158
   NetWare menu, 199-201
   PCONSOLE, 658
   PRINTCON, 383-389, 658
   PRINTDEF, 374-383, 658
   SALVAGE, 660
   SESSION, 661
   SETPASS (set password), 225-226

SHGEN, 157-180
SYSCON (System Configuration), 197-227, 662
USERDEF, 262-263, 663, 681-687
VOLINFO, 663

V

VAP (value added process), 38-39, 577
VAP command, 663
variables, login scripts, 428-436
VERIFY command, 454-455
VERSION command, 540, 663
VOLINFO command, 497-499, 663
VOLUME command, 552
  console command, 552
volume
  disk, 144-149
  information, 117, 298
    statistics, 527-528
VOLUMES command, 663
VREPAIR command, 664

W

WAIT command, 447
  login scripts, 447
WHOAMI command, 664
WordPerfect, 637-642
workgroup manager, 198
  adding, 224
  removing, 224
workgroups, 223-225
workstations, 16
WRITE, 664
  command, 438-441
  directory rights, 230-231, 236-237
  file rights, 234
WRITE AUDIT file attribute, 267-270
  login scripts, 438-441

Z

zero wait states, 43

More Computer Knowledge from Que